SPECIALTY COOKBOOKS

GARLAND REFERENCE LIBRARY
OF THE HUMANITIES
(VOL. 1297)

SPECIALTY COOKBOOKS
A Subject Guide

Volume I

Harriet Ostroff
Tom Nichols

GARLAND PUBLISHING, INC. • NEW YORK & LONDON
1992

© 1992 Harriet Ostroff and Tom Nichols
All rights reserved

Library of Congress Cataloging-in-Publication Data

Ostroff, Harriet, 1930–
   Specialty cookbooks : a subject guide / Harriet Ostroff, Tom Nichols.
      p. cm. — (Garland reference library of the humanities ; vol. 1297)
   Includes index.
   ISBN 0-8240-6947-1 (acid-free paper)
   1. Cookery—Bibliography. I. Nichols, Tom. II. Title.
III. Series.
Z5776.G2.O84   1992
[TX651]
016.6415—dc20   91-37398
                                                                           CIP

Printed on acid-free, 250-year-life paper
Manufactured in the United States of America

CONTENTS

Introduction	vii
Section I Abalone to Zucchini: Cookbooks for Specific Ingredients	3
Section II Appetizers, Waffles, and More: Cookbooks for Specific Dishes and Courses	339
Section III From Breakfast to Supper: Cookbooks for Specific Meals	512
Section IV Baking...Freezing...Stir-Frying: Cookbooks for Special Techniques	532
Author Index	569
Title Index	605

INTRODUCTION

We all eat to live; many of us love to eat; and some of us live to eat. The pleasure of eating is usually enhanced by modifying the food we eat. Directions for the preparation of food were transmitted from one person to another from the time humans first tried to alter the taste of the wild food available to them. Cookbooks have been in existence since the beginning of recorded history. There are probably very few homes in the industrialized world today that do not contain at least one cookbook.

Although we still roast meat over a fire, we now call it barbecue. Our knowledge about foods and their effect on us has greatly increased since ancient times and the world has become more and more complex every year. Like other printed books, cookbooks reflect our complex society and our desire to keep up with advancing technology. Since cooking and eating are both vital and pleasurable, it should come as no surprise that large numbers of many different kinds of cookbooks are published annually. However, there are very few comprehensive or current guides to the numerous cookbooks available in bookstores and libraries. This is particularly true for the many specialized cookbooks that appear each year.

It is our aim to provide a catalog of recently published cookbooks that have been written on a variety of specialized topics. These books reflect a wide range of approaches and were written to satisfy various needs.

The number of cookbooks published in the last decade is so large that it was impossible to provide information about all of them in one volume. Therefore, general cookbooks, ethnic and regional cookery, and some categories of specialized cookbooks could not be listed in this volume.

The specialized cookbooks included in Volume I comprise a subject as well as chronological list of English language titles published from 1980 to 1990 in the United States, United Kingdom, Canada, and other English-speaking countries. Also included are those titles known to be in print regardless of publication date and in a few instances the only known cookbook found on a specific subject (e.g. papaws). This first volume is divided into four broad sections: specific ingredients (e.g. eggplants), types of dishes (e.g. desserts), specific meals (e.g. breakfast), and cooking techniques (e.g. baking).

Volume II will cover additional specialized topics such as special equipment, special diets, the cook's special needs, and miscellaneous special conditions.

In compiling this guide, we have used as our foundation bibliographic citations from the Library of Congress computerized catalogs, other national catalog databases, publisher's announcements, newspaper and periodical reviews of cookbooks, the *British National Bibliography*, and many other sources. Excluded from this guide are references to any newspaper and magazine articles, sources rich in cooking information, but too numerous and difficult to cite. We have also excluded audiovisual materials on cookery.

Although every effort was made to be as comprehensive and accurate as possible, we realize that omissions and errors were bound to occur. Since time did not permit us to examine all the 4,500 titles found, the citations listed do not address the quality of the publication. We welcome comments and suggestions from the users of this bibliography in order that future revisions will be more complete.

HOW TO USE THIS GUIDE

It is important for the users of this guide to familiarize themselves with the four section headings listed in the table of contents. Within each section is an alphabetical subject listing of cookbooks pertinent to that section's categories. Under each topical heading are citations listed by date of publication, arranged alphabetically by titles within a given year. Each entry is numbered. The headings assigned are as specific as possible, so the reader should look under Eggplants first in Section I, the ingredient section, instead of under the more general term: Vegetables. In addition, cross references at the end of each heading have been provided to and from the more specific and broader terms. With the exception of combination categories (i.e. fruits and vegetables, soups and salads, etc.), cookbooks that cover more than one topic are listed in

Introduction

only one category with references to the appropriate entry number from the other relevant categories. Cookbooks intended for children are listed last under a given category.

Each citation includes the full title of the work, statements of authorship and responsibility, edition statements, publication facts (place, publisher, date), and a brief physical description of the book (number of pages, presence of illustrations). We have also included information on whether the work was published in a series, and the presence of an index. The punctuation used is a modification of the International Standard Book Description (ISBD). A slash / separates the title from the statements of responsibility; a colon : precedes the subtitle and always follows the place of publication; parentheses ( ) enclose series statements. There are numerous notes that provide additional information such as the number of recipes in some cases. In many instances, we were able to provide the complete bibliographic history of the item including original titles, American and British titles, and dates of original publication. Prices of books were not included because such information becomes obsolete very quickly. Finally, we have provided author and title indexes to all the citations.

Abbreviations used in this guide

c1985	copyright date
ca.	circa (approximately)
Co.	Company
Corp.	Corporation
Dept.	Department
ed.	edition
enl.	enlarged
Govt.	Government
illus.	illustrations
Ltd.	Limited
n.p.	no place of publication
p.	page(s)
Pub.	Publishing
rev.	revised
v. or vol.	volume

Geographic abbreviations outside the United States

Alta.	Alberta
B.C.	British Columbia
Eng.	England
Man.	Manitoba
N.B.	New Brunswick
N.S.W.	New South Wales
N.Z.	New Zealand
N.T.	Northern Territory
N.W.T.	Northwest Territories
N.S.	Nova Scotia
Ont.	Ontario
P.E.I.	Prince Edward Island
Qld.	Queensland
R.O.C.	Republic of China
Sask.	Saskatchewan
Scot.	Scotland
S. Aust.	South Australia
W.I.	West Indies
Yukon	Yukon Territory

OBTAINING THE BOOKS

It is our hope that these citations will not only reflect the recent publishing history of specialty cookbooks but will also assist users in obtaining the books that meet their specific needs. This may not be an easy task. Cookbooks go out of print fairly quickly. Consulting a library is a good first step. While no library will have all of the books included in this guide, most larger libraries have access to national cataloging data bases such as OCLC or RLIN, which can determine the location of the item. If your library does not have the item, perhaps they will order it for you through interlibrary loan. While at the library, one can also check in *Books in Print* for addresses and telephone numbers of the publishers in case you are interested in buying the cookbook. The *Cumulative Book Index* (C.B.I.) and *Whitakers Books in Print* (for British books) also have lists of publishers and addresses. Many cookbooks are published by the author and may be purchased by writing directly to him or her. When addresses have not been provided by either this guide or Books in Print,

Introduction xi

it may be possible to find an address by consulting telephone books or city directories. Libraries frequently have collections of out-of-town telephone books. A good bookstore, particularly those specializing in cookbooks, may have many of the books and can provide assistance in obtaining a book, even if they don't have it in stock. If none of these sources work, perhaps an out-of-print bookdealer can offer assistance.

Harriet Ostroff and Tom Nichols
September 1991

Specialty Cookbooks

SECTION I

ABALONE TO ZUCCHINI
COOKBOOKS FOR SPECIFIC INGREDIENTS

Abalone

1. Crab & Abalone: West Coast Ways with Fish & Shellfish / Shirley Sarvis; designed & illustrated by Tony Calvello. Indianapolis, Ind.: Bobbs-Merrill, 1968. 160 p., illus.

see also broader category: Shellfish

Alligator Pears *see* Avocados

Almond Paste

2. Almond Paste Recipe Book / California Almond Growers Exchange. Sacramento, Calif.: The Exchange, 1982. 1 booklet.

Almonds

3. The New Treasury of Almond Recipes / Blue Diamond, the Almond People. Sacramento, Calif.: California Almond Growers Exchange, 1980. 1 v. Includes 100 recipes for salads, main dishes, vegetables, and desserts.

4. The Little Almond Cookbook / Mary L. Green. Denver, Colo.: Giftstar, 1984. ca. 10 p., illus. (Little Cookbooks).

5. New Almond Cookery / by Michelle Schmidt. New York: Simon and Schuster, c1984. 193 p., colored illus. Includes index.

see also broader category: Nuts

Aloe Vera

6. Cooking with the Vegetable Aloe Vera: v. I / by Jim Matney, Ann Matney, Jeannette Sanders, Joanne White. Clovis, Calif. (1510 Escalon, Clovis 93612): Matney, c1981. 40 p.

Amaranth

7. Allergy Recipes: Baking with Amaranth / Marge Jones. Deerfield, Ill.: Mast Enterprises, Inc., 1983. 17 p.

see also broader category: Grains

Anchovies

8. The Tomatoes, Cheese, and Anchovies Cookbook / Lillian Langseth-Christensen and Carol Sturm Smith; illustrations by Lillian Langseth-Christensen. New York: Walker, 1967. 96 p., illus.

see also broader category: Fish

Apple Butter

9. Sweet 'n' Slow: Apple Butter, Cane Molasses, and Sorghum Syrup Recipes / Patricia B. Mitchell. Rev. ed. Chatham, Va.: P.B. Mitchell, c1989. 37 p.

Apples

10. Apple Orchard Cook Book / Janet M. Christensen and Betty Bergman Levin. Stockbridge, Mass.: Berkshire Traveller Press, c1978. 155 p. Includes index.

11. One Hundred and One Apple Recipes / Carole Eberly. East Lansing, Mich.: Eberly Press, 1978. 48 p., illus.

Apples *(Continued)*

12. The Apple Cookbook / by Kyle D. Fulwiler. Seattle, Wash.: Pacific Search Press, c1980. 107 p. Includes index.

13. All American Apple Cookbook / by Sharon Kay Alexander and Kay Fairbairn. Santa Ana, Calif.: ABC Enterprises, c1982. 102 p., illus. Includes index.

14. Apples for Every Season / Jo Ann Aamodt. Stillwater, Minn. (6428 Manning Ave. North, Stillwater 55082): Aamodt Apple Farm, c1982. 105 p., illus. Includes index. Cover title: Cooking with Apples Every Season: A Collection of Favorite Recipes from the Aamodt Family.

15. The Apple Book / Jane Simpson and Gill MacLennan; illustrated by Cherry Denman. London, Eng.: Bodley Head, 1984. 160 p., illus. (some colored). Includes index.

16. The Apple Cookbook / Olwen Woodier; illustrations compiled or drawn by Andrea Gray and Leslie Fry. Pownal, Vt.: Garden Way Pub., c1984. 156 p., illus. Includes index.

17. Apple Magic / Marina Boudreau. Silver Spring, Md.: American Cooking Guild, 1984. 56 p.

18. Apples: Uses for the Whole Apple, with Recipes & Suggestions / Recycling Consortium. Houston, Tex.: Prosperity & Profits, 1984. 14 p.

19. From the Apple Orchard: Recipes for Apple Lovers: A Collection of Recipes for Apple Lovers Everywhere / by Lee Jackson; cover, illustrations, and calligraphy by Ione Pearson. 1st ed. Maryville, Mo.: Images Unlimited, c1984. 163 p., illus. More than 150 recipes. Includes index. Also published in Great Britain: London, Eng.: W.H. Allen, 1985.

20. Georgia Apple Recipes. Atlanta, Ga.: Georgia Apple Commission, ca. 1984. 20 p., illus.

Specialty Cookbooks

Apples *(Continued)*

21. The Little Apple Cookbook / Mary L. Green. Denver, Colo.: Giftstar, 1984. ca. 10 p., illus. (Little Cookbooks).

22. Making Apple Pies & Crusts / by Phyllis Hobson. Pownal, Vt.: Storey Communications, 1984, c1975. 62 p., illus. Includes index. Cover title: Garden Way Publishing's Making Apple Pies & Crusts. Reprint. Originally published: Making Homemade Apple Pies & Crusts. Charlotte, Vt.: Garden Way Pub., c1975.

23. The Apple Connection: Apple Cookery with Flavour, Fact and Folklore, from Memories, Libraries and Kitchens of Old and New Friends, and Strangers / compiled at Cranberrie Cottage in Granville Centre, Nova Scotia, by Beatrice Ross Buszek. Halifax, N.S.: Nimbus Pub., 1985. 204 p., illus. (some colored). Includes index.

24. The Big, Fat, Red, Juicy Apple Cookbook / edited by Judith Bosley. Middleton, Mich.: Grand Books, c1985. ca. 100 p.

25. Pick Your Own Apples, Oranges, and Pears: Locations with Apple, Orange, and Pear Recipes / Center for Self Sufficiency, Research Division Staff. Houston, Tex.: Prosperity & Profits, 1985. 50 p.

26. A is for Apple: Some Information About the Church Family Orchard of the Watervliet, N.Y. Shaker Community / text prepared by Elizabeth Shaver; illustrations by Elizabeth Lee. Albany, N.Y.: The Shaker Heritage Society, 1986. 36 p., illus. Includes bibliography.

27. Apple Garnishing: With Full-Color Photos and Step-by-Step Instructions / Harvey Rosen, Kevin O'Malley. Elberon, N.J.: International Culinary Consultants, c1986. 95 p., illus. (some colored).

28. Apple Sampler / Jan Siegrist. Shelburne, Vt.: New England Press, 1986. 250 p., illus.

Apples *(Continued)*

29. Apples, Apples, Apples / Judith Comfort and Kathy Chute. 1st ed. Toronto, Ont.: Doubleday Canada; Garden City, N.Y.: Doubleday, 1986. 300 p., illus. Includes indexes.

30. Maine Apples, Blue Ribbon Recipes: Delicious, Nutritious & Really Good. Augusta, Me.: Maine Bureau of Agricultural Marketing, 1987? 9 p.

31. Apples Everyday / Thelma B. Cooper. Williamsport? Pa.: T.B. Cooper, c1988. 72 p., illus. Includes index.

32. Country Cooking with A-peel: A Treasury of Apple Cookery, Over 300 Ways to Use Fresh & Dried Apples / Margaret Gubin. Juneau, Wis. (N7160 County Highway I, Juneau 53039): Country Cupboard Pub., c1988. 269 p., illus. (some colored). Includes index.

33. A Harvest of Apples / Ruth Ward. Harmondsworth, Eng.: Penguin, 1988. 263 p.

34. Apple Country Cooking: Apple Recipes, Anecdotes, and a Commemoration of Johnny Appleseed / Patricia B. Mitchell. Chatham, Va.: P.B. Mitchell, c1989. 37 p. (Patricia B. Mitchell Foodways Publications).

35. Apple-Lovers' Cook Book / by Shirley Munson and Jo Nelson. Phoenix, Ariz.: Golden West Publishers, c1989. 119 p., illus.

see also broader category: Fruits

Apricots

36. California Apricot Growers' Favorite Recipes. Walnut Creek, Calif.: California Apricot Advisory Board, 1980. 36 p.

37. The Little Apricot Cookbook / Mary L. Green. Denver, Colo.: Giftstar, 1984. ca. 10 p., illus. (Little Cookbooks).

Apricots *(Continued)*

38. The Complete Apricot Cookbook / Gerry Adams. Kennewick, Wash. (Rte. 11, Box 11295, Kennewick 99337): Adams Place, c1985. 104 p. Includes index.

39. A Glut of Apricots & Peaches / Ann Carr. London, Eng.: Merehurst, 1988. 92 p.

40. Lots of 'Cots: Cooking with Apricots / compiled by Rita Gennis; illustrations, Sari Gennis. Carmichael, Calif.: Ben Ali Books, c1988. 62 p., illus. (some colored). 100 recipes.

see also broader category: Fruits

Artichokes

41. The Little Artichoke Cookbook / Mary L. Green. Denver, Colo.: Giftstar, 1984. ca. 10 p., illus. (Little Cookbooks).

42. The Artichoke Cookbook / Patricia Rain. Berkeley, Calif.: Celestial Arts, c1985. 174 p., illus. More than 100 recipes. Includes index.

see also broader category: Vegetables

Asparagus

43. Asparagus: A Miscellany of Gastronomic and Horticultural Information and Therapeutic Remedies / Jane Wilton-Smith & Maria Donkin; drawings by Bear. Salisbury, Eng.: Stylus, 1986. 24 p., illus. (The Good Table).

44. Asparagus, All Ways--Always / Cookbook Committee, Glenda Hushaw and others; illustrations by Bill Kobus. Souvenir ed. Stockton, Calif. (46 W. Fremont St., Stockton 95202): Stockton Asparagus Festival, c1986. 149 p., illus. 150 recipes. Includes index.

Specific Ingredients

Asparagus *(Continued)*

45. The Asparagus Cookbook / by the Stockton Asparagus Festival. Berkeley, Calif.: Celestial Arts, 1987. 148 p. Includes index.

see also broader category: Vegetables

Avocados

46. The Little Green Avocado Book / Linda Doeser. New York: St. Martin's Press, 1983, c1981. 60 p., illus.

47. The Amazing Avocado / by Leah Leneman; illustrated by Ian Jones. Wellingborough, Eng.: Thorsons, c1984. 96 p., illus. (A Thorsons Wholefood Cookbook). Includes index.

48. The Little Avocado Cookbook / Mary L. Green. Denver, Colo.: Giftstar, 1984. ca. 10 p., illus. (Little Cookbooks).

49. The Avocado Lovers' Cookbook / Joyce Carlisle. Berkeley, Calif.: Celestial Arts in association with Blue Ribbon Publishers, c1985. 140 p., illus. More than 150 recipes. Includes index.

50. Avocado Recipes, etc. / Teri Gordon. Austin, Tex. (10901 Rustic Manor Lane, Austin 78750): T. Gordon, c1987. 164 p., illus. ca. 300 recipes. Includes index.

51. A Glut of Avocados / Ann Carr. London, Eng.: Merehurst, 1988. 92 p.

see also entry 2286; and broader category: Fruits

Bacon

52. The Best of Bacon Cookbook / edited by Mary Norwak & Emma Manderson. London, Eng.: Quiller, 1987. 144 p.

see also broader category: Pork

Bananas

53. Green Banana Recipes / compiled by Compañía Bananera de Costa Rica. Golfito, Costa Rica: Compañía Bananera de Costa Rica, 198-. 70 p. Cover title: All You Need Is Under the Peel.

54. Bananas by the Bunch: A Book of Favorite Recipes / compiled by Edith M. VeuCasovic, her family, and friends. Bexar, Ark.: E.M. VeuCasovic, c1982. 116 p., illus. Includes index.

55. Banana Cookbook / Reba E. Shepard. London, Eng.: Macmillan, 1986. 96 p., illus. Includes index.

56. The Banana Book / by Dana Yuen Black; with illustrations by Teresa San Miguel and Dover Publications. Hilo, Hawaii: Petroglyph Press, c1988. 53 p., illus. Includes index.

CHILDREN'S COOKBOOKS

57. The Great Banana Cookbook for Boys and Girls / by Eva Moore; illustrated by Susan Russo. New York: Clarion Books, c1983. 48 p., illus. Presents eleven simple recipes to use with a bunch of bananas, starting with the firmest fruit and working to the ripest.

see also broader category: Fruits

Specific Ingredients

Barley

58. The Best of Barley / written by Illa Darlene Thompson. 1st ed. Melfort, Sask.: I.D. Thompson, 1987. 106 p., 14 p. of colored plates.

see also Green Barley Juice; *and broader category:* Grains

Basil

59. The Basil Book / Marilyn Hampstead; illustrations by Isadore Seltzer; basil drawings by Maggie LaNoue. New York: Pocket Books, c1984. 148 p., illus. Includes index. "Long Shadow Books."

see also broader category: Herbs

Bean Curd *see* Tofu

Beans

60. The Bean Cookbook / Tess Mallos. Leicester, Eng.: Windward, c1980. 128 p., illus. (some colored). Includes index.

61. Bean Cookery / Sue & Bill Deeming. Tucson, Ariz.: HP Books, c1980. 160 p., illus. Includes index.

62. Growing and Cooking Beans / by John E. Withee; illustrated by Ray Maher; cover photo by Frank Cordelle. 1st ed. Dublin, N.H.: Yankee, 1980. 143 p., illus. Includes index.

63. Bean Feast / Pamela Westland. London, Eng.: Granada, 1981. 189 p. (A Mayflower Book). Includes index.

64. Beans & Peas / by Inez M. Krech. 1st ed. New York: Primavera Books/Crown, c1981. 64 p.

Beans *(Continued)*

65. The Bean Cookbook: Dry Legume Cookery / by Norma S. Upson. Seattle, Wash.: Pacific Search Press, c1982. 153 p. Includes index.

66. Bean Cuisine / Janet Horsley; illustrated by Andrew Pomeroy. Dorchester, Eng.: Prism, 1982. 89 p., illus. Includes index.

67. Cooking with Dried Beans / by Sara Pitzer. Pownal, Vt.: Garden Way Pub., c1982. 32 p., illus. (Garden Way Bulletin; A-77).

68. Dried Beans & Grains / by the editors of Time-Life Books. Alexandria, Va.: Time-Life Books; Morristown, N.J.: School and library distribution by Silver Burdett, c1982. 176 p., illus. (The Good Cook, Technique & Recipes). Includes indexes.

69. Explore the Magic World of California Beans with Jack Beanstalk M.B.A. (master of bean arts). Dinuba, Calif.: Dry Bean Advisory Board, 1982. 15 p., illus.

70. Beans in My Boots / Hoppie Stibolt. Memphis, Tenn.: S.C. Toof & Co., 1983. 28 p., illus.

71. The Little Bean Book / Judy Ridgway. Loughton, Eng.: Piatkus, 1983. 60 p., illus.

72. The Little Brown Bean Book / by David Eno; illustrated by Clive Birch. Enl., rev. and reset ed. Wellingborough, Eng.: Thorsons, 1983. 55 p., illus. Includes index. Originally published in 1978.

73. Bean Banquets, from Boston to Bombay: 200 International, High-Fiber, Vegetarian Recipes / by Patricia R. Gregory; illustrations by Robert G. Gregory; foreword by Fred W. Rio. Santa Barbara, Calif.: Woodbridge Press, c1984. 238 p., illus. Includes index.

Beans *(Continued)*

74. Bean Cuisine / Nan Tupper Chapman. Toronto, Ont.: Rebecca Clarkes Pub., 1984. 208 p., illus. Includes indexes.

75. Beanfest / Rose Elliot. Rev. and expanded ed. London, Eng.: Fontana, 1985. 127 p., illus. Includes index.

76. Spilling the Beans: Into These Recipes. Frazee, Minn.: Red River Edible Bean Growers Assoc., 1987. 10 p., illus.

77. Western Bean Cookery: Recipes, Menus, Information / Robert W. Wolfe. Ellington, Conn. (P.O. Box 322, Ellington 06029): Action Foods, c1987. 43 p., illus. Includes index.

78. The WIC Bean Book. Jefferson City, Mo.: Special Supplemental Food Program for Women, Infants and Children (WIC), Dept. of Health, 1987? 29 p., illus.

79. The All-American Bean Book / F.H. "Ted" Waskey; illustrations by Martin Berman. New York: Simon & Schuster, c1988. 207 p., illus. More than 125 recipes. Includes index. "A Fireside Book."

80. The Brilliant Bean / Sally and Martin Stone. Toronto; New York: Bantam Books, 1988. 276 p. 175 recipes. Includes index.

81. Healthy Bean Dishes / Cecilia J. Au-Yeung. Cincinnati, Ohio: Seven Hills Book Distributors, 1988. 128 p., illus. (Chopsticks Recipes). In Chinese and English.

82. Better Bean Microwave Recipes: And More. Whitby, Ont.: Stokely-Van Camp of Canada, c1989. 28 p.

83. The Little Bean Book / by Margie F. Tyler. Brandon, Miss.: Quail Ridge Press, 1989. 104 p. Includes index.

84. Jean's Beans: Favorite Recipes from Around the World / Jean Hoare. Rev. ed. Port Coquitlam, B.C.: The Spirit of Cooking Pub., 1990. ca. 130 p.

Beans *(Continued)*

85. The Little Bean Cookbook / Patricia Stapley; illustrations by Jennie Oppenheimer. New York: Crown, 1990. 64 p., colored illus. 20 recipes with nutrition information for each.

86. More Than Soup: Bean Cookbook / by Anna Aughenbaugh. Fort Collins, Colo.: Starlite Publications, 1990. 102 p. 112 recipes.

    see also entries 903, 1331, 1667, 1908; Soybeans; *and broader category:* Legumes

Bear Meat

87. Bears in My Kitchen: An Exclusive Collection of Black Bear Recipes / by Carol Suddendorf. 1st ed. Bovey, Minn. (Makwa Guide Service, Rt. 2, Box 304C-1, Bovey 55709): C. Suddendorf, c1988. 131 p. Includes index.

    see also broader category: Game

Beef

88. The All Beef Cookbook / recipes compiled and tested by the American National CowBelles. New York: Benjamin Co.; Distributed by Scribner, 1973. 223 p., colored illus.

89. Quick and Easy Ways with Beef. Toronto, Ont.: Beef Information Centre, 1982. 7 p.

90. Beef & Veal. Newton Abbot, Eng.: David & Charles, c1983. 63 p., illus. (some colored). (Kitchen Workshop). Includes index. Translation of: Okse- of Kalvekjott.

91. Beef Sounds Good, Good Value Cookbook. Toronto, Ont.: Beef Information Centre, 1983 or 4. 16 p.

Beef *(Continued)*

92. Beef Sounds Good, on a Barbecue. Toronto, Ont.: Beef Information Centre, 1983. 15 p.

93. Florida CowBelles Cookbook / compiled and edited by Carolyn Kempfer and Sarah K. Childs; calligraphy and drawings by Jayne M. Masaro. Fort Pierce, Fla.: Plaza Press, 1983. 164 p., illus.

94. Beef & Veal Menus. Alexandria, Va.: Time-Life Books, 1984. 105 p., illus. (some colored). (Great Meals in Minutes). Includes index.

95. Dear James Beard: Recipes and Reminiscing from Your Friends and the Beef Industry Council. Chicago, Ill.: The Council, c1984. 47 p., colored illus.

96. The Epicure's Book of Steak and Beef Dishes / Marguerite Patten. London, Eng.: Treasure, 1984, c1979. 168 p., illus. (some colored). Includes bibliography and index.

97. Beef Dishes / text, Hae Sung Hwang, [and others]; translator, Miyoung Kim Lee. Seoul, Korea: Ju Bu Saeng & Hak Won, 1985. 62 p., colored illus. (Korean Card Cook; 2).

98. A Cowboy's Cookbook / by T.L. Bush; with the photographs of Erwin E. Smith. Austin, Tex.: Texas Monthly Press, c1985. 104 p., illus. Includes index. "Photographs from the Erwin E. Smith Collection of Range Life Photographs, Library of Congress."

99. Making the Most of Beef & Veal / Robert Carrier. London, Eng.: Marshall Cavendish, 1985. 112 p., colored illus. (Robert Carrier's Kitchen). Includes index.

100. The Steakhouse Cookbook: A Collection of the Best Recipes from the Great Steakhouses of the U.S. / by Joan and Joe Foley. New York: Freundlich Books: Distributed by Scribner, c1985. 152 p., illus. Includes index.

Specialty Cookbooks

Beef *(Continued)*

101. Beef, Light Lean Beef Recipes for Contemporary Lifestyles / by Karen Chase & Tracy Bell; illustrated by Karen Chase. Calgary, Alta.: C & B Communications, 1986. 175 p., colored illus. Includes index.

102. Beef Recipe Round-up / Julie Steeves, editor. Kamloops, B.C.: B.C. CattleBelles, 1986. 217 p., illus. (some colored). Includes index.

103. The Maine-Anjou Association Cookbook / North American Maine-Anjou Association. Burnstown, Ont.: General Store Pub., c1986. 132 p., illus. Includes index.

104. The New Look of Beef / by Kathleen Crowley. Toronto, Ont.: Grosvenor House Press, c1986. 175 p., 10 leaves of colored plates. Includes indexes. "All recipes in this cookbook conform to the Canadian Heart Foundation's nutritional guidelines, which attempt to reduce the likelihood of heart disease by limiting fat content in the diet."

105. Beef. Toronto, Ont.: Grolier, 1987. 108 p., colored illus. (Microwave Magic; 1). Includes index.

106. Beef: King of the American Dinner Table / written and edited by Vicki Kyler. Jefferson City, Mont.: V. Kyler, c1987. 340 p.

107. Fresh Ways with Beef & Lamb / by the editors of Time-Life Books. Alexandria, Va.: Time-Life Books, c1987. 144 p., colored illus. (Healthy Home Cooking). Includes index.

108. Beef II. Toronto, Ont.: Grolier, 1988. 110 p., colored illus. (Microwave Magic; 8).

109. The Art of Cooking with Certified Angus Beef: A Collection of Recipes by Distinguished Chefs. West Salem, Ohio: Published by Culinaire for Certified Angus Beef, 1989. 80 p., colored illus.

Specific Ingredients

Beef *(Continued)*

110. Beef and Veal. Toronto, Ont.: Grolier, 1989. 1 v. (Creative Cook; 1).

111. The Beef Lover's Guide to Weight Control and Lower Cholesterol / by Chriss McNaught; illustrated by Jerry Palen. 1st ed. The Woodlands, Tex.: Portfolio Pub. Co., c1989. 236 p., illus. (some colored). More than 200 recipes. Includes index.

112. Fresh Ways with Beef & Veal / by the editors of Time-Life Books. Alexandria, Va.: Time-Life Books, 1989. 144 p., colored illus. (Healthy Home Cooking). Includes index.

113. James McNair's Beef Cookbook / photography by Patricia Brabant. San Francisco, Calif.: Chronicle Books, c1989. 96 p., colored illus. 40 recipes. Includes index.

114. How Steak Is Done: The A.1. Cookbook. East Hanover, N.J.: Nabisco Foods Co., c1990. 13 p., colored illus. 25 recipes.

see also Ground Meat; *and broader category:* Meat

Beef Jerky

115. Beef Jerky Recipes for in the Home or on the Trail / by Jeffrey A. Goodsell, William H. Nelson. Bradford, Pa. (P.O. Box 2395, Bradford 16701): Human Interest Publishers, c1984. 19 p., illus.

see also broader category: Beef

Beer

116. Cooking with Beer / by Hunter Edmunds. Timberlea, N.S.: Timberlea Press, c1980. 31 p., illus.

18 *Specialty Cookbooks*

Beer *(Continued)*

117. Cooking with Beer / Annette Ashlock Stover and the Culinary Arts Institute staff; Edward G. Finnegan, executive editor; book designed and coordinated by Charles Bozett; illustrations by Seymour Fleishman; photos. by Zdenek Pivecka. New York: Culinary Arts Institute, c1980. 96 p., illus. Includes index.

118. A Taste of the West from Coors / editor, Anita Krajeski. Des Moines, Iowa (Locust at 17th, Des Moines 50336): Meredith Pub. Services, c1981. 96 p., illus. (some colored). Includes indexes.

119. The Little Beer Cookbook / Mary L. Green. Denver, Colo.: Giftstar, 1984. ca. 10 p., illus. (Little Cookbooks).

120. Cooking with Beer / Angela Mayes, editor. Aylesbury, Eng.: Goodchild, 1986. 96 p., illus. (The Good Cook Series).

121. Cooking with Beer: In the Spirit of Things / Barbara L. Lacy. Dallas, Tex.: Golightly Publications, 1987. 56 p., illus.

122. Brew Cuisine: Cooking with Beer / by Judith Gould and Ruth Koretsky. Toronto, Ont.: Summerhill Press; New York: Distributed by Sterling Pub. Co., c1989. 192 p., illus. Includes index.

123. Great Cooking with Beer / by Jack Erickson. Reston, Va.: RedBrick Press, 1989. 146 p., illus.

see also broader category: **Liquors**

Berries

124. The Berry Cookbook / Carol Katz; illustrations by Judith Fast. New York: Butterick Pub., 1980. 176 p., illus. Includes index.

Berries *(Continued)*

125. Growing and Cooking Berries / by Mary W. Cornog; illustrated by Ray Maher. 1st ed. Dublin, N.H.: Yankee, 1980. 141 p., illus. Includes index.

126. Northwestern Wild Berries / J.E. Underhill. 2nd ed. Saanichton, B.C.: Hancock House, 1980. 96 p., colored illus. Includes bibliography and index.

127. Summer Berries / Elizabeth Baird. Toronto, Ont.: J. Lorimer, 1980. 128 p. (Great Canadian Recipes). Includes index.

128. The Berry Book: The Illustrated Home Gardener's Guide to Growing and Using Over 50 Kinds and 300 Varieties of Berries / by Robert Hendrickson. 1st ed. Garden City, N.Y.: Doubleday, 1981. 259 p., illus.

129. Alaska Wild Berry Guide and Cookbook / by the editors of Alaska Magazine; illustrations by Virginia Howie. Anchorage, Alaska: Alaska Northwest Pub. Co., c1982. 201 p., illus. (some colored). Includes indexes.

130. Berried Treasures Cookbook: Just Possibly the Most Scrumptious Collection of Berry Recipes Ever Assembled / by Elaine Jauman; cover and illustrations by Photo Offset Printing. Rev. ed. Escanaba, Mich.: Kitchen Treasures, 1983, c1982. 128 p., illus. Includes index.

131. More Berried Treasures, and Other Good Pickin's / by Elaine Jauman; cover and illustrations by Photo Offset Printing. Escanaba, Mich.: Kitchen Treasures, c1983. 128 p., illus.

132. The Berry Cookbook / by Henry R. Lorenzo; illustrated by Suzanne L. Leonard. San Francisco, Calif.: Easy Banana Press, c1984. 93 p., illus. Includes index. "A Terrier Book."

Specialty Cookbooks

Berries *(Continued)*

133. Berries Beautiful: An All-Season Cookbook for Lovers of Strawberries and Raspberries / by Carol Kutzli Olson. Spy Hill, Sask.: C. Olson Pub., 1985. 110 p., colored illus. Includes index.

134. The Berry Cookbook / by Kyle D. Fulwiler. 2nd ed., rev. and enl. Seattle, Wash.: Pacific Search Press, c1985. 117 p. Includes index.

135. Pick Your Own Blueberries, Raspberries, and Other Berries: Locations with Berry Recipes / Center for Self Sufficiency, Research Division Staff. Houston, Tex.: Prosperity & Profits, 1985. 50 p.

136. It's the Berries!: Exotic and Common Recipes / by Liz Anton and Beth Dooley. Pownal, Vt.: Storey Communications, c1988. 156 p. Includes index. "A Gardening Way Publishing Book."

137. Berries: Cultivation, Decoration, and Recipes / text by Mary Forsell; photographs by Tony Cenicola; foreword by Rosemary Verey; design by Liz Trovato. New York: Bantam Books, 1989. 288 p., ca. 200 colored photos. Includes indexes.

138. Berries: A Cookbook / Robert Berkley; photographs by Eric Jacobson. New York: Simon & Schuster, c1990. 120 p., illus. 50 recipes. "A Fireside Book." Includes guide to mail-order sources for a variety of berries.

139. The New England Berry Book: Field Guide & Cookbook / Bob Krumm. Camden, Me.: Yankee Books, c1990. 110 p., 16 p. of plates, illus (some colored). Includes bibliography and index.

see also specific kinds of berries: Blackberries, Blueberries, Cranberries, Huckleberries, Raspberries, Strawberries; *and broader category:* Fruits

Bisquick

140. Betty Crocker's Creative Recipes with Bisquick. Minneapolis, Minn.: General Mills, c1980. 96 p., colored illus. Includes index.

141. Bisquick Classics Collection. Minneapolis, Minn.: General Mills, 1989. 91 p., colored illus. (Betty Crocker Creative Recipes; no. 30). Includes index.

Blackberries

142. Blackberry Delights: A Blackberry Connoisseur's Specialty Cookbook / Lynda L. Harter; illustrations by Darlene Kuppersmith. Rev. 2nd ed. Bend, Or.: Maverick Publications, c1990. 98 p., illus. Includes index.

see also broader category: Berries

Blackfish

143. Blackfish-Tautog / by R. Marilyn Schmidt. Barnegat Light, N.J.: Barnegat Light Press, 1989. 24 p.

see also broader category: Fish

Blueberries

144. Blueberry Cookbook. Plymouth, Ind.: Love Inc., 198-. 1 v.

145. The Blueberry Connection: Blueberry Cookery with Flavour, Fact, and Folklore, from Memories, Libraries, and Kitchens of Old and New Friends and Strangers / compiled by Beatrice Ross Buszek. 2d ed. Brattleboro, Vt.: S. Greene Press, c1980. 209 p., illus.

Specialty Cookbooks

Blueberries *(Continued)*

146. Blueberry Thrills / by Katherine Knapp Aho. [n.p.]: K.K. Aho, c1981 (Walla Walla, Wash.: Eastgate Printing) 100 p. Includes index.

147. Favorite Blueberry Recipes: from Ryan's Berry Farm / compiled by Tom Ryan, Tyra Clogh. Frankford, Del.: T. Ryan, 1984. 105 p., illus. Includes index.

148. All About Blueberries / by R. Marilyn Schmidt. 1st ed. Barnegat Light, N.J.: Pine Barrens Press, 1985. 1 v. (various pagings). 101 recipes.

149. Basically Blue: A Collection of Blueberry Recipes / Fern Walker. Carp, Ont.: Gai-Garet Design & Publication, 1986. 76 p., colored illus.

150. A Taste of Blueberries / Gail Anderson. York, Pa.: Wellspring, c1986. 14 p. 14 recipes.

151. Blueberry Sampler: A Collection of Fresh Blueberry Recipes / by Jan Siegrist. Shelburne, Vt.: New England Press, 1988. 48 p., illus.

see also broader category: Berries

Bluefish

152. Secrets of Bluefishing / by D.W. Bennett. Killingworth, Conn.: Hancock House, c1982. 72 p., illus. (Hancock House Fishing Series).

153. Bluefish / by R. Marilyn Schmidt. Barnegat Light, N.J.: Barnegat Light Press, 1989. 24 p.

Specific Ingredients 23

Bluefish *(Continued)*

154. The Bluefish Cookbook / Greta Jacobs & Jane Alexander; illustrated by Wezi Swift. 4th ed., rev. and expanded. Chester, Conn.: Globe Pequot Press, c1990. ca. 105 p., illus. Includes index.

see also broader category: Fish

Bouillon Cubes

155. Bouillon is Basic: Wyler's New Idea Book. Columbus, Ohio: Borden, Inc., 1980. 1 booklet.

156. Bring Out the Basic: Wyler's New Idea Book. Columbus, Ohio: Borden, Inc., 1983. 1 booklet. 157 recipes.

Bran

157. The Cooking with Bran Cookbook. Minnetonka, Minn.: Cy DeCosse, Inc., 1984. 1 v., photos.

see also Oat Bran; *and broader category:* Grains

Brandy

158. Stan Jones' Cooking with the Christian Brothers Brandy / by Stan Jones; with photography by John Guarente. Los Angeles, Calif.: Bar Guide Enterprises, c1982. 190 p., colored illus. Includes index.

159. California Brandy Cuisine: Celebrating 200 Years of California Brandy / by Malcolm Hebert. San Francisco, Calif.: Wine Appreciation Guild, c1984. 124 p., illus. Includes index.

see also broader category: Liquors

Specialty Cookbooks

Bread Crumbs

160. The Humble Crumb / Elizabeth Jones. London, Eng.: Lion, 1989. 128 p.

Broccoli

161. The Gardens for All Book of Cauliflower, Broccoli & Cabbage / by Dick and Jan Raymond. Burlington, Vt.: Gardens for All, 1984, c1980. 31 p., illus.

see also broader category: Vegetables

Brown Rice

162. The New Age Brown Rice Cookbook / compiled by Gail Pierce; illustrated by Gail Pierce & Richard Pierce. Carmel, Calif.: Sea-Wind Press, c1982. 171 p., illus. Includes index.

163. The Little Brown Rice Book / by David Eno; illustrated by Clive Burch. Enl., rev. and reset ed. Wellingborough, Eng.: Thorsons, 1983. 56 p., illus. Includes index.

164. Brown Rice Cookbook: Traditional World-Wide Western Recipes / by Jacques and Yvette De Langre. Magalia, Calif.: Happiness Press, 1984. 32 p., illus.

165. The Brown Rice Cookbook / Gail Pierce. London, Eng.: W.H. Allen, 1985. 153 p.

166. The Brown Rice Cookbook: A Selection of Delicious Wholesome Recipes / by Craig and Ann Sams. Rochester, Vt.: Healing Arts Press, c1988. 98 p. Includes index. Reprint. Originally published: New York: Thorsons: Distributed by Inner Traditions International, 1983.

Brown Rice *(Continued)*

167. Genmai: Brown Rice for Better Health / Eiwan Ishida; translated by Frederic P. Metreaud. Briarcliff Manor, N.Y.: Japan Publications, 1988. 256 p.

see also broader category: Rice

Buckwheat Groats

168. Wolff's Buckwheat Cookbook. Penn Yan, N.Y.: Birkett Mills, 1980? 35 p., colored illus. ca. 50 recipes.

see also broader category: Grains

Buckwheat Noodles *see* Soba

Buffalo

169. Buffalo Cookbook / Judi Hebbring. Custer, S.D.: National Buffalo Association, 1981. 33 p.

170. Buffalo at Steak / Ann Oakland. Boulder, Colo.: One Percent, 1983. 32 p., illus.

171. Buffalo Cook Book, Buffalo Meat / editor, Kim Dowling. Fort Pierre, S.D.: National Buffalo Association, c1989. 32 p.

see also broader category: Game; Meat

Bulgur *see* Wheat

Buttermilk

172. Cooking with Sour Cream and Buttermilk / by staff home economists, Culinary Arts Institute, Melanie De Proft, director, and others; illustrated by Davi Botts. Chicago, Ill.: Culinary Arts Institute, 1973. 68 p., illus.

   see also broader category: Dairy Products

Cabbage

173. Of Cabbages and the King: The World Cabbage Cookbook / by Eloise Paananen; illustrated by Brant Parker. White Hall, Va.: Betterway Publications, c1984. 189 p., illus. (some colored). Includes index.

174. Cabbage: Cures to Cuisine / by Judith M. Hiatt. Happy Camp, Calif.: Naturegraph, 1989. 80 p., illus. Includes bibliography.

175. Alaskan Grown Cabbage: More than Just Sauerkraut / by Ellen Ayotte. Rev. Fairbanks, Alaska, University of Alaska, Cooperative Extension Services, 1990. 11 p., illus.

   see also entry 161; and broader category: Vegetables

Cake Mixes

176. Bake Shop in a Book / Duncan Hines. Cincinnati, Ohio: Proctor & Gamble Co., 1980. 1 loose leaf vol., colored illus. 242 recipes for desserts and snacks. Includes index.

177. Pillsbury Plus Recipe Cookbook, v. 2. Minneapolis, Minn.: Pillsbury Co., 1980. 48 p.

178. Baking with American Dash / Duncan Hines. Cincinnati, Ohio: Proctor & Gamble Co., 1985. 1 booklet.

Cake Mixes *(Continued)*

179. Duncan Hines Celebrates Baking. New York: Beekman House, 1990. 96 p., colored illus. More than 80 recipes. Includes index.

see also Cakes *(Section II)*

Calamari *see* Squid

Canned Chicken

180. No Fuss Chicken Recipe Booklet / Swanson Chunk Chicken. Camden, N.J.: Campbell Soup Co., 1980. 1 booklet.

see also broader categories: Canned Foods; Chicken

Canned Fish

181. The Canned Fish Cookbook / Lillian Langseth-Christensen and Carol Sturm Smith; line drawings by Lillian Langseth-Christensen. Walker large print ed. New York: Walker, 1984, c1968. 96 p., illus. Includes index.

see also entries 1928, 1929, 1932, 2296-2298; and broader categories: Canned Foods; Fish

Canned Foods

182. The New New Can-Opener Cookbook / Poppy Cannon. New York: Crowell, 1968. 314 p. First published in 1951 under title: The Can-Opener Cookbook.

183. The Easy Can Opener Cookbook / William I. Kaufman. Old Tappan, N.J.: Hewitt House, 1969. 160 p.

Canned Soups

184. Cooking with Confidence in Your Microwave: A Campbell Cookbook. Camden, N.J.: Campbell Soup Co., 1980. 1 v., colored illus.

185. The Creative Cook: A Campbell Cookbook. Camden, N.J.: Campbell Soup Co., 1980. 1 v., colored illus.

186. The International Cook. Camden, N.J.: Campbell Soup Co., 1980. 1 v., colored illus. 142 recipes from 30 different countries. Includes glossary and index.

187. Most for the Money Main Dishes: A Campbell Cookbook. Camden, N.J.: Campbell Soup Co., 1980. ca. 130 p., colored illus.

188. Campbell's Creative Cooking with Soup. New York: Beekman House: Distributed by Crown Publishers, c1985. 224 p., colored illus. More than 19,000 mix and match recipes. Includes index.

189. Campbell's Creative Cooking with Soup. 4th ed, New York: Beekman House: Distributed by Crown Publishers, c1985. 96 p., colored illus. More than 10,000 mix and match recipes. Includes index. "This edition is an abridged version of Campbell's Creative Cooking with Soup (1985)."

see also broader category: Canned Foods; *and* Soups *(Section II)*

Carob

190. Cooking with Carob: The Healthful Alternative to Chocolate / by Frances Sheridan Goulart. Charlotte, Vt.: Garden Way, c1980. 32 p., illus. (Garden Way Bulletin; A-48). Includes bibliography.

191. The Carob Way to Health: All-Natural Recipes for Cooking with Nature's Healthful Chocolate Alternative / Frances Sheridan Goulart. New York: Warner Books, c1982. 147 p.

Specific Ingredients

Carob *(Continued)*

192. Juel Andersen's Carob Primer: A Beginner's Book of Carob Cookery / Robin Clute, Juel Andersen, with Sigrid Andersen. Berkeley, Calif. (833 Bancroft Way, Berkeley, Calif. 94701): Creative Arts Communications, 1983. 56 p., illus. Includes index.

193. The Carob Cookbook / by Lorraine Whiteside; illustrated by Ian Jones. Rev., enl. and reset. Wellingborough, Eng.: Thorsons, 1984. 192 p., illus. (A Thorsons Wholefood Cookbook). Includes index.

194. The Here's Health Alternative Chocolate Book / Janette Marshall. London, Eng.: Century, 1986. 128 p., 20 p. of plates; illus. (some colored). Includes index.

195. Carob Cookbook / Tricia Hamilton. 1st ed. Santa Fe, N.M.: Sunstone Press, c1989. ca. 140 p. Includes index.

see also broader category: Natural Foods

Carrots

196. The Carrot Cookbook / by Ann Saling; drawings by Darci Covington. 3rd ed. Edmonds, Wash.: Ansal Press, 1980. ca. 160 p., illus. Includes index.

197. Carrot Cookbook / Lynn and Bob Barry. Prescott, Ark.: Barry Pub. Co., c1981. 92 p., illus. (Encyclopedia of Fresh Vegetable Cooking; v. 1). Includes index.

198. The Gourmet Carrot Cookbook. Howey-in-the-Hills, Fla.: Central Florida Wildlife Adoption Society, 1984. 98 p., illus. (some colored). Includes indexes.

Carrots *(Continued)*

199. The Carrot Cookbook / by Audra and Jack Hendrickson. 1st ed. Pownal, Vt.: Storey Communications, c1986. 171 p., illus. Includes index. "A Garden Way Publishing Book."

    see also broader category: Vegetables

Cashews

200. The Little Cashew Cookbook / Mary L. Green. Denver, Colo.: Giftstar, 1984. ca. 10 p., illus. (Little Cookbooks).

    see also broader category: Nuts

Catfish

201. The Catfish Cookbook / edited by Barry Fast. Charlotte, N.C.: East Woods Press, c1982. 126 p., illus. Includes index.

    see also broader category: Fish

Cauliflower

see entry 161; and broader category: Vegetables

Caviar

202. All About Caviar / by R. Marilyn Schmidt. Barnegat Light, N.J.: Barnegat Light Press, 198-. 32 p. 23 recipes.

203. Caviar! Caviar! Caviar! / by Gerald M. Stein, with Donald Bain. 1st ed. Secaucus, N.J.: L. Stuart, c1981. 220 p., illus. (some colored).

Caviar *(Continued)*

204. Caviar / Susan R. Friedland. 1st ed. New York: Scribner, c1986. 152 p. 100 recipes. Includes index.

see also broader category: Fish

Cereals *see* **Grains**

Cheese

205. The World of Cheese / Evan Jones. 1st ed. New York: Knopf: Distributed by Random House, 1976. 298 p., illus. Includes bibliography and index.

206. Complete Cheese Cookbook / Kraft Foods. New York: Benjamin Co., 1977. 1 v., illus.

207. Good Food Ideas Cheese Cookbook from Kraft. New York: Benjamin Co., 1977. 244 p., illus. (some colored). Includes index.

208. Cheese Cookery / Doris McFerran Townsend. Tucson, Ariz.: HP Books, c1980. 160 p., illus. (some colored). Includes index.

209. Cooking with Cheese / Mary Berry; illustrations by Laura Potter. London, Eng.: Batsford, 1980. 144 p., illus. Includes index.

210. Sargento Cheese Recipe Booklet. Plymouth, Wis.: Sargento Cheese, 1980. 1 booklet.

211. Velveeta Cookbook. Glenview, Ill.: Kraft, Inc., 1980. 1 booklet. 40 recipes.

212. The Wonderful World of Cheese. Chicago, Ill.: American Dairy Association, 1980. 20 p. 36 recipes.

Specialty Cookbooks

Cheese *(Continued)*

213. Good Ideas Keep Popping Up: 40 Delicious Velveeta Recipes, Volume II. Glenview, Ill.: Kraft, Inc., 1981. 1 booklet.

214. Cheese & Wine Anytime / Kraft. Saratoga, Calif.: P. Masson, c1982. 176 p., colored illus. Includes index.

215. Cheese Sweets and Savories: Pies, Cheesecakes, Quiches, Appetizers / by Steve Sherman. 1st ed. Brattleboro, Vt.: S. Greene Press, c1982. 166 p. Includes index.

216. Cooking with Cheese. New York: Culinary Arts Institute, c1982. 79 p., 8 p. of colored plates. (Adventures in Cooking Series). Includes index.

217. The Country Mouse: A Cookbook for Cheese Lovers / by Sally Walton and Faye Wilkinson; illustrated by Tupper Davidson. Brandon, Miss.: Quail Ridge Press, c1983. 79 p., illus. (some colored). (The Quail Ridge Press Cookbook Series). Includes index.

218. Mad About Cheddar / Angela Clubb. Toronto, Ont.: Clarke Irwin, c1983. 88 p., illus. Includes index.

219. Making the Most of Cheese / Judy Ridgway. Newton Abbot, Eng.: David & Charles, c1983. 48 p., illus. Includes index.

220. Winning Ways with Cheese. Paulton, Eng.: Purnell, 1983. 120 p., colored illus. Includes index.

221. The Betty Jane Wylie Cheese Cookbook / drawings by Heather Delfino, Bob Paul, and Richard Whyte. Toronto, Ont.: Oxford University Press, 1984. 182 p., illus. Includes index.

222. Liberty Cookbook: Say Cheese Please!: 50 Recipes / by Norene Gilletz; illustrated by Davina Davis. Brossard, Que.: Liberty Brand Products, c1984. 112 p., illus. In English and French.

Cheese *(Continued)*

223. The Little Cheese Cookbook / Mary L. Green. Denver, Colo.: Giftstar, 1984. ca. 10 p., illus. (Little Cookbooks).

224. Mad About Pastas & Cheese / by Jacqueline Heriteau; illustrations by Woodleigh Hubbard. New York: Perigee Books, 1984. 63 p., illus. Includes index.

225. The Cheese Book / Vivienne Marquis and Patricia Haskell with an additional chapter by Laurence Senelick. Rev. ed. New York: Simon and Schuster, c1985. 336 p. "A Fireside Book." Includes index.

226. Creative Cheese Cookery: Making and Cooking with Rennet-free Cheeses / Jo Marcangelo. Rochester, Vt.: Thorsons Pub. Group, 1985. 128 p. Probably an earlier edition of: Vegetarian Cheese Cookery (entry 236).

227. Pasta & Cheese: The Cookbook / by Henry A. Lambert. New York: Pocket Books, c1985. 223 p., illus. ca. 200 recipes. Includes index.

228. A Pocket Book on Cheese: A Natural Food and a Versatile Ingredient / Shirley Gill. London, Eng.: Octopus, 1985. 96 p., colored illus. Includes index.

229. Polly-O Cooking with Cheese Cookbook. Mineola, N.Y.: Pollio Dairy Products Corp., c1985. 79 p., colored illus. Includes index.

230. Cheese / James McNair; photography by Patricia Brabant. San Francisco, Calif.: Chronicle Books, 1986. 95 p., colored illus. Includes indexes.

231. Cheese: How to Choose, Serve & Enjoy / by the editors of Sunset Books and Sunset Magazine. 1st ed. Menlo Park, Calif.: Lane Pub. Co., c1986. 96 p., colored illus. Includes index.

Cheese *(Continued)*

232. Cheese Cheese: From Everyday to Gourmet Cookbook / M.J. Butterfield. Burnstown, Ont.: General Store Pub. House, c1986. 84 p., illus. (some colored). Includes index.

233. Cheese Please! / edited by Judith Bosley; designed and illustrated by Jill Ellen Parling. Middleton, Mich.: Grand Books, c1986. ca. 100 p., illus. Includes index.

234. The Complete Cheese Cookbook / Judy Ridgway. London, Eng.: Piatkus, 1986. 224 p., colored illus. Includes index.

235. The Ideal Cheese Book / Edward Edelman and Susan Grodnick; preface by Barbara Kafka; illustrations by Ippy Patterson. 1st ed. New York: Harper & Row, c1986. 253 p., illus. More than 130 recipes. Contains information on buying international cheeses. Includes index.

236. Vegetarian Cheese Cookery: Making and Using Rennet-free Cheeses / Jo Marcangelo; illustrated by Kim Blundell. Wellingborough, Eng.; Rochester, Vt.: Thorsons Pub. Group; New York: Distributed by Sterling Pub. Co., 1987, c1985. 160 p., 8 p. of plates, illus. (some colored). "A Thorsons Wholefood Cookbook." Includes index. Probably a later edition of: Creative Cheese Cookery (entry 226).

237. Better Homes and Gardens Cheese Recipes / editor, Rosemary C. Hutchinson. 1st ed. Des Moines, Iowa: Meredith Corp., c1988. 46 p., illus. (some colored). Includes index.

238. British Country Cheeses: From Devon Garland to Danbydale / Pamela Westland. London, Eng.: Ward Lock, 1988. 144 p.

239. Classic Cheese Cookery / Peter Graham. Harmondsworth, Eng.: Penguin, 1988. 401 p.

Specific Ingredients

Cheese *(Continued)*

240. American Country Cheese: Cooking with America's Specialty and Farmstead Cheeses / Laura Chenel and Linda Siegfried; foreword by Evan Jones. Reading, Mass.: Addison-Wesley, 1989. 288 p., illus. More than 100 recipes. Includes index.

241. Cheese and Cheese Making. London, Eng.: W.I. Books, 1989. 160 p.

242. The Cheese Cookbook / Pam Cary. Marlborough, Eng.: Crowood, 1989. 160 p.

243. James McNair's Cheese Cookbook / photography by Patricia Brabant. San Francisco, Calif.: Chronicle Books, c1989. 96 p., colored illus. 40 recipes. Includes index. Possibly a later ed. of the author's Cheese, published in 1986 (entry 230).

244. A Gourmet's Guide to Cheese / by Carol Timperley & Cecilia Norman; photography by Graham Tann. Los Angeles, Calif.: HP Books, 1990. 120 p., more than 100 colored photos. Includes index.

245. Velveeta Creative Cooking. New York: Beekman House: Distributed by Crown Publishers: 1990. 96 p., colored photos. Includes index.

see also entries 8, 563, 2347, 4409; and Cheese and Eggs; *specific kinds of cheese*: Cream Cheese, Goat Cheese, Ricotta Cheese, Yogurt Cheese; *and broader category:* Dairy Products

Cheese and Eggs

246. Eggs & Cheese / by the editors of Time-Life Books. Alexandria, Va.: Time-Life Books, c1980. 176 p., illus. Includes index.

247. Egg and Cheese Cookbook / Jane Todd. London, Eng.: Hamlyn, 1981. 128p., illus. (some colored). Includes index.

Cheese and Eggs *(Continued)*

248. Ideals Egg and Cheese Cookbook / by Darlene Kronschnabel. Milwaukee, Wis.: Ideals Pub. Corp., 1982. 64 p., colored illus. Includes index.

249. Eggs & Cheese. Newton Abbot, Eng.: David & Charles, c1983. 64 p., colored illus. (Kitchen Workshop). Includes index. Translation of: Egg og Osteretter.

250. Egg & Cheese Menus. Alexandria, Va.: Time-Life Books, 1984. 105 p., illus. (some colored). (Great Meals in Minutes). Includes index.

251. Famous Brands Cooking with Eggs and Cheese. St. Louis, Mo.: Brand Name Pub. Corp., 1986. ca. 128 p., colored illus. (Famous Brands Cookbook Library). Includes index.

252. Eggs and Cheese. Toronto, Ont.: Grolier, 1988. 110 p., illus. (Microwave Magic; 16). Includes index.

253. Egg & Cheese Dishes / Mary Cadogan, Barbara Logan. London, Eng.: Treasure, 1989, c1981. 64 p., colored illus. (Good Cook's Recipe Collection).

see also Cheese; Eggs

Cherries

254. 101 Cherry Recipes / by Carole Eberly; cover and illustrations by Gerry Wykes. Lansing, Mich.: Eberly Press, c1984. 47 p., illus.

255. Cherries Galore: A Cookbook / edited by Clara Eschmann. 1st ed. Macon, Ga.: Macon Telegraph and News, c1984. 206 p., illus. Includes index.

256. The Little Cherry Cookbook / Mary L. Green. Denver, Colo.: Giftstar, 1984. ca. 10 p., illus. (Little Cookbooks).

Cherries *(Continued)*

257. Cherry Time! / compiled and edited by Judith Bosley; cover design & illustrations by Jill Ellen Parling; airbrush artist, Joseph P. Baldino. Middleton, Mich.: Grand Books, c1989. 1 v., illus.

   see also broader category: Fruits

Chicken

258. Family Circle Great Chicken Recipes / edited by Nancy A. Hecht; designed by William Schulein. Rev. ed. New York: New York Times Co., 1972. 168 p., illus.

259. 141 and One-Half Chinese-Style Chicken Recipes / by Lonnie Mock. Walnut Creek, Calif.: Alpha Gamma Arts, 1980. 190 p., illus. Includes index.

260. The Chicken Cookbook / Anne Mason. London, Eng.: Corgi, 1980. 183 p. Includes index.

261. A Chicken for Every Pot: San Francisco's Famous Chicken Diet / by Rudolf E. Noble; featuring 100 delectable, low-calorie chicken recipes. Santa Monica, Calif.: Delphi Books, 1980. 128 p., illus.

262. Chicken Only, Only Chicken / by Ferdie Blackburn. 1st ed. New Ipsich, N.H.: Fowl Play, 1980. 82 p., illus. Includes index.

263. Land O Lakes Chicken & Seafood Cookbook. Arden Hills, Minn.: Land O Lakes, 1980. 1 booklet. 50 recipes.

264. The Chicken and the Egg Cookbook / Maria Luisa Scott and Jack Denton Scott. Toronto, Ont.; New York: Bantam Books, 1981. 518 p., illus. Includes index.

Chicken *(Continued)*

265. The Chicken Cookbook / by Sophie Kay and the editors of Consumer Guide. New York: Fawcett Columbine, c1981. 160 p., colored illus. Includes index.

266. Chicken Favorites / by Mary Kay Hollander; illustrated by Alice Harth. San Francisco, Calif.: Owlswood Productions, c1981. 63 p., illus. Includes index.

267. The Super Chicken Cookbook / Iona Nixon. New York: Ventura Books, 1982. 128 p.

268. Chicken & Game Hen Menus. Alexandria, Va.: Time-Life Books, 1983. 104 p., colored illus. (Great Meals in Minutes). Includes index.

269. Chicken Cookery / by Ceil Dyer. Tucson, Ariz.: HP Books, c1983. 160 p., colored illus. Includes index.

270. How the World Cooks Chicken / H.J. Muessen. 1st Scarborough Books ed. New York: Stein and Day, 1983, c1982. 404 p. 375 recipes. Includes index.

271. New Ways to Enjoy Chicken / by Stanley Wolf; photographs by Glen Millward. 1st ed. Concord, Calif.: Nitty Gritty Productions, c1983. 183 p., 24 p. of plates, illus. (some colored). Includes index.

272. Betty Crocker's Chicken Cookbook / illustrator, Ray Skibinski. New York: Golden Press; Racine, Wis.: Western Pub. Co., c1984. 96 p., illus. (some colored). Includes index.

273. The Chicken Cookbook / by the editors of the Consumer Guide. New York: Beekman House: Distributed by Crown Publishers, c1984. 160 p., colored illus. Includes index.

Specific Ingredients 39

Chicken *(Continued)*

274. The Chicken and Egg Cookbook / Lillian Langseth-Christensen and Carol Sturm Smith; illustrations by Lillian Langseth-Christensen. Walker large print ed. New York: Walker, 1984, c1967. 96 p., illus. Includes index.

275. The Chicken Gourmet / Ferdie Blackburn. 1st U.S. ed. New York: St. Martin's Press, 1984, c1980. 82 p., illus. Includes index.

276. Chicken Just for You! / editor, Pat Teberg. Springdale, Ark.: Tyson, c1984. 160 p., illus. (some colored). Includes index.

277. How to Succeed with Chicken Without Even Frying / by Barbara S. Rosenberg; edited by Frances Rosenberg Hendrick; illustrated by Alice H. Balterman. Cincinnati, Ohio: MarLance, c1984. 204 p., illus. Includes index.

278. The Little Chicken Cookbook / Mary L. Green. Denver, Colo.: Giftstar, 1984. ca. 10 p., illus. (Little Cookbooks).

279. Best-Ever Chicken Recipes / by Christine Koury. Woodbury, N.Y.: Barron's, c1985. 64 p., colored illus. (Easy Cooking). Includes index.

280. Chicken Breasts: 116 New and Classic Recipes for the Fairest Part of the Fowl / by Diane Rozas. 1st ed. New York: Harmony Books, c1985. 96 p. (A Particular Palate Cookbook). Includes index.

281. Chicken! Chicken! Chicken! Lynn Mendelson's First Cookbook. Vancouver, B.C.: Whitecap Books, 1985. 128 p., illus. 121 recipes. Includes index. "A David Robinson Book."

282. The Complete Book of Chicken Wings / by Joie Warner. 1st U.S. ed. New York: Hearst Books, c1985. 112 p., illus. 70 recipes. Includes index.

Specialty Cookbooks

Chicken *(Continued)*

283. Episcopal Chicken: A Cookbook Containing a Variety of Chicken Recipes from the Episcopal Church Women, Diocese of Southern Virginia. Norfolk, Va. (600 Talbot Hall Rd., Norfolk 23505): For copies, write to ECW-Cookbook, 1985. 118 p.

284. Just Chicken / Thomas Hinde & Cordelia Chitty. 1st English language ed. Woodbury, N.Y.: Barron's, 1985. 128 p., illus. 100 recipes from 24 countries. Includes index.

285. Perfect Cooking with Chicken / Bernice Hurst. Twickenham, Eng.: Hamlyn, 1985. 32 p., illus. Originally published: Reading, Eng.: Elvendon, 1982, under title: The Perfect Chicken.

286. 365 Ways to Cook Chicken / Cheryl Sedaker. 1st ed. New York: Harper & Row, c1986. 224 p. "A John Boswell Associates Book." Includes index.

287. Better Homes and Gardens Fast-Fixin' Chicken. 1st ed. Des Moines, Iowa: Meredith Corp., c1986. 80 p., colored illus. More than 80 recipes. Includes index.

288. The Count Dracula Chicken Cookbook / Jeanne Youngson. New York: Dracula Press, 1986. 64 p.

289. Madam LaZong's Chicken Breast Recipes / Text and illustrations by Cheryl Bennett. Long Beach, Calif. (P.O. Box 30117 Long Beach 90853): Bennett, 1986. 1 v., illus. Includes fictitious stories and true recipes.

290. 101 Quick Ways with Chicken / Judy Ridgway. London, Eng.: Piatkus, 1987. 124 p., colored illus. Includes index.

291. Chicken / by James McNair; photography by Patricia Brabant. San Francisco, Calif.: Chronicle Books, c1987. 96 p., colored illus. Includes index.

Chicken *(Continued)*

292. Chicken: One Hundred One Ways to Cook Your Bird / Janice M. Fukuhara. Aurora, Colo.: Kelci's, 1987. 230 p., illus.

293. Chicken Expressions / by Normand Leclair, Red Rooster Tavern. Warwick, R.I.: Dome Pub., c1987. 67 p., illus.

294. Fowl Play: A Chicken Lover's Cookbook / Judie Rawson. Santa Ana, Calif.: EZ Cookin', 1987. 176 p., illus.

295. Quick & Easy Microwaving Chicken / Microwave Cooking Institute. 1st Prentice Hall Press ed. New York: Prentice Hall Press, 1987, c1986. 96 p. (Quick & Easy Microwaving Library; 2). Includes index.

296. The Best Chicken Recipes / Lorna Ellsworth. Los Angeles, Calif. (515 Deane Ave. 90043): L.C. Ellsworth, 1988. 56 p., illus.

297. The Chicken for Every Occasion Cookbook / Helen Studley and the editors of Consumer Reports Books. Mount Vernon, N.Y.: Consumers Union, c1988. 192 p., 49 line drawings. 95 recipes. Includes index.

298. Chicken on the Run: Fast & Easy Recipes Using Boneless Chicken Breasts / by Leslie Bloom; edited by Marian Levine. Silver Spring, Md.: American Cooking Guild, 1988. 64 p., illus. (Collector's Series).

299. Best Recipes for Chicken. 1st Prentice Hall Press ed. New York: Prentice Hall Press, c1989. 112 p., illus. (some colored). More than 100 recipes. (Betty Crocker's Red Spoon Collection). Includes index.

300. The Chic Chicken Book / Deborah L. Rebollo. New York: Carlton Press, 1988. 240 p.

Chicken *(Continued)*

301. Chicken 'n Quick Fixin's. Minneapolis, Minn.: Pillsbury Co., 1989. 93 p., colored illus. More than 100 recipes. (Classic Pillsbury Cookbooks; #102).

302. The Chicken Little Cookbook / Martha Harvey. Burnstown, Ont.: General Store Pub. House, 1989. 1 v.

303. Creative Chicken. London, Eng.: Treasure, 1989. 128 p. (Great Cooking Made Easy).

304. Entertaining Chicken / Pamela S. Kenney. Topeka, Kan.: Kenney Publications, 1989. 50 p., illus.

305. Great Chicken Dishes / by Jane Novak. New York: Weathervane Books: Distributed by Crown, 1989, c1974. 263 p. Includes index. Reprint. Originally published: Treasury of Chicken Cookery. New York: Harper & Row, c1974.

306. The New Complete Book of Chicken Wings / by Joie Warner. Rev. ed. Toronto, Ont.: Little, Brown/Flavour Publications, 1989. 111 p., illus.

307. Award-Winning Chicken Recipes. Lincolnwood, Ill.: Publications International, 1990. 96 p., colored illus. (Favorite Recipes; v. 5, no. 23). Includes index.

308. The Chicken Cook Book / Wendy Veale. New York: Gallery Books, W.H. Smith Publishers, 1990. 96 p., illus., colored photos. 100 recipes. Includes index.

309. Cooking with the Chicken Breast: Delicious Main Dishes Starring the Delectable Skinless & Boneless White Meat / Stephen M. Lehrer. Cincinnati, Ohio: Madeira-Hudson Pub. Co., 1990. 222 p., illus. Includes index.

Specific Ingredients

Chicken *(Continued)*

310. More Chicken Breasts: 94 New and Classic Recipes for the Fairest Part of the Fowl / by Diane Rozas. 1st ed. New York: Harmony Books, c1990. 96 p. "A Particular Palate Cookbook." Includes index.

see also Canned Chicken; *and broader category:* Poultry

Chili Peppers *see* Peppers

Chives

see entries 876, 1606; and broader category: Herbs

Chocolate

311. The Seven Chocolate Sins: A Devilishly Delicious Collection of Chocolate Recipes / Ruth Moorman & Lalla Williams. Brandon, Miss.: Quail Ridge Press, c1979. 79 p., illus. 175 recipes.

312. The "Exclusively Chocolate" Cookbook / Pauline G. Child. Diamond Bar, Calif.: PGC Publications, c1980. 205 p., illus. Includes index.

313. The Kake Brand Cookbook / Jess Mitchell. Cambridge, Eng.: Martin Books, 1980. 95 p., colored illus.

314. Maida Heatter's Book of Great Chocolate Desserts / drawings by Toni Evins. 1st ed. New York: Knopf: Distributed by Random House, 1980. 428 p., illus. Includes index.

315. In Praise of Chocolate / Paul A. Lawrence; edited by Cleo Linn. San Anselmo, Calif.: PAL Press, c1981. 80 p., illus. (Positive Health Library). Includes bibliography.

Chocolate *(Continued)*

316. Mountains of Chocolate / Martin Johner and Gary Goldberg; illustrated by Wendy Mansfield. New York (23 East 92nd St., New York 10028): I. Chalmers Cookbooks, c1981. 48 p., illus.

317. The Perfect Chocolate Dessert. Skokie, Ill.: Consumer Guide, c1981. 32 p., colored illus. (Perfect Cookbooks).

318. The Big Chocolate Cookbook / by Gertrude Parke. New York: A & W Pub., 1982, c1968. 325 p. Includes index.

319. Hershey's Chocolate Memories Through the Years Cookbook: Sweets and Treats Since 1895 / nostalgia author, Nao Hauser; designer, Tom Gawle; editor, Cecily R. Hogan. Racine, Wis.: Western Pub. Co., c1982. 96 p., illus.

320. Ideals Hershey's Chocolate and Cocoa Cookbook. Milwaukee, Wis.: Ideals Pub. Corp., c1982. 64 p., colored illus. Includes index.

321. The Joy of Chocolate / Judith Olney, with Ruth Klingel. Woodbury, N.Y.: Barron's, c1982. 182 p., 12 p. of plates, illus. (some colored). ca. 100 recipes. Includes index.

322. Cadbury's Cocoa Recipes. Birmingham, Eng. (P.O. 171, Franklin House, Bournville, Birmingham B30 2NA): Cadbury Typhoo Ltd., 1983? 20 p., illus. (some colored).

323. Cadbury's Novelty Cookbook / Patricia Dunbar. London, Eng.: Hamlyn, 1983. 128 p., illus. (some colored). Includes index.

324. Chocolate Artistry: Techniques for Molding, Decorating, and Designing with Chocolate / Elaine Gonzalez. Chicago, Ill.: Contemporary Books, c1983. 221 p., illus. Includes index.

325. The Chocolate Book / by Susanne LeRiche, Catherine Sharpe, Diana McDougall. Milton, Ont.: Our Place Publications, 1983, c1982. 40 p., illus.

Specific Ingredients 45

Chocolate *(Continued)*

326. Chocolate, Chocolate, Chocolate / Barbara Myers. 1st ed. New York: Rawson Associates, c1983. 293 p. Includes index. Also published: New York: Penguin Books, 1984.

327. Chocolate Cookery / Mable Hoffman. London, Eng.: Hamlyn, 1983, c1978. 124 p., illus. (some colored). Includes index. Originally published: Mable Hoffman's Chocolate Cookery. Tucson, Ariz.: HP Books, c1978.

328. Chocolate Desserts. Los Angeles, Calif.: Knapp Press, c1983. 91 p. (The Bon Appétit Kitchen Collection). Includes index.

329. Ghirardelli Original Chocolate Cookbook / by Phyllis Larsen. Rev. 2d ed. San Leandro, Calif.: Ghirardelli Chocolate Co./Mariposa Press, c1983. 156 p., illus.

330. Pamella Asquith's Ultimate Chocolate Cake Book. 1st ed. New York: Holt, Rinehart and Winston, c1983. 239 p., 8 p. of plates, illus. (some colored). 124 recipes. Includes index.

331. Recipes from the Third Annual Chocolate Tasting Fair / Shelter Against Violent Environments, Inc. Fremont, Calif.: Shelter Against Violent Environments, Inc., 1983. 55 p., illus.

332. Topsy and Tim's Chocolate Cook Book / Jean Adamson. Glasgow, Scot.: Blackie, c1983. 24 p., colored illus.

333. The Ultimate Chocolate Cake and 110 Other Chocolate Indulgences / Helge Rubinstein. 1st American ed. New York: Congdon & Weed: Distributed by St. Martin's Press, 1983, c1982. 333 p., illus. First published in 1982 under title: The Chocolate Book. Includes indexes.

334. Better Homes and Gardens Chocolate. 1st ed. Des Moines, Iowa: Meredith Corp., c1984. 96 p., colored illus. Includes index.

Chocolate *(Continued)*

335. The Book of Chocolate / Patricia Lousada. London, Eng.: Ebury, 1984. 48 p., colored illus.

336. Cadbury's Creative Chocolate Cookbook / Patricia Dunbar. London, Eng.: Hamlyn, 1984. 240 p., illus. (some colored). Includes index. Reprint of 1978 ed.

337. Chocolate / Jennie Reekie. London, Eng.: Ward Lock, 1984. 80 p., illus. (some colored). Includes index. Adapted from: The Ultimate Chocolate Cookbook. 1983.

338. The Chocolate and Coffee Cookbook / Lillian Langseth-Christensen and Carol Sturm Smith; illustrations by Lillian Langseth-Christensen. Walker large print ed. New York: Walker, 1984, c1967. 96 p., illus. Includes index.

339. Chocolate Cooking / edited by Judy Ridgway. New York: Gallery Books, 1984. 77 p., illus. Includes index. On cover: The Color Book of Chocolate Cooking.

340. The Diabetic Chocolate Cookbook / Mary Jane Finsand; foreword by James D. Healy. New York: Sterling, c1984. 160 p. Includes index.

341. The Gourmet's Guide to Chocolate / Lesly Berger. 1st Quill ed. New York: Quill, 1984. 128 p., illus. "A Quarto Book ... produced and prepared by Quarto Marketing Ltd." Includes index.

342. Hershey's Chocolate Treasury. New York: Golden Press, 1984. 286 p., colored illus. Includes index.

343. The Little Chocolate Cookbook / Mary L. Green. Denver, Colo.: Giftstar, 1984. ca. 10 p., illus. (Little Cookbooks).

344. Madame Chocolate's Book of Divine Indulgences / Elaine Sherman. Chicago, Ill.: Contemporary Books, 1984. 212 p., colored illus. Includes index.

Chocolate *(Continued)*

345. The Ultimate Chocolate Cookbook / Jennie Reekie. New York: Exeter Books: Distributed by Bookthrift, 1984. 112 p., colored illus. Includes index. Originally published: London, Eng.: Ward Lock, 1983.

346. Woman's Day Chocolate Lovers' Cookbook / by Marlene K. Connor & the editors of Woman's Day. 1st ed. New York: Crown Publishers, c1984. 154 p. Includes index.

347. Bakers Book of Chocolate Riches. Kankakee, Ill.: General Foods Corp., c1985. 112 p., colored photos. 100 chocolate and coconut recipes.

348. Betty Crocker's Chocolate Cookbook. 1st. ed. New York: Random House, c1985. 96 p., illus. (some colored). Includes index.

349. Le Chocolat / Martine Jolly; translated and adapted by Philip and Mary Hyman. 1st American ed. New York: Pantheon Books, c1985. 149 p., illus. (some colored). 126 recipes. Includes index. Translation of: Le chocolat.

350. The Chocolate Book / Valerie Barrett. London, Eng.: Apple, c1985. 128 p., illus. (some colored). (A Quintet Book). Includes index.

351. The Chocolate Book / Anne Hodges; illustrated by Graham Palfrey-Rogers. London, Eng.: Kato Press, 1985. 79 p., illus. (some colored). Includes index.

352. Chocolate Cooking / text by Denise Jarrett-Macauley; photography by Peter Barry. New York: Exeter Books: Distributed by Bookthrift, 1985. 64 p., colored illus. Includes index.

Chocolate *(Continued)*

353. Chocolate Crazy / Sylvia Balser Hirsch. New York: New American Library, 1985, c1984. 204 p. 150 recipes. Reprint. Originally published: New York: Macmillan; London: Collier Macmillan, c1984.

354. The Chocolate Cookbook / by Juliette Elkon Hamelecourt. New York: Macmillan Pub. Co., c1985. 214 p., illus. More than 200 recipes. Includes index. "A Bobbs-Merrill Book."

355. Chocolate Delights / Cathy Gill. Tucson, Ariz.: HP Books, c1985. 80 p., colored illus. (Creative Cuisine). Includes index.

356. Chocolate Fantasies: A Chocolate Lover's Fun Kit / by Verne Ricketts; illustrated by Hazel Croner. Baltimore, Md.: Lieba, c1985. 128 p., illus. (some colored).

357. Chocolate Lovers Cookbook / Audrey Ellis. New York: Exeter Books: Distributed by Bookthrift, 1985. 192 p., colored illus. Includes index.

358. Chocolate Quick Fix: Recipes You Can Make in 15 Minutes or Less / from the editors of Chocolate News; edited by Milton Zelman & Jeannine Winquist. Silver Spring, Md.: American Cooking Guild, 1985. 56 p., illus. (Collector's Series).

359. Chocolate Recipes / compiled by the Vernon Community Arts Council. Vernon, B.C.: The Council, 1985. 41 p.

360. Hershey's Timeless Desserts. Nashville, Tenn.: Ideals Pub. Corp., c1985. 80 p., colored illus. Includes index.

361. Chocolate! / Carolyn Humphries. New York: Gallery Books, c1986. 92 p., colored illus. Includes index.

362. Chocolate Cookery / Mitzie Wilson and Nichola Palmer. Twickenham, Eng.: Hamlyn, 1986. 64 p., colored illus. Includes index.

Chocolate *(Continued)*

363. The Chocolate Lover's Cookbook / by Billie Little. Los Angeles, Calif.: Medallion Books, c1986. 220 p. Includes index.

364. Chocolate Mousse and Other Fabulous Chocolate Creations / by Betty Malosow Potter. Chanhassen, Minn.: New Boundary Design, 1986. 220 p. 145 recipes. Includes index.

365. Chocolate Sensations / Faye Levy. Tucson, Ariz.: HP Books, 1986. 205 p., 100 colored photos. More than 200 recipes. Cover title: Faye Levy's Chocolate Sensations.

366. Famous Brands Chocolate Classics. St. Louis, Mo.: Brand Name Pub. Corp., 1986. ca. 128 p., colored illus. (Famous Brands Cookbook Library). Includes index.

367. Festive Chocolate: Recipes / by Peter G. Rose; illustrations by Sandra Baenen. White Plains, N.Y.: Peter Pauper Press, c1986. 64 p., colored illus.

368. The Little Chocolate Book / Jennie Reekie. London, Eng.: Piatkus, c1986. 60 p., illus.

369. Nuts About Chocolate: Recipes / by Susan Mendelson & Deborah Roitberg. New York: Sterling Pub. Co., 1986, c1983. 106 p., colored illus. Includes index.

370. Chocolate Delights / Mary Berry. London, Eng.: Sphere, 1987, c1985. 90 p. 60 recipes. Includes index. Originally published: London, Eng.: Piatkus, 1985.

371. Chocolate Fantasies. Birmingham, Ala.: Oxmoor House, c1987. 79 p., illus. More than 200 recipes. Includes index.

372. Whitman's Chocolate Cookbook / edited by Marian Hoffman. New York: Crescent Books: Distributed by Crown Books, 1987. 124 p., colored photos. Includes index.

Chocolate *(Continued)*

373. Best Kept Secrets of Chocolate Drinks & Life / written by Antoinette Trainer. New York: Starbud Press, c1988. 102 p. Contains 72 recipes for drinks made with chocolate; accompanied by poems and personal recollections. Includes index.

374. The Chocolate Cookbook / by Culinary Arts Institute. New York: Dover Publications, 1988. 47 p., illus. 218 recipes. "A republication of the work originally published by Culinary Arts Institute, Chicago, Ill., in 1955. Includes index.

375. Chocolate Cookbook / William I. Kaufman. New York: Bart Books, 1988. 168 p.

376. Chocolate Cooking / Cathy Gill. London, Eng.: Hamlyn, 1988, c1984. 84 p. (Cooking for Today).

377. Chocolate Fantasies: Live Your Chocolate Fantasies While Savoring the 67 Best Chocolate Recipes in America / Honey and Larry Zisman. New York: Pocket Books, c1988. 143 p. Includes indexes.

378. Fantasy Chocolate Desserts / by Robert Lambert; photography by Patricia Brabant. San Francisco, Calif.: Chronicle Books, c1988. 108 p., colored illus. Includes indexes.

379. The Great American Chocolate Cookbook. Nashville, Tenn.: Favorite American Press: Great American Opportunities, Inc., 1988. 128 p., illus. Includes index.

380. Hershey's Simply Chocolate: A Selection of Quick and Easy Recipes from the Hershey Kitchens. Hershey, Pa.: Hershey Foods Corp., 1988. 96 p., colored photos. More than 150 recipes.

381. Lady Macdonald's Chocolate Book. London, Eng.: Ebury, 1988. 96 p.

Specific Ingredients

Chocolate *(Continued)*

382. Marshall Field's Frango Chocolate Cookbook. Chicago, Ill.: Contemporary Books, c1988. 176 p., 14 p. of colored plates. Includes index.

383. Polly Pinder's Chocolate Cookbook. Tunbridge Wells, Eng.: Search Press, 1988. 144 p., illus.

384. Chocolate / Janice Murfitt. London, Eng.: Macdonald Orbis, 1989. 160 p.

385. Chocolate: A Healthy New Image! / by Donna M. Ortman. Regina, Sask.: Sweet Dreams Pub., 1989. 118 p., illus. (some colored).

386. Glorious Chocolate / Mary Goodbody and the editors of Chocolatier Magazine. New York: Simon & Schuster, 1989. ca. 400 p., illus. Includes index.

387. Hershey's Chocolate Cookbook. Lincolnwood, Ill.: Publications International, 1989. 96 p., colored illus. Includes index.

388. Hershey's Chocolate Recipe Collection: A Selection of Recipes from the Hershey Kitchens. Hershey, Pa.: Hershey Foods Corp., c1989. 32 p., colored photos. More than 90 recipes.

389. Hershey's Fabulous Desserts. Lincolnwood, Ill.: Publications International, 1989. 200 p., ca. 135 colored photos. 230 recipes. Includes index.

390. A Passion for Chocolate / Maurice and Jean-Jacques Bernachon; translated and adapted for the American kitchen by Rose Levy Beranbaum; edited by Maria Guarnaschelli; designed by Richard Oriolo. New York: W. Morrow, 1989. 257 p., 20 colored photos. 107 recipes. Translation of: La passion du chocolat.

Specialty Cookbooks

Chocolate *(Continued)*

391. Solid Chocolate / by Patsy and Ole Swendson; handwritten by Marcia Barr. San Antonio, Tex.: Printed by Nilam Photocopy Co., 1989. 116 p., illus.

392. The Sporting a Healthier Image for Chocolate Cookbook / Donna M. Ortman. Regina, Sask.: Sweet Dreams Pub., 1989. This title was never published. The book was published under the title: Chocolate: A Healthy New Image (entry 385).

393. The Wicked Chocolate Book / Mary Norwak. London, Eng.: Gollancz, 1989. 160 p.

394. Chocolate: The Chocolate Lover's Guide to Complete Indulgence / Jill Norman. Bantam ed. New York: Bantam Books, 1990. 41 p. (The Bantam Library of Culinary Arts). Includes index. Dorling Kindersley edition published in Great Britain in 1989.

395. Chocolate Lovers IV. Minneapolis, Minn.: Pillsbury Co., 1990. 93 p., colored illus. More than 100 recipes. (Classic Pillsbury Cookbooks; #108).

396. Cocolat: Extraordinary Chocolate Desserts / by Alice Medrich; photographs by Patricia Brabant. New York: Warner Books, c1990. 208 p., 50 colored photos.

397. A Gourmet's Guide to Chocolate / by Lesley Mackley & Carole Handslip; photography by Sue Atkinson. Los Angeles, Calif.: HP Books, 1990. 120 p., colored photos. Includes index.

398. Growing Up on the Chocolate Diet: A Memoir with Recipes / Lora Brody. Lexington, Mass.: S. Greene Press, Pelham Books; New York: Distributed by Viking Penguin, 1990. 253 p. 84 recipes. Includes index. Originally published: Boston, Mass.: Little, Brown, c1985; reprinted: New York: Holt, 1986. This edition contains a new chapter published in 1990.

Chocolate *(Continued)*

399. In Love with Chocolate: 85 Best Recipes. Minneapolis, Minn.: General Mills, 1990. 91 p., colored illus. (Betty Crocker Creative Recipes; no. 41). Includes index.

400. The Pillsbury Chocolate Lovers Cookbook. New York: Doubleday, c1990. 144 p., colored illus. More than 200 recipes for chocolate cookies, brownies, cakes, pies, and candy. Includes index.

401. The Taste of Chocolate / Patricia Dunbar. London, Eng.: Simon & Schuster, 1990. 128 p.

CHILDREN'S COOKBOOKS

402. Hershey's Kidsnacks. Chicago, Ill.: Children's Press, c1984. 63 p., colored illus.

403. The Kids' Book of Chocolate / by Richard Ammon. 1st ed. New York: Atheneum, 1987. 74 p., illus. Includes bibliography and index. A history of chocolate, a discussion of the processing of cacao into chocolate products, recipes, suggestions for related places to visit, and chocolate lore, jokes, and poems.

404. Chocolate, Chocolate, Chocolate: The Complete Book of Chocolate / Sonia Black & Pat Brigandi. New York: Scholastic, Inc.: 1989. 1 v.

see also Chocolate Chips; White Chocolate; *and specific dishes using chocolate in Section II:* Cakes, Candy, Cookies, Desserts, *etc.*

Chocolate Chips

405. In the Chips: The Complete Chocolate Chip Cookbook / Peggy Mellody and Linda Rosenbloom. 1st ed. New York: Rawson Associates, c1985. 260 p. ca. 300 recipes. Includes index.

see also Chocolate Chip Cookies *(Section II); and broader category:* Chocolate

Cider

406. The Cider Book / Lila Gault and Betsy Sestrap. Seattle, Wash.: Madrona Publishers, c1980. 166 p. Includes index.

407. A Taste of Cider / Shirley Harrison; illustrations by Graeme Jenner. Newton Abbot, Eng.: North Pomfret, Vt.: David & Charles, c1982. 96 p., illus. Includes index.

see also broader categories: Beverages *(Section II); and* Liquors

Cilantro *see* Coriander

Cinnamon

408. The Cinnamon Cook Book / by Ferrilyn Michele Welsh; illustrated by Howard J. Currens. [United States]: Welsh Enterprises, c1982. 147 p., illus.

409. The Little Cinnamon Cookbook / Mary L. Green. Denver, Colo.: Giftstar, 1984. ca. 10 p., illus. (Little Cookbooks).

see also broader category: Spices

Specific Ingredients 55

Citrus Fruits

410. Citrus Recipes: A Collection of Favorites from the Citrus Belt / compiled by Al Fischer and Mildred Fischer; cover and artwork by Jerry Reynolds. Phoenix, Ariz.: Golden West Publishers, c1980. 126 p., illus. Almost 300 recipes. Includes index.

411. The Citrus Cookbook / Josephine Bacon; illustrations by Nancy Simonds. Harvard, Mass.: Harvard Common Press, c1983. 162 p., illus. Includes index.

412. The Sunshine Cookbook. Lakeland, Fla.: Florida Dept. of Citrus, 1983. 1 booklet, illus.

413. Citrus Recipes from Florida Restaurants. Lakeland, Fla.: Florida Dept. of Citrus, 1985. 16 p., illus.

414. Florida Citrus Cookbook / editor, Elizabeth Speir, contributing editor, William Schemmel. Atlanta, Ga.: Marmac Pub. Co.; Gretna, La.: Distributed by Pelican Pub. Co., c1985. 192 p., colored illus. Includes index.

415. Orange Fantasia / compiled and edited by Suzanne and Hugh Conrod; with guest chefs Karen Ghent and Jim Meade. Dartmouth, N.S.: Cookbook World, c1985. 96 p., illus. (Cookbook World Series). Includes index. Cover subtitle: Citrus Recipes to Put You into Orbit.

416. Cooking with Sunshine: Recipes from the Sunkist Kitchens. 1st ed. New York: Atheneum, 1986. 341 p., 8 p. of plates, illus. (some colored). Includes index.

417. Citrus Fruits / editor, Virginia Siewertsen; ethnobotany of the Citrus by Lois and Harold Birnbaum; introduction by Virginia Siewertsen. Lawai, Kauai, Hawaii (P.O. Box 340, Lawai, Kauai, Hawaii 96765): Na Lima Kokua, for the benefit of the Pacific Tropical Botanical Garden, c1987. 68 p., illus. Cover has subtitle: Uses and Recipes.

Citrus Fruits *(Continued)*

418. A Glut of Citrus Fruit / Ann Carr. London, Eng.: Merehurst, 1988. 92 p.

419. Surprising Citrus: A Cookbook / by Audra and Jack Hendrickson; edited by Constance Oxley. Pownal, Vt.: Storey Communications, c1988. 160 p., illus. "A Garden Way Publishing Book." Includes index.

CHILDREN'S COOKBOOKS

420. Citrus Fruits / Susan Wake; illustrations by John Yates. Minneapolis, Minn.: Carolrhoda Books, 1990, c1989. 32 p., illus. Includes index. Describes several citrus fruits, their importance, and their histories and presents several recipes.

see also specific citrus fruits: Lemons, Oranges, etc.; *and broader category:* Fruits

Clams

421. The Clam Lover's Cookbook / by William G. Flagg. 3rd ed. Croton-on-Hudson, N.Y.: North River Press; New York: Distributed by Dodd, Mead, c1983. 142 p.

422. Clambakes Sans Sand in Pots & Woks / Robert H. Robinson. Georgetown, Del.: Sussex Prints, Inc., 1983. 48 p.

423. No Ordinary Clam Book: A Cookbook / by May H. Davis; cover and illustrations by Lois Ireland. Suquamish, Wash. (P.O. Box 910, Suquamish 98392): Megan Publications, c1983. 103 p., illus.

424. Soft Shell Clams-Steamers / by R. Marilyn Schmidt. Barnegat Light, N.J.: Barnegat Light Press, 1985. 12 p.

Specific Ingredients 57

Clams *(Continued)*

425. The Compleat Clammer / Christopher R. Reaske; illustrated by Suzanne T. Reaske. New York: N. Lyons Books, c1986. 152 p., illus. Includes index.

426. Hard Clams / by R. Marilyn Schmidt. Barnegat Light, N.J.: Barnegat Light Press, 1988. 24 p.

427. How to Catch Clams by the Bushel! / by Tom Schlichter; illustrations by Vincent Piazza. Tarrytown, N.Y.: Northeast Sportsman's Press; Harrisburg, Pa.: Stackpole Books, c1990. 98 p., illus.

see also broader category: Shellfish

Cocoa *see* **Chocolate**

Coconuts

428. Coconut: The Tree of Life / Carolyn Meyer; illustrated by Lynne Cherry. New York: Morrow, 1976. 96 p., illus.

429. Coconut = Niu: Uses and Recipes / by Na Lima Kokua. Lawai, Hawaii: Na Lima Kokua, 1980. 28 p., illus. "For the benefit of the Pacific Tropical Botanical Garden."

430. Coconut: Uses for the Entire Coconut, with Recipes & Suggestions / Cookbook Consortium. Houston, Tex.: Prosperity & Profits, 1984. 14 p.

see also entry 347; and broader category: Fruits

Coffee

431. Coffee / Suzanne Taylor Moore; illustrator, Mary McCrea. Tarzana, Calif.: Moore/Taylor/Moore Pub. Co., 1974. 144 p., illus.

432. The Coffee Lover's Handbook / researched by Cathy Ford; edited by Dona Sturmanis; illustrations by Moira Weinreich. Vancouver, B.C.: Intermedia, 1979. 119 p., illus.

433. 100 Coffee Dishes / Susan Locke and Heather Lambert. London, Eng.: Octopus, 1983. 64 p., illus. (some colored). Includes index.

434. Coffee for Every Occasion: A Recipe Collection for the Coffee Lover, Connoisseur and Novice / by Elisabeth Kloepper. Vancouver, B.C.: Seawalk Enterprises, c1984. 127 p., illus.

435. The Little Coffee Cookbook / Mary L. Green. Denver, Colo.: Giftstar, 1984. ca. 10 p., illus. (Little Cookbooks).

436. The Community Kitchens Complete Guide to Gourmet Coffee / John DeMers. New York: Simon and Schuster, c1986. 251 p., illus. ca. 100 recipes. Contains information on coffee beans and roasts, preparation of coffee, and recipes for accompanying dishes. Includes bibliography and index.

see also entry 338; and Beverages *(Section II)*

Conch

437. The Conch Book / by Dee Carstarphen. [n.p.]: Pen and Ink Press; Miami, Fla.: Distributed by Banyan Books, c1982. 73 p., illus. Includes bibliography.

438. Cooking Conch / by Nixon Griffis, John Clark, Catherine Lochner Clark. New York: Griffis Foundation; Miami, Fla.: PRIDE, c1983. 59 p., illus.

see also broader category: Shellfish

Specific Ingredients 59

Condensed Milk

439. Delicious Desserts Made Easy with Eagle Brand Sweetened Condensed Milk. Columbus, Ohio: Borden, Inc.: 1982. 28 p., colored illus. 50 recipes.

440. Classic Desserts. Columbus, Ohio: Borden, Inc.: 1986. 128 p., colored illus. More than 200 recipes using Eagle Brand Sweetened Condensed Milk.

441. Simply Delicious Desserts: With Eagle Brand Sweetened Condensed Milk. Columbus, Ohio: Borden, Inc.: 1989. 1 spiral bound v., colored photos. More than 150 recipes.

see also broader category: Milk

Condiments

442. Condiments: The Art of Buying, Making, and Using Mustards, Oils, Vinegars, Chutneys, Relishes, Sauces, Savory Jellies, and More / Kathy Gunst; illustrations by Keiko Narahashi. New York: G.P. Putnam's, c1984. 258 p., illus. 75 recipes. Includes index.

443. Bert Greene's Kitchen Bouquets: A Cookbook Celebration of Aromas and Flavors / illustrations by the author; design by Barbara DuPree Knowles. 1st [rev.] Fireside ed. New York: Simon & Schuster, 1986, c1979. 425 p., illus. 400 recipes using 28 different flavors. Includes index. Reprint. Originally published: Chicago, Ill.: Contemporary Books, 1979.

444. Indian Chutneys, Raitas, Pickles & Preserves / by Michael Pandya; illustrated by Paul Turner. Wellingborough, Northamptonshire; New York: Thorsons Pub. Group, 1986., illus. 176 p. Includes index.

445. Sable & Rosenfeld, Elegant Entertaining Cookbook / by Myra Sable. New York: Bantam Books, 1986. 400 p. Includes index.

Specialty Cookbooks

Condiments *(Continued)*

446. Paradise Preserves: Condiments of Hawaii: A Collection of Kamaaina Condiments; with a special section on curries / by Yvonne Neely Armitage; drawings by Lorna Armitage Cabato and Paul Douglas Armitage. Kailua, Hawaii: Press Pacifica, c1987. 126 p., illus. Includes index.

447. The Art of Accompaniment: Making Condiments / Jeffree Sapp Brooks. San Francisco, Calif.: North Point Press, 1988. 237 p.

448. Condiments!: Chutneys, Relishes, and Table Sauces / by Jay Solomon. Freedom, Calif.: Crossing Press, 1990. 128 p. Includes index. (Specialty Cookbook Series).

see also entries 957, 1087; Spices; Chutney; Pickles and Relishes; and Sauces *(Section II);* Canning and Preserving *(Section IV); and names of specific condiments, e.g.* Mustard, Vinegar, *etc.*

Coriander

449. Cooking with Cilantro / W. Lee Gay. Houston, Tex.: Houston Pub. Co., c1987. 78 p. Includes index.

see also broader category: Herbs

Corn

450. The Book of Corn Cookery: One Hundred and Fifty Recipes Showing How to Use This Nutritious Cereal and Live Cheaply and Well / by Mary L. Wade. Glenwood, Ill.: Meyerbooks, c1979. 105 p.

451. The Gardens for All Book of Corn / by Dick and Jan Raymond. Burlington, Vt.: Gardens for All, c1980. 31 p., illus.

Specific Ingredients

Corn *(Continued)*

452. Corn Means Tamales, Corn on the Cob, Tortillas, etc., etc. / by Rosina. Cortez, Colo.: Mesa Verde Press, c1985. 28 leaves, illus.

453. Corn: Meals & More / by Olwen Woodier. Pownal, Vt.: Storey Communications, 1987. 172 p., illus. "A Garden Way Publishing Book." Includes index.

454. American Corn / Maria Polushkin Robbins. New York: St Martin's Press, 1989. ca. 140 p., illus. 80 recipes.

455. Corn: Uses for Corn, with Recipes & Suggestions / Recycling Consortium. Houston, Tex.: Prosperity & Profits, 1989. ca. 14 p.

456. James McNair's Corn Cookbook / photography by Patricia Brabant. San Francisco, Calif.: Chronicle Books, 1990. 96 p., colored illus. 35 recipes. Includes index.

see also broader category: Vegetables

Corn Oil

457. A Diet for the Young at Heart: Great Eating for Everyone from Mazola. Englewood, N.J.: Best Foods, 1984. 1 booklet.

Corn Syrup

458. The Karo Cook Book: Recipe Collector's Edition. Englewood, N.J.: Best Foods, 1981. 128 p.

Cottonseed Meal

459. Cottonseed Cookery / edited by Rhonda Simmons. College Station, Tex.: Texas A & M University, 1981? 48 p., illus.

Crabs

460. How to Catch a Crab / William R. Poppke. Chelsea, Mich.: Scarborough House, 1977. 1 v., illus.

461. How to Catch Crabs by the Bushel!: The Manual of Sport Crabbing / by Jim Capossela; recipes created, tested, and compiled with the generous assistance of Josephine Capossela. 2nd print. 1982 rev. Tarrytown, N.Y.: Northeast Sportsman's Press, 1982, c1981. 64 p., illus. Revised and expanded edition.

462. The Art of Catching & Cooking Crabs / Lynette L. Walther. Georgetown, Del.: Sussex Prints, c1983. 94 p., illus. (A Shellfish Series Cookbook).

463. The Crab: Finding It, Catching It & Cooking It / by Tom Bailey. Nyack, N.Y.: Rockcom Enterprises Publications, c1985. 68 p., illus.

464. The Official Crab Eater's Guide / Whitey Schmidt. Alexandria, Va.: M. Hartnett Press, 1985, c1984. 260 p., illus. A guide to more than 275 eating establishments and seafood markets in the Chesapeake Bay area, together with recipes. Includes index.

465. Blue Crab / by R. Marilyn Schmidt. Barnegat Light, N.J.: Barnegat Light Press, 1986. 16 p.

466. The Compleat Crab and Lobster Book / Christopher R. Reaske; illustrated by Suzanne T.R. Crocker. New York: Lyons & Burford, c1989. 150 p., illus. Includes bibliography and index.

see also entry 1; and broader category: Shellfish

Specific Ingredients

Cranberries

467. Cranberries / Pinelands Folklife Project. Washington, D.C.: American Folklife Center, Library of Congress, 1984. 32 p., colored illus. 23 recipes. Includes bibliography.

468. The Cranberry Connection: Cranberry Cookery With Flavour, Fact, and Folklore, from Memories, Libraries, and Kitchens of Old and New Friends and Strangers / compiled by Beatrice Ross Buszek. Halifax, N.S.: Nimbus Pub. Ltd., c1984. 208 p., illus. Includes bibliography.

469. All-Time Favorite Cranberry Recipes. Plymouth, Mass.: Ocean Spray Cranberries, Inc., 1985? 32 p., illus.

470. Cranberry Cookery / by R. Marilyn Schmidt. 1st ed. Barnegat Light, Long Beach Island, N.J.: Pine Barrens Press; Cranbury, N.J.: Orders, Barnegat Light Press, c1985. 120 p. 118 recipes.

471. Something Cranberry / by Jill Baker; illustrated by Robin Strand. Oak Park, Ill. (P.O. Box 1432, Oak Park 60304): Brandison Press, c1986. 77 p., illus. "123 easy recipes for breads, desserts, salads, accompaniments, and more." Includes index.

see also broader category: Berries

Crappie

472. Crappie Cookbook: from Lake to Table / Steve L. Wunderle. 1st ed. Carterville, Ill.: Wunderle Outdoor Books, 1987. 69 p., illus. Includes index.

see also broader category: Fish

Crawfish

473. Crawfish House Cookbook. New Orleans, La.: B. Hoffpauer, c1984. 146 p.

474. About Crawfish & Easy to Prepare Recipes / Louise Klebba, Scott Moore. Beaumont, Tex.: Kinko's, c1987. 33 leaves.

see also broader category: Shellfish

Crayfish *see* Crawfish

Cream

475. Cooking with Cream--the Versatile Ingredient / Phyllis M. Letellier. Greybull, Wyo. (Shell Rte. Box 23, Greybull 82426): P.M. Letellier, 1983. 76 p., illus.

see also broader category: Dairy Products

Cream Cheese

476. The Phabulous Philly Cookbook / Kraft Limited. Paris, Ont.: Kraft, c1985. 20 p., illus. Issued also in French under title: Le Philly fantastique en cuisine.

477. Philadelphia Cream Cheese Cookbook. Lincolnwood, Ill.: Publications International, c1988. 200 p., colored illus.

478. Philadelphia Cream Cheese Summer Sensations: All New Recipes. Lincolnwood, Ill.: Publications International, 1990. 96 p., colored illus. (Favorite Recipes; v. 5, no. 21). Includes index.

see also entry 3079; and broader category: Cheese

Specific Ingredients 65

Cucumbers

479. Book of Cucumbers, Melons, & Squash / edited by the staff of the National Gardening Magazine; illustrations by Elayne Sears & Lyn Severance. Rev. ed. New York: Villard Books, 1987. 86 p., illus. Originally published as: The Gardens for All Book of Cucumbers, Melons, Squash / by Dick and Jan Raymond. Burlington, Vt.: Gardens for All, c1979.

see also broader category: Vegetables

Curry

480. The Complete Curry Cookbook / Charmaine and Reuben Solomon; photography by Reg Morrison and Ray Joyce; edited by Peita Royle. New York: McGraw-Hill, 1981, c1980. 126 p., illus. Includes index.

481. Curries and Oriental Cookery / Josceline Dimbleby. 2nd (rev.) impression. Cambridge, Eng.: Published for J. Sainsbury Limited by Woodhead-Faulkner, 1981. 96 p., illus. (some colored). (A Sainsbury's Cookbook).

482. Cooking with Curry / Renu Arora. Tokyo, Japan: Shufunotomo Co., Ltd.; C.E. Tuttle, 1982. 96 p., illus.

483. The Hamlyn Curry Cookbook / Meera Taneja. London, Eng.: Hamlyn, c1982. 128 p., illus. (some colored). Includes index.

484. Indian Curries / Michael Pandya. Cardiff, Wales: Preeti, c1982. 48 p., illus. Includes index.

485. Curry Every Sunday / Lawrence M. Prescott & Ellen G. Prescott; illustrations by Han Winn. White Hall, Va.: Betterway Publications, c1984. 191 p., illus. Includes index and bibliography.

Specialty Cookbooks

Curry *(Continued)*

486. Juel Andersen's Curry Primer: A Grammar of Spice Cookery / by Juel Andersen with Sigrid Andersen. Berkeley, Calif.: Creative Arts Communications, c1984. 63 p., illus. Includes index.

487. International Curry Cooking / N. Maheswari Devi; food photography, Yim Chee Peng. Petaling Jaya, Selangor, Malaysia: Eastern Universities Press, 1984. 155 p., illus. (some colored). Includes index.

488. Exotic Curries / Saroj Hadley. London, Eng.: Octopus, 1985. 78 p., colored illus. (The Kitchen Companion). Cover title: 100 Recipes for Exotic Curries. Includes index. Reprint of the 1983 ed.

489. The Little Curry Book / Pat Chapman. London, Eng.: Piatkus, 1985. 64 p., illus.

490. The Perfect Curry / Bernice Hurst; illustrated by Glynis Overton. Twickenham, Eng.: Hamlyn, 1985. 31 p., illus. Originally published: Reading, Eng.: Elvendon, 1983.

491. Indian Vegetarian Curries / Harvey Day; illustrated by Clive Birch; food preparation, styling and colour photography by Paul Turner and Sue Pressley. Wellingborough, Eng.: Thorsons, 1987, c1982. 128 p., illus. (some colored). Includes index. Originally published in 1982 under title: Indian Curries.

492. The Curry Club Favourite Restaurant Curries / Pat Chapman. London, Eng.: Piatkus, 1988. 192 p.

493. The Book of Curries & Indian Foods / Linda Fraser. Los Angeles, Calif.: HP Books, 1989. 120 p., colored photographs. More than 100 recipes. Includes index.

see also entry 446; and broader category: Spices

Specific Ingredients 67

Dairy Products

494. Great Cooking with Dairy Products / prepared and produced by Ridge Press. New York, Benjamin Co., 1973. 160 p., illus. At head of title: Sealtest. "A Benjamin Company/Rutledge Book."

495. Shopwell's Dairy Lovers' Cookbook: Featuring Daitch Dairy Products / by June Roth. New York: Dorison House Publishers, c1976. 143 p., illus. Includes index.

496. The Art of Cheesemaking / by Anne Nilsson; English translation and editing by Kerstin A. Shirokow, Steven E. Hegaard. Santa Barbara, Calif.: Woodbridge Press Pub. Co., c1979. 157 p., illus.

497. Anytime is Dairytime, It's a Snap!: 42 Super, Good & Easy Recipes. Toronto, Ont.: Dairy Bureau of Canada, 1980? 15 p., illus. Issued also in French under title: C'est toujours le temps pour les produits laitiers.

498. Making Cheeses, Butters, Cream, and Yogurt at Home: How to Make the Most of Your Milk Supply / by Patricia Cleveland-Peck. Wellingborough, Eng.: Thorsons, 1980. 127 p., illus. Includes index and bibliography.

499. Dairy Food Cookery. Tucson, Ariz., HP Books; Los Angeles, Calif., Knudsen Corp, 1981, c1977. 176 p., colored illus. Includes index. Formerly entitled: Cooking for Compliments.

500. The Complete Dairy Foods Cookbook: How to Make Everything from Cheese to Custard in Your Own Kitchen / by E. Annie Proulx and Lew Nichols; editor, Charles Gerras; original art, Jean Gardner and Jerry O'Brien; book design by Jerry O'Brien. Emmaus, Pa.: Rodale Press, c1982. 296 p., illus. 150 recipes using buttermilk, cheese, cream, milk, and yogurt. Includes index.

Specialty Cookbooks

Dairy Products *(Continued)*

501. Whisk It, Beat It, Cook It, Eat It!: Easy Recipes Using Dairy Products / prepared by the National Dairy Council; written by Sheila McEnery. Stevenage, Eng.: Publications for Companies, 1982. 96 p., illus. (some colored).

502. Making Cheese and Butter / Phyllis Hobson. Pownal, Vt.: Storey Communications, 1984. 45 p., illus. (Country Kitchen Library). "A Garden Way Publishing Book."

503. Cooking with Yoghurt: Delicious Recipes Made with Cultured Milk, Yoghurt, Sour Cream, Buttermilk, Soft Cheeses / Elaine Hallgarten. London, Eng.: Apple, c1985. 175 p., colored illus. "A Quintet Book." Includes index.

504. The Avalon Dairy Cookbook / by Linda Black-Crowley. Vancouver, B.C.: Black Publications, c1986. 159 p., illus. Includes index.

505. The Daring Dairy Cookbook. Boston, Mass.: Dorison House Publishers, c1986. 144 p., colored illus. Includes index.

506. Give Yourself a Treat! Granby, Que.: Agropur, 1986? 112 p., illus. Issued also in French under title: De l'entrée au dessert.

507. Wisconsin Dairy Country Recipes: A Collection from America's Dairyland / photographs, Wisconsin dairy scene by Grant Heilman Photography, food photographs by deGennaro Associates; food stylists, Mable Hoffman and Susan Brown Draudt. Madison, Wis.: Dairy Farmers of Wisconsin, Wisconsin Milk Marketing Board, c1986. 128 p., colored illus. Includes index.

508. Cheese and Dairy Sampler: A Collection of Dairy Foods Recipes / by Jan Siegrist. Shelburne, Vt.: New England Press, 1988. 48 p., illus.

Dairy Products *(Continued)*

509. Our Dairy Specialties: A Collection of Dairy Recipes from Illinois Dairy Farmers and Illinois Dairy Farm Wives. El Paso, Ill.: American Dairy Association of Illinois, c1988. 350 p. Includes index.

    see also specific dairy products: Buttermilk, Cheese, Cream, Milk, Yogurt

Dandelions

510. The Dandelion: Uses for the Whole Dandelion, with Recipes & Suggestions / Recycling Consortium. Houston, Tex.: Prosperity & Profits, 1984. 14 p.

    see also broader category: Flowers

Dates

511. Cooking with Dates. Toronto, Ont.: J.S. Khazzam, c1984. 40 p., illus. In English and French. French title: Recettes aux dattes.

512. Sphinx Ranch Date Recipes / compiled by Rick I. Heetland. Phoenix, Ariz.: Golden West Publishers, c1986. 128 p., illus. Includes index.

    see also broader category: Dried Fruits

Daylilies

513. The Delightful Delicious Daylily / by Peter A. Gail. Cleveland Heights, Ohio: Goosefoot Acres Press, 1989. 24 p.

    see also broader category: Flowers

Deer *see* Venison

Dogfish

514. The Dogfish Cookbook / by Russ Mohney; drawings by the author. Seattle, Wash.: Pacific Search Books, c1976. 108 p. Includes index.

see also broader category: Fish

Dried Beans *see* Beans

Dried Fruits

515. Dried Fruit / Robert Dark. Wellingborough, Eng.: Thorsons, 1982. 96 p.

516. Cooking and Baking with Dried Fruit / by Rita Greer; illustrated by the author. Wellingborough, Eng.: Thorsons, 1984. 192 p., illus. Includes index.

see also specific kinds of dried fruits: Dates, Prunes, Raisins; *and broader category:* Fruits

Dried Soup Mix

517. Souped up Recipes from Lipton. Englewood Cliffs, N.J.: T.J. Lipton, Inc., 1980. 128 p.

518. Lipton Creative Cookery. Englewood Cliffs, N.J.: T.J. Lipton, Inc., 1987. 1 v.

see also Bouillion Cubes; *and* Soups *(Section II)*

Specific Ingredients

Duck

519. Answering the Call to Duck Cookery: The Gourmet's and Hunter's Cookbook of Wild and Domestic Duck / Chandler S. Cheek. Biloxi, Miss. (P.O. Box 6597, Biloxi 39532): Answering The Call, c1985. 160 p., illus. Includes index.

520. Turkey & Duck Menus. Alexandria, Va.: Time-Life Books, c1985. 104 p., colored illus. (Great Meals in Minutes). Includes index.

see also broader category: Poultry

Earthworms

521. The Nobody Loves Me Cookbook / B. Gayle (Turner) Beadle, Gordon C. Beadle. Denver, Colo. (235 S. Decatur St., Denver 80219): Mad River Press, c1982. 40 p., illus.

Eels

522. The Anglers' Cookbook: Trout, Salmon, and Eel / Stewart Reidpath. Wellington, N.Z.: A.H. & A.W. Reed, 1973. 87 p.

see also broader category: Fish

Eggplants

523. The Eggplant Cookbook / by Norma S. Upson. Seattle, Wash.: Pacific Search Press, c1979. 154 p. Includes index.

524. Aubergine: A Miscellany of Gastronomic Delights and Horticultural Information / Jane Wilton-Smith & Maria Donkin; drawings by Bear. Salisbury, Eng.: Stylus, c1986. 24 p., illus. (The Good Table).

Eggplants *(Continued)*

525. Book of Eggplant, Okra & Peppers / edited by the staff of the National Gardening Magazine; illustrations by Elayne Sears & Lyn Severance. Rev. ed. New York: Villard Books, 1987. 87 p., illus. First ed. published as: The Gardens for All Book of Eggplant, Okra & Peppers / by Dick and Jan Raymond. 1979.

see also broader category: Vegetables

Eggs

526. The Fine Art of Egg, Omelet & Souffle Cooking / editor, Carol D. Brent; art director, Dick Collins; photography by Bill Miller. Chicago, Ill.: Tested Recipe Publishers; Garden City, N.Y.: Book trade distribution by Doubleday, 1970. 80 p., colored illus. (Gourmet International).

527. American Egg Board Food Service Manual: The Incredible Edible Egg. Park Ridge, Ill.: American Egg Board, 1980? 61 leaves, illus.

528. Classic Egg Dishes. Wilmington, Del.: Dupont, 1980. 64 p., colored illus.

529. A Carton Full of Texas Eggs: Plus Answers to Often Asked Questions About Eggs and Egg Cooking. Austin, Tex.: Texas Dept. of Agriculture, 1981? 12 p., illus.

530. The Egg Primer. Willowdale, Ont.: Ontario Egg Producers' Marketing Board, 1981? 22 p., illus.

531. Eggcyclopedia. Park Ridge, Ill.: American Egg Board, c1981. 50 p., illus.

532. Entertaining with Eggs / compiled by the Canadian Egg Marketing Agency. Markham, Ont.: PaperJacks, 1981. 191 p., 8 p. of colored plates.

Specific Ingredients 73

Eggs *(Continued)*

533. Every Day - Serve Eggs - Some Way / Elna Miller. Logan, Utah: Utah State University Cooperative Extension Service, 1981. 21 p., illus.

534. The Michael Field Egg Cookbook / edited by Joan Scobey. 1st ed. New York: Holt, Rinehart and Winston, 1981, c1980. 209 p., illus. "An Owl Book." Includes index.

535. Ova Easy: Egg Recipes You'll Flip Over / by Maxine Saltonstall; drawings by Wayne Mayfield. Honolulu, Hawaii: Bess Press; Mercer Island, Wash.: Available for distribution through Peanut Butter Pub.; Orange, Calif.: Distributed by Career Pub., c1982. 129 p. Includes index.

536. The Complete Book of Egg Cookery / Ann Seranne; illustrations by Lauren Jarrett. New York: Macmillan; London, Eng.: Collier Macmillan, c1983. 219 p., illus. Includes index.

537. Eggsinstead. 3rd ed. Willowdale, Ont.: Ontario Egg Producers' Marketing Board, 1983. 32 p., colored illus. Includes index.

538. The Little Brown Egg Book / by David Eno; illustrated by Clive Burch. Enl., rev. and reset ed. Wellingborough, Eng.: Thorsons, 1983. 56 p., illus. Includes index.

539. Making the Most of Eggs / Judy Ridgway. Newton Abbot, Eng.: David and Charles, c1983. 48 p., illus. Includes index.

540. The Little Egg Cookbook / Mary L. Green. Denver, Colo.: Giftstar, 1984. ca. 10 p., illus. (Little Cookbooks).

541. The Other Half of the Egg / by Ann Chilcote. Santa Fe, N.M.: Lightning Tree, c1984. 80 p.

542. A Pocket Book on Eggs: Appetizing Ways with Everyone's Favourite Food / Shirley Gill. London, Eng.: Octopus, 1984. 96 p., illus. (some colored). Includes index.

Eggs *(Continued)*

543. Eggs Only / by Sylvie Zebroff, Petra Zebroff, Leslie Kaip. Vancouver, B.C.: Fforbez Publications, c1985. 62 p., illus.

544. Microegg Meets the Munch Bunch: A Microwave Cookbook / brought to you by the Canadian Egg Marketing Agency. Ottawa, Ont.: Canadian Egg Marketing Agency, 1985. 27 p., illus. (some colored).

545. The Separate Egg: Recipes for Yolks and Whites / Pat Kery and Pat Field. 1st ed. New York: St. Martin's Press, c1985. 96 p., illus. Recipes for whites and recipes for yolks bound back to back.

546. Eggs by the Dozen: 12 Easy Egg Recipes. Willowdale, Ont.: Consumer Services & Public Relations, Ontario Egg Producers' Marketing Board, 1986? 15 p.

547. The Humpty Dumpty Cook Book: Or, What to Do with Them Once They're Broke / Joseph M. Joeb. Tampa, Fla.: American Studies Press, 1986. 33 p.

548. The Elegant Economical Egg Cookbook / by Lou Seibert Pappas; drawings by Marion Seawell. San Francisco, Calif.: 101 Productions; New York: Distributed to the book trade in U.S. by the Scribner Book Co., 1987?, c1976. 191 p. Originally published under title: Egg Cookery. Includes index.

549. The Little Egg Book / Jenny Ridgwell. London, Eng.: Piatkus, 1987. 64 p., illus.

550. Eggs: Uses for the Egg, with Recipes & Suggestions / Recycling Consortium. Houston, Tex.: Prosperity & Profits, 1989. ca. 14 p.

551. The Well Cooked Egg / Ann Carr. London, Eng.: Simon & Schuster, 1989. 96 p.

Eggs *(Continued)*

552. Exclusively Eggs / M.J. Butterfield. Burnstown, Ont.: General Store Pub. House, 1990. 1 v.

CHILDREN'S COOKBOOKS

553. Eggs / Dorothy Turner; illustrated by John Yates. Minneapolis, Minn.: Carolrhoda Books, 1989. 32 p., colored illus. Includes index.

see also Cheese and Eggs; *entries 264, 274; and specific dishes using eggs in Section II:* Omelets, Souffles, etc.

Elk

554. Elegant Elk, Delicious Deer / Judy Barbour; line illustrations by Cindy Garetson. 1st ed. Palacios, Tex.: Paul Peters Studio, 1978. 194 p., illus. Includes index.

555. The Incipient Elk Hunter: How to Hunt, Butcher, Preserve, and Prepare Elk / Mort Arkava; illustrated by Dayl Fredrickson. Rev. ed. Missoula, Mont.: Mountain Press Pub. Co., 1983, c1976. 112 p., illus.

see also broader category: Game

English Muffins

556. Thomas' Best: Thomas' Collection of Family Favorites Featuring Award Winning Recipes. Totowa, N.J.: S.B. Thomas, Inc., 1989. 1 booklet.

Filo Dough

557. Filo File for Filophiles / Billie Venturatos Andersson; illustrations by Leslie Bruning. New Orleans, La.: Andesign, c1985. 95 p., illus. Includes index.

558. The Art of Filo Cookbook: International Entries, Appetizers & Desserts Wrapped in Flaky Pastry / by Marti Sousanis; illustrated by Masayo Suzuki. Berkeley, Calif.: Aris Books; Reading, Mass.: Addison-Wesley Pub. Co., 1988. 143 p., illus. 60 recipes for fillings. Includes index.

see also broader category: Pastry *(Section II)*

Fish

559. Fish / by the editors of Time-Life Books. Alexandria, Va.: Time-Life Books; Morristown, N.J.: School and library distribution by Silver Burdett Co., 1979. 176 p., illus. (The Good Cook, Techniques & Recipes). Includes index.

560. New Fish Cookery / Marika Hanbury Tenison. London, Eng.: Granada, 1980, c1979. 256 p. (A Mayflower Book). Includes index.

561. A Fine Kettle of Fish / Michael Smith. London, Eng.: BBC, 1981. 46 p.

562. Fish Cookery with Magimix: Recipes Written for Food Processors / by Marika Hanbury Tenison. Sunbury, Eng. (Hanworth Rd., Sunbury, Middlesex): 1CTC, 1981. 31 p.

563. Fresh Ideas for Fish 'n Poultry. Glenview, Ill.: Kraft, Inc., 1981. 1 booklet. Recipes for main dishes using grated cheeses.

564. Keeping the Catch / Kenn and Pat Oberrecht. Tulsa, Okla.: Winchester Press, c1981. 227 p., illus.

Specific Ingredients 77

Fish *(Continued)*

565. A Kettle of Fish: Salt Water Fishes of the Mid-Atlantic Coast / text and illustrations by Lisa M. Beard; introduction by Dennis M. Allen. Stone Harbor, N.J.: Wetlands Institute, c1981. 48 p., illus. Includes bibliography.

566. 500 Recipes for Fish Dishes / by Marguerite Patten. London, Eng.: Hamlyn, 1982, c1965. 96 p. Includes index.

567. The Adventurous Fish Cook / George Lassalle. London, Eng.: Papermac, 1982, c1976. 236 p., illus. Includes index.

568. Cleaning & Cooking Fish / by Sylvia Bashline. Minnetonka, Minn. (5700 Green Circle Drive, Minnetonka 55343): Publication Arts, c1982. 160 p., colored illus. (The Hunting & Fishing Library). Includes index.

569. A Fish Feast / by Charlotte Wright; illustrated by Mike Foster. Seattle, Wash.: Pacific Search Press, 1982. 199 p., illus. Includes index.

570. Fish for Health: Low Calorie Fish Recipes. Dublin, Ire. (Hume House, Ballsbridge, Dublin 4): An Bord Iascaigh Mhara, 1982? 7 p., illus.

571. The Chef Recommends: A Selection of the Finest Fish Recipes in South Lakeland / compiled by Cumbria Seafoods. Preston, Eng.: Lakeland, c1983. 104 p. Includes index.

572. The Fish Recipe Book / Marika Hanbury Tenison. Cambridge, Eng.: Woodhead-Faulkner for J. Sainsbury, 1983. 96 p., illus. (some colored). (A Sainsbury Cookbook).

573. Freshwater Fisherman's Companion / Paul C. Baumann, James Jaeger; illustrated by Kandis Elliot. New York: Van Nostrand Reinhold, c1983. 215 p., illus. Includes indexes.

Fish *(Continued)*

574. The Frugal Fish: 300 Delicious Recipes for All Seasons / by Robert Ackart. 1st ed. Boston, Mass.: Little, Brown, c1983. 308 p., illus. Includes index.

575. The Microwave Fish Cookbook / Val Collins. Newton Abbot, Eng.: North Pomfret, Vt.: David & Charles, c1983. 120 p., illus. (some colored). Includes index.

576. North American Game Fish Cookbook / Bill & Anita Mabbutt; illustrated by Dana Sloan and Scott Fife. Vancouver, B.C.: Douglas & McIntyre, c1983. 188 p., illus. Includes index.

577. Paula Smith & Dorothy Seaman's It's All Fish: The Kosher Way to Cook Gourmet. West Hartford, Conn.: Jetsand Publishers, c1983. 286 p. Includes index.

578. Smoked Fish Recipes from Pinneys Smokehouses. Annan, Eng.: Pinneys Smokehouses, 1983. 70 p., illus. (some colored). Includes index.

579. The Fish Cookbook / Frederick E. Kahn. New York: Nautilus Communications; Aurora, Ill.: Distributed by Caroline House, c1984. 164 p., illus. Includes index.

580. Fishing in the West: A Guide to Alberta, Saskatchewan, and Manitoba / David Carpenter. Saskatoon, Sask.: Western Producer Prairie Books, 1984. 185 p., illus., maps. Includes bibliography.

581. Fixin' Fish: A Guide to Handling, Buying, Preserving, and Preparing Fish / Jeffrey Gunderson; illustrated by Leanne Alexander-Witzig. 2nd ed. Minneapolis, Minn.: University of Minnesota Press for the University of Minnesota Sea Grant Extension Program, c1984. 56 p., illus.

582. Hundreds of the Best Recipes from The Art of Fish Cookery / Milo Miloradovich. New York: Bantam Books, 1984, c1963. 214 p., illus.

Fish *(Continued)*

583. Juel Andersen's Seafood Primer: A Practical Book of Fish Cookery / by Shirley LaMere with Sigrid Andersen. Berkeley, Calif.: Creative Arts Communications, c1984. 64 p., illus. Includes index.

584. The Simply Seafood Cookbook of East Coast Fish / R. Marilyn Schmidt. 2nd ed. Barnegat Light, N.J.: Barnegat Light Press, 1984? ca. 185 p., illus. 175 recipes for 55 fish and batters, marinades, sauces, and stuffings. Includes index.

585. Classic Fish Dishes / Myra Street. London, Eng.: Apple, c1985. 128 p., colored illus. (A Quintet Book). Includes index.

586. Floyd on Fish / Keith Floyd. London, Eng.: British Broadcasting Corp. in association with Absolute Press, 1985. 112 p., illus. (some colored). Includes index.

587. Strictly Fish Cookbook / by Babe and Charlie Winkelman. 1st ed. Brainerd, Minn.: Babe Winkelman Productions, 1985. 258 p., illus. Includes index.

588. Better Homes and Gardens Fresh Fish Cook Book. 1st ed. Des Moines, Iowa: Meredith Corp., c1986. 96 p., illus. (some colored). Includes index.

589. Catchin' & Cookin' Freshwater Fish / by Jan Nalepa; drawing by Jan Nalepa. New York: Simon & Schuster, c1986. 60 p., illus. "A Fireside Book."

590. The Complete Fish Cookbook / Dan and Inez Morris. Rev. ed. / edited by Rosalyn Badalamenti. New York: Macmillan, c1986. 436 p., illus. "A Bobbs-Merrill Book." Includes index.

591. Delicious Fish / Claire MacDonald. London, Eng.: Grafton: 1986. 208 p., illus. Includes index.

Fish *(Continued)*

592. Dr. Bob Shipp's Guide to Fishes of the Gulf of Mexico / by Robert L. Shipp. Dauphin Island, Ala.: Dauphin Island Sea Lab, 1986. 256 p., illus. (some colored). Includes index.

593. Fish / Christian Teubner. 1st English-language ed. Woodbury, N.Y.: Barron's, 1986, c1985. 96 p., colored illus. Includes index. Translation of: Fisch.

594. Fish and Meat. Pleasantville, N.Y.: Reader's Digest Assn., c1986. 192 p., colored illus. (The Reader's Digest Good Health Cookbooks). Includes index.

595. Fish Dishes of the Pacific from the Fishwife / by Shirley Rizzuto; illustrations by Leslie Hata; editing by Sylvia Rodgers. 1st ed. Honolulu, Hawaii (P.O. Box 25413, Honolulu 96825): Hawaii Fishing News, c1986. 157 p., illus.

596. Fish on the Grill: More Than 70 Elegant, Easy, and Delectable Recipes / Barbara Grunes and Phyllis Magida. Chicago, Ill.: Contemporary Books, c1986. 114 p., illus. (some colored). Contains recipes for 30 types of fish and seafood. Includes index.

597. Gray's Fish Cookbook: A Menu Cookbook / by Rebecca Gray with Cintra Reeve; photography by Frank Foster; watercolors by Thomas Aquinas Daly. South Hamilton, Mass.: GSJ Press, 1986. 216 p., illus. (some colored). Includes index.

598. Let's Cook Fish: Complete Guide to Fish Cookery. New York: Gordon Press, 1986. 55 p., illus.

599. Saucing the Fish / Shirley King; illustrated by Rodica Prato. New York: Simon and Schuster, c1986. 320 p., illus. Includes index.

600. Wheeler's New Fish Cookery. London, Eng.: Ebury, 1986. 112 p., illus. (some colored). Includes index.

Fish *(Continued)*

601. 104 Ontario Game Fish Recipes / by Darryl Choronzey. Wiarton, Ont.: Ontario Fisherman Publications, 1987. 78 p., illus.

602. Cooking with Fish / Elizabeth Cornish. New York: Gallery Books, c1987. 73 p., colored illus. 49 recipes. (The Microwave Library). Includes index.

603. F for Fish / Anne Williams. London, Eng.: Dent, 1987. 203 p., illus. (some colored). (Healthright). Includes index.

604. A Feast of Fish / Ian McAndrew. London, Eng.: Macdonald, 1987. 224 p., colored illus. Includes index.

605. The Fish Course / Susan Hicks. London, Eng.: BBC Books, 1987. 304 p.

606. Fresh Fish Cookbook. New York: Exeter Books, c1987. 96 p., illus. (some colored). Includes index.

607. The Good Fat Diet / Robert Gold and Kerry Rose-Gold. Toronto, Ont.; New York: Bantam Books, 1987. 195 p. Includes index.

608. International Fish Cookbook / Nina Froud and Tamara Lo. New York: Hippocrene Books, 1987. 240 p.

609. James Beard's New Fish Cookery: A Revised and Updated Edition of James Beard's Fish Cookery / illustrations by Earl Thollander. New York: Warner Books, 1987, c1976. 495 p., illus. Includes index. Reprint. Originally published: Boston, Mass.: Little, Brown, c1976.

610. Microwave Fish Cookbook / Janet Smith. London, Eng.: Ebury, 1987. 128 p.

611. The New Fish Cookbook / Janet Horsley. London, Eng.: Futura, 1987. 188 p. Includes index.

Fish *(Continued)*

612. The Omega-3 Breakthrough: The Revolutionary, Medically-Proven Fish Oil Diet Including Menu Plans & Recipes / by Julius Fast; developed by Philip Lief Group, Inc. Tucson, Ariz.: Body Press, c1987. 228 p. Includes bibliography.

613. The Angler's Only Cookbook: A Fantastic Guide to Preparing Game Fish / by Darryl Choronzey. Wiarton, Ont.: Ontario Fisherman Publications, 1988. 164 p., illus.

614. Anton Mosimann's Fish Cuisine. London, Eng.: Macmillan, 1988. 256 p., illus. (some colored). Includes index. Also published in 1990 by Papermac, London, Eng.

615. The Compleat McClane: A Treasury of A.J. McClane's Classic Angling Adventures / A.J. McClane; edited and with an introduction by John Merwin. 1st ed. New York: E.P. Dutton, c1988. 404 p. "Truman Talley Books." Includes index.

616. Cooking with Fish / Rosamond Man. London, Eng.: Hamlyn, 1988, c1986. 80 p. (Cooking for Today).

617. Family Fish Cookbook: Easy-to-Use Recipes for Tasty Fish Favourites / Roz Denny. Cambridge, Mass.: Martin Books, 1988. 94 p.

618. Fish. Toronto, Ont.: Grolier, 1988. 110 p., colored illus. (Microwave Magic; 5). Includes index.

619. Fish / Robyn Wilson. London, Eng.: Sphere, 1988. 236 p.

620. Fish Steaks and Fillets: 83 Recipes for Serving up the Catch of the Day / by Michele Scicolone. 1st ed. New York: Harmony Books, c1988. 96 p., illus. (A Particular Palate Cookbook). Includes index.

621. How to Hook and Cookbook / Mike Sakamoto. Honolulu, Hawaii: Bess Press, 1988. 192 p., illus.

Fish *(Continued)*

622. Microwave Fish Cooking / Kate Whiteman. London, Eng.: Macdonald, 1988. 128 p.

623. The National Trust Book of Fish Cookery / Sara Paston-Williams. London, Eng.: The Trust, 1988. 224 p., illus. Includes index.

624. Simply Fish / Jenny Baker; illustrated by Madeleine Baker. London, Eng.: Faber, 1988. 333 p., illus. Includes index.

625. Bill Saiff's Rod & Reel: Recipes for Hookin' & Cookin' / WNPE-TV, Channel 16. Nashville, Tenn.: Favorite Recipes Press, 1989. 120 p.

626. Eat Fish, Live Better: How to Put More Fish and Omega-3 Fish Oils Into Your Diet for a Longer, Healthier Life / Anne M. Fletcher. 1st ed. New York: Harper & Row, c1989. 378 p. More than 75 reduced-fat-and-calorie recipes. Includes index.

627. The Fish in My Life: Cooking and Eating Fish for Health and Happiness / George Lassalle; illustrated by Harriet Lasalle. London, Eng.: Macmillan, 1989. 277 p., illus. Includes bibliography and index.

628. Gourmet Fish on the Grill: More Than 90 Easy Recipes for Elegant Entertaining / Phyllis Magida and Barbara Grunes. Chicago, Ill.: Contemporary Books, c1989. 192 p. Includes index.

629. The Northeast Saltwater Fisherman's International Cookbook / Sal Agliano; edited by Bob Rhodes. Point Pleasant, N.J.: Ocean Sport Fish, 1989. 132 p., illus. (The Fisherman Library).

630. The Angler's Guide to Fish as Food / adapted from material written by Robert J. Learson, John D. Kaylor, and the staff of the National Marine Fisheries Service Gloucester Laboratory; adapted and edited by Ian Dore; illustrations by Karen Swift. Huntington, N.Y.: Osprey Books, c1990. 1 v., illus.

Fish *(Continued)*

631. Anton Mosimann's Fish Cuisine. London, Eng.: Papermac, 1990. 256 p., illus. (some colored). Includes index. Also published in 1989 by Macmillan, London, Eng.

632. Fishing for Buffalo: A Guide to the Pursuit, Lore and Cuisine of Buffalo, Carp, Mooneye, Gar, and Other "Rough" Fish / Rob Buffler, Tom Dickson. Minneapolis, Minn.: Culpepper Press, c1990. 197 p., illus., maps. Includes bibliography.

633. Making the Most of Your Catch: An Angler's Guide / Ian Dore. New York: Van Nostrand Reinhold, c1990. 162 p., illus. Includes bibliography and index.

CHILDREN'S COOKBOOKS

634. Fishing Is for Me / text and photos. by Art Thomas. Minneapolis, Minn.: Lerner Publications Co., c1980. 46 p., illus. (The Sports for Me Books). Kevin and his friend Virgil explain the techniques of fishing, equipment, bait, kinds of fish, and preparing fish for cooking.

see also Canned Fish; Fish and Game; Frozen Fish; *specific kinds of fish:* Anchovies, Blackfish, Bluefish, Catfish, Caviar, Crappie, Dogfish, Eels, Flounder, Halibut, Mackerel, Mahi-Mahi, Monkfish, Orange Roughy, Pollock, Salmon, Sardines, Shad, Shark, Tilefish, Trout, Tuna, and Weakfish; *and broader categories:* Seafood; *and* Sushi *(Section II)*

Fish and Game

635. European Recipes for American Fish & Game / by David Backus. Oshkosh, Wis.: Willow Creek Press, c1978. 110 p., illus. (European Classic Series).

636. The Encyclopedia of Wild Game Cleaning and Cooking / Pat Billmeyer. Danville, Pa.: A. Billmeyer Cars Pub., c1979. 116 p. Includes index.

Fish and Game *(Continued)*

637. Collins' Backroom Cooking Secrets: Wild Game, Fish, and Other Savories / by Tom Collins; foreword by Ron Schara; illustrations by Dennis Anderson. 1st ed. Minneapolis, Minn.: Waldman House Press, c1980. 253 p., illus. Includes index.

638. Recipes of the Wild: Complete Game Cookery / by Terry Griffith. Memphis, Tenn.: Wimmer Bros. Fine Printing and Lithography, c1980. 93 p., illus. (Cookbooks of Distinction). Includes index.

639. Wild Game Cook Book. Winnipeg, Man.: Gateway Pub. Co., c1980. 2 v., illus.

640. Dominique's Famous Fish, Game & Meat Recipes / Dominique D'Ermo. Washington, D.C.: Acropolis Books, c1981. 126 p., illus. Includes index.

641. Newest, Easiest, Most Exciting Recipes and Menus for Fish and Game Cooking Using Standard Kitchen Equipment Plus Energy-Saving Crockpots, Pressure Cookers, Outdoor Grills, Microwave and Convection Ovens / Joan Cone. McLean, Va.: EPM Publications, 1981. 382 p. Spine title: Fish and Game Cooking. Includes index.

642. Care & Cooking of Fish & Game / John Weiss. Tulsa, Okla.: Winchester Press, c1982. 252 p., illus. Includes index.

643. Cooking Wild Game & Fish Mississippi Style: A Treasury of Unique Recipes for the Sportsman / by Billy Joe Cross. Rev. ed. Clinton, Miss. (P.O. Box 171, Clinton 39056): B.J. Cross, c1982. 160 p., illus.

644. Rocky Mountain Cache: A Western Wild Game Cookbook / Sharon Duffala. 1st ed. Boulder, Colo.: Pruett, c1982. 80 p., illus. Includes index.

Fish and Game *(Continued)*

645. Wild Country All Game and Fish Recipes: A Collection of Over 115 Recipes: Big Game, Small Game, Fish, Dressings, Marinades, Brines / by Jay Jaxson. Shoreview, Minn.: Wild Country Innovations, 1982. 85 p.

646. The Complete Encyclopedia of Wild Game & Fish Cleaning & Cooking / by Pat Billmeyer. Danville, Pa.: Yesnaby Publishers, 1983. 3 v., illus. Includes indexes. Contents: v.1. Big Game. v.2. Small Game. v.3. Fish, Fowl, Reptiles & Survival.

647. Complete Fish and Game Cookery of North America / Frances MacIlquham; special photography by Sylvia and Jim Bashline; decorative drawings by E.B. Sanders. Tulsa, Okla.: Winchester Press, c1983. 304 p., illus. (some colored). Includes index.

648. Cooking the Sportsman's Harvest II. Pierre, S.D.: South Dakota Dept. of Game, Fish, and Parks, 1983. 120 p., illus.

649. The L.L. Bean Game and Fish Cookbook / Angus Cameron and Judith Jones; illustrations by Bill Elliott. New York: Random House, c1983. 475 p., illus. Includes index.

650. Wild Game and Country Cooking: Recipes for the Sportsman and Gourmet / by Timothy Manion. [n.p.]: Manion Outdoors; Oconomowoc, Wis.: printing by C.W. Brown, 1983. 199 p., illus. Includes index.

651. Beaver Tails and Dorsal Fins: Wild Meat Recipes / by G. Lamont Burley; illustrations by Joe Borril. Menominee, Mich.: G.L. Burley, c1984. 50 p., illus.

652. Cooking the Wild Harvest / by J. Wayne Fears; illustrated by David Wright. Merrillville, Ind.: ICS Books; Harrisburg, Pa.: Distributed by Stackpole Books, c1984. 183 p., illus.

Fish and Game *(Continued)*

653. Classic Game Cookery / compiled for the Game Conservancy by Julia Drysdale. London, Eng.: Macmillan, 1984, c1975. 223 p., illus. Originally published: Glasgow, Scot.: Collins, 1975 under title: The Game Cookery Book.

654. The Wild Game and Fish Cookbook / by Jim Bryant; drawings by Lea Carmichael. Boston, Mass,: Little, Brown, c1984. 207 p., illus. Includes index.

655. Fish, Poultry and Game. London, Eng.: Reader's Digest Association, c1985. 104 p., illus. (some colored). (The Reader's Digest Good Health Cookbooks). Includes index.

656. Microwave Game & Fish Cookbook: Quick, Convenient Recipes for Concocting the Tastiest, Juiciest, Most Succulent Wild Meat and Fish Meals You've Ever Eaten / Paula J. Del Giudice. Harrisburg, Pa.: Stackpole Books, c1985. 191 p., illus. More than 200 recipes. Includes index.

657. Alice Hunter's North Country Cookbook / Alice Hunter. Yellowknife, N.W.T.: Outcrop, c1986. 85 p., colored illus. Includes index.

658. Cooking Over Coals: Preparing Fish and Game in the Field / Mel Marshall. Rev. ed. Lexington, Mass.: S. Greene Press; New York: Distributed by Viking Penguin, 1986. 361 p., illus. Includes index. "A Penguin Original."

659. Game in Season: The Orvis Cookbook / by Romi Perkins; introduction by Gene Hill; illustrated by Judy Sgantas. Piscataway, N.J.: New Century Publishers, c1986. 231 p., illus. "Nick Lyons Books." Includes index.

660. 99 Game and Fish Dishes with 33 Colour Photographs / Mari Lajos, Károly Hemző. Budapest, Hungary: Corvina, 1987. 64 p., colored illus. Translated from the Hungarian.

Fish and Game *(Continued)*

661. Colorado Catch Cookbook: Wild Game and Fish Recipes. Denver, Colo.: Colorado Division of Wildlife, c1987. 154 p., illus. Issued in cooperation with the Colorado Wildlife Federation.

662. Cy Littlebee's Guide to Cooking Fish & Game: Missouri Recipes / compiled by Werner O. Nagel; illustrations by Jim Keller. Jefferson City, Mo.: Missouri Dept. of Conservation, 1987 printing, c1981. 144 p., illus.

663. The Derrydale Cook Book of Fish and Game / by Louis P. De Gouy. Wautoma, Wis.: Willow Creek Press, 1987. v. 2. Cover title: The Derrydale Fish Cook Book. Reprint. Originally published: New York: Derrydale Press, 1937. (v. 2).

664. Fish and Fowl Cookery: The Outdoorsman's Home Companion / by Carol Vance Wary with William G. Wary. Woodstock, Vt.: Countryman Press, c1987. 194 p., illus.

665. The Game and Fish Menu Cookbook: A Country Collection / by Timothy E. Manion; illustrated by Sharon Anderson. 1st ed. New York: Weidenfeld & Nicolson, c1987. 304 p., illus. Includes index.

666. Game for All: With a Flavour of Scotland / Nichola Fletcher. London, Eng.: V. Gollancz, 1987. 208 p., illus. Includes index.

667. Going Wild / Urban Gaida and Martin Marchello. Sartell, Minn.: Watab Marketing, c1987. 240 p., illus. "A guide to field dressing, butchering, sausage-making & cooking wild game & fish." Includes index.

668. Going Wild: Recipes from the Great Outdoors / Linda Braun, Barbara Cox-Lloyd. Saskatoon, Sask.: Western Producer Prairie Books, c1987. 108 p. Includes index.

669. The Real Bill Bannock Cookbook / by Bill Bannock. The Pas, Man.: New North Ventures, c1987. 135 p., illus.

Fish and Game *(Continued)*

670. Easy Recipes for Wild Game and Fish / by Ferne Holmes. Phoenix, Ariz.: Golden West, c1988. 160 p., illus. More than 200 recipes. Includes index.

671. Getting the Most from Your Game and Fish: A Complete Field Manual for the North American Sportsman / written and illustrated by Robert Candy. Putney, Vt.: A.C. Hood, 1988?, c1978. 278 p., illus. Includes bibliography and index. Reprint. Originally published: Charlotte, Vt.: Garden Way Pub., c1978.

672. The Sporting Wife: A Guide to Game and Fish Cooking / edited by Barbara Hargreaves. London, Eng.: Gollancz, 1988. 336 p., illus. "Incorporating in one volume, with revisions, The Sporting Wife and The Compleat Angler's Wife."

673. Outdoor Life's Complete Fish and Game Cookbook / by A.D. Livingston; drawings by Dolores Santoloquido. Danbury, Conn.: Outdoor Life Books, c1989. 440 p. Includes index.

674. Uncle Russ Chittenden's Good Ole Boys Wild Game Cookbook, or, How to Cook 'Possum and Other Varmints Good. Paducah, Ky.: Image Graphics: Copies ordered from Collector Books, 1989. 126 p., illus. (some colored).

675. Gourmet Game: Recipes and Anecdotes from Around the World / Philippa Scott; illustrations by Francesca Pelizzoli. New York: Simon and Schuster, c1990. 160 p., colored illus. More than 160 recipes for fish and game. First published in 1989 in Great Britain by Barrie & Jenkins Ltd., London. Includes index.

676. Wild & Famous Fish & Game Cookbook / George Manthei. Utica, N.Y.: North Country Books, 1990. 124 p., illus. Contains 25 recipes for fish, 17 for deer, 16 for ducks and geese, 5 for frogs, 10 for bear, boar, buffalo, and rabbit, and 17 for small game birds.

see also Fish; Game

Flounder

677. Flounder and Other Flat Fish / by R. Marilyn Schmidt. Barnegat Light, N.J.: Barnegat Light Press, 1987. 20 p.

see also broader category: Fish

Flour

678. Flour Cooking, Naturally / Jo Smith. London, Eng.: Hutchinson, 1980. 128 p., illus. (some colored). Includes index.

679. Purity All-Purpose Flour Cook Book / Anna Lee Scott. Toronto, Ont.: Maple Leaf Mills, 1982. 215 p., illus. (some colored). Includes index. Previously published: Purity Cook Book. Saint John, N.B.: Maple Leaf Mills, 197-.

680. Favorite Gold Medal Flour Recipes. Minneapolis, Minn.: General Mills, 1987. 91 p., colored illus. (Betty Crocker Creative Recipes; no. 6). Includes index.

see also Grains; *specific dishes using flour in Section II, e.g.* Bread; Cakes; Cookies; Pastry; etc.; and Baking *(Section III)*

Flowers

681. A Book of Flowers / by June Hildebrand. New York: Claremount Press, c1981. 71 p., illus. (some colored). "Printed in a limited edition to 200 signed and numbered copies."

682. A Worldly Taste of Seasonings, Herbs and Flowers / written and illustrated by L. Wallace Harvey. Churchville, N.Y.: School of Fine Cookery, c1981. 390 p., illus. (The School of Fine Cookery Encyclopedia; v. 1). Includes index.

683. Cooking with Flowers / Zack Hanle; illustrated by Donald Hendricks. New York: I. Chalmers Cookbooks, c1982. 48 p., illus.

Flowers *(Continued)*

684. Living with the Flowers: A Guide to Bringing Flowers into Your Daily Life / by Denise Diamond; illustrations by Patricia Waters. 1st ed. New York: Morrow, 1982. 293 p., illus. Includes index.

685. The New England Butt'ry Shelf Almanac: Being a Collation of Observations on New England People, Birds, Flowers, Herbs, Weather, Customs, and Cookery of Yesterday and Today / Mary Mason Campbell; illustrated by Tasha Tudor. Brattleboro, Vt.: S. Greene Press, c1982. 302 p., illus. (some colored). Includes index.

686. A Book of Fruits and Flowers: First Published in 1653 and Here Reproduced in Facsimile / with an introduction by C. Anne Wilson. London, Eng.: Prospect Books, 1984. 49 p., illus.

687. Edible Flowers / Claire Clifton; illustrated by Glynn Boyd Harte. New York: McGraw-Hill, c1984. 94 p., colored illus. Includes bibliography and index.

688. The Forgotten Art of Flower Cookery / Leona Woodring Smith; drawings by Liz Thompson. Gretna, La.: Pelican Pub. Co., 1985, c1973. 180 p. Includes index. Reprint. Originally published: 1st ed. New York: Harper & Row, 1973.

689. Cooking with Flowers / Jenny Leggatt. 1st American ed. New York: Fawcett Columbine, 1987. 142 p., colored photos. More than 150 recipes. Includes bibliography and index.

690. On Flowers / by Kathryn Kleinman and Sara Slavin; photography, Kathryn Kleinman; styling, Sara Slavin; text, Linda Peterson; design, Michael Mabry; food, Amy Nathan. San Francisco, Calif.: Chronicle Books, c1988. 159 p., colored illus.

Flowers *(Continued)*

691. A Bouquet of Flowers: Sweet Thoughts, Recipes, and Gifts from the Garden, with "The Language of Flowers" / by Barbara Milo Ohrbach. New York: C.N. Potter, 1990. 56 p. More than 130 hand-colored engravings.

692. Flowers in the Kitchen: A Bouquet of Tasty Recipes / Susan Belsinger; photography by Joe Coca. Loveland, Colo.: Interweave Press, c1990. 1 v., illus.

693. Flowery Food & Drink / Jenny Leggatt. London, Eng.: Piatkus, 1990. 64 p.

see also specific flowers: Dandelions, Daylilies, Roses

Fowl
see **Chicken; Duck; Fowl and Game; Pheasants; Poultry; Turkey**

Fowl and Game

694. Southern Wildfowl and Wild Game Cookbook / by Jan Wongrey; illustrated by Laura Peck. 2nd ed. Lexington, S.C.: Sandlapper Pub., c1976. 163 p., illus. Includes index.

695. Rolf's Collection of Wild Game Recipes / by Rolf A. Pederson. Montevideo, Minn.: Rolf's Gallery, c1982-1983. v. 1: Upland Game Birds. 154 p., illus. Includes bibliography. v. 2: Waterfowl.

696. Making the Most of Chicken, Poultry & Game / Robert Carrier. London, Eng.: Marshall Cavendish, 1985. 112 p., colored illus. (Robert Carrier's Kitchen). Includes index.

697. The Poultry and Game Cookbook / Jill Graham. London, Eng.: Hamlyn, 1985. 255 p., colored illus. Includes index.

Specific Ingredients

Fowl and Game *(Continued)*

698. The WI Book of Poultry and Game / Pat Hesketh. London, Eng.: WI Books, 1985. 96 p., illus. Includes index.

699. Game: The Art of Preparation and Cooking of Game and Game Fowl / by Klaus Wöckinger. Calgary, Alta.: N and C Pub., 1988. 196 p., colored illus. Includes index.

700. Ian McAndrew on Poultry and Game. New York: Nostrand Reinhold, 1989. 232 p., illus. (some colored).

see also Game; Poultry

Frankfurters

701. Hot Dog! / by Robert Fischer; photos by the author; illustrations by Steve Gregg. New York: J. Messner, c1980. 64 p., illus. Includes index.

702. I Love Hot Dogs: 120 Frank Recipes / recipes by Pat Thompson; cartoons by Dan Youra. Port Ludlow, Wash.: Still News Press, c1982. 119 p., illus. Includes index.

703. Nathan's Famous Hot Dog Cookbook / by Murray Handwerker. New York: Gramercy: Distributed by Crown Publishers, 1983, c1968. 95 p., illus. "A Lou Reda Book." Includes index.

704. Cooking Frankly: Hot Dog Cuisine / Wallace Baljo, Jr. Pullman, Wash.: Clipboard Publications, 1989? 175 p., illus.

see also broader category: Meat; Sausages

Frozen Fish

705. Trust the Gorton's Fisherman for Delicious Recipe Ideas. Gloucester, Mass.: Gorton's, 1983. 1 booklet.

Frozen Fish *(Continued)*

706. Secrets of the Sea: The Fresh Appeal of Frozen Fish / Rose Murray. Toronto, Ont.: Grosvenor House Press, 1989. 94 p., 8 p. of colored plates. Includes index.

see also broader category: Fish

Frozen Vegetables

707. The Birds Eye Magic Moments in Minutes Cookbook. White Plains, N.Y.: General Foods, 1980. 1 booklet. Includes chicken, hamburger, and tuna one-dish dinners.

see also broader category: Vegetables

Fructose

708. The Fructose Cookbook / by Minuha Cannon; illustrations by Eloise Pope. Charlotte, N.C.: East Woods Press, c1979. 128 p., illus. Includes index.

709. Sweets Without Guilt: The Fructose Dessert Cookbook / by Minuha Cannon; illustrations by Laurie Graybeal. Charlotte, N.C.: East Woods Press, c1980. 150 p., illus. Almost 200 recipes. Includes index.

710. Cooking with Fructose / Anita Byrd. New York: Arco, c1981. 147 p. Includes index.

Fruits

711. Cooking with Fruit / Mary Norwak. New York: Dover Publications, 1974. 160 p. First published: Albuquerque, N.M.: Transatlantic Arts, 1960.

Fruits *(Continued)*

712. How to Use Hawaiian Fruit / Agnes Alexander. Hilo, Hawaii: Petroglyph, 1974.

713. The No-Cooking Fruitarian Recipe Book / by Sheila Andrews; drawings by Graham Lester. Wellingborough, Eng.: Thorsons Publishers, 1975. 96 p., illus. Includes index.

714. Maurice's Tropical Fruit Cook Book / by Maurice de Verteuil. St. Petersburg, Fla.: Great Outdoors, c1979. 79 p., illus.

715. All Maine Fruit Cookbook / compiled and edited by Loana Shibles and Annie Rogers; illustrations by James Kingsland. Camden, Me.: Down East Books, c1980. 186 p., illus. Includes index. "No. 3 of a new series."

716. Better Homes and Gardens All-Time Favorite Fruit Recipes / editors, Joanne Johnson, Bonnie Lasater. 1st ed. Des Moines, Iowa: Meredith Corp., c1980. 96 p., colored illus. Includes index.

717. The Fruit Cookbook / Suzanne Topper. New York: Avon, 1980. 315 p., illus. (Flare Books).

718. Recipes from the Mangrove Country of the Everglades. Everglades City, Fla.: Collier County Public Schools, Everglades City High School, Prop Roots Organization, c1980. 58 p., illus. (Prop Roots; v. 1).

719. The Book of Fruit and Fruit Cookery / Paul Dinnage; illustrations by Meg Rutherford. London, Eng.: Sidgwick and Jackson, 1981. 277 p., illus.

720. Fruits of the Desert / by Sandal English, food editor. Tucson, Ariz.: Arizona Daily Star, c1981. 181 p., illus. Includes index.

721. Enjoy B.C. Brand Fruit the Diabetic Way / by Elaine Johnston. 1st ed. Kelowna, B.C.: B.C. Tree Fruits, 1982. 40 p., 18 p. of plates, illus. (some colored).

Fruits *(Continued)*

722. Fruit Desserts. New York: Golden Press, c1982. 64 p., colored illus. (A Betty Crocker Picture Cookbook; 7). "Selected from Betty Crocker's Step-by-step receipe cards."

723. The Pocket Book of Fruit & Nut Cooking / Gwyneth Ashmore. London, Eng.: Evans, 1981. 128 p., illus. Includes index.

724. Tropical Fruit Desserts (and Other Good Things!) / by Beverly Kling Mohlenbrock. St. Petersburg, Fla.: Outdoors Pub. Co., c1981. 72 p., illus. Includes index.

725. Tropical Fruit Recipes: Rare and Exotic Fruits / Rare Fruit Council International. Rev. ed. Miami, Fla.: Rare Fruit Council International: Distributed by Banyan Books, 1981. 180 p., illus. (some colored).

726. Cooking with Fruit and Preserving / edited by Ruth Farnsworth. London, Eng.: M. Cavendish Books, 1982, c1977. 64 p., illus. Includes index.

727. The Natural Fruit Cookbook / by Gail L. Worstman. Seattle, Wash.: Pacific Search Press, c1982. 155 p. Includes index.

728. Cooking with Fruit / Marion Gorman; editor, Charles Gerras. Emmaus, Pa.: Rodale Press, c1983. 332 p., illus. Includes index.

729. A Fruit Cookbook / Gillian Painter. London, Eng.: Hodder and Stoughton, 1983. 367 p., illus. Includes index.

730. Fruit Fare / Mary Berry. London, Eng.: Sphere, 1983, c1982. 204 p. Includes index.

731. Fruits / by the editors of Time-Life Books. Alexandria, Va.: Time-Life Books, c1983. 176 p., illus. (some colored). (The Good Cook, Techniques & Recipes). Includes indexes.

Fruits *(Continued)*

732. Jane Grigson's Fruit Book / illustrated by Yvonne Skargon. Harmondsworth, Eng.: Penguin, 1983, 1982. 508 p., illus. Includes index.

733. One Hundred and One Fruit Recipes / Carole Eberly. East Lansing, Mich.: Eberly Press, 1983. 48 p., illus.

734. Rose Elliot's Book of Fruits. London, Eng.: Fontana, 1983. 64 p., illus. Includes index.

735. South African Fruit Cooking & Preserving / Magdaleen van Wyk; photography, Richard Wege Photography (Natal). 1st ed. Cape Town, South Africa: C. Struik, 1983. 153 p., illus.

736. Taste Niagara: 200 Recipes to Celebrate 200 Years of Agriculture in Niagara / written and compiled by Garcia Janes; illustrated by Liisa Harju for the Preservation of Agricultural Lands Society. St. Catharines, Ont.: The Society, c1983. 150 p., illus. Includes bibliography and index.

737. Wild Fruits: An Illustrated Field Guide & Cookbook / Mildred Fielder. Chicago, Ill.: Contemporary Books, c1983. 271 p., illus. Includes indexes.

738. But I Love Fruits / George Ohsawa & Jacques De Langre. New York: Happiness Press, 1984. 1 v., illus.

739. Fresh Fruit Drinks / by Lorraine Whiteside; color photography by the author, line drawings by Ian Jones. 1st U.S. ed. New York: Thorsons Publishers, 1984. 128 p., Includes index.

740. The Fruit and Nut Book / Helena Radecka. New York: McGraw-Hill, c1984. 256 p., illus. (some colored). "A Phoebe Phillips Editions Book." Includes index.

Fruits *(Continued)*

741. The Fruit Cookbook / Frederick E. Kahn; edited by Carla Neville Ciofalo. New York: Nautilus Communications; Aurora, Ill.: Distributed by Caroline House, c1984. 125 p., illus. (Preparing Food the Healthy Way Series). Includes index.

742. A-Z of Favorite Fruits. New York: Arco, 1985. 72 p., colored illus. Includes index.

743. Cooking with Fruits & Wines / Pietro Corsi. 1st ed. Los Angeles, Calif.: Phoenix Printing and Design, 1985, c1983. 209 p., illus. (some colored). Includes index.

744. Fruit / Pamela Westland. London, Eng.: Bell & Hyman, 1985. 93 p., illus. (some colored). (New & Natural). Includes index.

745. Fruit for the Home and Garden / Leslie Johns & Violet Stevenson; illustrated by Marianne Yamaguchi. North Ryde, N.S.W.: Angus & Robertson, 1985, c1979. 252 p., 12 p. of plates, illus. (some colored). First published in 1979 as: The Complete Book of Fruit.

746. A Guide to Market Fruits of Southeast Asia / by Karen Phillipps and Martha Dahlen. Quarry Bay, Hong Kong: South China Morning Post Ltd., Publications Division, c1985. 131 p., colored illus. Includes index.

747. The Complete Book of Fruit: An Illustrated Guide to Over 400 Species and Varieties of Fruit from All Over the World / Dick Pijpers, Jac. G. Constant, Kees Jansen. New York: Gallery Books, c1986. 179 p., illus. Includes index.

748. Fabulous Fruit Desserts: Their Preparation, Presentation & Creation / by Terence Janericco; color photographs by James Scherer; line drawings by Anne Vadeboncoeur. 1st ed. Dublin, N.H.: Yankee Books, c1986. 296 p., illus. (some colored). ca. 600 recipes. Includes index.

Fruits *(Continued)*

749. Cooking with BC Fruit: Tame & Wild / by Bette McClure Capozzo. Prince George, B.C.: BeeCap Pub., 1987. 153 p., illus. Includes index.

750. The Little Exotic Fruit Book / Susan Fleming. London, Eng.: Piatkus, 1987. 64 p., illus.

751. Fruit Desserts! / by Dorothy Parker; edited by Andrea Chesman. Freedom, Calif.: Crossing Press, c1987. 175 p., illus. Includes index.

752. Fruit from Your Garden / Liz Brand; illustrated by Rosemary Wise. London, Eng.: Unwin Hyman, 1987. 87 p., illus. (some colored).

753. Introspection by Observation: The 3-R's of Fruitful Living (Rhyme, Reason, Recipe) / Wm. Du Bois Carlyle. Sacramento, Calif.: Word Dynamics Concept, c1987. 112 p., illus. Includes index.

754. Pamella Z. Asquith's Fruit Tart Cookbook / illustrations by the author. New York: Weathervane Books: Distributed by Crown Publishers, 1987, c1982. 141 p., illus. Reprint. Originally published: New York: Harmony Books, c1982. Includes index.

755. The Sugarless Cookbook: Cooking with the Natural Sweetness of Fruit / by Nellie G. Hum; photography by Patricia Holdsworth. Ottawa, Ont.: Hum Pub., 1987, c1985. 111 p., colored photos. Includes index.

756. Exotic Fruits A-Z / Josephine Bacon. London, Eng.: Xanadu, 1988. 128 p.

757. Fabulous French Fruit Cuisine: Gourmet French Fruit Recipes from a Master Chef / Jean Conil and Fay Franklin. Wellingborough, Eng.: Thorsons Pub. Group; New York: Distributed by Sterling Pub. Co., 1988. 160 p., illus. (some colored). Includes index.

Fruits *(Continued)*

758. The Fresh Fruit Cookbook: New Ways with Traditional Favourites / Pam Cary. Marlborough, Eng.: Crowood Press, 1988. 192 p., illus. Includes index.

759. Fruit / Amy Nathan; photographs by Kathryn Kleinman. San Francisco, Calif.: Chronicle Books, c1988. 144 p., colored illus. 50 recipes. Includes index.

760. The Old-Fashioned Fruit Garden: The Best Way to Grow, Preserve and Bake with Small Fruit / Jo Ann Gardner. Halifax, N.S.: Nimbus Pub., c1989. 140 p., illus. Includes bibliography and index.

761. Sunburst Tropical Fruit Co. Cookbook / written by Nita Grochowski; illustrated by Melani Meo. 2nd ed. Pineland, Fla.: Mondongo Pub. Co., 1988, c1987. 80 p., 8 leaves of plates, illus. (some colored). Includes index.

762. Sweets Without Sugar / Thérèse Duval, Renata Drouin. Scarborough, Ont.: McGraw-Hill Ryerson, 1989. 135 p., colored illus.

763. A Gourmet's Guide to Fruit / Judy Bastrya & Julia Canning; photography by David Johnson. Los Angeles, Calif.: HP Books, 1990. 120 p., colored photos. Includes index.

see also entries 686, 890; Fruits and Vegetables; Natural Foods; *and specific fruits:* Apples, Apricots, Avocados, Bananas, Berries, Cherries, Citrus Fruits, Dried Fruits, Kiwifruit, Papaws, Peaches, Persimmons, Pineapples, Plums, Prunes, Rhubarb; *and specific dishes using fruits in Section II:* Desserts; Pies; etc.

Fruits and Vegetables

764. The Greengrocer Cookbook / Joe Carcione; introduction by Peter Carcione. Millbrae, Calif.: Celestial Arts, 1975. 246 p.

Fruits and Vegetables *(Continued)*

765. The Home Gardener's Cookbook / Clare Walker and Gill Coleman. Harmondsworth, Eng.: Penguin, 1980. 362 p. (Penguin Handbooks). Includes index.

766. The Fresh Fruit and Vegetable Book / produced by Celebrity Kitchen, Inc., in cooperation with United Fresh Fruit and Vegetable Association. New York: Barnes & Noble, 1981, c1980. 320 p., illus. Includes index.

767. Microwave Cooking, Fruits & Vegetables / from Litton. Minneapolis, Minn.: Publication Arts, Inc., c1981. 160 p., colored illus.

768. The Microwave Fruit & Vegetable Cookbook / Val Collins. Newton Abbot, Eng.: David & Charles, c1981. 120 p., illus. (some colored). Includes index.

769. Microwaving Fruits & Vegetables / by Barbara Methven and Sara Jean Thoms; photographers, Michael Jensen, Buck Holzemer, Ken Greer. Minnetonka, Minn. (5700 Green Circle Dr., Minnetonka, 55343): Publication Arts, c1981. 160 p., colored illus. (Microwave Cooking Library). Includes index. Also published as: Fruits & Vegetables.

770. New Ways with Fresh Fruit and Vegetables / Pamela Dixon. London, Eng.: Faber, 1981, c1973. 224 p. Includes index.

771. Forbidden Fruits & Forgotten Vegetables: A Guide to Cooking with Ethnic, Exotic, and Neglected Produce / by George and Nancy Marcus; photography by Will Brown. 1st ed. New York: St. Martin's Press, 1982. 146 p., illus. Includes indexes.

772. Mama's Fruits & Vegetables Cookbook / by Judy Ivey. Birmingham, Ala.: J. Ivey?, c1982. 84 p.

Fruits and Vegetables *(Continued)*

773. Good Food Gardening / Peter Seabrook; photographs by Michael Warren; cookery by Pamela Dotter. London, Eng.: Elm Tree Books, 1983. 128 p., colored illus. Includes index.

774. The Gourmet Garden: How to Grow Vegetables, Fruits, and Herbs for Today's Cuisine / Theodore James, Jr. 1st ed. New York: Dutton, c1983. 236 p., illus. Includes index.

775. Grow it, Cook it / by Jacqueline Heriteau; illustrated by David M. Hunter. Rev. ed. New York: Perigee Books, c1983. 320 p., illus. Includes index. Rev. ed. of: The How to Grow and Cook it Book of Vegetables, Herbs, Fruits, and Nuts. 1970. "A GD/Perigee Book."

776. The Old Cape Farmstall Cookbook / Judy Badenhorst, Glenda Moody & Sarah Seymour. 1st ed. Cape Town, South Africa: D. Nelson, 1983. 95 p., illus. (some colored). Includes index.

777. Cooking Against Cancer / by Suezanne Tangerose Orr. Springfield, Ill.: C.C. Thomas, c1984. 131 p. Includes index.

778. Fancy Fruits and Extraordinary Vegetables: A Guide to Selecting, Storing & Preparing / by Sandra Conrad Strauss; illustrated by Wardell Parker. New York: Hastings House, c1984. 224 p., illus. Includes index.

779. The Green Thumb Harvest / Johanna and Patricia Halsey; with illustrations by Dennis Snyder; foreword by Craig Claiborne. 1st ed. New York: Vintage Books, 1984. 274 p., illus. "A Vintage Original." Includes index.

780. The Creative Gardener's Cookbook. Nashville, Tenn.: Ideals, c1985. 366 p., colored illus. Translation of: Das Grosse Garten- und Kochbuch. Includes index.

Fruits and Vegetables *(Continued)*

781. Food from Your Garden: All You Need to Know to Grow, Cook and Preserve Your Own Fruit and Vegetables. London, Eng.: Reader's Digest Association, 1985, c1977. 380 p., illus. (some colored). Includes index.

782. Home Gardener's Month-by-Month Cookbook / Marjorie Page Blanchard. Pownal, Vt.: Storey Communications, 1985 printing, c1974. 208 p., illus. "Garden Way Publishing Book." Includes index. Originally published: Home Gardener's Cookbook. Charlotte, Vt.: Garden Way Pub. Co., 1974.

783. Perfect Cooking with Exotic Fruit & Vegetables / Elisabeth Lambert Ortiz. Twickenham, Eng.: Hamlyn, 1985, c1983. 31 p., illus.

784. Fresh from the Garden: Time Honored Recipes from the Readers of Texas Gardener / edited by Rita Miller; design and illustrations, Don Mulkey. Waco, Tex.: Texas Gardener Press, c1986. 224 p., colored illus. Includes index.

785. The Fruits of the Earth: Vegetable & Fruit Recipes / Adrian Bailey; paintings by Graham Rust. Topsfield, Mass.: Salem House, 1986. 128 p., illus. (some colored). Includes index.

786. Home Is My Garden / Dorothy Hammond Innes; drawings by Brenda Moore. Glasgow, Scot.: Fontana, 1986, c1984. 1 v., illus. Includes index.

787. Kitchen Garden Heritage / Barbara Fairweather. Glencoe, Scot.: Glencoe and North Lorn Folk Museum, 1986. 64 p.

788. The New Harvest / Lou Seibert Pappas and Jane Horn; photographs by Renee Lynn, drawings by Pamela Manley. San Francisco, Calif.: 101 Productions, c1986. 138 p., illus. (some colored). Includes index.

Specialty Cookbooks

Fruits and Vegetables *(Continued)*

789. Queer Gear: How to Buy & Cook Exotic Fruits & Vegetables / Carolyn Heal and Michael Allsop; illustrated by Brian Dear. London, Eng.: Century, 1986. 200 p., illus. Includes index.

790. The Summer Cook's Book: A Guide to Planting, Harvesting, Storing, Canning, Freezing and Cooking Popular Fruits and Vegetables / Brenda Cobb. Charlottetown, P.E.I.: Ragweed Press, 1986. 192 p., illus. Includes index.

791. Uncommon Fruits & Vegetables: A Commonsense Guide / Elizabeth Schneider; illustrations by Soun Vannithone. 1st ed. New York: Harper & Row, c1986. 546 p., illus. 400 recipes. Includes index.

792. Barry Ballister's Fruit and Vegetable Stand: A Complete Guide to the Selection, Preparation, and Nutrition of Fresh Produce. Woodstock, N.Y.: Overlook Press, c1987. 455 p., illus. More than 300 recipes with descriptions of more than 175 varieties. Includes index.

793. Exotic Fruits & Vegetables / text by Jane Grigson; illustrations by Charlotte Knox. 1st American ed. New York: H. Holt, 1987, c1986. 128 p., colored illus. Includes index.

794. Fruit and Vegetables of the World: Complete with Preparation, Notes, and Recipes / John Goode, Carol Willson. Melbourne, Australia: Lothian, 1987. 205 p., illus. Includes indexes.

795. The Pick Your Own Cook Book / Ann Nicol. London, Eng.: Threshold, c1987. 176 p., illus. Includes index.

796. Rodale's Garden-Fresh Cooking: Hundreds of Ways to Cook, Serve, and Store Your Favorite Fresh Vegetables and Fruits: Text and Recipes / by Judith Benn Hurley. Emmaus, Pa.: Rodale Press, c1987. 218 p., colored illus. Includes index.

Fruits and Vegetables *(Continued)*

797. Sunset Fresh Produce / by the editors of Sunset Books and Sunset Magazine; research & text, Joan Griffiths, Mary Jane Swanson. Menlo Park, Calif.: Lane Pub. Co., c1987. 128 p., colored illus. Includes index.

798. A Bumper Crop / Anne Williams. London, Eng.: Dent, 1988. 176 p., illus. (Healthright). Includes index.

799. Farmers Market Cookbook / Susan F. Carlman. 1st ed. Chicago, Ill: Chicago Review Press, c1988. 210 p., illus. Includes index.

800. Home Grown / Denys De Saulles. London, Eng.: Macmillan, 1988. 240 p., illus.

801. Okanagan Harvest: Favorite Fruit and Vegetable Recipes / edited and compiled by Delver and Weston. Vernon, B.C.: DVA Pub., 1988. 197 p., colored illus. Includes indexes.

802. Fresh: A Greenmarket Cookbook / by Carol Schneider. New York: Panache Press, 1989. 192 p., 36 full-page colored photos. 180 recipes. Includes index.

803. The Fruit, Herbs & Vegetables of Italy: An Offering to Lucy, Countess of Bedford / Giacomo Castelvetro; translated with and introduction by Gillian Riley; foreword by Jane Grigson. London, Eng.: British Museum, Natural History; New York: Viking, 1989. 175 p., colored illus. Includes bibliography and index.

804. International Produce Cookbook & Guide: Recipes Plus Buying & Storage Information / by Marlene Brown. Los Angeles, Calif.: HP Books, 1989. 160 p., 38 colored photos. More than 75 recipes. Includes index.

Fruits and Vegetables *(Continued)*

805. Ordinary and Extraordinary Fruits & Vegetables: Nutritional Information, Selected Recipes and Tidbits from the T.V. Series "A Minute in the Kitchen with Mary" / by Mary Zenorini Silverszweig. Haverstraw, N.Y. (Rte 9W, Haverstraw 10927): South Mountain Press, c1989. 130 p. Includes index.

806. The Gourmet Garden: The Fruits of the Garden Transported to the Table / Geraldene Holt; photographs by Hugh Palmer. 1st United States ed. Boston, Mass.: Little, Brown, c1990. 192 p., colored photos. "A Bulfinch Press Book."

807. Pete Luckett's Cookbook & Guide to Fresh Fruits & Vegetables / Kathleen Robinson with Pete Luckett. Tucson, Ariz.: Fisher Books, c1990. ca. 275 p. Includes index. Reprint. Originally published: Pete Luckett's Complete Guide to Fresh Fruits & Vegetables. Fredericton, N.B.: Goose Lane Editions, 1990.

808. The World Wide Selection of Exotic Produce / Julia Richardson. Saint-Lambert, Que.: Heritage, 1990. 1 v. Issued also in French under title: Fruits et légumes exotiques du monde entier.

see also Fruits; Natural Foods; Raw Foods; Vegetables; Pickles and Relishes *(Section II); and* Canning and Preserving *(Section IV)*

Game

809. Wild Game Cook Book / Martin Rywell. Saratoga Springs, N.Y.: Buck Hill Associates, 1952. 74 p.

810. Game is Good Eating / John Willard. 4th rev. ed. Billings, Mont. (3119 Country Club Circle, Billings 59102): J.A. Willard, 1970? 111 p., illus.

Game *(Continued)*

811. Wild Game Cookbook / edited by L. W. "Bill" Johnson. New York: Benjamin Co., 1970. 174 p., colored illus. "A Benjamin Company/Rutledge Book."

812. Game Cookery / with Felipe Rojas-Lombardi; introduction by George Plimpton; drawings by Bill Goldsmith. Newtown Square, Pa.: Harrowood Books, 1973, c. 1972. 31 p., illus.

813. Easy Game Cooking: 124 Savory, Home-tested, Money-saving Recipes and Menus for Game Birds and Animals / Joan Cone. McLean, Va.: EPM Publications; Distributed by Hawthorn Books, New York, 1974. 140 p., illus.

814. Lyman's Wild Gourmet: A Game Cookbook / by Barbara Jo Hayden & Richard Pietschmann; C. Kenneth Ramage, editor; Robert D. Hayden, associate editor; illustrated by Fred Treadgold. Middlefield, Conn.: Lyman Publications, c1976. 256 p., illus. Cover title: The Wild Gourmet. Includes index.

815. Easy Game Cookery / by Phyllis Hobson. Charlotte, Vt.: Garden Way, c1980. 32 p., illus. (Garden Way Publishing Bulletin; A-56).

816. Game Cookery: Preparation, Freezing, Cooking and Recipes of Game. Brinscall, Eng.: Countryside Publications, 1980. 120 p., illus. Cover title: The Complete Guide to Game Cookery.

817. The Great Southern Wild Game Cookbook / by Sam Goolsby; designed by Mike Burton. Gretna, La.: Pelican Pub. Co., 1980. 191 p., illus. Includes index.

818. 49 North Cooks Wild: Wild Game Cookbook and Outdoor Manual / by Kim H. Bennett. 1st venture, 2nd run. Edmonton, Alta.: 49 North Pub., 1981. 130 p., illus. (some colored). Includes indexes. Published in 1980 under title: North Cooks Wild!

Game *(Continued)*

819. The Wild Game Cookbook of Idaho / Lucas L. Stone. 1st ed. Boise, Idaho: Highcountry Books, 1981. 66 p., illus. Includes index.

820. Wildlife Chef. 2nd ed., rev. and enl. Lansing, Mich. (Box 30235, Lansing 48909): Michigan United Conservation Clubs, c1981. 106 p., illus.

821. Game Cookbook / by Charles E. Stuart; photography, Gary Schleicher; edited by R.L. Hardy Jr. Middleburg, Va. (P.O. Box 432, Middleburg 22117): Country Publishers, c1982. 142 p., colored illus.

822. Home Cookbook of Wild Meat and Game / Bradford Angier. Harrisburg, Pa.: Stackpole Books, 1982, c1975. ca. 192 p., illus. Previously published as: Home Book of Cooking Venison and Other Natural Meats. 1975. Includes index.

823. The Hunter's Game Cookbook / by Jacqueline E. Knight. New York: New Century, 1982. 295 p., illus. Includes index.

824. North American Wild Game Cookbook / Bill & Anita Mabbutt. Moscow, Idaho: Solstice Press, c1982. 212 p., illus. Includes index.

825. Our Wild Harvest: Sowing, Reaping, Cooking, Eating / by Rolf A. Pederson. Montevideo, Minn.: Rolf's Gallery, 1982. 174 p., illus.

826. Wild Game Cookbook for Beginners & Experts / by Joseph Lamagna. Yonkers, N.Y.: J. Lamagna, c1982. 48 p., illus.

827. Fair Game: A Hunter's Cookbook / Jane Hibler; illustrated by Sandra Ciarrochi. New York: I. Chalmers Cookbooks, c1983. 84 p., illus. (Great American Cooking Schools).

828. The Laird's Kitchen / Winnie Stewart. Great Britain: W. Stewart, 1983. 87 p. Includes index.

Game *(Continued)*

829. NAHC Wild Game Cookbook. Minneapolis, Minn.: North American Hunting Club, 1983-1990. illus. Published annually.

830. Sylvia Bashline's Savory Game Cookbook / Sylvia G. Bashline. Harrisburg, Pa.: Stackpole Books, c1983. 176 p. Includes index.

831. You and Your Wild Game / Ray A. Field, Carolyn A. Raab. Bozeman, Mont.: Cooperative Extension Service, Montana State University, 1983. 74 p., illus. Includes recipe index.

832. After the Hunt Cookbook / Ducks Unlimited. Nashville, Tenn.: Favorite Recipes Press, c1984. 199 p., illus. (some colored). Includes indexes.

833. Dress 'em Out / by James A. Smith; illustrations by Susan Gilbert. South Hackensack, N.J.: Stoeger Pub. Co., c1984. 255 p., illus. Includes index.

834. The Game Gourmet / Ron Wood. Calgary, Alta.: Great North Wood Pub., c1984. 188 p., 20 p. of plates, illus. (some colored).

835. Gray's Wild Game Cookbook: A Menu Cookbook / by Rebecca Gray. South Hamilton, Mass.: GSJ Press, 1984. 219 p., illus. (some colored). 198 recipes. Includes index.

836. To Hell with Gravy!: Gourmet Wild Game Tastes from Simple Recipes with Favorite Recipes from Outdoor People Like You / by Glenn and Judy Helgeland. 1st ed. Mequon, Wis.: Target Communications Corp., c1984. 120 p., illus. Includes index.

837. Alaska Trappers Cookin' Book / R.A. Self. Sitka, Alaska (288 Kogwonton, Sitka 99835): Woodsmoke Outfitters, c1985. 96 p., illus. Includes index.

838. Cooking for Your Hunter / by Miriam L. Jones; illustrated by Angela Jones, cover photo by Larry D. Jones. Springfield, Or.: Wilderness Sound Productions, 1985. 180 p., illus.

Game *(Continued)*

839. Country Cooking: Featuring Foods Wild and Domestic / by Helen Hale. Elgin, Pa.: Allegheny Press, c1985. 112 p., illus. Includes index.

840. The Game Cookbook / Geraldine Steindler. Rev. & expanded. South Hackensack, N.J.: Stoeger Pub. Co., c1985. 288 p., illus. Includes index.

841. The Meat Hunter / John L. Yarbrough. San Antonio, Tex.: Quality Pub. Co., c1985. 161 p., illus.

842. The New Texas Wild Game Cookbook: A Tradition Grows / Judith & Richard Morehead; with woodcut illustrations by Barbara Mathews Whitehead. Austin, Tex.: Eakin Press, 1985. 83 p., illus. Rev. ed. of: The Texas Wild Game Cookbook. 1st ed. 1972.

843. Perfect Cooking with Game / Veronica Heath. Twickenham, Eng.: Hamlyn, 1985, c1983. 31 p., illus.

844. The Game Cookbook / Colin Brown. London, Eng.: Souvenir, 1986, c1985. 202 p., illus. (some colored). Includes index. Originally published: North Ryde, N.S.W.: Methuen Australia, 1985.

845. Game Cookery / Angela Humphreys. Newton Abbott, Eng.; North Pomfret, Vt.: David & Charles, c1986. 176 p., illus. Includes index.

846. Pioneer Heritage Wild Game Cookbook: Old-Fashioned Frontier Favorites / by Jack French. Jupiter, Fla.: Realco Pub., c1986. 415 p., illus. Includes index.

847. The Venison Cookbook: More Than 200 Tested Recipes for Deer, Elk, Moose, and Other Game / Jim and Lois Zumbo. New York: Prentice Hall Press, c1986. 214 p. Includes index.

Game *(Continued)*

848. Wild Game Cookbook / by John A. Smith. New York: Dover Publications, c1986. 137 p., illus.

849. Dressing & Cooking Wild Game / text by Teresa Marrone; recipes by Annette & Louis Bignami and others. Minnetonka, Minn.: Cy DeCosse; New York: Distributed by Prentice Hall Press, c1987. 160 p., colored illus. (The Hunting & Fishing Library). Includes index.

850. Mountain Indian Recipes: Game and Side Dishes / by Frances Gwaltney. Cherokee, N.C.?: F. Gwaltney, c1987. 32 p., illus.

851. Game. Toronto, Ont.: Grolier, 1988. 110 p., colored illus. (Microwave Magic; 17). Includes index.

852. Game Cookery in America and Europe / by Raymond R. Camp; drawings by Richard Harrington. Los Angeles, Calif.: HP Books, 1988, c1983. 176 p. Reprint. Previously published: Buffalo, N.Y.: Wild Duck Press, c1983. Includes index.

853. A Game for All Seasons: A Hunter's Complete Handbook to Southwest Game Cooking / by Doris Dorough Sigler. Texas?, 1988? 91 p., illus. Includes index.

854. Wild Game Cookbook / compiled by Jim Dempsey; illustrated by Wayne Horne. Phoenix, Ariz.: UCS Press, c1988. 156 p. Includes index.

855. Wild Game Cookery: The Hunter's Home Companion / Carol Vance Wary. Rev. and expanded ed. Woodstock, Vt.: Countryman Press, c1988. 207 p., illus.

856. Wildlife Harvest Game Cookbook: Collection of Favorite Recipies [sic] from North America's Hunting Resorts and Game Farms / editors, John M. Mullin, Peggy Mullin Boehmer. Completely rev. ed. Goose Lake, Iowa: Wildlife Harvest Publications, 1988. 199 p., illus. (some colored). Includes index.

Game *(Continued)*

857. The Complete Guide to Game Care & Cookery / by Sam Fadala. Rev. and expanded ed. Northfield, Ill.: DBI Books, c1989. 320 p., illus.

858. Game Cookery / Patricia Lousada. London, Eng.: Murray, 1989. 224 p., illus.

859. Game in Good Taste: A Feast of Recipes for Wild Game / Ann Gorzalka. Glendo, Wyo.: High Plains Press, 1989. 160 p., illus.

860. Minnesota Game Warden's Cookbook / edited by Minnesota Conservation Officers Association Staff. Fargo, N.D.: Prairie House, 1989. 140 p., illus.

861. Mrs. Beeton's Game Cookery. London, Eng.: Ward Lock, 1989. 176 p., colored illus.

862. Nicola Cox on Game Cookery / with wine by Simon Cox. London, Eng.: V. Gollancz in association with P. Crawley, 1989. 224 p., illus. (some colored). Includes index.

863. Savoring the Wild. Helena, Mont.: Falcon Press, c1989. 96 p., illus. "Recipes and food preparation hints from employees of the Montana Dept. of Fish, Wildlife, and Parks and others."

864. Texas Wild Game Recipes Cookbook / Dale H. and Phyllis M. Robertson. Bryan, Tex.: Keepem Running, 1989. 215 p.

865. Variety with Venison and Other Wild Game / recipes by Delores Green and Connie White; marinating and preparation by Connie White; cover and illustrations by Terry Groner. Jackson, Mich. (2108 Spring Arbor Rd., Jackson 49203): Green & White Pub. Co., c1989. 95 p., illus. Includes index.

Game *(Continued)*

866. The Game Cookbook / Carolyn Little. Wiltshire, Eng.: Crowood Press; North Pomfret, Vt.: Distributed by David & Charles, 1990. 224 p., illus. Includes index.

867. New Game Cuisine: Selected Menus and Suggested Wines / by Janet Hazen; wine notes by Brian St. Pierre; photography by Joyce Oudkerk Pool; design by Thomas Ingalls. San Francisco, Calif.: Chronicle Books, c1990. 127 p., colored illus. Contains 29 menus, including sauces, side dishes, and suggestions. Includes bibliographical references and index.

868. Northeast Upland Hunting Guide / Jim Capossela. Tarrytown, N.Y.: Northeast Sportsman's Press; Harrisburg, Pa.: Stackpole Books, c1990. 189 p., illus.

see also Fish and Game; Fowl and Game; *specific kinds of game:* Bear Meat, Buffalo, Elk, Opossum, Rabbit, Venison; *and broader category:* Meat

Gamebirds

see entry 268; **Fish and Game; Fowl and Game; Game; Pheasants; Poultry**

Garlic

869. A Passion for Garlic / Penny Drinkwater and Elaine Self. London, Eng.: Duckworth, 1980. 128 p. Includes bibliography and index.

870. The Little Garlic Book / Rosamond Richardson. 1st U.S. ed. New York: St. Martin's Press, c1982. 60 p., illus.

871. Garlic: 101 Savory and Seductive Recipes, Along with Fascinating Facts and Folklore / Sue Kreitzman. 1st ed. New York: Harmony Books, c1984. 128 p., illus. Includes index.

Garlic *(Continued)*

872. Garlic Cookery / by Martha Rose Shulman; illustrated by Rita Greer. 1st U.S. ed. New York: Thorsons Publishers: Distributed to the trade by Inner Traditions International, 1984. 192 p., illus. (some colored). Includes bibliography and index. A revised ed. of Garlic Cookery combined with the author's Herb and Honey Cookery was published as: Gourmet Vegetarian Feasts. Rochester, Vt.: Thorsons Pub. Group, 1987 and reprinted in 1990 by Healing Arts Press, Rochester, Vt.

873. Perfect Cooking with Garlic / Sally Lavis. Twickenham, Eng.: Hamlyn, 1985, 1982. 31 p., illus.

874. Garlic for Health! and for Taste! / by Vishwa Lamba. Ottawa, Ont.: Impel Pub., c1986. 52 p., illus.

875. Garlic Gourmet: Garlic, It's [sic] History, Growing, and 100 Recipes for It's [sic] use / by Joan Nelson. Redding, Calif.: J. Nelson, c1986. 89 p., illus. Includes index.

876. Glorious Garlic: A Cookbook / by Charlene A. Braida; illustrations by Cindy McFarland. 1st ed. Pownal, Vt.: Garden Way Pub., c1986. 188 p., illus. Includes index.

877. Lilies of the Kitchen: Recipes Celebrating Onions, Garlic, Leeks, Shallots, Scallions, and Chives / Barbara Batcheller; with a foreword by Wolfgang Puck; illustrations by Lauren Jarrett. 1st ed. New York: St. Martin's Press, c1986. 262 p., illus. Includes index.

878. The Official Garlic Lovers Handbook / by Lloyd John Harris and Lovers of the Stinking Rose. Berkeley, Calif.: Aris Books, c1986. 144 p.

879. Willacrick Farm French Giant Elephant Garlic Cookbook / by Bernadine Ferguson in association with Will & Mary Wilcox; graphic design and illustration by Jim Shubin. Templeton, Calif. (P.O. Box 599, Templeton 93465): The Farm, c1986. 142 p.

Garlic *(Continued)*

880. The Complete Garlic Lovers' Cookbook: From Gilroy, Garlic Capital of the World. Berkeley, Calif.: Celestial Arts, c1987. 349 p., illus., map. "Available for the first time in one volume all the recipes from The Garlic Lovers' Cookbooks (Volumes I & II) plus the prize-winning entries from the Great Garlic Cookoffs." Includes index.

881. The Book of Garlic / by Lloyd J. Harris; line drawings by Licita Fernandez; collages by Lloyd J. Harris. Berkeley, Calif.: Aris Books; Reading, Mass.: Addison-Wesley Pub. Co., 1988, c1979. 286 p. More than 100 recipes. Contains information on the history, folklore, and medicinal properties of garlic.

882. The Great Garlic Cookbook / Sophie Hale. London, Eng.: Apple Press, 1989. 128 p., illus. Also published: Secaucus, N.J.: Chartwell, c1986.

see also entry 1606; and broader category: Herbs

Gelatin

883. Amazing Magical Jell-O Brand Desserts / illustrations, Seymour Chwast; photography, Arnold Rosenberg. White Plains, N.Y.: General Foods Corp., c1977. 95 p., colored illus. "Plus magic tricks by Marvello the Great." Includes index.

884. Knox Gelatine Cookbook / prepared and produced by Rutledge Books. New York: Benjamin Co., c1977. 128 p., illus. (some colored). Includes index.

885. The Gelatin Cook Book / Manuela Soares. New York: Dorchester Pub. Co., 1978. 1 v. Leisure Books.

886. Woman's Day Gelatin Cookery / by Carole Collier. New York: Simon and Schuster, c1979. 256 p. Includes index.

Gelatin *(Continued)*

887. The Jell-O Gelatin Salad Selector. White Plains, N.Y.: General Foods Corp., 1980. 1 booklet.

888. Sinlessly Sweet Recipes. Englewood Cliffs, N.J.: Knox Gelatine Co., 1980. 1 booklet. Recipes from Knox Unflavored Gelatine and Sweet 'N Low sugar substitute.

889. Joys of Jell-O Brand Gelatin. 1st ed. White Plains, N.Y.: General Foods Corp., c1981. 128 p., colored illus. Includes index.

890. Light'n Fruity Pies from Jell-O Jelly Powder. Port Credit, Ont.: General Foods, 1981. 16 p., colored illus.

891. The Sea Vegetable Gelatin Cookbook and Field Guide / Judith Cooper Madlener. Santa Barbara, Calif.: Woodbridge Press, c1981. 154 p., illus. (some colored). Includes bibliography.

892. The Grand Performer: Knox Unflavored Gelatine. Englewood Cliffs, N.J.: Knox Gelatine Co., 1982. 1 v. (spiral bound), 24 colored photos. 123 recipes for main dishes, salads, desserts, and appetizers.

893. Jell-O Brand Fun and Fabulous Recipes: From Jell-O Gelatins & Puddings. New York: Beekman House: Distributed by Crown Publishers, c1988. 216 p., colored illus.

894. The Jell-O Pages Recipe Book. White Plains, N.Y.: General Foods Corp., 1988. 1 booklet.

895. New Joys of Jell-O. Lincolnwood, Ill.: Publications International, c1990. 224 p., colored illus. More than 150 recipes. Includes index.

see also Desserts *(Section II)*; Molded Foods *(Section II)*

Specific Ingredients 117

Ginger

896. The Ginger Cookbook / by Anne Ager. Pinner: Vantage Books; London, Eng.: Distributed by Hale, 1976. 144 p., illus. Includes index.

897. Ginger East to West: The Classic Collection of Recipes, Techniques and Lore / by Bruce Cost. Rev. and expanded. Reading, Mass.: Addison-Wesley, 1989. ca. 192 p. 90 recipes. Includes bibliography and indexes. "Aris Books."

see also broader category: Spices

Gluten

898. How to Make All the "Meat" You Eat Out of Wheat: International Gluten Wheat "Meat" Cookbook / by Nina and Michael Shandler. 1st ed. New York: Rawson, Wade Publishers, c1980. 241 p. Includes index.

899. The Gluten Book / LeArta Moulton. Rev. ed. Provo, Utah: Gluten Co., c1981. 165 p., illus. Includes index.

see also broader category: Wheat

Goat Cheese

900. Chevre!: The Goat Cheese Cookbook / Laura Chenel, Linda Siegfried. Reading, Mass.: Addison-Wesley, 1990. illus. 119 p.

see also broader category: Cheese

Specialty Cookbooks

Goat Milk

901. The Collectors Goat Milk Cook Book: Better Health with a Natural Health Food... / illustrations by Linda Mohn, JoAnn Mohn. Detroit Lakes, Minn. (Rt. 3 Box 214, Detroit Lakes 56501): J. Mohn, 1982? 150 p., illus.

see also broader category: Milk

Goats

902. Chevon (Goat Meat) Recipes. Scottsdale, Ariz.: Printed by Dairy Goat Journal, 1981? 41 p., illus.

see also broader category: Meat

Grains

903. The Book of Whole Grains: The Grain-by-Grain Guide to Cooking, Growing, and Grinding Whole Cereals, Nuts, Peas, and Beans / Marlene Anne Bumgarner; illustrations by Maryanna Kingman. New York: St. Martin's Press, c1976. 334 p., illus. More than 250 recipes. Includes bibliography and index.

904. Cooking with Love & Cereal / Betty McMichael with Karen McDonald. 1st ed. Chappaqua, N.Y.: Christian Herald Books, c1981. 223 p., illus. Includes index.

905. Fiber & Bran Better Health Cookbook / Cory SerVaas, Charlotte Turgeon & Frederic Birmingham. Abridged ed. New York: Bonanza Books: Distributed by Crown Publishers, 1981, c1977. 296 p., illus. At head of title: The Saturday Evening Post. Includes index. Reprint. Originally published: Indianapolis, Ind.: Curtis Pub. Co., 1977.

906. Whole Grains: Grow, Harvest, and Cook Your Own / Sara Pitzer. Charlotte, Vt.: Garden Way Pub., c1981. 169 p., illus.

Grains *(Continued)*

907. Cooking with Wholegrains / by Ellen and Vrest Orton. New York: Gramercy Pub. Co.: Distributed by Crown Publishers, 1982, c1951. 64 p. Includes index.

908. The Good Grains / by the editors of Rodale Books. Emmaus, Pa.: Rodale Press, c1982. 96 p., illus. (Rodale's High Health Cookbook Series). Includes index.

909. How Do We Eat It? / Deborah Pedersen Vanderniet. Salt Lake City, Utah: Deseret Book Co., c1982. 54 p. Includes index.

910. Sheryl & Mel London's Creative Cooking with Grains & Pasta / editor, Charles Gerras. Emmaus, Pa.: Rodale Press, c1982. 308 p., illus. (some colored). Includes index.

911. The Whole Grain Recipe Book / Marlis Weber. Wellingborough, Eng.: Thorsons, 1983. 160 p. Translation of: Mit Vollkorn Kochen, and Vollkorn Backbuch.

912. Better Homes and Gardens Cooking with Whole Grains. 1st ed. Des Moines, Iowa: Meredith Corp., c1984. 96 p., illus. (some colored).Includes index.

913. Cooking with Grains, Nuts and Seeds. 2nd ed. Wellingborough, Eng.: Thorsons, 1984. 128 p. Previous ed. published as: Grains, Nuts and Seeds, 1978.

914. Classic Indian Vegetarian and Grain Cooking / Julie Sahni; illustrations by Richard Pfanz. 1st ed. New York: Morrow, c1985. 511 p., illus. More than 200 recipes. Includes index.

915. The War Eagle Mill Wholegrain Cookbook / by Zoe Medlin Caywood; illustrated by Donn Frantz. 5th ed. Rogers, Ark.: Z.M. Caywood, 1985, c1976. 65 p., illus.

Specialty Cookbooks

Grains *(Continued)*

916. Wholegrains: Cereals for Essential Fibre / Sally Parsonage. Nottingham, Eng.: Boots, c1985. 64 p., illus. (some colored). (Boots Healthy Eating Guides). Includes index.

917. The Wholemeal Kitchen / Miriam Polunin; illustrated by Ian Jones; colour photograhy by John Welburn Associates. Wellingborough, Eng.: Thorsons, 1985. 127 p., illus. (some colored). Includes index.

918. Grains and Fibres for Optimum Health / by Helga Lambrecht. Duncan, B.C.: Lambrecht Publications, 1986. 212 p., illus. Includes indexes. Also published: Winnipeg, Man.: Gateway Pub. Co., 1986.

919. Can I Make One? London, Eng.: Temple House, 1987. 55 p.

920. Grain Gastronomy: A Cook's Guide to Great Grains from Couscous to Polenta / Janet Fletcher. Berkeley, Calif.: Aris Books, 1988. 112 p. Includes index.

921. The Grains Cookbook / Bert Greene; illustrations by Norman Green. New York: Workman Pub., c1988. 403 p., illus. 500 recipes for 15 different grains. Includes index.

922. The Complete Whole Grain Cookbook / by Carol Gelles. New York: Donald Fine, 1989. 514 p. Includes bibliography and index. "How to buy, prepare and cook all high-fiber grains, including over 400 recipes from soups to desserts."

923. Amazing Grains: Creating Vegetarian Main Dishes with Whole Grains / Joanne Saltzman. Tiburon, Calif.: H.J. Kramer, c1990. 202 p., illus.

924. Great Grains / Linda Drachman and Peter Wynne; in consultation with Lynne Hill. New York: Simon & Schuster, c1990. 160 p. (Feed Your Family Right). "A Fireside Book."

Specific Ingredients   121

Grains *(Continued)*

925. The Stone Age Diet: Grains and Greens / Patrick White. Atlanta, Ga.: Humanics New Age, 1990. 156 p., illus.

 see also entries 69, 1148, 1571; Flour; Granola; Natural Foods; *and specific grains:* Amaranth, Buckwheat Groats, Oats, Rice, Triticale, Wheat

Granola

926. The Granola Cookbook / by Eric Meller and Jane Kaplan. New York: Arco, 1973. 182 p., illus.

 see also broader category: Grains

Grapes

see entry 1710; and broader category: Fruits

Green Barley Juice

927. Green Barley Essence: The Ideal "Fast Food" / Yoshihide Hagiwara; adapted and edited by Doug Smith & Dan McTague; introduction by Richard A. Passwater; preface by William H. Lee. New Canaan, Conn.: Keats Pub., c1985. 147 p., illus. Translation of: Kyoi No Kenkogen Bakuryokuso.

Greens

928. Greene on Greens / Bert Greene; illustrations by Norman Green. New York: Workman Pub., c1984. 432 p., illus. Includes index. Also published: Wellingborough, Eng.: Equation, 1987.

Greens *(Continued)*

929. Book of Lettuce & Greens / edited by the staff of National Gardening Magazine; illustrations by Elayne Sears & Lyn Severance. Rev. ed. New York: Villard Books, 1987, c1985. 87 p., illus. Originally published: The Gardens for All Book of Lettuce & Greens / by Dick and Jan Raymond. Burlington, Vt.: Gardens for All, c1979.

see also entries 963, 2205, 2498; and broader categories: Vegetables; *and* Salads *(Section II)*

Ground Meat

930. Great Ground-Beef Recipes / by Family Circle food staff, with Anne M. Fletcher; drawings by Grambs Miller. Rev. ed. New York: Family Circle, 1971. 168 p., illus. (some colored). Cover title: Family Circle Great Ground-Beef Recipes. The 1966 ed. by G.M. White, published under the same title; the 1972 ed. published under title: The International Gourmet Uses of Ground Beef. "A New York Times Company Publication."

931. Creative Hamburger Cookery: 182 Unusual Recipes for Casseroles, Meat Loaves, and Hamburger. New York: Dover Publications, 1974, c1951. 120 p. Reprint of the ed. published by Greenberg, New York, under title: The Burger Book.

932. Better Homes and Gardens All-Time Favorite Hamburger & Ground Meat Recipes. 1st ed. Des Moines, Iowa: Meredith Corp., c1980. 96 p., colored illus. Includes index.

933. Ground Beef Favorites / by Barbara Swift Brauer; illustrated by Maryanne Regal Hoburg. San Francisco, Calif.: Owlswood Productions, c1981. 63 p., illus. Includes index.

934. Ground Meat Cookbook / Naomi Arbit & June Turner. Milwaukee, Wis.: Ideals, 1981. 64 p., illus.

Ground Meat *(Continued)*

935. Farm Journal's Ground Beef Roundup: More Than 100 Casseroles, Soups, Stews and Skillet Specialities / by the food editors of Farm Journal. Philadelphia, Pa.: Farm Journal, 1982. 121 p. Includes index.

936. The Ground Meat Cookbook / illustrations by Karen Rolnick. New York: Culinary Arts Institute, c1982. 80 p., illus. (some colored). (Adventures in Cooking Series). Includes index.

937. Marvelous Meals with Mince / Josceline Dimbleby. Cambridge, Eng.: Woodhead-Faulkner for J. Sainsbury Ltd., 1982. 96 p., colored illus. (A Sainsbury Cookbook).

938. Ground Beef Cookbook. Nashville, Tenn.: Favorite Recipes Press, c1983. 167 p., illus. Includes index. "Favorite recipes of home economics teachers."

939. The New 365 Ways to Cook Hamburger and Other Ground Meat / by Doyne and Dorothy Nickerson; with drawings by Lauren Rosen. 1st ed. Garden City, N.Y.: Doubleday, 1983. 215 p. Includes index. Rev. ed. of: 365 Ways to Cook Hamburger, 1960.

940. The Ground Meat Cookbook / Frederick E. Kahn. New York: Nautilus Communications; Aurora, Ill.: Distributed by Caroline House, c1984. 151 p., illus. Includes index.

941. Ground Beef Sounds Good, Around the World. Toronto, Ont.: Beef Information Centre, 1984. 16 p.

942. The Little Hamburger Cookbook / Mary L. Green. Denver, Colo.: Giftstar, 1984. ca. 10 p., illus. (Little Cookbooks).

943. Mighty Mince Cookbook / Jane Todd. London, Eng.: Hamlyn, 1984, c1980. 127 p., illus. (some colored). Includes index.

944. Betty Crocker's Hamburger Cookbook. Rev. ed. New York: Golden Press, c1985. 96 p., colored illus. Includes index.

Ground Meat *(Continued)*

945. Better Homes and Gardens Bigger Better Burgers / editor, Linda Henry. 1st ed. Des Moines, Iowa: Meredith Corp., c1986. 80 p., illus. (some colored). Includes index.

946. Minced Beef Cookbook / Carole Cooper; edited by Mary Norwak. London, Eng.: Foulsham, c1986. 96 p., illus. (some colored). Includes index.

947. The Burger Book / Honey and Larry Zisman. 1st ed. New York: St. Martin's Press, c1987. 110 p. Includes index.

948. Quick & Easy Microwaving Ground Beef / developed by the kitchens of the Microwave Cooking Institute. New York: Prentice Hall Press, c1987. 96 p., colored illus. Includes index.

949. Ground Beef Microwave Meals / by Barbara Methven. Minnetonka, Minn.: C. DeCosse Inc., c1990. 158 p., colored illus. (Microwave Cooking Library). Includes index.

see also entry 3719; Frankfurters; Sausages; *and broader category:* Meat

Ground Turkey

950. Ground Turkey Lover's Cookbook / by Helen L. Garcia; illustrations by Denise E. Garcia. 1st ed. West Linn, Or.: Cedar Island Press, c1987. 127 p., illus. Includes index.

951. The Ground Turkey Cookbook: Great Recipes for the Practical at Heart / Kristine H. Templeman. Winchester, Mass. (388 Cambridge St., Winchester 01890): Advantage/Aurora Publications, c1989. 96 p.

see also Ground Meat; Turkey

Halibut

952. Alaskan Halibut Recipes / Cecilia Nibeck. Anchorage, Alaska: AK Enterprises, 1989. 200 p., illus.

see also broader category: Fish

Ham

953. The Ham Book: A Comprehensive Guide to Ham Cookery / by Monette R. Harrell and Robert W. Harrell, Jr.; illustrations by Nancy Simpson Hoke. Norfolk, Va.: Donning Co., 1977. 224 p., illus. Includes index.

954. 80 Quick 'n Easy Polish Ham Recipes. New York: Atalanta Corp., 1980. 1 booklet.

955. A Ham for All Seasons / Bettie Clark. Shelburne, Vt.: New England Press, 1985. 128 p., illus.

see also broader category: Pork

Herbs

956. Better Health with Culinary Herbs / Ben Charles Harris. Barre, Mass.: Barre Publishers, 1971. 163 p.

957. Culinary Herbs and Condiments / by M. Grieve. New York: Dover Publications, 1971. 209 p.

958. Culinary and Salad Herbs: Their Cultivation and Food Values, with Recipes / by Eleanour Sinclair Rohde; drawings by Hilda M. Coley. New York: Dover Publications, 1972. 106 p., illus. Reprint of the 1940 ed.

959. Mastering Herbalism: A Practical Guide / by Paul Huson; illustrated by the author. New York: Stein and Day, 1974. 371 p., illus. Includes bibliography and index.

Specialty Cookbooks

Herbs *(Continued)*

960. Twenty-two Common Herbs and How to Use Them / by Ruth N. Allen and Charles F. Allen; drawings by Hope Day. New ed. Boston, Mass.: Branden Press, 1974, c1968. 61 p., illus. Includes index.

961. Herbs for the Kitchen / by Irma Goodrich Mazza. 3rd ed. rev. Boston, Mass.: Little, Brown, c1975. 366 p., illus. Includes index.

962. Cooking and Curing with Mexican Herbs: Recipes and Remedies Gathered in Muzquiz, Coahuila / by Dolores L. Latorre; with woodcut illustrations by Barbara Mathews Whitehead. Austin, Tex.: Encino Press, c1977. 178 p., illus. Includes bibliography and index.

963. A Cook's Guide to Growing Herbs, Greens, and Aromatics / by Millie Owen; illustrations by Karl Stuecklen. 1st ed. New York: Knopf; Distributed by Random House, 1978. 263 p., illus. Includes index.

964. Herbal Recipes / compiled by Clarence Meyer. Glenwood, Ill.: Meyerbooks, 1978. 1 v., illus.

965. Minnie Muenscher's Herb Cookbook / by Minnie Worthen Muenscher; with illustrations by Elfriede Abbe. Ithaca, N.Y.: Comstock Pub. Associates, 1978. 241 p., illus. Includes indexes.

966. All Good Things Around Us: A Cookbook and Guide to Wild Plants and Herbs / written by Pamela Michael; illustrated by Christabel King. 1st American ed. New York: Holt, Rinehart, and Winston, c1980. 240 p., illus.

967. Country Herbal / Lesley Gordon. 1st American ed. New York: Mayflower Books, c1980. 208 p., illus. Includes index.

968. Country Kitchen Recipes with Herbs / Maurice Hanssen. Wellingborough, Eng.: Thorsons, 1980. 32 p., illus. (Country Kitchen Recipes).

Herbs *(Continued)*

969. Health, Happiness, and the Pursuit of Herbs / by Adele Dawson; with drawings by Robin Rothman. Brattleboro, Vt.: S. Greene Press, c1980. 278 p. Includes index.

970. Herb Book / Arabella Boxer, Philippa Back. New York: Octopus/Mayflower, c1980. 224 p. colored illus. Includes index.

971. Italian Herb Cooking / by Lolita Daneo Moore. 3d ed. Richboro, Pa.: Richboro Press, 1980. 199 p., illus. Includes index.

972. New Wave in Cooking: Light and Simple Microwave Cookery: Also Featuring Low-Sodium Information / by Sherri Spector. Studio City, Calif. (P.O. Box 1622, Studio City, Calif. 91403): Leoram Productions; Hollywood, Calif. (1626 N. Wilcox Ave., Suite 427, Hollywood, Calif. 90028): Distributed by S & S Productions, c1980. 112 p., illus.

973. Park's Success with Herbs / by Gertrude B. Foster and Rosemary F. Louden; with photographs by the authors and the staff photographers of the Geo. W. Park Seed Co. Greenwood, S.C.: G.W. Park Seed Co., c1980. 192 p., illus. (some colored). Includes index.

974. Encyclopedia of Herbs and Herbalism / edited by Malcolm Stuart. New York: Crescent Books: Distributed by Crown, 1981, c1979. 304 p., illus. (some colored). Includes indexes. Reprint. Originally published: London, Eng.: Orbis Pub., c1979.

975. A Multitude of Mints / compiled by Guy Cooper & Gordon Taylor; preface by Elizabeth David. London, Eng.: Herb Society in association with Juniper Press, 1981. 48 p., illus. Includes bibliography.

976. The Star Herbal / Robert H. Menzies; illustrated by Gale Matthews. Rev. ed. Millbrae, Calif.: Celestial Arts, 1981, c1977. 206 p., illus. Includes bibliography and index.

Herbs *(Continued)*

977. Happy Eating Recipe Book / Twin City Herb Society. Lenexa, Kan.: Cookbook Publishers, 1982. 167 p., illus.

978. The Herb Book: An A-Z of Useful Plants / Elizabeth Peplow; illustrated by Rodney Shackell. London, Eng.: W.H. Allen, c1982. 176 p., illus. Includes bibliography.

979. Herbs, from Cultivation to Cooking / compiled by Herb Society of Greater Cincinnati. Gretna, La.: Pelican Pub. Co., 1982, c1979. 240 p., illus. Includes index.

980. Herbs, Health, and Cookery / by Claire Loewenfeld and Philippa Back. 1982 ed. New York: Gramercy Pub. Co.: Distributed by Crown, 1982, c1967. 320 p. Originally published: Herbs for Health and Cookery. Includes index.

981. The Two-in-One Herb Book / illustrated by Linda Diggins. New Canaan, Conn.: Keats Pub., 1982. 202 p., illus. (Keats Living with Herbs). Includes index. Contents: Herbs for Better Body Beauty / by Alyson Huxley. Herbs for Cooking, Cleaning, Canning and Sundry Household Chores / by Philippa Back.

982. Cooking with Chinese Herbs / Terry Tan; photographs by Andrew Merewether. Singapore: Times Books International, c1983. 119 p., illus. (some colored).

983. Cooking with the Healthful Herbs: Over 300 No-Salt Ways to Great Taste and Better Health / Jean Rogers. Emmaus, Pa.: Rodale Press, c1983. 278 p., illus. Includes index.

984. A Herb Cookbook / Gillian Painter. Auckland, N.Z.: London, Eng.: Hodder and Stoughton, 1983. 427 p., illus. Includes index.

985. Herbs for All Seasons / Rosemary Hemphill. London, Eng.: Angus & Robertson, 1983, c1972. 200 p., illus. Includes bibliography and index.

Herbs *(Continued)*

986. Illustrated Book of Herbs / Gilda Daisley; with illustrations by Ingrid Jacob. New York: American Nature Society Press, 1983, c1982. 128 p., illus. (some colored). Includes index.

987. Margaret Roberts' Book of Herbs: The Medicinal and Culinary Uses of Herbs in South Africa / illustrated by Joan van Gogh. Bergvlei, South Africa: J. Ball, 1983. 159 p., 32 p. of plates, illus. (some colored). Includes bibliography and index.

988. Summer Delights: Cooking with Fresh Herbs: 60 Recipes from Ravenhill Herb Farm, Saanichton. Saanichton, B.C.: The Farm, 1983? 60 p. Includes index.

989. Cooking with Herbs / Susan Belsinger, Carolyn Dille. New York: Van Nostrand Reinhold, c1984. 261 p., 8 p. of plates, illus. (some colored). "A CBI Book." Includes index.

990. Dooryard Herbs / by Linda Ours Rago; illustrator, Evalina Manucy Stowell; editor, Susan G. Knott. 1st ed. Shepherdstown, W.Va.: Carabelle Books, c1984. 139 p., illus. Includes index.

991. Growing Vegetables & Herbs: With Recipes for the Fresh Harvest / by the garden and landscape staff, Southern Living Magazine. Birmingham, Ala.: Oxmoor House, c1984. 272 p., illus. (some colored). Includes index.

992. Herbs: Their Cultivation and Usage / John and Rosemary Hemphill. Poole, Eng.: Blandford Press; New York: Distributed in the U.S. by Sterling Pub. Co., 1984, c1983. 128 p., colored illus. Includes bibliography and index.

993. How to Herb Book: Let's Remedy the Situation / by Velma J. Keith and Monteen Gordon. Pleasant Grove, Utah: Mayfield Pub., 1984. 256 p. Includes bibliography and index.

Specialty Cookbooks

Herbs *(Continued)*

994. A Kitchen Herbal: Making the Most of Herbs for Cookery and Health / Maurice Mességué with Madeleine Peter; translated by Fay Sharman; with drawings by Yvonne Skargon. London, Eng.: Pan in association with Collins, 1984. 255 p., illus. Includes index. Originally published: London, Eng.: Collins, 1982. Translation of: Mon herbier de cuisine.

995. Practical Herb Gardening with Recipes / by Bryan H. Bunch; illustrations by Leslie Tierney. 1st ed. Blue Ridge Summit, Pa.: Tab Books, c1984. 207 p., illus. "A Hudson Group Book." Includes index.

996. The Roman Cookery of Apicius: A Treasury of Gourmet Recipes & Herbal Cookery / translated and adapted for the modern kitchen by John Edwards. Point Roberts, Wash.: Hartley & Marks, c1984. 322 p., illus. Includes bibliography and index. Translation of: De Re Coquinaria.

997. Atlanta Herb Sampler / presented "for use and delight" by the Chattahoochee Unit of the Herb Society of America. 2nd ed., rev. / editor, Mary Bowler Miller. Atlanta, Ga.: The Unit, 1985. 187 p., illus.

998. Better a Dinner of Herbs / by Byron Herbert Reece. Atlanta, Ga.: Cherokee Pub. Co., 1985. 220 p. Reprint. Originally published: New York: Dutton, 1950.

999. The Book of Herbs / editor, Renny Harrop; designer, Caroline Dewing; illustrated by Caroline Austin. New York: Exeter Books: Distributed by Bookthrift, 1985. 152 p., illus. (some colored). Includes index.

1000. The Book of Herbs / Kay N. Sanecki. Seacaucus, N.J.: Chartwell Books, c1985. 127 p., illus.

1001. Cook Gourmet Everyday / by Dee Cox; cartoon illustrations by Den DeSota. Huntington Beach, Calif.: Lifestyle Systems, 1985. 74 p., illus. Includes index.

Herbs *(Continued)*

1002. Cooking with Culinary Herbs / by Kelly Stelzer and John Stelzer. 3rd ed. Roseburg, Or.: Creative Images, 1985. 132 p.

1003. Culinary Herbs: A Potpourri / James A. Duke; illustrated by Peggy-Ann K. Duke. Owerri, Nigeria; New York: Trado-Medic Books, 1985. 195 p., illus. Includes bibliography and index.

1004. Herb and Honey Cookery / by Martha Rose Shulman; illustrated by Rita Greer. 1st U.S. ed. New York: Thorsons: Distributed to the trade by Inner Traditions International, 1985. 191 p., 8 leaves of plates, illus. (some colored). Includes index. A revised ed. of Herb and Honey Cookery combined with the author's Garlic Cookery was published as: Gourmet Vegetarian Feasts. Rochester, Vt.: Thorsons Pub. Group, 1987 and reprinted in 1990 by Healing Arts Press, Rochester, Vt.

1005. Herbs: Gardens, Decorations, and Recipes / by Emelie Tolley and Chris Mead; text by Emelie Tolley; photographs by Chris Mead. New York: C.N. Potter: Distributed by Crown, c1985. 244 p., 450 colored photos. Includes index.

1006. Herbs for the Home and Garden / Shirley Reid. North Ryde, N.S.W.: Angus & Robertson, 1985. 132 p., 8 leaves of plates, illus. (some colored). Includes bibliography and index.

1007. Herbs Today: Recipes, Gardening, Crafts / by Bertha Reppert. Minneapolis, Minn.: Dillon Press, c1985. 1 v. Includes index.

1008. Hobbying with Herbs: A Month-by-Month Guide / Phyllis V. Shaudys. Washington Crossing, Pa.: Pine Row Publications, c1985. 210 p., illus. Includes index.

1009. A Little Book of Recipes for Cooking with Herbs: A Gallimaufry of Herbal Flavours / Shirley & Michael Scott. Blo' Norton Hall, Eng.: M.G. Scott, 1985. 14 p.

Specialty Cookbooks

Herbs *(Continued)*

1010. Macmillan Treasury of Herbs: A Complete Guide to the Cultivation and Use of Wild and Domesticated Herbs / Ann Bonar; illustrations, Sue Wickison; special photography, Simon Butcher. New York: Macmillan, c1985. 144 p., illus. (some colored). Includes index.

1011. Nancy Enright's Canadian Herb Cookbook; illustrations by Eila Hooper Ross. Toronto, Ont.: Lorimer & Co., 1985. 146 p., illus. Includes index.

1012. Perfect Cooking with Herbs / Janet Corran. Twickenham, Eng.: Hamlyn, 1985, c1982. 31 p., illus.

1013. Growing and Using Herbs with Confidence: Recipes, Gardening, Crafts / Bertha Reppert; illustrated by Marjorie L. Reppert and Margaret S. Browne. Mechanicsburg, Pa.: Remembrance Press, c1986. 268 p., illus. Includes bibliography and index.

1014. Herbal Delights: Botanical Information and Recipes for Cosmetics, Remedies and Medicines, Condiments and Spices, and Sweet and Savory Treats for the Table / by Mrs. C.F. Leyel; with drawings by M.E. Rivers-Moore. New York: Gramercy Pub. Co.: Distributed by Crown Publishers, 1986. 429 p., illus. Includes indexes. Reprint. Originally published: Boston, Mass.: Houghton Mifflin, 1938.

1015. Pleasure of Herbs: a Month-by-Month Guide to Growing, Using, and Enjoying Herbs / by Phillis V. Shaudys. 1st ed. Pownal, Vt.: Storey Communications, c1986. 275 p., illus. "A Garden Way Publishing Book." Includes index.

1016. Summer Delights: Cooking with Fresh Herbs / by Noel Richardson, with illustrations by J. Ward Harris. Vancouver, B.C.: Whitecap Books, 1986. 128 p., illus. "A David Robinson Book." Includes bibliography and index.

Herbs *(Continued)*

1017. Herb Garden Cookbook / Lucinda Hutson; photography by Cooke Photographics. Austin, Tex.: Texas Monthly Press, c1987. 278 p., colored illus. 150 recipes. Contains information on planting, harvesting, and cooking. Includes index.

1018. Herbal Secrets from a Kenya Garden / Bee Stephenson. Nairobi, Kenya: Kenway Publications, 1987. 88 p., illus. (some colored).

1019. Herbs Are Good Companions: To Vegetables in the Garden: To Cooks in the Kitchen / by Adelma Grenier Simmons. Coventry, Conn.: Caprilands Pub. Co., 1987. 144 p., illus.

1020. Herbs Through the Seasons at Caprilands / Adelma Grenier Simmons; photographs by Randa Bishop. Emmaus, Pa.: Rodale Press, c1987. 192 p., illus. (some colored).

1021. How to Grow and Use Herbs / Ann Bonar and Daphne MacCarthy. London, Eng.: Ward Lock, 1987. 96 p., illus. (some colored). (Concorde Gardening). Includes index.

1022. The New Herb Cook Book: From the Kitchens and Gardens of the Southern Ontario Unit, Herb Society of America / edited by Beatrice Jeanneret; drawings by Susan Hamilton. Toronto, Ont.: Southern Ontario Unit, Herb Society of America, c1987. 123 p., illus. Includes index.

1023. Southern Herb Growing / Madalene Hill & Gwen Barclay, with Jean Hardy. Fredericksburg, Tex.: Shearer Pub., 1987. 196 p., colored illus. Includes indexes.

1024. The Complete Book of Herbs / Lesley Bremness. New York: Viking Studio Books, c1988. 288 p., illus. (some colored). 75 recipes and instructions on harvesting and preserving herbs. Includes bibliogrpahy and index.

Herbs *(Continued)*

1025. Cooking with Herbs / Patricia Lousada. Exeter, Eng.: Webb & Bower, 1988. 96 p., illus. (some colored). (Culpeper Guides). Includes index.

1026. A Dooryard Herb Cookbook / by Linda O. Rago. Charleston, W. Va.: Pictorial Histories Pub. Co., c1988. 128 p. Includes index. Possibly a later version of Dooryard Herbs, published in 1984 (entry 990).

1027. Herbal Fare / Carolyn Martindale, editor; Irene Yelton and Barbara Crook, chairpersons, Cookbook Committee; Diane Strudwick, coordinator. Youngstown, Ohio: Holborn Herb Growers Guild, 1988. 269 p., illus.

1028. It's About Thyme!: An Herb Manual and Cookbook of Herb and Non-Herb Recipes / by Marge Clark; illustrations by Doan Helms. West Lebanon, Ind.: M. Clark, c1988. 271 p., illus. Includes index.

1029. Kitchen Herbs: The Art and Enjoyment of Growing Herbs and Cooking with Them / Sal Gilbertie; photographs by Joseph Kugielsky; culinary text and recipes by Frances Towner Giedt. Toronto, Ont.; New York: Bantam Books, 1988. 251 p., colored illus. ca. 125 recipes. Includes index.

1030. Old Ways Rediscovered / compiled, written & illustrated by Clarence Meyer; selected & edited by David C. Meyer. Glenwood, Ill.: Meyerbooks, c1988. 142 p., illus. "Material for this book originally appeared in the Herbalist Almanac, in the annual issues published from 1954 through 1978." Includes index.

1031. Season to Taste / Jeannette Ferrary, Louise Fiszer; illustrated by Lauren Jarrett. New York: Simon and Schuster, c1988. 396 p., illus. Includes index.

1032. Secret Ingredients / Michael Roberts. Toronto, Ont.; New York: Bantam Books, 1988. 279 p. Includes index.

Herbs *(Continued)*

1033. Cooking with Herbs / by Emelie Tolley and Chris Mead. New York: C.N. Potter: Distributed by Crown Publishers, 1989. 312 p., ca. 400 color photos. More than 200 recipes. Includes index.

1034. Herbs / Simon and Judith Hopkinson; photographs by Deni Bown. 1st American ed. Chester, Conn.: Globe Pequot Press, c1989. 144 p., illus. (some colored), maps. (Classic Garden Plants). Includes bibliography and index.

1035. Jeanne Rose's Herbal Guide to Food: Eating Healthy the Herbal Way / illustrated by Michael S. Moore; with John Hulburd. Berkeley, Calif.: North Atlantic Books, c1989. 252 p., illus. Includes bibliography.

1036. Recipes from a French Herb Garden / Geraldene Holt. New York: Simon and Schuster, c1989. 159 p., 70 colored photos. 120 recipes. Includes index.

1037. Aromatic Herbs: How to Use Them in Cooking and Seasoning Foods / Jill Norman. Bantam ed. New York: Bantam Books, 1990. 41 p., colored illus. (The Bantam Library of Culinary Arts). Includes index.

1038. From Seed to Serve: A Beginner's Guide to Growing & Using Herbs / Leanna Kay Potts. Joplin, Mo. (717 Glenview, Joplin 64801): Potts, 1990. 153 p., illus. More than 150 recipes. "Includes seeds, directions, garden plan, and lots of recipes."

1039. Herbal Treasures: Inspiring Month-by-Month Projects for Gardening, Cooking, and Crafts / by Phyllis V. Shaudys. Pownal, Vt.: Storey Communications, c1990. 288 p., line drawings. Includes bibliography and index.

1040. Herbs: A Connoisseur's Guide / Susan Fleming. New York: Crescent Books: Distributed by Crown Publishers, c1990. 112 p., illus. (some colored). Includes index.

Herbs *(Continued)*

1041. Herbs in Healthy Home Cooking / by Jessica Houdret. Garden City Park, N.Y., Avery, 1990. 159 p. More than 100 recipes using 25 basic herbs. "An Ashgrove Book."

1042. Herbs & Cooking / Ann Lovejoy, guest editor. Brooklyn, N.Y.: Brooklyn Botanic Garden, 1990. 96 p. illus. (Plants and Gardens; v. 45, no. 4).

1043. The Windowsill Herb Garden / by John Prenis; Elizabeth Corning Dudley, editor; Alice Joy Carter, consulting editor, food. Philadelphia, Pa.: Running Press, c1990. 96 p., illus.

1044. Winter Pleasures / Noel Richardson; edited by Elaine Jones; line drawings by Andrew Yeoman. Vancouver, B.C.: Whitecap Books, c1990. 131 p., illus. On cover: Herbs and Comfort Cooking. Includes bibliography.

CHILDREN'S COOKBOOKS

1045. Thyme for Kids / Leanna K. Potts & Evangela Potts. Joplin, Mo. (717 Glenview, Joplin 64801): Potts, 1990. 84 p., illus. "Includes planting instructions, recipes, and seeds."

see also entries 685, 774, 803, 2510, 2515, 2532, 2690, 2698; Herbs and Spices; Herbal Teas *(Section II);* Pestos *(Section II); specific herbs:* Basil, Garlic, *etc.; and broader category:* Natural Foods

Herbs and Spices

1046. All You Need to Know About Herbs & Spices / by G.B. Woodin. Mount Vernon, N.Y.: Peter Pauper Press, 1970. 62 p., illus.

1047. From Caravan to Casserole: Herbs and Spices in Legend, History, and Recipes / Malvina W. Liebman. Miami, Fla.: E. A. Seemann Pub., c1977. 160 p., illus. Includes index.

Specific Ingredients 137

Herbs and Spices *(Continued)*

1048. Salt-Free Cooking with Herbs & Spices / June Roth; foreword by S.K. Fineberg. Chicago, Ill.: Contemporary Books, 1977. 204 p., illus. Includes index.

1049. Herbs and Spices / by Jan Kybal; illustrated by Jirina Kaplicka; translated by Olga Kuthanova. London, Eng.: Hamlyn, c1980. 224 p., illus. (some colored). (A Hamlyn Colour Guide). Translated from the Czech. Includes index.

1050. Spices and Herbs, Lore & Cookery / Elizabeth S. Hayes; illustrations by J.M. Yeatts. New York: Dover Publications, 1980, c1961. 266 p., illus. Reprint of the ed. published by Doubleday, Garden City, N.Y., under title: Spices and Herbs Around the World. Includes index.

1051. Cooking with Spices & Herbs / Dina Zimmerman. Stanford, Calif.: Institute of Vedic Science, 1981. 28 p.

1052. Spices, Salt and Aromatics in the English Kitchen / Elizabeth David. Repr. with revisions. Harmondsworth, Eng.: Penguin, 1981, c1970. 277 p. (Penguin Handbooks). Includes bibliography and index.

1053. Stay Slim with Herbs and Spices / Elizabeth Peplow; illustrated by Yvonne Skargon. London, Eng.: Darton, Longman & Todd, 1981. 120 p., illus. Includes bibliography and index.

1054. Using Herbs & Spices / Mala Young. Newton Abbot, Eng.: David & Charles, c1981. 48 p., illus. (Health Food Cooking). Includes index.

1055. The Complete Book of Herbs & Spices / Sarah Garland. 1982 ed. New York: Bookthrift, 1982, c1979. 288 p., illus. (some colored). Includes bibliography and index. Reprint. Originally published: New York: Viking Press, 1979 (A Studio Book).

Herbs and Spices *(Continued)*

1056. Herbs, Spices & Flavorings / by Doris McFerran Townsend. Tucson, Ariz.: HP Books, c1982. 160 p., colored illus. Includes index. Cover title: How to Cook with Herbs, Spices & Flavorings.

1057. Herbs, Spices, and Flavorings / Tom Stobart. Woodstock, N.Y.: Overlook Press, 1982. 320 p., illus. (some colored). Includes indexes.

1058. The Complete Book of Spices: Their Medical, Nutritional, and Culinary Uses / John Heinerman; introduction by Henry Heimlich. New Canaan, Conn.: Keats Pub., c1983. 183 p., illus. Includes bibliography and index.

1059. Durkee Spice and Herb Cookbook / Ideals. Milwaukee, Wis.: Ideals Pub. Corp., c1983. 64 p., colored illus. Includes index.

1060. Herbs and Spices / Amy Cockburn. Exeter, Eng.: Webb & Bower, 1983. 47 p., colored illus. (A Webb & Bower Miniature).

1061. Herbs and Spices of the World / by Hermie Kranzdorf; photography, Norman M. Kranzdorf. Exton, Pa.: Schiffer Pub., c1983. 205 p., colored illus. Includes index.

1062. A Pinch of This, a Grain of That: The Creative Guide to Herbs & Spices / Geraldine Lacerte-Neumann. Ottawa, Ont.: Deneau, 1983. 89 p.

1063. The Book of Herbs & Spices / John & Rosemary Hemphill. New York: Gallery Books, 1984. 128 p., 13 p. of colored plates. Includes bibliography and index.

1064. Cooking with Herbs and Spices / Craig Claiborne; drawings by Alice Golden. New ed. New York: Harper & Row, c1984. 339 p. More than 600 recipes. Rev. ed. of: Cooking with Herbs & Spices. 1970. Includes index.

Herbs and Spices *(Continued)*

1065. Encyclopedia of Herbs, Spices, and Flavourings / Arabella Boxer and others; photography, Laurie Evans and Charlie Stebbings; illustrations, Claire Davies and others. New York: Crescent Books: Distributed by Crown Publishers, 1984. 207 p., colored illus. Includes index.

1066. Herbs and Spices of the Bible: How to Grow and Use Them / by Marian Maeve O'Brien. St. Louis, Mo.: CBP Press, c1984. 125 p., illus. A revision and enlargement of The Bible Herb Book. Includes index.

1067. Cooking with Herbs & Spices / Sallie Morris. London, Eng.: Octopus, 1985. 79 p., colored illus. (The Kitchen Companion). Includes index.

1068. Herbs & Spices / Sonia Allison. London, Eng.: Bell & Hyman, 1985. 93 p., illus. (some colored). (New & Natural). Includes index.

1069. Herbs and Spices: A Guide to Culinary Seasoning / Waverley Root and others; edited by Waverley Root. New and rev. ed. New York: Alfred van der Marck Editions, c1985. 133 p., illus. (some colored). Includes index.

1070. The Penguin Book of Herbs and Spices / Rosemary Hemphill. Harmondsworth, Eng.: Penguin, 1985, c1966. (Penguin Handbook). Includes bibliography and index. Originally published in 2 v. as: Fragrance and Flavour, London, Eng.: Angus and Robertson, 1960 and: Spices and Savour, London, Eng.: Angus and Robertson, 1965.

1071. Salt-Free Herb Cookery / by Edith Stovel; illustrations by Cindy McFarland. Pownal, Vt.: Garden Way Pub., c1985. 31 p., illus. (Garden Way Publishing Bulletin; A-97).

1072. Traditional Herb & Spice Cookery / Jack Santa Maria; illustrations by John Spencer. London, Eng.: Rider, 1985. 186 p., illus. Includes bibliography and index.

Herbs and Spices *(Continued)*

1073. Cooking with Herbs & Spices. 1st U.S. and Canadian ed. Woodbury, N.Y.: Barron's, 1986, c1984. 160 p., colored illus. (Step-by-Step Cooking Series). Includes index.

1074. Growing and Using Herbs and Spices / Milo Miloradovich. New York: Dover Publications, 1986. 231 p., illus. Reprint. Originally published: The Home Garden Book of Herbs and Spices. Garden City, N.Y.: Doubleday, 1952. Includes index.

1075. The Herb & Spice Cookbook: A Seasoning Celebration / Sheryl & Mel London; photography by the Rodale Press Dept. Emmaus, Pa.: Rodale Press, c1986. 306 p., illus. (some colored). Includes index.

1076. Herb Grower's Guide: Cooking, Spicing & Lore / John Prenis. Philadelphia, Pa.: Running Press, c1986. 96 p., illus.

1077. Low-Salt Cookery: 100 Healthy & Delicious Main Dishes. Tuscon, Ariz.: HP Books, c1986. 79 p., colored illus. (Creative Cuisine). Includes index.

1078. Of Tarragon, Thyme & Tauvirg: Delectable Cooking with Herbs & Spices / Lois O'Connor. Rev. ed. Alfred, N.Y.: Scriptorium Press, 1986. 1 v.

1079. Book of Herbs & Spices: Recipes, Remedies, and Lore / Gail Duff; illustrated by Cherry Denman. Topsfield, Mass.: Salem House Publishers, 1987. 121 p., colored illus. Includes indexes.

1080. Cooking with Herbs & Spices / compiled by Judith Ferguson. New York: Colour Library Books, c1987. 64 p., colored illus. Includes index.

1081. Herb & Spice Handbook / writer, Karen Miles; editor, Chris D. Baker. 3d ed. Norway, Iowa: Frontier Cooperative Works, c1987. 196 p., illus. Includes bibliography and index.

Herbs and Spices *(Continued)*

1082. Cookery Magic with Spices and Herbs / by Priscilla Grijalva. Las Cruces, N.M.: New Mexico State University, Cooperative Extension Service, 1988. 12 p.

1083. Margaret Roberts Cooks with Herbs & Spices. 1st ed. Johannesburg, South Africa: Southern Book Publishers, 1988. 267 p., 28 p. of colored plates. Includes index.

1084. Cooking with Herbs and Spices / by Milo Miloradovich. New York: Dover Publications, 1989, c1950. 320 p. Reprint. Originally published: The Art of Cooking with Herbs and Spices. 1st ed. Garden City, N.Y.: Doubleday, 1950.

1085. A Gourmet's Guide to Herbs and Spices / Mary Trewby; photography by David Johnson. Los Angeles, Calif.: HP Books, 1989. 120 p. More than 100 colored photos. Includes index.

1086. Herb Cuisine with Added Spice / Mary Lea Jabara; edited and illustrated by Carol Lee Hill. Wichita, Kan.: From The Studio, 1989. 102 p., illus.

1087. The Complete Book of Herbs, Spices, and Condiments: From Garden to Kitchen to Medicine Chest / Carol Ann Rinzler. New York: Facts on File, c1990. 199 p., illus. Includes bibliography and index.

1088. The Spice of Vegetarian Cooking: Ethnic Recipes from India, China, Mexico, Southeast Asia, the Middle East, and Europe / Martha Rose Shulman. Rochester, Vt.: Healing Arts Press; New York?: Distributed to the book trade in the U.S. by AIDC, c1990. 240 p. Includes bibliography and index. Reprint. Originally published: Spicy Vegetarian Feasts. Wellingborough, Eng.; New York: Thorsons, 1986.

see also Herbs; Spices

Honey

1089. The Honey Cookbook / Juliette Elkon. 1st ed. New York: Knopf, 1955. 162 p.

1090. Bee Prepared with Honey: 140 Delicious Honey Recipes Plus a Guide to Backyard Beekeeping / Arthur W. Andersen. Bountiful, Utah: Horizon Publishers, c1975. 144 p., illus. Includes index and bibliography.

1091. Honey Recipes from Amana. Iowa City, Iowa: Penfield, 1978. 32 p.

1092. The Wonderful World of Honey: The Only Nutrition-Wise Sugarless Cookbook, Beauty Aids & Preventive Medicine / Joe M. Parkhill. Berryville, Ark.: Country Bazaar Pub. Co., 1978. 160 p.

1093. Putting It Up with Honey: A Natural Foods Canning and Preserving Cookbook / by Susan Geiskopf; illustrated by Linda Cleaver. Ashland, Or.: Quicksilver Productions, c1979. 224 p., illus. Includes index.

1094. A Book of Honey / Eva Crane. New York: Scribner, 1980. 193 p., illus. Includes bibliography and index.

1095. The Book of Honey / Claude Francis & Fernande Gontier; illustrated by Stephen Zinkus. London, Eng.: Hale, 1981, c1979. 175 p., illus. Includes index.

1096. Cooking with Honey / by Joanne Barrett; illustrations by Nancy Anisfield. Pownal, Vt.: Garden Way Pub., c1981. 32 p., illus. (Garden Way Publishing Bulletin; A-62).

1097. The Healthy Taste of Honey: Bee People's Recipes, Anecdotes, & Lore / Larry James Lonik. Virginia Beach: Donning, c1981. 159 p., illus. Includes bibliography and index.

Specific Ingredients   143

Honey (Continued)

1098. Here's to You Honey!: The Book That Takes up Where the World of Honey Leaves off / Joe M. Parkhill. Berryville, Ark.: Country Bazaar Pub., 1981. 166 p.

1099. Honey / Isha Mellor; illustrated by Rodney Shackell. 1st ed. New York: Congdon & Lattes: Distributed by St. Martin's Press, 1981, c1980. 80 p., illus. Reprint of the edition published by W. H. Allen, London, Eng.

1100. A Honey of a Cookbook: Featuring Recipes Using Texas Honey. Austin, Tex.: Texas Dept. of Agriculture, 1981. 13 p.

1101. The Sunshine Larder: Using Honey to Preserve the Natural Goodness of Summer's Bounty / by Susan Geiskopf. Wellingborough, Eng.: Thorsons, 1981, c1979. 157 p., illus. Includes index.

1102. A Taste of Honey / Boris Wittich; line drawings and design Peter Haillay; translation by Sara Moncur. Sherborne, Eng.: Alphabooks, 1981. 92 p. Translation of: Rund um den Honig.

1103. The Honey Kitchen / edited by Dadant & Sons. New York: Scribner, 1982, c1980. 192 p., illus. Includes index.

1104. A Honey of a Cookbook / by the Alberta Beekeepers' Association. Edmonton, Alta.: Alberta Beekeepers' Association, 1982. 94 p., colored illus. Includes indexes.

1105. Wonderful World of Bee Pollen / Joe M. Parkhill. Berryville, Ark.: Country Bazaar Pub. Co., c1982. 128 p., illus. Includes index.

1106. Gale's Honey Book / Bridget Jones. London, Eng.: Hamlyn, c1983. 128 p., illus. (some colored).

1107. Honey: God's Gift for Health and Beauty / by Joe M. Parkhill with Sandi Knode. Berryville, Ark.: Country Bazaar Pub. Co.; Clarkson, Ky.: Sold by the Walter T. Kelly Co., c1983. 152 p.

Honey *(Continued)*

1108. Honey: Natural Food and Healer / by Janet Bord. 2nd ed. rev., enl. and reset. Melbourne, Australia: Science of Life; Wellingborough, Eng.: Thorsons, distributor, 1983. 96 p. Includes index.

1109. Honey & Spice: A Nutritional Guide to Natural Dessert Cookery / written and illustrated by Lorena Laforest Bass. Ashland, Or.: Coriander Press, c1983. 339 p., illus.

1110. Honey Delights: Cooking with Honey and Whole Wheat Flour: Over 250 Sugarless Recipes / by Katherine Partain; illustrated by David Partain. San Diego, Calif.: San Diego Pub. Co., c1983. 149 p., illus.

1111. Cooking with Honey / by Judy Powers. Silver Spring, Md.: American Cooking Guild, 1984. 64 p., illus. (Collector's Series).

1112. The Little Honey Book / Mavis Budd. London, Eng.: Piatkus, 1984. 60 p., illus.

1113. The Little Honey Cookbook / Mary L. Green. Denver, Colo.: Giftstar, 1984. ca. 10 p., illus. (Little Cookbooks).

1114. Good and Wholesome Honey Recipes / American Honey Institute. New York: Dover Publications, 1985. 105 p. 322 recipes. Slightly altered republication of the following two pamphlets published by the American Honey Institute, Madison, Wis.: Old Favorite Honey Recipes (1945) and New Favorite Honey Recipes (1947).

1115. Honey: Pure and Natural Energy / Daphne Metland. Nottingham, Eng.: Boots, c1985. 64 p., illus. (some colored). (Boots Health Eating Guides). Includes index.

1116. A Honey of a Cookbook, vol. II / by the Alberta Beekeepers' Association. Edmonton, Alta.: Alberta Beekeepers' Association, 1986. 94 p., colored illus. Includes index.

Honey *(Continued)*

1117. Honey Recipes / coordinated by Annabelle Derden Selph. Durham, N.C.: North Carolina State Beekeepers Association: N.C. Agricultural Extension Service, Durham County, 1986. 135 p., illus. Includes indexes.

1118. Ontario Honey Recipe Book. Bayfield, Ont.: Ontario Beekeepers' Association, 1986. 66 p. Includes index.

1119. American Honey Institute's Old Favorite Honey Recipes and the Honey Recipes Book of the Iowa Honey Producers Association. Glenwood, Ill.: Meyerbooks, c1988. 89 p., illus. Includes index.

1120. Honey Microwave Cookery Recipes / by Barbara Dalby. Mytholmroyd, Eng.: Northern Bee Books, 1988? 16 p.

1121. New Honey & Yogurt Recipes / Rena Cross. Rev. and updated ed. London, Eng.: Foulsham, c1988. 128 p.

1122. Cooking with Love and Honey / Nancy Hoag. 1st ed. Greensboro, N.C.: Tudor Publishers, 1989. 168 p. Contains information on storage of honey and using it for non-food purposes.

CHILDREN'S COOKBOOKS

1123. The Honey Book / by Lucille Recht Penner; illustrated with photos. and old prints arranged by Ronnie and Herman. New York: Hastings House, c1980. 160 p., illus. Includes indexes. An introduction to the importance of honey throughout history and around the world, including discussions of its composition and how it is produced, gathered, sold, and used. Includes a number of recipes for cosmetics and food dishes.

Specialty Cookbooks

Honey *(Continued)*

1124. Friendly Bees, Ferocious Bees / by Mona Kerby. New York: F. Watts, 1987. 96 p., illus. Includes bibliography and index. Describes the physical characteristics, habits, and natural environment of honeybees and Africanized bees. Also discusses beekeeping and includes recipes using honey.

see also entries 1004, 3212, 3568

Horse Meat

1125. Le Cheval a Toutes les Sauces ... et en 50 Recettes / François Lubrina, Annie et Christian d'Orangeville; illustrations de Gerard Frischeteau. Montreal, Que.: Editions Quebec-Amerique, c1975. 142 p., illus. Includes index.

see also broader category: Meat

Hot Dogs *see* Frankfurters

Hot Peppers *see* Peppers

Huckleberries

1126. The Huckleberry Book / by 'Asta Bowen; with illustrations by Karen Leigh Noice. Helena, Mont.: American Geographic Pub., c1988. 90 p., illus. "All about the West's most treasured wild berry, from botany to bears, mountain lore to recipes."

see also broader category: Berries

Insects

1127. Entertaining with Insects: or, The original Guide to Insect Cookery / Ronald L. Taylor, Barbara J. Carter; illustrated by John Gregory Tweed. Santa Barbara, Calif.: Woodbridge Press Pub. Co., c1976. 160 p., illus. Includes index.

Jalapeños

1128. Cooking with Jalapeños / by Jeff and Greg Schnell. Wylie, Tex. (P.O. Box 641, Wylie 75098): Distributor, Schnell Enterprises, c1987. 63 p. Includes index.

see also broader category: Peppers

Jams

1129. Smucker's Cookbook / prepared and produced by Rutledge Books. New York: Benjamin Co., 1976. 128 p., illus. Includes index. "A Benjamin Company/Rutledge Book."

1130. Cooking with Jam / Henry R. Lorenzo; edited by Charles R. Graham. San Francisco, Calif.: Easy Banana Productions, 1990. 68 p.

Kasha *see* Buckwheat Groats

Kiwifruit

1131. Recipes for Kiwifruit Lovers / by Mary Beutel; illustrations by Wayne Spurgeon, cover photo. by Richard Klein. Gridley, Calif.: Kiwi Growers of California, c1975. 63 p., illus. Title on cover: Kiwifruit Recipes.

1132. Kiwifruit Collection: Cookbook / Brennan, McGeough, Smith. Sidney, B.C.: Island Directories, 1989. 93 p., illus.

see also broader category: Fruits

Kudzu

1133. The Book of Kudzu: A Culinary & Healing Guide / William Shurtleff & Akiko Aoyagi; illustrated by Akiko Aoyagi. Wayne, N.J.: Avery Pub. Group, c1985. 102 p., illus. Includes index.

1134. The Kudzu Cookbook: You Don't Eat It: It Eats You! / Carole S. Marsh. Bath, N.C.: Gallopade Pub. Group, 1987. 1 v.

Lamb

1135. The Great British Lamb Guide: All You Need to Know to Make the Most of Your British Lamb. London, Eng. (5 St. John's Sq., Smithfield, EC1M 4DE): Applied Creativity on behalf of the Meat Promotion Executive of the Meat and Livestock Commission, c1980. 34 p., colored illus.

1136. Lamb / by the editors of Time-Life Books. Alexandria, Va.: Time-Life Books, c1981. 176 p., colored illus. Includes index.

1137. Black Sheep Newsletter Cookbook / compiled and edited by Sachiye Jones. Eugene, Or.: Black Sheep Press, c1982. 79 p., illus.

1138. Lamb in Family Meals / prepared by Human Nutrition Information Service. Slightly rev. Washington, D.C.: U.S. Dept. of Agriculture; For sale by the Supt. of Documents, U.S. Government Printing Office, 1982. 21 p., illus. (Home and Garden Bulletin; no. 124). Includes index.

1139. Lamb & Mutton. Newton Abbot, Eng.: David & Charles, 1983. 64 p. (David & Charles Kitchen Workshop). Translation of: Lammekjott.

1140. Making the Most of Lamb & Pork / Robert Carrier. London, Eng.: Marshall Cavendish, 1984. 112 p., colored illus. (Robert Carrier's Kitchen). Includes index.

Specific Ingredients

Lamb *(Continued)*

1141. Fresh Ways with Lamb / by the editors of Time-Life Books. Alexandria, Va.: Time-Life Books, c1988. 144 p., colored illus. (Healthy Home Cooking Series). Includes index.

see also entries 107, 2320; and broader category: Meat

Leeks

1142. First You Take a Leek: Recipes with a Gourmet Touch / recipes, Maxine J. Saltonstall; illustrations, Wayne Mayfield. 1st ed. Rutland, Vt.: C.E. Tuttle Co., 1970. 59 p., illus.

1143. The Leek Cookbook / Mary Hamilton. 1st ed. Seattle, Wash.: Madrona Publishers, c1982. 121 p., illus. Includes index.

1144. Potter County Leek Cookbook / created and illustrated by Dottie Bajor. Coudersport, Pa.: Leader Pub. Co., c1990. 78 p., illus.

see also entries 877, 1606; and broader category: Vegetables

Legumes

1145. The Bean & Lentil Cookbook: Colourful, Inexpensive and Highly Nutritious Pulse Recipes: Includes Sweet Dishes / by Pamela Dixon; illustrated by Clive Birch. Wellingborough, Eng.: Thorsons, 1982, c1980. 128 p., illus. Includes index. Originally published as: Pulse Cookery, 1980.

1146. Rose Elliot's Book of Beans and Lentils. London, Eng.: Fontana Paperbacks, 1984. 63 p., illus. Includes index.

1147. Basically Beans: New Ways with Beans, Pulses and Lentils / Daphne Metland. Nottingham, Eng.: Books, c1985. 64 p., illus. (some colored). Includes index.

Legumes *(Continued)*

1148. Grains, Beans & Pulses / Mary Norwak. London, Eng.: Bell & Hyman, 1985. 93 p., illus. (some colored). (New & Natural). Includes index.

1149. The Perfect Pulses: Cooking with Alberta Beans, Peas, Lentils. Lethbridge, Alta.: Pulse Growers Association of Alberta, 1985. 32 p., colored illus.

1150. Wholefood Cookery with Beans, Peas and Lentils / Tess Mallos. Sydney, Australia: Lansdowne, c1985. 128 p., illus. Includes index.

1151. Beans, Nuts and Lentils / by Sarah Brown. London, Eng.: Dorling Kindersley, 1986. 96p., colored illus. (Sainsbury's Healthy Eating Cookbooks).

1152. The Amazing Legume: Cooking with Lentils, Beans and Peas / by Alice Jenner. Woodstock, N.Y.: Overlook Press: Distributed by Viking, 1989. 134 p., illus. Includes index.

see also specific legumes: Beans, Lentils, Peas, Soybeans, etc.; *and broader category:* Vegetables

Lemon Juice

1153. Create a Difference: The ReaLemon Cookbook. Columbus, Ohio: Borden, Inc., 1980. 1 booklet. "69 recipes for appetizers, meat and seafood main dishes, soups, salads, beverages, and desserts," using reconstituted lemon juice.

see also broader category: Lemons

Specific Ingredients 151

Lemons

1154. The Golden Lemon: A Collection of Special Recipes / Doris Tobias and Mary Merris. 1st ed. New York: Atheneum, 1978. 210 p. Includes index.

1155. The Compleat Lemon: A Cookbook / by Chris Casson and Susan Lee; illustrations by Kimble Mead. 1st ed. New York: Holt, Rinehart and Winston, c1979. 142 p., illus. Includes index.

1156. Pass the Salt: Put Flavor Into Low Sodium Diets with Sunkist Lemons / Phyllis Ullman. Van Nuys, Calif.: Consumer Services, Sunkist Growers, Inc., 1982. 15 p., illus.

1157. The Little Lemon Cookbook / Mary L. Green. Denver, Colo.: Giftstar, 1984. ca. 10 p., illus. (Little Cookbooks).

1158. Lemon: Uses for the Entire Lemon, with Recipes & Suggestions / Recycling Consortium. Houston, Tex.: Prosperity & Profits, 1989. 14 p.

1159. Lemon Twist: No Salt Added Cookbook: Zesty and Zingy Lemon Recipes, Garnishes, and Menus / by Ree. 1st ed. Arcadia, Calif.: Nutrition Unlimited Publications, c1989. 204 p., illus.

see also Lemon Juice; *and broader category:* Citrus Fruits

Lentils

1160. Dry Peas and Lentils / by Betty Lowe Janson; design and art, Betty Lowe Janson; editor, Susan Hughes; food photography, Steve Connor, Craig Sweat. Latah, Wash.: B.L. Janson, c1982. 208 p., illus. (some colored). Includes index. Cover title: Cooking with the "Protein Twins" Dry Peas and Lentils.

see also broader category: Legumes

Lettuce *see* Greens

Lime Juice

1161. ReaLime Recipe Booklet. Columbus, Ohio: Borden, Inc., 1981. Includes recipes for beverages and other dishes using reconstituted lime juice. 1 booklet.

Liquors

1162. Homemade Liqueurs / Dona and Mel Meilach. Chicago, Ill.: Contemporary Books, c1979. 222 p., illus. Contains recipes for dozens of liqueurs and for dishes using them. Includes bibliography and indexes.

1163. Cooking with Wines and Spirits--and Beer and Cider Too / by Elaine Hallgarten. London, Eng.: Published by Hodder & Stoughton in association with The Good Food Club, c1980. 224 p., colored illus. Includes indexes.

1164. Morey Amsterdam's Cookbook for Drinkers: Or, Betty Cooker's Crock Book, Over 100 Great Recipes Made with Booze / Morey Amsterdam. Santa Monica, Calif.: Delphi Information Sciences Corp., c1980. 113 p. (Delphi Books). Includes index. Another ed. published under title: Morey Amsterdam's Benny Cooker Crock Book for Drinkers.

1165. Carousing in the Kitchen: Creative Cooking Using Spirits / Linda Taylor Anderson. Melbourne, Fla. (5885 Crane Rd., Melbourne 32901): Good Times Productions, c1981. 147 p., illus. Includes indexes.

1166. Spirited Cooking: With Liqueurs, Spirits and Wine / Sonia Allison. Newton Abbot, Eng.: David & Charles, c1981. 136 p., illus. (some colored). Includes index.

Liquors *(Continued)*

1167. The 80 Proof Cookbook: An Introduction to Cooking with High Spirits / Mary Anne & Frank Cullen. 1st ed. New York: St. Martin's Press, 1982. 125 p.

1168. Cordial Cookery / by Marjorie White. Maplewood, N.J.: Hammond, c1982. 154 p. Includes index.

1169. Grand Finales: Desserts and Sweets Flavored with Liqueurs, Rums, and Brandies / Dick Taeuber. Woodbury, N.Y.: Barron's, c1982. 234 p., 8 leaves of plates, colored illus. Includes index.

1170. Mr. Boston Cordial Cooking Guide. New York: Warner Books, c1982. 138 p., 16 p. of plates, colored illus. More than 170 recipes. Includes index.

1171. Mr. Boston Spirited Dessert Guide. New York: Warner Books, 1982. 120 p., 16 p. of plates, colored illus. More than 130 recipes. Includes index.

1172. Cooking with Booze / J.L. Nichols. San Diego, Calif.: Joed Originals of California, 1984. 1 v.

1173. Desserts with Spirit! / Robert Carmack, Gino Cofacci; introduction by James Beard. 1st ed. New York: Atheneum, 1985. 227 p. ca. 100 recipes. Includes index.

1174. The Spirit of Cooking: Spectacular Dishes Using Champagne, Wine, Spirits and Liqueurs / by Paul Warwick. Port Coquitlam, B.C.: Spirit of Cooking Pub., 1985. 110 p., colored illus. Includes index.

1175. Homemade Cream Liqueurs / Dona and Mel Meilach. Chicago, Ill.: Contemporary Books, c1986. 150 p., illus. Contains recipes for making liqueurs and for foods and drinks using them.

Liquors *(Continued)*

1176. The Boozy Chef / Suzanne Dixon-Hudson. Kensington, N.S.W.: Bay Books Pty Ltd., 1988. 128 p.

1177. Salute to the Great American Chefs: B & B/Benedictine Liqueurs Anniversary Cookbook. Elmsford, N.Y.: Benjamin Co., c1988. 222 p., illus (some colored). Includes indexes.

1178. The Best of the Spirit of Cooking / by Paul Warwick. Port Coquitlam, B.C.: Spirit of Cooking Pub., 1989. 64 p. Includes recipes using beer, wine, champagne, spirits, and liqueurs.

1179. Classic Liqueurs: The Art of Making and Cooking with Liqueurs / by Cheryl Long and Heather Kibbey. Lake Oswego, Or.: Culinary Arts Ltd., c1990. 128 p.

see also specific liquors: Beer, Brandy, Cider, Rum, Whiskey, Wine

Lobsters

1180. The Book of the Lobster: An Informal Account of What He Is and What He Is Not, How He Is Caught, and How He Is Cooked and Eaten, with 43 Recipes / written and illustrated by Joy V. Dueland. Somersworth, N.H.: New Hampshire Pub. Co., 1973. 214 p., illus.

1181. Diving for Crayfish in South Africa: A Guide to the South African Rock Lobster and its Capture / Colin Vary; drawings by Margo Branch. 1st ed. Cape Town, South Africa: C. Struik, 1983. 112 p., 16 p. of plates, illus. (some colored). Includes index.

1182. The Little Lobster Cookbook / Mary L. Green. Denver, Colo.: Giftstar, 1984. ca. 10 p., illus. (Little Cookbooks).

Specific Ingredients

Lobsters *(Continued)*

1183. How to Make Love to a Lobster / Marjorie Harris and Peter Taylor; illustrations by Geoffrey Moss. Toronto, Ont.: Macmillan of Canada, 1988. 166 p., illus.

1184. The Lobster Almanac / by Bruce Ballenger. 1st ed. Chester, Conn.: Globe Pequot Press, c1988. 217 p., illus.

1185. Largely Lobster: Making the Most of Lobster / Julie V. Watson. Halifax, N.S.: Nimbus Pub., c1989. 96 p., illus. Includes index.

1186. North American Lobster / by R. Marilyn Schmidt. Barnegat Light, N.J.: Barnegat Light Press, 1989. 24 p.

1187. A Lobster in Every Pot: Recipes and Lore / edited by Susan K. White; designed and illustrated by Majo Keleshian. Camden, Me.: Yankee Books, 1990. 192 p., illus. More than 100 recipes.

see also entry 466; and broader category: Shellfish

Macadamia Nuts

1188. The Marvelous Macadamia Nut / by Rebecca Buyers with Helen Caivano, Catherine Johnson, and Joann Carroll Linden; illustrations by Marc Rosenthal. New York: Irena Chalmers Cookbooks, c1982. 84 p., colored illus.

see also broader category: Nuts

Macaroni *see* **Pasta**

Mackerel

1189. Mackerel: Atlantic-King-Spanish / by R. Marilyn Schmidt. Barnegat Light, N.J.: Barnegat Light Press, 1989. 24 p.

see also broader category: Fish

Mahi-Mahi

1190. Mahi-Mahi / by R. Marilyn Schmidt. Barnegat Light, N.J.: Barnegat Light Press, 1988. 16 p.

see also broader category: Fish

Mangos

1191. Mangos, Mangos, Mangos: Recipes and Art from Hawaii / by Marilyn R. Harris; illustrated by Charlene K. Smoyer. Honolulu, Hawaii: M.R. Harris, c1989. 231 p., illus.

see also broader category: Fruit

Maple Sugar and Syrup

1192. The Sugar Bush Connection: Maple Cookery--"Sweet Water" Folklore--Sugaring off Facts, Sucre d'Erable Recettes Delicieuses / compiled by Beatrice Ross Buszek. Halifax, N.S.: Nimbus Pub., 1984. 202 p., illus. Includes bibliography and index.

1193. The Maple Syrup Baking and Dessert Cookbook / by Ken Haedrich; with lettering and illustrations by Ginger Brown. Rumney, N.H.: American Impressions Book Co., c1985. 46 p., illus.

1194. Microwaved Maple / by Pamela Davy and Shirley Deugo. Almonte, Ont.: SAP, c1987. 202 p., illus.

Specific Ingredients

Maple Sugar and Syrup *(Continued)*

1195. Primitive Maple-Sugaring and Cookery; The Maple Tree and Indian Legends; New and Nostalgic Recipes / Deone R. Wood. Menomonie, Wis.: West Wind Graphics, 1987. 34 p., illus. ca. 55 recipes.

1196. The Maple Syrup Cookbook / by Ken Haedrich; illustrations by Anna Rich. Pownal, Vt.: Storey Communications, 1989. 134 p., illus. More than 100 recipes. "A Garden Way Publishing Book." Includes index.

1197. Cooking with Maple Syrup: A Collection of Recipes / by A.E. Nelson & R. Smith Nelson. Winston-Salem, N.C.: A. Nelson (1039 Beecher Road, Winston-Salem 27104), 1990. 1 v.

CHILDREN'S COOKBOOKS

1198. Sugar Bush: Making Maple Syrup / by Nancy Hatch Gokay; art by Theresa Deeter. Hillsdale, Mich.: Hillsdale Educational Publishers, c1980. 32 p., illus. Text and illustrations describe the process of making maple syrup, one of America's oldest crops. Also includes projects and recipes.

Margarine

1199. The Parkay Margarine Cookbook / from Kraft. New York, N.Y.: Benjamin Co., c1980. 160 p., illus. (some colored). Includes index.

Marijuana

1200. Cooking with Marijuana / Evelyn Schmevelyn. Kent, Wash.: Pacific Pipeline, 1976. 67 p., illus.

1201. Marijuana Food: A Handbook for Marijuana Extract Cooking / Bill Drake. New York: Simon and Schuster, c1981. 160 p., illus. Includes index.

Specialty Cookbooks

Marine Algae

1202. Juel Andersen's Sea Green Primer: A Beginner's Book of Sea Weed Cookery / by Richard Ford, Juel Andersen with Sigrid Andersen. Berkeley, Calif.: Creative Arts Book Co., c1983. 63 p., illus. Includes index.

1203. Low Calorie, High Nutrition Vegetables from the Sea to Help You Look and Feel Better / by Seibin Arasaki and Teruko Arasaki. 1st ed. Tokyo, Japan: Japan Publications; New York: Distributor, U.S., Kodansha International/USA, through Harper & Row, 1983. 196 p., illus. (some colored).

1204. Seaweed and Vegetables. Tokyo, Japan: JOIE; Brisbane, Calif.: Distributed by JP Trading, c1984. 100 p., illus. (most colored). (Quick & Easy Nutritious Japanese Cooking, no. 2).

1205. Sea Vegetables: Harvesting Guide & Cookbook / Evelyn McConnaughey. Happy Camp, Calif.: Naturegraph Publishers, c1985. 239 p., illus. Includes index.

1206. Cooking with Sea Vegetables: A Collection of Naturally Delicious Dishes Using to the Full the Bountiful Harvest of the Oceans / by Peter and Montse Bradford; illustrated by Sue Reid. 1st U.S. ed. Rochester, Vt.: Healing Arts Press; New York: Distributed in the U.S. by Harper and Row, 1988, c1985. 144 p., illus. Includes index. Reprint. Originally published: New York: Thorsons Publishers, 1985.

see also entry 891

Mayonnaise

1207. That Amazing Ingredient: Mayonnaise!: Recipes in the Tradition of Hellmann's and Best Foods Mayonnaise/ copywriter, Miranda Craig; prop coordinator Hal Walter; illustrator, Joan Blume. Montreal, Que.: Best Foods Division, Canada Starch, 1981, c1979. 128 p., illus. Includes index. Issued also in French under title: Les délices de la mayonnaise!

Mayonnaise *(Continued)*

1208. Hellmann's Real Mayonnaise Seasonal Cookbook. Esher, Eng. (Claygatte House, Esher, Surrey KT10 9PN): Hellmann's Real Mayonnaise CPC (United Kingdom) Ltd., 1982. 20 p., colored illus. Includes index.

1209. Hellmann's Mayonnaise Best Foods: Over 100 Ways to Bring Out the Best. Lincolnwood, Ill.: Publications International, 1990. 96 p., colored illus. (Favorite Recipes; v. 5, no. 19). Includes index.

Mead

1210. All About Mead / S.W. Andrews. Mytholmroyd, Eng.: Northern Bee Books, c1982. 95 p.

see also broader category: Liquors

Meat

1211. The Meat Board Meat Book / by Barbara Bloch; with an introduction by Julia Child. New York: McGraw-Hill, c1977. 224 p., illus. "A Benjamin Company Book." Includes index.

1212. Microwaving Meats / by Barbara Methven; photographers, Michael Jensen, Ken Greer. Minnetonka, Minn.: Publication Arts, c1979. 158 p., colored illus. (Microwave Cooking Library). Includes index.

1213. The Bisto Book of Meat Cookery / Sonia Allison. Newton Abbot, Eng.: David & Charles, 1980. 128 p., illus. (some colored). Includes index.

1214. Buying and Cooking Meat / Mary Reynolds. Cambridge, Eng.: Published for J. Sainsbury Ltd. by Woodhead-Faulkner, 1980. 40 p., illus. (some colored). (Sainsbury's Food Guides, no. 3).

Meat *(Continued)*

1215. Carol Wright's Complete Meat Cookery: Choosing, Cooking, Carving. London, Eng.: Granada, 1980. 222 p., illus. (A Mayflower Book). Includes index.

1216. Lessons on Meat. 7th ed., rev. Chicago, Ill.: National Live Stock and Meat Board, 1980. 86 p., illus. (some colored).

1217. The Lobel Brothers' Meat Cookbook / Leon and Stanley Lobel, with Jon Messmann. New York: Cornerstone Library, c1980. 255 p. Includes index.

1218. Make it with Meat: Recipes with British Meat / photography by Melvin Grey. London, England (5 St. John's Square, Smithfield, EC1M 4DE): Meat Promotion Executive of the Meat and Livestock Commission, 1981. 16 p., colored illus.

1219. Meat Meals in Minutes. New York: Benjamin Co., c1981. 128 p., colored illus. Includes indexes.

1220. Meats, Including Poultry & Seafood. Nashville, Tenn. (P.O. Box 77, Nashville 37202): Favorite Recipes Press, c1981. 127 p., illus. (Favorite Recipes of Home Economics Teachers). Includes index.

1221. Armadillo Cook-off Cookbook: A Texas Original / Sam Lewis. Huntsville, Tex.: M & M Designs, 1982? 41 p.

1222. A Little Meat Goes a Long Way: 200 Kitchen-tested, Salt-free Recipes That Prove You Can Cut Down on Meat Without Sacrificing Flavor or Nutrition / by Nancy Albright; editor, Charles Gerras; assistant editor, Carol Munson; illustrations, Susan Rosenberger. Emmaus, Pa.: Rodale Press, c1982. 234 p., illus. Includes index.

1223. Meats from Amish and Mennonite Kitchens / collected and edited by Phyllis Pellman Good and Rachel Thomas Pellman. Lancaster, Pa.: Good Books, 1982. 32 p. (Pennsylvania Dutch Cookbooks).

Meat *(Continued)*

1224. All Canadian Meat Book. Toronto, Ont.: Fitzhenry & Whiteside in association with Agriculture Canada, c1983. 96 p., illus. (some colored).

1225. How to Buy More Meat for Less Money / by Bill Pizzico. 1st ed. Philadelphia, Pa. (2900 Lewis Tower Bldg., Philadelphia 19102): Direct Response Network Venture 51, c1983. 78 p., illus.

1226. Beef, Veal, Lamb & Pork. Los Angeles, Calif.: Knapp Press, c1984. 120 p., colored photos. (Cooking with Bon Appétit). More than 200 recipes from Bon Appétit magazine. Includes index.

1227. Meat Dishes in the International Cuisine / conceived and created by Rene Kramer; editor, John Fuller. London, Eng.: Virtue, 1984. 1058 p., colored illus. Includes index. Translation of: Fleischgereichte in der Internationale Kuche.

1228. The Quick Meats Cookbook / Lillian Langseth-Christensen and Carol Sturm Smith; illustrations by Lillian Langseth-Christensen. Walker large print ed. New York: Walker, 1984, c1967. 96 p., illus. Includes index.

1229. The Southern Heritage Beef, Veal & Lamb Cookbook. Birmingham, Ala.: Oxmoor House, c1984. 143 p., illus. (some colored). (The Southern Heritage Cookbook Library). Includes index.

1230. Better Homes and Gardens Favorite Meat Recipes. 1st ed. Des Moines, Iowa: Meredith Corp., c1985. 92 p., illus. (some colored). Includes index.

1231. Healthful Korean Cooking: Meats & Poultry / by Noh Chin-hwa; copyreader, Shirley A. Dorow. Elizabeth, N.J.: Hollym International Corp., 1985. 76 p., colored illus. Includes indexes.

Meat *(Continued)*

1232. Making the Most of Meat: A New Zealand Cookbook / Jan Bilton. Rev. and updated ed. Christchurch, N.Z.; London, Eng.: Whitcoulls, 1985. 102 p., colored illus. Includes index.

1233. Meat Dishes. London, Eng.: Reader's Digest Association, c1985. 104 p., illus. (some colored). (The Reader's Digest Good Health Cookbooks). Includes index.

1234. Meats and Sauces / Jehane Benoît. Saint-Lambert, Que.: Heritage, 1985. 110 p., colored illus. (Encyclopedia of Microwave Cooking; 1). Includes index. Issued also in French under title: Les viandes et leurs sauces.

1235. Prairie Farmer Meat Cookbook / Mitzi Ayala. Lombard, Ill.: Wallace-Homestead Book Co., c1985. 173 p., illus. Includes index.

1236. Famous Brands Meat Cookbook. St. Louis, Mo.: Brand Name Pub. Corp., 1986. 128 p., colored illus. (Famous Brands Cookbook Library). Includes index.

1237. Meat Dishes / edited by Susan Dixon. London, Eng.: Ward Lock, 1986. 63 p., illus. (some colored). (Mrs. Beeton's Home Cooking). Contains recipes selected from Mrs. Beeton's Cookery and Household Management.

1238. The New Book of Meat Cookery / Mary Berry. London, Eng.: Futura, 1986, c1981. 268 p. Includes index. Cover title: Mary Berry's New Book of Meat Cookery. Originally published: London, Eng.: Queen Anne Press in association with Oxo, 1981.

1239. The WI Book of Meat Cookery: Over 100 Recipes Tried and Tested by the Women's Institute / Angela Mottram. London, Eng.: Ebury, 1986. 96 p., illus. Includes index.

Meat *(Continued)*

1240. American Charcuterie: Recipes from Pig-by-the-Tail / Victoria Wise in collaboration with James "Chooch" Potenziani & Arayah Jenanyan. New York: Penguin Books, 1987, c1986. 300 p., illus. Includes bibliography and index. Reprint. Originally published: New York: Viking, 1986.

1241. Cooking with Meat / Veronica Bull. New York: Gallery Books, c1987. 73 p., colored illus. (Microwave Library). Includes index.

1242. Eating Meat and Staying Healthy / Josephine Levy-Bacon; photographer, David Burch. 1st U.S. ed. Woodbury, N.Y.: Barron's Educational Series, 1987. 256 p. "A Quarto Book." Includes index.

1243. Jack Ubaldi's Meat Book: A Butcher's Guide to Buying, Cutting, and Cooking Meat / by Jack Ubaldi and Elizabeth Crossman; illustrated by Mario Piazza. New York: Macmillan, c1987. 294 p., illus. 200 recipes. Includes index.

1244. Better Homes and Gardens Fast-Fixin' Meat Recipes. 1st ed. Des Moines, Iowa: Meredith Corp., c1988. 79 p., colored illus. Includes index.

1245. The Complete Meat Cookbook / Angela Mottram. London, Eng.: Bay Books, 1988. 304 p.

1246. Meat & Game Cookery / Naomi Wise, writer; Peggy Waldman, editor; Chris Shorten, photographer. San Ramon, Calif.: Chevron Chemical Co., c1988. 127 p., colored illus. (California Culinary Academy Series). Includes index.

1247. The Meat and Potatoes Cookbook / Maria Luisa Scott & Jack Denton Scott. 1st ed. New York: Farrar, Straus & Giroux, 1988. 388 p., illus. More than 400 recipes. Includes index.

Meat *(Continued)*

1248. Secrets of Italian Meat and Poultry Dishes / general editor, Beverly LeBlanc. London, Eng.: Macdonald Orbis, 1988. 95 p. Includes index.

1249. Great Meat Cookery / edited by Tony de Angeli. London, Eng.: Hamlyn, 1989. 160 p.

1250. Meat and Game Cookbook / Annette Wolter. New York: Crescent Books, 1989. 123 p., 160 colored photos. More than 150 recipes. (Grand Cook's Library). Includes index. Originally published under the title: Fleisch.

1251. Meat & Potatoes Too. Minneapolis, Minn.: General Mills, 1989. 91 p., colored illus. (Betty Crocker Creative Recipes; no. 31). Includes index.

1252. The Lobel Brothers' Complete Guide to Meat / Leon and Stanley Lobel. Philadelphia, Pa.: Running Press, 1990. 436 p., illus. 75 recipes. Contains information on selection, storage, and preparation of meat and a discussion of cholesterol. Includes index.

see also entries 594, 640; and specific meats: Beef, Buffalo, Game, Ground Meat, Lamb, Pork, Variety Meats, Veal

Melons

1253. Melon Garnishing / Harvey Rosen. Neptune, N.J.: TFH Publications, 1985. 192 p., illus.

1254. The Annapolis Diet / Karen Gibson. 1st ed. New York: St. Martin's Press, c1985. 226 p. Includes index.

see also entries 479, 1710; specific melons: Watermelons; *and broader category:* Fruits

Milk

1255. Cook Milk in Any Flavour You Like. Toronto, Ont.: Ontario Milk Marketing Board, 1980? 1 v., illus. (some colored). Includes index.

1256. Georgia Milk Recipes. Atlanta, Ga.: Georgia Agricultural Commodity Commission for Milk, 1983? 20 p., illus.

see also entry 2695; and broader category: Dairy Products

Mince Meat

1257. The Touch of Taste. Columbus, Ohio: Borden's, Inc., 1980. 1 booklet. Contains recipes for None Such mince meat.

Miso

1258. The Book of Miso / William Shurtleff & Akiko Aoyagi; illustrated by Akiko Aoyagi. Soquel, Calif.: Autumn Press, c1976-1980. 2 v., illus. Vol. 2, published by New-age Foods Study Center, Lafayette, Calif., has title: Miso Production.

see also broader category: Soybeans

Molasses

1259. Country Kitchen Recipes with Molasses / Maurice Hanssen. Wellingborough, Eng.: Thorsons, 1980. 32 p., illus. (Country Kitchen Recipes).

1260. My Favorite Molasses Recipes / Estelle B. Nickell. West Liberty, Ky. (Box 335, West Liberty 41472): E.B. Nickell; Shawnee Mission, Kan. (P.O. Box 7306, Shawnee Mission 66207): Circulation Service, c1981. 160 p., 16 p. of plates, illus. (some colored). Includes index.

see also entries 9, 2457, and 3212

Monkfish

1261. All About Monkfish / by R. Marilyn Schmidt. Barnegat Light, N.J.: Barnegat Light Press, 1984. 24 p.

see also broader category: Fish

Moose

1262. The Moose: From Forest to Table. 3rd ed. Montreal, Que.: National Meat Institute, 1983. 216 p., illus.

see also broader category: Game

Morels

1263. The Curious Morel: Mushroom Hunters' Recipes, Lore & Advice / Larry Lonik. Royal Oak, Mich.: RKT Pub., c1984. 134 p., illus. Includes index.

1264. Roon: A Tribute to Morel Mushrooms / Paul Chelgren, Jerry Petermeier, John Ratzloff; foreword by Peter Wahlstrom. Long Lake, Minn.: Cabin Pub., 1985. 66 p., illus. (some colored). "Photography and text copyright by John Ratzloff."

1265. Malfred Ferndock's Morel Cookbook / Peter Leach and Anne Mikkelsen, editors. Dennison, Minn.: Ferndock Pub., c1986. 117 p., illus.

1266. Morelling: The Joys of Hunting & Preparing Morel Mushrooms / parts I and II by Margaret M. Evans, part III by Nettie Lou Samuels; drawings by Elizabeth Weber. Santa Barbara, Calif.: Fithian Press, 1987. 92 p., illus.

see also broader category: Mushrooms

Mushrooms

1267. Oft Told Mushroom Recipes / by members of Puget Sound Mycological Society. 1st ed. Seattle, Wash.: Puget Sound Mycological Society, 1969. 178 p., illus.

1268. Some Edible Mushrooms and How to Cook Them / Nina Faubion. Edited by L. K. Phillips. 2d ed. Portland, Or.: Binford & Mort, 1972, c1964. 198 p., illus.

1269. Toadstools, Mushrooms, Fungi: Edible and Poisonous; One Thousand American Fungi; How to Select and Cook the Edible; How to Distinguish and Avoid the Poisonous, with Full Botanic Descriptions / by Charles McIlvaine and Robert K. Macadam. Rev. ed. Barton, Vt.: Something Else Press, 1973. 729 p., illus. "Toadstool poisons and their treatment, instructions to students, recipes for cooking, etc., etc." Includes index. Reprint of the 1902 ed. published by Bowen-Merrill, Indianapolis, Ind.

1270. Mushroom Recipes / collected by Andre L. Simon; introduction by F.C. Atkins. New York: Dover Publications, 1975. 54 p. Reprint of the 1951 ed. published by Newman Neame, London, Eng. under title: Mushrooms Galore.

1271. Cooking with Exotic Mushrooms / Kay Shimizu. Tokyo, Japan: Shufunmoto Co., Ltd.; Rutland, Vt.: C.E. Tuttle, 1977. 60 p., illus.

1272. Fresh Ideas with Mushrooms: 112 Delicious Recipes from Country Stand Fresh Mushrooms / from Checkerboard Kitchens, Ralston Purina Company; with additional recipes by Barbara Bloch. New York: Benjamin Co., 1977, c1978. 128 p., illus. Includes index.

1273. Mushroom Matings: The Best in Mushroom Cookery / Jean Granger. San Francisco, Calif.: Cragmont Publications; Thornwood, N.J.: Distributed by Caroline House Publishers, c1978. 63 p., illus. Includes index.

Mushrooms *(Continued)*

1274. Wild Mushroom Recipes / by Carole Eberly; cover and illustrations by Toni Gorkin. East Lansing, Mich.: Shoestring Press, c1979. 63 p., illus. Includes index.

1275. Mushroom Cookery / by Jo Mueller. Charlotte, Vt.: Garden Way, c1980. 32 p., illus. (Garden Way Bulletin; A-40).

1276. Mushrooms, Wild and Edible: A Seasonal Guide to the Most Easily Recognized Mushrooms / Vincent Marteka. 1st ed. New York: Norton, c1980. 290 p., 8 leaves of plates, illus. (some colored). Includes index.

1277. Wild Mushrooms Worth Knowing / by Ansel Hartley Stubbs; illustrated with color photographs and with drawings by Chester E. Moore. 1st ed. Kansas City, Mo.: Lowell Press, 1980. 135 p., illus. Includes bibliography and index. Previous ed. published with title: Wild Mushrooms of the Central Midwest.

1278. The Mushroom Lover's Cookbook / by William G. Flagg. Croton-on-Hudson, N.Y.: North River Press; New York: Distributed by Everest House, 1981. 143 p.

1279. A Judge Judges Mushrooms / by Samuel R. Rosen; illustrations by Joan Rosen. Nashville, Ind.: Highlander, c1982. 92 p., illus. Contains general information about edible and poisonous mushrooms and 17 recipes.

1280. The Mushroom Basket: A Gourmet Introduction to the Best Common Wild Mushrooms of the Southern Rocky Mountains, with Applications Throughout the Northern Hemisphere, and Tidbits of Mushroom Lore from Europe, Russia, and China / Andrew L. March, Kathryn G. March. Bailey, Colo.: Meridian Hill Publications, c1982. 161 p., 8 p. of plates, illus. (some colored). Includes index.

1281. Mushrooms, Mushrooms: Appetizers, Main Dishes, Casseroles, Side Dishes, Salads. Hellam, Pa.: Wellspring, 1982. 36 p.

Mushrooms *(Continued)*

1282. Wild Mushroom Recipes / by Members of Puget Sound Mycological Society. Seattle, Wash.: Pacific Search Press, 1982. 178 p., illus. First published 1979.

1283. The Little Mushroom Book / Rosamond Richardson. Loughton, Eng.: Piatkus, 1983. 62 p., illus.

1284. The Mushroom Feast / Jane Grigson; illustrations by Yvonne Skargon. Harmondsworth, Eng.; New York: Penguin Books, 1983, c1975. 305 p., illus. Includes index.

1285. Cooking Your Own Mushrooms / Jo Mueller; illustrations by Jo Mueller and Cathy Baker. Pownal, Vt.: Garden Way Pub., 1984 printing, c1976. 174 p., illus. Includes bibliography and index.

1286. The Little Mushroom Cookbook / Mary L. Green. Denver, Colo.: Giftstar, 1984. ca. 10 p., illus. (Little Cookbooks).

1287. Mad about Mushrooms / by Jacqueline Heriteau; illustrations by Woodleigh Hubbard. New York: Putnam Pub. Group, c1984. 63 p., illus. "A GD/Perigee Book." Includes index.

1288. Mushrooms Are Marvelous / James Barber. Vancouver, B.C.: Douglas & McIntyre, 1984. 104 p., colored illus. Includes index.

1289. 101 Favorite Mushroom Recipes / Duane R. Lund. Staples, Minn.: Adventure Publications, c1985. 69 p., illus.

1290. Celebrating the Wild Mushroom: A Passionate Quest / Sara Ann Friedman; illustrations by Diana Jacobs. 1st ed. New York: Dodd, Mead, c1986. 265 p., illus. Contains information on the identification of mushrooms and mushroom folklore.

1291. The Edible Mushroom: A Gourmet Cook's Guide / Margaret Leibenstein; illustrations by Monika Bittman. 1st ed. New York: Fawcett Columbine, 1986. 205 p., illus. Includes index.

Specialty Cookbooks

Mushrooms *(Continued)*

1292. Joe's Book of Mushroom Cookery / Jack Czarnecki; wild mushroom photography by Joseph L. Czarnecki; food photography by Sally Shenk Ullman; food styling by Barbara Fritz. 1st ed. New York: Atheneum, 1986. 340 p., colored illus. More than 300 recipes from the proprietor of Joe's Restaurant, Reading, Pa. Includes menu plans and index.

1293. The Mushroom Lover's Cookbook: Recipes / collected by the American Association of University Women, Wilmington, Delaware Branch. Wilmington, Del. (1800 Fairfax Blvd., Wilmington 19803): The Branch, 1987. 60 p., illus.

1294. A Passion for Mushrooms / Antonio Carluccio. Topsfield, Mass.: Salem House Publishers, 1989. 192 p. Includes index.

1295. Wild About Mushrooms: A Cookbook for Feasters and Foragers / Louise Freedman with William Freedman and the Mycological Society of San Francisco; illustrations by Teeda LoCodo; scientific advisors, Harry Thiers, Fred Stevens. Reading, Mass.: Addison-Wesley Pub. Co., 1989, c1987. 239 p., illus. 150 recipes. Aris Books. Includes bibliography and index.

1296. A Gourmet's Book of Mushrooms & Truffles / by Jacqui Hurst, Lyn Rutherford. Los Angeles, Calif.: HP Books, 1990. 1 v.

see also entries 2535, 2594; *and* Morels

Mussels

1297. The Mussel Cookbook / Sarah Hurlburt; drawings by Edith Allard. Cambridge, Mass.: Harvard University Press, 1979, c1977. 169 p., illus. Includes index.

1298. Cultured Mussel Cookbook: How to Buy, Store and Cook the Cultured Blue Mussel / by Julie V. Watson. Tantallon, N.S.: Four East Publications, 1986. 62 p., illus.

Specific Ingredients 171

Mussels *(Continued)*

1299. Mussels / by R. Marilyn Schmidt. Barnegat Light, N.J.: Barnegat Light Press, 1989. 24 p.

see also broader category: Shellfish

Mustard

1300. The Mustard Cookbook / by Sally and Martin Stone. New York: Avon, c1981. 234 p. Includes index.

1301. The Little Mustard Book / David Mabey. London, Eng.: Piatkus, 1984. 60 p., illus.

1302. Gulden's Makes Good Food Taste Great: Cookbook / senior editor, Barbara Bloch. Elmsford, N.Y.: Benjamin; Ronks, Pa.: Order from Gulden's Recipe Book, c1985. 124 p., illus. (some colored). Includes index.

1303. Perfect Cooking with Mustard / Ayee Mendes da Costa. Twickenham, Eng.: Hamlyn, 1985. 31 p., illus. Originally published: Goring-on-Thames: Elvendon, 1982.

1304. The Plain & Fancy Mustard Cookbook / Rita Calvert. Charlotte, N.C.: East Woods Press, c1986. 143 p. Includes index.

1305. Gourmet Mustards: How to Make and Cook with Them / Helene Sawyer. Lake Oswego, Or.: Culinary Arts, c1987. 63 p., illus. Contains recipes for creating 20 different mustards. Includes index.

1306. Grey Poupon: Spring Collection Cookbook. East Hanover, N.J.: Nabisco Brands, 1989. 1 booklet.

see also entry 4409; and broader category: Condiments

Specialty Cookbooks

Natural Foods

1307. The Natural Foods Blender Cookbook / Frieda H. Nusz. New Canaan, Conn.: Keats Pub., 1972. 227 p.

1308. Good Food Naturally: How to Grow It, Cook It, Keep It / John B. Harrison; introduction by Beatrice Trum Hunter. New Canaan, Conn.: Keats Pub., 1973, c1972. 116 p., illus. Includes bibliography and index.

1309. The Liberated Man's Natural Foods Cookbook / Michael Bambiger. 1st ed. Port Washington, N.Y.: Ashley Books, 1974. 240 p. Includes index.

1310. Super Natural Cookery: Recipes for Vegetarian Gourmets / Jim Corlett; illustrations by Dave Colin. Washington, D.C.: Acropolis Books, 1975, c1974. 96 p., illus. Includes index.

1311. The New Life Cookbook: Based on the Health and Nutritional Philosophy of the Edgar Cayce Readings / by Marceline A. Newton; introduction by Hugh Lynn Cayce. Virginia Beach, Va.: Donning, c1976. 176 p. Includes index.

1312. The Moosewood Cookbook: Recipes from Moosewood Restaurant, Ithaca, New York / compiled, edited, illustrated, and hand-lettered by Mollie Katzen. Berkeley, Calif.: Ten Speed Press, c1977. 221 p. Includes index. Rev. ed. of: The Moosewood Cookbook. c1974.

1313. Cooking Naturally: An Evolutionary Gourmet Cuisine of Natural Foods / by John R. Calella; illustrations by Pedro J. Gonzalez. Berkeley, Calif.: And/Or Press, 1978. 112 p., illus. Includes index.

1314. Eydie Mae's Natural Recipes / Eydie Mae Hunsberger and Chris Loeffler. San Diego, Calif.: Production House Publishers, c1978. 168 p., illus. Includes index.

Natural Foods *(Continued)*

1315. Nutrition Survival Kit: A Natural Foods Recipe and Reference Guide / Kathy Dinaburg and D'Ann Ausherman Akel. San Francisco, Calif.: Panjandrum Press, 1978, c1976. 248 p., illus.

1316. Natural Food Cookery / by Eleanor Levitt; drawings by Carol Nelson. New York: Dover Publications, 1979, c1971. 320 p., illus. Reprint of the ed. published by Hearthside Press, Great Neck, N.Y., under title: The Wonderful World of Natural-Food Cookery. Includes index.

1317. Step-by-Step to Natural Food: Cancer Prevention Through the Holistic Way of Eating / by Diane Campbell; illustrated by Mary E. Sandifer. Clearwater, Fla.: CC Publishers, c1979. 216 p., illus. Includes bibliography and index.

1318. Aldonna's Wholesome Delights: Food, Its Preparation, and Recipes / by Aldonna Kaulius-Barry. 1st ed., May 1980. Caledon East? Ont.: The Author, 1980. 61 p. Includes bibliography.

1319. Cooking the Natural Way / Gail Duff. New York: Exeter Books: Distributed by Bookthrift, 1980. 152 p., colored illus. Includes index.

1320. Crown Valley Natural Food Reserve Cookbook. Laguna Niguel, Calif. (27751 La Paz, Laguna Niguel 92677): Crown Valley Products, c1980. 152 p., illus. Includes index.

1321. Dr. Pfeiffer's Total Nutrition / Carl C. Pfeiffer and Jane Banks. New York: Simon and Schuster, 1980. 191 p. Includes indexes.

1322. Easy Whole-Food Recipes: For Wholesome, Healthful, and Delicious Meals, Naturally / by Elinor Wunderlich. St. Petersburg, Fla.: Johnny Reads, c1980. 80 p., illus. Includes index.

Natural Foods *(Continued)*

1323. Eating Naturally: Recipes for Food with Fibre / Maggie Black and Pat Howard. London, Eng.; Boston, Mass.: Faber & Faber, 1980. 148 p. Includes index.

1324. Eating What Grows Naturally / Martin & Kathlyn Gay; illustrated by Brian "Woodie" Byrn. South Bend, Ind.: and books, c1980. 137 p., illus.

1325. The Electric Vegetarian: Natural Cooking the Food Processor Way / Paula Szilard, Juliana J. Woo. Boulder, Colo.: Johnson Pub. Co., c1980. 214 p., illus. Includes index.

1326. Feasting Naturally from Your Own Recipes / by Mary Ann Pickard; foreword by Lendon H. Smith. Lenexa, Kan.: Cookbook Publishers; Harrison, Ark.: Distributed by Southern Star, c1980. 155 p., illus. Includes index.

1327. Friends of the Earth Cookbook / Veronica Sekules; illustrated by Donna Muir. Harmondsworth, Eng.: Penguin, 1980. 192 p., illus. Includes bibliography and index.

1328. From God's Natural Storehouse: Practical Alternatives to Cooking with Junk / Yvonne G. Baker. Elgin, Ill.: D.C. Cook Pub. Co., c1980. 185 p. Includes bibliography and index.

1329. The GNC Gourmet Vitamin Cookbook: With Directions for Conventional and Microwave Cooking / Myra Cameron; introduction by Beatrice Trum Hunter. Pivot original health book ed. New Canaan, Conn.: Keats Pub., 1980. 299 p. "A Keats/GNC Original Health Book." Includes index.

1330. The Garden of Eternal Swallows: A Natural Foods Cookbook / Karen Elizabeth Gordon; decorated by Barry Zaid. Boulder, Colo.: Shambhala; New York: Distributed in the U.S. by Random House, 1980. 163 p. Includes indexes.

Specific Ingredients 175

Natural Foods *(Continued)*

1331. Grains! Beans! Nuts! / by David Scott; illustrated by Steve Hardstaff. London, Eng.: Rider, 1980. 264 p., illus. Includes bibliography and index.

1332. Kripalu Kitchen: A Natural Foods Cookbook & Nutritional Guide / by JoAnn Levitt (Parimala), Linda Smith (Chitra), Christine Warren (Sukanya); illustrations by Sukanya. Summit Station, Pa.: Kripalu Publications, c1980. 253 p., illus.

1333. Make it Light: Natural Whole Food Recipes for Everyone / drawings, Elaine Green; cover and logo, Larry Kirk. Boardman, Ohio: Nature's Nook, c1980. 308 p., illus. Includes index.

1334. The Natural Fast Food Cookbook / by Gail L. Worstman; edited by Betsy Rupp Fulwiler. Seattle, Wash.: Pacific Search Press, c1980. 142 p. Includes index.

1335. Organic Cooking for (Not-So-Organic) Mothers / Marlene Anne Bumgarner; illustrated by Maryanna Kingman and Jean McManis; preface by Lendon H. Smith; edited by Sue Olson. Morgan Hill, Calif.: Chesbro Press, c1980. 165 p., illus. Includes index.

1336. Simple Food for the Good Life: An Alternative Cookbook / by Helen Nearing. New York: Delacorte Press/Eleanor Friede, c1980. 309 p.

1337. We Love Your Body / Lani Miller and Diane Rodgers; illustrated by Joanie Oliver. Seattle, Wash.: Morse Press, c1980. 256 p., illus.

1338. Wholefood for Beginners: Easy Recipes and Hints / by Brenda Evans. Oulton, Eng.: Teecoll, 1980. 81 p., illus. Includes index.

Natural Foods *(Continued)*

1339. The Wholefoods Cookbook / Caroline Liddell; illustrated by Sharon Finmark. London, Eng.: Coronet, 1980. 240 p., illus. Includes index.

1340. The Yoga Way Cookbook: Natural Vegetarian Recipes. 4th ed. Honesdale, Pa.: Himalayan International Institute of Yoga Science and Philosophy, 1980. 249 p., illus. Includes index.

1341. The All Natural Seed & Grain Cookbook / by Darcy Williamson; co-author, John Allgair. Bend, Or.: Maverick Publications, c1981. 153 p. Includes index.

1342. The Back to Eden Cookbook / the Jethro Kloss family, Promise Kloss Moffett, and Doris Kloss Gardiner; illustrated by Daniel Guild. Loma Linda, Calif.: Back To Eden Books, c1981. 158 p., illus. "Based on the work of the late Jethro Kloss, published under the supervision of Promise Kloss Moffett and Doris Kloss Gardiner." Includes index.

1343. The Book of Whole Foods: Nutrition & Cuisine / Karen MacNeil. 1st ed. New York: Vintage Books, 1981. 356 p. Includes bibliographical references and indexes.

1344. Bragg Health Food Cook Book / by Paul C. Bragg and Patricia Bragg. Santa Barbara, Calif.: Health Science, 1981. 402 p., illus. Includes index.

1345. Cashews and Lentils, Apples and Oats: From the Basics to the Fine Points of Natural Foods Cooking with 233 Superlative Recipes / Diana Dalsass. Chicago, Ill.: Contemporary Books, c1981. 301 p., illus. Includes index.

1346. Come and Get It: A Natural Foods Cookbook for Children / recipes and calligraphy by Kathleen M. Baxter; illustrations by Mimi Orlando. 3rd ed. Ann Arbor, Mich.: Children First Press, 1981, c1978. 128 p., illus.

Specific Ingredients 177

Natural Foods *(Continued)*

1347. Cooking with Vitamins / by Martha Oliver. New Canaan, Conn.: Keats Pub., c1981. 210 p., illus. "A Keats Health Book." Includes index.

1348. Diet for a Small Island / by Patrick and Shirley Rivers. Wellingborough, Eng.: Turnstone Press, 1981. 255 p., illus. Includes index.

1349. Food of My Friends: The Best Meals in Town / Judith Shepard. Sagaponack, N.Y.: Permanent Press, c1981. 134 p., illus. Includes index.

1350. The Free Cookbook: Free of Additives, Refined Sugar, Chocolate, Preservatives, Salicylates / by June Mack Maffin. Delta, B.C.: J. Maffin, 1981. 100 p. Includes index.

1351. Getting Your Kids to Eat Right: A Daily Program for Giving Your Children the Vitamins and Nutrients They Need in the Foods They Love / Barbara Richert. New York: Cornerstone Library, 1981. 190 p. Includes bibliography and index.

1352. The Global Kitchen: The Authoritative Reference on Cooking, Seasoning, and Dieting with Ethnic and Natural Foods / Karen Gail Brooks and Gideon Bosker. Kansas City, Mo.: Andrews and McMeel, c1981. 505 p.

1353. Great Tasting Health Foods / by R. Rodale and the staff of Prevention Magazine. Emmaus, Pa.: Rodale, 1981. 77 p.

1354. The Harrowsmith Cookbook / by the editors & readers of Harrowsmith Magazine; compiled from the private recipe collections of the editors, readers, contributors and staff of Harrowsmith. v. 1: Classic & Creative Cuisine. Camden East, Ont.: Camden House, c1981. 1 v., illus. (some colored). Includes index.

Specialty Cookbooks

Natural Foods *(Continued)*

1355. The Healthy Gourmet Cookbook: How to Use Natural Foods Deliciously / by Barbara Bassett; illustrated by Felix Sanchez. Carson City, Nev.: Bestways Magazine, Inc., 1981. 193 p., illus. Includes index.

1356. Holistic H.E.L.P. Handbook: Learn by Doing, Survival / by Stanley Steven Kalson. 4th ed. rev. & expanded. Phoenix, Ariz.: International Holistic Center, c1981. 96 p., illus. Includes bibliography.

1357. Kathy Cooks--Naturally / by Kathy Hoshijo. San Francisco, Calif.: Harbor Pub.; New York: Distributed by Putnam, c1981. 495 p., illus. Includes index.

1358. Mrs. Cottrell's Stretching-the-Food-Dollar Cookbook / by Edyth Young Cottrell. Santa Barbara, Calif.: Woodbridge Press Pub. Co., 1981. 127 p. "Incorporates Stretching the Food Dollar and Supplement to Stretching the Food Dollar."

1359. The Real Food Cookbook: Wholefood Recipes for Healthy Nutrition / by Vivien Quick and Clifford Quick. 2nd ed., rev., enl., and reset. Wellingborough, Eng.: Thorsons Publishers, 1981. 160 p., illus. Includes index. Rev., enl., and reset ed. of: Everywoman's Wholefood Cookbook. 1974.

1360. Runner's World Natural Foods Cookbook / by Pamela Hannan. Mountain View, Calif.: Runner's World Books: [Distributed by] Anderson World, c1981. 284 p. Includes index.

1361. The Sainsbury Book of Wholefood Cooking / Carole Handslip. London, Eng.: Published exclusively for J. Sainsbury Ltd. by Cathay Books, 1981. 91 p., colored illus. Includes index.

1362. The Sunday Times Guide to the World's Best Food / Michael Bateman, Caroline Conran, Oliver Gillie; illustrations by Susan J. Curtis; photography by Christine Hanscomb. London, Eng.: Hutchinson, 1981. 246 p., illus., 8 p. of plates (some colored). Includes indexes.

Specific Ingredients 179

Natural Foods *(Continued)*

1363. The 20-Minute Natural Foods Cookbook / by Sharon Claessens; design, Barbara Field. Emmaus, Pa.: Rodale Press, c1982. 230 p. Includes index.

1364. Cooking Naturally for Pleasure and Health / by Gail C. Watson; illustrations by Gail C. Watson and Dover Publications. Davie, Fla.: Falkynor Books, c1982. 242 p., illus. Includes index.

1365. The Food Sleuth Handbook / Sandra K. Friday and Heidi S. Hurwitz; foreword by Leonard Grauer. 1st ed. New York: Atheneum, 1982. 294 p., illus.

1366. For the Love of Food: The Complete Natural Foods Cookbook / Jeanne Martin; illustrations by Robert Penny. 1st ed. New York: Ballantine, c1982. 365 p., illus. Includes index.

1367. The Good Life Natural Cooking from Teresa Kennedy Moore's Kitchen: Low Fat, Low Sodium, Low Sweetener. Abingdon, Va.: C.T.K. Moore, c1982. 292 p. in various pagings.

1368. The Healthy Gourmet International Cookbook: Great Natural Recipes from Around the World / by Barbara Bassett; illustrated by Felix Sanchez. Carson City, Nev.: Bestways Magazine, Inc., 1982. 148 p., illus. Includes index.

1369. Low-Cost Natural Foods / by the editors of Rodale Books. Emmaus, Pa.: Rodale Press, c1982. 96 p., illus. (Rodale's High Health Cookbook Series). Includes index.

1370. The Natural Baby Food Cookbook / Margaret Elizabeth Kenda and Phyllis S. Williams. Updated and fully rev. New York: Avon, c1982. 217 p. Includes bibliography and index.

1371. The Natural Gourmet / written and illustrated by Cindy Panton; cover and chapter introductions by Nikola Warnock. Kitimat, B.C.: Natural Gourmet Pub., c1982. 325 p., illus. Includes index.

Natural Foods *(Continued)*

1372. Nature's Bounty for Your Table: A How to Do It Book with Scores of Recipes / Duane R. Lund. Staples, Minn.: Nordell Graphic Communications, c1982. 126 p., illus.

1373. The New York Times New Natural Foods Cookbook / Jean Hewitt. New York: Times Books, c1982. 438 p., illus. Includes index. Rev. ed. of: The New York Times Natural Foods Cookbook. 1972, c1971.

1374. Through Thick & Thin: An Adventure in Whole Food Cooking / by Kay Huberty; illustrations by Nina Ruth Price. Birmingham, Mich. (6216 Hills Dr., Birmingham 48010): K. Huberty, c1982. 1 v., illus. Includes index.

1375. The Wholefood Book / George Seddon, Jackie Burrow. London, Eng.: Artists House, 1982. 240 p., illus. (some colored). Includes indexes.

1376. The Book of Whole Meals: A Seasonal Guide to Assembling Balanced Vegetarian Breakfasts, Lunches, & Dinners / Annemarie Colbin. 1st Ballantine Books trade ed. New York: Ballantine Books, 1983. 231 p., illus. Includes index.

1377. The Busy People's Naturally Nutritious, Decidedly Delicious Fast Foodbook / Sharon Elliot's recipes; Sandy Haight's drawings. New York: Sterling Pub., 1983, c1977. 117 p., illus. Includes index. Reprint. Originally published: Palo Alto, Calif.: Fresh Press, 1977.

1378. Cooking Kosher: The Natural Way / by Jane Kinderlehrer. Middle Village, N.Y.: Jonathan David Publisher, c1983. 346 p., illus. Includes index.

1379. Everybody's Natural Foods Cookbook / Andrea Jacobs with Ruth Barsky & friends; illustrated by Lorena Laforest Bass. Mill Valley, Calif.: Whatever Pub.; Berkeley, Calif.: Distributed to the trade by Network, Inc., c1983. 142 p., illus. Includes index.

Natural Foods *(Continued)*

1380. Fast & Natural Cuisine: A Complete Guide to Easy Vegetarian and Seafood Cooking / by Susann Geiskopf and Mindy Toomay; illustrated by Chris Rose-Merkle. Ashland, Or.: Quicksilver Productions, c1983. 255 p., illus. Includes index.

1381. Good Food Naturally: The Healthy Living Cookbook / Heather and Zune Bampfylde. London, Eng.: Collins, 1983. 173 p., illus. (some colored). Includes index.

1382. The Good Health Cook Book / Jackie Burrow, Mary Norwak, Angela Kay. London, Eng.: Octopus, 1983. 239 p., illus. (some colored). Includes index.

1383. Gourmet Food Naturally / Heather and Zune Bampfylde. New York: Larousse, c1983. 176 p., illus. (some colored). Includes index.

1384. Healthy Cooking on the Run / by Elaine Groen, Irene Rapp. Concord, Calif.: Nitty Gritty Productions, c1983. 191 p., illus. (some colored). (A Nitty Gritty Cookbook). Includes index.

1385. The Healthy Peasant Gourmet: How to Enjoy and Thrive on a Pennies-a-Day Diet Based on Whole Seed & Grain / by Don Ridgeway. Palo Alto, Calif.: Earth Basics Press, c1983. 237 p. in various pagings, illus. Includes index.

1386. Home-Made: And at a Fraction of the Cost / Polly Pinder. Tunbridge Wells, Eng.: Search Press Ltd., in association with Sterling Pub., 1983. 125 p., illus. (some colored). Includes index.

1387. The Joy of Cooking Naturally / by Peggy Dameron. 1st ed. Orlando, Fla.: Graphic House; Bowman, Calif.: The Joy of Cooking Naturally, distributor, c1983. 144 p. Includes index.

Natural Foods *(Continued)*

1388. Kid Power: A Recipe Book of Easy-to-Fix Natural Foods Kids Love (Grown-Ups Too!) / by Irene E. Sabotin and Norene R. Terry; illustrations by Laura M. Terry. Lexington, Ky.: Thoroughbred Press, c1983. 125 p., illus.

1389. The Low-Cost No-Fuss, All-Natural, Food Guide for Students and (Other Desperate People) / by Scott Knickelbine; cartoons by Debra Lovelien. Manitowoc, Wis.: Natural Press; Chicago, Ill: Distributed by Contemporary Books, c1983. 142 p., illus.

1390. More Food of My Friends: Their Favorite Recipes / Judith Shepard. Sag Harbor, N.Y.: Permanent Press, c1983. 164 p.

1391. The Natural Foods Epicure: The No Salt, No Sugar, No Artificial Ingredients, All Natural Foods Cookbook / by Nancy Albright; editor, Charles Gerras; illustrations by Chris Magadini & Joe Charnoski; special contributions by Rita Reemer and others. Emmaus, Pa.: Rodale Press, 1983?, c1977. 408 p., illus. Includes index. Also published in 1977 and 1986 as: Rodale's Naturally Great Foods Cookbook (entry 1484).

1392. The Natural Health Cookbook / Dorothy Hall & Carol Odell. London, Eng.: Angus & Robertson, 1983, c1982. 241 p., 8 p. of plates, illus. (some colored). Includes index.

1393. Nature's Banquet / Living Springs Retreat. Harrisville, N.H.: MMI Press, 1983. 133 p.

1394. Nature's Kitchen: A Treasury of Natural Foods: Information & Recipes for Disease Prevention the Wholistic Way / Donald R. Whitaker and Barbara Durham Flournoy; foreword by Kenneth and Gloria Copeland. Lufkin, Tex. (P.O. Box 1117, Lufkin 75901): Nature's Kitchen, c1983. 269 p., illus. Includes bibliography and index.

Natural Foods *(Continued)*

1395. Nikki & David Goldbeck's American Wholefoods Cuisine: Over 1300 Meatless, Wholesome Recipes, from Short Order to Gourmet. New York: New American Library, c1983. 580 p., illus. Includes index. Also published in Great Britain as: The Complete Wholefood Cuisine. Wellingborough, Eng.: Thorsons, 1984.

1396. The Official Eating to Win Cookbook: Super Foods for Super Athletic Performance / Frances Sheridan Goulart. New York: Stein and Day, 1983. 287 p.

1397. The Real Food Cookbook / Ethel H. Renwick; drawings by Martha Bentley. New Canaan, Conn.: Keats Pub., 1983?, c1978. 272 p., illus. (A Keats/Pivot Health Book) Reprint. Originally published: Grand Rapids, Mich.: Zondervan, c1978. Includes index.

1398. The Shaklee Family Favorites Cookbook / editor, Phyllis Benjamin; photographer, Joel Glenn; illustrations, Michael Mercado; prepared and produced by the Benjamin Company. Elmsford, N.Y.: Benjamin Co., c1983. 415 p., illus. (some colored). Includes index.

1399. Sunset Quick Meals -- with Fresh Foods / by the editors of Sunset Books and Sunset Magazine; research & text, Elaine Woodard, Claire Coleman, Joan Griffiths; illustrations, Sharron O'Neil; photography, Nikolay Zurek. 1st ed. Menlo Park, Calif.: Lane Pub. Co., c1983. 96 p., colored illus. Includes index.

1400. A Way of Eating for Pleasure and Health / Michael Blate; recipes by Gail C. Watson; foreword by Barry Sultanoff. Davie, Fla.: Falkynor Books, c1983. 136 p., illus. (The G-Jo Institute Fabulous Foods Series).

1401. Whole Meals / Marcea Weber. Dorchester, Eng.: Prism, c1983. 174 p., illus. (some colored). Includes index.

Natural Foods (Continued)

1402. The Wholefood Cookery Course / Janette Marshall. Wellingborough, Eng.: Thorsons, 1983. 128 p.

1403. The Wholefoods Menu Book: A Month of Healthy Menus and Recipes for "Normal" People / Barbara Frazier; with assistance from Jean Frazier; monoprint drawings by Kristina Mickelic. Huntington Station, N.Y.: Lifestyle Series, c1983. 159 p., illus. Includes index.

1404. The Wholegrain Recipe Book: Baking and Cooking the Healthy Way / by Marlis Weber; translated from the German by Amanda Pask; line illustrations by Clive Birch. Wellingborough, Eng.: Thorsons, c1983. 176 p., 8 leaves of plates, illus. (A Thorsons Wholefood Cookbook). Includes index.

1405. Asian Food Feasts / Sigrid M. Shepard; illustrated by Margaret V. Putnam. [n.p.]: Solstice Press, 1984, c1977. 451 p., illus. Includes index. Published in 1976 under title: The Thursday Night Feast and Good Meals Cookbook.

1406. Autumn's Country Heritage Cookbook / by Autumn Donna Irene Hagen. Coeur d'Alene, Idaho (P.O. Box 1816, Coeur d'Alene 83814): Caribou Pub. Co., c1984. 194 p., illus. Includes index.

1407. Bandwagon to Health: The All-Natural Way to Eat, Think, and Exercise / by Elizabeth and Elton Baker. Saguache, Colo.: Drelwood Publications: Distributed by Communication Creativity, c1984. 207 p. Includes index.

1408. Cooking for Your Baby the Natural Way / Laraine Toms. American ed. New York: Sterling Pub. Co., 1984. 128 p. Includes index.

Specific Ingredients 185

Natural Foods *(Continued)*

1409. Country Life Recipes. Harrisville, N.H.: MMI Press, c1984. 105 p., illus. Cover title: Country Life Natural Foods, Something Better: Nutrition Seminar Cookbook. Spine title: Country Life Natural Foods Cookbook. Includes index. No animal products were used in these recipes from the Country Life Vegetarian Restaurant Kitchens.

1410. Deliciously Low: A Gourmet Guide to Low-Salt, Low-Fat, Low-Cholesterol, Low-Sugar Cooking / Harriet Roth; foreword by John W. Farquhar. London, Eng.: Century, c1984. 228 p. Includes index.

1411. Don't Tell 'em It's Good for 'em / Nancy Baggett, Ruth Glick, and Gloria Kaufer Greene. New York: Times Books, c1984. 307 p., illus. Includes index.

1412. Evelyn Findlater's Wholefood Cookery Course. London, Eng.: Muller, 1984. 159 p., illus. (some colored). (A Charles Herridge Book). Includes index. Originally published in 1983.

1413. Fitness from Food / Miriam Armstrong. Christchurch, N.Z.; London, Eng.: Whitcoulls, 1984. 88 p., illus. Includes index.

1414. The Fresh Foods Country Cookbook / from the editors and staff of the Mother Earth News. Hendersonville, N.C.: Mother Earth News, 1984. 188 p., colored illus. Includes index.

1415. Golda Sirota's Love Food: Gourmet Recipes for Holistic Health: More Than a Cookbook / illustrations by Noel Pugh. 1st limited ed. Topanga, Calif.: Living Loving Learning Center, c1984. 142 p., illus.

1416. Health Food, Fruit and Nuts, Seafood. Tokyo, Japan: JOIE; Brisbane, Calif.: Distributed by JP Trading, c1984. 100 p., illus. (most colored). (Quick & Easy Nutritious Japanese Cooking; no. 3).

Natural Foods *(Continued)*

1417. Healthy Cooking / by Sharon Claessens. Emmaus, Pa.: Rodale Press, c1984. 168 p., colored illus. (The Prevention Total Health System). Includes index.

1418. Into the Mouths of Babes: A Natural Foods Cookbook for Infants & Toddlers / by Susan Tate Firkaly. White Hall, Va.: Betterway Publications, c1984. 168 p., illus. Includes index.

1419. The Natural Foods Recipe Book: 800 Low-Calorie Dishes to Help you Lose Weight / Helen Brassel; foreword by William P. Castelli. New York: Arco Pub., c1984. 305 p. Includes index.

1420. The No Weenie Cookbook: Nutritious and Excitable Recipes for Weekend Camping / by Judy Moll. Rossland, B.C.: J. Moll, c1984. 120 p., illus. Includes bibliography.

1421. People Power: Natural Food Favorites for the Whole Family / by Irene Sabotin; illustrated by Norene Terry. Lexington, Ky.: Thoroughbred Press, c1984. 149 p., illus.

1422. A Practical Guide to Health Foods: Recognizing, Preparing and Cooking Natural Foods / Pamela Westland. London, Eng.: Columbus, 1984. 127 p., colored illus. Includes index.

1423. Rasoi: Over 250 Delicious Vegetarian Recipes / Madhvi Dikshit. New Delhi, India: Hind Pocket Books, c1984. 147 p., 8 leaves of colored plates.

1424. Recipes from the Weimar Kitchen. Rev. 1984 ed. Weimar, Calif.: Weimar Institute, c1983. 144 p.

1425. The Romance of West Coast Cooking / Judie Curle; illustrated by Ursula Medley. Galiano Island, B.C.: Scarab Publications, 1984. 1 v., illus. Includes index. [Publication of this book has not been verified].

Natural Foods *(Continued)*

1426. Whole Foods for the Whole Family: La Leche League International Cookbook / edited by Roberta Bishop Johnson. New York: New American Library, 1984, c1981. 338 p., illus. "A Plume Book." Includes index. Originally published: Franklin Park, Ill.: La Leche League International, 1981.

1427. The Wholefood Party Cookbook: A Wealth of Original Ideas for Super Party Catering for All Occasions / by Janette Marshall. New York: Thorsons Publishers: Distributed to the trade by Inner Traditions International, c1984. 192 p., illus. (some colored). Includes index. Published in 1986 under title: Thorsons Guide to Entertaining with Wholefood (entry 1488).

1428. The ABC of Natural Cooking / by Karen Zebroff and Pegge Gabbott. Vancouver, B.C.: Fforbez Enterprises, c1985. 178 p. illus.

1429. California State Grange Recipes Are Naturally Good Eating. Nashville, Tenn.: Favorite Recipes Press, c1985. 199 p., illus. (some colored). Includes index.

1430. Colin Spencer's Vegetarian Wholefood Cookbook. London, Eng.: Panther, 1985, c1983. 177 p. Includes index. Published in 1983 and 1990 under title: Good and Healthy (entry 1551).

1431. The Complete Book of Natural Foods / David Carroll. New York: Summit Books, c1985. 269 p., illus. Includes index.

1432. The Complete Health Food Cookbook. New York: Exeter Books, 1985. 88 p., colored illus.

1433. Cooking Naturally: Wholefood Cuisine with Flair and Finesse / Maria Middlestead; illustrations by Linda C. Simpson. London, Eng.: Hodder and Stoughton, 1985. 263 p., illus.

1434. The Cranks Recipe Book / David Canter, Kay Canter, Daphne Swann. London, Eng.: Panther, 1985, c1982. 256 p., 8 p. of plates, illus. (some colored). Includes bibliography and index.

Natural Foods *(Continued)*

1435. Eat Well: Stay Healthy / Pamela Westland. London, Eng.: Hamlyn, 1985. 184 p., illus. Includes index.

1436. Evelyn Findlater's Natural Foods Primer: A Beginner's Guide to Choosing and Using Wholefoods / illustrated by Paul Kesteven. Wellingborough, Eng.: Thorsons, 1985. 112 p., illus. (A Thorsons Wholefood Cookbook). Includes index.

1437. The Fibre-Plan Cookbook / Myra Street. London, Eng.: Apple, c1985. 128 p., colored illus. (A Quintet Book). Includes index.

1438. Food for Health and Vitality: Wholefoods Cookbook / Sarah Bounds. London, Eng.: Ward Lock, 1985. 128 p., illus. Includes index.

1439. A Good Cook -- Ten Talents / by Frank J. Hurd and Rosalie Hurd. Rev. new ed. Chisholm, Minn. (Box 86 A, Chisholm 55719): Hurd, c1985. 368 p., 14 p. of plates, illus. (some colored). Spine title: Ten Talents. Includes index.

1440. Good Health Cookbook / Mary-Lou Arnold. London, Eng.: Bay, c1985. 96 p.

1441. Good Healthy Food / Gail Duff. Harmondsworth, Eng.: Penguin, 1985. 188 p.

1442. Gourmet Health Recipes: For Life Extension and Vital, Healthy Living to 120 / Paul Bragg, Patricia Bragg. Santa Barbara, Calif.: Health Science, 1985. 448 p.

1443. Journey for Health / Theo Koufas with Bernard Shapiro. Lakeland, Fla.: National Health Institute, c1985. 302 p., illus. Includes index.

1444. Joy of Wellness Cookbook / by Beverly Ryder. Madison, Wis.: B. Ryder, c1985. 280 p., illus. Includes index.

Specific Ingredients

Natural Foods *(Continued)*

1445. Making Your Own Home Proteins: Tofu, Tempeh, Soft Cheeses, Yoghurt, and Sprouted Seeds / Evelyn Findlater. London, Eng.: Century, 1985. 151 p., illus. Includes index.

1446. The Microwave Wholefood Cookbook / Val Collins. Newton Abbot, Eng.: David & Charles, 1985. 121 p., illus. (some colored). Includes index.

1447. A Mountain Harvest Cookbook / Roberta Sickler; illustrated by Jeff Jones. Garden City, N.Y.: Doubleday, 1985. 226 p., illus. Includes index.

1448. The Natural Cookbook / Gail Duff. London, Eng.: Marshall Cavendish, c1985. 57 p., illus.

1449. The Natural Foods Cookbook / by Marlis Weber; translated from the German by Amanda Pask. Wellingborough, Eng.: Thorsons, 1985. 192 p., illus. Includes index. Translation of: Naturkuche Gesund & Lecker.

1450. Natural Foods Cookbook: Vegetarian Dairy-Free Cuisine / by Mary Estella. 1st ed. Tokyo, Japan; New York: Japan Publications, 1985. 250 p., illus. (some colored). Includes index and bibliography.

1451. The Natural Foods Healthy Baby Cookbook / by Carol Hunter. Wellingborough, Eng.: Thorsons, 1985. 176 p., illus. Includes index.

1452. New Food / Helene Hodge; foreword by Pat Phoenix. London, Eng.: Columbus, 1985. 176 p., colored illus. Includes index.

1453. Perfect Cooking with Wholefoods / Margaret Ellicott. Twickenham, Eng.: Hamlyn, 1985, c1983. 31 p., illus.

1454. A Pocket Book on Pure Food: Healthy Eating Without Additives / recipes by Marie Green and Pauline Hemmings. London, Eng.: Octopus, 1985. 96 p.

Natural Foods *(Continued)*

1455. Survival Gardening Cookbook / John A. Freeman. 1st ed. Rock Hill, S.C.: John's Press, c1985. 102 p., illus. Includes bibliography and index.

1456. The Taste of Health: The BBC Guide to Healthy Cooking / edited by Jenny Rogers. London, Eng.: British Broadcasting Corp., 1985. 293 p., 16 p. of plates, illus. (some colored). Includes bibliography and index.

1457. Vegetarian Cooker-Top Cookery: Quick and Easy Meat-Free Meals / by Pamela Brown; illustrated by Kim Blundell. Rev. and reset. Wellingborough, Eng.: Thorsons, 1985. 128 p., illus. (Nature's Way). Includes index. "Published in co-operation with the Vegetarian Society of the U.K." First published 1978.

1458. Whole Foods Cookery: The Easy Basics / by Beverly White. Seattle, Wash.: Distributed by Food Learning Center, c1985. 252 p., illus. Includes index.

1459. The Whole Foods Experience: Everybody's Guide to Better Eating / by Ellen Sue Spivack. Berkeley, Calif.: Ross Books, c1985. 248 p., illus. Includes bibliography and index.

1460. The Wholefoods Book / Margaret Slack and Valerie Gustard. Warley, Eng.: Tetradon, 1985. 108 p., illus. Includes index.

1461. The WI Book of Wholefood Cookery / Margaret Hanford. London, Eng.: WI Books, 1985. 96 p., illus. Includes index.

1462. The World Almanac Guide to Natural Foods / Shirley Ross. New York: World Almanac Publications: Distributed in the United States by Ballantine Books, 1985. 246 p. Includes index.

1463. The All Natural International Vegetarian Entree Cookbook / Darcy Williamson. Bend, Or.: Maverick Publications, 1986. 160 p., illus. (The All Natural Cookbook Series).

Specific Ingredients

Natural Foods *(Continued)*

1464. Body and Soul: The Wholefood Cookery Book / Katharine Jones; consultant, Diana Lamplugh. Sparkford, Eng.: Oxford Illustrated, c1986. 140 p., colored illus. Includes index.

1465. A Child's Garden: Health & Vegetarianism for Children / Suzanne C. Jennings. ?, Eng.: Ari, 1986. 40 p. Includes bibliography.

1466. Cooking with Natural Foods As You Search for Abundant Health / Muriel Beltz. 7th ed. Hermosa, S.D.: Black Hills Health & Education Center, 1986. 127 p., illus. Includes index.

1467. Cuisine Naturelle / by Anton Mosimann; photographs by John Lee; illustrations by Jane Human. 1st American ed. New York: Atheneum, 1986. 263 p., illus. (some colored). Includes index.

1468. Demiveg: The New Style of Cookery That Is Not Quite Vegetarian: Exciting Recipes for Our Changing Lifestyle / Richard Cawley; photography by Trevor Richards. London, Eng.: Orbis, 1986. 160 p., colored illus. Includes index.

1469. Feed Your Family the Healthier Way / Mary Berry. London, Eng.: Sphere, 1986, c1985. 192 p. Includes index. Originally published: London, Eng.: Piatkus, 1985.

1470. Happiness is Junk-Free Food: Fight Hyperactivity and Other Food Allergies with Quick and Easy Healthy Meals for All the Family / by Janet Ash and Dulcie Roberts; illustrated by Kim Blundell. Wellingborough, Eng.: Thorsons, 1986. 272 p., illus. Includes bibliography and index.

1471. Healthy Eating / Susanna Tee. London, Eng.: Ebury, 1986. 192 p., colored illus. At head of title: Good Housekeeping. Includes index.

1472. Healthy Eating on a Low Budget / Maggie Black. Poole, Eng.: Blandford, 1986. 160 p. Includes bibliography and index.

Natural Foods *(Continued)*

1473. The Healthy Gourmet / Caroline Waldegrave. London, Eng.: Grafton, 1986. 192 p., illus. Includes index.

1474. The Here's Health Wholefood Cookery Course: Step-by-Step Guidelines for Preparing a Wide Range of Delicious Wholefood Menus / by Janette Marshall and Sarah Bounds; photography by John Welburn Associates. Wellingborough, Eng.: Thorsons, 1986. 119 p., colored illus. Includes index. First published 1983.

1475. The Holistic Cook / Janet Hunt. Wellingborough, Eng.: Thorsons, 1986. 222 p., illus. Includes bibliography and index.

1476. It's Only Natural: No Added Sugar, Salt, Fats, Low Cholesterol Cooking / Suzanne Porter. Newton Abbot, Eng.: David & Charles, 1986, c1985. 112 p., illus. (some colored). Includes index.

1477. Lean Cuisine / Anne Ager. London, Eng.: Octopus, 1986. 144 p., colored illus. Includes index.

1478. Natural Foods East and West / Gail Savina and Alan White; drawings by Ulysses Labajo. Philippines?: ZIKR Publications, 1986, c1985. 58 p., illus. Includes index.

1479. Natural Remedies, Recipes & Realities / by Marci Cunningham. 1st ed. Gibbon Glade, Pa.: Backwoods Books, 1986. 184 p., illus. Includes bibliography.

1480. Nature's Kitchen: The Complete Guide to the New American Diet / by Fred Rohe; illustrations by Donna Wright. Rev. ed. Pownal, Vt.: Storey Communications, c1986. 491 p., illus. "A Garden Way Publishing Book." Includes bibliography and index. Rev. ed. of: The Complete Book of Natural Foods.

1481. The Neal Yard Bakery Wholefood Cookbook / Rachel Haigh. London, Eng.: Dorling Kindersley, c1986. 160 p., 16 p. of plates, illus. (some colored). Includes index.

Specific Ingredients

Natural Foods *(Continued)*

1482. Off the Shelf: The Healthfood Shopper's Brandname Cookbook / Evelyn Findlater. London, Eng.: Century, 1986. 252 p., 20 p. of plates, illus. (some colored). Includes index.

1483. Recipes for Healthy Eating / Yvonne Dewhurst and Gillian Lockie. London, Eng.: Heinemann Educational, 1986. 1 v. (loose-leaf).

1484. Rodale's Naturally Great Foods Cookbook: The Best Foods to Use and How to Use Them in Over 400 Original Recipes / by Nancy Albright; illustrations by Chris Magadini & Joe Charnoski. New York: Weathervane Books: Distributed by Crown Publishers, 1986, c1977. 408 p., illus. Includes index. Reprint. Also published in 1983? as: The Natural Foods Epicure (entry 1391).

1485. Simple Foods for the Pack / by Claudia Axcell, Diana Cooke, and Vikki Kinmont. Completely rev., 1st rev. ed. San Francisco, Calif.: Sierra Club Books, c1986. 256 p., illus. Rev. ed. of: Simple Foods for the Pack / by Vikki Kinmont & Claudia Axcell, 1976. Includes index.

1486. Suzanne's Natural Food Cookbook / Suzanne Marquardt; foreword by David Dodson. Hantsport, N.S.: Lancelot Press, 1986. 127 p., illus. Includes bibliography and index.

1487. Take the E Out of Eating / Felicity Jackson. London, Eng.: Windward, c1986. 124 p.

1488. Thorsons Guide to Entertaining with Wholefood / Janette Marshall. London, Eng.: Treasure, 1986, c1984. 192 p., illus. (some colored). Includes index. Originally published in 1984 under title: The Wholefood Party Book (entry 1427).

1489. Whole Foods for Whole People / Lucy Fuller. 4th rev. ed. Harrisville, N.H.: MMI Press, 1986. 92 p., illus.

Natural Foods *(Continued)*

1490. Wholefood Cooking / Carole Handslip. London, Eng.: Octopus, 1986, c1981. 91 p., colored illus. (The Kitchen Library). Includes index.

1491. Wholefood for the Whole Family / by Sue Scott. Kingswood, Eng.: Paperfronts, c1986. 192 p., illus. Includes index.

1492. The All Natural Baby Cookbook / Judith A. Stoffer. Bend, Or.: Maverick, c1987. 186 p.

1493. America's Favorites, Naturally / by Victoria P. Cavalier. 1st ed. Aberdeen, S.D.: Melius & Peterson Pub., c1987. 163 p., 9 p. of plates, illus. (some colored). Includes index.

1494. The Champneys Cookbook / recipes by Mark Hickman with Danielle Truman; photographs by Christopher Cormack. Enfield, Eng.: Guinness, c1987. 128 p., colored illus. Includes index.

1495. Cook it Light / Jeanne Jones. New York: Macmillan; London, Eng.: Collier Macmillan, c1987. 279 p., 8 p. of plates, illus. (some colored). Includes bibliography and index.

1496. Cooking Without Additives / Jill McWilliam. London, Eng.: Octopus in association with Bejam, 1987. 80 p., colored illus. Includes index.

1497. The Demiveg Cookbook / David Scott. London, Eng.: Bloomsbury, 1987. 176 p.

1498. Experiencing Quality: A Shopper's Guide to Whole Foods / by Margaret M. Wittenberg; illustrated by David Paul Butler. Austin, Tex.: Whole Foods Market, c1987. 310 p., illus. Includes index.

Natural Foods *(Continued)*

1499. Fast and Easy Vegetarian Cooking: Time-Saving Recipes for All Occasions / by Janet Hunt. Wellingborough, Eng.: Thorsons, 1987. 128 p., 8 p. of plates, illus. (some colored). Originally published in 1982 under title: Simple and Speedy Wholefood Cooking.

1500. Feast for Health / Colin Spencer. London, Eng.: Dorling Kindersley, 1987. 166 p.

1501. Fresh from the Country: The Natural Foods Cookbook / Susan Restino. Toronto, Ont.: Key Porter Books, 1987. 200 p., illus. Includes index.

1502. The Good Health Cookery Book. London, Eng.: Hodder & Stoughton [for] Consumers' Association, 1987, c1986. 272 p., illus. (some colored). Includes index.

1503. Gourmet Whole Foods: Vegetarian & Macrobiotic Cuisine / Rachel Albert; introduction by Karl Mincin; illustrated by Rebecca Rickabaugh; edited by Evelyn Roehl. Seattle, Wash.: Grain of Salt Pub., c1987. 176 p., illus. Includes indexes.

1504. International Whole Meals / Gai Stern. Bridport, Eng.: Prism, c1987. 196 p., illus. (Nature & Health Books). Includes index. Originally published in Australia in 1986.

1505. Kim Williams' Cookbook & Commentary: A Seasonal Celebration of Good Food for Mind & Body. Tucson, Ariz.: Knight-Ridder Press, 1987, c1983. 165 p., illus. Reprint. Originally published: Missoula, Mont.: Bitterroot Educational Resources, c1983. Includes index.

1506. More Taste of Life / Julie Stafford. London, Eng.: Sphere, 1987. 179 p., 16 p. of plates.

1507. More with Less Cookbook / Doris Longacre. 2nd ed. Tring, Eng.: Lion, 1987, c1981. 239 p. (A Lion Paperback). Includes index.

Natural Foods *(Continued)*

1508. The Natural Cook: Exciting Recipes for Healthy Eating / by Lorna Rhodes and Zune Bampfylde. London, Eng.: Sackville, 1987. 144 p., colored illus. Includes index.

1509. The Natural Cuisine of Georges Blanc / photography by Christopher Baker; recipes translated and tested by Tina Ujlaki and Charles Pierce. 1st ed. New York: Stewart, Tabori & Chang; New York: Distributed by Workman Pub., c1987. 318 p., colored illus. Includes index.

1510. The Natural Entertainer: The Healthy Way to Delicious Food / Evelyn Findlater. London, Eng.: Century, 1987. 192 p., illus. (Century Paperbacks). Includes index.

1511. New Recipes from Moosewood Restaurant / the Moosewood Collective. Berkeley, Calif.: Ten Speed Press, c1987. 302 p., 14 leaves of plates, colored illus. ca. 100 recipes. Includes index.

1512. A New Way of Eating / Marilyn Diamond. London, Eng.: Bantam, 1987. 156 p.

1513. Once Upon a Recipe: Delicious, Healthy Foods for Kids of All Ages / Karen Greene; design by Anna Marie Heinz and Karen Greene. New Hope, Pa.: New Hope Press, 1987. 96 p., colored illus. Includes index.

1514. Patty Cakes / Patricia Sharrigan. Boise, Idaho: Pacific Press Pub. Association, c1987. 96 p., illus.

1515. Power Food / James McNair. London, Eng.: Angus & Robertson, 1987. 119 p.

1516. Scarista Style: A Free-Range and Humane Approach to Cooking and Eating / by Alison Johnson. London, Eng.: V. Gollancz, 1987. 167 p.

Natural Foods *(Continued)*

1517. Simply Healthy: No Added Sugar, Salt, Fats, Low Cholesterol Cooking: Pritikin-Style Cooking / by Suzanne Porter. Newton Abbot, Eng.: David & Charles, c1987. 132 p. Includes index.

1518. Under the Influence of Bright Sunbeams: Centuries of Natural Cuisine in Recipes for Today / by China De Burnay; illustrated by Dandi Palmer; photography by Sue Atkinson. Rochester, Vt.: Thorsons; New York: Distributed in the U.S. by Harper & Row, c1987. 240 p., illus. Includes bibliography and index.

1519. The Well-Filled Cupboard: Everyday Pleasures of the Canadian Home and Garden with Over 200 Recipes / Mary Alice Downie and Barbara Robertson. Toronto, Ont.: Lester & Orpen Dennys Publishers, 1987. 228 p. Includes index.

1520. Cooking for Health. Toronto, Ont.: Grolier, 1988. 110 p., colored illus. (Microwave Magic; 19). Includes index.

1521. Cooking for Health II. Toronto, Ont.: Grolier, 1988. 109 p., colored illus. (Microwave Magic; 21). Includes index.

1522. Cooking for Kids the Healthy Way: Wholesome Recipes with Child-Appeal / Joanna Pay. London, Eng.: Optima, 1988. 125 p., illus. (some colored). Includes index.

1523. Evelyn Findlater's Wholefood Cookery School. London, Eng.: Optima, 1988. 160 p.

1524. Fresh Thoughts on Food / Lynda Brown. London, Eng.: Dorling Kindersley, 1988. 176 p. Includes index.

1525. Hurricane Kitchen: How to Cook Healthy, Foods for Large Groups and Institutions / Rick Perry; illustrations by Douglas Alvord. Augusta, Me.: L. Tapley, c1988. 172 p., illus. Includes index.

Natural Foods *(Continued)*

1526. Living Well: Eight Fundamental Principles for Developing a Healthy Lifestyle / Dale and Kathy Martin. Brentwood, Tenn.: Wolgemuth & Hyatt, c1988. 249 p.

1527. New Ways to Eat Well / Susan Tomnay. London, Eng.: Bay, c1988. 96 p.

1528. Second Bite of the Cherry / Alan Stewart and Margaret Jackson. London, Eng.: Optima, 1988. 224 p.

1529. A Self-Sufficient Larder / Mike Foxwell. London, Eng.: Optima, 1988. 160 p.

1530. Starting Over: Learning to Cook with Natural Foods / Delia Quigley, Polly Pitchford. Summertown, Tenn.: Book Pub. Co., c1988. 143 p., 8 p. of plates, illus. (some colored). Includes index.

1531. A Texas Family's Cookbook / Joseph Lowery with Donald R. Counts, and Kathryn O'C. Counts. New York: Weathervane Books: Distributed by Crown Publishers, 1988, c1985. 231 p., illus. Reprint. Originally published: Austin, Tex.: Texas Monthly Press, 1986. Includes index.

1532. To Everything There Is a Season / by Margaret E. Tucker. Independence, Mo.: International University Press, 1988. 221 p., illus.

1533. The Wholefood Catalog: A Complete Guide to Natural Foods / written and illustrated by Nava Atlas. 1st ed. New York: Fawcett Columbine, 1988. 212 p., illus. More than 200 recipes. Includes index.

1534. Eat Well, Stay Well / Marguerite Patten. London, Eng.: Hamlyn, 1989. 160 p.

Specific Ingredients

Natural Foods *(Continued)*

1535. Food Combining for Health / Doris Grant & Jean Joice; foreword by Sir John Mills; illustrated by Rita Greer. Rochester, Vt.: Healing Arts Press; New York: Distributed to the trade in the U.S. by Harper and Row Publishers, c1989. 248 p., illus. Reprint. Originally published: Rochester, Vt.: Thorsons Publishers, c1987.

1536. Good Housekeeping Eating for a Healthy Skin / Alix Kirsta. London, Eng.: Ebury, 1989. 160 p.

1537. Good Housekeeping Wholefood Cookery / Gail Duff. Rev. ed. London, Eng.: Ebury, 1989. 248 p.

1538. Healthy Eating / Jenny Ridgwell & Judy Ridgway. Oxford, Eng.: Oxford University Press, 1989. 112 p.

1539. A Household Legacy / Amanda Goodfellow. London, Eng.: Brewhouse Traditional & Wholefood Co., 1989. 408 p.

1540. Judy Brown's Guide to Natural Foods Cooking / by Judy Brown and Dorothy R. Bates. Summertown, Tenn.: Book Pub. Co., c1989. 159 p., colored illus. Includes index.

1541. Light Fantastic: Health-Conscious Entertaining / by Janice Kenyon; cover drawing and design by Deborah Brennan; photography by E. Ross Henry. Victoria, B.C.: Kachina Press, c1989. 256 p., colored illus. Includes bibliography and index.

1542. Natural Foods and Good Cooking / Kathy Cituk with John Finnegan. Mill Valley, Calif.: Elysian Arts, c1989. 119 p.

1543. The Natural Gourmet: Delicious Recipes for Healthy Balanced Eating / Annemarie Colbin. 1st ed. New York: Ballantine Books, c1989. 322 p., illus. Includes bibliography and index.

1544. The Not-Strictly Vegetarian Cookbook / by Lois Fishkin & Susan DiMarco. Tucson, Ariz.: Fisher Books, 1989. ca. 242 p., illus. Includes index.

Natural Foods *(Continued)*

1545. Rodale's Basic Natural Foods Cookbook / editor, Charles Gerras; collaborating editors and text authors, Camille Cusumano and Carol Munson; editorial assistant, Camille Bucci. 1st Fireside ed. New York: Simon & Schuster, 1989, c1984. 899 p., illus. Includes index.

1546. Taste of Life Cookbook: 200 Low Cholesterol Easy to Make Healthy Life Style Recipes / Julie Stafford. Long Beach, Calif.: Australia in Print, c1989. 147 p., 16 p. of colored plates, illus. Originally published: Richmond, Vic.: Greenhouse, 1983; London, Eng.: Souvenir, 1985.

1547. Whole Foods Kitchen Journal / Bernie Kuntz. Redmond, Wash.: Elfin Cove Press, c1989. 389 p., illus. More than 200 recipes. Includes index.

1548. The WI Book of Healthy Family Cookery. London, Eng.: Ebury, 1989. 256 p.

1549. Working Chef's Cookbook for Natural Whole Foods / Jackson F. Blackman. 1st ed. Morrisville, Vt.: Central Vermont Publishers, c1989. 344 p., illus.

1550. The Caboodle Cookbook: Quality Cooking for, with or by Kids / recipes by Lisa Cestnik; illustrations by Jay Cestnik; nutrition analysis by Ellen Desjardins. 1st ed. Toronto, Ont.: Caboodle, 1990. 81 p., illus. (some colored). Includes bibliography.

1551. Good and Healthy / Colin Spencer. London, Eng.: Robson, 1990. 183 p. Previously published in 1983 under title: Good and Healthy and in 1985 under title: Colin Spencer's Vegetarian Wholefood Cooking (entry 1430).

1552. Healing with Whole Foods: Includes The Art of Cooking and Grains and Vegetables: Food as Medicine for the Body and Mind / Evergreen Foundation Staff. Berkeley, Calif.: North Atlantic Books, 1990. 450 p., illus.

Natural Foods *(Continued)*

1553. The Microwave Gourmet Healthstyle Cookbook / Barbara Kafka. London, Eng.: Barrie and Jenkins, 1990. 512 p.

1554. The National Trust Book of Healthy Eating / Sarah Edington. London, Eng.: National Trust, 1990. 160 p.

1555. Sundays at Moosewood Restaurant: Ethnic and Regional Recipes from the Cooks at the Legendary Restaurant / by the Moosewood Collective. New York: Simon and Schuster, c1990. 733 p., illus. "A Fireside Book." Includes bibliographical references and index.

1556. Thorsons Green Cookbook / Sarah Bounds. Wellingborough, Eng.: Thorsons, 1990. 159 p.

1557. The Wholefood Harvest Cookbook / Rachel Hunt. Shaftesbury, Eng.: Broadcast Books, 1990. 160 p.

CHILDREN'S COOKBOOKS

1558. Peter Rabbit's Natural Foods Cookbook / by Arnold Dobrin; illustrated by Beatrix Potter. New York: F. Warne, c1977. 112 p., illus. (some colored). Includes recipes for sandwiches, soups, salads, and desserts with hints on cooking techniques and handling kitchen equipment.

1559. The Down to Earth Cookbook / Anita Borghese; illustrated by Ray Cruz. Rev. ed. New York: Scribner, c1980. 144 p., illus. Includes index. Recipes for breakfast, lunch, supper, dessert, and snack time featuring natural foods such as whole grain flour, dried fruits, honey, nuts, and seeds.

1560. Junk Food, Fast Food, Health Food: What America Eats and Why / by Lila Perl. New York: Houghton Mifflin/Clarion Books, c1980. 182 p. Includes index and bibliography. Explores 20th-century American eating patterns and includes a selection of recipes reflecting contemporary tastes.

Natural Foods *(Continued)*

1561. Loaves and Fishes: A "Love Your Neighbor" Cookbook / Linda Hunt, Marianne Frase, Doris Liebert. Scottdale, Pa.: Herald Press, 1980. 168, 9 p., illus. (some colored). ca. 120 recipes. Includes index and bibliography. A cookbook emphasizing eating one's fair share of healthful food in a world of limited resources.

1562. Stuffin' Muffin: Muffin Pan Cooking for Kids / by Strom Scherie; foreword by Norma C. Konefal; illustrated by Dave Ferry. Avon, Conn.: Young People's Press, c1981. 91 p., illus. Includes index. Recipes for meat, vegetable, salad, muffin, and dessert dishes, using healthful ingredients and made in muffin pans.

1563. The Kitchen Crew: A Children's Wholefood Cookery Book / Stephanie Lashford; illustrated in colour by Adrian Obertelli and in black and white by Fraser May. Bath, Eng.: Ashgrove Press, 1989. 72 p.

see also entries 1674, 3162, 3176, 3188, 3221, 3260, 3277, 3295, 3296, 3302, 3312, 3359, 3397, 3413, 3444, 3448, 3611, 3715, 3746, 3879, 3882, 3892, 3911, 4041, 4063, 4126, 4133, 4207, 4228, 4240, 4241, 4260; and specific kinds of natural foods: Carob, Fruits, Grains, Herbs, Honey, Legumes, Nuts, Raw Foods, Seeds, Sprouts, Vegetables, Wild Foods, *etc.*

Noodles *see* **Pasta**

Nuts

1564. Nut Cookbook from Planters. Winston-Salem, N.C.: Planters Lifesavers Co., 1980. 1 booklet.

1565. Nuts! Nuts! Nuts! / by Ann Mason Norton. Jonesboro, Ark.: Handy Andy Industries, 1980. 230 p.

Nuts *(Continued)*

1566. The Little Nut Book / Rosamond Richardson. Loughton, Eng.: Piatkus, 1983. 60 p., illus.

1567. Seed and Nut Cookery / Margaret C. Eastman. 1st ed. Brattleboro, Vt.: Stephen Greene Press, c1982. 136 p. Includes index.

1568. The Book of Edible Nuts / Frederic Rosengarten, Jr. New York: Walker, 1984. 384 p., illus. Includes indexes.

1569. The Nutlovers' Cookbook / by Shirl Carder. Berkeley, Calif.: Celestial Arts, c1984. 165 p., illus. ca. 200 recipes. Includes index.

1570. Nuts! / Sonia Allison. London, Eng.: Bell & Hyman, 1984. 96 p.

1571. Cooking with Nuts & Cereals / Judy Ridgway; line drawings by Sue Sharples. London, Eng.: Century, 1985. 118 p., illus. (The Vegetarian Library). Includes index.

see also entries 723, 740, 903, 913, 1151; specific nuts: Almonds, Macadamia Nuts, Peanuts, Pecans, Pine Nuts, Walnuts; *and broader category:* Natural Foods

Oat Bran

1572. Cooking with Oat Bran: Giving Your Heart a Treat! Armstrong, B.C.: Rogers Foods, 1988? 40 p.

1573. The Hodgson Mill Oat Bran Cookbook and Guide to Reducing Blood Cholesterol / copy edited by Meredith Holmes, Donna Jean Morris; indexed by Mary Ward. Cleveland, Ohio (P.O. 770563, Cleveland 44107): M. Ward Enterprises, c1988. 104 p.

Oat Bran *(Continued)*

1574. Cooking with Oat Bran: Recipes to Live By / by Pat Amsden. Brentwood Bay, B.C.: AMS Publishers, c1989. 125 p.

1575. The Fast & Easy Oat Bran Cookbook / by Jeanette Egan. Los Angeles, Calif.: HP Books, 1989. 48 p. 35 recipes. Includes index. "Cholesterol reducing recipes for breakfast, lunch, and dinner."

1576. The Oat and Wheat Bran Health Plan / Dina R. Jewell and C. Thomas Jewell. New York: Bantam Books, c1989. 279 p.

1577. The Oat Bran Baking Book: 85 Delicious, Low-Fat, Low-Cholesterol Recipes / Nancy Baggett and Ruth Glick. Chicago, Ill.: Contemporary Books, 1989. 144 p. Includes index.

1578. The Oat Bran Cookbook / Kitty and Lucian Maynard. Nashville, Tenn.: Rutledge Hill Press, c1989. 160 p., illus. 160 recipes. Includes index.

1579. Oat Bran Recipes / Shirley Lorenzani Sperry. New Canaan, Conn.: Keats Pub., 1989. 31 p.

1580. Oat Cuisine / Bobbie Hinman; illustrations by Vonnie Crist. Rocklin, Calif.: Prima Pub. and Communication: Distributed by St. Martin's Press, 1989. 289 p., illus. "Over 200 delicious recipes to help you lower your cholesterol level."

1581. Quaker Oat Bran Cookbook / Lincolnwood, Ill.: Publications International, 1989. 96 p., colored illus. Includes index.

1582. Quaker Oat Bran Favorite Recipes. Chicago, Ill.: Quaker Oats Co., Food Division, 1990. 1 booklet.

see also broader category: Oats

Oats

1583. Fantastic Oatmeal Recipes / compiled by Wilma Ramp. Iowa City, Iowa: Penfield Press, c1981. 60 p. Includes index.

1584. Staffordshire Oatcake Recipe Book / Eleanor Fishman. Eng.: J.H. Brookes, c1984. 31 p.

1585. The Oatcake Cookbook / Steve Dixon; illustrated by Marc Burnett; photography by Bernard Staig-Graham. Newcastle-under-Lyme, Eng.: Upsetter Press, c1985. 47 p., illus.

1586. Eats with Oats: The New Soluble Fibre Cookbook / Janette Marshall. London, Eng.: Foulsham, 1986. 128 p., illus. (some colored).

1587. Oat Cuisine / Pamela Westland. Salem, N.H.: Salem House Publishers, 1986. 96 p.

1588. The Oat Cookbook / Mary Cadogan and Shirley Bond. London, Eng.: Optima, 1987. 127 p., illus. (some colored). (Positive Health Guide). Includes index.

1589. The Low-Cholesterol Oat Plan: Over 300 Delicious and Innovative Recipes for the Miracle Food / Barbara Earnest and Sarah Schlesinger. 1st ed. New York: Hearst Books, c1988. 352 p. More than 300 recipes. Includes bibliography and index.

see also Granola; Oat Bran; *and broader category:* Grains

Offal *see* Variety Meats

Okra

1590. Kenner O.K.R.A. Festival Cookbook. Kenner, La.: City of Kenner, 1984. 108 leaves.

see also entry 525; and broader category: Vegetables

Olives and Olive Oil

1591. Home Pickling of Olives / prepared by Reese Vaughn. Rev. Berkeley, Calif.: Division of Agricultural Sciences, University of California, 1980. 11 p. (Leaflet; 2758)

1592. Olives and Olive Oil for the Gourmet: 100 Recipes of Foods Made with Olives and Olive Oil / by George F. Steffanides. [n.p.] Steffanides, 1980. 48 p., illus.

1593. The Feast of the Olive: Cooking with Olives & Olive Oil / by Maggie Blyth Klein; illustrated by the author. Berkeley, Calif.: Aris Books, c1983. 223 p., illus. Includes index.

1594. The Itinerant Ripe Olive. Fresno, Calif.: California Olive Industry, 1984. More than 40 recipes.

1595. Simply Elegant: Entertaining Ideas from Lindsay Olives. Lindsay, Calif. (P.O. Box 848, Lindsay 93247): Lindsay International, c1985. 96 p., colored illus. Includes index.

1596. With a Touch of Olive Oil from Spain / Asoliva; recipes by Susy Umlauff. Madrid, Spain: Olive Oil Exporters Association of Spain, 1987. 52 p., colored illus.

1597. The Essential Olive Oil Companion / Anne Dolamore. Topsfield, Mass.: Salem House Publishers, 1989. 160 p., illus. (some colored).

1598. Olive Oil from Italy: The Natural Tastemaker, a Brief History and Recipes / by Ed Giobbi. New York: Italian Trade Commission, 1989. 16 p., illus. 14 recipes.

1599. The Low Cholesterol Olive Oil Cookbook: More than 200 Recipes, the Most Delicious Way to Eat Healthy Food / by Sarah Schlesinger and Barbara Earnest. New York, N.Y.: Villard Books, 1990. 429 p. Includes bibliography and index.

Specific Ingredients 207

Onions

1600. The Onion Cookbook / Jean Bothwell; with illustrations by Margaret Ayer. New York: Dover Publications, 1976, c1950. 166 p., illus. Unabridged and corrected republication of the work originally published by Hastings House, New York, in 1950 under title: Onions Without Tears.

1601. Know Your Onions / Kate Hastrop; illustrations by Joyce Tuhill. Feltham, Eng.: Hamlyn, 1980. 296 p., illus. (Hamlyn Kitchen Library). Includes index.

1602. Onions / by Inez M. Krech. 1st ed. New York: Primavera Books/Crown, c1981. 64 p. Includes index.

1603. The Original Vidalia Onion Cookbook / recipes compiled and tested by Pam McIntyre. Vidalia, Ga.: Vidalia Chamber of Commerce, c1981. 84 p., illus. Includes index.

1604. Georgia Cooking with Sweet Vidalia Onions / Evelyn Carroll-McLemore Rogers; illustrations by Jean Greer. 1st ed. Vidalia, Ga. (P.O. Box 736, Vidalia 30474): E.C. Rogers, 1982. 200 p., illus.

1605. The Little Onion Cookbook / Mary L. Green. Denver, Colo.: Giftstar, 1984. ca. 10 p., illus. (Little Cookbooks).

1606. The Elegant Onion: The Art of Allium Cookery / Betty Cavage. Pownal, Vt.: Storey Communications, c1987. 156 p. 100 recipes using onions, leeks, shallots, scallions, garlic, and chives. "A Garden Way Publishing Book." Includes index.

see also entry 877; and broader category: Vegetables

Opossums

1607. Possum Cookbook: America's Magnificent Marsupials Made Famous by Fact & Fancy & Dozens of Ways to Cook Them / by E.W. Carswell; illustrated by Frank Roberts. A rev. ed. Bonifay, Fla.: Taylor Publications, c1981. 65 p., illus. Includes bibliography.

see also broader category: Game

Orange Roughy

1608. Orange Roughy / by R. Marilyn Schmidt. Barnegat Light, N.J.: Barnegat Light Press, 1988. 24 p.

see also broader category: Fish

Oranges

1609. Just Oranges: A Collection of 785 Orange Recipes / compiled by Mr. and Mrs. A. T. Weaver, Jr. Lake Placid, Fla.: Weaver, 1977. 246 p. Includes index.

1610. The Orange Cook Book / Reginald L. Muir, editor; Dianne Carole Fogle, associate editor; Humberto O'Cadiz, design and illus. Santa Ana, Calif.: De la Maison de Muir, c1977. 208 p. Includes index.

1611. The Little Orange Cookbook / Mary L. Green. Denver, Colo.: Giftstar, 1984. ca. 10 p., illus. (Little Cookbooks).

1612. Orange: Uses for the Whole Orange, with Recipes & Suggestions / Recycling Consortium. Houston, Tex.: Prosperity & Profits, 1989. 14 p.

see also entry 25; and broader category: Citrus Fruits

Oysters

1613. The Louisiana Oyster / revised by Ronald Dugas. Baton Rouge, La.: Louisiana Dept. of Wildlife and Fisheries, 1982. 33 p., illus. (Wildlife Education Bulletin; no. 32).

1614. Ode to the Oysters / compiled by Joan and Doug Adams. Lenexa, Kan.: Cookbook Publishers; Gulf Breeze, Fla.: Orders to J. and D. Adams, c1983. 71 p., illus. Includes index.

1615. Oyster Cookery / by Sharon Montoya-Welsh, Marjorie Speare-Yerxa; illustrations by Kathie Crabb. Oysterville, Wash. (P.O. Box 624 Oysterville 98641): Shoalwater Kitchen, c1984. 153 p., illus. Spine title: Oysters. Includes index.

1616. Oysters: A Culinary Celebration / Joan Reardon, Ruth Ebling. Orleans, Mass.: Parnassus Imprints, c1984. 264 p., 16 p. of plates, illus. (some colored). 240 recipes. Includes index.

1617. The Celebrated Oysterhouse Cookbook: Valuable Recipes, Curiously Illustrated. Allentown, Pa.: F.J. Parks. Copies may be obtained from Parks' Seafood, c1985. 64 p., illus. (some colored).

1618. Eastern Oysters / by R. Marilyn Schmidt. Barnegat Light, N.J.: Barnegat Light Press, 1986. 16 p.

1619. Oysters: A Connoisseur's Guide & Cookbook / recipes by Lonnie Williams; text by Karen Warner; color photographs by Lisa Blevins; food styling by Stevie Bass. San Francisco, Calif.: 101 Productions: Distributed to the book trade in the U.S. by Macmillan, c1987. 96 p., illus. (some colored). 100 recipes. "Published in cooperation with Pacific Heights Bar & Grill." Includes index.

1620. Consider the Oyster / M.F.K. Fisher. San Francisco: North Point Press, 1988, c1941. 76 p.

Oysters *(Continued)*

1621. Oyster Cookery / Joe Daniels. Fort Ludlow, Wash.: Olympic Pub., 1988. 64 p.

see also broader category: Shellfish

Papaws

1622. Papino Papaws Please: Original Ways to Update Your Menu / by Juliet Oosthuizen. Pretoria, South Africa: Muller en Retief, 1972. 62 p. colored illus.

see also broader category: Fruits

Pasta

1623. The Complete Book of Pasta / Enrica and Vernon Jarratt; introduction by the late Andre L. Simon. New York: Dover Publications, 1977, c1975. 365 p., illus. Translation of: 230 Modi di Cucinare la Pasta. Includes indexes.

1624. Pasta Cookery / by Sophie Kay. Tucson, Ariz.: HP Books, c1979. 160 p., colored illus. Includes index.

1625. 99 Ways to Cook Pasta / Flora and Robert Alda; with a preface by Alan Alda; illustrations by Sidonie Coryn. New York: Macmillan, c1980. 148 p., illus. Includes index.

1626. Pasta / by the editors of Time-Life Books. Alexandria, Va.: Time-Life Books; Morristown, N.J.: School and library distribution by Silver Burdett Co., c1980. 176 p., illus. Includes indexes.

1627. Sunset Pasta Cook Book / by the editors of Sunset Books and Sunset Magazine. 1st ed. Menlo Park, Calif.: Lane Pub. Co., c1980. 96 p., illus. Includes index.

Pasta *(Continued)*

1628. Pasta and Noodles / by Merry White; drawings by Edward Koren. New York: Penguin Books, 1981. 280 p., illus. Reprint of the 1976 ed. published by Basic Books, New York, under title: Noodles Galore. Includes index.

1629. Pasta Cookbook / Myra Street. London, Eng.: Hamlyn, 1981, c1974. 80 p., illus. (some colored). Includes index.

1630. Pasta Cooking / Jacques Harvey; with the collaboration of Alfredo of the world-famous restaurant Alfredo l'Originale of Rome; recipes translated by Rose G. Formiconi; illustrations by Bill Goldsmith. Toronto, Ont.: Coles, c1981. 301 p., illus. Includes index. Previously published as: 365 Ways to Cook Pasta. Garden City, N.Y.: Doubleday, 1974.

1631. Pasta Italian Style / Patricia Lousada. Cambridge, Eng.: Woodhead-Faulkner for J. Sainsbury Ltd., 1981. 96 p., illus. (some colored). (A Sainsbury Cookbook).

1632. The Joy of Pasta / translation by Fulvia Dassi; photographs by Adamo Photographer; drawings by Salvatore Cibelli; paintings by Mario Jetti. Gessate? Italy: SIMAC, c1982. 222 p., illus. (some colored). (SIMAC'S Cuisine Collection). Includes indexes.

1633. Pasta! Cooking It, Loving It / Carlo Middione; illustrated by Donald Hendricks. New York: I. Chalmers Cookbooks, c1982. 84 p., illus. (Great American Cooking Schools).

1634. Beard on Pasta / by James Beard. 1st ed. New York: Knopf: Distributed by Random House, 1983. 236 p., illus. Includes index.

1635. The Joy of Pasta / by Joe Famularo & Louise Imperiale. Woodbury, N.Y.: Barron's, c1983. 200 p., 32 p. of plates, illus. (some colored). More than 100 recipes. Includes index.

Pasta *(Continued)*

1636. Making the Most of Pasta / Judy Ridgway. Newton Abbot, Eng.: David & Charles, 1983. 48 p., illus. Includes index.

1637. Pasta Menus. Alexandria, Va.: Time-Life Books, c1983. 104 p., illus. (some colored). (Great Meals in Minutes). Includes index.

1638. Positively Pasta / by Sandra Bartiromo; illustrations by Mary Long. Hermosa Beach, Calif.: Silver Seas Press, c1983. 50 p., illus.

1639. Quick & Easy Pasta Recipes / by Coleen and Bob Simmons. Concord, Calif.: Nitty Gritty Productions, c1983. 191 p., illus. (some colored). Includes index.

1640. The Harrowsmith Pasta Cookbook / by the editors & readers of Harrowsmith Magazine; editor, Pamela Cross; associate editor, Alice Pitt. Camden East, Ont.: Camden House Pub., 1984. 151 p., illus. (some colored). Includes index.

1641. Nika Hazelton's Pasta Cookbook. 1st ed. New York: Ballantine Books, 1984. 164 p., illus. Includes index.

1642. Pasta / Anne Ager. London, Eng.: Ward Lock, 1984. 80 p., illus. (some colored). Includes index.

1643. Pasta and Rice Italian Style / Efrem Funghi Calingaert, Jacquelyn Days Serwer; drawings by Paulette Dickerson. New York: New American Library, 1984, c1983. 304 p., illus. "A Plume Book." Includes index. Recipes for pasta, risotto, and gnocchi to be used in high-fiber, low-fat meatless meals with vegetables, seafood, and cheese.

1644. The Pasta Book / Audrey Ellis. London, Eng.: Piatkus, 1984. 96 p., illus. Includes index.

Pasta (Continued)

1645. The Pasta Book: Home-Made Pasta, Filled Pasta and Pasta Sauces / Simonetta Lupi Vada. London, Eng.: Columbus, 1984. 190 p., colored illus. Includes index. Translation of: Pasta e Sughi.

1646. The Pasta Diet / Elisa Celli. New York: Warner Books, c1984. 256 p. Includes index.

1647. Pasta for Pleasure / Moyra Bremner and Liz Filippini. London, Eng.: Fontana, 1984. 304 p., illus. (some colored). (A Fontana Original). Includes index.

1648. The Pasta Salad Book / Nina Graybill and Maxine Rapoport. Washington, D.C.: Farragut Pub. Co., 1984. 174 p.

1649. Pasta with a Flair / by Katherine DeDomenico Reichert; food stylist, Stevie Bass; photographer, George Sellend. Minneapolis, Minn.: Dillon Press, c1984. 160 p., colored illus. Includes index.

1650. Perfect Pasta / Valentina Harris. 1st U.S. ed. New York: W. Morrow, 1984. 160 p., illus. (some colored). More than 300 recipes. Includes index.

1651. Rose Elliot's Book of Pasta. London, Eng.: Fontana Paperbacks, 1984. 64 p., illus. Includes index.

1652. Step-by-Step Pasta Cookbook (and More). Secaucus, N.J.: Chartwell Books, c1984. 384 p., illus. (some colored). More than 200 recipes. Adapted from: Cucinare Oggi by Simonetta Lupi Vada.

1653. The Classic Book of Pasta / Vincenzo Buonassisi; translated by Elisabeth Evans. London, Eng.: Futura, 1985, c1976. 361 p., illus. Includes index. Translation of: Il Codice della Pasta.

Pasta *(Continued)*

1654. Cold Pasta / James McNair; photography by Tom Tracy. San Francisco, Calif.: Chronicle Books, 1985. 96 p., colored illus. 33 recipes. Includes index.

1655. Exotic Pasta: 70 New Recipes for Very Different Pasta Dishes / by Rossella de Angioy; illustrations by Angela Chidgey. Boston, Mass.: Faber and Faber, c1985. 92 p., illus. (some colored). Includes index.

1656. The New Complete Book of Pasta: An Italian Cookbook / by Maria Luisa Scott and Jack Denton Scott; with photographs of Italy by Samuel Chamberlain and drawings by Melvin Klapholz. 1st ed. New York: Morrow, c1985. 448 p., illus. 390 recipes. Includes index and glossary. Reissue of the book written in 1968 with 54 additional recipes.

1657. The Pasta Book / by Luigi Veronelli. New York: St. Martin's Press, 1985. 188 p., colored photos. Includes index.

1658. Pasta Plus / introduced by Luigi Veronelli; compiled by Simonetta Lupi Vada. London, Eng.: Collins, 1985. 190 p., colored illus. Includes index. Translation of: Il Libro della Pasta.

1659. Perfect Cooking with Pasta / Bernice Hurst; illustrations by Ronald Hurst. Twickenham, Eng.: Hamlyn, 1985. 32 p., illus. Originally published in 1981 under the title: The Perfect Pasta.

1660. The Power of Pasta / Olwen Woodier. Pownal, Vt.: Storey Communications, 1985. 154 p., illus. ca. 100 recipes. "A Garden Way Publishing Book."

1661. Umberto's Pasta Book / Umberto Menghi. Vancouver, B.C.: Whitecap Books, 1985. 173 p., colored illus. Includes index. "Arranged by shape of pasta under the Italian name."

Pasta *(Continued)*

1662. Famous Brands Pasta Dishes. St. Louis, Mo.: Brand Name Pub. Corp., 1986. ca. 128 p., colored illus. (Famous Brands Cookbook Library). Includes index.

1663. The Glorious Noodle: A Culinary Tour Around the World / Linda Merinoff; maps and decorations by Glenn Wolff. New York: Poseidon Press, c1986. 367 p., illus. More than 200 recipes. Includes bibliography, glossary, and index.

1664. How to Make Pasta One Hundred and One Different Ways / by Armand Tambouri. Canandaigua, N.Y.: Park Ave. Publications, c1986. 95 p.

1665. The Pasta-Lover's Diet Book / by June Roth. 1st Collier Books ed. New York: Macmillan; London, Eng.: Collier Macmillan, 1986, c1984. 218 p. "A Bobbs-Merrill Book." Includes recipes for low calorie sauces, a two-week diet, and index.

1666. Pasta Salads! / by Susan Janine Meyer. Trumansburg, N.Y.: Crossing Press, c1986. 146 p. 77 recipes. (Specialty Cookbook Series). Includes index.

1667. Pastas, Rice and Dried Beans / Jehane Benoît. Saint-Lambert, Que.: Heritage, 1986. 1 v. (Encyclopedia of Microwave Cooking; 7). Includes index. Issued also in French under the title: Pâtes alimentaires, riz et fèves sèches.

1668. Better Homes and Gardens Pasta. 1st ed. Des Moines, Iowa: Meredith Corp., c1987. 128 p., colored illus. (Great Cooking Made Easy). Includes index.

1669. The Book of Pasta / Lesley Mackley; photography by Jon Stewart. Tucson, Ariz.: HP Books, c1987. 120 p., colored illus. Includes index.

Specialty Cookbooks

Pasta *(Continued)*

1670. Great Pasta Dishes / Antonio Piccinardi; photographs, Emilio Fabio Simion; drawings, Ezio Giglioli. New York: International Culinary Society; Distributed by Crown Publishers, 1987. 191 p., illus. (some colored). 122 recipes. Includes index. "Translated from the Italian by Elaine Hardy." Published in England in 1987 under the title: Taste of Pasta.

1671. Pasta & Budget Cooking / Pol Martin. Montreal, Que.: Brimar, c1987. 64 p., colored illus. Includes index.

1672. Pasta and Other Special Salads / Ceil Dyer. New York: Simon & Schuster, c1987. 194 p., illus. "A Fireside Book." Includes index.

1673. Pasta Classica: The Art of Italian Pasta Cooking / Julia della Croce. San Francisco, Calif.: Chronicle Books, c1987. 160 p., illus. (some colored). Includes index.

1674. Pasta Dishes: Recipes from Around the World Using Versatile Natural Ingredients / Janet Hunt. New ed. Wellingborough, Eng.: Thorsons, 1987. 128 p., colored illus.

1675. Pasta Perfect / Anna Del Conte. 1st ed. in U.S. Garden City, N.Y.: Doubleday, 1987, c1986. 80 p., colored illus. (Conran Cookbooks). Includes index.

1676. Pure Pasta / Rosamond Richardson. London, Eng.: Ebury Press, 1987. 128 p.

1677. 365 Ways to Cook Pasta / Marie Simmons. 1st ed. New York: Harper & Row, c1988. 236 p. "A John Boswell Associates Book." Includes index.

1678. Asian Vegetarian Feast: Tempting Vegetable & Pasta Recipes from the East / Ken Hom. 1st ed. New York: W. Morrow, c1988. 222 p., illus. Includes index.

Pasta *(Continued)*

1679. Bugialli on Pasta / by Giuliano Bugialli; illustrations by Glenn Wolff; photographs by John Dominis. New York: Simon and Schuster, c1988. 363 p., illus. (some colored). Includes index.

1680. Cooking with Pasta & Fine Sauces: Original Italian Family Recipes / by Alfredo Croce and John Sunzeri; edited by Elizabeth Croat and John Sunzeri. Saratoga, Calif. (18597 McCory Avenue, Saratoga 95070): A. Croce, 1988.

1681. The New Pasta Cookbook / Joanne Glynn. London, Eng.: Bay Books, 1988? 97 p.

1682. Pasta and Rice. London, Eng.: Hamlyn, 1988. 96 p.

1683. Pasta and Rice. Toronto, Ont.: Grolier, 1988. 110 p., colored illus. (Microwave Magic; 12). Includes index. Translation of: Pâtes and rize.

1684. Pasta Fresca / Viana La Place and Evan Kleiman; illustrations by Ann Field. 1st ed. New York: Morrow, c1988. 270 p., illus. (some colored). Includes index.

1685. Pasta Presto: 100 Fast & Fabulous Pasta Sauces / Norman Kolpas. Chicago, Ill.: Contemporary Books, c1988. 124 p. Includes index.

1686. Pastability / Lizzie Spender; illustrations by Karen Kerridge. New York: Ecco Press, 1988, c1987. 153 p., illus. Reprint. Includes index. Originally published: London, Eng.: Faber and Faber, 1987.

1687. Secrets of Italian Pasta: Over 100 Authentic Pasta Recipes / general editor, Beverly LeBlanc. London, Eng.: Macdonald Orbis, 1988. 95 p., illus. Includes index.

Pasta *(Continued)*

1688. Anna Teresa Callen's Menus for Pasta. New York: Weathervane Books: Distributed by Crown Publishers, 1989, c1985. 256 p., illus. 53 menus for 4-course meals centering around pasta. Includes index.

1689. Asian Pasta: A Cook's Guide to the Noodles, Wrappers, and Pasta Creations of the East / by Linda Burum. Reading, Mass.: Addison-Wesley Pub., 1989, c1985. 225 p. Includes index. Reprint. Originally published: Berkeley, Calif.: Aris Books, 1985. "Guide to the noodles, wrappers and pasta creations of the East."

1690. The Authentic Pasta Book / Fred Plotkin. 1st Fireside ed. New York: Simon & Schuster, 1989, c1985. ca. 318 p., illus. Includes index.

1691. Pasta al Dente-Recipes from All the Regions of Italy / by Alberta Nocentini. Port Washington, N.Y.: Ashley Books, 1989. 1 v., illus.

1692. Sensational Pasta / by Faye Levy. Los Angeles: HP Books, 1989. 192 p. 18 colored photos. Includes index.

1693. Best Recipes for Pasta. 1st ed. New York: Prentice Hall, c1990. 112 p. (Betty Crocker's Red Spoon Collection). Includes index.

1694. James McNair's Pasta Cookbook / photography by Patricia Brabant. San Francisco, Calif.: Chronicle Books, c1990. 96 p., colored illus. Includes index.

1695. A Passion for Pasta / by Polly Clingerman. Gaithersburg, Md.: American Cooking Guild, 1990. 64 p., illus. (Collector's Series).

Pasta *(Continued)*

1696. Pasta: Creating, Celebrating and Saucing! Exotic Recipes from Over 20 Countries / by Constance Jones. Los Angeles, Calif.: HP Books, 1990. 144 p., ca. 100 colored photos. Includes menus and guides to entertaining.

1697. Pasta: Recipes for Today / San Giorgio. Hershey, Pa.: Hershey Foods Corp., 1990. 1 booklet, colored photos. More than 50 recipes.

1698. Pasta International / Gertrude Harris. San Ramon, Calif.: Chevron Chemical Co., 1990. 192 p., illus. Includes index. First published in 1978 by 101 Productions, San Francisco, Calif.

1699. Sunset Fresh Ways with Pasta / by the editors of Sunset Books and Sunset Magazine; research & text, Cynthia Scheer; illustrations, Susan Jaekel. 1st ed. Menlo Park, Calif.: Lane Pub. Co., 1990. 96 p., colored illus.

see also entries 224, 227, 910, 2395, 2660, 2803, 3866, 3876, 3877, 3983, 3990, 4003, 4194; and Pasta and Pizza

Pasta and Pizza

1700. Chez Panisse Pasta, Pizza & Calzone / by Alice Waters, Patricia Curtan & Martine Labro. 1st ed. New York: Random House, c1984. 196 p., illus. (some colored). Includes index.

1701. Pasta and Pizza. Los Angeles, Calif.: Knapp Press, c1985. 117 p., colored illus. Includes index.

1702. Wild About Pizza and Pasta / by Lois M. Cristofano. Woodbury, N.Y.: Barron's, c1985. 86 p., colored illus. Includes index.

Specialty Cookbooks

Pasta and Pizza *(Continued)*

1703. Italian Delights / Christian Teubner; color photographs by Christian Teubner; translation by Tom Snow. 1st English language ed. Woodbury, N.Y.: Barron's, 1986, c1984. 96 p., illus. Includes index. Translation of: Pizza und Pasta Variationen.

1704. Pizza and Pasta / Susan Conte. Twickenham, Eng.: Hamlyn, 1986. 173 p., illus. (some colored). Includes index.

1705. Pizzas, Pasta and Pancakes / by Ian Burleigh. London, Eng.: Dorling Kindersley, 1986. 96 p., illus. (Sainsbury's Healthy Eating Cookbooks). Includes index.

1706. Pasta & Pizza with Pizazz. Minneapolis, Minn.: Pillsbury Co., 1988. 93 p., colored illus. More than 100 recipes. (Classic Pillsbury Cookbooks; #91).

see also Pasta; Pizza *(Section II)*

Peaches

1707. The Passion for Peaches Cookbook / compiled and edited by Gail McPherson; cover design and ink drawings by Roman Kudipal. New Park, Pa.: Passion for Peaches Pub., c1976. 192 p., illus. Includes index.

1708. Georgia Peach Recipes. Atlanta, Ga.: Georgia Peach Commission, 1983? 20 p., illus.

1709. The Peach Sampler / compiled by Eliza Mears Horton; edited by Anna Hicks. 1st ed. Lexington, S.C.: At Home Enterprises (367 Millstream Road, Lexington 29072): Additional copies, The Peach Sampler, c1983. 195 p., illus. Includes index.

Peaches *(Continued)*

1710. Pick Your Own Peaches, and Grapes: Locations with Peach, Melon, and Grape Recipes / Center for Self Sufficiency, Research Division Staff. Houston, Tex.: Prosperity & Profits, 1985. 50 p.

1711. Peaches 'n Cream / compiled and edited by Brenda McKnight. 1st ed. Austin, Tex.: Eakin Press, c1988. 197 p., illus. 400 recipes. Includes index.

see also entry 39; and broader category: Fruits

Peanut Butter

1712. The 3-in-1 Cook Book: Featuring Unique Yogurt, Zucchini, and Peanut Butter Recipes / by Helen O. Dandar, Emil B. Dandar. 1st ed. Penndel, Pa.: Sterling Specialties Cookbooks, c1980. 100 p., illus. Includes index.

1713. The Great American Peanut Butter Book: A Book of Recipes, Facts, Figures, and Fun / Larry and Honey Zisman. 1st ed. New York: St. Martin's Press, 1985. 130 p., illus. More than 100 recipes.

1714. Peanut Butter Madness: An Exciting Collection of Proven Taste-Tempting Recipes / by Betty J. Brass. Newton, Kan.: Mennonite Press, c1986. 174 p., illus. Includes index.

1715. Peanut Butter Plus. Waverly, Iowa (507 Industrial St., Waverly 50677): Printed by G & R Pub. Co., 1987? 83 p., illus. Includes index.

1716. The Ultimate Peanut Butter Cookbook / by Arthur Boze. Los Angeles, Calif.: Hillcrest Pub. Co., c1987. 118 p. Includes index.

1717. The "I Love Peanut Butter" Cookbook / William I. Kaufman. New York: Bart Books, 1988. 168 p.

222 Specialty Cookbooks

Peanut Butter *(Continued)*

1718. The I Love Peanut Butter Cookbook: How To Do More Amazing Things with America's Favorite Food Than You Ever Dreamed Possible! / by Mike Fuzzetti & Steve Monaco. San Diego, Calif.: Sunsponges, 1988. 75 p., illus.

1719. The Big Little Peanut Butter Cookbook: 50 Recipes for Delicious, Easy-to-Make Desserts, Snacks, & Sandwiches / Norman Kolpas. Chicago, Ill.: Contemporary Books, c1990. 84 p. Includes index.

Peanuts

1720. The Peanut Cookbook / by Dorothy C. Frank. 1st ed. New York: C. N. Potter: Distributed by Crown Publishers, c1976. 110 p. Includes index.

1721. Peanut One Goes to Washington: The Peanut Cook Book: Including Jimmy & Rosalynn's Favorite Recipes / Cynthia & Jerome Rubin. Charlestown, Mass.: Emporium Publications, c1976. 64 p.

1722. Complete Peanut Cook-Book from the Peanut Museum, Plains, Georgia: Over 125 Recipes on How to Prepare Peanuts. Plains, Ga.: The Museum, c1977. 47 leaves.

1723. Gourmet Goobers / by Frank Foster. San Angelo, Tex.: D.J. Designs, c1977. 69 p., illus. Includes index.

1724. The Great American Peanut Book / Sandra Fenichel Asher; illustrations by Jo Anne Metsch Bonnell. New York: Tempo Books, c1977. 190 p., illus.

1725. Hugh Carter's Peanut Cook-Book: Over 125 Recipes Using the Very Nutritious Peanut. Decatur, Ga.: Ken-Dor, c1977. 47 leaves, illus. Copyright by K. M. Bayne. Edition (c1976) published under title: Peanutty Food.

Peanuts *(Continued)*

1726. Popcorn and Peanuts / by Julianne Lemon; illustrated by Mike Nelson. Concord, Calif.: Nitty Gritty Productions, c1977. 90 p., illus. Includes index.

1727. It's Easy to Be a Gourmet with Peanuts: The Good Buys in Many Ways. Madill, Okla.: Oklahoma Peanut Commission, 198-. 29 p., illus.

CHILDREN'S COOKBOOKS

1728. The First American Peanut Growing Book / Kathy Mandry. 1st ed. New York: Random House, c1976. 82 p., illus. "A Subsistence Press Book." As published, accompanied by a sample (1 unshelled unroasted peanut mounted on card 8 x 16 cm.). Includes index. Gives instructions for growing peanuts indoors and outdoors and includes peanut recipes, history, lore, and trivia.

1729. The Peanut Cookbook / by Natalie Donna; illustrated by Robert Quackenbush. New York: Lothrop, Lee & Shepard Co., c1976. 55 p., colored illus. Includes index. Recipes using peanuts and peanut butter and featuring natural foods. Includes peanut butter soup, peanut butter pie, peanut burger, and peanut granola.

see also entry 1730; and broader category: Nuts

Pears

see entry 25; and broader category: Fruits

Specialty Cookbooks

Peas

1730. The Gardens for All Book of Peas & Peanuts / by Dick and Jan Raymond. Burlington, Vt.: Gardens for All, c1981. 31 p., illus.

see also entries 64, 903, 1160; and broader categories: Legumes; Vegetables

Pecans

1731. The Pecan Lovers' Cookbook / compiled by Carol Lee Miller. Natchez, Miss.: Myrtle Bank Publishers; Waterproof, La. (Rte. 2, Box 139, Waterproof 71375): Order from Plantation Pecan and Gift Co., 1980. 78 p. More than 150 recipes. Includes index.

1732. The Great American Cookbook: Featuring Pecans--America's Favorite Nut / editors, Rebecca H. Johnson, Sharon K. Rousseau. Atlanta, Ga.: National Pecan Marketing Council, c1984. 158 p., illus. (chiefly colored). Includes index.

1733. Pecans, From Soup to Nuts! / by Keith Courrege. Natchitoches, La.: Cane River Pecan Co., c1984. 54 p.

1734. Cooking with Pecans: Texas in a Nutshell / Terry Scott Bertling. 1st ed. Austin, Tex.: Eakin Press, c1986. 142 p., illus. Includes index.

1735. Pecan Lovers' Cook Book / by Mark Blazek. Phoenix, Ariz.: Golden West Publishers, c1986. 120 p. More than 150 recipes. Includes index.

1736. Cooking with Pecans / Smith College Club of New York City. New York: Smith College Club of New York City, 1987. 89 p.

see also broader category: Nuts

Specific Ingredients 225

Pepper

1737. Mr. Dudley's Peppermill Cookbook / Peggy Treadwell. Los Angeles, Calif.: D. Kebow, c1970. 180 p., illus.

see also broader category: Spices

Peppers

1738. Green Chili: A Cookbook / by Bette Shannon. Tucson, Ariz.: Treasure Chest Publications, 1981. 89 p., illus. Includes index.

1739. The Little Pepper Book / Michelle Berriedale-Johnson. 1st U.S. ed. New York: St. Martin's Press, c1982. 60 p., illus.

1740. The Little Pepper Cookbook / Mary L. Green. Denver, Colo.: Giftstar, 1984. ca. 10 p., illus. (Little Cookbooks).

1741. Hot Stuff: A Cookbook in Praise of the Piquant / Jessica B. Harris. 1st ed. New York: Atheneum, 1985. 278 p., illus. Includes index.

1742. The Hot Pepper Cookbook / recipes by Ingrid N. Fawcett. 2nd rev. ed. Port Coquitlam, B.C.: Chile Pepper Co., 1986, c1981. 64 p. Includes index.

1743. Peppers: A Miscellany of Gastronomic and Horticultural Information and Therapeutic Remedies / Jane Wilton-Smith & Maria Donkin; drawings by Bear. Salisbury, Eng.: Stylus, c1986. 24 p., illus. (The Good Table).

1744. Peppers Hot & Chile: A Cook's Guide to Chile Peppers from California, the Southwest, Mexico, and Beyond / Georgeanne Brennan and Charlotte Glenn. Reading, Mass.: Aris Books, c1988. 108 p., illus. (Kitchen Edition). Includes indexes.

1745. Peppers, Hot and Sweet: Over 100 Recipes for All Tastes / by Beth Dooley. Pownal, Vt.: Storey Communications, c1990. 160 p. Includes index.

Peppers *(Continued)*

1746. The Whole Chile Pepper Book: With Over 150 Hot and Spicy Recipes / by Dave DeWitt and Nancy Gerlach; illustrated by Cyd Riley. 1st ed. Boston, Mass.: Little, Brown, c1990. 373 p., illus. 150 recipes. Includes bibliography and index. Contains information on the history and lore of chile peppers and how to grow them.

see also entry 525; Jalapeños; *and broader category:* Vegetables

Persimmons

1747. People Pleasing Persimmon Recipes / compiled by Marie A. Filut. Leawood, Kan.: Circulation Service; Napa, Calif.: Copies, Persimmon Recipes, 1985. 38, 34, A-D p., illus. Includes index.

see also broader category: Fruits

Pheasants

1748. The Pheasant Cook / Tina Dennis and Rosamond Cardigan. Wiltshire, Eng.: Crowood, 1988. 128 p.

see also broader categories: Fowl and Game; Game; Poultry

Pie Fillings

1749. A Comstock Year Full of Special Event Treats. Rochester, N.Y.: Curtice-Burns, Inc., 1982. 1 booklet. 62 recipes using Comstock pie fillings.

Specific Ingredients 227

Pine Nuts

1750. The Piñon Pine: A Natural and Cultural History / Ronald M. Lanner; with a section on pine-nut cookery by Harriette Lanner. Reno, Nev.: University of Nevada Press, 1981. 208 p., illus. Includes index.

see also broader category: Nuts

Pineapples

1751. How to Grapple with the Pineapple: From Planting Pineapple Tops to Baking Upside-Down Cakes / by Helen Rosenbaum. New York: Hawthorn Books, c1975. 129 p., illus. Includes index.

1752. Just Pineapples: A Collection of 751 Pineapple Recipes from Plantation Paradise, the Pineapple Farm / compiled by Mr. and Mrs. A. T. Weaver, Jr. Lake Placid, Fla.: Weaver, 1976. 335 p.

1753. The Little Pineapple Cookbook / Mary L. Green. Denver, Colo.: Giftstar, 1984. ca. 10 p., illus. (Little Cookbooks)

see also broader category: Fruits

Plums

1754. Plum Crazy: A Book About Beach Plums / Elizabeth Post Mirel; drawings by Betty Fraser. 1st ed. New York: C. N. Potter; Distributed by Crown Publishers, 1973. 144 p., illus.

1755. A Glut of Plums / Ann Carr. London, Eng.: Merehurst, 1988. 92 p.

see also entry 2286; and broader category: Fruits

Poi

see entry 2242

Pollock

1756. Portraits with Pollock / U.S. Bureau of Commercial Fisheries. Chicago, Ill.: National Marketing Services Office; for sale by the Supt. of Docs., U.S. Govt. Print. Off., Washington, D.C., 1970. 28 p., illus. (Fishery Market Development Series; no. 16).

see also broader category: Fish

Popcorn

1757. Popcorn Cookery. Sea Cliff, N.Y.: Carbooks, Inc., 1980. 1 v. 200 recipes.

1758. Bang!: The Explosive Popcorn Recipe Book / Robert T. Brucken. New York: Ballantine Books, c1983. 142 p. 200 recipes.

1759. The Popcorn Lover's Book / Sue Spitler & Nao Hauser. Chicago, Ill.: Contemporary Books, c1983. 90 p., illus. More than 100 recipes. Includes index.

1760. For Popcorn Lovers Only / Diane Pfeifer; illustrations by Clark Taylor. Marietta, Ga.: Strawberry Patch; Atlanta, Ga.: Marmac Pub. Co., c1987. 153 p., illus.

1761. The Popcorn Plus Diet / Joel Herskowitz. New York: Pharos Books: Distributed in the U.S. by Ballantine Books, 1987. 160 p., illus. Includes index.

see also entry 1726

Pork

1762. The Complete Pork Cookbook / Louise Sherman Schoon and Corrinne Hardesty. New York: Stein and Day, 1977. 296 p., illus. Includes index.

1763. The Art of Making Sausages, Pâtés, and Other Charcuterie / by Jane Grigson; illustrated with drawings by M.J. Mott. New York, Knopf, 1980. 349 p., illus. Includes index. "Formerly published in hardcover as The Art of Charcuterie." First published in 1967 under title: Charcuterie & French Pork Cookery.

1764. Pork / by the editors of Time-Life Books. Alexandria, Va.: Time-Life Books, c1980. 179 p., illus. Includes index.

1765. Today's Pork Goes to School: Recipes and Helpful Information for School Food Service Directors. Des Moines, Iowa: National Pork Producers Council, 1981. 6 p., illus., 7 recipe cards in pocket.

1766. Pork in Family Meals / prepared by Human Nutrition Information Service. Rev. Washington, D.C.: U.S. Dept. of Agriculture; For sale by the Supt. of Documents, U.S. Government Printing Office, 1982. 33 p., illus. (Home and Garden Bulletin; no. 160). Includes index.

1767. Oscar Mayer Celebration Cookbook: 1883-1983, 100 Years of Dedication to the Kid in All of Us. Milwaukee, Wis.: Ideals Pub. Corp., c1983. 64 p., illus. (some colored). Includes index.

1768. Pork, Ham & Bacon. Newton Abbot, Eng.: David & Charles, c1983. 64 p., illus. (some colored). (Kitchen Workshop). Includes index. Translation of: Svinekjott.

1769. Pork Facts: Consumer Information / produced by National Pork Producers Council. Rev. Des Moines, Iowa: NPPC, 1984. 31 p., illus.

Specialty Cookbooks

Pork *(Continued)*

1770. Pork, Perfect Pork / Canadian Pork Council. Saskatoon, Sask.: Western Producer Prairie Books, 1983. 189 p., colored illus. Includes index.

1771. Ribs: Over 80 All-American and International Recipes for Ribs and Fixings / by Susan R. Friedland. 1st ed. New York: Harmony Books, c1984. 125 p., illus. Includes index.

1772. The Southern Heritage All Pork Cookbook. Birmingham, Ala.: Oxmoor House, c1984. 143 p., illus. (some colored). (The Southern Heritage Cookbook Library). Includes index.

1773. Pork & Ham Menus. Alexandria, Va.: Time-Life Books, 1985. 105 p., colored illus. (Great Meals in Minutes). Includes index.

1774. The Professional Chef's Book of Charcuterie: Pâtés, Terrines, Timbales, Galantines, Sausages, and Other Culinary Delights / T.G. Mueller. New York: CBI Books, c1987. 276 p., illus. (some colored). Includes index.

1775. British Charcuterie / Jennie Reekie. London, Eng.: Ward Lock, 1988. 144 p.

1776. Fresh Ways with Pork / by the editors of Time-Life Books. Alexandria, Va.: Time-Life Books, c1988. 144 p., colored illus. (Healthy Home Cooking). Includes index.

1777. Pork. Toronto, Ont.: Grolier, 1988. 110 p., colored illus. (Microwave Magic; 4). Includes index. Translation of: Le Porc.

1778. The Professional Charcuterie Series: Basic Techniques / Marcel Cottenceau, Jean-François Deport, and Jean-Pierre Odeau. New York: Van Nostrand Rheinhold, 1990. 2 v. (304 p. each), illus. v. 1: Hams, sausages, sausage specialties, black puddings, white puddings, rilettes and rillons, confits and smoked products. v. 2: Liver-based pâtés, etc. Includes index. Translation of: Traité de charcuterie artisanale.

Pork *(Continued)*

1779. The Useful Pig / Roberta Wolfe Smoler. 1st ed. New York: Harper & Row, 1990. 288 p., illus. Includes index.

see also entry 140; Bacon; Ham; Sausages; *and broader category:* Meat

Potatoes

1780. The Caterers' Guide to Potatoes. London, Eng.: Potato Marketing Board in association with the Army Catering Corps, 1980. 36 p.

1781. Fifty Delightfully Different Ways to Cook Potatoes / by Eleanor Goetz. Montchanin, Del.: Montchanin Press, c1980. 38 p., illus. Cover title: Potatoes, Potatoes. Includes index.

1782. The Great Potato Cookbook / by Maria Luisa Scott and Jack Denton Scott. New York: Bantam Books, 1980. 316 p., illus. Includes index.

1783. The Noble Potato / Princess Weikersheim. London, Eng.: Hutchinson, 1980. 128 p.

1784. The Potato Cookbook / Gwen Robyns. London, Eng.: Pan, 1980. 140 p., illus. Includes index.

1785. Potato Cookery / by Tom Hoge. Edinburgh, Scot.: Harris, 1980. 270 p. Includes index.

1786. The Spud Book: 101 Ways to Cook Potatoes / compiled by James Houston Turner; illustrations by Chris Jansson. Solana Beach, Calif.: Seven Seven Search Publications, c1980. 132 p., illus.

1787. Appealing Potatoes / Princess Weikersheim; illustrated by Martin Williams. London, Eng.: Hutchinson, 1981. 96 p., illus. Includes index.

Potatoes *(Continued)*

1788. Growing and Cooking Potatoes / by Mary W. Cornog; illustrated by Ray Maher. 1st ed. Dublin, N.H.: Yankee, 1981. 143 p., illus. Includes index.

1789. Potatoes / by Inez M. Krech. 1st ed. New York: Primavera Books/Crown, c1981. 64 p. Includes index.

1790. Texas Potatoes: They Belong in Any Diet. Austin, Tex.: Texas Dept. of Agriculture, 1981. 7 p.

1791. The All-American Potato Cookbook / editor, Julie Hogan. Elmsford, N.Y.: Benjamin Co., c1982. 160 p., illus. (some colored). Includes index.

1792. Stuffed Spuds: 100 Meals in a Potato / Jeanne Jones. New York: M. Evans, c1982. 132 p. Includes index.

1793. Great British Potato Recipes: 101 Ways with Britain's Favourite Vegetable. London, Eng.: Potato Marketing Board, 1983. 223 p., colored illus.

1794. Making the Most of Potatoes / Judy Ridgway. Newton Abbot, Eng.: David & Charles, c1983. 48 p., illus. Includes index.

1795. One Potato, Two Potato: A Cookbook / by Constance Bollen and Marlene Blessing. Seattle, Wash.: Pacific Search Press, c1983. 167 p., illus. Includes index.

1796. The Little Potato Cookbook / Mary L. Green. Denver, Colo.: Giftstar, 1984. ca. 10 p., illus. (Little Cookbooks).

1797. One Potato, Two Potato, Three Potato--Four: The Potato Cookbook / by Thos. G. Godfrey. Elkhorn, Wis.: T.G. Godfrey, 1984? 74 leaves.

1798. A Pocket Book on Potatoes: The Vegetable That Makes a Meal / Rhona Newman. London, Eng.: Octopus, 1984. 96 p., illus. (some colored). Includes index.

Potatoes *(Continued)*

1799. Potato Cookery / Linda Collister. London, Eng.: Hamlyn, 1984. 128 p., illus. (some colored). (Hamlyn Cookshelf Series). Includes index.

1800. Cooking in Style with British Potatoes. London, Eng.: Potato Marketing Board, 1985. 10 p., colored illus.

1801. Down to Earth with British Potatoes. London, Eng.: Potato Marketing Board, 1985. 10 p., colored illus.

1802. The Gardens for All Book of Potatoes. Burlington, Vt.: Gardens for All, 1985, c1980. 26 p., illus.

1803. The Incredible Potato: A Cookbook and History / by Agnes Toews-Andrews. Trumpeter, Alta.: Toews-Andrews Pub., 1985. 158 p. Includes index.

1804. The Noble Spud / Judy Wells and Rick Johnson. Markham, Ont.; New York: Penguin Books, c1985. 160 p., 4 leaves of colored plates, line drawings. Includes index.

1805. Potato Potential: All Eyes Turn to Potatoes / compiled by Isaac R. Horst. Mt. Forest, Ont.: I.R. Horst, 1985. 35 p.

1806. Small Potatoes: A Potato Cookbook from the Luther Burbank Home & Gardens. Santa Rosa, Calif. (P.O. Box 1678, Santa Rosa 95402): Luther Burbank Home & Gardens, c1985. 122 p., illus.

1807. Spuds / Brenda Bell. Chicago, Ill.: Contemporary Books, c1985. 73 p., 12 p. of plates, colored illus. 50 stuffed potato recipes. Includes index.

1808. Wild about Potatoes / by Marie Bianco. Woodbury, N.Y.: Barron's, c1985. 91 p., colored illus. Includes index.

Potatoes *(Continued)*

1809. The Maine Potato Cookbook: World Collection of Recipes / compiled by Paul Maureau of Masardis, Maine; text by Shirlee Connors Carlson. Madawaska, Me.: Valley Pub. Co., 1986? 92 p., illus. Reprint. Originally published: 150 Potato Recipes. Camden, Me.: Town Crier, 1982.

1810. The Potato Experience: Wonderful Ways with Potato Outers and Innards: recipes, illustrations, calligraphy, and hand-lettering / by Lisa Tanner. Berkeley, Calif.: Ten Speed Press, c1986. 245 p., illus. Includes index.

1811. The "Trust in British Potatoes" Recipe Book. London, Eng.: Potato Marketing Board, 1986. 96 p., colored illus. Includes index.

1812. The World of Potatoes / by Wilma G. van Kersbergen. Marcy, N.Y.: Vans Co., distributor, c1986. 109 p.

1813. The Complete Idaho Potato Cookbook / by Elaine Prescott, SanDee Scherer; illustrated by SanDee Scherer. Blackfoot, Idaho: Modern Print.; Pingree, Idaho: May order from Wholistic Enterprises, c1987. 91 p., illus.

1814. The Little Potato Book / compiled by Susan Fleming. London, Eng.: Piatkus, 1987. 64 p., illus.

1815. One Potato, Two Potato: A Cookbook and More / Janet Reeves. Charlottetown, P.E.I.: Ragwood Press, 1987. 244 p. Includes index.

1816. Pot Luck: Potato Recipes from Ireland / Nell Donnelly; with illustrations by Jimmy Burns. Dublin, Ire.: Wolfhound, 1987. 96 p., illus.

1817. The Unique Potato Salad Cookbook / Vera Klein. 1st ed. Seattle, Wash.: Entrepreneurial Workshops Publications, c1987. 152 p. More than 250 recipes. Includes index.

Potatoes *(Continued)*

1818. Deliciously Different. London, Eng.: Potato Marketing Board, 1988. 10 p.

1819. A Taste of Summer. London, Eng.: Potato Marketing Board, 1988. 10 p.

1820. Everyday Recipes with Home Grown Potatoes. London, Eng.: Potato Marketing Board, 1989. 15 p.

1821. The Great Potato Cookbook / Jennifer Steel. Tunbridge Wells, Eng.: Search Press, 1989. 144 p.

1822. James McNair's Potato Cookbook / photography by Patricia Brabant. San Francisco, Calif.: Chronicle Books, c1989. 96 p. 35 recipes, each accompanied by a colored photograph.

1823. Potatoes: Uses for the Whole Potato, with Recipes & Suggestions / Recycling Consortium. Houston, Tex.: Prosperity & Profits, 1989. ca. 14 p.

1824. Potatoes: 68 Delicious Recipes for Everyone's Favorite Vegetable / by Sue Kreitzman. 1st ed. New York: Harmony Books, c1989. 96 p., illus. Includes index.

1825. Cooking with Potatoes / Dorothy Parker. Pownal, Vt.: Garden Way Pub.; Storey Communications, 1990. 1 v.

1826. In Praise of the Potato: Recipes from Around the World / Lindsey Bareham. Woodstock, N.Y.: Overlook Press, 1990. 320 p. Contains information on buying and storage of potatoes and its history and folklore. Includes bibliography and index.

1827. Please Pass the Potatoes: Appealing Recipes / from the Society of St. Andrew; compiled and edited by Marian Buchanan. Big Island, Va.: St. Andrew Press, c1990. 160 p., illus.

see also entries 1247, 1251; and broader category: Vegetables

Poultry

1828. Poultry / by the editors of Time-Life Books. Alexandria, Va.: Time-Life Books, c1979. 176 p., illus. (The Good Cook, Techniques & Recipes). Includes index.

1829. Chicken and Poultry Cookbook / by Hank Meadows. Milwaukee, Wis.: Ideals Pub. Corp., c1980. 64 p., illus. (chiefly colored). Includes index.

1830. The Hamlyn Chicken Cookbook / Elizabeth Pomeroy. Rev. and updated ed. London, Eng.: Hamlyn: 1981. 127 p., illus. (some colored). Includes index. Previous ed. published as: Chicken Cookbook. 1973.

1831. Chinese Poultry Cooking / Stella Lau Fessler; illustrated by Janet Nelson. New York: New American Library, c1982. 278 p., illus. "A Plume Book." Includes index.

1832. Poultry and Game Birds / edited by Georgia Orcutt and Sandra Taylor; illustrated by Pamela Carroll. 1st ed. Dublin, N.H.: Yankee, c1982. 143 p., illus. (The Flavor of New England). Includes index.

1833. Poultry in Family Meals / prepared by Human Nutrition Information Service. Rev. Washington, D.C.: U.S. Dept. of Agriculture; For sale by the Supt. of Documents, U.S. Government Printing Office, 1982. 29 p., illus. (Home and Garden Bulletin; no. 110). Includes index.

1834. Poultry Dishes. Newton Abbot, Eng.: David & Charles, c1983. 64 p., colored illus. (Kitchen Workshop). Includes index. Translation of: Fjaerkre.

1835. The Southern Heritage Plain and Fancy Poultry Cookbook. Birmingham, Ala.: Oxmoor House, c1983. 143 p., illus. (some colored). (The Southern Heritage Cookbook Library). Includes index.

Poultry *(Continued)*

1836. Chicken & Poultry Cookbook. London, Eng.: Marshall Cavendish, c1984. 58 p., colored illus.

1837. The More Than Chicken Cookbook / Sara Pitzer. Pownal, Vt.: Garden Way Pub., c1984. 139 p., illus. More than 100 recipes. Includes index.

1838. Poultry. Los Angeles, Calif.: Knapp Press, c1984. 120 p., 16 p. of plates, illus. (some colored). (Cooking with Bon Appétit). Includes index.

1839. The Poultry Cookbook / Frederick E. Kahn. New York: Nautilus Communications; Aurora, Ill.: Distributed by Caroline House, c1984. 155 p., illus. Includes index.

1840. Chicken and Fowl / text copyright by Joshua Morris, Inc.; illustrations, A/S Hjemmet. New York: Modern Pub., c1985. 64 p., colored illus. (Home Cooking Library).

1841. Chicken & Other Poultry / Julie Renaud, Jane Horn, writers; Sally W. Smith, editor; Bob Montesclaros, photographer. San Francisco, Calif.: Ortho Information Services, c1985. 128 p., colored illus. (California Culinary Academy Series). Includes index.

1842. Chicken and Poultry. 1st U.S. and Canadian ed. Woodbury, N.Y.: Barron's, 1985. 160 p., illus. (some colored). More than 100 recipes. (Step-by-Step Cooking Series). Includes index. "Special feature: 30-page illustrated supplement with tips on buying, preparing, cooking, and carving poultry."

1843. Perfect Poultry: More Than 200 Recipes and Dozens of Tips for Making Delicious Meals with Chicken and Turkey / the editors of Family Circle; foreword by Jean Hewitt. 1st ed. New York: Times Books, c1985. 254 p., illus. Includes index.

Poultry *(Continued)*

1844. Potpourri of Poultry & Seafood Favorites: Favorite Recipes of Home Economics Teachers. Nashville, Tenn.: Favorite Recipes Press, c1985. 128 p., illus. Includes index.

1845. Poultry and Sauces / Madame Jehane Benoît. Saint-Lambert, Que.: Heritage, 1985. 102 p., 8 leaves of plates, illus. (Heritage+Plus). (Encyclopedia of Microwave Cooking; 4). Includes index. Cover title: Poultry, Stuffing and Sauces. Issued also in French under title: Les volailles et leurs sauces.

1846. Prairie Farmer Poultry Cookbook / Mitzi Ayala. Lombard, Ill.: Wallace-Homestead Book Co., c1985. 127 p., illus. Includes index.

1847. Reader's Digest, the Creative Kitchen: Poultry. 1st ed. Montreal, Que.: Reader's Digest Association (Canada), c1985. 148 p., illus. (some colored). Includes index.

1848. Better Homes and Gardens Poultry / editor, Barbara Atkins; photographers, Michael Jensen and Sean Fitzgerald. 1st ed. Des Moines, Iowa: Meredith Corp., c1986. 128 p., illus. (some colored). (Great Cooking Made Easy). Includes index.

1849. Famous Brands Chicken & Poultry. St. Louis, Mo.: Brand Name Pub. Corp., 1986. ca. 128 p., colored illus. (Famous Brands Cookbook Library). Includes index.

1850. Fresh Ways with Poultry / by the editors of Time-Life Books. Alexandria, Va.: Time-Life Books, c1986. 144 p., colored illus. (Healthy Home Cooking). Includes index.

1851. Microwaving Poultry & Seafood / by Barbara Methven. Minnetonka, Minn.: Cy DeCosse, c1986. 159 p., colored illus. (Microwave Cooking Library). Includes index.

Poultry *(Continued)*

1852. Poultry Dishes / edited by Susan Dixon. London, Eng.: Ward Lock, 1986. 63 p., illus. (some colored). (Mrs. Beeton's Home Cooking). Contains recipes selected from Mrs. Beeton's Cookery and Household Management.

1853. Sunset Fresh Ways with Chicken / by the editors of Sunset Books and Sunset Magazine. 1st ed. Menlo Park, Calif.: Lane Pub. Co., c1986. 96 p., colored illus. Includes index.

1854. Poultry. Toronto, Ont.: Grolier, 1987. 110 p., colored illus. (Microwave Magic; 2). Includes index. Translation of: La Volaille.

1855. Poultry II. Toronto, Ont.: Grolier, 1988. 110 p., colored illus. (Microwave Magic; 7). Includes index. Translation of: La Volaille II.

1856. Beard on Birds / by James Beard. New York: Warner Books, 1989. 194 p. More than 200 recipes. Includes index. Rev. ed. of: James Beard's Fowl and Game Bird Cookery, 1979.

1857. Chicken and Poultry / William A. Pizzico and Gina Marie Corporation. New York: Modern Pub. Division of Unisystems, Inc., 1989. 64 p., illus. (some colored). (Convenient Cooking). Includes index.

1858. Poultry on the Grill / by Phyllis Magida and Barbara Grunes. New York: Dell Pub., 1989. 191 p., illus.

1859. The Complete Poultry Cookbook / by Lonnie Gandara with Peggy Fallon. Los Angeles, Calif.: HP Books, 1990. 160 p., illus. (some colored). Includes index.

1860. Poultry and Game Birds / Lyn Hall. London, Eng.: Pavilion, 1990. 160 p. (Class in the Kitchen).

see also entries 563, 655, 664, 1220, 1231, 1248; Fowl and Game; *and specific kinds of poultry:* Chicken, Duck, Turkey

Prunes

1861. The Original All Prune Recipe Book / author, Dolores F. Schoen. Yuba City, Calif. (697 Palorca, Yuba City 95991): D.F. Schoen, 1988. 67 p., illus. Cover title: California, Prune Bowl of the U.S.A. Includes index.

1862. The Prune Gourmet / Donna Rodnitzky, Ellie Densen, JoGail Wenzel. San Francisco, Calif.: Chronicle Books, c1989. 232 p. 150 recipes.

see also broader category: Dried Fruits

Pudding Mixes

see entry 893

Pulse foods *see* Legumes

Pumpkin

1863. Old-Fashioned Pumpkin Recipes: Halloween Treats. Nashville, Ind.: Bear Wallow Books, c1979. 32 p., illus.

1864. Pumpkin Corner / by Estelle K. Abernathy. Herndon, Va.: Strawberry Patchworks, 1979. 160 p., illus. "A collection of recipes, facts, and fables."

1865. The Pumpkin Eaters Cook Book: First of a Series / Rosemary Smithson. Madison, Wis.: R. Smithson, c1980. 80 p.

1866. Pumpkin Cookbook / compiled by R.L. Gilberg; illustrations by M. Gilberg. 1st ed. Newcastle, Calif.: Gilmar Press: Distributed by Gilmar Enterprise, c1982. 120 p., illus.

1867. The Great Pumpkin Cookbook: A Harvest of Libby's Favorite Recipes. New York: Rutledge Books, c1984. 128 p., colored illus. Includes index.

Pumpkin *(Continued)*

1868. The Great Pumpkin Cookbook / Norma Upson; illustrated by Eileen Vollertsen. 2nd ed. Bend, Or.: Maverick Publications, 1985. 154 p., illus. Includes bibliography and index.

1869. Pumpkin, Pumpkin!: Lore, History, Outlandish Facts, and Good Eating / compiled, edited, written, and otherwise attended to by Anne Copeland MacCallum; artwork by Diane Nelson Palmore. San Pedro, Calif.: Heather Foundation, 1986. 203 p., illus. First edition published in San Pedro, Calif., 1984. Includes bibliography.

1870. Pumpkins & Squashes: A Miscellany of Gastronomic and Horticultural Information / Jane Wilton-Smith & Maria Donkin; drawings by Bear. Salisbury, Eng.: Stylus, c1986. 24 p., illus. (The Good Table).

1871. The Best of the Pumpkin Recipes Cookbook / edited by Helen & Emil Dandar. Penndel, Pa. (P.O. Box 16, Penndel 19047): Sterling Specialties Cookbook, c1989. 120 p.

CHILDREN'S COOKBOOKS

1872. The All-Around Pumpkin Book / by Margery Cuyler; illustrated by Corbett Jones. New York: Holt, Rinehart and Winston, c1980. 95 p., illus. Presents little-known facts about and recipes and craft projects using pumpkins. Also includes planting and cultivation hints and suggested carving techniques.

see also entry 2599; and broader category: Vegetables

Rabbits

1873. New Domestic Rabbit Cook Book. Bloomington, Ill.: American Rabbit Breeders Association, 198-. 22 p.

Rabbits *(Continued)*

1874. Rabbit, a Taste of Tradition!: A Collection of Delicious Recipes. Fredericton, N.B.: N.B. Rabbit Breeders Association, 198-? 16 p., illus. Text in English and French.

1875. Rabbits for Food and Profit / edited by Lee Schwanz; recipe editor, Kathleen Schwanz. Brookfield, Wis. (Box 363, Brookfield 53005): Farmer's Digest, c1982. 160 p., illus. Chiefly concerned with the raising of rabbits but contains a chapter with 36 recipes using rabbit meat.

1876. The Complete Rabbit Cook Book / by Jimmy Manteris and Cindy Buchmann. 1st ed. Bellaire, Tex. (4800 Maple, Bellaire 77401): Gulf Coast Rabbits, 1983. 116 p.

see also broader category: Game

Raisins

1877. The Sun Maid Cookbook: Brought to You by Sun Maid Growers of California; color photography, Walter Storck. New York: Benjamin Co., c1980. 126 p., illus. Includes index.

see also broader category: Dried Fruits

Raspberries

1878. Raspberry Tyme / Leonard "Ty" Garraghan. Merriam, Kans.: Raspberry Tyme, 198-. 1 v.

1879. Mad about Raspberries & Strawberries / by Jacqueline Heriteau; illustrations by Woodleigh Hubbard. New York: Putnam Pub. Group, c1984. 62 p., illus. "A GD/Perigee Book." Includes index.

see also broader category: Berries

Raw Foods

1880. Feasting on Raw Foods: Featuring Over 350 Healthful No-cook Recipes for Every Part of a Meal--from Appetizers Through Main Course Dishes to Desserts / edited by Charles Gerras; special contributions, Nancy Arobone and others; recipes, readers of Organic Gardening Magazine and Carole Collier plus Linda Gilbert and others; book design, Carol Stickles; illustrations, Robert Pennise. Emmaus, Pa.: Rodale Press, c1980. 323 p., illus. Includes index.

1881. The Uncook Book: Raw Food Adventures to a New Health High / by Elizabeth & Elton Baker. [n.p.]: Drelwood Publications; Saguache, Colo.: Distributed by Communication Creativity, c1980. 208 p., illus. Includes index.

1882. Living Medicine: The Healing Properties of Plants / by Mannfried Pahlow; introduction by Karl Heinz Caspers; translated from the German by Linda Sonntag. Wellingborough, Eng.: Thorsons, 1980. 96 p., illus. (some colored). Includes index. Translation of: Heilpflanzen Heute.

1883. The Book of Raw Fruit and Vegetable Juices and Drinks / William H. Lee. New Canaan, Conn.: Keats Pub., c1982. 177 p. (A Pivot Original Health Book). Includes index.

1884. The Complete Raw Juice Therapy / by Susan E. Charmine. 1st U.S. ed. New York: Thorsons Publishers: Distributed to the trade by Inner Traditions International, 1983. 128 p., illus. Includes index.

1885. Raw Energy Recipes / Leslie and Susannah Kenton. London, Eng.: Century, 1985. 60 p., colored illus. Includes index.

1886. Helping Hand: 8-Day Diet Programs for People Who Care About Wellness / by Henry L.N. Anderson. Pacific Palisades, Calif.: Publius Pub. and Productions; Inglewood, Calif.: Distributed by Associated Family Counselors, c1986. 117 p., illus.

Raw Foods *(Continued)*

1887. The Raw Food Cookbook / Jennie Reekie. London, Eng.: Kingswood, 1986. 152 p., illus. Includes index.

1888. Raw Foods / by Sarah Brown. London, Eng.: Dorling Kindersley, 1986. 96 p., illus. (Sainsbury's Healthy Eating Cookbooks).

1889. Vegetable Juice Therapy: How to Get Relief from Drug Addiction and Other Maladies / N.N. Saha. 1st ed. Calcutta, India: Firma KLM, 1988. 119 p.

see also Natural Foods; Sprouts

Rhubarb

1890. The Rhubarb Cookbook / by Pamela Gilsenan Wubben. Boulder, Colo.: One Percent Pub., c1979. 65 p., illus.

1891. Rhubarb Renaissance: A Cookbook / by Ann Saling; illustrated by Darci Covington. 3rd ed. New York: Ansal Press, 1980? 159 p., illus. Includes index.

1892. Rhubarb Recipes: A Collection / by Gayle. Cedar, Minn. (21730 Cedar Dr. N.W., Cedar 55011): Gayle's Collections, c1981. 79 p.

1893. Rhubarb for Good Measure / Jocelyne Kidston. Kapuskasing, Ont.: Penumbra Press, c1987. 77 p. Includes index.

1894. R-r-rhubarb: From Soups to Nuts / by Camille McDonald. Chicago, Ill.: C. McDonald, c1988. 33 p.

1895. Rhubarb / by Sharon Fohring and Marion Batten. Waterloo, Ont.: Batten-Fohring Books, c1989. 82 p., illus.

see also broader category: Fruits

Rice

1896. Rice and Spice: Rice Recipes from East to West / Phyllis Jervey. Rutland, Vt.: C.E. Tuttle Co., 1957. 200 p., illus. Reprinted.

1897. Rice Recipes from Around the World / Tomi Egami. 1st ed. Tokyo, Japan: Kodansha International, 1966. 122 p., illus. (part colored). Reprinted.

1898. The East-West Book of Rice Cookery / by Marian Tracy; illustrated by Marguerite Burgess. New York: Dover Publications, 1976. 148 p., illus. "Unabridged and unaltered republication of the work originally published in 1952 by the Viking Press."

1899. Rice Cookery. Sea Cliff, N.Y.: Carbooks, Inc., 1980. 1 v. 231 recipes.

1900. Making the Most of Rice / Judy Ridgway. Newton Abbot, Eng.: David and Charles, c1983. 48 p., illus. Includes index.

1901. The Little Rice Book / Judy Ridgway. London, Eng.: Piatkus, 1984. 59 p., illus.

1902. At the Dainty Rice Sign / Jehane Benoît. Lachine, Que.: Editions héritage, 1985. 42 p., colored illus.

1903. The Complete Rice Cookbook / Myra Street. London, Eng.: Apple, c1985. 128 p., colored illus. Includes index.

1904. The American Rice Cookbook / Alex Barker. Cambridge, Eng.: Martin Books published in association with the US Rice Council, 1986. 96 p., illus.

1905. The Rice Diet Report: How I Lost Up to 12 Pounds a Week on the World-Famous Weight-Loss Plan / Judy Moscovitz. New York: G.P. Putnam's Sons, 1986. 242 p.

Rice *(Continued)*

1906. Cooking with Great American Chefs. Houston, Tex.: Uncle Ben's, Inc., 1987. 1 booklet.

1907. James McNair's Rice Cookbook / photography by Patricia Brabant. San Francisco, Calif.: Chronicle Books, c1988. 96 p., colored illus. Includes index.

1908. Official Rice & Dry Bean Cookbook: 1988. Williams, Calif.: Published by International Rice Festival & Dry Bean Jubilee, 1988. 40 p. Cover title: 77 Ways to Use Rice & Beans.

1909. Risotto: A Taste of Milan / Constance Arkin Del Nero and Rosario Del Nero; illustrations by Constance Arkin Del Nero. New York: Harper & Row, c1988. 120 p., illus. Contains anecdotes. Includes index.

1910. Rice: A Cookbook / Maria Luisa Scott and Jack Denton Scott. Mount Vernon, N.Y.: Consumers Union, 1989, c1988. 368 p. 250 recipes. (Consumer Reports Books). Includes index.

1911. Rice: A Food for All Seasons / compiled by Harold Deane Thomason Akins. Savannah, Ga.: H.D. Akins, c1989. 254 p., illus. On cover: A collection of 600 favorite recipes.

1912. Risotto / Judith Barrett & Norma Wasserman; illustrations by Norma Wasserman. 1st Collier Books ed. New York: Collier Books, 1989, c1987. 336 p., illus. "More than 100 recipes for the classic rice dish of Northern Italy." Includes index.

1913. Wild About Rice / by Marie Bianco. New York: Barron's, c1989. 96 p., colored photos. Includes index.

1914. Minute Rice: Fast, Fabulous Meals. New York: Beekman House; Distributed by Crown Publishers, 1990. 96 p., colored illus. More than 100 recipes, more than 30 of which have microwave directions. Includes index.

Rice *(Continued)*

CHILDREN'S COOKBOOKS

1915. Rice / Lynne Merrison; illustrations by John Yates. Minneapolis, Minn.: Carolrhoda Books, 1990, c1989. 32 p., colored illus. (Foods We Eat). Describes rice, the history of its cultivation, and the part it plays in human health and diet. Contains several recipes. Includes index. First published: East Sussex, Eng.: Wayland, 1989.

see also entries 1643, 1667, 1682, 1683, 2395; Brown Rice; Wild Rice

Rice Flour

1916. Delicious and Easy Rice Flour Recipes: Gluten-Free: A Sequel to Gourmet Food on a Wheat-Free Diet / by Marion N. Wood; with a foreword by Margaret B. Salmon. Springfield, Ill.: C.C. Thomas, 1981. 160 p.

1917. The Joy of Gluten-Free Cooking / by Juanita Kisslinger; illustrated by Phillip Kisslinger. Rev. ed. Sidney, B.C.: Kisslinger Publications, 1987? 117 p., illus. Includes index. Also published under title: The Rice Flour Cookbook.

see also broader category: Grains

Ricotta Cheese

1918. Ricotta Recipes from Polly-O: Wonderful Ideas for the Most Versatile Cheese. Mineola, N.Y.: Pollio Dairy Products Corp., 1989. 1 booklet.

see also broader category: Cheese

Roses

1919. Rose Recipes from Olden Times / Eleanour Sinclair Rohde; decorated by Helen Kapp. New York: Dover Publications, 1973. 94 p. Reprint of the 1939 ed. published by Routledge, London, Eng., under title: Rose Recipes.

1920. Julia Clements Book of Rose Arrangements. New York: Arco Pub., 1984. 127 p., illus. (some colored). Includes index.

1921. Roses: Uses for the Rose, with Recipes & Suggestions / Recycling Consortium. Houston, Tex.: Prosperity & Profits, 1989. ca. 14 p.

see also broader category: **Flowers**

Rum

1922. The Rum Cookbook / by Willa M. Hoffman. Los Angeles, Calif.: Price Stern/Sloan Publishers, 1972. 79 p.

1923. The Rum Cookbook / Alex D. Hawkes. New York: Drake Publishers, 1973, c1972. 64 p., colored illus.

1924. Trader Vic's Rum Cookery and Drinkery / by Victor J. Bergeron, assisted by Shirley Sarvis; illustrations by Jane Walworth. 1st ed. Garden City, N.Y.: Doubleday, 1974. 229 p., illus.

1925. Stan Jones' Cooking with Bacardi Rum / by Stan Jones; with photography by John Guarente. Los Angeles, Calif.: Bar Guide Enterprises, c1982. 191 p., colored illus. Includes index.

1926. Caribbean Rum Book. Basingstoke, Eng.: Macmillan, 1985. 40 p., illus.

see also broader category: **Liquors**

Saffron

1927. Mediterranean Gold: The Historical Romance of Saffron, the World's Most Precious Spice, and an International Guide to Culinary Alchemy / Virginia Anne Strong-Church, Jennifer Church. Pleasant Hill, Calif. (2248 Morello Blvd., Pleasant Hill 94523): Strong-Church Enterprises, c1980. 96 p., illus.

see also broader category: Spices

Salmon

1928. Canned Salmon Delicacies / by Lola M. Cremeans. Rev. Fairbanks, Alaska: University of Alaska Cooperative Extension Service, 1981. 9 leaves.

1929. How to Improve Your Cooking with Canned Salmon: A Collection of Tasty, Inexpensive Salmon Dishes / by Rhonda Bilton. Detroit, Mich.: J. Stuart Pub. Co., c1981. 47 p., illus. Includes index.

1930. Smoking Salmon & Trout: Plus Pickling, Salting, Sausaging & Care / by Jack Whelan. Bowser, B.C.: Aerie Pub., c1982. 230 p., illus.

1931. Pacific Northwest Salmon Cookbook / Curt & Margie Smitch, Ron & Ellie Wagner. Olympia, Wash.: Northwest Resources, c1985. 164 p. Includes index.

1932. Simply Salmon: Fresh, Frozen and Canned / Linda Martinson. Seattle, Wash.: Lance Publications, 1986. 138 p.

1933. James McNair's Salmon Cookbook / photography by Patricia Brabant. San Francisco, Calif.: Chronicle Books, c1987. 96 p., illus. (some colored). ca. 35 recipes. Includes indexes.

1934. Salmon: International Chefs' Recipes / compiled by Willy Wyssenbach. New York: St. Martin's Press, 1987. 126 p.

Salmon *(Continued)*

1935. The Salmon Cookbook / by Jerry Dennon. 2nd ed. Seattle, Wash.: Pacific Search Press, 1987. 127 p., illus. Includes index.

1936. Salmon Is King: 250 Recipes for His Royal Highness / compiled and edited by Michael T. Skumavc; produced and marketed by Richard F. "Dick" Skumavc. Brainerd, Minn.: Lakes Area Speciality [sic] Recipes, RMS Enterprises, c1987. 202 p., illus. Includes index.

1937. Salmon Recipes / Cecilia G. Nibeck; illustrations, Barbara Lavallee. Anchorage, Alaska: AK Enterprises, c1987. 190 p., 3 leaves of plates, colored illus.

1938. Fresh Salmon / by R. Marilyn Schmidt. Barnegat Light, N.J.: Barnegat Light Press, 1988. 24 p.

1939. Ontario Salmon Fishing / by Darryl Choronzey. Wiarton, Ont.: Ontario Fisherman Publications, c1989. 168 p., illus. At head of title: All the Facts, How To, When To, and Where To for Ontario Salmon Fishing.

see also entry 522; and broader category: Fish

Sardines

1940. Steinbeck's Street, Cannery Row / by Maxine Knox and Mary Rodriguez. San Rafael, Calif.: Presidio Press, c1980. 97 p., illus.

see also broader category: Fish

Sausages

1941. The Sausage Book: Quick and Easy Recipes Anyone Can Make: New, Economical, and Excitingly Different Ways of Making Sausage / by a professional sausagemaker. Minneapolis, Minn.: Masterpiece Sausage Recipes, c1979. 120 p., illus.

1942. The Homemade Sausage Cookbook / Bertie Mayone Selinger and Bernadine Sellers Rechner; illustrations by Edward W. Rechner and Joel Rak; photographs by Bernadine M. Rechner. Chicago, Ill.: Contemporary Books, c1982. 184 p., illus. Includes index.

1943. The Sausage-Making Cookbook / Jerry Predika. Harrisburg, Pa.: Stackpole Books, c1983. 182 p., illus. Includes index.

1944. Sausages & Mince. Newton Abbot, Eng.: David & Charles, 1983. 64 p. (David & Charles Kitchen Workshop). Translation of: Kjottfarse- og Polseretter.

1945. 50th Anniversary Cookbook. West Point, Neb. (126 W. Grant, West Point 68788): Wimmer's Meat Products, c1984. 117 p., colored illus. Includes index.

1946. Sausages / David Mabey. London, Eng.: Piatkus, 1984. 95 p. Includes index.

1947. The Art and Secrets of Making Bratwurst the Old Fashion Way / by Mr. Bratwurst Meats & Sausages Ltd. Edmonton, Alta.: Mr. Bratwurst, c1986. 52 p., illus.

1948. Antony & Araminta Hippisley Coxe's Book of Sausages. Rev. and enl. ed. London, Eng.: V. Gollancz in association with P. Crawley, 1987. 250 p. Includes indexes.

Sausages *(Continued)*

1949. Great Sausage Recipes and Meat Curing / by Rytek Kutas; with sketches by Christine Engla Eber. New York: Macmillan; London, Eng.: Collier Macmillan, c1987. 503 p., illus. Includes index. Reprint. Originally published: Buffalo, N.Y.: Sausage Maker, c1984.

1950. Home Sausage Making / by Charles G. Reavis. Rev. ed. Pownal, Vt.: Storey Communications, c1987. 168 p., illus. "A Garden Way Publishing Book." Includes index.

1951. The Savory Sausage: A Culinary Tour Around the World / by Linda Merinoff; illustrations by Glenn Wolff. New York: Poseidon Press, c1987. 416 p., illus. Includes index.

1952. Cooking with Fresh Sausage / Charles Reavis. Pownal, Vt.: Garden Way Pub., c1988. 32 p. (Garden Way Publishing Bulletin; A-107).

1953. Jimmy Dean 20th Anniversary Recipe Book. Dallas, Tex.: Jimmy Dean Meat Co., 1989. 1 booklet.

1954. Hot Links & Country Flavors: Sausages in American Regional Cooking / by Bruce Aidells and Denis Kelly. 1st ed. New York: Knopf, 1990. 359 p., illus. 200 recipes, including 60 regional dishes. Includes index.

see also entries 1763, 1774, 1778; Frankfurters; *and broader categories:* Ground Meat; Meat; Pork

Scallions

see entries 866, 1606

Specific Ingredients 253

Scallops

1955. Scallops / by R. Marilyn Schmidt. Barnegat Light, N.J.: Barnegat Light Press, 1987. 20 p.

see also broader category: Shellfish

Sea Vegetables *see* Marine Algae

Seafood

1956. How to Smoke Seafood Florida Cracker Style / by Ted Dahlem. St. Petersburg, Fla.: Great Outdoors, c1971. 44 p., illus.

1957. Long Island Seafood Cook Book / by J. George Frederick; recipes edited by Jean Joyce. New York, Dover Publications, 1971. 324 p. Reprint of the 1939 ed.

1958. Maryland Seafood Cookbook. Annapolis, Md.: Seafood Marketing Authority, Dept. of Economic and Community Development, 1972-1982. 3 v., illus. (chiefly colored).

1959. Southern Fish and Seafood Cookbook / by Jan Wongrey. 3d ed. Lexington, S.C.: Sandlapper Pub., 1975. 141 p., illus.

1960. Preparing and Cooking Various Seafoods: Salmon, Halibut, Shrimp, Oysters, & Clams. Seattle, Wash.: Shorey Book Store, 1976. 61 p., illus. Facsimile reproduction of 5 U.S. Fish and Wildlife Service publications from their Test Kitchen Series, originally published from 1951? to 1956. Contents.--How to Cook Salmon / by Kathryn L. Osterhaug and Rose G. Kerr.--How to Cook Halibut / by Kathryn L. Osterhaug and Rose G. Kerr.--How to Cook Shrimp / by Jean Burtis and Rose G. Kerr.--How to Cook Oysters / by Rose G. Kerr and Jean Burtis.--How to Cook Clams / by Kathryn Osterhaug and Rose G. Kerr.

Seafood *(Continued)*

1961. The Encyclopedia of Fish Cookery / by A.J. McClane; photography by Arie deZanger; designed by Albert Squillace. 1st ed. New York: Holt, Rinehart and Winston, c1977. 511 p., 695 colored photos. 352 recipes. Includes index.

1962. The Seafood Book: A Complete Cook's Guide to Preparing and Cooking Fish and Shellfish / by Shirley Ross; illustrations by Beth Cannon. New York: McGraw-Hill, 1978, c1977. 177 p., illus. Includes index.

1963. Starchild & Holahan's Seafood Cookbook / Adam Starchild and James Holahan. Seattle, Wash.: Pacific Search Press, c1978. 228 p. Includes index.

1964. Fish and Shellfish: In the International Cuisine / editor, A.E. Simms; assistant editor, Mabel Quin; preface by John Fuller. New York: Van Nostrand Reinhold, 1979. 504 p., illus. Includes indexes.

1965. Mystic Seaport's Seafood Secrets Cookbook / edited by Ainslie Turner. Mystic, Conn.: Mystic Seaport Museum, 198? 246 p., illus. More than 400 recipes.

1966. The American Heritage Book of Fish Cookery / by Alice Watson Houston; drawings by James Houston. New York: American Heritage Pub. Co.; Book trade distribution by Scribner's, c1980. 224 p., illus. Includes indexes.

1967. Better Homes and Gardens All-Time Favorite Fish & Seafood Recipes / editor, Marcia Stanley. 1st ed. Des Moines, Iowa: Meredith Corp., c1980. 96 p., illus. Includes index.

1968. Catch 'em, Hook 'em, and Cook 'em / by Bunny Day; drawings by Grambs Miller. New York: Gramercy Pub. Co., 1980. 277 p., illus. Originally published in 2 v. by Doubleday, Garden City, N.Y., the 1st published in 1961 under title: Catch 'em and Cook 'em; the 2nd published in 1962 under title: Hook 'em and Cook 'em. Includes indexes.

Seafood *(Continued)*

1969. Food From the Seashore / by Kendall McDonald; line drawings by Kevin McDonald. London, Eng.: Pelham, 1980. 126 p., illus. Includes index.

1970. Gulf Fare: Favorite Seafood Recipes / compiled by Iris Garden Club of Wakulla County. Panacea, Fla.: The Club, 1980. 76 p., illus.

1971. McClane's North American Fish Cookery / A.J. McClane; photos. by Arie deZanger. 1st ed. New York: Holt, Rinehart and Winston, c1980. 242 p., illus. Includes index.

1972. The Waterfront Cookbook: Secrets of San Francisco Restaurant Chefs / Joseph Orlando. Rev. ed. San Francisco, Calif.: California Living Books, c1980. 140 p., illus. (A California Living Book). Includes index.

1973. The Beachcomber's Handbook of Seafood Cookery / Hugh Zachary; illustrated by Claude Howell. Winston-Salem, N.C.: J.F. Blair, 1981, c1969. 208 p., illus.

1974. Chinese Seafood Cooking / Stella Lau Fessler; illustrated by Janet Nelson. New York: New American Library, c1981. 308 p., illus. "A Plume Book." Includes index.

1975. The Complete South African Fish & Seafood Cookbook / Alicia Wilkinson. Johannesburg, South Africa: Central News Agency, c1981. 192 p., 24 p. of plates, illus. (some colored). Includes index.

1976. A Different Kettle of Fish: Traditional Seafood Recipes from Down East Kitchens. 1st ed. Halifax, N.S.: Book Room, c1981. 65 p., colored illus. Includes index.

1977. Dock to Dish: What to Do with a Fish: Long Island Seafood Secrets. Wildwood, N.J.: Eat More Fish, 1981. 34 p., illus.

Seafood *(Continued)*

1978. Fish and Shell-fish / editor, A.E. Simms; assistant editor, Mabel Quin; preface by John Fuller. 2nd rev. ed. London, Eng.: Virtue, 1981, c1973. 504 p., illus. Includes index. Translation by Steve Combes and John Galleymore of the 1969 French edition conceived, designed, and produced by René Kramer of Castagnola, Switzerland. Possibly a later ed. of: Fish and Shellfish, published in 1979 (entry 1964).

1979. Fish and Shellfish for Your Table / Charles E. Eshbach and Kirby M. Hayes. Honolulu, Hawaii: Cooperative Extension Service, College of Tropical Agriculture and Human Resources, University of Hawaii at Manoa, 1981. 1 v. Adapted by Frank B. Thomas for use in Hawaii.

1980. The Fish Book / Jeffrey A. Fisher; illustrations by John Silverio. Buchanan, N.Y.: Emerson Books, c1981. 128 p., illus.

1981. Island Cookery: Seafood Specialties and Alltime Favourites from Quadra Island British Columbia / Quadra Island Child Care Society. Quadra Island, B.C.: Ptarmigan Press, c1981. 214 p., illus. Includes index.

1982. Mediterranean Seafood / Alan Davidson. 2nd ed. Baton Rouge, La.: Louisiana State University Press, 1981. 432 p., illus. "A handbook giving the names in seven languages of 150 species of fish, with 50 crustaceans, molluscs and other marine creatures, and an essay on fish cookery, with over 200 recipes from the Mediterranean and Black Sea countries". Includes bibliography and indexes.

1983. The Seafood Kitchen / Judy Ridgway. London, Eng.: Ward Lock, 1981. 165 p., illus. (some colored). Includes index.

1984. The Family Cookbook for Fishes and Seafoods Recipes / by Connie Sta Maria. Manila, Philippines: Philippine Book Co., c1982. 138 p.

Specific Ingredients 257

Seafood *(Continued)*

1985. The Great East Coast Seafood Book / Yvonne Young Tarr; illustrations by Pat Stewart. 1st ed. New York: Vintage Books, c1982. 394 p., illus. Includes index.

1986. Hooked on Seafood / by Nana Whalen; interior illustrations by Debra McNabb Meteyer. Silver Spring, Md.: WRC Pub., c1982. 64 p., illus.

1987. Nova Scotia Seafood Cookery: From Canada's Atlantic Playground: The Fabled Bounty of the Deep. Halifax, N.S.: Province of Nova Scotia, Dept. of Fisheries, 1982. 167 p.

1988. Recipes of the Deep: Complete Fish and Seafood Cookery, Microwave and Conventional Methods / Terry Griffith. Memphis, Tenn.: Wimmer Bros. Fine Printing and Lithography, c1982. 94 p., illus. Includes index.

1989. Simple Sanibel Seafood / compiled by Margaret H. Greenberg and Nancy J. Olds. Sanibel Island, Fla.: Available from The Island Book Nook, c1982. 48 p., illus.

1990. 32 Seafood Dishes / by Marie Bianco. Woodbury, N.Y.: Barron's, c1983. 63 p., colored illus. (Easy Cooking). Includes index.

1991. Buying and Cooking Fish and Seafood / Marika Hanbury Tenison. Cambridge, Eng.: Published for J. Sainsbury by Woodhead-Faulkner, c1983. 32 p., illus. (Sainsbury's Food Guides; no. 12).

1992. The Canadian Fish Cook Book! / A. Jan Howarth. Vancouver, B.C.: Douglas & McIntyre in co-operation with the Dept. of Fisheries and Oceans and the Canadian Govt. Pub. Centre, Supply and Services Canada, c1983. 287 p., illus. (some colored). Includes index.

Seafood *(Continued)*

1993. Chinese Seafood / author, Tuan-hsi Shou; photographer, Kun-hung Lin; translator, Dah-Wen F. Ba. 1st ed. Taipei, Taiwan, R.O.C.: Hilit Pub. Co., 1983. 114 p., colored illus. (Highlight's Culinary Series).

1994. The Complete Fish Cookbook / by Jan Howarth. New York: St. Martin's Press, 1983. 287 p., illus. (some colored). Includes index.

1995. The Complete Seafood Book / James Wagenvoord and Woodman Harris. New York: Macmillan; London, Eng.: Collier Macmillan, c1983. 192 p., illus. "A James Wagenvoord Studio, Inc. Book." Includes indexes.

1996. Fish & Shellfish. Newton Abbot, Eng.: David & Charles, 1983. 64 p., colored illus. (Kitchen Workshop). Includes index. Translated from the Norwegian.

1997. The Fish & Shellfish Cookbook / illustrated by Sally Sisson Anderson. New York: Culinary Arts Institute, c1983. 80 p., illus. (some colored). (Adventures in Cooking Series). Includes index.

1998. Fish Without Fuss: Seafood Simplified / by Ginny Lentz for Golden Dipt Company. St. Louis, Mo.: Golden Dipt Co., c1983. 95 p., colored illus. Includes index.

1999. The Frank Davis Seafood Notebook / Frank Davis; foreword by Paul Prudhomme. Gretna, La.: Pelican Pub. Co., 1983. 272 p., illus. Includes index.

2000. Seafood. Los Angeles, Calif.: Knapp Press, c1983. 118 p., 16 p. of plates, colored illus. (Cooking with Bon Appétit). Includes index.

2001. Seafood Cookery from Prince Edward Island / by Julie Watson. Charlottetown, P.E.I.: Ragwood Press, 1983. 192 p. Includes index.

Seafood *(Continued)*

2002. Simply Seafood, Seafood Cookery Made Easy: Basics for Selection and Preparation of Seafood from the Gulf of Mexico to the Atlantic Provinces, with Recipes for Saltwater and Freshwater Fish and Shellfish / by Vicki Emmons. Freeport, Me.: DeLorme Pub. Co., c1983. 220 p., illus.

2003. A Taste of the Tropics / Joyce Wells; illustrations by John Doak. 1st ed. Markham, Ont.: PaperJacks, c1983. 150 p., illus. Includes index.

2004. The Underwater Gourmet: The Great Seafood Book: Best Seafood Recipes from Florida's Best Restaurants / Joyce LaFray-Young, Susan Shepard, Laura DeSalvo. 1st ed. St. Petersburg, Fla.: LaFray Pub. Co., c1983. 311 p., illus. (Famous Florida!).

2005. The Best of Marjorie Standish Seafood Recipes / Marjorie Standish. 1st ed. Portland, Me.: Gannett Books, c1984. 62 p., illus.

2006. Chinese Seafood / author, Huang Su-huei; translator, Lai Yen-jen; editor, Gloria C. Martinez; photographers, Aki Ohno, Wu Hua-sheng. Monterey Park, Calif.: Wei-Chuan's Cooking; Taipei, Taiwan, R.O.C.: Distributed by Sun-Chuan Pub. Co., c1984. 101 p., colored illus.

2007. Cooking Fish and Shellfish / Ruth A. Spear. 1st Ballantine Books ed. New York: Ballantine Books, 1984, c1980. 464 p., illus. Reprint. Originally published: Garden City, N.Y.: Doubleday, c1980. Includes index.

2008. Easy & Elegant Seafood / Jane Franke Hibler; color photos by Mike Henley. Portland, Or.: Frank Amato Publications, 1984. 142 p., illus.

Seafood *(Continued)*

2009. Fish & Seafood / by the editors of Consumer Guide. New York: Beekman House: Distributed by Crown Publishers, c1984. 80 p., illus. (some colored). (Favorite Brand Name Recipes). Includes index.

2010. Fish & Shellfish Menus. Alexandria, Va.: Time-Life Books, c1984. 105 p., illus. (some colored). (Great Meals in Minutes). Includes index.

2011. The Fish-lovers' Cookbook: More than 300 Kitchen-Tested Recipes / by Sheryl and Mel London; editor, Charles Gerras; illustration, Lutz Schmidt; photography, Carl Doney. Emmaus, Pa.: Rodale Press, 1984, c1980. 411 p., illus. Includes index.

2012. Free From the Sea: The South African Seafood Cookbook / Lannice Snyman and Anne Klarie. Cape Town, South Africa: Don Nelson, 1984. 134 p., illus. (some colored). First published 1979. "A complete alphabetical guide to the identification and preparation of South African fish, shellfish and molluscs."

2013. Fresh Seafood, the Commercial Buyer's Guide: Buying, Choosing, Handling, and Using Fresh Fish and Shellfish / Ian Dore. Huntington, N.Y.: Osprey Books, c1984. 375 p., illus. (Osprey Seafood Handbooks). Includes bibliography and indexes.

2014. The Gourmet's Guide to Fish and Shellfish / Ken Anderson. 1st Quill ed. New York: Quill, 1984. 128 p., illus. "A Quarto Book." Includes index.

2015. The Great Taste of Virginia Seafood: A Cookbook and Guide to Virginia Waters / written and edited by Mary Reid Barrow, with Robyn Browder; interior art by Connie Johnson. 1st ed. Hampton, Va.: GB Pub., 1984. 274 p., illus. (some colored). Includes index.

Seafood *(Continued)*

2016. Mad About Fish & Seafood / by Jacqueline Heriteau; illustrations by Woodleigh Hubbard. New York: Perigee Books, 1984. 63 p., illus. Includes index.

2017. Pacific Fresh: A Seafood Cookbook of Appetizers, Soups, Sauces, Salads, Entrées, and Casseroles, Including a Guide to Buying, Storing, Cleaning, and Cooking Seafood / by Maryana Vollstedt. Eugene, Or.: Cookbook Factory, 1984. 126 p., illus. Cover title: Pacific Fresh Seafood Cookbook.

2018. The Rappahannock Seafood Cookbook / compiled and edited by Rappahannock Community College. Warsaw, Va.: Rappahannock Community College Educational Foundation, Inc., 1984. 157 p. Includes index.

2019. Seafood Celebration: In Commemoration of Prince Rupert's 75th Birthday. Prince Rupert, B.C.: Prince Rupert 75th Birthday Committee, 1984. 143 p., colored illus.

2020. The Seafood Cookbook / Frederick E. Kahn. New York: Nautilus Communications, c1984. 152 p. (Preparing Food the Healthy Way Series). Includes index.

2021. Seafood Favorites / recipes from authors and staff of International Marine Pub. Co. Camden, Me.: The Company, c1984. 118 p., illus. Includes index.

2022. The Seafood Heritage Cookbook / Adam Starchild. 1st ed. Centreville, Md.: Tidewater Publishers, c1984. 182 p. Includes index.

2023. The Southern Heritage Sea and Stream Cookbook. Birmingham, Ala.: Oxmoor House, c1984. 143 p., illus. (some colored). (The Southern Heritage Cookbook Library). Includes index.

Seafood *(Continued)*

2024. American Seafood Cooking: The Best of Regional Recipes / George Kerhulas. New York: Exeter Books, 1985. 223 p., illus. (some colored). Includes index.

2025. Annette Annechild's Seafood Wok / Annette Annechild with Captain BJ; illustrated by Cristina Eisenberg. New York: Pocket Books, c1985. 157 p., illus. "A Wallaby Book." Includes index.

2026. A Cape Cod Seafood Cookbook / Margaret Deeds Murphy; drawings by Harold Durand White. Orleans, Mass.: Parnassus Imprints, c1985. 157 p., illus. Includes index.

2027. Catch of the Day: Southern Seafood Secrets / Ginny Lentz. Charlotte, N.C.: East Woods Press, 1985. 123 p., illus.

2028. Edible? Incredible! / text, photographs and scientific material by Virginia Pill and Marjorie Furlong. 5th ed. Seattle, Wash.: Pill Enterprises, 1985. 73 p., colored illus. Includes index.

2029. Fish & Shellfish / Lonnie Gandara, writer; Anne Coolman, Jill Fox, editors; Jackson Vereen, photographer. San Francisco, Calif.: Ortho Information Services, c1985. 128 p., colored illus. (California Culinary Academy Series). Includes index.

2030. Fish and Their Sauces / Jehane Benoît. Saint-Lambert, Que.: Heritage, 1985. 110 p., illus. (Encyclopedia of Microwave Cooking; 3). Issued also in French under the title: Les poissons et leurs sauces.

2031. The Harrowsmith Fish & Seafood Cookbook / by the editors & readers of Harrowsmith Magazine. Camden East, Ont.: Camden House, c1985. 235 p., illus. Includes index.

2032. Icelandic Seafood: Chef's Choice / edited by Sigmar B. Hauksson; translator, Paul Richardson. Reykjavik, Iceland: Matur & Menning, 1985. 85 p., illus.

Seafood *(Continued)*

2033. Living Off the Sea / Charles White; technical illustrations by Nelson Dewey; fish drawings by Chris Sherwood. Vancouver, B.C.: Special Interest Publications, 1985. 126 p., illus. (BC Outdoors Saltaire Series).

2034. Perfect Cooking with Seafood / Jennifer Stead. Twickenham, Eng.: Hamlyn, 1985, c1983. 31 p., illus.

2035. Seafood As We Like It / Anthony Spinazzola and Jean-Jacques Paimblanc; illustrations by Janet Cummings Good. 1st ed. Chester, Conn.: Globe Pequot Press, c1985. 477 p., illus. More than 250 recipes. Includes index.

2036. Sunshine Coast Seafood: A Collection of Recipes Using Locally Available Seafood / Grace Taylor, Wendy Rogers, Lauren Armstrong. Delta, B.C.: G. Taylor, 1985. 127 p., illus. Includes index. Also published: Halfmoon Bay, B.C.: Arbutus Bay Publications, 1985.

2037. All-Maine Seafood Cookbook / compiled and edited by Loana Shibles and Annie Rogers, with new recipes compiled by Raquel Boehmer. 2nd ed. Camden, Me.: Down East Books, 1986. 187 p., illus. Includes index.

2038. Better Homes and Gardens Fish & Seafood / editor, Gerald M. Knox; fish and seafood contributing editor, Lorene Frohling. 1st ed. Des Moines, Iowa: Meredith Corp., c1986. 128 p., colored illus. (Great Cooking Made Easy). Includes index.

2039. Cooking the Shore Catch / R. Marilyn Schmidt. Barnegat Light, N.J.: Barnegat Light Press, c1986. 132 p., illus. Includes index.

2040. Famous Brands Fish & Seafood Cookbook. St. Louis, Mo.: Brand Name Pub. Corp., 1986. ca. 128 p., colored illus. (Famous Brands Cookbook Library). Includes index.

Seafood *(Continued)*

2041. Fish & Seafood / written by Judith Ferguson. Guildford, Eng.: Coombe Books, c1986. 64 p., illus. Includes index.

2042. Fishing for Compliments / Jan Keeshen. San Luis Obispo, Calif.: Creative Cuisine, 1986. 1 v. Subtitle on cover: Creative Seafood Cuisine. Includes index. [Publication of this book has not been verified].

2043. Fresh Ways with Fish & Shellfish / by the editors of Time-Life Books. Alexandria, Va.: Time-Life Books, c1986. 144 p., colored illus. (Healthy Home Cooking). Includes index.

2044. From Sea & Stream / Lou Seibert Pappas; illustrations by Marinell & Robert Harriman. San Francisco, Calif.: 101 Productions; New York: Distributed in the U.S. by Macmillan, c1986. 144 p., illus. Rev. ed. of: International Fish Cookery. c1979. Includes index.

2045. Great Seafood Dishes / Antonio Piccinardi; translated from the Italian by Elaine Hardy. New York: Crescent Books, 1986. 191 p., illus. (some colored). Translation of: Piatti de mare. Includes index.

2046. Jean Conil's French Fish Cuisine: Gourmet French Fish Recipes / from Jean Conil with Fay Franklin; colour photography and styling by Paul Turner and Sue Pressly. Wellingborough, Eng.: Thorsons, 1986. 192 p., illus. (some colored). Includes index.

2047. A Louisiana Seafood Cookbook / recipes from Louisiana Sea Grant. Baton Rouge, La.: Louisiana Sea Grant, Center for Wetlands Resources, Louisiana State University, 1986. 99 p. Includes index.

2048. The New Zealand Fish and Shellfish Cookbook / Heather Currie, Susan Marris, Jennifer Brasted; New Zealand Fishing Industry Board. Christchurch, N.Z.; London, Eng.: Whitcoulls, 1986. 152 p., illus. (some colored). Includes index.

Seafood *(Continued)*

2049. The Seafish Cookbook / Susan Hicks. Twickenham, Eng.: Hamlyn in association with the Sea Fish Industry Authority, 1986. 192 p., illus. (some colored). Includes index.

2050. The Seafood Cookbook: Classic to Contemporary / Pierre Franey & Bryan Miller; illustrations by Lauren Jarrett. 1st ed. New York: Times Books, c1986. 296 p., 9 p. of plates, illus. 300 recipes. Includes index.

2051. Seafood Secrets: A Nutritional Guide to Seafood / R. Marilyn Schmidt. 2nd ed. Barnegat Light, N.J.: Barnegat Light Press, c1986. 120 p., illus. Includes index.

2052. The Stephen Yan's Seafood Wokbook / Stephen Yan. Toronto, Ont.: Key Porter Books, 1986. 162 p., colored illus. Includes index.

2053. 101 Simple Seafood Recipes / by Pam and Bill Collins. Edmonds, Wash.: Alaska Northwest Pub. Co., c1987. 148 p., illus. Includes index.

2054. The Cape Cod Seafood Cookbook / Noel W. Beyle. Orleans, Mass.: First Encounter Press, 1987. 48 p., illus.

2055. Alaska's Seafood Cookbook. Juneau, Alaska: Alaska Seafood Marketing Institute, 1987? 60 p., illus.

2056. Ann Clark's Fabulous Fish: Easy and Exciting Ways to Cook and Serve Seafood / by Ann Clark. New York: New American Library, c1987. 250 p. 200 recipes. Includes index.

2057. Bargain Seafoods: How to Cook the Underutilized Species / R. Marilyn Schmidt. Barnegat Light, N.J.: Barnegat Light Press, c1987. 92 p.

Seafood *(Continued)*

2058. Fish and Shellfish / by George Lassalle; illustrated by Alan Cracknell. 1st American ed. New York: Pantheon Books, 1987. 93 p., colored illus. (A Pantheon Classic Cookbook). Reprint. Originally published: London, Eng.: Walker Books, 1986. Includes index.

2059. Great Seafood Recipes from the Grand Central Oyster Bar & Restaurant / introduction by Jerome Brody; illustrated by Richard Sommers. New York: Crown Publishers, 1987, c1977. 192 p., illus. Includes index. Previously published as: The Grand Central Oyster Bar & Restaurant Seafood Cookbook.

2060. Grilled Fish and Seafood / Pol Martin. Montreal, Que.: Brimar, c1987. 64 p. (Smart & Simple Cooking).

2061. Predominantly Fish: New Interpretations for Cooking Fish and Shellfish / Nancy Longo. Baltimore, Md.: Fissurelle Publishers, c1987. 121 p., illus. Includes index.

2062. Quick & Easy Microwaving Seafood / Microwave Cooking Institute. Minnetonka, Minn.: Cy DeCosse, 1987. 96 p., illus. Includes index.

2063. Seafood Adventures from the Gulf and South Atlantic / edited and prepared by Bertha V. Fontaine and Sue Turner, Annette Reddell, and the Virginia Seafood Council. Tampa, Fla.: Gulf and South Atlantic Fisheries Development Foundation, 1987. 72 p., illus. (some colored). "This publication was partially supported by the Economic Development Administration, National Marine Fisheries Service and Coastal Plains Regional Commission."

2064. Seafood and Health / Joyce A. Nettleton. Huntington, N.Y.: Osprey Books, c1987. 234 p. Includes indexes.

2065. Seafood Microwave Cookery / Joanna Farrow. London, Eng.: Grub Street, 1987. 128 p. Includes index.

Seafood *(Continued)*

2066. Seafood Smoking / R. Marilyn Schmidt. Barnegat Light, N.J.: Barnegat Light Press, 1987. 58 p., illus. Includes index.

2067. Seashore Entertaining / Naomi Black. Philadelphia, Pa.: Courage Books, c1987. 144 p., colored illus. Includes bibliography and index.

2068. The Umberto Menghi Seafood Cookbook / by Umberto Menghi with Ron Lammie. Toronto, Ont.: Key Porter Books, c1987. 200 p., colored illus. Includes index.

2069. The WI Book of Fish and Seafood: Over 100 Recipes Tried and Tested by the Women's Institute / Mary Norwak; illustrated by Vanessa Luff. London, Eng.: Ebury Press, 1987. 96 p., illus. Includes index.

2070. Barbecuing Atlantic Seafood / by Julie Watson. Halifax, N.S.: Nimbus, 1988. 100 p., illus. Includes index.

2071. Better Homes and Gardens Fish & Seafood. 1st ed. Des Moines, Iowa: Meredith Corp., c1988. 48 p., colored illus. Includes index.

2072. The California Seafood Cookbook: A Cook's Guide to the Fish and Shellfish of California, the Pacific Coast, and Beyond / by Isaac Cronin, Jay Harlow, and Paul Johnson; illustrated by Amy Portschuk. Reading, Mass.: Addison-Wesley, 1988, c1983. 288 p., illus. "Aris Books." Includes index.

2073. The Chesapeake Bay Fish & Fowl Cookbook: A Collection of Old and New Recipes from Maryland's Eastern Shore / by Joan and Joe Foley. New York: Weathervane Books: Distributed by Crown Publishers, 1988, c1981. 175 p., illus. Includes index. Reprint. Originally published: New York: Macmillan, 1981.

2074. Dave Hopfer's Fresh-water Fish Cookbook: With Crayfish and Sauces. Turner, Or.: Dave Hopfer Enterprises, c1988. 1 v.

Seafood *(Continued)*

2075. The Edible Seashore: Pacific Shores Cookbook & Guide / Rick M. Harbo. Surrey, B.C.: Hancock House, c1988. 62 p., colored illus. Includes index.

2076. English Seafood Dishes / Richard Stein. Harmondsworth, Eng.: Penguin, 1988. 288 p.

2077. A Feast of Fishes / by Elizabeth H. Bray and others; illustrations by Judith Dufour Love. 1st ed. Chester, Conn.: Globe Pequot Press, 1988. 310 p., illus. More than 250 recipes. On spine: New England Aquarium. Includes index.

2078. The Fish Book: A Seafood Menu Cookbook / by Kelly McCune; designed by Thomas Ingalls; photography by Victor Budnik; food styling by Sandra Cook. 1st ed. New York: Perennial Library, c1988. 126 p., colored illus. More than 30 recipes and 25 menus. Includes index.

2079. The Fishmonger Cookbook: From a New England Neighborhood Fish Market: An Expert's Guide to Selecting, Preparing, Cooking, & Serving the Very Best Fish & Seafood / by Dorothy Batchelder. 1st ed. Dublin, N.H.: Yankee Books, c1988. 320 p., illus. Includes index.

2080. Gourmet Seafood Entrees / William A. Pizzico, Gina Marie Corporation. New York: Modern Pub., Division of Unisystems Inc., 1988. 64 p., illus. (Convenient Cooking). Includes index.

2081. The Great American Seafood Cookbook / by Susan Herrmann Loomis; illustrations by Jamie Hogan; preparation illustrations by Wendy Wray. New York: Workman Pub., 1988. 320 p., illus. 250 recipes. At head of title: From Sea to Shining Sea. Includes index.

2082. The Jewel Lake Seafood Market Cookbook / Linette Hoglund; illustrations by Glenn Wolff. New York: Simon & Schuster, c1988. 221 p., illus. "A Fireside Book." Includes index.

Specific Ingredients

Seafood *(Continued)*

2083. The Joy of Seafood / Patrice Boely. New York: Barron's, c1988. 210 p., 46 p. of plates, illus. (some colored). Includes index.

2084. Just Hooked / compiled and tested by Gaye Hansen. North Vancouver, B.C.: G. Hansen, c1988. 60 p.

2085. The Legal Sea Foods Cookbook / George Berkowitz and Jane Doerfer; illustrations by Bruce Hutchinson. 1st ed. New York: Doubleday, 1988. 182 p., illus. Includes index.

2086. The Lighthouse Cookbook / Anita Stewart. Madeira Park, B.C.: Harbour Pub., c1988. 150 p., illus.

2087. An Ocean of Flavor: The Japanese Way with Fish and Seafood / Elizabeth Andoh; illustrated by Isabel Samaras. 1st ed. New York: Morrow, c1988. 272 p., illus. Includes index.

2088. Off the Hook: A Cook's Tour of Coastal Connecticut / presented by the Junior League of Stamford-Norwalk, Inc.; illustrations by Amy Lamb. 1st ed. Darien, Conn.: JLSN Books, 1988. 214 p., illus. Includes index.

2089. Raquel's Main Guide to New England Seafoods / Raquel Boehmer; illustrated by Brian A. Hubbard. Monhegan Island, Me.: Seafood Soundings Press, c1988. 32 p., illus.

2090. Seafood. Toronto, Ont.: Grolier, 1988. 110 p., colored illus. (Microwave Magic; 6). Includes index.

2091. Southern Seafood Classics: The Official Cookbook of the Southeastern Fisheries Association. Atlanta, Ga.: Peachtree Publishers, c1988. 272 p., illus. (some colored). Includes index.

2092. The Summertime Cookbook / editorial consultants, Sandra Madsen, Claudia O'Brien; photographer, Ashley Mackevicius. Los Angeles, Calif.: California Magazines, c1988. 123 p., colored illus. (Look & Cook Library). Includes index.

Seafood *(Continued)*

2093. The Taste of Seafood / Antonio Piccinardi. Exeter, Eng.: Webb & Bower, 1988. 191 p.

2094. 1001 Nights of Seafood Delights / by Elaine Blohm Jordan. 1st ed. LaGrange, Ga.: Jordan Ink Pub. Co., c1989. 208 p., illus. Includes index.

2095. The Best of Thai Seafood / editor, Richard Goldrick. 2nd ed. Bangkok, Thailand: Nidda Hongwiwat: Distributed by Index Book Promotion & Service, 1989. 192 p., chiefly colored illus. Includes bibliography.

2096. Catch of the Day: A Fish Cookbook / Carol Cutler and the editors of Consumer Reports Books. Mount Vernon, N.Y.: Consumers Union of United States, c1989. 224 p. More than 100 recipes. Contains information on buying, storing, cleaning, and filleting.

2097. The Complete Book of American Fish and Shellfish Cookery / Elizabeth Bjornskov; with illustrations by the author. New York: Weathervane Books: Distributed by Crown, 1989, c1984. 481 p., 126 line drawings. More than 680 recipes. Reprint. Originally published: New York: A.A. Knopf, 1984. Includes index.

2098. Dock to Dish: What to Do with a Fish: New England Seafood Secrets. Wildwood, N.J. (P.O. Box 1287, Wildwood 08260): Lored Enterprises, c1989. 34 p., illus.

2099. Favorite Seafood Recipes: A Complete Guide to Seafood Buying, Storage and Preparation / by Sally Murphy Morris. 1st ed. Concord, Calif.: Nitty Gritty Productions, 1989, c1983. 183 p., 24 p. of plates, illus. (some colored). Includes index.

2100. Fish & Seafood Made Easy. Washington, D.C.: U.S. Dept. of Commerce, National Fish & Seafood Promotional Council, 1989. 28 p., colored illus.

Seafood *(Continued)*

2101. Glorious Fish in the Microwave / Patricia Tennison. Chicago, Ill.: Contemporary Books, c1989. 336 p., illus. More than 200 recipes.

2102. The Health-Lover's Guide to Super Seafood: 250 Delicious Ways to Enjoy the Ultimate in Natural Nutrition / Tom Ney; photography by the Rodale Press Photography Department. Emmaus, Pa.: Rodale Press, c1989. 282 p., illus. (some colored). ca. 250 recipes. Includes index.

2103. Light-Hearted Seafood: Tasty, Quick, Healthy / Janis Harsila and Evie Hansen. Richmond Beach, Wash.: National Seafood Educators, 1989. 159 p. 100 recipes.

2104. No-Salt Seafood: All the Flavor without the Salt / by Joyce Taylor. Raleigh, N.C.: UNC Sea Grant College Program, 1989. 35 p., illus. (UNC Sea Grant Publication; 89-07).

2105. North Atlantic Seafood / Alan Davidson. New York: Harper & Row, 1989. 512 p., illus. Includes bibliography and index.

2106. The Official Fulton Fish Market Cookbook / Bruce Beck; photographs by Richard Lord. 1st ed. New York: Dutton, c1989. 381 p., 8 p. of plates, colored illus. More than 150 recipes. Includes index.

2107. Outdoor Cooking and Grilled Fish / by Pol Martin. New York: Eclair Pub. International, 1989. 128 p., colored illus. Includes index.

2108. Sea to Shore: Caribbean Charter Yacht Recipes: A Cook's Guide to Fish Cookery / author and publisher, Jan Robinson; illustrator/cartoonist, Raida Ahmad. Charlotte, N.C.: For copies write to Ship to Shore, 1989, c1988. 288 p. More than 250 fish and shellfish recipes from 80 international Caribbean charter yacht chefs.

Specialty Cookbooks

Seafood *(Continued)*

2109. Seafood: A Connoisseur's Guide and Cookbook / Alan Davidson; illustrations by Charlotte Knox; edited and designed by Mitchell Beazley International Ltd. New York: Simon and Schuster, c1989. 208 p., 80 watercolor paintings. 145 recipes. Includes index.

2110. Seafood Cookery: Nutritious and Delicious / Shizuko Yoshida. Briarcliff Manor, N.Y.: Japan Publications, 1989. 176 p. 93 recipes.

2111. Seafood Cooking for Your Health / by Shizuko Yoshida. 1st ed. Tokyo, Japan; New York: Japan Publications; New York: Distributors, United States, Kodansha International, c1989. 147 p., illus. (some colored). Includes index.

2112. Seafood Lover's Cookbook. Minneapolis, Minn.: General Mills, 1989. 91 p., colored illus. (Betty Crocker Creative Recipes; no. 35). Includes index.

2113. Seafood Sampler / Jan Siegrist. Shelburne, Vt.: New England Press, 1989. 48 p., illus.

2114. Sunset Fish & Shellfish / by the editors of Sunset Books and Sunset Magazine. 1st ed. Menlo Park, Calif.: Lane Pub. Co., c1989. 128 p., colored illus. Includes index.

2115. Sunset Seafood Cook Book / by the editors of Sunset Books and Sunset Magazine; illustrations, John Lytle, Susan Jaekel; photography, Tom Wyatt. 5th ed. Menlo Park, Calif.: Lane Pub. Co., c1989. 96 p., illus. (some colored). More than 120 recipes. Includes index.

2116. Best Recipes for Fish and Shellfish. 1st ed. New York: Prentice Hall, c1990. 112 p., illus. (chiefly colored). (Betty Crocker's Red Spoon Collection). Includes index.

Seafood *(Continued)*

2117. The Compleat Fish Cook: 100 Delicious Recipes for Grilling, Sautéing, Broiling, Panfrying, Smoking, and More / Barbara Grunes and Phyllis Magida. Chicago, Ill.: Contemporary Books, Inc., c1990. 152 p. Includes index.

2118. The Complete Cookbook of American Fish and Shellfish / Jean F. Nicolas. 2nd ed. New York: Van Nostrand Reinhold, c1990. 480 p., illus. Includes index.

2119. Fish: The Basics / Shirley King; illustrations by Glenn Wolff. New York: Simon & Schuster, 1990. 464 p., illus. Contains information about more than 150 different kinds of fish and shellfish. Includes bibliography and index.

2120. Fish and Seafood / Annette Wolter. New York: Crescent Books, 1990. 125 p., 150 colored photos. 150 recipes. (Good Cook's Library). Includes index. Published originally under the title: Fisch.

2121. The Great Book of Seafood Cooking / Giuliana Bonomo; photographs by Riccardo Marsialis. New York: International Culinary Society, 1990, c1989. 319 p., 200 colored illus. More than 500 recipes. Includes index. Translated from the Italian by Sara Harris.

2122. Revised Seafood Secrets: A Nutritional Guide to Seafood / R. Marilyn Schmidt. Barnegat Light, N.J.: Barnegat Light Press, 1990? 121 p., illus. Includes index.

2123. Seafood: A Collection of Heart-Healthy Recipes / Janis Harsila & Evie Hansen. 2nd ed., newly rev. & expanded. Richmond Beach, Wash.: National Seafood Educators, 1990. 276 p., illus. Includes bibliography and index. "Recipes for good health & weight loss."

2124. Seafood Menus for the Microwave: Full-Course Meals in a Flash / Julie V. Watson. Halifax, N.S.: Nimbus Pub., c1990. 81 p., illus. Includes index.

Seafood *(Continued)*

2125. Seafood of Australia & New Zealand: A Comprehensive Guide to Its Preparation and Cooking / John Goode and Carol Willson; photographs by Per Ericson. North Ryde, N.S.W., Australia: Angus & Robertson, 1990. 181 p.

2126. The Wainscott Seafood Shop Cookbook / Beth Harris with John Haessler. New York: Random House, 1990. 288 p., illus. 250 recipes from Beth Harris's eastern Long Island fish market and gourmet shop. Includes index.

see also entries 263, 1220, 1380, 1416, 1844, 1851; Fish; Shellfish

Seeds

see entries 913, 1567, 2202; specific seeds: Sesame Seeds, *etc.; and broader category:* Natural Foods

Sesame Seeds

2127. Juel Andersen's Sesame Primer: A Compendium of Sesame Seed Cookery / Juel Andersen with Sigrid Andersen. Berkeley, Calif.: Creative Arts Communications, c1983. 63 p., illus. Includes index.

Shad

2128. Shad and Shad Roe / by R. Marilyn Schmidt. Barnegat Light, N.J.: Barnegat Light Press, 1989. 24 p.

see also broader category: Fish

Shallots

see entries 877, 1606

Specific Ingredients 275

Sharks

2129. The Shark Cookbook / by Paula Andersen; with illustrations by Mark Bryan. Santa Barbara, Calif.: Water Table Press; Berkeley, Calif.: Distributed by Book People, 1975. 55 p., illus. Includes index.

2130. Shark, Sea Food of the Future: Gourmet Sea Food Cook-Book: Excellent for any Catch of the Day / by Eddy Hovey; artwork, Gary McGee; photography, Barry Edmonds. 1st ed. Grand Blanc, Mich.: Sea Harvest Press, c1980. 112 p., illus. Includes index.

2131. Cook's Book: A Guide to the Handling and Eating of Sharks and Skates / by Sid F. Cook; illustrated by Dawn Conway. Corvallis, Or.: G.A. Bonham: Distributor, Cook's Book, c1985. 106 p., illus. "A GAB Books Publication." Includes index.

2132. Mako Shark / by R. Marilyn Schmidt. Barnegat Light, N.J.: Barnegat Light Press, 1985. 20 p.

see also broader category: Fish

Shellfish

2133. Molluscan Melange, or, All About Edible Molluscs Around the World, with Numerous Recipes for Their Preparation / by Alex Roth, Jr. Tamuning, Guam: Aljemasu Enterprises, 1980. 148 p., illus. Includes index.

2134. The Complete Shellfisherman's Guide / David Tedone; illustrated by Art Ciccone. Old Saybrook, Conn.: Peregrine Press, c1981. 199 p., illus., maps. Includes index.

2135. Savory Shellfish Recipes of the Shore / Joanne van Roden. Hellam, Pa.: Wellspring, c1981. 36 p., illus.

Shellfish *(Continued)*

2136. The Shellfish Cookbook: The Definitive Shellfish Cookbook with More Than 200 New and Traditional Recipes / by Arthur and Nancy Hawkins. New York: Hastings House, c1981. 213 p., illus. Includes index.

2137. Shellfish Heritage Cookbook: A Collection of Old Prints, Photographs & Current Recipes / compiled by Robert H. Robinson. Georgetown, Del. (115 N. Race St., Georgetown 19947): Shellfish Digest Series, c1981. 1 v., illus. (Shellfish Digest; v. 4, no. 7). Includes index.

2138. Secrets of Potfishing / by Edward R. Riccuiti. Killingworth, Conn.; Surrey, B.C.: Hancock House, c1982. 75 p., illus. (Hancock House Fishing Series).

2139. Shellfish / by the editors of Time-Life Books. Alexandria Va.: Time-Life Books; Morristown, N.J.: School and library distribution by Silver Burdett, c1982. 176 p., illus. (some colored). (The Good Cook, Techniques & Recipes). Includes index.

2140. The Essential Book of Shellfish / by Robert H. Robinson. Cockeysville, Md.: Liberty Pub. Co., 1983. 153 p., illus. Includes index.

2141. Marine Mollusks of Cape Cod / text by Donald J. Zinn; illustrations by Terry Ellis. 1st ed. Brewster, Mass.: Cape Cod Museum of Natural History, 1984. 78 p., illus. Includes index.

2142. The Simply Seafood Cookbook of East Coast Shellfish / by R. Marilyn Schmidt. 2nd ed. Barnegat Light, N.J.: Barnegat Light Press, c1984? 159 p., illus. 180 recipes. Includes index.

2143. Cooking with Oysters and Other Shellfish / compiled and edited by George and Marianne Preston in celebration of the 1985 Oyster Festival. East Norwich, N.Y. (P.O. Box 103, East Norwich 11732): Cuisine Avec Panache, c1985. 66 p., illus. Includes index.

Shellfish *(Continued)*

2144. How to Catch Shellfish / by Charles White; illustrated by Nelson Dewey. Updated. Vancouver, B.C.: Special Interest Publications, c1985. 144 p., illus. (BC Outdoors Saltaire Series).

2145. Shellfish Cookery: Absolutely Delicious Recipes from the West Coast / by John Doerper. Seattle, Wash.: Pacific Search Press, c1985. 269 p., illus. Includes index.

2146. Shellfish: The Art of Shellfish Cookery with an Illustrated Directory / Anton Mosimann, Holger Hofmann. 1st U.S. ed. New York: Hearst Books, 1987. 206 p., illus. (some colored). Includes index. Translation of: Das Grosse Buch der Meeresfruchte.

2147. Heaven on the Half Shell: Edible Treasures from the Sea / Tom Chapman. San Francisco, Calif.: Chronicle Books, 1988. 1 v. Includes index. [Publication of this book has not been verified].

2148. Shellfish on the Grill: More Than 80 Easy and Delectable Recipes for Lobster, Shrimp, Scampi, Scallops, Oysters, Clams, Mussels, Crab, and More / Phyllis Magida and Barbara Grunes. Chicago, Ill.: Contemporary Books, c1988. 138 p., illus. Includes index.

2149. Shellfish: 85 Recipes for Lobsters, Shrimps, Scallops, Crabs, Clams, Mussels, Oysters, and Squid / by Michele Scicolone. New York: Harmony Books, 1989. 96 p., illus. "A Particular Palate Cookbook." Includes index.

2150. A Gourmet's Guide to Shellfish / Mary Cadogan; photography by David Gill. Los Angeles, Calif.: HP Books, 1990. 120 p., 280 colored photos.

Shellfish *(Continued)*

2151. Howard Mitchell's Clams, Mussels, Oysters, Scallops, & Snails. Orleans, Mass.: Parnassus Imprints, c1990. 215 p. Includes index.

see also specific kinds of shellfish: Abalone, Clams, Conch, Crabs, Crawfish, Lobsters, Mussels, Oysters, Scallops, Shrimp, Snails; *and broader category:* Seafood

Sherry

2152. Sherry, the Golden Wine of Spain / Cork Millner. White Hall, Va.: Betterway Publications, c1984. 153 p., illus. (some colored). ca. 24 drink recipes and ca. 36 food recipes. Includes indexes.

see also broader category: Wine

Shortening

2153. Crisco's Good Cooking Made Easy Cookbook. Cincinnati, Ohio: Proctor and Gamble, Inc., 1980. 1 booklet.

Shrimp

2154. The Little Shrimp Cookbook / Mary L. Green. Denver, Colo.: Giftstar, 1984. ca. 10 p., illus. (Little Cookbooks).

2155. The Shrimp Lover's Cookbook / by William G. Flagg. Croton-on-Hudson, N.Y.: North River Press: Distributed by Dodd, Mead, c1984. 114 p., illus.

2156. The Art of Catching and Cooking Shrimp / Lynette L. Walther. Georgetown, Del.: Sussex Prints, 1986. 120 p., illus.

Shrimp *(Continued)*

2157. Shrimp / by Jay Harlow; photography by Victor Budnik; food styling by Karen Hazarian. San Francisco, Calif.: Chronicle Books, 1989. 116 p., colored illus. More than 60 recipes. Includes bibliography and index.

2158. Simply Shrimp! / by R. Marilyn Schmidt. Barnegat Light, N.J.: Barnegat Light Press, 1989. 132 p., illus. Includes index.

2159. Simply Shrimp / Glenn Day. Freedom, Calif.: Crossing Press, 1990. 180 p., illus. ca. 120 recipes. Includes index.

see also broader category: Shellfish

Skates

see entry 2132

Snails

2160. A Guide to Common Whelks / text by Arnold G. Eversole and William D. Anderson; illustrations by D. Bryan Stone III; recipes by Donna S. Florio. Charleston, S.C.: South Carolina Sea Grant Consortium, c1985? 25 p., illus. Includes bibliography.

2161. To Cook a Snail / Roy and Phyll Groves. Colwyn Bay, Wales: Snail Centre, c1988. 112 p.

see also broader category: Shellfish

Soba (Buckwheat Noodles)

2162. The Book of Soba / James Udesky, with a foreword by William Shurtleff. 1st ed. Tokyo, Japan; New York: Kodansha International, c1988. 166 p., illus. (some colored). Includes index.

see also broader category: Pasta

Sour Cream

see entry 172; and broader category: Dairy Products

Sourdough

2163. Adventures in Sourdough Cooking and Baking / Charles D. Wilford. South San Francisco, Calif.: Gold Rush Sourdough Co., 1971. 275 p., illus.

2164. The Complete Sourdough Cookbook for Camp, Trail, and Kitchen: Authentic and Original Sourdough Recipes from the Old West / by Don and Myrtle Holm. Caldwell, Idaho: Caxton Printers, 1972. 136 p., illus.

2165. Alaska Sourdough / Ruth Allman. Anchorage, Alaska: Alaska Northwest Pub. Co., 1976. 190 p., illus.

2166. Sourdough Cookin' / by Dean Tucker. Salt Lake City, Utah: Hawkes Pub. Co., c1976. 72 p.

2167. Sourdough Cookery. Sea Cliff, N.Y.: Carbooks, Inc. 1980. 1 v. "220 breads, rolls, pancakes and more."

2168. Sourdough Cookery / by Rita Davenport. Tucson, Ariz.: HP Books, c1981. 160 p., colored illus. Later ed. of: Rita Davenport's Sourdough Cookery. Includes index.

Sourdough *(Continued)*

2169. Sourdough Breads and Coffee Cakes: 104 Recipes Using Homemade Starters / by Ada Lou Roberts; drawings by Françoise Webb. New York: Dover Publications, 1983, c1967. 192 p., illus. Reprint. Originally published: Breads and Coffee Cakes with Homemade Starters from Rose Lane Farm. New York: Hearthside Press, 1967. With minor updated corrections. Includes index.

2170. World Sourdoughs From Antiquity / Ed Wood. Cascade, Idaho: Sinclair Pub., c1989. 362 p., illus. Includes index.

see also Bread *(Section II)*

Soy Sauce

2171. The Kikkoman Cookbook: Your Way to Better Flavor! Tokyo, Japan: Kikkoman Shoyu Co.; New York: Distributed by Van Nostrand Reinhold Co., c1973, 1977 printing. 80 p., illus.

see also broader category: Soybeans

Soybeans

2172. Soybean Cookery / by Virg and Jo Lemley. 2nd ed. Cave Junction, Or.: Wilderness House, c1975. 56 p., illus.

2173. Super Soy!: Delicious Protein Without Meat / Barbara Farr. New Canaan, Conn.: Keats Pub., c1976. 151 p. (A Pivot Book). Includes bibliography and index.

2174. Using Tofu, Tempeh & Other Soyfoods in Restaurants, Delis & Cafeterias / William Shurtleff & Akiko Aoyagi. Lafayette, Calif.: Soyfoods Center, c1982. 1 v., illus.

Specialty Cookbooks

Soybeans *(Continued)*

2175. The Magic of Tofu and Other Soybean Products / by Jane O'Brien; illustrations by Niall Morris and Clive Birch. 1st U.S. ed. New York: Thorsons Publishers, 1983. 128 p., illus. Includes index.

2176. The Book of Soybeans: Nature's Miracle Protein / by Tokuji Watanabe with Asako Kishi. 1st ed. Tokyo, Japan; New York: Japan Publications; New York: Distributors, U.S., Kodansha International/USA through Harper & Row, 1984. 191 p., illus. 120 recipes using miso, soy milk, tofu, and other soy foods. Includes information on the history of soy products and index.

2177. Soy for the 21st Century / by Lois Yoder; illustrations by Edna Searles. Washington, D.C.: Nu-Soy Publishers, 1984. 80 p., illus. Includes index.

2178. Soybeans and Soybean Products. Tokyo, Japan: JOIE; Brisbane, Calif.: Distributed by JP Trading, c1984. 116 p., illus. (most colored). (Quick & Easy Nutritious Japanese Cooking; no. 1).

2179. Tofu, Tempeh, & Other Soy Delights: Enjoying Traditional Oriental Soyfoods in American-Style Cuisine / Camille Cusumano. Emmaus, Pa.: Rodale Press, c1984. 261 p., illus. More than 200 recipes. Includes index.

2180. Soya Foods Cookery / Leah Leneman. London,Eng.; New York: Routledge & Kegan Paul, 1988. 145 p., illus. "Published in the USA in association with Methuen." Includes index.

see also specific foods made from soybeans: Miso, Soy Sauce, Tempeh, Tofu; *and broader category:* Legumes

Spaghetti *see* **Pasta**

Spaghetti Squash

2181. The Vegetable Spaghetti Cookbook: How to Grow & How to Cook Spaghetti Squash / by Derek Fell & Phyllis Shaudys. Washington Crossing, Pa.: Pine Row Publications, c1982. 96 p., illus. Includes index.

see also broader category: Squash

Spices

2182. Seasonings Cookbook for Quantity Cuisine / edited by Jule Wilkinson. Boston, Mass.: CBI Pub. Co., c1980. 273 p., illus. Includes index.

2183. Better Homes and Gardens Hot & Spicy Cooking / editor, Jill Burmeister. 1st ed. Des Moines, Iowa: Meredith Corp., c1984. 96 p., colored illus. Includes index.

2184. Cynthia Wine's Hot & Spicy Cooking / Cynthia Wine. Toronto, Ont.; New York: Penguin Books, 1984. 160 p., 8 p. of plates, illus. (some colored).

2185. The Fiery Cuisines: The World's Most Delicious Dishes / Dave DeWitt and Nancy Gerlach. 1st ed. New York: St. Martin's Press, 1984. 229 p. 200 recipes. Includes index.

2186. The Little Brown Spice Book / Rachael Holme. Wellingborough, Eng.: Thorsons, 1984. 56 p.

2187. Spices of the World Cookbook by McCormick / prepared and tested in the kitchens of McCormick. 2nd ed. New York: McGraw-Hill, 1984. 448 p., illus. 1964 ed. prepared by Mary Collins and published under title: The McCormick Spices of the World Cookbook. Includes indexes.

Spices *(Continued)*

2188. Cooking with Spices / Carolyn Heal and Michael Allsop; 16 colour photographs by Charles Pocklington; 100 line drawings by Ann Collingridge. London, Eng.: Panther, 1985, c1983. 416 p., illus. Includes index.

2189. Hot & Spicy: Unusual, Innovative Recipes from the World's Fiery Cuisines / Marlena Spieler. 1st ed. Los Angeles, Calif.: J.P. Tarcher; New York: Distributed by St. Martin's Press, c1985. 230 p., illus. Includes index.

2190. Some Like it Hotter: The Official Cookbook of the Galvanized Gullet / Geraldine Duncann. San Francisco, Calif.: 101 Productions; New York: Distributed to the book trade in the U.S. by Scribner, c1985. 168 p., 8 p. of plates, illus. (some colored). Includes index.

2191. Totally Hot! / Michael Goodwin, Charles Perry, Naomi Wise. New York: Doubleday, 1986. 270 p., illus. "A Dolphin Book." "The ultimate hot pepper cookbook." Includes index.

2192. The Book of Hot & Spicy Foods / Louise Steele; photography by Paul Grater. Tucson, Ariz.: HP Books, c1987. 120 p., colored illus. Includes index.

2193. The Hot and Spicy Cookbook / Sophie Hale. Secaucus, N.J.: Chartwell Books, 1987. 128 p., colored illus.

2194. Hotter than Hell: Hot & Spicy Dishes from Around the World / Jane Butel. Tucson, Ariz.: HP Books, c1987. 208 p., illus. Includes index.

2195. Cooking with Old Bay: Award Winning Recipes Featuring Old Bay Seasoning / edited by Marian Levine. Silver Spring, Md.: American Cooking Guild, 1989. 64 p., illus. (Collector's Series; v. 27).

Spices *(Continued)*

2196. Fire and Spice: The Cuisine of Sri Lanka / by Heather Jansz Balasuriya and Karin Winegar; illustrated by Susan Friesen. New York: McGraw-Hill, c1989. 227 p., illus. Includes index.

2197. The Hot and Spicy Cookbook / Moira Hodgson. New York: Prentice Hall Press, 1989. 304 p., illus. Originally published: New York: McGraw-Hill, c1977. Includes index.

2198. Light & Spicy / Barbara Gibbons. 1st ed. New York: Harper & Row, c1989. 192 p., photos. More than 300 recipes. Includes index. "A Roundtable Press Book."

2199. Complete Book of Spices: A Practical Guide to Spices & Aromatic Seeds / Jill Norman. London, Eng.: Dorling Kindersley, 1990. 160 p., illus. Includes index. Also published: Montreal, Que.: R D Press, 1990. To be published in 1991 by New York: Viking Studio Books.

2200. Spices, Condiments, and Seasonings / Kenneth T. Farrell. 2nd ed. New York: Van Nostrand Reinhold, c1990. 414 p., illus. "An Avi Book." Includes bibliography and index.

2201. Spices: Roots & Fruit / Jill Norman. Bantam ed. Toronto, Ont.; New York: Bantam Books, 1990. 41 p., colored illus. (The Bantam Library of Culinary Arts). Includes index.

2202. Spices--Seeds & Barks: Their Use in Flavoring Traditional and Exotic Dishes / Jill Norman. Toronto, Ont.; New York: Bantam Books, 1990. 41 p., colored illus. (The Bantam Library of Culinary Arts). Includes index.

2203. Sweet Flavorings / Jill Norman. Bantam ed. Toronto, Ont.; New York: Bantam Books, 1990. 41 p., colored illus. (The Bantam Library of Culinary Arts). Includes index.

see also entries 1896, 2640; Herbs and Spices; *and specific spices:* Cinnamon, Coriander, Pepper, Saffron

Spirulina

2204. The Spirulina Cookbook: Recipes for Rejuvenating the Body / Sonia Beasley. Boulder Creek, Calif.: University of the Trees Press, c1981. 184 p., illus. Includes index.

see also broader category: Marine Algae

Sprouts

2205. Love the Sunshine in with Sprouts! A Guide to Growing Sprouts and Baby Greens Plus Simple Recipes and Seed Storage for Biogenic Living / by Sita Ananda; illustrated by Peter Joyes. Corvallis, Or. (P.O. Box 1718, Corvallis 97339): Better Health For Life, c1982. 130 p., illus. Includes index.

2206. The Complete Sprouting Book: A Guide to Growing and Using Sprouted Seeds / by Per and Gita Sellmann; translated from the Swedish by Kit Zweigbergk and Palden Jenkins. Wellingborough, Eng.: Thorsons, 1984. 128 p., illus. (Nature's Way Series). Includes bibliography and index. Translation of: Allt om Groddar. Originally published in 1981.

2207. The Sprouting Book / Ann Wigmore. Wayne, N.J.: Avery Pub. Group, c1986. 116 p., illus. Includes index.

see also broader category: Natural Foods; Vegetables

Squash

2208. Squash / Rachel Bard and Caroline Kellogg; drawings by Rik Olson. San Francisco, Calif.: 101 Productions; New York: Distributed in the United States by Scribner, c1977. 96 p., illus. (Edible Garden Series). Includes index.

2209. The Squash Cookbook / Yvonne Young Tarr. 1st Vintage Books ed. New York: Vintage Books, 1978. 223 p., illus. Includes index.

Squash (Continued)

2210. Fifty Squash Recipes / Debby Cochran. Thurmont, Md.: D. Cochran, 1981. 1 v., illus.

2211. James McNair's Squash Cookbook / photography by Patricia Brabant; artworks by Alan May. San Francisco, Calif.: Chronicle Books, c1988. 96 p. 35 recipes. Includes index.

see also entries 479, 1870, 2599; Spaghetti Squash; *and broader category:* Vegetables

Squid

2212. Squid / by R. Marilyn Schmidt. Barnegat Light, N.J.: Barnegat Light Press, 1980. 20 p.

2213. And More Squid / by R. Marilyn Schmidt. Barnegat Light, N.J.: Barnegat Light Press, 1985. 20 p.

2214. Calamari Cookbook: Exploring the World's Cuisines with Squid / by Joseph Schultz & Beth Regardz; illustrated by Beth Regardz. Berkeley, Calif.: Celestial Arts, c1987. 135 p., illus. Includes index.

2215. The International Squid Cookbook / by Isaac Cronin; designed and illustrated by Jeanne Jambu. Reading, Mass.: Addison-Wesley Pub. Co., 1988, c1981. 96 p., illus. 50 recipes. "Aris Books."

see also broader category: Seafood

Steak *see* Beef

Strawberries

2216. Strawberry Patchwork / Susan A. McCreary. Fayetteville, N.C.: Strawberry Patchworks, 1977. 104 p., illus.

2217. From the Strawberry Patch / by Sharon Kay Alexander. Santa Ana, Calif. (2521-F N. Grand Ave., Santa Ana 92701): ABC Enterprises, c1980. 110 p., illus.

2218. Best of Strawberries: A Strawberry Cookbook / by Elizabeth Schwartz; interior artwork by Robert J. Schwartz, Jr.. Orange, Va.: Green Publishers, c1981. 88 p.

2219. Strawberry Sportcake: A Recipe Collection Using the Strawberry, Naturally, in All of Its Forms / by Susan A. McCreary. Fayetteville, N.C.: Strawberry Patchworks, c1982. 88 p., illus.

2220. Strawberries: Recipes for America's Favorite Fruit / compiled & edited by Nana Whalen; illustrations by Jim Haynes. Silver Spring, Md.: WRC Pub., c1983. 64 p., illus.

2221. Strawberry Delights / by Joy Cummings & Gerald Sykes. 1st ed. West Chester, Pa. (P.O. Box 1957, West Chester 19380): J. Cummings and G. Sykes, c1983. 101 p. Includes index.

2222. The Little Strawberry Cookbook / Mary L. Green. Denver, Colo.: Giftstar, 1984. ca. 10 p., illus. (Little Cookbooks).

2223. The Strawberry Connection: Strawberry Cookery with Flavour, Fact and Folklore, From Memories, Libraries and Kitchens of Old and New Friends, and Strangers / compiled by Beatrice Ross Buszek. Halifax, N.S.: Nimbus Pub., 1984. 212 p., illus. (some colored). Includes bibliography and index.

2224. The Compleat Strawberry / Stafford Whiteaker. 1st American ed. New York: Crown Publishers, 1985. 128 p., illus. (some colored). More than 70 recipes. Discusses the strawberry in art and poetry and contains herbal remedies and gardening tips. Includes index.

Strawberries *(Continued)*

2225. Simply Strawberries / by Sara Pitzer; illustrations by Elayne Sears. Pownal, Vt.: Garden Way Pub., c1985. 123 p., illus. More than 100 recipes.

2226. Strawberry Sampler: A Collection of Fresh Strawberry Recipes / by Jan Siegrist. Shelburne, Vt.: New England Press, c1985. 46 p., illus.

2227. Something Strawberry / Jill Baker. Oak Park, Ill.: Brandison Press, 1987. 84 p.

2228. A Glut of Strawberries & Soft Fruit / Ann Carr. London, Eng.: Merehurst, 1988. 92 p.

see also entry 1879; and broader categories: Berries; Fruits

Striped Bass

2229. Striped Bass on the Fly: A Guide to California Waters / Russell D. Chatham; illustrations by the author. 1st ed. San Francisco, Calif.: Examiner Special Projects, 1977. 96 p., illus.

see also broader category: Fish

Suet

2230. Atora Family Suet Cookery / Roz Denny. Cambridge, Mass.: Martin, 1982. 96 p., colored illus.

Sugar

2231. The Sweet Touch in Family Cooking / compiled by Eva Rush. Cambridge Mass.: Dorison House Publishers, c1978. 144 p., illus. Includes index.

Sun-Dried Tomatoes

2232. Cooking with Sun-Dried Tomatoes / written by Lois Dribin and Denise Marina; illustrated by Susan Ivankovich. Tucson, Ariz.: Fisher Books, c1990. 160 p., illus. Includes index.

2233. Sun-Dried Tomatoes! / Andrea Chesman. Freedom, Calif.: Crossing Press, c1990. 138 p. 75 recipes. (Specialty Cookbook Series). Includes index.

see also broader category: Tomatoes

Sunflower Oil

2234. The Cooking Lite, Feeling Right Cookbook. Fullerton, Calif.: Hunt-Wesson Foods, Inc., 1980. 1 booklet.

Sweet Potatoes

2235. Shirley's Cajun Yam Cuisine: 25 Prize Winning Recipes / Shirley Meche. Opelousas, La.: Meche, c1982. 43 p., illus.

2236. Sweet Potato = 'Uala: Uses and Recipes. Lawai, Hawaii: Na Lima Kokua, 1983. 24 p., illus. "For the benefit of the Pacific Tropical Botanical Garden." Includes bibliography.

2237. The Exotic Yam: The Golden Vegetable Specialty Cookbook / by Hollie White. Beaumont, Tex.: F.D. Larkin, 1988, c1983. 260 p. Includes index.

2238. The Sweet Potato Cookbook / by Franklin W. Martin, Ruth M. Ruberte, and Jose L. Herrera; artwork, Ann Winterbotham. North Fort Myers, Fla. (17430 Durrance Rd., North Fort Myers 33917): Educational Concerns for Hunger Organization, c1989. 86 p.

see also broader category: Potatoes

Swordfish

2239. Swordfish / by R. Marilyn Schmidt. Barnegat Light, N.J.: Barnegat Light Press, 1986. 12 p.

see also broader category: Fish

Syrups

see entry 9; and Corn Syrup; Maple Sugar and Syrup

Tabasco Sauce

2240. 16 Classic Recipes. Avery Island, La.: McIlhenny Co., 1985. 38 colored illus. 1 booklet.

Taro

2241. Taro (Kalo): Uses and Recipes / by Na Lima Kokua. Rev. Lawai, Hawaii: Pacific Tropical Botanical Garden, 1982, c1977. 20 p., illus. Includes bibliography.

2242. Cooking with Taro and Poi / Anna Seabury Pereira. Honolulu, Hawaii: A.S. Pereira, 1983. 56 p., illus. Includes index.

see also broader category: Vegetables

Tautog *see* Blackfish

Tea

2243. The Tea Lover's Handbook / written and illustrated by Moira Weinreich. Vancouver, B.C.: Intermedia Press, 1980. 184 p., illus.

Tea *(Continued)*

2244. Being Social with Tea. Etobicoke, Ont.: Tea Council of Canada, 1981. 11 p., illus.

see also broader category: Beverages *(Section II);* and Afternoon Teas *(Section III)*

Tempeh

2245. Tempeh Cookery / by Colleen Pride; illustrators, Jeanne Purviance, Gregory Lowry; photography, Michael Bonnickson. Summertown, Tenn.: Book Pub. Co., 1984. 127 p., illus. (some colored). Includes index.

2246. Tempeh Production: A Craft and Technical Manual / William Shurtleff & Akiko Aoyagi; illustrated by Akiko Aoyagi. 2nd ed. Lafayette, Calif.: Soyfoods Center, 1986. 176 p., illus. Rev. ed. of: The Book of Tempeh. Vol. 2. 1st ed. 1980. Includes index.

2247. The Tempeh Cookbook / by Dorothy R. Bates. Summertown, Tenn.: Book Pub. Co., c1989. 96 p. Includes index.

see also broader category: Soybeans

Tequila

2248. The Tequila Book / Marion Gorman & Felipe P. de Alba. Chicago, Ill.: Regnery, c1976. 184 p., illus. Includes index.

2249. Stan Jones' Cooking with Tequila Sauza / by Stan Jones; with photography by John Guarente; recipes prepared by Monette. Los Angeles, Calif.: BarGuide Enterprises, c1979. 192 p., colored illus. Includes index.

see also broader category: Liquors

Tilefish

2250. Tilefish / by R. Marilyn Schmidt. Barnegat Light, N.J.: Barnegat Light Press, 1985. 16 p.

see also broader category: Fish

Tofu

2251. Tofu Goes West: Recipes / by Gary Landgrebe; illustrations by Seraphina Landgrebe. 1st ed. Palo Alto, Calif.: Fresh Press, 1978. 114 p., illus. Includes bibliography and index.

2252. The Great American Tofu Cookbook / Patric[i]a Gaddis McGruter; illustrated by Stephanie Fleischer. Brookline, Mass.: Autumn Press; Westminster, Md.: Distributed by Random House, c1979. 124 p., illus. Includes index.

2253. The Tofu Cookbook / Cathy Bauer & Juel Andersen; woodcuts by David Frampton. Emmaus, Pa.: Rodale Press, c1979. 188 p., illus. Includes index.

2254. Tofu: Everybody's Guide / by Stephen (Snehan) Cherniske; with foreword by Sandra McLanahan; illustrations by Sue Thompson. East Woodstock, Conn.: Mother's Inn Center for Creative Living, c1980. 90 p., illus. Includes index.

2255. Cook with Tofu / Christina Clarke; illustrations, Marcia Smith. New York: Avon, c1981. 223 p., illus. "A Madison Press Book." Includes index.

2256. Cooking with Tofu / by Mary Anna DuSablon; illustrations by Sue Storey. Pownal, Vt.: Garden Way Pub., c1981. 32 p., illus. (Garden Way Publishing Bulletin; A-74).

2257. The Incredible Tofu Cookbook, California Style / Mavis Immegart & Patti Jon Dansby. Yorba Linda, Calif.: M. Immegart: P.J. Dansby, 1981. 129 p., illus.

Tofu *(Continued)*

2258. Tofu at Center Stage / recipes by Gary Landgrebe; illustrations by Seraphina Landgrebe. 1st ed. Palo Alto, Calif.: Fresh Press, 1981. 110 p., illus. Includes index.

2259. Juel Andersen's Tofu Fantasies: A Cookbook of Incomparable Desserts. Berkeley, Calif.: Creative Arts Book Co., c1982. 76 p., illus. "A Creative Arts Communications Book." Includes index.

2260. Juel Andersen's Tofu Kitchen / Juel Andersen; illustrations by Juel Andersen. New York: Bantam, 1982, c1981. 210 p., illus. Includes index.

2261. Quick and Easy Tofu Cook Book / Yukiko Moriyama. Tokyo, Japan: JOIE, c1982. 104 p.

2262. Tofu Cookery: Soups, Salads, Snacks, Main Dishes, and Desserts / Fusako Holthaus. 1st ed. Tokyo, Japan; New York: Kodansha International; New York : Distributed by Harper & Row, c1982. 159 p., illus. Includes index.

2263. The Book of Tofu: Protein Source of the Future--Now! / William Shurtleff & Akiko Aoyagi; illustrated by Akiko Aoyagi. Berkeley, Calif.: Ten Speed Press, c1983, 433 p., illus. "A Soyfoods Center Book." Includes index.

2264. Tofu: Not Just for the Health of It / by Jana. Charlottesville, Va.: JANA, c1983. 169 p., illus. Includes index.

2265. Juel Andersen's Tofu Primer: A Beginner's Book of Bean Cake / by Juel Andersen, Sigrid Andersen. Berkeley, Calif.: Creative Arts Communications, c1984. 63 p., illus. Includes index.

2266. Nutritional Cooking with Tofu / Christine Y. C. Liu. Ann Arbor, Mich.: Graphique Pub., c1984. 167 p., illus. Includes bibliography and index.

Tofu *(Continued)*

2267. The International Tofu Cookery Book / Leah Leneman. London, Eng.; New York: Routledge & K. Paul in association with Methuen, 1986. 122 p., illus. Includes index.

2268. The Secrets of Tofu / Christopher and Jean Conil. London, Eng.: Foulsham, c1986. 128 p., illus. (some colored). Includes index.

2269. Tofu: A New Way to Healthy Eating / Linda Lee Barber & Junko Lampert. London, Eng.: Century Hutchinson, 1986. 128 p., colored illus.

2270. The Tofu Cookbook: Recipes for Traditional and Modern Cooking / Junko Lampert. San Francisco, Calif.: Chronicle Books, 1986, c1983. 96 p., illus. (some colored). Includes index.

2271. Tofu Quick & Easy / by Louise Hagler. Summertown, Tenn.: Book Pub. Co., c1986. 96 p., illus. (some colored). Includes index.

2272. The Little Tofu Book / Linda Sonntag. London, Eng.: Piatkus, 1987. 60 p., illus.

2273. Tofu Magic: Zero to Low Cholesterol and Low Sodium Recipes / Julia Weinberg; editor, Terry Stewart. Los Angeles, Calif.: Cookwrite Pub., 1988. 64 p., illus.

2274. The Tofu Book: The New American Cuisine / John Paino & Lisa Messinger. Garden City Park, N.Y.: Avery Pub. Group, c1990. 160 p., illus. More than 150 recipes. Includes bibliographical references and index.

2275. Tofu Cookery / by Louise Hagler. Rev. ed. Summertown, Tenn.: Book Pub. Co., c1990. ca. 160 p., illus. (some colored). Includes index.

Tofu *(Continued)*

2276. The Tofu Gourmet / by L. Barber & J. Lampert. Tokyo, Japan: Shufunotomo/Japan Publications; New York: Distributed by Kodansha International/USA through Harper & Row, 1990, c1984. 129 p., colored illus. Includes index.

see also broader category: Soybeans

Tomato Paste

2277. Hunt's Tomato Paste Recipe Collection / from the home economists of the Hunt-Wesson kitchens. New York: Rutledge Books, c1977. 128 p., colored illus. Includes index.

see also broader category: Tomatoes

Tomatoes

2278. A Tomato Cookbook / Mike Michaelson. Rev. ed. edited by Ian Wilkes and Stella Hazlewood. Hornchurch, Eng.: I. Henry, 1980. 140 p. Includes index. Previous ed. published as: The Great Tomato Cookbook. Chicago, Ill.: Great-Lakes Living Press, 1975.

2279. All About Tomatoes / written by Walter L. Doty and A. Cort Sinnes; edited by Susan M. Lammers; illustrations, Ron Hildebrand; photography, William Aplin, Clyde Childress, Michael Landis. Rev. ed. San Francisco, Calif.: Ortho Books, c1981. 96 p., colored illus. Includes index. Rev. ed. of: All About Tomatoes / written, edited, and designed by the editorial staff of Ortho Books. c1976.

2280. Tomatoes / Ingrid N. Fawcett. Port Moody, B.C.: I. Fawcett, c1981. 28 p. (Keremeos Harvest).

2281. Tomatoes / by Inez M. Krech. 1st ed. New York: Primavera Books/Crown, c1981. 64 p. Includes index.

Tomatoes *(Continued)*

2282. Garden Way's Red & Green Tomato Cookbook / Janet Ballantyne; photographs by Erik Borg; illustrations by Elayne Sears. Charlotte, Vt.: Garden Way Pub., c1982. 158 p., illus. Includes index.

2283. Tomatoes / written by Walter L. Doty, A. Cort Sinnes; contributing writers, Annette C. Fabri, Susan M. Lammers; illustrations by Ron Hildebrand. Mount Vernon, Va.: American Horticultural Society, c1982. 144 p., colored illus. "Portions of this volume previously appeared in the Ortho book All About Tomatoes." Includes index.

2284. The Little Tomato Cookbook / Mary L. Green. Denver, Colo.: Giftstar, 1984. ca. 10 p., illus. (Little Cookbooks).

2285. The Great American Tomato Book: The One Complete Guide to Growing and Using Tomatoes Everywhere / Robert Hendrickson. 1st Scarborough Books ed. New York: Stein and Day, 1984, c1977. 226 p., illus. Includes index. Reprint. Originally published: New York: Doubleday, 1977.

2286. Pick Your Own Tomatoes, Plums, and Avocadoes: Locations with Tomato, Plum, and Avocado Recipes / Center for Self Sufficiency, Research Division Staff. Houston, Tex.: Prosperity & Profits, 1985. 50 p.

2287. The Amazing Tomato Cookbook / Mary-Lou Arnold and others. London, Eng.: Bay Books, 1987. 96 p.

2288. Book of Tomatoes / edited by the staff of the National Gardening Magazine; illustrations by Elayne Sears & Lyn Severance. Rev. ed. New York: Villard Books, 1987, c1985. 87 p., illus.

see also entry 8; Sun-Dried Tomatoes; *and broader category:* Vegetables

Triticale

2289. Triticale Cook Book / by TritiRich Products Ltd.; photographed and designed by Rakesh Syal. Winnipeg, Man.: TritiRich Products, c1979. 139 p., colored illus. Includes index.

2290. Triticale New Harvest Recipes: A Collection of Recipes from Our Triticale Kitchens. Winnipeg, Man.: TritiRich Products, 1982, c1981. 163 p., illus. Includes index.

see also broader category: Grains

Trout

2291. The All Trout Cookbook / written, compiled, developed, and photographed by Rick Taylor; illustrated by Carol Knapp. Grand Junction, Colo.: Vista Grande, c1979. 77 p., illus.

2292. The Trout Cookbook / Patricia Ann Hayes. Wiltshire, Eng.: Crowood Press, 1989. 144 p.

see also entry 522; and broader category: Fish

Truffles

2293. The Cookbook of North American Truffles / The North American Truffling Society, Inc. Corvallis, Or. (PO Box 296, Corvallis 97339): The Society, c1987. 89 p., illus. Includes index.

see also broader category: Mushrooms

Tuna

2294. The Tuna Cookbook / Sheila Metcalf. 1st ed. Garden City, N.Y.: Doubleday, 1972. 175 p.

Tuna *(Continued)*

2295. Tempting Tuna Cookbook / prepared by Rutledge Books; edited by Kitchen Consultants. New York: Supermarket Book Co., c1976. 128 p., illus. "A Benjamin Company/Rutledge Book." At head of title: Chicken of the Sea. Includes index.

2296. Chicken of the Sea Tuna Recipes. St. Louis, Mo.: Ralston Purina, 1980. 1 booklet.

2297. Souper Tuna Cook Book. Camden, N.J.: Campbell Soup Co., 1981. 100 p., illus. More than 125 recipes featuring Campbell soups and Chicken of the Sea tuna.

2298. Charlie the Tuna's Recipe Booklet. Long Beach, Calif.: Star Kist Seafood Co., 1985. 1 booklet.

2299. Fresh Tuna / by R. Marilyn Schmidt. Barnegat Light, N.J.: Barnegat Light Press, 1986. 10 p.

2300. Love That Tuna and Other Gamefish: A Complete Outer Banks Cookbook / Carmen Gray and Dorothy Hope. Kitty Hawk? N.C.: C&D Pub., 1987. 46 p.

see also Canned Fish; *and broader category:* Fish

Turkey

2301. The Great Year-Round Turkey Cookbook / Anita Borghese; instruction drawings by Yaroslava Mills; decorative drawings by Dorothy Zahra Hurley. New York: Stein and Day, c1979. 288 p., illus. Includes index.

2302. Lisa Bacon's Complete Turkey Cookbook. Granada Hills, Calif.: L. Weeks Pub., c1979. 155 p., illus. Includes index.

Turkey *(Continued)*

2303. The Year-Round Turkey Cookbook: Guide to Delicious, Nutritious Dining with Today's Versatile Turkey Products / Barbara Gibbons. 1st McGraw-Hill ed. New York: McGraw-Hill, c1980. 185 p., colored illus. Includes index.

2304. The Twelve Days of Turkey / by Christine Allen; illuminations by Michael Kluckner. Vancouver, B.C.: Consolidated Merriment, c1981. 47 p., illus.

2305. Talkin' Turkey: Sarah Rawls' Year-round Turkey Recipes. St. Louis, Mo.: Pet, Inc., 1982. 1 booklet.

2306. Discover Turkey: Year-Round Recipes for Parts and Leftovers. Champaign, Ill.: Family Room Press, 1983. 24 p.

2307. Turkey All Year / Susan O. Byrne; Barbara M. Mueller, illustrations. Arlington, Va. (P.O. Box 7122, Arlington 22207): Barclay-Ramsey Associates, c1984. 104 p., illus.

2308. The Woman's Day Book of Great Turkey Feasts / by Kim Honig & the editors of Woman's Day. 1st ed. New York: Crown, c1984. 122 p., illus. Includes index.

2309. Let's Talk Turkey: Gourmet Recipes / by Mary Ann Trombold; drawings by Margo Peterson. Mercer Island, Wash.: Year-Round Press, c1985. 173 p., illus.

2310. Talking About Turkey: How to Buy, Store, Thaw, Stuff, and Prepare Your Holiday Bird. Slightly rev. Washington, D.C.: U.S. Dept. of Agriculture, 1987. 20 p., illus. (Home and Garden Bulletin; no. 243).

2311. Chef Wolfe's New American Turkey Cookery / Ken Wolfe, Olga Bier; illustrations by Amy Pertschuk; photographs by Marshall Berman; edited and recipes tested by Maggie Blyth Klein. Reading, Mass.: Aris Books, 1989, c1984. ca. 155 p., illus.

Specific Ingredients 301

Turkey *(Continued)*

2312. Fresh Turkey Ideas. Minneapolis, Minn.: General Mills, 1990. 92 p., colored illus. (Betty Crocker Creative Recipes; no. 46). Includes index.

2313. Turkey: The Magic Ingredient / Coleen Simmons & Robert Simmons. San Leandro, Calif.: Bristol Pub. Enterprises, 1990. 160 p., illus.

2314. The Turkey Cookbook / Rick Rodgers. 1st Perennial Library ed. New York: Harper Collins, 1990. 288 p. Contains recipes for turkey parts, turkey breasts, ground turkey, and turkey cutlets. Includes index.

see also entry 520; Ground Turkey; *and broader categories:* Fowl and Game; Poultry

Vanilla

2315. Vanilla Cookbook / Patricia Rain; photographs by Benjamin H. Kaestner, III. Berkeley, Calif.: Celestial Arts, c1986. 124 p., 8 p. of plates, illus. More than 100 recipes. Includes index.

see also broader category: Condiments

Variety Meats

2316. Innards and Other Variety Meats / by Jana Allen and Margaret Gin. San Francisco, Calif.: 101 Productions; Distributed by Scribner, New York, 1974. 144 p. illus.

2317. Special Offal. London, Eng. (5 St. John's Sq., Smithfield, EC2M 4DE): Meat Promotion Executive of the Meat and Livestock Commission, 1981. 16 p., colored illus.

Variety Meats *(Continued)*

2318. Variety Meats / by the editors of Time-Life Books. Alexandria, Va.: Time-Life Books, c1982. 176 p., illus. (some colored). (The Good Cook, Techniques & Recipes). Includes index.

see also broader category: Meat

Veal

2319. Veal Cookery / Craig Claiborne, Pierre Franey; drawings by Barbara Fiore; photos. by Bill Aller. 1st ed. New York: Harper & Row, c1978. 229 p., illus. (some colored). Includes index.

2320. Veal and Lamb. Toronto, Ont.: Grolier, 1988. 110 p., colored illus. (Microwave Magic; 8). Includes index. Translation of: Veau et agneau.

see also entries 94, 99, 110, 112; and broader category: Meat

Vegetables

2321. The Home Garden Cookbook: From Seed to Plate / Ken & Pat Kraft. No. Hollywood, Calif.: Wilshire Book Co., 1972, c1970. 297 p., colored illus.

2322. Vegetable Bounty / Annette Gohlke. Milwaukee, Wis., Reiman Associates, 1975. 60 p.

2323. Nika Hazelton's Way with Vegetables: The Unabridged Vegetable Cookbook / drawings by Shelly Sacks. New York: M. Evans, c1976. 381 p., illus. 250 recipes. Includes index.

Vegetables *(Continued)*

2324. Too Many Tomatoes ... Squash, Beans, and Other Good Things: A Cookbook for When Your Garden Explodes / Lois M. Burrows & Laura G. Myers. 1st ed. New York: Harper & Row, c1976. 287 p., illus. More than 475 recipes. Contains information on storing, canning, freezing, and handling. Includes index. Reprinted as a paperback in 1991.

2325. Garden to Table / Bruce Johnstone. St. Paul, Minn.: McGill/Jensen, 1978. 148 p., colored illus.

2326. Vegetables / by the editors of Time-Life Books. Alexandria, Va.: Time-Life Books; Morristown, N.J.: School and library distribution by Silver Burdett, c1979. 176 p., illus. (The Good Cook, Techniques & Recipes). Includes index.

2327. The Versatile Vegetable. Ithaca, N.Y.: Division of Nutritional Sciences, State University of New York at Cornell University, 198-. 50 p., illus.

2328. 500 Recipes for Vegetables and Salads / Moya Maynard. Feltham, Eng.: Hamlyn, 1980. 96 p. Includes index.

2329. The Best Vegetable Recipes from Woman's Day / by the editors of Woman's Day. Boston, Mass.: Houghton Mifflin Co., 1980. 216 p. Includes index.

2330. Buying and Cooking Vegetables / Mary Norwak. Cambridge, Eng.: Published for J. Sainsbury Ltd. by Woodhead-Faulkner, 1980. 40 p., illus. (Sainsbury's Food Guides; no. 4).

2331. Cooking with Vegetables: Original Recipes / by Marika Hanbury Tenison; illustrations by John Miller. London, Eng.: Cape, 1980. 284 p., illus. Includes index.

2332. A Feast of Vegetables / by Rena Cross; edited by Mary Norwak. London, Eng.: Foulsham, c1980. 96 p., illus. (From a Country Kitchen). Includes index.

Specialty Cookbooks

Vegetables *(Continued)*

2333. The Gardener's Kitchen: A Guide for Preparing Fresh Vegetables / John and Grace Corry. Tulsa, Okla.: Winchester Press, c1980. 160 p., illus. Includes index.

2334. A Passion for Vegetables: Recipes from European Kitchens / Vera Gewanter. New York: Viking Press, 1980. 328 p. Includes index.

2335. Vegetable Cookery / Frances Naldrett; illustrated by Heather Sherratt. Sevenoaks, Eng.: Teach Yourself Books, 1980. 151 p., illus. (Teach Yourself Books). Includes index.

2336. Vegetables the Italian Way / by Teresa Gilardi Candler; illustrations by John Murphy. New York: McGraw-Hill, c1980. 236 p., illus. Includes indexes.

2337. Versatile Vegetables / by Katherine Hayes Greenberg and Barbara Kanerva Kyte; illustrated by Alice Harth. San Francisco, Calif.: Owlswood Productions, c1980. 62 p., illus. Includes index.

2338. Wild Green Vegetables of Canada / Adam F. Szczawinski, Nancy J. Turner. Ottawa, Ont.: National Museum of Natural Sciences; Chicago, Ill.: Distributed by University of Chicago Press, c1980. 179 p., illus. (some colored). (Edible Wild Plants of Canada; no. 4 0705-3967) "Catalogue no. NM95-40/4." Includes index.

2339. The Covent Garden Cookbook / Marie Stone. London, Eng.: Allison and Busby, 1981, c1974. 253 p., illus. Includes bibliography and index.

2340. Feed Your Family with Love / Titia Sotebeer. Cobalt, Ont.: Highway Book Shop, c1981. 175 p. (Highway Book Shop Large Print; no. 3). On cover: A Cookbook for Vegetarians.

Vegetables *(Continued)*

2341. Gourmet Gardening: 48 Special Vegetables You Can Grow for Deliciously Distinctive Meals / by the editors of Organic Gardening Magazine; edited by Anne Moyer Halpin; illustrations by Cynthia Hellyer. Emmaus, Pa.: Rodale Press, c1981. 243 p., illus. Includes index. Abridged from: Unusual Vegetables.

2342. Jane Grigson's Vegetable Book: With a New Introduction, Glossary and Table of Equivalent Weights and Measures for the American Edition / illustrated by Yvonne Skargon. Harmondsworth, Eng.: Penguin, 1981, c1979. 618 p., illus. (Penguin Handbooks). Includes index.

2343. Kerr's Country Kitchen / Vivian and Don Kerr; illustrations by Marta Cone and Vivian Kerr. Old Saybrook, Conn.: Peregrine Press, c1981. 160 p., illus. Includes index.

2344. Mother Earth's Hassle-free Vegetable Cookbook / by Joel Rapp; illustrations by Marvin Rubin. New York: Avon, c1981. 211 p., illus. Includes index.

2345. Rootcrops, Your Cookmate / a project of the Development Academy of the Philippines. Quezon City, Philippines: New Day Publishers, 1981. 106 p.

2346. Southern Vegetable Cooking / by Jon [i.e. Jan] Wongrey; illustrated by Kathryn Morse Howard. 1st ed. Lexington, S.C.: Sandlapper Store, c1981. 158 p., illus. Includes index.

2347. Variations of Vegetables. Glenview, Ill.: Kraft, Inc., 1981. 1 v. Recipes for side dishes, salads, and main dishes using fresh, canned, or frozen vegetables and Kraft grated parmesan cheese.

2348. Vegetable Cooking of All Nations / edited by Florence Schwartz; illustrated by Mary Norton. 1981 ed. New York: Gramercy Pub. Co.: Distributed by Crown Publishers, 1981, c1973. 282 p., illus. Includes index.

Vegetables *(Continued)*

2349. Vegetables & Salads / Mala Young; illustrated by Susan Neale. Newton Abbot, Eng.: David & Charles, c1981. 48 p., illus. (Health Food Cooking).

2350. The Best of Jenny's Kitchen: Cooking Naturally with Vegetables / Jennifer Raymond. New York: Avon, 1982, c1980. 180 p. Includes index.

2351. Home Gardening Wisdom / Dick and Jan Raymond. Charlotte, Vt.: Garden Way Pub., c1982. 303 p., illus. Includes index.

2352. The Mostly Vegetable Menu Cookbook / Nancy B. Katz; illustrations by Kari Ann Pagnano. New York: Grosset & Dunlap, c1982. 223 p., illus. Includes index.

2353. Roots & Tubers: A Vegetable Cookbook / by Kyle D. Fulwiler. Seattle, Wash.: Pacific Search Press, c1982. 101 p. Includes index.

2354. Vegetable Cookery / Lou Seibert Pappas. Tucson, Ariz.: HP Books, c1982. 192 p., colored illus. Includes index.

2355. Vegetable Gardening Encyclopedia / by the editors of Consumer Guide. New York: Galahad Books, 1982. 384 p., illus. Includes index.

2356. Vegetables / editors Anne Moyer and Gillian Andrews. Aylesbury, Eng.: Rodale Press, 1982. 255 p., illus. (some colored). (Rodale's Good Food Kitchen). Includes index. Originally published: Emmaus, Pa.: Rodale Press, 1977 under title: The Green Thumb Cookbook.

2357. Vegetables in Family Meals: A Guide for Consumers / prepared by Human Nutrition Information Service. Slightly rev. Washington, D.C.: U.S. Dept. of Agriculture; For sale by the Supt. of Documents, U.S. Government Printing Office, 1982. 28 p., illus. (Home and Garden Bulletin; no. 105).

Vegetables *(Continued)*

2358. The Victory Garden Cookbook / by Marian Morash; in collaboration with Jane Doerfer; principal photography by Bill Schwob; additional photography by James Scherer. 1st ed. New York: Knopf, 1982. 374 p., colored illus. More than 800 recipes. Includes index.

2359. Adam's Luxury and Eve's Cookery; or, The Kitchen-Garden Display'd: In Two Parts. Facsim. ed. London, Eng.: Prospect Books, 1983. 216 p. Reprint. Originally published: London, Eng.: Printed for R. Dodsley; sold by M. Cooper, 1744.

2360. Chinese Vegetarian Dishes / author, Tuan-hsi Shou; photographers, Kun-hon Lin and Jenn-yu Chen; translator Chun-chi Chen and Li-min Yang. 2nd ed. Taipei, Taiwan, R.O.C.: Hilit Pub. Co., 1983. 119 p., colored illus. (Highlight's Culinary Series). Translation of: Shu Tsai Su Tsai Shih Pu.

2361. The Complete Vegetable Cookbook / Dolores Casella; illustrated by Alba Corrado. Port Washington, N.Y.: D. White, c1983. 229 p., illus. Includes index.

2362. Fresh Garden Vegetables / Libby Hillman; illustrated by Joan Blume. 1st ed. New York: Harper & Row: Chalmers Cookbooks, 1983. 84 p., illus.

2363. Lois Burpee's Gardener's Companion and Cookbook / edited by Millie Owen; illustrated by Parker Leighton. 1st ed. New York: Harper & Row, c1983. 248 p., illus. Includes index.

2364. The Pleasure of Vegetables / Elizabeth Ayrton. Harmondsworth, Eng.: Penguin, 1984, c1983. 189 p. (Penguin Handbooks). Includes index. Originally published: London, Eng.: Allen Lane, 1983.

Specialty Cookbooks

Vegetables *(Continued)*

2365. A Popular Guide to Chinese Vegetables / Martha Dahlen, Karen Phillipps. 1st American ed. New York: Crown Publishers, c1983. 113 p., colored illus. "Originally written and published in Hong Kong as two volumes entitled A Guide to Chinese Market Vegetables and A Further Guide to Chinese Market Vegetables." Includes index.

2366. Rose Murray's Vegetable Cookbook / illustrations by Eila Hopper Ross. Toronto, Ont.: J. Lorimer, 1983. 151 p., illus. Includes index.

2367. The Southern Heritage Vegetables Cookbook. Birmingham, Ala.: Oxmoor House, c1983. 143 p., illus. (some colored). (The Southern Heritage Cookbook Library). Includes index.

2368. Sunset Vegetable Cook Book / by the editors of Sunset Books and Sunset Magazine. 2nd ed. Menlo Park, Calif.: Lane Pub. Co., c1983. 96 p., illus. (some colored). Includes index.

2369. Vegetable Dishes. Newton Abbot, Eng.: David & Charles, c1983. 64 p., colored illus. (Kitchen Workshop). Includes index. Translation of: Gronnsaker.

2370. The Vegetable Lover's Cookbook / Shauna Cooney Brenner, Deborah Shields Smoot. Chicago, Ill.: Contemporary Books, c1983. 180 p., illus. Includes index.

2371. The Versatile Vegetable Cookbook / Dolores Riccio and Joan Bingham; illustrations by Ruth Hartshorn. New York: Van Nostrand Reinhold, c1983. 184 p., illus. Includes index.

2372. All Color Book of Vegetable Dishes. New York: Arco Pub., 1984. 82 p., colored illus. ca. 80 recipes. Includes index.

2373. Easy Gourmet Vegetables & Salads: A Step-by-Step Guide / edited by Charlotte Turgeon. New York: Beekman House, c1984. 75 p., illus.

Vegetables *(Continued)*

2374. Farm Journal's Best-Ever Vegetable Recipes: A Fresh Approach to Main Dishes, Appetizers, and Snacks, Soups, Salads, and Desserts--with 400 Never-Fail Recipes / by the food editors of Farm Journal. Philadelphia, Pa.: Farm Journal, Inc.; Garden City, N.Y.: Distributed to the trade by Doubleday, c1984. 278 p., 8 p. of plates, illus. Includes index.

2375. Garden Way's Joy of Gardening Cookbook / by Janet Ballantyne with Andrea Chesman and Dottie Rankin; photographs by Didier Delmas. Troy, N.Y.: Garden Way, c1984. 322 p., colored illus. Includes index.

2376. The Vegetable Book: How to Grow and Cook Your Own Vegetables / Terence Conran and Maria Kroll; paintings by Faith Shannon. London, Eng.: Treasure, 1984, c1976. 96 p. Includes index.

2377. Vegetable Menus. Alexandria, Va.: Time-Life Books, c1984. 104 p., colored illus. (Great Meals in Minutes). Includes index.

2378. A World of Vegetable Cookery: An Encyclopedic Treasury of Recipes, Botany, and Lore of the Vegetable Kingdom / Alex D. Hawkes; illustrations by Bill Goldsmith. Rev. ed. New York: Simon and Schuster, c1984. 283 p., illus. Includes indexes.

2379. 100 Vegetable Dishes / Sue Locke. London, Eng.: Octopus, 1985. 64 p., colored illus. Includes index.

2380. A-Z of Vegetable Variety. New York: Arco, 1985. 72 p., colored illus. Includes index.

2381. The Classic Vegetable Cookbook / by Ruth Spear; illustrated by Grambs Miller. 1st ed. New York: Harper & Row, c1985. 424 p., illus. More than 450 recipes for 42 vegetables. Includes index.

Vegetables *(Continued)*

2382. Classic Vegetable Cookery / Arto der Hartounian. London, Eng.: Ebury, 1985. 175 p., illus. (some colored). Includes index.

2383. The Complete Vegetable Cookbook, Including Nutritious Main Dishes. Nashville, Tenn.: Favorite Recipes Press, c1985. 128 p., illus. (Favorite Recipes of Home Economics Teachers). Includes index.

2384. A Cook's Garden / Jan Mahnken. Woodstock, Vt.: Countryman Press, c1985. 195 p., illus. Includes indexes.

2385. Eat Your Vegetables! More than 200 Irresistible Recipes from the authors of Don't Tell 'em It's Good for 'em / Nancy Baggett, Ruth Glick, and Gloria Kaufer Greene. 1st ed. New York: Times Books, c1985. 306 p., illus. 220 recipes. Includes index.

2386. Famous Brands Great Vegetable Dishes. St. Louis, Mo.: Brand Name Pub. Corp., c1985. 128 p., colored illus. (Famous Brands Cookbook Library). Includes index.

2387. French Vegetable Cookery: Traditional and Regional Recipes / Patricia Bourne. London, Eng.: Macdonald, 1985. 256 p., colored illus. Includes index.

2388. Fresh Ideas for Vegetable Cooking / by Georgia Machala Massie. Dallas, Tex.: Fresh Ideas, c1985. 355 p., illus. (some colored). Includes index.

2389. John Tovey's Feast of Vegetables: The Perfect Accompaniment to Any Meal. London, Eng.: Century, 1985. 240 p., illus. (some colored). Includes index.

2390. Making the Most of Vegetables / Robert Carrier. London, Eng.: Marshall Cavendish, 1985. 112 p., colored illus. (Robert Carrier's Kitchen). Includes index.

Vegetables *(Continued)*

2391. Vegetable Magic / by Sheilah Kaufman; edited by Martina Boudreau. Silver Spring, Md.: American Cooking Guild, 1986. 64 p., illus.

2392. Vegetables / Elizabeth Brand. London, Eng.: Bell & Hyman, 1985. 94 p., illus. (some colored). (New & Natural). Includes index.

2393. Vegetables / text, Delphine Hirasuna; design, Kit Hinrichs; photography, Tom Tracy; recipes, Diane J. Hirasuna. San Francisco, Calif.: Chronicle Books, c1985. 143 p., illus. (some colored). Includes index.

2394. Vegetables: The New Main Course Cookbook / Joe Famularo, Louise Imperiale. Woodbury, N.Y.: Barron's, c1985. 284 p., 32 p. of colored photos. Includes index.

2395. Vegetables, Pasta, and Rice. London, Eng.: Reader's Digest Association, c1985. 104 p., illus. (The Reader's Digest Good Health Cookbooks). Includes index.

2396. Better Homes and Gardens Microwave Vegetables. 1st ed. Des Moines, Iowa: Meredith Corp., c1986. 80 p., illus. (some colored). Includes index.

2397. The Complete Book of Vegetables: An Illustrated Guide to Over 400 Species and Varieties of Vegetables from All Over the World / Tjerk Buishand, Harm P. Houwing, Kees Jansen. New York: Gallery Books, 1986. 180 p., illus. (some colored). Includes index. "Adapted from the Dutch by Multimedia Publications. Translation: AGET Language Services, London."

2398. The Fragrant Vegetable: Simple Vegetarian Delicacies from the Chinese / Martin Stidham. 1st ed. Los Angeles, Calif.: J.P. Tarcher; New York: Distributed by St. Martin's Press, c1986. 224 p., illus. Includes index.

Vegetables *(Continued)*

2399. Fresh Ways with Vegetables / by the editors of Time-Life Books. Alexandria, Va.: Time-Life Books, c1986. 144 p., colored illus. (Healthy Home Cooking). Includes index.

2400. Judy Gorman's Vegetable Cookbook: More than 400 Superb Recipes for Preparing 78 Different Kinds of Fresh Vegetables, with Guidelines for Selecting and Storing from the Author of The Culinary Craft / by Judy Gorman. 1st ed. Dublin, N.H.: Yankee Books, c1986. 416 p., illus. Includes index.

2401. New Chinese Vegetarian Cookery / Kenneth Lo. London, Eng.: Fontana, 1986. 176 p. Includes index.

2402. This Is the Way My Garden Grows and Comes into the Kitchen / Barbara Dodge Borland; drawings by Lilly Langotsky. 1st ed. New York: Norton, c1986. 158 p., illus. Includes index.

2403. Vegetable Cookery / P. Maruska and L. Nodl; photography by O. Davidova and S. Nemec; translated by Dana Habova. Twickenham, Eng.: Hamlyn, c1986. 227 p., colored illus. Includes index. Translated from the Czech.

2404. Vegetable Dishes / edited by Susan Dixon. London, Eng.: Ward Lock, 1986. 63 p., illus. (some colored). (Mrs. Beeton's Home Cooking). Contains recipes selected from Mrs. Beeton's Cookery and Household Management.

2405. The Vegetable Year Cookbook / Judy Ridgway. London, Eng.: Futura, 1986, c1985. 172 p., illus.

2406. Vegetables. London, Eng.: Ward Lock, 1986. 64 p., illus. (Mrs. Beeton's Mini Series).

2407. Vegetables / Christian Teubner; translation and Americanization by Patricia Connell. 1st English-language ed. Woodbury, N.Y.: Barron's, 1986, c1985. 96 p., colored illus. (Cooking Magic). Includes index. Translation of: Gemuse.

Specific Ingredients 313

Vegetables *(Continued)*

2408. Vegetables and Desserts. 1st ed. Pleasantville, N.Y.: Reader's Digest Association; New York: Distributed by Random House, c1986. 192 p., illus. (Reader's Digest Good Health Cookbooks).

2409. Vegetables and Their Sauces: Microwave / Madame Jehane Benoît. Saint-Lambert, Que.: Heritage, 1986. 135 p., 16 p. of plates, illus. (some colored). (Encyclopedia of Microwave Cooking; 5). Includes index. Issued also in French under title: Les legumes et leurs sauces.

2410. Veggie Mania / by Cathy Prange and Joan Pauli. Kitchener, Ont.: Muffin Mania Pub., c1986. 76 p.

2411. Better Homes and Gardens Vegetables / editor, Gerald M. Knox. 1st ed. Des Moines, Iowa: Meredith Corp., c1987. 128 p., colored illus. (Great Cooking Made Easy). Includes index.

2412. The Bristol Recipe Book: Over 150 Recipes from the Cancer Help Kitchen / Sadhya Rippon; foreword by Penny Brohn; illustrated by Emma Rippon. London, Eng.: Century, 1987. 150 p., illus. "From the Bristol Cancer Help Centre." Includes index.

2413. Cooking with Vegetables / Elizabeth Corning. New York: Gallery Books, 1987. 73 p., illus. (some colored). (Microwave Library). Includes index.

2414. Glorious Vegetables in the Microwave / Patricia Tennison. Chicago, Ill.: Contemporary Books, c1987. 282 p., illus. (some colored). More than 250 recipes for 50 vegetables. Includes index.

2415. The Little Exotic Vegetable Book / Rosamond Richardson. London, Eng.: Piatkus, 1987. 64 p., illus.

Vegetables *(Continued)*

2416. Recipes from a Kitchen Garden / by Renee Shepherd. 1st ed. Felton, Calif.: Shepherd's Garden, c1987. 92 p., illus. (Shepherd's Garden Seeds). Includes index.

2417. Vegetable Creations / Faye Levy; illustrations by Maureen Jensen; photograms by Bill Westheimer. 1st ed. New York: E.P. Dutton, c1987. 364 p., 8 p. of plates, illus. (some colored). (Fresh from France). Includes index.

2418. The Vegetarian Handbook / Gary Null. 1st ed. New York: St. Martin's Press, c1987. 266 p. Includes index.

2419. The WI Book of Vegetables and Salads: Over 100 Recipes Tried and Tested by the Women's Institute / Maggie Black; illustrated by Vanessa Luff. London, Eng.: Ebury Press, 1987. 96 p., illus. Includes index.

2420. The Art of the Kitchen Garden / Ethne Clarke. London, Eng.: Joseph, c1988. 168 p., illus.

2421. Cooking from the Garden / Rosalind Creasy. San Francisco, Calif.: Sierra Club Books, c1988. 547 p., colored illus. 180 recipes. Includes index.

2422. The Early Summer Garden / by Perla Meyers; photography by Simon Metz; food styling by Michael di Beneditto. New York: Simon & Schuster, c1988. 125 p., illus. (some colored). "A Fireside Book." Includes index.

2423. Exotic Vegetables A-Z / by Josephine Bacon. Topsfield, Mass.: Salem House, 1988. 128 p. Includes index.

2424. Fast and Healthy Ways to Cook Vegetables / by Penny Noepel. Pownal, Vt.: Storey Communications, c1988. 32 p. (Garden Way Publishing Bulletin; A-105).

2425. A Glut of Courgettes & Marrows / Ann Carr. London, Eng.: Merehurst, 1988. 91 p.

Vegetables *(Continued)*

2426. A Glut of Tomatoes & Salad Vegetables / Ann Carr. London, Eng.: Merehurst, 1988. 92 p.

2427. Mediterranean Vegetable Cooking / Rena Salaman. London, Eng.: Fontana, 1988. 212 p., illus. Includes index.

2428. The New American Vegetable Cookbook: The Definitive Guide to America's Exotic & Traditional Vegetables / Georgeanne Brennan, Isaac Cronin & Charlotte Glenn; illustrated by Amy Pertschuk. Reading, Mass.: Addison-Wesley Pub. Co., 1988, c1985. 318 p., illus. Recipes for 200 vegetables. "Aris Books." Includes index.

2429. Plain & Fancy Vegetables. Minneapolis, Minn.: General Mills, 1988. 91 p., colored illus. (Betty Crocker Creative Recipes; no. 16). Includes index.

2430. The Spring Garden / by Perla Meyers; photography by Simon Metz; food styling by Michael di Beneditto. New York: Simon & Schuster, c1988. 125 p., illus. (some colored). "A Fireside Book." Includes index.

2431. Vegetables. Toronto, Ont.: Grolier, 1988. 110 p., colored illus. (Microwave Magic; 13). Includes index.

2432. The Well-Flavored Vegetable: Novel and Traditional Vegetable Recipes from Japan / Eri Yamaguchi. Tokyo, Japan; New York: Kodansha International, 1988, c1987. 134 p., illus. Includes index.

2433. Beans, Greens and Other Things / Doris B. Cain. Port O'Connor, Tex.: D.B. Cain, 1989. 1 v.

2434. Broccoli & Company: Over 100 Healthy Recipes for Broccoli, Brussels Sprouts, Cabbage, Cauliflower, Collards, Kale, Kohlrabi, Mustard, Rutabaga, and Turnip / by Audra and Jack Hendrickson. Pownal, Vt.: Storey Communications, c1989. 144 p., illus. "A Garden Way Publishing Book." Includes index.

Vegetables *(Continued)*

2435. The Cook's Garden: Growing and Using the Best-Tasting Vegetable Varieties / by Shepherd and Ellen Ogden; illustrated by Karl Stuecklen. Emmaus, Pa.: Rodale Press, 1989, c1988. 230 p., illus. More than 50 recipes. Includes index.

2436. The Food-Lover's Garden / Angelo M. Pellegrini; illustrated by Grambs Miller. New York: N. Lyons Books, 1989, c1970. 253 p., illus. Originally published: New York: Knopf, 1970.

2437. From Vegetables with Love / by Siri Ved Kaur Khalsa. Los Angeles, Calif.: G.T. International/Arcline Publications, c1989. 221 p., illus.

2438. Microwave Vegetable Cooking / Judy Jackson. London, Eng.: Macdonald / Orbis, 1989. 128 p.

2439. Vegetables the French Way: A Classic Repertoire of New and Traditional Gallic Recipes / Jack Santa Maria; illustrated by Oliver Caldecott. 1st U.S. ed. Rochester, Vt.: Healing Arts Press, 1989. 160 p., illus. Rev. ed. of: The French Way with Vegetables.

2440. Versatile Vegetables. London, Eng.: Treasure, 1989. 128 p.

2441. All About Vegetables / created and designed by the editorial staff of Ortho Books; written by Walter L. Doty; revision editor, Anne Reilly; illustrator, Ron Hildebrand. Updated, expanded ed. for the 90's. San Francisco, Calif.: Ortho Books, c1990. 144 p., illus. Includes index.

2442. The Cook 's Garden / Lynda Brown. London, Eng.: Century, 1990. 256 p.

2443. From a Breton Garden: The Vegetable Cookery of Josephine Araldo / Josephine Araldo, Robert Reynolds; with illustrations by Gary Bukovnik. Reading, Mass.: Addison-Wesley Pub. Co., 1990. 353 p., illus. 200 recipes. Includes index.

Vegetables *(Continued)*

2444. A Gourmet's Guide to Vegetables / Louise Steele; photographed by David Gill. Los Angeles, Calif.: HP Books, 1990. 120 p., colored illus.

2445. Great Vegetables from the Great Chefs / Baba S. Khalsa; introduction by M.F.K. Fisher. San Francisco, Calif.: Chronicle Books, c1990. 394 p., illus.

2446. Winter Harvest Cookbook: How to Select and Prepare Fresh Seasonal Produce All Winter Long / Lane Morgan. Seattle, Wash.: Sasquatch Books, c1990. 280 p. Includes bibliography and index.

CHILDREN'S COOKBOOKS

2447. Vegetables: An Illustrated History with Recipes / Elizabeth Burton Brown; drawings by Marisabina Russo. Englewood Cliffs, N.J.: Prentice-Hall, c1981. 216 p., illus. Includes bibliography and index. Discusses the origin of such popular vegetables as the cucumber and radish and provides recipes.

2448. Vegetables and Salads / S.J.A. de Villiers and Eunice van der Berg; illustrated by Marita Johnson. Milwaukee, Wis.: G. Stevens, c1985. 32 p., colored illus. "First published in It's Fun to Cook." Introduction to vegetables and salads. Includes index.

2449. Vegetables / Susan Wake; illustrated by John Yates. Minneapolis, Minn.: Carolrhoda Books, 1990, c1989. 32 p., illus. Includes index. Describes different types of vegetables, their history, how they are grown, and their role in human diet and health and provides recipes.

see also entries 991, 1204, 1678; Fruits and Vegetables*; specific vegetables:* Artichokes, Asparagus, Beans, Broccoli, Cabbage, Carrots, Corn, Cucumbers, Eggplants, Greens, Leeks, Legumes, Mushrooms, Okra, Onions, Peas, Peppers, Potatoes, Pumpkin, Squash, Taro, Tomatoes, Zucchini, *etc.; and broader category:* Natural Foods

Venison

2450. The Venison Book: How to Dress, Cut Up, and Cook Your Deer / Audrye Alley Gorton; illustrated by George Daly. Brattleboro, Vt.: Stephen Greene Press, 1957. 78 p., illus.

2451. The Venison Handbook / Brad Sagstetter. Houston, Tex.: Larksdale, 1981. 80 p., illus.

2452. 101 Ways to Fix Venison / Gene L. Skramstad. Kalispell, Mont.: Hunters Guide and Cookbook, c1983. 112 p.

2453. More Than a Trophy / Dennis Walrod. Harrisburg, Pa.: Stackpole Books, c1983. 267 p., illus. Includes index.

2454. Venison: The Monarch of the Table / by Nichola Fletcher. Auchtermuchty, Scot.: N. Fletcher, c1983. 63 p., illus.

2455. Venison--from Field to Table / John Weiss; drawings by Harry Schaare. New York: Outdoor Life Books; Harrisburg, Pa.: Distributed to the trade by Stackpole Books, c1984. 365 p., illus. Includes index.

2456. Mountain Man Cookbook: Venison and Other Recipes / by Thomas L. Canino. 1st ed. Littleton, Colo.: TLC Enterprises, 1985. 99 p., illus.

see also entry 554; and broader category: Game

Vinegar

2457. The Cider Vinegar and Molasses Recipe Book / by Maurice Hanssen. Wellingborough, Eng.: Thorsons, 1976. 64 p., illus. Includes index.

2458. Virtues of Vinegar: Best Vinegar Recipes and Household Hints. Atlanta, Ga.: The Vinegar Institute, 198-. 17 p., illus.

Specific Ingredients 319

Vinegar *(Continued)*

2459. Flavored Vinegars: Herb and Fruit / R. Marilyn Schmidt. Barnegat Light, N.J.: Pine Barrens Press, 1989. 58 p., illus. Directions for 32 different vinegars and 16 recipes for using them. Includes index.

2460. Gourmet Vinegars: How to Make and Cook with Them / Marsha Peters Johnston. Lake Oswego, Or.: Culinary Arts, 1989. 64 p., illus. Contains recipes for creating 57 different vinegars. Includes index.

see also entry 4409; and broader category: Condiments

Walnuts

2461. California Walnuts: Talk of the Town: A Collection of Delicious Recipes, Menus, and Tips Featuring America's Favorite Nut. Sacramento, Calif.: Walnut Marketing Board, c1984. 35 p. Includes index.

see also broader category: Nuts

Watermelon

2462. Watermelon: Uses for the Watermelon, with Recipe Suggestions / Recycling Consortium. Houston, Tex.: Prosperity & Profits, 1989. 14 p.

see also broader category: Fruits

Weakfish

2463. Weakfish-Sea Trout / by R. Marilyn Schmidt. Barnegat Light, N.J.: Barnegat Light Press, 1989. 24 p.

see also broader category: Fish

Wheat

2464. The Classic Wheat for Man Cookbook: More than 300 Delicious and Healthful Ways to Use Stoneground Whole Wheat Flour / written and compiled by Vernice Rosenvall, Mabel H. Miller, Dora D. Flack; design and illustrations by Walt Woesner. New ed. Santa Barbara, Calif.: Woodbridge Press Pub. Co., c1975. 229 p., illus. Includes index. Published in 1952 and 1966 under title: Wheat for Man.

2465. Wheat Flowers: Recipes for Lovers of Healthy Bodies, Clear Minds and Pure Hearts / by Mac Schaffer & Printer Bowler. Big Fork, Mont.: Heartland Communications, c1977. 44 p., illus.

2466. Cooking with Stone Ground Flour / by Arlene Kovash and Marcie Anderson; illustrations by Dorothy Hagerty. Dallas, Or.: Itemizer Observer, c1979. 48 p., illus. Includes index.

2467. Bulgur Wheat Recipes. Logan, Utah: Utah State University Cooperative Extension Service, 1981. 41 p., illus.

2468. How to Cook and Use Whole Kernel Wheat / Flora Bardwell. Logan, Utah: Utah State University Cooperative Extension Service, 1981. 13 p., illus.

2469. The Wholegrain, Health-Saver Cookbook / Miriam Polunin, with Lorraine Bacchus, Martina Hiley, and Carol Hunter; drawings by Eric Rose. New Canaan, Conn.: Keats Pub., 1982, c1977. 138 p., illus. (A Keats/Pivot Health Book). Includes index.

2470. Wheat, Farm to Feast: A Collection of Wheat Recipes / by Juanita Dietz; illustrated by Sharla White. Fort Benton, Mont.: J. Dietz: Can be obtained from Farm to Feast, c1984. 97 p., illus. Includes index.

Specific Ingredients 321

Wheat *(Continued)*

2471. Ethnic Is Now: Ethnic Wheat Foods for Today's Consumer. Bismarck, N.D.: North Dakota Wheat Commission, 1985? 23 p., illus. Issued in cooperation with the Wheat Foods Council and the National Association of Wheat Growers Foundation.

2472. Fabulous Fiber Fixings. Manhattan, Kan.: Kansas Wheat Commission, 1986? 10 p.

2473. Whole Wheat Cookery: Treasures from the Wheat Bin / compiled by Howard and Anna Ruth Beck. 1st ed. Halstead, Kan. (R.R. #1, Box 64, Halstead 67056): Wheat Bin, Inc., c1986. 165 p. Includes index.

2474. Cooking with Seitan: Delicious Natural Foods from Whole Grains / by Barbara and Leonard Jacobs. 1st ed. Tokyo, Japan; New York: Japan Publications, 1987. 240 p., illus. Includes bibliography and index.

see also entry 1100, 1576; Gluten; Wheat Germ; *and broader category:* Grains

Wheat Germ

2475. Naturally Good Wheat Germ Cookbook. New York: Avon, c1974. 144 p., colored illus. On spine: Naturally Good Kretschmer Wheat Germ Cookbook. Includes index.

see also broader category: Wheat

Wheatgrass

2476. The Wheatgrass Book / Ann Wigmore. Wayne, N.J.: Avery Pub. Group, c1985. 126 p., illus. "How to grow and use wheatgrass to maximize your health and vitality." Includes 10 recipes, bibliography, and index.

Whiskey

2477. The Bourbon Cookbook / by Tom Hoge. Harrisburg, Pa.: Stackpole Books, 1975. 288 p., illus. Includes index.

2478. Jack Daniel's The Spirit of Tennessee Cookbook / Lynne Tolley, Pat Mitchamore. Nashville, Tenn.: Rutledge Hill Press, c1988. 192 p., illus. (some colored). 350 recipes. Spine title: Jack Daniel's Cookbook. Includes index.

2479. Cooking with Scotch Whisky / Rosalie Gow. Edinburgh, Scot.: Gordon Wright, 1990. 96 p.

2480. Jack Daniel's Hometown Celebration Cookbook, volume 2 / Pat Mitchamore; with recipes edited by Lynne Tolley. Nashville, Tenn.: Rutledge Hill Press, c1990. 192 p., colored photos. 350 recipes. Contains stories of American life. Includes index. Spine title: Jack Daniel's Cookbook, volume 2.

2481. That Special Touch: A Cookbook / by Sandra Davis. Springfield, Ky.: Special Touch Pub., c1990. 132 p., colored illus. Includes index.

see also broader category: Liquors

White Chocolate

2482. White Chocolate / Janice Wald Henderson. Chicago, Ill.: Contemporary Books, 1989. 220 p., colored illus. 80 recipes. Includes index.

see also broader category: Chocolate

Wild Boar

2483. The European Wild Boar Cookbook = La cuisson du sanglier / Louis Joseph Gautron. St. Claude, Man.: Bridge-Hill Books, c1986. 55 p., illus. Text in English. Includes index.

see also broader category: Game

Wild Foods

2484. Edible and Useful Plants of California / by Charlotte Bringle Clarke. Berkeley, Calif.: University of California Press, c1977. 280 p., illus. (some colored). (California Natural History Guides; 41). Includes indexes.

2485. Wild Foods: A Beginner's Guide to Identifying, Harvesting and Cooking Safe and Tasty Plants from the Outdoors / text and photos. by Laurence Pringle; illustrations by Paul Breeden. New York: Four Winds Press, c1978. 182 p., illus. A guide to identifying, collecting, and preparing twenty wild plants commonly found in and around fields, forests, and streams. Includes bibliography and index.

2486. Wild Foods Cookery: Concerning the Simple Preparation of Edible Wild Things for Consumption / prepared by John Tomikel. California, Pa.: Allegheny Press, c1978. 94 p. Includes index.

2487. The Bounty of the Earth Cookbook: How to Cook Fish, Game, and Other Wild Things / Sylvia G. Bashline. New York: Winchester Press, c1979. 266 p. Includes index.

2488. Edible? Incredible! Pondlife / by Marjorie Furlong & Virginia Pill. Happy Camp, Calif.: Naturegraph Publishers, c1980. 95 p., illus. Includes index.

Specialty Cookbooks

Wild Foods *(Continued)*

2489. Hedgerow Cookery / Rosamond Richardson; illustrations by Molly Hyde. Harmondsworth, Eng.: Penguin, 1980. 250 p., illus. (some colored). (Penguin Handbooks). Includes bibliography and index.

2490. The Natural World Cookbook: Complete Gourmet Meals from Wild Edibles / Joe Freitus; completely illustrated by Salli Haberman, cover photo. by Randy Hill; edited and designed by Pamela B. Haran. Washington, D.C.: Stone Wall Press; Brattleboro, Vt: Distributed by the S. Greene Press, c1980. 283 p., illus. Includes index.

2491. The Wild Palate: A Serious Wild Foods Cookbook / Walter and Nancy Hall; illustrations by David Frampton; designed by Joan Peckolick. Emmaus, Pa.: Rodale Press, c1980. 374 p., illus. Includes index.

2492. Guide to Northeastern Wild Edibles / written and photographed by E. Barrie Kavasch. Vancouver, B.C.; Blaine, Wash.: Hancock House, c1981. 64 p., colored illus. Includes index.

2493. The Weed Eater's Cook Book: How to Identify and Make Tasty Dishes of Common Weeds / Cora G. Chase; illustrations, Margaret Jamieson, Myrtle Cragun. 2nd ed. Burley, Wash. (P.O. Box 103, Burley 98322): Coffee Break Press, c1981. 65 p., illus. Includes bibliography and index.

2494. The Countryside Cookbook: Recipes & Remedies / Gail Duff; illustrated by Linda Garland, with line illustrations by Roger Garland. New York: Van Nostrand Reinhold Co., 1982. 191 p., illus. (some colored). Includes index.

2495. Edible Wild Plants: A Guide to Collecting and Cooking / by Ellen Elliott Weatherbee and James Garnett Bruce. 2nd ed. Ann Arbor, Mich.: E.E. Weatherbee: J.G. Bruce, c1982. 127 p., illus. Includes index. Rev. ed. of: Edible Wild Plants of the Great Lakes Region. 1979.

Wild Foods *(Continued)*

2496. Field Guide to North American Edible Wild Plants / by Thomas S. Elias and Peter A. Dykeman. New York: Outdoor Life Books: Distributed to the trade by Van Nostrand Reinhold, c1982. 286 p., illus. (some colored). Includes indexes.

2497. A Foraging Vacation / by Raquel Boehmer; illustrations by Anne Kilham. Camden, Me.: Down East Books, c1982. 127 p., illus. Includes index.

2498. Wild Greens and Salads / Christopher Nyerges; illustrations by Janice Fryling. Harrisburg, Pa.: Stackpole Books, c1982. 204 p., illus. More than 200 recipes. Includes index.

2499. The Wild, Wild Cookbook: A Guide for Young Wild-Food Foragers / by Jean Craighead George; illustrated by Walter Kessell. 1st ed. New York: Crowell, c1982. 182 p., illus. Includes index.

2500. Deliciously Decadent: A Garden of Wild Culinary Delights / Judie Curle; illustrated by Ursula Medley. Galiano Island, B.C.: Scarab Publications, c1983. 177 p., illus. Includes bibliography and index.

2501. Nature's Wild Harvest / Eric Soothill & Michael J. Thomas. Poole, Eng.: Blandford, 1983. 160 p., illus. (some colored). Includes bibliography and index.

2502. Wildlife Vittles / compiled by Isaac R. Horst. Mt. Forest, Ont.: I.R. Horst, c1983. 117 p. Includes four poems by Esther Horst.

2503. Eating Wild Plants / Kim Williams; illustrations by Toby Tobias. Rev. ed. Missoula, Mont.: Mountain Press Pub. Co., c1984. 140 p., illus. Includes index.

Wild Foods *(Continued)*

2504. Harvesting the Northern Wild: A Guide to Traditional and Contemporary Uses of Edible Forest Plants of the Northwest Territories / Marilyn Walker; plant illustrations by Linda Fairfield. Yellowknife, N.W.T.: Outcrop, c1984. 224 p., illus. Includes index.

2505. The Wild Flavor: Delectable Wild Foods to be Found in Field and Forest and Cooked in Country Kitchens / by Marilyn Kluger; illustrated by Mary Azarian. 1st ed. Los Angeles, Calif.: J.P. Tarcher; Boston, Mass.: Distributed by Houghton Mifflin, 1984. 285 p., illus. Includes index. Reprint. Originally published: New York: Coward, McCann & Geoghegan, 1973.

2506. Billy Joe Tatum's Wild Foods Field Guide and Cookbook / edited by Helen Witty; plant drawings by Jim Blackfeather Rose. New York: Workman Pub. Co., 1985, c1976. 276 p., illus. Includes index. Later ed. of: Billy Joe Tatum's Wild Foods Cookbook and Field Guide, 1976.

2507. Lawn Food Cook Book: Groceries in the Backyard / Linda Runyon; drawings by Linda Runyon. Warrensburg, N.Y.: Runyon Institute, c1985. 46 p., illus.

2508. Plant Lore of an Alaskan Island / Frances Kelso Graham and the Ouzinkie Botanical Society; illustrations by Sandra Coen. Anchorage, Alaska: Alaska Northwest Pub. Co., c1985. 194 p., illus. Includes index.

2509. A Survival Acre: 50 Northeastern Wild Foods & Medicines: A Basic Guide / Linda Runyon; drawings by Linda Runyon. Saranac Lake, N.Y.: Chauncy Press, c1985. 43 p., illus.

2510. A Country Harvest: An Illustrated Guide to Herbs and Wild Plants, Including Delicious Recipes, Herbal Remedies and Beauty Treatments / by Pamela Michael; illustrated by Christabel King. London, Eng.: Peerage, 1986. 240 p., colored illus. Includes bibliography and index. Originally published in 1980 under title: All Good Things Around Us.

Wild Foods *(Continued)*

2511. Wild and Free: Cooking from Nature: 100 Recipes & Folklore of Nature's Harvest / Cyril and Kit O Ceirin. Dublin, Ire.: O'Brien, 1986. 58 p., illus. Includes index. Reprint of 1978 ed.

2512. Wild Food / Roger Phillips; research by Nicky Foy; assisted by Jacqui Hurst; layout by Jill Bryan. 1st ed. Boston, Mass.: Little, Brown, c1986. 192 p., colored illus. Includes index.

2513. Wild Foods of Appalachia / William H. Gillespie. Morgantown, W. Va.: Seneca Books, c1986. 159 p., illus.

2514. Wild Foods of the Desert Cookbook / Darcy Williamson. Bend, Or.: Maverick Publications, c1986. 206 p., illus., maps. Includes bibliography and index.

2515. The Wild Plant Companion: A Fresh Understanding of Herbal Food and Medicine / by Kathryn G. March and Andrew L. March. Bailey, Colo.: Meridian Hill Publications, c1986. 166 p., illus. Includes index.

2516. The Wildfoods Cookbook / Joy O.I. Spoczynska; illustrated by Kenneth H. Poole. London, Eng.: W.H. Allen, 1986, c1985. 272 p., illus. Includes bibliography and index.

2517. Bill & Bev Beatty's Wild Plant Cookbook / by Bill Beatty; illustrations by Bev Beatty. Happy Camp, Calif.: Naturegraph Publishers, c1987. 174 p., illus. Includes indexes.

2518. A Practical Guide to Edible & Useful Plants: Including Recipes, Harmful Plants, Natural Dyes & Textile Fibers / by Delena Tull. Austin, Tex.: Texas Monthly Press, c1987. 518 p., 16 p. of plates, illus. (some colored). Includes index.

Wild Foods *(Continued)*

2519. Stalking the Wild Asparagus / by Euell Gibbons; with illustrations by Margaret F. Schroeder; including a remembrance of the author by John McPhee. 25th anniversary ed. Putney, Vt.: A.C. Hood; Woodstock, Vt.: Distributed by the Countryman Press, 1987, c1962. 303 p., illus. Reprint. Originally published: New York: D. McKay, 1962. Includes index.

2520. The Tumbleweed Gourmet: Cooking with Wild Southwestern Plants / Carolyn J. Niethammer; illustrations by Jenean Thomson. Tucson, Ariz.: University of Arizona Press, c1987. 229 p., illus. Includes index.

2521. The Rural and Native Heritage Cookbook. Toronto, Ont.: Totem Books, 1987. 1 v., illus. Includes index.

2522. Wild Plums in Brandy: Wild Foods Cookery / by Sylvia Boorman. Toronto, Ont.: McGraw-Hill Ryerson, c1987. 194 p., illus. Includes index.

2523. The Basic Essentials of Edible Wild Plants & Useful Herbs / by Jim Meuninck; illustrations by Peggy Duke. Merrillville, Ind.: ICS Books, c1988. 66 p., illus.

2524. Edible Wild Plants: A Guide to Natural Foods / Roy Genders. New York: Van der Marck Editions, c1988. 208 p., illus. (some colored). Includes index.

2525. Hedgerow Harvest / Jan Orchard. Wiltshire, Eng.: Crowood, 1988. 96 p.

2526. How to Prepare Common Wild Foods / by Darcy Williamson. Bend, Or.: Maverick Publications, 1988, c1978. 102 p., illus. Includes index.

Wild Foods *(Continued)*

2527. Thistle Greens and Mistletoe: Edible and Poisonous Plants of Northern California / text and illustrations by James Wiltens. Berkeley, Calif.: Wilderness Press, c1988. 160 p., illus. Includes index. Reprint. Originally published: Plants Your Mother Never Told You About. Saratoga, Calif.: Deer Crossing Wilderness Camp, 1986.

2528. Wild Foods / Avril Rodway; with illustrations by Zane Carey. London, Eng.: B. Trodd, 1988. 128 p., illus. (chiefly colored).

2529. Exploring Nature's Uncultivated Garden / by Deborah Lee. 2nd ed. Takoma Park, Md.: Havelin Communications, 1989. 195 p., illus. Includes bibliography and index.

2530. Food from the Countryside / Leon and Sylvia Olin. London, Eng.: Bishopgate, c1989. 108 p.

2531. Southeastern Wildlife Cookbook: A Collection of Recipes for Sea and Freshwater Food, Large and Small Game, and Savory Oddities from the Wild / from the publishers of South Carolina Wildlife Magazine. Columbia, S.C.: University of South Carolina Press, c1989. 224 p. More than 300 recipes. Contains nutritional charts comparing wild and domestic meats. Originally published as: The South Carolina Wildlife Cookbook. Columbia, S.C.: South Carolina Wildlife and Marine Resources Dept., Information and Public Affairs Division, c1981.

2532. Stalking the Healthful Herbs / Euell Gibbons; with drawings of plants by Raymond W. Rose. Putney, Vt.: A.C. Hood, 1989. 303 p. Includes index. Reprint. Originally published: New York: D. McKay, 1966.

2533. Wild Food Cookbook / Frances Hamerstrom; illustrated by Elva Hamerstrom Paulson. 1st ed. Ames, Iowa: Iowa State University Press, 1989. 126 p., illus. More than 175 recipes. Includes index.

Wild Foods *(Continued)*

2534. Wild Foods Cookbook / by Cathy Johnson; research assistant, Harris Johnson. Lexington, Mass.: Stephen Greene Press, 1989, illus. 224 p. Includes index.

2535. The Wild Taste: Plant & Mushroom Recipes for the Knowledgeable Cook / Kathryn G. March and Andrew L. March; photography and line drawings by Kathryn G. March. Bailey, Colo.: Meridian Hill Publications, c1989. 312 p., illus.

2536. Edible Wild Plants of Pennsylvania and Neighboring States / by Richard J. Medve and Mary Lee Medve; illustrations by Kimball S. Erdman. University Park, Pa.: Pennsylvania State University Press, c1990. 242 p., illus.

see also entries 126, 737, 966, 1274, 1276, 1277, 1282, 1290, 1294, 2338, 2670, 2690, 3572; and Natural Foods

Wild Rice

2537. Wild Rice for All Seasons Cookbook / by Beth Anderson; illustrations by Jan Anderson. Minneapolis, Minn. (5501 Londonderry Rd., Minneapolis 55436): Minnehaha Pub., 1981, c1977. 173 p., illus. Includes index.

2538. 101 Favorite Wild Rice Recipes / Duane R. Lund. Staples, Minn.: Adventure Publications, c1983. 76 p., illus.

2539. Wild Rice, Star of the North: 150 Minnesota Recipes for a Gourmet Grain / the 1006 Summit Avenue Society. New York: McGraw-Hill, c1986. 188 p., illus. Includes index.

2540. The Best of Wild Rice Recipes / by Beatrice Ojakangas. Cambridge, Minn.: Adventure Publications, 1989. 93 p.

Wild Rice *(Continued)*

2541. Naturally Wild Rice: Delicious, Nutritious, Easy & Elegant Recipes / by Cheryl Cardiff. La Ronge, Sask.: Naturally Wild Pub., 1990. 62 p.

see also broader categories: Grains; Rice

Wine

2542. The Standard Wine Cookbook / by Anne Director. Berkeley, Calif.: Ross Books, 1979. 192 p. (Culinary Arts Series). Includes index.

2543. Culinary Creations: A Collection of Michigan Wine Recipes / courtesy of Michigan wineries and the Michigan Grape and Wine Industry Council. Lansing, Mich.: 198-. 32 p., illus.

2544. The Champagne Cookbook: Add Some Sparkle to Your Cooking and Your Life / by Malcolm R. Hebert; illustrations, Susann Ortega. San Francisco, Calif.: Wine Appreciation Guild, c1980. 124 p., illus. Includes index.

2545. The Wine Book / James Wagenvoord. New York: Quick Fox, c1980. 127 p., illus. (some colored). Includes index.

2546. Favorite Recipes of California Winemakers / collected by Wine Advisory Board, editor, Lee Hecker; artist, Judy Hibel. San Francisco, Calif.: Wine Appreciation Guild, 1981. 128 p., illus. Includes index.

2547. New Adventures in Wine Cookery / by California Winemakers; illustrations by Susann Ortega. San Francisco, Calif.: Wine Appreciation Guild, c1981. 123 p., illus. Includes index.

2548. Country Winemaking & Wine Cookery / Muriel Hooker Mackay. Newton Abbot, Eng.; North Pomfret, Vt.: David & Charles, c1982. 143 p., illus. Includes index.

Wine *(Continued)*

2549. The Odyssey Cookbook: A Culinary Cruise / by Malcolm R. Hebert. San Francisco, Calif.: Wine Appreciation Guild, c1982. 124 p., illus. Includes index.

2550. Wine in Everyday Cooking: Cooking with Wine for Family and Friends / by Patricia Ballard; edited by Pamela Kittler. San Francisco, Calif.: Wine Appreciation Guild, 1982. 122 p., illus. Includes index.

2551. California Wine Lovers' Cookbook / by Malcolm Hebert. San Francisco, Calif.: Wine Appreciation Guild with Wine Institute, c1983. 174 p. Includes index.

2552. Wine / by the editors of Time-Life Books. Alexandria, Va.: Time-Life Books; Morristown, N.J.: School and library distribution by Silver Burdett, c1983. 176 p., colored illus. (The Good Cook, Techniques & Recipes). "A Buyer's Guide to Selecting Wine" and "A Catalogue of Well-Known Wines" (4 p.) inserted. Includes indexes.

2553. Life with Wine: A Self-Portrait of the Wine Business in the Napa and Sonoma Valleys, plus 100 recipes that go with the product / interviews by Nancy Chirich; drawings by John Simpkins. Oakland, Calif.: 'Ed-it Productions, c1984. 189 p., illus. Includes index.

2554. The Little Wine Cookbook / Mary L. Green. Denver, Colo.: Giftstar, 1984. ca. 10 p., illus. (Little Cookbooks).

2555. Spirited Cooking: An Introduction to Wines in the Kitchen / Robert Ackart. 1st ed. New York: Atheneum, 1984. 364 p. More than 250 recipes. Includes index.

2556. Wine, Food & the Good Life: Recipes Celebrating 50 Years of Family Winemaking / Arlene Mueller, Dorothy Indelicato. San Francisco, Calif.: Wine Appreciation Guild, c1985. 140 p., illus. Includes index.

Wine *(Continued)*

2557. Adventures in Wine Cookery / edited by Donna Bottrell [and others]. 2nd ed. San Francisco, Calif.: Wine Appreciation Guild, 1986. 144 p., illus.

2558. Epicurean Recipes of California Winemakers / by Wine Advisory Board; editor, David R. Wilcox; food editor, Marjorie L. Lumm; book design and illustrations, Nancy J. Kennedy. New ed. Blue Earth, Minn.: Piper Pub., Inc. 1986. 128 p., illus. Includes indexes.

2559. The Frugal Gourmet Cooks with Wine / Jeff Smith; illustrations by Gary Jacobsen; with articles on tasting and selecting wine by Corbet Clark. 1st ed. New York: Morrow, c1986. 447 p., illus. More than 400 recipes. Includes index.

2560. The Pleasures of Wine with Food. San Francisco, Calif.: Wine Institute, c1986. 29 p., illus.

2561. Vintner's Choice / Hilde Gabriel Lee. 1st ed. Berkeley, Calif.: Ten Speed Press, c1986. 381 p., illus. Includes indexes.

2562. Winemakers Cookbook: Culinary Adventures with America's Premier Vintners / Lou Seibert Pappas; photography by Renee Lynn. San Francisco, Calif.: Chronicle Books, 1986. 108 p., colored illus. Includes index.

2563. Cooking with Wine / John Pearse; edited by John Warde. Buckingham, Pa.: Buckingham Wine Press, 1987. 100 p., illus.

2564. The Cook's Wine Book: A Guide to Pairing Wine with Food, Recipes and Suggestions / edited by Fritz and Mary Nordengren. Des Moines, Iowa: Wine Society, 1987. 112 p.

2565. Easy Recipes of California Winemakers / production editor, Frances W. Hewlett; editor, Marjorie Kent Jacobs. San Francisco, Calif.: California Wine Advisory Board, 1987. 128 p., colored illus.

Wine *(Continued)*

2566. Gourmet Wine Cooking the Easy Way / Wine Advisory Board staff; edited by David R. Wilcox. 3rd ed. San Francisco, Calif.: Wine Appreciation Guild, 1987. ca. 130 p., illus. (part colored).

2567. Fine Wine in Food / by Patricia Ballard; edited by Jill Goddard. San Francisco, Calif.: Wine Appreciation Guild, 1988. 156 p., illus. Includes index.

2568. Betty Crocker's Cooking with American Wine. 1st ed. New York: Prentice Hall, c1989. 112 p., colored illus. Includes index.

2569. Cooking with Wine & Spirits: A Collection of Easy & Elegant Recipes / edited by Barbara Brusehaber Dvorak. San Diego, Calif.: PCI Publications, c1990. 149 p.

see also entries 214, 743; Sherry; *and broader category:* Liquors

Worcestershire Sauce

2570. Lea & Perrins Appetizer, Soup, Main Dish, Vegetable, and Salad Cookbook. [n.p.] Supermarket Book Co., c1975. 128 p., colored illus. "A Rutledge Book." Includes indexes.

see also broader category: Condiments

Yeast

2571. New and Easy Yeast Recipes. Milwaukee, Wis.: Universal Food Corp., 1980. 24 p.

2572. Fleischmann's Bake-it-easy Yeast Book. East Hanover, N.J.: Nabisco Brands, 1982. 1 booklet.

2573. Quick and Easy Yeast Recipes / by Kate Easlea. Southampton, Eng.: Paul Care, 1982. 52 p. Includes index.

Specific Ingredients

Yeast *(Continued)*

2574. Meal-in-a-Loaf Cookbook. East Hanover, N.J.: Nabisco Brands, 1986. 1 booklet.

2575. Your First 100 Recipes for Nutritional Yeast / by M.J. Haines. Axminster, Eng.: Tytherleigh Press, 1986. 99 leaves, colored illus. Includes index.

see also Breads *(Section II);* Baking *(Section IV)*

Yogurt

2576. The Complete Book of Yogurt / Shaun Nelson-Henrick. New York: Macmillan, c1980. 324 p. Includes index.

2577. Cooking with Yogurt / Beth Cockburn-Smith. London, Eng.: Hamlyn, 1980. 128 p., illus. (some colored). Includes index.

2578. Country Kitchen Recipes with Yogurt / Maurice Hanssen. Wellingborough, Eng.: Thorsons, 1980. 32 p., illus. (Country Kitchen Recipes).

2579. The Yogurt Cookbook / by Shona Crawford Poole and Jasper Partington. London, Eng.: Octopus Books, 1980. 92 p., illus. (chiefly colored). Includes index.

2580. Yogurt Cookery. Sea Cliff, N.Y.: Carbooks, Inc., 1980. 1 v. 200 recipes. Includes directions for making your own yogurt.

2581. Cooking with Yogurt / Olwen Woodier. Charlotte, Vt.: Garden Way Pub., c1981. 32 p., illus. (Garden Way Bulletin; A-86).

2582. Dannon Yogurt Cookbook. New York: Bonanza: Distributed by Crown Publishers, c1982. 63 p., colored illus. At head of title: Ideals.

Yogurt *(Continued)*

2583. Cooking with Yogurt / Sister Berthe. Toronto, Ont.: McClelland and Stewart, c1983. 278 p., 28 p. of colored plates.

2584. The Yoghurt Book: Food of the Gods / Arto der Haroutunian. Harmondsworth, Eng.: Penguin, 1983. 205 p. Includes index.

2585. Warm Weather Recipes Featuring Yogurt / by Susan George; illustrations, Susan George. St. Petersburg, Fla.: LaFray Young Pub. Co., c1985. 73 p., illus. Includes index.

2586. The Peninsula Farm Yogurt Cookbook / by Sonia Jones; illustrations by Jennie Prish. Porters Lake, N.S.: Pottersfield Press, c1988. 83 p., illus. (Cookbooks with Culture Series; #1).

see also entries 1121, 1712; Yogurt Cheese; *and broader category:* Dairy Products

Yogurt Cheese

2587. Not Just Cheesecake!: The Low-Fat, Low-Cholesterol, Low-Calorie Great Dessert Cookbook / Marilyn Stone, Shelley Melvin, Charlie Crawford; foreword by Gail Kauwell. Gainesville, Fla.: Triad Pub. Co., c1988. 142 p. 100 recipes. Includes index.

2588. Snack to Your Heart's Content!: The Low-Fat, Low-Cholesterol, Low-Calorie Quick & Easy Cookbook / Shelley Melvin and Marilyn Stone; foreword by Gail Kauwell. Gainesville, Fla.: Triad Pub Co., 1990. 192 p. 150 recipes.

see also broader categories: Cheese; Yogurt

Zucchini

2589. Zucchini Cookery / by Virg and Jo Lemley. Enl. ed. Cave Junction, Or.: Wilderness House, c1976. 56 p., illus.

2590. Cooking with Zucchini / by Janet Lewis and Barbara Plumb. Duluth, Minn.: Country Garden Press, c1980. 170 p.

2591. Harriet's Zucchini Lovers' Cookbook / by William Boot; cover design and chapter illustrations by Lenio S. Pereira. Forest Hills, N.Y.: Harriet's Kitchen, c1981. 213 p., illus. Includes index.

2592. Mickey's Zucchini Recipes / Leona Mickey Nault. Winnipeg, Man.: Gateway Pub., c1983. 110 p., illus.

2593. The Zucchini Cookbook / by Paula Simmons. 3rd ed., rev. & enl. Seattle, Wash.: Pacific Search Press, c1983. 130 p., illus. Includes index.

2594. The Best of Zucchini Time/Mushroom Time / Maxine Plastino. Livermore, Calif.: Plastino, c1984. 200 p. Combined ed. of the author's Zucchini Time, and Mushroom Time.

2595. The Zucchini Monster Cookbook / by John Muller; illustrations by Rebecca Whittaker Miller. Sebastopol, Calif.: J. Muller/Great Housekeeping, c1984. 59 p., colored illus.

2596. Bette McClure Capozzo Presents Just Zucchini Cook Book / edited by Charlotte Barber. Prince George, B.C.: Bee Cap Pub., c1986. 95 p.

2597. The Zucchini Cook Book: Over 207 Zucchini Recipes from Soups to Desserts / by Helen O. and Emil B. Dandar. Penndel, Pa.: Sterling Specialties Cookbooks, c1986. 52 p.

Specialty Cookbooks

Zucchini *(Continued)*

2598. Best of the "Fest": Selected "Cook Them Zukes" Cooking Contest Recipes, 1983-1986. Hayward, Calif.: Hayward Zucchini Festival, c1987. 77 p. "A joint venture of the Hayward Zucchini Festival and Soroptimist International of Hayward."

2599. Fabulous Cooking with Zucchini, Pumpkin and Squash / Anne Katherine Kowbel. 1st ed. Saskatoon, Sask.: Fabulous Cooking, 1987. 112 p., colored illus. Includes index.

2600. The Best of the Zucchini Recipes Cookbook: Blue Ribbon Recipes from Around the Country / edited by Helen & Emil Dandar. Penndel, Pa.: Sterling Specialties Cookbooks, c1989. 126 p., illus. Includes index.

2601. The New Zucchini Cookbook / by Nancy C. Ralston and Marynor Jordan. Rev. ed. Pownal, Vt.: Storey Communications, c1990. 170 p., illus. "A Garden Way Publishing Classic." Includes index. Revision of: Garden Way's Zucchini Cookbook. 1977.

2602. Zucchini from A to Z / by Ellen Ayotte, and rev. by Marguerite Stetson. Fairbanks, Alaska: University of Alaska, Cooperative Extension Service, 1990. 13 p., illus.

see also entry 1712; and broader category: Vegetables

SECTION II

APPETIZERS, WAFFLES, AND MORE COOKBOOKS FOR SPECIFIC DISHES AND COURSES

Appetizers

2603. Hors d'Oeuvres: Favorite Recipes from the Embassy Kitchens. Tokyo, Japan; Rutland, Vt.: C.E. Tuttle Co., 1959. 104 p., illus.

2604. Cocktails & Hors d'Oeuvres / by Ina C. Boyd; illustrated by Mike Nelson. Concord, Calif.: Nitty Gritty Productions, c1978. 88 p., illus.

2605. The Big Beautiful Book of Hors d'Oeuvres / Julia Weinberg. New York: Butterick Pub., c1980. 176 p., illus. Includes index.

2606. Canapés--Appetizers--for Your Party / these recipes collected by Creations Lac Brome of Knowlton; editors, Mary Bruce, Angela Kerrigan. 1st ed. Knowlton, Que.: Creations Lac Brome of Knowlton, 1980. 104 p., illus. Includes index.

2607. The Frozen Hors d'Oeuvre Cookbook: You've Got It Made / by Jane Keyes; illustrations by Jane Breit. New York: Hasting House, c1980. 214 p., illus. Includes index.

2608. The Pocket Book of Simple Starters. London, Eng.: Evans Bros., 1980. 127 p.

2609. Variations on a Starter / Jean Conil. Loughton, Eng.: Piatkus, 1980. 144 p.

2610. Hors d'Oeuvres / the Sir Mortimer B. Davis Jewish General Hospital Auxiliary; illustrated by Robert de Bellefeuille. Montreal, Que.: The Auxiliary, 1981. 59 p., illus.

Specialty Cookbooks

Appetizers *(Continued)*

2611. Just for Starters: A Treasury of 350 of the World's Best Hors d'Oeuvres and Appetizers / Gloria Edwinn. New York: Viking Press, 1981. 255 p., illus. Includes index.

2612. Appetizers. Los Angeles, Calif.: Knapp Press, c1982. 119 p., colored illus. (Cooking with Bon Appétit). Includes index.

2613. Appetizers, Salad Dressings, and Salads / Geraline B. Hardwick and Robert L. Kennedy. Boston, Mass.: CBI Pub. Co., c1982. 360 p., illus. (some colored). (Fundamentals of Quality Food Preparation). Includes index.

2614. Beginning Again: More Hors d'Oeuvres. Cincinnati, Ohio: Rockdale Ridge Press, 1982, c1981. 224 p., illus. Includes index.

2615. Chinese Appetizers and Garnishes / Huang Su-huei; translator, Chen Chang-yen; photographers, Aki Ohno, T.S. Wang, Lin Kun Hon. Alhambra, Calif.: Distributed by Wei-chuan's Cooking, 1982. 151 p., illus. (some colored).

2616. Hors d'Oeuvre / by the editors of Time-Life Books. Alexandria, Va.: Time-Life Books; Morristown, N.J.: School and library distribution by Silver Burdett, c1982. 176 p., illus. (some colored). (The Good Cook Technique & Recipes). Includes index.

2617. In the Beginning: A Collection of Hors d'Oeuvres. 12th ed., enl. and rev. Cincinnati, Ohio: Rockdale Ridge Press, 1982, c1975. 201 p., illus. Includes indexes.

2618. Sunset Hors d'Oeuvres: Appetizers, Spreads & Dips / by the editors of Sunset Books and Sunset Magazine. Menlo Park, Calif.: Lane Pub. Co., 1982, c1976. 80 p., illus. Includes index.

2619. 101 Pretentious Hors d'Oeuvres / G.H. Crown. 1st ed. Chicago, Ill.: Chicago Review Press, c1983. 112 p., illus. Includes index.

Specific Dishes and Courses 341

Appetizers *(Continued)*

2620. Hors d'Oeuvres Everybody Loves / Mary Leigh Furrh and Jo Barksdale. Brandon, Miss.: Quail Ridge Press, 1983. 79 p.

2621. I Can't Cook Starters / Sonia Allison. London, Eng.: Elm Tree, 1983. 64 p.

2622. The Appetizer Cookbook / Frederick E. Kahn; edited by William Wright. New York: Nautilus Communications, c1984. 142 p. Includes index.

2623. Easy & Elegant Hors d'Oeuvres: An Encore Performance / by Nonnie Cameron and Diane Phillips. Silver Spring, Md.: American Cooking Guild, 1984. 56 p., illus. (Collector's Series).

2624. Easy Appetizers / by Kim Upton and Bev Bennett. Woodbury, N.Y.: Barron's, c1984. 64 p., colored illus. (Easy Cooking). Includes index.

2625. For Starters / Ingeborg Pertwee; photography by John Barrett; line drawings by John Spencer. Kingswood, Eng.: World's Work, c1984. 272 p., illus. (some colored).

2626. Great Beginnings: Hors d'Oeuvres, Appetizers, Soups, Salads / Marion McCristall; illustrations, Sheila Bensley. Surrey, B.C.: Happy Hostess Cooking Co., c1984. 113 p., illus. Includes index.

2627. Hors-d'Oeuvres / Carla Homan & Joyce Palmer. Edmonton, Alta.: Hurtig, 1984. 112 p., colored illus. More than 100 recipes.

2628. Martha Stewart's Hors d'Oeuvres: The Creation and Presentation of Fabulous Finger Foods / Martha Stewart; photographs by Peter Bosch; recipes and styling with Sara Foster. 1st ed. New York: C.N. Potter: Distributed by Crown Publishers, c1984. 165 p., colored illus. More than 150 recipes. Includes index.

Appetizers *(Continued)*

2629. The International Appetizer Cookbook / by Sonia Uvezian. New York: Fawcett Columbine, c1984. 450 p., 8 p. of plates, illus. (some colored). Includes index.

2630. The Joy of Cocktails & Hors d'Oeuvre / by Bev Bennett & Kim Upton. Woodbury, N.Y.: Barron's, c1984. 218 p., 32 p. of plates, colored illus. 75 recipes for alcoholic and non-alcoholic drinks; 125 food preparation recipes. Includes index.

2631. Microwave Cuisine Cooks Appetizers / Millie Delahunty. Garden City, N.Y.: Microwave Cuisine, 1984. 32 p., illus.

2632. Oriental Appetizers / Yukiko and Bob Haydock. 1st ed. New York: Holt, Rinehart and Winston, c1984. 145 p., illus. (some colored). Includes index.

2633. America's Best Appetizers / JoNett Butler and Bea Farwell. Clinton, Iowa: Butler-Farwell, 1985. 220 p., illus.

2634. Appetizers & Hors d'Oeuvres / Hallie Donnelly, Janet Kessel Fletcher, writers; Joel Glenn, photographer. San Francisco, Calif.: California Culinary Academy: Inquiries to Ortho Books, Chevron Chemical Co., c1985. 128 p., colored illus. More than 180 recipes. (Easy & Elegant Meals). Includes index.

2635. Hors d'Oeuvre and Canapés / by James Beard. 1st Quill ed., Classic ed. New York: Quill, c1985. 206 p. Includes index. Originally published: New York: M. Barrows, 1963.

2636. Mary Blair's Hors d'Oeuvre Cookbook: A Complete Guide to Hors d'Oeuvre Cookery and Festive Menus / by Mary Blair. New York: Freundlich Books, c1985. 433 p., 12 p. of plates, illus. (some colored). Includes index.

2637. The Perfect Starter / Bernice Hurst; illustrations by Ronald Hurst. Twickenham, Eng.: Hamlyn, 1985. 32 p., illus. (The Perfect Series). Originally published in 1979.

Appetizers *(Continued)*

2638. The Book of Appetizers / June Budgen; photography by Per Ericson. Tucson, Ariz.: HP Books, c1986. 128 p., colored illus. Includes index.

2639. Entertaining with Appetizers. Tucson, Ariz.: HP Books, c1986. 80 p., colored illus. Includes index.

2640. Fiery Appetizers: Seventy Spicy Hot Hors d'Oeuvres: A "Fiery Cuisines" Cookbook / by Dave DeWitt and Nancy Gerlach; illustrations by Cyd Riley. 1st ed. New York: St. Martin's Press, c1986. 87 p., illus. Includes index.

2641. First Course Dishes / edited by Susan Dixon. London, Eng.: Ward Lock, 1986. 63 p., illus. (some colored). (Mrs. Beeton's Home Cooking). Contains recipes selected from Mrs. Beeton's Cookery and Household Management.

2642. Hors d'Oeuvres: Easy Elegance / Laurene Morley; edited by Diane Morley Petruzzini. Two Rivers, Wis.: Creative Cookery, c1986. 105 p.

2643. Starters with Style / Arabella Boxer. London, Eng.: Conran Octopus, 1986. 80 p., colored illus. Includes index. Published in the U.S. under title: Fashionable First Courses (entry 2646).

2644. Appetizers and Salads / Pol Martin. Montreal, Que.: Brimar, c1987. 64 p., colored illus. (Smart & Simple Cooking). Includes index.

2645. Best Little Hors d'Oeuvres in Kansas / by Betty M. May. Olathe, Kan.: Cookbook Publishers, c1987. 82 p.

2646. Fashionable First Courses / Arabella Boxer. 1st ed. in U.S. Garden City, N.Y.: Doubleday, 1987, c1986. 80 p., colored illus. (Conran Cookbooks). Includes index. Originally published under title: Starters with Style (entry 2643).

Appetizers *(Continued)*

2647. Fast & Fabulous Hors d'Oeuvres / by Polly Clingerman; edited by Marian Levine. Silver Spring, Md.: American Cooking Guild, 1987. 64 p., illus. (Collector's Series; v. 21).

2648. Starters as a Main Meal / Mary-Lou Arnold and others. London, Eng.: Bay Books, 1987? 96 p.

2649. Antipasto Feasts: Variations on an Italian Theme with Aperitivi and Sweets / Karen A. Lucas and Lisa Wilson. Berkeley, Calif.: Aris Books, 1988. 120 p., illus. (Kitchen edition). Includes index.

2650. Appetizers / Mable & Gar Hoffman; photography, deGennaro Associates. Rev. ed. Los Angeles, Calif.: HP Books, c1988. 160 p., colored illus. Cover title: Mable Hoffman's Appetizers. Includes index.

2651. Canapés / Berit Vinegrad. London, Eng.: Macdonald Orbis, 1988. 160 p. (Tempting Treats).

2652. The Complete Book of Starters / Yve Menzies. London, Eng.: Hale, 1988. 320 p.

2653. Fast & Flashy Hors d'Oeuvres / Michele Braden. Washington, D.C.: Acropolis Books, c1988. 320 p., illus. (some colored). 275 recipes. Includes index.

2654. Fresh Ways with Appetizers / by the editors of Time-Life Books. Alexandria, Va.: Time-Life Books, c1988. 144 p., colored illus. (Healthy Home Cooking). Includes index.

2655. The Hors d'Oeuvre Book / Coralie Castle; illustrations by Karen Lynch. Rev. ed. San Ramon, Calif.: Chevron Chemical Co., 1988. 241 p., illus. (some colored). More than 450 recipes and 350 variations. Includes index. Originally published: Hors d'Oeuvre etc. San Francisco, Calif.: 101 Productions, 1973.

Appetizers *(Continued)*

2656. Openers / by Amy Nathan; photographs by Kathryn Kleinman; text by Jo Mancuso. San Francisco, Calif.: Chronicle Books, c1988. 139 p., colored illus. Includes index.

2657. Secrets of French Hors d'Oeuvres / general editor, Beverly LeBlanc. London, Eng.: Macdonald, 1988. 96 p., colored illus. Includes index.

2658. Best Recipes for Appetizers. 1st Prentice Hall Press ed. New York: Prentice Hall Press, c1989. 112 p., colored illus. More than 100 recipes. (Betty Crocker's Red Spoon Collection). Includes index.

2659. Primi Piatti / by Christopher Styler; illustrations by Scott Baldwin. 1st ed. New York: Harper & Row, c1989. 300 p., illus. 196 recipes. Includes index.

2660. Appetizers: Soups, Spreads, Salads, Hors d'Oeuvre, Pastas and Much More / Bonnie Stern. Mississauga, Ont.: Random House Canada, 1990. 168 p., illus. Includes index.

2661. The Book of Great Hors d'Oeuvre / Terence Janericco. Updated and expanded. New York: Van Nostrand Reinhold, 1990. 776 p., illus. Includes index.

2662. Holiday Appetizers. Des Moines, Iowa: Meredith Corp., 1990. 104 p., colored illus. 150 recipes. (Better Homes and Gardens Creative Ideas). Includes index. "Better Homes and Gardens Special Interest Publications."

2663. Hors d'Oeuvres: Festive and Elegant Party Menus / by Norman Kolpas. Los Angeles, Calif.: HP Books, 1990. 141 p., 75 colored photos. Contains instructions for planning party meals consisting of appetizers and 14 menus for appetizer buffets. Includes index.

Appetizers *(Continued)*

2664. Sunset Appetizers / by the editors of Sunset Books and Sunset Magazine; research & text, Sue Brownlee; photographers, Darrow M. Watt, Tom Wyatt, Nikolay Zurek. 2nd ed. Menlo Park, Calif.: Lane Pub. Co., 1990. 96 p., colored illus. Includes index. First ed. published in 1984.

see also entries 3945, 3956, 3963, 3966; and Dips

Appetizers and Desserts

2665. Before & After: A Cookbook of Appetizers and Desserts / American Association of University Women, New Brunswick Area Branch. Iowa Falls, Iowa: General Pub. and Binding; Washington, D.C.: Available from AAUW, 1981. 94 p., illus.

2666. Great Beginnings & Happy Endings: Hors d'Oeuvres and Desserts for Standing Ovations / by Renny Darling. Beverly Hills, Calif.: Royal Pub. Co., Book Division, Recipes-of-the-Month-Club, c1981. 262 p., illus. Includes index.

2667. The Chosen: Appetizers & Desserts / edited by Marilyn Stone; illustrated by Lea Gabbay. Gainesville, Fla.: Triad Pub. Co., c1982. 208 p., illus. (The Chosen Cookbook Series). Includes index. Recipes selected from 120 Jewish cookbooks.

2668. Cooking Among Friends: A New Collection of More Than 170 Delicious Hors d'Oeuvres and Desserts. Columbia, Md.: Among Friends; Cockeysville, Md.: Distributed by Liberty Pub. Co., 1983. 93 p., illus.

2669. Simple Feasts: Appetizers, Main Dishes & Desserts / Marilee Matteson. Boston, Mass.: Houghton Mifflin, 1983. 249 p., illus. (some colored). Includes index.

Appetizers and Desserts *(Continued)*

2670. The Friends of the Essex Youth Orchestras Present Overtures & Encores: Being a Collection of Quick and Easy Recipes for Starters & Puds. West Hanningfield, Eng.: The Friends, c1985. 62 p., illus. Includes index.

2671. Appetizers, Salads and Desserts / by Pol Martin. New York: Eclair Pub. International, 1989. 128 p. Includes index.

see also Desserts

Appetizers and Snacks

2672. Oriental Snacks and Appetizers / Jacki Passmore. Sydney, Australia; London, Eng.: Lansdowne, 1981. 128 p., colored illus. Includes index.

2673. Favorite Brand Name Recipes: Appetizers, Dips & Party Snacks / by the editors of Consumer Guide. New York: Beekman House: Distributed by Crown Publishers, c1982. 80 p., colored illus. Includes index.

2674. Hors d'Oeuvres and Party Snacks. New York: Golden Press, c1982. 64 p., colored illus. (A Betty Crocker Picture Cookbook; 8).

2675. Wok Appetizers and Light Snacks / by Gary Lee; photographs by Glen Millward; illustrations by Mike Nelson; edited by Jackie Walsh. Concord, Calif.: Nitty Gritty Productions, c1982. 182 p., illus. (some colored). Includes index.

2676. Cocktail Party Nibbles / Helen O'Leary. Newton Abbot, Eng.; North Pomfret, Vt.: David & Charles, c1984. 64 p., illus. Includes index.

Specialty Cookbooks

Appetizers and Snacks *(Continued)*

2677. Vegetarian Snacks and Starters / by Janet Hunt; illustrated by Ian Jones. Wellingborough, Eng.: Thorsons in co-operation with the Vegetarian Society of the United Kingdom, 1984. 128 p., illus. Includes index.

2678. Better Homes and Gardens Anytime Appetizers. 1st ed. Des Moines, Iowa: Meredith Corp., c1985. 96 p., illus. (some colored). ca. 100 recipes. Includes index.

2679. Just a Bite / Polly Tyrer. New York: Prentice Hall Press, 1986. 160 p., colored illus. Includes index.

2680. Nibble Mania / by Cathy Prange and Joan Pauli; sketches by Miriam Stanbury. Kitchener, Ont.: Muffin Mania Pub., 1986, c1983. 66 p., illus.

2681. Better Homes and Gardens After-School Cooking. 1st ed. Des Moines, Iowa: Meredith Corp., c1987. 96 p., colored illus. Includes index.

2682. Better Homes and Gardens Super Snacks / editor, Rosemary C. Hutchinson. 1st ed. Des Moines, Iowa: Meredith Corp., c1987. 46 p., illus. (some colored). Includes index.

2683. Diabetic Snack & Appetizer Cookbook / Mary Jane Finsand; foreword by James D. Healy; edited by Laurel Ornitz. New York: Sterling Pub. Co., c1987. 160 p. Includes index.

2684. Oriental Appetizers & Light Meals / Susan Fuller Slack. Los Angeles, Calif.: HP Books, c1987. 160 p., colored illus.

2685. Quick & Easy Microwaving Snacks & Appetizers / developed by the kitchens of the Microwave Cooking Institute. New York: Prentice-Hall, c1987. 96 p., colored illus. Includes index.

2686. Appetizers and Side Dishes. Toronto, Ont.: Grolier, 1988. 110 p., colored illus. (Microwave Magic; 15). Includes index.

Appetizers and Snacks *(Continued)*

2687. Microwaving Light Meals & Snacks / by Barbara Methven. Minnetonka, Minn.: Cy DeCosse, c1988. 159 p., colored illus. (Microwave Cooking Library). Includes index.

see also Snacks; Tapas

Bagels

2688. Bagelmania: The "Hole" Story / Connie Berman & Suzanne Munshower. Tucson, Ariz.: HP Books, c1987. 126 p., illus. "An Ultra Communications and Mountain Lion Book." Includes index.

2689. The Bagel Book / by Marilyn & Tom Bagel; illustrations by Donna Ward. Bethesda, Md.: Poppyseed Press, c1989. 114 p., illus. 100 recipes. Includes index.

see also broader category: Bread

Beverages

2690. A Country Cup: Old and New Recipes for Drinks of All Kinds Made from Wild Plants and Herbs / Wilma Paterson. London, Eng.: Pelham Books, 1980. 88 p., illus. (some colored).

2691. Drinks & Snacks / Mala Young; illustrated by Susan Neale. Newton Abbot, Eng.: David & Charles, c1981. 48 p., illus. (Health Food Cooking).

2692. The Non-drinker's Drink Book: A Guide to Mixing Non-alcoholic Drinks / Gail Schioler. Toronto, Ont.: Personal Library; Rexdale, Ont.: Distributed by Wiley, c1981. 159 p., illus. Includes index.

Beverages *(Continued)*

2693. The Book of Coffee and Tea: A Guide to the Appreciation of Fine Coffees, Teas, and Herbal Beverages / Joel, David, and Karl Schapira; illustrated by Meri Shardin. 2nd ed. New York: St. Martin's Press, c1982. 323 p., illus. Includes index.

2694. Drinks for All Seasons / Babs Honey. Wakefield, Eng.: EP, 1982. 96 p., illus. (some colored). Includes index.

2695. Tootie Frootie: Milk Drinks for Children / prepared by the National Dairy Council; illustrations by Gerry Greaves. Stevenage, Eng.: Publications for Companies, 1982. 16 p., illus. (some colored).

2696. 100 Luscious Diet Drinks / by Naomi Koshkin and Millicent Brower. New York: Simon and Schuster, c1983. 110 p. "A Fireside Book." Includes index.

2697. Beverages / by the editors of Time-Life Books. Alexandria, Va.: Time-Life Books, c1983. 176 p., colored illus. (The Good Cook, Techniques & Recipes). Contains recipes for alcoholic and non-alcoholic drinks. Includes indexes.

2698. Country Wines & Cordials: Wild Plant & Herbal Recipes for Drinks Old & New / Wilma Paterson. Ware, Eng.: Omega Books, 1983. 88 p., illus. (some colored). Includes bibliography.

2699. Drinks without Liquor: For Bashes, Beaches, BBQs and Birthdays / by Jane Brandt; illustrations by Jerry Joyner. New York: Workman Pub., 1983. 143 p., illus. Includes index.

2700. In Search of the Wild Dewberry: Making Beverages, Teas, and Syrups from Wild Ingredients / Steven A. Krause; illustrations by Robert W. Freckmann. Harrisburg, Pa.: Stackpole Books, c1983. 276 p., illus. Includes index.

2701. Non-alcoholic Cocktails / Anne Jesper. Weybridge, Eng.: Whittet, 1983. 96 p.

Beverages *(Continued)*

2702. The Beverage Cookbook / Frederick E. Kahn; edited by William Wright. New York: Nautilus Communications, c1984. 119 p., illus. Includes index.

2703. Alcohol-free Entertaining: Come for Mocktails / Patsy Anne Bickerstaff, Bill Seay. White Hall, Va.: Betterway Publications, 1985. 159 p., illus. Includes index.

2704. Liquid Sunshine, Naturally Yours / by Elizabeth Quinn. Lisburn, Eng. (13 Ardis Ave., Lisburn, Co. Antrim, BT28 3PX): B.Q. Publications, c1985. 131 p., illus. Includes index.

2705. Entertaining Without Alcohol / by Dorothy Crouch. London, Eng.: Arlington, 1986, c1985. 208 p., illus. Includes index.

2706. Good Spirits: Alcohol-free Drinks for All Occasions / by Marie Simmons and Barbara J. Lagowski. New York: New American Library, c1986. 160 p., 8 p. of plates, illus. (some colored). "A Plume Book." Includes indexes.

2707. The Non-alcoholic Cocktail Book / David Bevan. London, Eng.: Ebury, 1986. 64 p., illus. (some colored). Includes index.

2708. One for the Road: Vogue Guide to Non-alcoholic Drinks / Henry McNulty. Twickenham, Eng.: Hamlyn, 1986. 96 p., colored illus. Includes index.

2709. Claire's Cocktails & Party Drinks / Claire Attridge. London, Eng.: MacDonald Orbis, 1987. 42 p., colored illus. Includes index.

2710. The Hot Drink Book / Noni Scott. ?, Eng.: Bath Street, 1988. 96 p.

352   Specialty Cookbooks

Beverages *(Continued)*

2711.   The Non-alcoholic Pocket Bartender's Guide / by Jill Cox; illustrations by Allan Drummond. New York: Simon & Schuster, c1988. 136 p., illus. (some colored). "A Fireside Book." First published in 1988 in Great Britain by Mitchell Beazley Publishers, London, Eng., under title: The Mitchell Beazley Pocket Guide to Non-alcoholic Drinks.

2712.   The Savoy Food and Drink Book / edited by Alison Leach. Topsfield, Mass.: Salem House Publishers, 1988. 224 p., illus. (some colored). Includes index.

2713.   A Gourmet's Guide to Coffee & Tea / by Lesley Mackley and Carole Handslip. Los Angeles, Calif.: HP Books, 1989. 120 p., colored illus. More than 50 recipes. Includes index.

2714.   New and Classic Cocktails Without Alcohol / Robert Sutton and Keith Pointing. Eng.: Stacy, 1989. 128 p.

see also entries 373, 693, 739, 1161, 1883, 1889, 2604, 2630, 3012, 3454, 3851, 3887, 3919; and specific drinks: Herbal Teas

Biscuits

2715.   A Batch of Biscuits / by Kathleen M. Nichol. Vancouver, B.C.: Bottesini Press: G. Soules, distributor, 1984. 57 p. Includes index.

2716.   Biscuits and Scones: 62 Recipes, from Breakfast Biscuits to Homey Desserts / by Elizabeth Alston. 1st ed. New York: C.N. Potter: Distributed by Crown, c1988. 106 p., illus. Includes index.

2717.   Butter 'em While They're Hot!: Original Recipes for Delicious Biscuits, Muffins, etc. / Patricia B. Mitchell. Rev. ed. Chatham, Va.: P.B. Mitchell, c1989. 37 p.

see also Cookies; *and broader category:* Bread

Specific Dishes and Courses 353

Biscuits (British) *see* Cookies

Blintzes *see* Crepes and Pancakes

Bread

2718. Mexico: Her Daily & Festive Breads / Barbara Howland Taylor; illustrations arranged by the author and photographed by Merle G. Wachter; edited by Ruth S. Lamb. Claremont, Calif.: Creative Press, 1969. 98 p., illus.

2719. The Barmy Bread Book / Jane Nordstrom. Santa Fe, N.M.: Lightning Tree, 1974. 80 p.

2720. Bread Baking / by Lou Seibert Pappas; illustrated by Mike Nelson. Concord, Calif.: Nitty Gritty Productions, 1975. 183 p., illus. Includes index.

2721. Bread, Being a Thorough Compendium of More Than 100 Recipes & Directions for Mixing, Kneading, Covering, Letting Rise, & Baking the Staff of Life ... / by Sarah Morgan. Austin, Tex.: Encino Press, 1975. 103 p. Includes index.

2722. Breads of Many Lands / Florence Laffal. Essex, Conn.: Gallery Press; Harrisburg, Pa.: Distributed by Stackpole Books, 1975. 128 p., illus. Includes index.

2723. Homemade Breads / Annette Gohlke. Milwaukee, Wis.: Reiman Associates, 1977. 64 p.

2724. Bake Breads from Frozen Dough / by Sylvia Ogren. 2nd ed. Minneapolis, Minn.: Dillon Press, 1979. 127 p., illus. Includes index.

2725. The Garden Way Bread Book: A Baker's Almanac / Ellen Foscue Johnson. Charlotte, Vt.: Garden Way Pub., c1979. 192 p., illus. Includes index.

Bread *(Continued)*

2726. Whole Wheat Bread Recipes / by Daniel D. Stuhlman; illustrated by M.J. Stuhlman. Chicago, Ill.: Bet Yoatz Library Services, 1979. 14 p., illus.

2727. A Short Course with King Arthur Flour in Baking with Yeast. Norwich, Vt.: King Arthur Flour Co., 198-. 36 p., illus. Includes recipes for basic hearth bread, pita bread, English muffins, pizza, sticky buns, rye bread, bagels, oatmeal bread, anadama bread, and brioche.

2728. Baking Country Breads and Pastries / Rosemary Wadey; line drawings by Denys Baker; colour photographs by John Lee. North Pomfret, Vt.: David & Charles, 1980. 191 p., illus. (some colored).

2729. Breadmaking and Yeast Cookery / Doreen Chetwood. Aylesbury, Eng.: Shire Publications, 1980. 48 p., illus.

2730. The Cornell Bread Book: 54 Recipes for Nutritious Loaves, Rolls & Coffee Cakes / Clive M. McCay & Jeanette B. McCay. Rev. and enl. version. New York: Dover Publications, 1980. 27 p., illus. Previous eds. published in 1955, 1961, and 1973 as: You Can Make Cornell Bread.

2731. Festive Breads of Easter / Norma Jost Voth; illustrations by Ellen Jane Price. Scottdale, Pa.: Herald Press, 1980. 79 p., illus. Includes index.

2732. Food Processor Bread Book / by the editors of Consumer Guide; author, Beatrice Ojakangas. New York: Simon and Schuster, c1980. 160 p., illus. Includes index.

2733. Helen Groll's Homemade Bread, Fun and Foolproof. Stafford, Va.: Northwoods Press, c1980. 58 p., illus. Includes index.

2734. Janice Murray Gill's Canadian Bread Book. Toronto, Ont.: McGraw Hill Ryerson, c1980. 224 p., illus. (some colored). Includes bibliography and index.

Bread *(Continued)*

2735. More Barmy Breads: Little Breads & Tea Loaves / Jane Nordstrom. Santa Fe, N.M.: Lightning Tree, 1980. 80 p.

2736. Beard on Bread / James Beard; drawings by Karl Stuecklen. New York: Ballantine, 1981, c1973. 206 p., illus. Includes index. Originally published: New York: Knopf, 1973.

2737. Breads / by the editors of Time-Life Books. Alexandria, Va.: Time-Life Books; Morristown, N.J.: School and library distribution by Silver Burdett Co., c1981. 176 p., illus. Includes index.

2738. Breads: Favorite Recipes of Home Economics Teachers. Nashville, Tenn.: Favorite Recipes Press/Nashville EMS, c1981. 127 p. Includes index.

2739. Breads & Biscuits / by Linda Campbell Franklin. New York: Tree Communications, c1981. 128 p., illus. (some colored). (An Old Fashioned Keepbook). At head of title: Good Home Cooking. Includes index.

2740. Breads, Rolls, and Pastries / edited by Georgia Orcutt and Sandra Taylor; illustrated by Pamela Carroll. 1st ed. Dublin, N.H.: Yankee, Inc.: Peterborough, N.H.: Yankee Books, distributor, c1981. 143 p., illus. (The Flavor of New England). Includes index.

2741. The Cake Shop Bread Book / by Jack and Patti Feder. Merlin, Or.: C & S Associates, c1981. 47 p., illus.

2742. How to Book of Bread [and] Breadmaking / Malcolm Holloway. London, Eng.: Blandford Press; New York: Distributed in the U.S. by Sterling Pub. Co., 1981. 95 p., illus. (some colored). Includes index.

Bread *(Continued)*

2743. The New Book of Favorite Breads from Rose Lane Farm / by Ada Lou Roberts; drawings by Edward J. Roberts. New York: Dover Publications, 1981, c1970. 192 p., illus. Reprint. Originally published: New York: Hearthside Press, 1970. Includes index.

2744. A Passion for Bread: The Art & Fun of Whole Grain Baking / by Ken Haedrich; hand lettered by Sandy Knieriem; illustrations by Dana Estrich. Plainfield, N.J.: American Impressions Book Co., c1981. 94 p., illus.

2745. Red Star Centennial Bread Sampler / written & compiled in honor of a century of service to the homemakers and bakers of America. Milwaukee, Wis.: Universal Foods Corp., c1981. 216 p., illus. (some colored). Includes index.

2746. Spotlight on Bread / prepared by home economics specialists at the Ontario Ministry of Agriculture and Food. Toronto, Ont.: The Ministry, 1981. 60 p., illus.

2747. Baking Your Own: Recipes and Tips for Better Breads / Marilyn M. Moore. Hoopeston, Ill.: Prairie Craftsman, c1982. 96 p., illus.

2748. Barron's the Festive Bread Book / by Kathy Cutler. Woodbury, N.Y.: Barron's, c1982. 224 p., colored illus. Includes index.

2749. Bountiful Bread: Basics to Brioches / Lynn Kutner; illustrated by Maceo Mitchell. New York: I. Chalmers Cookbooks, c1982. 84 p. (Great American Cooking Schools).

2750. Breads from Many Lands / Lois Lintner Sumption and Marguerite Lintner Ashbrook; with pencil drawings by Amelia Reinmann. New York: Dover; London, Eng.: Constable, 1982. 248 p., illus. Includes bibliography and index. Originally published in 1948 under the title: Breads and More Breads.

Specific Dishes and Courses

Bread *(Continued)*

2751. English Bread and Yeast Cookery / Elizabeth David; illustrations by Wendy Jones. American ed., with notes by Karen Hess. New York: Penguin Books, 1982. 592 p., illus. Includes bibliography and index.

2752. Make Bread-in-a-Bag with Texas Wheat Flour. Austin, Tex.: Texas Dept. of Agriculture, 1982? 4 p.

2753. Miriam B. Loo's Fresh-from-the-Oven Breads. Colorado Springs, Colo.: Current, Inc., 1982. 92 p.

2754. The Sunday Times Book of Real Bread / Michael Bateman and Heather Maisner. Aylesbury, Eng.: Rodale Press, 1982. 336 p., illus. (some colored). Includes bibliography and index.

2755. Baking Better Breads / by Rachael Holme; illustrated by Clive Birch. Wellingborough, Eng.: Thorsons, 1983. 128 p., illus. (A Thorsons Wholefood Cookbook). Includes index.

2756. Basically Bread / Marilyn Barbe. Ailsa Craig, Ont.: M. Barbe, 1983. 127 p., illus.

2757. Bread & Yeast Cookery. Newton Abbot, Eng.: David & Charles, c1983. 64 p., colored illus. (Kitchen Workshop). Includes index. Translated from the Norwegian.

2758. The Bread Winners Cookbook / compiled by Mel London; editor, Charles Gerras; line drawings, Donald Breter; color photography, Carl Doney; additional photography, Mitchell T. Mandel. 1st Fireside ed. New York: Simon and Schuster, 1983, c1979. 365 p. More than 200 recipes. Previously published as: Bread Winners, 1979.

2759. Bread without Tears / Donna Thacker; illustrated by David Shaw; edited by Patricia McColl Bee. 1st ed. Ottawa, Ont.: D.A. Cameron, c1983. 83 p., illus.

Bread *(Continued)*

2760. Breads / by Sharon Tyler Herbst. Tucson, Ariz.: HP Books, c1983. 176 p., colored illus. Includes index.

2761. The Complete Bread Book / Lorna Walker & Joyce Hughes. London, Eng.: Hamlyn, 1983. 185 p., illus. (some colored). Includes index.

2762. Festive Breads of Christmas / Norma Jost Voth; illustrated by Ellen Jane Price. Scottdale, Pa.: Herald Press, 1983. 104 p., illus. Includes index.

2763. The Little Brown Bread Book / by David Eno; illustrated by Clive Birch. Enl., rev. and reset ed. Wellingborough, Eng.: Thorsons, 1983. 56 p., illus. Includes index.

2764. Loaf Magic / by Mary Carey, Debbie Peirce, Nancy Smith. Kitchener, Ont.: Published and distributed by Loaf Magic, c1983. 50 p., illus.

2765. Making the Most of Bread / Judy Ridgway. Newton Abbot, Eng.: David & Charles, c1983. 48 p., illus. Includes index.

2766. The New York Times Bread and Soup Cookbook / Yvonne Tarr Young. New York: Times Books, 1983, c1972. 436 p., illus. Includes index.

2767. No Knead Baking with Fermipan / written by Deborah Collingwood. Merritt, B.C.: D. Collingwood, c1983. 30 p., illus. (some colored). Includes index.

2768. Rose Elliot's Book of Breads. London, Eng.: Fontana, 1983. 63 p., illus. Includes index.

2769. Smell That Bread: In Search of the Ultimate Loaf / D'Oyly Rochfort. Winlaw, B.C.: Polestar, 1983. 117 p., illus. Includes index.

Specific Dishes and Courses   359

Bread *(Continued)*

2770. Sonia Allison's Bread Book. Loughton, Eng.: Piatkus, 1983. 95 p., illus. Includes index.

2771. The Southern Heritage Breads Cookbook. Birmingham, Ala.: Oxmoor House, 1983. 143 p., illus. (some colored). (The Southern Heritage Cookbook Library). Includes index.

2772. The Book of Great Soups, Sandwiches, and Breads / Terence Janericco. New York: Van Nostrand Reinhold, c1984. 246 p. "A CBI Book." Includes index.

2773. Bread and Breakfasts / by Jeanne and John Hall. 1st ed. Wabasha, Minn. (333 W. Main St. Wabasha 55981): Convertinns, c1984. 232 p., illus. Includes indexes.

2774. The Bread & Cake Cookbook / Frederick E. Kahn; edited by William Wright. New York: Nautilus Communications, c1984. 138 p., illus. Includes index.

2775. Bread Baking Made Easy / Dora D. Flack; photography by Borge B. Andersen; food stylist, Janet Schaap. Salt Lake City, Utah: Bookcraft, c1984. 101 p., illus. (some colored). Includes index.

2776. Bread Winners Too: The Second Rising / Mel London. Emmaus, Pa.: Rodale Press, c1984. 336 p., illus. Includes index.

2777. The Churche's [sic] Banquet: A Collection of Tested Recipes for Bread, Cakes & Biscuits / edited by Oonagh Goode; illustrated by Susan Hsuan. Watford, Eng.: O. Goode, 1984. 59 p., illus. Includes index.

2778. Great Whole Grain Breads / by Beatrice Ojakangas; illustrations by Susan Gaber. 1st ed. New York: Dutton, c1984. 354 p., illus. Includes index.

Specialty Cookbooks

Bread *(Continued)*

2779. The Laurel's Kitchen Bread Book: A Guide to Whole-Grain Breadmaking / by Laurel Robertson, with Carol Flinders & Bronwen Godfrey. 1st ed. New York: Random House, c1984. 447 p., illus. Includes index.

2780. Making Whole-Grain Breads / by Phyllis Hobson. Pownal, Vt.: Storey Communications, 1984, c1974. 44 p., illus. Cover title: Garden Way Publishing's Making Whole-Grain Breads. Reprint. Originally published: Making Breads with Home-Grown Yeasts & Home-Ground Grains. Charlotte, Vt.: Garden Way Pub., 1974. Includes index.

2781. Sunset Breads: Step by Step Techniques / by the editors of Sunset Books and Sunset Magazine. 4th ed. Menlo Park, Calif.: Lane Pub. Co., c1984. 128 p., colored illus. Includes index.

2782. The WI Book of Bread and Buns / Mary Norwak. London, Eng.: Ebury, 1984. 96 p., illus. Includes index.

2783. The 60-Minute Bread Book and Other Fast-Yeast Recipes You Can Make in 1/2 the Usual Time / Nancy Baggett; illustrated by Linda Tunney. New York: Putnam, c1985. 325 p., illus. Includes index.

2784. America's Bread Book: 300 Authentic Recipes for America's Favorite Homemade Breads Collected on a 65,000-Mile Journey Through the Fifty United States / by Mary Gubser; illustrated by Pat Biggs. 1st ed. New York: Morrow, 1985. 495 p., illus. 325 recipes. Includes index.

2785. Betty Crocker's Breads. Rev. ed. New York: Golden Press, c1985. 96 p., colored illus. Includes index.

2786. Breads. Los Angeles, Calif.: Knapp Press, c1985. 118 p., 16 p. of plates, colored illus. (Cooking with Bon Appétit). Includes index.

Bread *(Continued)*

2787. Breads / Cynthia Scheer, writer and food stylist. San Francisco, Calif.: California Culinary Academy, c1985. 128 p., colored illus. (Easy & Elegant Meals). Includes index.

2788. Breads & Breadmaking / Mary Norwak. London, Eng.: Ward Lock, 1985. 80 p., illus. (some colored). Includes index.

2789. Carol Cutler's Great Fast Breads: 100 Choice Recipes-- Popovers to Panettone in Two Hours or Less. 1st ed. New York: Rawson Associates, c1985. 216 p., illus. Includes index.

2790. Famous Brands Breads, Quick Breads, & Coffee Cakes. St. Louis, Mo.: Brand Name Pub. Corp., 1985? 128 p., colored illus. (Famous Brands Cookbook Library). Includes index.

2791. Farm Journal's Homemade Breads: 250 Naturally Good Recipes / by the food editors of Farm Journal, Alice Joy Miller, editor; Joanne G. Fullan, assistant editor; Margaret C. Quinn, home economist. Philadelphia, Pa.: Farm Journal; Garden City, N.Y.: Distributed to the trade by Doubleday, c1985. 344 p., illus. Includes index.

2792. Homemade Breads / text copyright by Joshua Morris, Inc.; illustrations, A/S Hjemmet. New York: Modern Pub., c1985. 64 p., colored illus. (Home Cooking Library).

2793. Judith Olney on Bread / by Judith Olney; photographs by Vincent Lee. 1st ed. New York: Crown, c1985. 163 p., 16 p. of plates, illus. (some colored). 139 recipes. Includes index.

2794. Mary's Bread Basket and Soup Kettle / by Mary Gubser; drawings by Pat Biggs. 1st Quill ed. New York: Quill, 1985, c1974. 294 p., illus. Reprint. Originally published: New York: Morrow, 1975, c1974. Includes index.

2795. The Perfect Bread / Bernice Hurst; illustrations by Ronald Hurst. Twickenham, Eng.: Hamlyn, 1985, c1983. 32 p., illus. (The Perfect Series). Includes index.

Bread *(Continued)*

2796. The Book of Bread / Judith & Evan Jones; drawings by Lauren Jarrett. 1st Perennial Library ed. New York: Perennial Library, 1986, c1982. 384 p., illus. 240 recipes. Includes index.

2797. Bread & Beyond: Original Bread Recipes for Every Occasion / Beverley Sutherland Smith. London, Eng.: Orbis, 1986, c1985. 104 p., colored illus.

2798. Bread Bonanza / Kathy Bremer. Groton, Conn.: Bremer Books, 1986. 103 p.

2799. Breadcraft / Alan Littlewood. London, Eng.: Allison & Busby, 1986. 224 p., illus. Includes index.

2800. Breads / by Sarah Brown. London, Eng.: Dorling Kindersley, 1986. 96 p., colored illus. (Sainsbury's Healthy Eating Cookbooks).

2801. Breads & Muffins / Marion Ham [and others]. New York: A.D. Bragdon, 1986. 64 p., illus. (Munchie Books).

2802. The Breads of France and How to Bake Them in Your Own Kitchen / by Bernard Clayton, Jr. 1st Collier Books ed. New York: Collier Books, 1986, c1978. 284 p., photos. Includes index. Reprint. Originally published: Indianapolis, Ind.: Bobbs-Merrill, c1978.

2803. Florence Lin's Complete Book of Chinese Noodles, Dumplings and Breads / Florence Lin. 1st ed. New York: Morrow, c1986. 345 p., illus. Includes index.

2804. Fast Breads! / by Howard Early and Glenda Morris; edited by Andrea Chesman. Trumansburg, N.Y.: Crossing Press, c1986. 151 p., illus. (The Crossing Press Specialty Cookbook Series). Includes index.

Bread *(Continued)*

2805. The Tassajara Bread Book / Edward Espe Brown. Rev. and updated ed. Boston, Mass.: Shambhala; New York: Distributed in the U.S. by Random House, c1986. 145 p., illus.

2806. Baking and Bread / Mitzie Wilson and Nichola Palmer. London, Eng.: Hamlyn, 1987. 64 p.

2807. Bernard Clayton's New Complete Book of Breads / Bernard Clayton, Jr.; working drawings by Donnie Cameron. New York: Simon and Schuster, c1987. 748 p., illus. 300 recipes, including 200 revised and 100 new ones. Includes index. Rev. ed. of: The Complete Book of Breads. 1973.

2808. A Book of Welsh Bread / Bobby Freeman. Talybont, Wales: Y Lolfa, 1987. 47 p.

2809. Bread / Joan Wiener and Diana Collier. London, Eng.: Hale, 1987, c1973. 206 p., illus. Includes index. Originally published: Philadelphia, Pa.: Lippincott, 1973.

2810. The Bread Book / Audrey Ellison. New York: Gallery Books, c1987. 72 p., colored illus.

2811. Breads 2 / text and drawings by Polly Pinder. Tunbridge Wells, Eng.: Search, 1987. 32 p., illus.

2812. The Hallah Book: Recipes, History, and Traditions / Freda Reider. Hoboken, N.J.: Ktav, c1987. 88 p., illus.

2813. How to Make Sprouted Wheat Bread. Dudley, Mass.: Natural Food Institute (Box 185 WMB, Dudley 01570), 1987? 3 p., illus.

2814. The Wooden Spoon Bread Book: The Secrets of Successful Baking / by Marilyn M. Moore. 1st ed. New York: Atlantic Monthly Press, c1987. 418 p., illus. Includes bibliography and index.

Bread *(Continued)*

2815. Bread / by Beth Hensperger; photographs by Victor Budnik. San Francisco, Calif.: Chronicle Books, c1988. 160 p., colored illus. 130 recipes. Includes index.

2816. Breadspeed: Wonderful No-Knead Yeast Breads in Two Hours / Elma Schemenauer. Willowdale, Ont.: Farland Press, 1988. 95 p., illus.

2817. Cranks Breads & Teacakes / compiled by Daphne Swann. Enfield, Eng.: Guinness, c1988. 93 p., illus. Includes index.

2818. Judy Gorman's Breads of New England: From Biscuits to Bagels, Pizza to Popovers--More Than 500 Easy-to-Follow Recipes that Capture the Best of New England Home Baking / edited by Benjamin Watson. 1st ed. Dublin, N.H.: Yankee Books, c1988. 287 p., illus. Includes index.

2819. Old World Breads! / Charel Scheele. Freedom, Calif.: Crossing Press, c1988. 175 p. (Specialty Cookbook Series). Includes index.

2820. Rotis and Naans of India: Traditional and Exotic Recipes of Rotis, Vegetarian, and Non-Vegetarian Dishes / Purobi Babbar. Bombay, India: Vakils, Feffer and Simons, c1988. 240 p., colored illus.

2821. Yeast Bread and Rolls / by Pamela L. Brady. Rev. Little Rock, Ark.: University of Arkansas, Fayetteville, Cooperative Extension Service, 1988. 15 p., illus.

2822. Bake Your Own Bread / by Floss and Stan Dworkin; illustrations by Floss Romm Dworkin. Rev. and expanded. New York: New American Library, 1989. 252 p., illus. 100 recipes. "NAL books." Includes index. Rev. ed. of: Bake Your Own Bread and Be Healthier. 1st ed. c1972.

Bread *(Continued)*

2823. A Baker's Dozen of Daily Breads & More / by Paul Novak. Madison, Wis.: Only Connect Publications, 1989. 64 p. + 1 sound disc (9 min. : analog, 33 1/3 rpm, stereo.; 8 in.)

2824. The Book of Bread: From Pitta to Pizza / Julia Eccleshare and Martin Ursell. London, Eng.: Hamilton, 1989. 27 p.

2825. Loaves of Love: Wholegrain Yeast Breads / Patricia B. Mitchell. Chatham, Va. (P.O. Box 846, Chatham 24531): P.B. Mitchell, 1989. 37 p.

2826. Menus à Trois: The Soup, Bread, and Salad Cookbook / Julia Older and Steve Sherman. Lexington, Mass.: S. Greene Press; New York: Distributed by Viking Penguin, 1989, c1987. 249 p. Includes index. Contains directions for 50 three-part meals.

2827. Real Bread: A Fearless Guide to Making It / Maggie Baylis and Coralie Castle; drawings by Maggie Baylis. San Ramon, Calif.: Chevron Chemical Co., 1989. 240 p., illus. Includes index. Originally published: San Francisco, Calif.: 101 Productions, 1980.

2828. Rise to the Occasion with Yeast Breads / by Donald E. Fisher. Madison, Wis.: Wisconsin Unit of the Herb Society of America, c1989. 36 p., illus.

2829. Southern Born and Bread / Patricia B. Mitchell. 3rd ed. Chatham, Va.: P.B. Mitchell, 1989. 37 p. (Patricia B. Mitchell Foodways Publications).

Bread *(Continued)*

2830. Special and Decorative Breads / Roland Bilheux and others; under the direction of Jean Chazalon and Pierre Michalet; translated by Rhona Poritzky-Lauvand and James Peterson. Paris, France: CICEM (Compagnie internationale de consultation éducation et media; New York: Van Nostrand Reinhold, c1989. Vol. 1: Basic bread-making techniques, 46 special breads, fancy breads, Viennese breads, decorative breads (302 p., 1139 photos and illus.). Vol. 2: Traditional, regional, and special breads, fancy breads, Viennese pastries, croissants, brioches, decorative breads. (304 p., 1000 photos and illus., more than 80 recipes). Includes index. Translation of: Pains spéciaux et décorés.

2831. The Bread Book / Martha Rose Shulman. London, Eng.: Macmillan London, 1990. 288 p.

2832. The Bread Book: A Natural, Whole-Grain Seed-to-Loaf Approach to Real Bread / by Thom Leonard; foreword by Laurel Robertson. Brookline, Mass.: East West Health Books, 1990. 101 p., illus. Includes bibliography and index.

2833. Breadtime Stories: A Cookbook for Bakers / by Susan Cheney. Berkeley, Calif.: Ten Speed Press, 1990. ca. 280 p., illus. More than 200 recipes for breads and accompaniments. Includes indexes.

2834. Mary's Quick Breads, Soups, and Stews / Mary Gubser. Tulsa, Okla.: Council Oak Books, 1990. 288 p., illus. 196 recipes.

2835. Quick Breads: 63 Recipes for Bakers in a Hurry / by Beatrice A. Ojakangas. 1st ed. New York: C. Potter: Distributed by Crown, 1990. 128 p., illus. Includes index.

Bread *(Continued)*

CHILDREN'S COOKBOOKS

2836. Great Bread! The Easiest Possible Way to Make Almost 100 Kinds / Bernice Hunt; illustrated by Lauren Jarrett. Harmondsworth, Eng.; New York: Penguin Books, 1980, c1977. 121 p., illus. (A Penguin Handbook). Includes index. A brief history of bread, with a discussion of the traditional ingredients and baking methods, introduces a variety of recipes with the measurements given in both the metric and English system.

2837. Knead It, Punch It, Bake It! Make Your Own Bread / by Judith and Evan Jones; illustrated by Lauren Jarrett. 1st ed. New York: Crowell, c1981. 113 p., illus. Includes index. More than thirty recipes for baking all kinds and shapes of bread from hush puppies to bacon and peanut butter muffins.

2838. Shape It & Bake It: Quick and Simple Ideas for Children from Frozen Bread Dough / by Sylvia Ogren. Minneapolis, Minn.: Dillon Press, c1981. 106 p., illus. (Doing & Learning Books). Includes index. Helpful hints and drawings accompany step-by-step directions for making a variety of breads, dinner rolls, sweet rolls, coffee cakes, ethnic breads, and snack breads from frozen dough.

2839. The Breadbasket Cookbook / by Sue John; illustrated by Pat Butterworth and Charles Raymond. New York: Philomel Books, c1982. 29 p., colored illus. A guide to baking or buying bread and using it to make a variety of sandwiches for picnics, lunches, and snacks.

2840. Breads and Biscuits / S.J.A. de Villiers and Eunice van der Berg; illustrated by Marita Johnson. U.S. ed. Milwaukee, Wis.: G. Stevens, c1985. 31 p., colored illus. (First Cookbook Library). Includes index. "First published in It's Fun to Cook by Daan Retief Publishers." Introduces young chefs to the making of breads and biscuits.

Bread *(Continued)*

2841. Learning with Numbers: Bread and Cereal to Grow on / by Doris Cambruzzi and Claire Thornton; illustrations by Lorraine Arthur. Cincinnati, Ohio: Standard Pub., c1986. 32 p., colored illus. (What's Good for Me). Recipes and brief text introduce the breads and cereals which God has given us to nourish our bodies.

2842. Making Bread / Ruth Thomson; photography, Chris Fairclough. London, Eng.: New York: F. Watts, c1987. 32 p., illus. Describes with text and illustrations the process of making bread.

2843. Uncle Gene's Breadbook for Kids! Step-by-Step Instruction in the Art of Bread-Baking--Without the Use of Electrical Mixers / written and illustrated by Eugene Bove. Montgomery, N.Y.: Happibook Press, c1986. 64 p., colored illus. Illustrated, step-by-step instructions for baking a variety of yeast and quick breads. Also describes basic baking tools and techniques.

2844. Bread / Dorothy Turner; illustrations by John Yates. Minneapolis, Minn.: Carolrhoda Books, 1989, c1988. 32 p., colored illus. Includes index. First published in 1988 by Wayland Publishers, Hove, Eng. Describes how bread is produced, prepared, and eaten and presents some background history, as well as two recipes.

2845. Bread, Bread, Bread / by Ann Morris; photographs by Ken Heyman. New York: Lothrop, Lee & Shepard Books, 1989. 28 p., illus. Celebrates the many different kinds of bread and how it may be enjoyed.

see also entries 3111, 3690, 3997, 4013, 4409; specific kinds of breads: Bagels, Biscuits, Croissants, Muffins, Pita Bread, Pizza, Scones, Tortillas, etc.; Grains *(Section I);* Sourdough *(Section I);* Yeast *(Section I);* Baking *(Section IV)*

Brownies

2846. Brownie Recipes / edited by Carole Eberly; cover & illustrations by Gerry Wykes. E. Lansing, Mich.: Eberly Press, c1983. 189 p., illus.

2847. Recipes for Extra Brownie Points. Minneapolis, Minn.: General Mills, 1983. 1 booklet. Contains recipes using Betty Crocker Brownie Mix.

2848. The Brownie Experience: A Cookbook for Brownie-Lovers / recipes, illustrations, calligraphy, and hand-lettering by Lisa Tanner. Berkeley, Calif.: Ten Speed Press, c1984. 167 p., illus. Includes indexes.

2849. Brownies: Over 100 Scrumptious Recipes for More Kinds of Brownies Than You Ever Dreamed of / Linda Burum. New York: C. Scribner's, 1984. 128 p. Includes index.

2850. Wild About Brownies / by Barbara Albright & Leslie Weiner; color photographs by Karen Leeds. Woodbury, N.Y.: Barron's, c1985. 139 p., 7 leaves of plates. Includes index.

2851. Best-Ever Brownies: 76 Delicious Recipes / Joan Steuer and Rick Rodgers. Chicago, Ill.: Contemporary Books, c1990. 160 p. Step-by-step instructions.

see also broader category: Cookies

Cake Decoration

2852. The Wilton Way of Cake Decorating / edited by Eugene T. and Marilynn C. Sullivan. 1st ed. Chicago, Ill.: Wilton Enterprises, 1974-1979. 3 v., illus. (some colored). Vol. 3 has special title: The Uses of Tubes. Includes index.

2853. The Easy Way to the Fascinating Art of Cake Decorating / Betty Larsen Stauts. Glassboro, N.J.: St. Augeo Pub. Co., c1976. 203 p., illus.

Cake Decoration *(Continued)*

2854. Beautiful Bridal Cakes the Wilton Way / edited by Eugene T. and Marilynn C. Sullivan. Chicago, Ill.: Wilton Enterprises, c1978. 144 p., illus.

2855. Cake Design and Decoration / by L.J. Hanneman and G.I. Marshall. 4th ed. London, Eng.: Applied Science Publishers, 1978. 265 p., illus. Includes index.

2856. Modern Cake Decoration / by L.J. Hanneman. 2d ed. London, Eng.: Applied Science Publishers, 1978. 233 p., illus. Includes index.

2857. The Bride's Choice: Wedding Cakes from South Africa / Ria Meintjes; edited by Margie Smuts and Jackie Athey. 1st ed. Palos Verdes, Calif.: Continental Publications, 1979. 63 p., illus. (Creative Cake Series).

2858. Discover the Fun of Cake Decorating / edited by Eugene T. and Marilynn C. Sullivan. 1st ed. Woodridge, Ill.: Wilton Enterprises, c1979. 184 p., illus. Includes index.

2859. Celebrate! VI: The Wilton Annual for Cake Decorators / edited by Eugene T. and Marilynn C. Sullivan. Chicago, Ill.: Wilton Enterprises, c1980. 160 p., illus. Includes index.

2860. Lambeth Method of Cake Decoration and Practical Pastries: published expressly for the progressive baker, confectioner, pastry cook, and cake decorator / by Joseph A. Lambeth. Palos Verdes, Calif.: Continental Publications, c1980. 360 p., illus. Includes index.

2861. The Art of Decorating Cakes: The Cut Cone Method / by Leon F. Simmons. 3rd ed. San Diego, Calif.: Sea Lion Publications, 1981. 120 p., illus.

2862. Cake Calendar / Mary Beth Enderson. Carlsbad, Calif.: Continental Publications, c1981. 133 p., illus. (some colored).

Cake Decoration *(Continued)*

2863. Cake Decorating / edited by Mary Morris. London, Eng.: Octopus, 1981. 76 p., illus. (some colored). Includes index.

2864. Cake Decorating Book / Phyllis Magida; illustrations by William H. Jones. New York: Culinary Arts Institute, c1981. 80 p., colored illus. (Adventures in Cooking Series). Includes index.

2865. Cake Decorating Ideas & Designs / Louise Spencer; photography by John Andrew Fooks. New York: Sterling Pub., c1981. 176 p., illus. (some colored). Includes index.

2866. Party Cakes / James Winterflood. Carlsbad, Calif.: Continental Publications, c1981. 64 p., colored illus. (Continental's Creative Cake Series).

2867. The Wilton Book of Wedding Cakes. 2nd ed. Woodridge, Ill.: Wilton Enterprises, 1981, c1971. 112 p., colored illus.

2868. 101 Cake Designs / by Mary Ford. Bournemouth, Eng.: Mary Ford Cake Artistry Centre, c1982. 320 p., colored illus.

2869. Cake Designs and Ideas / designed and projected by Bill May and Kathleen Metcalfe. Preston, Eng.: Felicity Clare, c1982. 141 p., colored illus.

2870. Jane Asher's Party Cakes / photographs by Bryan Wharton; illustrations by Gerald Scarfe. London, Eng.: Pelham Books, 1982. 111 p., illus. (some colored).

2871. Better Homes and Gardens Creative Cake Decorating / editor, Jill Burmeister. 1st ed. Des Moines, Iowa: Meredith Corp., c1983. 96 p., illus. (some colored). Includes index.

2872. Cake Decorating Ornaments / by Norma Dunn. London, Eng.: Souvenir Press, 1983, c1979. 172 p., illus. (some colored). Includes index.

Cake Decoration *(Continued)*

2873. Celebrate! Wedding Cakes / edited by Eugene T. Sullivan, Marilynn C. Sullivan. 1st ed. Woodridge, Ill.: Wilton Enterprises, c1983. 192 p., colored illus.

2874. Celebrate! With Party Spectaculars from A to Z / edited by Eugene T. and Marilynn C. Sullivan. 1st ed. Woodridge, Ill.: Wilton Enterprises, c1983. 160 p., colored illus. Includes index.

2875. Farm Journal's Complete Cake Decorating Book: 100 Decorating Ideas Plus 200 Cake and Frosting Recipes / by the food editors of Farm Journal. Philadelphia, Pa.: Farm Journal; Garden City, N.Y.: Distributed to the trade by Doubleday, c1983. 172 p., illus. (some colored). Includes index.

2876. Floral Cake Decorating / Norma Dunn. New ed. London, Eng.: Souvenir Press, 1983, c1979. 172 p., illus. (some colored). Includes index.

2877. Free Hand Figure Piping: Step-by-Step Cake Decorating Guide / by John McNamara. Rev. Escondido, Calif.: McNamara Publications, 1983, c1974. 32 p., illus. (some colored).

2878. How to Air Brush Cakes-Arts-Crafts / Frances Kuyper. Pasadena, Calif. (432 Lola Ave., Pasadena 91107): F. Kuyper, c1983. 35 p., illus. (some colored).

2879. Betty Crocker's Cake Decorating with Cake Recipes for Every Occasion. 1st ed. New York: Random House, c1984. 160 p., colored illus. Includes index.

2880. The Book of Decorative Cakes / Gwyneth Cole. London, Eng.: Ebury, 1984. 47 p., illus. (some colored).

2881. Cake Icing and Decorating / Pamela Dotter. London, Eng.: Treasure Press, 1984, c1978. 80 p., illus. Includes index.

Cake Decoration *(Continued)*

2882. Cake Making & Decorating / Barbara Maher. New York: Exeter Books, 1984. 157 p., illus. Includes index.

2883. Celebration Cakes: Their Production and Decoration / Morris Howkins. 2nd ed. Barking, Eng.: Elsevier Applied Science Publishers, 1984. 223 p., illus. Reprint of the 1968 edition published by Maclaren, London, Eng.

2884. The Fine Art of Cake Decorating / Cile Bellefleur Burbidge. New York: Van Nostrand Reinhold, c1984. 225 p., illus. (some colored). "A CBI Book." Includes index.

2885. Flo Sez Have Fun with Cake and Icing / author, Florene (Flo) Ramboldt Shinn; illustrator, William Farnsworth. Fort Scott, Kan.: Sekan Publications Co.; Osage Beach, Mo.: Fancy Foods by Flo, c1984. 62 p., colored illus.

2886. John McNamara's Shaped & Cut-Out Cakes: The Easy, Professional Way. Escondido, Calif.: McNamara Publications, c1984. 38 p., illus. (some colored).

2887. The Magical Art of Cake Decorating / by Carole Collier. New York: Sedgewood Press, c1984. 168 p., illus. (some colored). Includes index.

2888. Mary Ford's Cake Designs: Another 101 with Step-by-Step Instructions. Bournemouth, Eng.: Mary Ford Cake Artistry Centre, c1984. 320 p., colored illus. Includes index.

2889. Wilton Celebrates the Rose in Cake and Food Decorating / Wilton Book Division Staff; co-editors, Marilynn C. Sullivan, Eugene T. Sullivan. Woodridge, Ill.: Wilton Enterprises, c1984. 63 p., colored illus. (A Wilton How-to Book).

2890. The All-Colour Cake Decorating Course / Elaine Macgregor. London, Eng.: Macdonald, 1985. 224 p., colored illus. Includes index.

Cake Decoration *(Continued)*

2891. Cake Decorating Simplified: The Roth Method / cakes and techniques by Lawrence M. Rosenberg; instructions edited by David Gamon; photography by Bart J. DeVito. New York: A.D. Bragdon Publishers: Distributed to the book trade by Dodd, Mead, c1985. 166 p., colored illus. 213 step-by-step photos. 63 cake and cookie designs.

2892. Cakes & Cake Decoration / text by Denise Jarrett-Macauley; photography by Peter Barry. New York: Exeter Books: Distributed by Bookthrift, c1985. 64 p., colored illus. Includes index.

2893. Creative Cake Baking and Decorating / Audrey Ellis. New York: Exeter, 1985. 192 p., illus. (some colored). Includes index.

2894. Decorating Cakes for Children's Parties / Polly Pinder. 1st American ed. New York: Holt, Rinehart, and Winston, 1985, c1984. 128 p., illus. (some colored). 31 cake designs.

2895. Fantastic Cakes / Sue Mann. London, Eng.: Century, 1985. 144 p., illus. Includes index.

2896. Birthday Cakes / Mary Ford. Bournemouth, Eng.: Mary Ford Cake Artistry Centre, c1986. 96 p.

2897. Cake Decor: New and Exciting Ideas for Modern Cake Decoration / Cynthia Lewis. 1st ed. Markham, Ont.: C. Lewis, 1986. 1 v., illus. (some colored).

2898. Cakes for Kids / by Sarah Stacey; photographs by Chris Ridley. London, Eng.: Elm Tree, 1986. 128 p., illus. (some colored).

2899. Creative Cake Decorating / Joanna Farrow. New York: Gallery Books, W.H. Smith Publishers, 1986. 72 p., colored photos.

Cake Decoration *(Continued)*

2900. Decorated Cakes / Mary Ford. Bournemouth, Eng.: Mary Ford Cake Artistry Centre, c1986. 96 p.

2901. Finishing Touches / Pat Ashby and Tombi Peck. Reprinted with amendments. London, Eng.: Merehurst, 1986. 143 p.

2902. Wedding Cakes / Mary Ford. Bournemouth, Eng.: Mary Ford Cake Artistry Centre, c1986. 96 p.

2903. Children's Party Cake Book. London, Eng.: Merehurst, 1987. 83 p.

2904. Classical Cake Decorating / Pam Leman. London, Eng.: Merehust, 1987. 96 p.

2905. Creative Party Cakes for Children / Angela Brown; illustrations by Ann Barrett; photographs by Mark Mason. London, Eng.: Foulsham, c1987. 60 p., illus. (some colored).

2906. Decorating Cakes for Special Occasions / Polly Pinder. Tunbridge Wells, Eng.: Search Press, 1987., c1985. 126 p., illus.

2907. Mrs. Mayo's How to Make a Wedding Cake / written and illustrated by Esther Murphy. 4th ed., rev. Denver, Colo.: Deco-Press Pub. Co., 1987. 141 p., illus. Includes index.

2908. The Practice of Royal Icing / by Audrey Holding; illustrated by John Holding. London, Eng.; New York: Elsevier Applied Science, c1987. 196 p., illus. (some colored). Includes index.

2909. Writing in Icing / Mary Ford. Bournemouth, Eng.: Mary Ford Cake Artistry Centre, c1987. 96 p.

2910. Cake Decorating: Wedding Designs / Lorraine Sorby-Howlett and Marian Jones. London, Eng.: Merehurst Press, 1988. 62 p., colored illus. Includes index. Originally published in 1986.

Cake Decoration *(Continued)*

2911. Cake Decorating for All Seasons: A Step-by-Step Guide / Lucy Poulton. London, Eng.: Merehurst Press, 1988. 112 p., colored illus. Includes index.

2912. Children's Party Cakes / Maxine Clark, Joanna Farrow, Kathy Man. London, Eng.: Macdonald Orbis, 1988. 119 p., colored illus. Includes index.

2913. Iced Follies / Jill Tipping. London, Eng.: Macdonald, 1988. 192 p.

2914. Novelty Cakes. London, Eng.: Hamlyn, 1988. 64 p.

2915. Woman and Home Celebration Cakes / editor, Sue Dobson. London?, Eng.: Woman and Home, c1988. 90 p.

2916. Cakemaking and Decoration / Lyn Hall. Topsfield, Mass.: Salem House Publishers, 1989. 1 v. (Lyn Hall's New Creative Cookery Course). Includes index. [Publication of this book has not been verified].

2917. Decorative Cakes / Rosemary Wadey, Janice Murfitt. London, Eng.: Hamlyn, 1989. 144 p.

2918. Hamlyn Cake Design and Decorating Course / edited by Suzy Powling. London, Eng.: Hamlyn, 1989. 222 p., colored illus. Includes index.

2919. The Icing on the Cake: Innovative Cakes for All Occasions / Greg Robinson, Max Schofield. New York: E.P. Dutton, 1989, c1988. 191 p., illus. (some colored). 30 projects and recipes for 4 different types of icings. Includes a section of designs to trace or enlarge. Originally published in Great Britain.

2920. Party Cakes: 50 Spectacular Cakes to Make, Ice, and Decorate / Virginia Welsh and Alison French. New York: Sterling Pub. Co., 1989, c1985. 128 p., colored illus. Originally published as: Cake Magic. London, Eng.: Conran Octopus Ltd., 1985.

Cake Decoration *(Continued)*

2921. Pretty Cakes: The Art of Cake Decorating / Mary Goodbody and Jane Stacey; contributing bakers, Ellen Baumwoll, Cheryl Kleinman, Lisa Cates & Janet Ross; photographs by David Arky. New York: International Culinary Society: Distributed by Crown Publishers, 1989, c1986. 192 p., illus. (part colored). Instructions for more than 50 cakes. Includes index. Reprint. Originally published: New York: Harper & Row, c1986.

2922. Lettering for Cake Decoration / by L.J. Bradshaw. London, Eng.: Merehurst Press; New York: Distributed by Sterling Pub. Co., 1989. 46 p., illus.

2923. Simply Elegant: More Techniques in Cake Design / Geraldine Randlesome. Richmond Hill, Ont.: Lesome Press, c1989. 96 p., illus. (some colored).

2924. Betty Crocker's Cake Decorating. 1st ed. New York: Prentice Hall, c1990. 160 p., illus.

2925. Cake Decorating: A Step-by-Step Guide to Making Traditional & Fantasy Cakes / Elaine MacGregor. New York: Crescent Books, 1990. 224 p. More than 650 colored photos. Includes step-by-step instructions for baking and decorating 38 cakes.

2926. Sugar Flowers from Around the World: An Inspirational Source Book for Sugarcraft Artists / Nicholas Lodge. London, Eng.: Merehurst, 1990. 144 p., illus. Contains directions for more than 45 flowers, primarily for wedding cakes. Includes patterns for templates.

see also Icings for Cake; *and broader category:* Cakes

Cakes

2927. Bundt Cakes / by Karen Plageman and Susan Herbert; illustrated by Lily Hollis. San Francisco, Calif.: Owlswood Productions, 1973. 63 p., illus.

Cakes *(Continued)*

2928. Cakes Aplenty / Annette Gohlke. Milwaukee, Wis.: Reiman Associates, 1975. 72 p.

2929. Geraldene Holt's Cake Stall. London, Eng.: Hodder and Stoughton, 1980. 24 p.

2930. Mile-high Cakes: Recipes for High Altitudes / by Klaus Lorenz and Willene Dilsaver. Rev. Fort Collins, Colo.: Colorado Agricultural Experiment Station, 1980. 28 p.

2931. Cakes / by the editors of Time-Life Books. Alexandria, Va.: Time-Life Books; Morristown, N.J.: School and library distribution by Silver Burdett, c1981. 176 p., illus. (some colored). (The Good Cook, Techniques & Recipes). Includes indexes.

2932. Creative Cakes / by Sheryn Smith. Winnipeg, Man.: Gateway Pub., c1981. 48 p., illus. Cover title: Love Enterprises Presents Creative Cakes.

2933. Festive Cakes of Christmas / Norma Jost Voth; illustrated by Ellen Jane Price. Scottdale, Pa.: Herald Press, 1981. 87 p., illus. Includes index.

2934. The Floris Book of Cakes / Christopher Floris. London, Eng.: Deutsch, 1981. 160 p., illus. (some colored). Includes index.

2935. Romantic and Classic Cakes / Rose Levy Beranbaum; illustrated by Jane Rosenberg. New York: I. Chalmers Cookbooks, c1981. 84 p., illus. (Great American Cooking Schools).

2936. Traditional Cakes / collected by Vera Segal. London, Eng.: Cottage, 1981. 32 p., illus.

2937. The Basics of Cake Baking, Decorating and Serving / by Lynette M. Middleton. Gresham, Or.: L.M. Middleton, c1982. 41 p., illus.

Specific Dishes and Courses 379

Cakes *(Continued)*

2938. Cake Crafts / by Sheryn Smith. Winnipeg, Man.: Gateway Pub., c1982. 62 p., 20 colored photos.

2939. The Good Cake Book / by Diana Dalsass; illustrated with linecuts by Lloyd Birmingham. New York: New American Library, c1982. 246 p., illus. Includes index.

2940. Recipes We Use at King John's Hunting Lodge / recipes by Marjorie Glentworth. Melksham, Eng.: Venton Educational, c1982, c1963. 96 p., illus. Includes index.

2941. Cakes, Icings, and Cheese Cakes: Quantity Baking Recipes / Nathan S. Cotton. Boston, Mass.: CBI Pub. Co., c1983. 303 p. Includes index.

2942. Classic Cake Recipes / illustrations by Karen Howitt. New York: Culinary Arts Institute, c1983. 80 p., colored illus. (Adventures in Cooking Series). Includes index.

2943. Cakes & Sponges. Newton Abbot, Eng.: David & Charles, 1983. 64 p. (David & Charles Kitchen Workshop). Translation of: Formkaker.

2944. Fast Cakes / Mary Berry. London, Eng.: Sphere, 1983, c1981. 207 p. Includes index.

2945. The Southern Heritage Cakes Cookbook. Birmingham, Ala.: Oxmoor House, c1983. 143 p., illus. (some colored). (The Southern Heritage Cookbook Library). Includes index.

2946. Cakes / Barbara Maher; illustrated by Thao Soun. Harmondsworth, Eng.: Penguin, 1984, c1982. 398 p., illus. (Penguin Handbooks). Includes bibliography and index.

2947. Cakes: A Book of Best British Recipes / Mary Norwak; illustrations by Prue Theobalds. London, Eng.: Batsford, 1984. 176 p., illus. Includes index.

Cakes *(Continued)*

2948. Cakes and Cake Decorating / Rosemary Wadey. New York: Gallery Books, 1984, c1979. 159 p., illus. (some colored). Includes index. First published: London, Eng.: Octopus Books, 1979.

2949. Country Cakes / Bevelyn Blair, author-editor. Columbus, Ga. (P.O. Box 7852, Columbus 31908): Blair of Columbus, 1984. 240 p., illus. More than 600 cake and cookie recipes, some more than 100 years old. Includes index.

2950. The Little Cake Cookbook / Mary L. Green. Denver, Colo.: Giftstar, 1984. ca. 10 p., illus. (Little Cookbooks).

2951. Party Cakes / Carole Handslip; foreword by Mary Berry. London, Eng.: Century, 1984. 1 v. (looseleaf), illus. (The Recipe Store). Includes index.

2952. Rose Elliot's Book of Cakes. London, Eng.: Fontana Paperbacks, 1984. 64 p., illus. Includes index.

2953. The Shadow Hill Book of Mix-Easy Cakes / written by Susan Ashby; illustrated by Pat Steiner. New Hope, Pa.: Woodsong Graphics, Inc., c1984. 63 p., illus. Includes index.

2954. 100 Great Cakes / edited by Judy Bugg. London, Eng.: Octopus, 1985. 64 p., illus. (some colored). Includes index.

2955. The Complete Cake Cookbook, Including Fancy Cakes & Frostings. Nashville, Tenn.: Favorite Recipes Press, c1985. 128 p., illus. (Favorite Recipes of Home Economics Teachers). Includes index.

2956. Gateaux and Torten / L.J. Hanneman. London, Eng.; New York: Elsevier Applied Science Publishers; New York: Sole distributor in the USA and Canada, Elsevier Science Pub. Co., c1985. 121 p., illus. Includes index.

Cakes *(Continued)*

2957. Magimix Cake Book / Tessa Hayward. Isleworth, Eng.: ICTC, 1985. 111 p., colored illus.

2958. Newnes All Colour Cake Making and Decorating / Stella Hartwell. Feltham, Eng.: Newnes, 1985. 191 p., colored illus. Includes index. Spine title: Cake Making and Decorating.

2959. O Taste and See: St. Thomas' Favourite Recipes / compiled by Patricia Lockett. Stockport, Eng. (c/o The Rectory, 25 Heath Rd., SK2 6JJ): St. Thomas' Parochial Church Council, 1985. 32 p.

2960. The Perfect Cake / Bernice Hurst; illustrations by Ronald Hurst. Twickenham, Eng.: Hamlyn, 1985. 32 p., illus. (The Perfect Series).

2961. Sugar Free Cakes and Biscuits: Recipes for Diabetics and Dieters / Elbie Lebrecht. Boston, Mass.: Faber and Faber, 1985. 128 p., illus. Includes index.

2962. The WI Book of Cakes / Lynn Mann. London, Eng.: Ebury, 1985. 96 p., illus. Includes index.

2963. Cream Cakes & Gateaux / Sue Ross. London, Eng.: Octopus, 1986, c1985. 93 p., colored illus. (The Kitchen Library). Includes index.

2964. Delicious Home-Made Petits Fours / Jean Montagard and Christiane Neuville; English version by Sarah Joyce. Tunbridge Wells, Eng.: Search, 1986. 32 p., colored illus. Includes index. Translated from the French.

2965. Harrods Book of Cakes & Desserts / by Pat Alburey. New York: Arbor House, 1986. 96 p., illus. (some colored). Includes index.

Cakes *(Continued)*

2966. Jewish Holiday Cakes: Kosher / Hana Shaulov; English translation, Ady Ginzburg. New York: Adama Books, c1986. 162 p., colored illus. Includes index.

2967. Victorian Cakes: A Reminiscence with Recipes / by Caroline B. King; introduction by Jill Gardner. Berkeley, Calif.: Aris Books; New York: Book trade distribution by Simon and Schuster, 1986, c1941. 240 p. More than 70 recipes. Contains anecdotes of life in Chicago in the 1880s. Includes index. Reprint. Originally published: Caldwell, Idaho: Caxton Printers, 1941.

2968. A Book of Welsh Country Cakes and Buns / Bobby Freeman. Talybont, Wales: Y Lolfa, 1987. 31 p.

2969. Cakes. Los Angeles, Calif.: Knapp Press, c1987. 118 p. (Cooking with Bon Appétit). Includes index.

2970. Claire's Cakes / Claire Attridge. London, Eng.: Macdonald Orbis, 1987. 45 p., colored illus. (Claire's Kitchen).

2971. Favourite Cakes / Jane Suthering. Mississauga, Ont.: Cupress, c1987. 79 p., colored illus. (A & P Creative Cooking Collection). Includes index.

2972. Festive and Novelty Cakes. London, Eng.: Merehurst, 1987. 80 p.

2973. Great American Cakes / Lorraine Bodger. New York: Warner Books, 1987. 176 p., illus. Includes index.

2974. More Fast Cakes / Mary Berry. London, Eng.: Sphere, 1987. 224 p., colored illus. Includes index.

2975. Supercook Cakes & Cake Decorating / Mandy Pryor. Cambridge, Eng.: Martin Books, 1987. 96 p., illus. Includes index.

Cakes *(Continued)*

2976. Western-Style Cakes / edited by Amy Ling. Hong Kong: Food Paradise Pub. Co., 1987. 91 p., illus. (some colored). Chinese and English.

2977. The Cake Bible / Rose Levy Beranbaum; edited by Maria D. Guarnaschelli; photographs by Vincent Lee; foreword by Maida Heatter. 1st ed. New York: W. Morrow, c1988. 555 p., 30 p. of plates, illus. (some colored). Includes index.

2978. Delia Smith's Book of Cakes. New ed. Sevenoaks, Eng.: Coronet, 1988, c1977. 191 p., illus. (some colored). Includes index.

2979. Fresh Ways with Cakes / by the editors of Time-Life Books. Alexandria, Va.: Time-Life Books, c1988. 144 p., colored illus. (Healthy Home Cooking). Includes index.

2980. A Piece of Cake / Susan G. Purdy; illustrated by Susan Martin. New York: Atheneum, 1988. 512 p., 150 line drawings. More than 380 recipes. Includes index.

2981. Cakes You Can Make: A Step-by-Step Illustrated Cookbook / Sachiko Moriyama. New York: Japan Publications Trading Co., Ltd., 1989. 48 p., colored photos and drawings of preparation steps for each recipe.

2982. Character Cakes / Sandy Garfield. London, Eng.: Sidgwick & Jackson, 1989. 96 p.

2983. Country Cakes: A Homestyle Treasury / Lisa Yockelson; illustrations by Wendy Wheeler. 1st ed. New York: Harper & Row, c1989. 160 p., illus. 45 recipes.

2984. Good Old-Fashioned Cakes / Susan Kosoff. New York: St. Martin's Press, 1989. 140 p., illus. More than 70 recipes. Includes index.

Cakes *(Continued)*

2985. Hamlyn All Colour Cakes and Baking. London, Eng.: Hamlyn, 1989. 140 p., illus.

2986. Mary Berry's New Cake Book. London, Eng.: Piatkus, 1989. 172 p.

2987. Company's Coming Cakes / by Jean Paré. 1st ed. Edmonton, Alta.: Company's Coming Pub., 1990. 156 p., colored illus.

2988. My Cake / Sheila Gore. London, Eng.: A.& C. Black, 1990. 26 p.

see also entries 2774, 2777, 2817, 3022; Cake Decoration; Cakes and Cookies; Cakes and Pastry; Cheesecake; Coffee Cakes; *and broader category:* Desserts

Cakes and Cookies

2989. Better Homes and Gardens All-time Favorite Cake & Cookie Recipes / editors, Diana Tryon, Elizabeth Woolever. 1st ed. Des Moines, Iowa: Meredith Corp., 1980. 96 p., illus. Includes index.

2990. Cookies and Cakes / edited by Jane Solmson. New York: Weathervane Books: Distributed by Crown Publishers, 1980. 64 p., colored illus. (Creative Cooking Institute Series). Includes index.

2991. Cookies, Cakes, and Pies. New York: Golden Press, c1982. 64 p., colored illus. (A Betty Crocker Picture Cookbook; 6).

2992. Cakes, Scones and Biscuits / by Rachael Holme. Wellingborough, Eng.: Thorsons, 1983. 128 p., illus. Includes index.

Cakes and Cookies *(Continued)*

2993. Cakes & Cookies / Mary Norwak. New York: Exeter, c1985. 80 p., illus. (some colored). (Ward Lock's Cookery Series). Includes index.

2994. 99 Biscuits and Cakes with 33 Colour Photographs / Mari Lajos, Károly Hemző. Budapest, Hungary: Corvina, 1987. 64 p., colored illus. Translated from the Hungarian.

2995. Classic Cakes and Cookies / by Barbara Maher; illustrated by Ken Laidlaw. 1st American ed. New York: Pantheon, 1987, c1986. 92 p., colored illus. (A Pantheon Classic Cookbook). Includes index. Reprint. Originally published: London, Eng.: Walker Book, 1986.

2996. Grandma Rose's Book of Sinfully Delicious Cakes, Cookies, Pies, Cheese Cakes, Cake Rolls & Pastries / Rose Naftalin. 1st Vintage Books ed. New York: Vintage Books, 1987, c1975. 255 p., illus. Includes index. Reprint. Originally published: New York: Random House, 1975.

2997. Cranks Cakes & Biscuits / compiled by Daphne Swann. London, Eng.: Guinness, c1988. 93 p., illus. Includes index.

2998. Mrs. Beeton's Complete Book of Cakes and Biscuits / consultant editor, Bridget Jones. London, Eng.: Ward Lock, 1989. 336 p., illus. (some colored).

see also Cake; Cookies

Cakes and Pastry

2999. 500 Recipes for Cakes & Pastries / by Catherine Kirkpatrick. London, Eng.: Hamlyn, 1982, c1963. 96 p., illus. Includes index.

3000. Cakes & Pastries / Christian Teubner, Jacques Charrette, Hannelore Blohm. 1st U.S. ed. New York: Hearst Books, c1983. 191 p., 500 illus. (some colored). Includes index.

Cakes and Pastry (Continued)

3001. Gateaux & Pastries. Newton Abbot, Eng.: David & Charles, c1983. 64 p., colored illus. (Kitchen Workshop). Includes index. Translation of: Dessertkaker.

3002. Traditional Cakes and Pastries / Barbara Maher. London, Eng.: Apple Press, 1984. 157 p., illus. (some colored). (A Quarto Book). Includes index.

3003. Cakes & Pastries / Olivia Erschen, writer and food stylist; Susan Lammers, editor; Patricia Brabant, photographer; Edith Allgood, illustrator. San Francisco, Calif.: California Culinary Academy: Chevron Chemical Co., c1985. 128 p., illus. (some colored). (Easy & Elegant Meals). Includes index.

3004. Cakes & Pies / Allen D. Bragdon; edited by Marion Ham. New York: A.D. Bragdon, 1985. 64 p., illus. (Munchie Books).

3005. Great Cakes & Pastries / Christian Teubner, Jacques Charrette, Hannelore Blohm. Twickenham, Eng.: Hamlyn, 1985, c1983. 191 p., illus. (some colored). Includes index.

3006. Cakes and Pastries Cookbook / Annette Wolter. New York: Crescent Books, 1989. 126 p., 140 colored photos. More than 150 recipes. (Good Cook's Library). Includes index. Published originally under the title: Kuchen und Torten.

see also Cakes; Pastry

Calzone

see entry 1700

Canapés *see* Appetizers

Candy

3007. Anita Prichard's Complete Candy Cookbook / by Anita Prichard; photographs by Martin Jackson. Bonanza 1981 ed. New York: Bonanza Books, 1981, c1978. 224 p., illus. Includes index.

3008. Candy / by the editors of Time-Life Books. Alexandria, Va.: Time-Life Books, c1981. 176 p., colored illus. (The Good Cook, Techniques & Recipes). Includes index.

3009. The Complete Wilton Book of Candy / edited by Eugene T. and Marilynn C. Sullivan. 1st ed. Woodbridge, Ill.: Wilton Enterprises, c1981. 176 p., colored illus. Includes index.

3010. Candy and Candy Molding Cookbook / by Mildred Brand. Milwaukee, Wis.: Ideals Pub. Corp, c1982. 64 p., illus. (some colored). Includes index.

3011. Chocolate and Candy Cookbook / Jan Morgan; with additional material by Rosemary Wadey; photographs by Anthony Kay; line drawings by Moira Shippard. New York: Arco Pub., 1982, c1979. 192 p., illus. (some colored).

3012. Candies, Beverages & Snacks: From Amish and Mennonite Kitchens / collected and edited by Phyllis Pellman Good and Rachel Thomas Pellman. Lancaster, Pa.: Good Books, c1983. 31 p. (Pennsylvania Dutch Cookbooks).

3013. Better Homes and Gardens Candy / editors, Linda Henry, Mary Jo Plutt. 1st ed. Des Moines, Iowa: Meredith Corp., c1984. 96 p., illus. (some colored). Includes index.

3014. Super Sweets: Easy-to-Make Recipes for Delicious Homemade Candy / Honey and Larry Zisman. 1st ed. New York: St. Martin's Press, c1984. 111 p., illus. Includes index.

3015. Candy Cookbook / Favorite Recipes Press. Nashville, Tenn.: Great American Opportunities, Inc., 1987. 95 p., illus. Includes index.

Candy *(Continued)*

3016. Candymaking / Kendrick & Atkinson. Tucson, Ariz.: HP Books, c1987. 160 p., colored illus. Includes index.

3017. Christmas Candy / edited by Glorya Hale. New York: Avenel Books, 1990. 1 v.

see also Candy and Cookies; Chocolate Candy; Marzipan; *and broader category:* Confectionery

Candy and Cookies

3018. Favorite Homemade Cookies and Candies. New York: Sedgewood Press: Distributed in the trade by Van Nostrand Reinhold, c1982. 192 p., illus. (some colored). Includes index.

3019. Cookies, Candies & Confections. Nashville, Tenn.: Favorite Recipes Press, 1986. 103 p., illus. (some colored). Includes index.

3020. Better Homes and Gardens Cookies & Candies. 1st ed. Des Moines, Iowa: Meredith Corp., c1987. 47 p., colored illus. (Better Homes and Gardens Test Kitchen). Includes index.

CHILDREN'S COOKBOOKS

3021. The Mother Goose Cookie-Candy Book / by Anne Rockwell. New York: Random House, c1983. 28 p., colored illus. A collection of recipes for cookies, cakes, and candies with a nursery theme including Peter Rabbit's Carrot Bars, Humpty Dumpty's Peanut Brittle, and the Queen of Hearts' Jam Tarts.

3022. Cookies, Cakes, and Candies / S.J.A. de Villiers and Eunice van der Berg; illustrated by Marita Johnson. U.S. ed. Milwaukee, Wis.: G. Stevens, c1985. 31 p., colored illus. "First published in It's Fun to Cook by Daan Retief Publishers." Includes index.

see also Candy; Cookies

Casseroles

3023. One Pot Meals / Margaret Gin; drawings by Rik Olson. San Francisco, Calif.: 101 Productions; New York: Distributed by Scribner, c1976. 192 p., illus. 230 recipes. Includes index. Reprint.

3024. The Complete International One-Dish Meal Cookbook for Everyday and Entertaining / Kay Shaw Nelson. New York: Stein and Day, 1979. 286 p. More than 260 recipes. Includes index.

3025. The Casserole Cookbook / Jackie Johnson and the Culinary Arts Institute staff; illustrations by Justin Wager, photos. by Zdenek Pivecka. New York: Culinary Arts Institute, c1980. 96 p., illus. Includes index. Previous ed. by staff home economists of the Culinary Arts Institute.

3026. Casseroles & Stews / Shelly Bolton. Salisbury, Zimbabwe: Graham Pub., 1980. 143 p. (Graham Cookery Library). Includes index.

3027. Great Casseroles! / by Karen Plageman; illustrated by Alice Harth; editor, Susan H. Herbert. San Francisco, Calif.: Owlswood Productions, c1980. 64 p., illus.

3028. Low, Slow, Delicious: Recipes for Casseroles and Electric Slow-Cooking Pots / Martha Lomask. London, Eng.; Boston, Mass.: Faber and Faber, 1980. 160 p., 8 p. of plates., illus. (some colored). Includes index.

3029. One Pot Cooking / Pamela Westland. London, Eng.: Fontana, 1980. 217 p. Includes index.

3030. Stews & Casseroles: Easy-to-Prepare Calorie Rated Recipes Based on the New Style Cookery / by Jean Conil and Daphne MacCarthy. Wellingborough, Eng.: Thorsons, 1980. 96 p., illus. Includes index.

Casseroles *(Continued)*

3031. Sunset Casserole Cook Book / by the editors of Sunset Books and Sunset Magazine; edited by Linda Brandt; photography, Nikolay Zurek. 3d ed. Menlo Park, Calif.: Lane Pub. Co., c1980. 96 p. Includes index. 1st-2d ed. (by Sunset) published under title: The Sunset Casserole Book.

3032. Woman's Own Book of Casserole Cookery. Rev. ed. London, Eng.: Hamlyn, 1980. 128 p. Includes index. Previous ed. by Jane Beaton, 1967.

3033. Just Casseroles / compiled by Gaye Hansen. North Vancouver, B.C.: Just Muffins, 1981. 115 p. (Just Series).

3034. New Casserole Cookery / Marian Tracy; illustrations by James and Ruth McCrea. New York: Penguin Books, 1981. 229 p., illus. Includes index. Originally published: New York: Viking Press, 1968.

3035. One-Pot Cooking / Su Cutts & Mary Morris. London, Eng.: Octopus, 1981. 141 p., colored illus. Includes index.

3036. Casseroles: From a Family Dinner to a Gala Celebration, Count on a Casserole. Nashville, Tenn.: Favorite Recipes Press/Nashville EMS, c1982. 127 p., illus. (Favorite Recipes of Home Economics Teachers). Includes index. Possibly another ed. of: Casseroles Cookbook (entry 3038).

3037. Casseroles: Range-Top and Oven. New York: Golden Press, c1982. 64 p., colored illus. (A Betty Crocker Picture Cookbook; 3). "Selected from Betty Crocker's step-by-step recipe cards."

3038. Casseroles Cookbook: A Variety of One-Dish Meals for Company or Family Menu Planning. Nashville, Tenn.: Favorite Recipes Press, c1982. 128 p., illus. Includes index. Possibly another ed. of: Casseroles (entry 3036).

Casseroles *(Continued)*

3039. Chinese Style Casserole Dishes Recipes / Li Tseng P'eng-chan chu. Hong-Kong: Vin shih t'ien ti' tsa chih se: Fa hsing che Wan li shu tien, 1982. 20 leaves. colored illus. In Chinese and English.

3040. Florence Lin's Chinese One-Dish Meals / Florence Lin. New York: Gramercy Pub. Co.: Distributed by Crown Publishers, 1982, c1978. 184 p. Includes index. Originally published: New York: Hawthorn Books, c1978.

3041. Sophie Kay's Casseroles and One-Dish Meals. Milwaukee, Wis.: Ideals Pub. c1982. 64 p., colored illus. Includes index.

3042. All-Occasion Casseroles Cookbook with Menus / Beta Sigma Phi International. Nashville, Tenn.: Favorite Recipes Press, c1983. 127 p., illus. Includes index.

3043. Beginner's Guide to Meatless Casseroles / by Ellen Sue Spivack. Rev. and expanded ed. Berkeley, Calif.: Ross Books, c1983. 47 p.

3044. Casserole Cookery / Good Housekeeping Institute. London, Eng.: Ebury, 1983. 128 p., illus. (some colored). Includes index.

3045. Casseroles & Stews. Newton Abbot, Eng.: David & Charles, c1983. 64 p., colored illus. (Kitchen Workshop). Includes index. Translation of: Gryteretter.

3046. Betty Crocker's Casserole Cookbook / director of photography, Remo Cosentino; illustrator, Tom Catania. New York: Golden Press; Racine, Wis.: Western Pub. Co., 1984. 96 p., colored illus. Includes index.

3047. The Casserole Cookbook / Jan Oldham. Ware, Eng.: Omega, 1984, c1977. 160 p., illus. (some colored). Includes index. Originally published: Summit Casserole Cookbook. Sydney, Australia: Summit, 1977.

Casseroles *(Continued)*

3048. Microwave Magic Casseroles / Jean Tweddle. Harris, Sask.: J. Tweddle, c1984. 108 p. Includes index.

3049. The One-Pot Cookbook / Lillian Langseth-Christensen and Carol Sturm Smith; illustrations by Lillian Langseth-Christensen. Large print ed. New York: Walker, 1984, c1967. 96 p., illus. Includes index.

3050. Better Homes and Gardens One-Dish Microwave Meals / editor, Lynn Hoppe. 1st ed. Des Moines, Iowa: Meredith Corp., c1985. 78 p., colored illus. Includes index.

3051. New Ideas for Casseroles / Beatrice Ojakangas. Tucson, Ariz.: HP Books, c1985. 160 p., colored illus. More than 300 recipes.

3052. One-Dish Meals. Los Angeles, Calif.: Knapp Press, c1985. 119 p., colored illus. (Cooking with Bon Appétit). Includes index.

3053. One-Dish Meals of Asia / written and illustrated by Jennifer Brennan. New York: Times Books, 1985. 372 p., illus. Includes bibliography and index.

3054. Pot Luck / Sonia Allison. London, Eng.: Futura, 1985, c1982. 192 p.

3055. Casseroles / by Jenni Fleetwood; editor, Annabel McLaren. New York: Gallery Books, c1986. 64 p., illus. (some colored). (Country Kitchen Cookbooks). Includes index.

3056. Casseroles and Bakes / by Christine Rycroft. London, Eng.: Dorling Kindersley, 1986. 96 p., illus. (Sainsbury's Healthy Eating Cookbooks). Includes index.

3057. Magnificent Casserole Cookbook / written & edited by Kathryn L. Ramsay. Richmond Hill, Ont.: Magnificent Cookbooks Pub., c1986. 124 p., colored illus.

Casseroles *(Continued)*

3058. Microwave Lite One-Dish Meals: Under 350 Calories / by the editors of Microwave Times. Chicago, Ill.: Contemporary Books, c1987. 166 p., illus. 150 recipes. Includes index.

3059. One Pot Meals / Gail Duff. London, Eng.: Hamlyn, 1987. 64 p.

3060. Better Homes and Gardens New Casserole Cook Book / editor, Mary Major. 1st ed. Des Moines, Iowa: Meredith Corp., c1988. 80 p., colored illus. (Better Homes and Gardens Test Kitchen). Includes index.

3061. Simmering Suppers: Classic & Creative One-Pot Meals from Harrowsmith Kitchens / edited by Rux Martin & JoAnne B. Cats-Baril. Charlotte, Vt.: Camden House, c1988. 240 p., illus. (some colored). "Compiled from the personal recipe collections of the editors, readers, contributors, and staff of Harrowsmith, the magazine of country life." Includes index.

3062. Canada Cooks!: Casseroles & Stews / by Eileen Dwillies. North Vancouver, B.C.: Whitecap Books, 1989. 160 p., colored illus.

3063. Hearty Winter Stews and Casseroles / Eileen Dwillies and others. Vancouver, B.C.: Opus Productions, c1989. 160 p., colored illus. (The Easy Gourmet; v. 3). Produced for Canada Safeway Ltd.

3064. 365 Easy One-Dish Meals / Natalie Haughton. New York: Harper & Row, 1990. 271 p.

3065. The Mennonite Girl Presents Ovenly Fare: 50 Recipes for Mennonite Casseroles from Mennonite Kitchens / compiled by Isaac R. Horst. Mt. Forest, Ont.: I.R. Horst, c1990. 32 p.

3066. One-Dish Meals / Mary Mouzar, Joanne Uhlman. Halifax, N.S.: Periwinkle, 1990. 1 v. (Kiss the Cook who Microwaves).

Casseroles *(Continued)*

3067. One-Pot Meals to Team with Warm Hearty Breads. Minneapolis, Minn.: Pillsbury Co., 1990. 93 p., colored illus. More than 100 recipes. (Classic Pillsbury Cookbooks; #109).

CHILDREN'S COOKBOOKS

3068. One Dish Meals / S.J.A. de Villiers and Eunice van der Berg; illustrated by Marita Johnson. U.S. ed. Milwaukee, Wis.: G. Stevens, c1985. 31 p., colored illus. "First published in It's Fun to Cook." Includes index. Introduction to one dish meals.

see also entry 935; Chili; Entrées; Stews

Cheesecake

3069. The Joy of Cheesecake / Dana Bovbjerg & Jeremy Iggers. Woodbury, N.Y.: Barron's, c1980. 200 p., 8 leaves of plates, illus. More than 100 recipes. Includes index.

3070. Say Cheesecake--and Smile / by Elvira Monroe. San Carlos, Calif.: Wide World Pub., c1981. 156 p.

3071. Cheesecake Madness / John J. Segreto. 1st Fireside ed. New York: Simon & Schuster, 1984, c1981. 189 p. More than 100 recipes. "A Fireside Book." Originally published: New York: Macmillan, 1981.

3072. Cheesecakes / Maggie Black. London, Eng.: Ward Lock, 1984. 80 p., colored illus. Includes index.

3073. The Little Cheesecake Cookbook / Mary L. Green. Denver, Colo.: Giftstar, 1984. ca. 10 p., illus. (Little Cookbooks).

3074. Cheesecake Only / book and illustrations by Ann B. Hutchinson. Littleton, Colo. (5842 S. Sheridan, Littleton 80123): Copies from Cheesecake Only, c1985. 81 leaves, illus. 105 recipes.

Cheesecake *(Continued)*

3075. Cheesecakes: Sweet & Savory / Barbara Maher. Tucson, Ariz.: HP Books, c1985. 80 p., colored illus. (Creative Cuisine). Includes index. Previously published as: Tempting Cheesecakes.

3076. The Perfect Cheesecake / Bernice Hurst; illustrations by Ronald Hurst. Twickenham, Eng.: Hamlyn, 1985. 32 p., illus. Includes index.

3077. Cheesecakes / Josephine Bacon. Twickenham, Eng.: Hamlyn, 1986. 64 p., colored illus. (Rainbow). Includes index.

3078. The Book of Cheesecakes / Steven Wheeler; photography by Paul Grater. Tucson, Ariz.: HP Books, 1988, c1987. 120 p., colored photos. 100 recipes. Includes index.

3079. Kraft Philadelphia Brand Cream Cheese Cheesecakes. Lincolnwood, Ill.: Publications International; New York: Distributed by Crown Publishers, 1989. 96 p., colored photos. 74 recipes.

3080. Cheesecake Extraordinaire / Mary H. Crownover. Dallas, Tex.: Taylor Pub., c1990. 160 p., 24 colored photos. More than 100 recipes.

3081. Mother Wonderful's Cheesecakes and Other Goodies / by Myra Chanin. Rev. ed. New York: H. Holt, c1990. 288 p. 82 recipes including 45 new ones for no-bake cheesecakes in addition to the traditional baked cheesecakes.

see also broader categories: Cakes; and Cheese *(Section I)*

Chili

3082. Chili Madness: A Passionate Cookbook / by Jane Butel; photos. by Jerry Darvin. New York: Workman Pub. Co., c1980. 94 p. More than 35 recipes. Includes index.

Specialty Cookbooks

Chili *(Continued)*

3083. The Great American Chili Book / Bill Bridges. 1st ed. New York: Rawson, Wade Publishers, c1981. 219 p. Includes index.

3084. The International Chili Society Official Chili Cookbook / by Martina and William Neely. 1st ed. New York: St. Martin's Press, c1981. 246 p. More than 100 recipes. Includes index.

3085. Recipes: The Great Oklahoma Congressional Chili Cook-off / sponsored by the Oklahoma State Society of Washington, D.C.; photographs by Dennis E. Caudill. Washington, D.C.: Oklahoma State Society of Washington, c1981. 38 p., illus.

3086. Chili-Lovers' Cook Book: Chili Recipes and Recipes with Chiles / compiled by Al Fischer and Mildred Fischer. Phoenix, Ariz.: Golden West Publishers, 1984, c1978. 131 p., illus. More than 300 recipes. Includes index.

3087. The Chili Cookbook / Bill Gunn. Twickenham, Eng.: Hamlyn, 1985. 128 p., illus. (some colored). (Hamlyn Cookshelf Series). Includes index.

3088. Just Another Bowl of Texas Red: Chili Con Carne, the Myth & the Makings / John Thorne. Castine, Me.: Jackdaw Press, 1985. 24 p.

3089. Wild About Chili / by Dotty Griffith. Woodbury, N.Y.: Barron's, c1985. 104 p., 7 leaves of plates, colored illus. 43 recipes. Includes index.

3090. The Manhattan Chili Co. Southwest-American Cookbook: A Spicy Pot of Chilies, Fixins', and Other Regional Favorites / Michael McLaughlin. 1st ed. New York: Crown Publishers, c1986. 120 p. 65 recipes. Includes index.

3091. New Mexico Favorites: Chile and Pecans. Rev. Las Cruces, N.M.: New Mexico State University, Las Cruces, Cooperative Extension Service, 1988. 8 p.

Chili (Continued)

3092. A Bowl of Red / Frank X. Tolbert. Dallas, Tex.: Taylor Pub. Co., 1989, c1988. 208 p. Reprint. Originally published: Garden City, N.Y.: Doubleday, 1972.

see also entry 4011; and Casseroles

Chocolate Candy

3093. Oh Truffles by Au Chocolat: Perfect Recipes for Every Choclate Lover's Fantasy / by Pam Williams and Rita Morin. New York: Stein and Day, 1984, c1983. 135 p., illus. (some colored). 78 recipes. Includes index.

3094. Sweet Seduction: Chocolate Truffles / Adrienne Welch; photographs by Bruce Wolf. 1st ed. New York: Harper & Row, c1984. 80 p., 8 p. of plates, colored illus. Includes index.

3095. Truffles and Other Chocolate Confections / Pamella Asquith. 1st ed. New York: Holt, Rinehart, and Winston, c1984. 120 p., illus. Includes index.

3096. Chocolate Truffles / by Carrie Huber; edited by Sheilah Kaufman. Silver Spring, Md.: American Cooking Guild, 1985. 64 p., illus. Directions for creating more than 30 variations of truffles.

3097. Inside Chocolate: The Chocolate Lover's Guide to Boxed Chocolates / Hal and Ellen Greenberg; photographs by Alan Porter. New York: H.N. Abrams, 1985. 79 p., colored illus. Includes index.

3098. The Book of Chocolates & Petits Fours / Beverley Sutherland Smith; photography by Philip Wymant. Tucson, Ariz.: HP Books, c1986. 128 p., colored illus. Includes index.

Chocolate Candy *(Continued)*

3099. Chocolate Candy: 80 Recipes for Chocolate Treats from Fudge to Truffles / by Anita Prichard. 1st ed. New York: Harmony Books, c1986. 95 p., illus. "A Particular Palate Cookbook." Includes index.

3100. Chocolates and Sweets / Marguerite Patten. Twickenham, Eng.: Hamlyn, 1986. 77 p., colored illus. (Hamlyn Kitchen Guides). Includes index.

3101. Delicious Home-Made Chocolates; With Recipes from the Famous Maison Bourdaloue, Paris / by Patrick Dalison and David Cotrez; English version by Sarah Joyce. Tunbridge Wells, Eng.: Search, 1986. 32 p., colored illus. Includes index. Translated from the French.

3102. The Dilettante Book of Chocolate and Confections / by Dana Taylor Davenport with Ruth Reed. 1st ed. New York: Perennial Library, c1986. 240 p., illus. Includes index.

3103. Harrods Book of Chocolates & Other Edible Gifts / by Gill Edden. New York: Arbor House, 1986. 96 p., colored illus. Includes index.

see also Chocolate *(Section I);* Fudge; *and broader category:* Candy

Chocolate Chip Cookies

3104. The 37 Best Chocolate Chip Cookies in America: The Winning Recipes in American Reflections' National Cookie Contest. Princeton, N.J.: Oceanic Press, c1980. 77 p.

3105. The Complete Chocolate Chip Cookie Book / by Bob & Suzanne Stat; illustrated by Richard Anderson. Wayne, Pa.: Banbury Books, c1982. 128 p., illus. (some colored). "A Dell/Banbury Book."

Chocolate Chip Cookies *(Continued)*

3106. The 47 Best Chocolate Chip Cookies in the World: The Recipes That Won the National Chocolate Chip Cookie Contest / by Larry and Honey Zisman. 1st ed. New York: St. Martin's Press, c1983. 86 p. Includes index.

3107. Making Chocolate Chip Cookies / Liz Martin. New York: Viking Kestrel, 1986. 22 p., illus. (Little Chef Series).

3108. The Search for the Perfect Chocolate Chip Cookie / compiled by Gwen Steege. Pownal, Vt.: Storey Communications, c1988. 140 p. "A Storey Publishing Book." Includes index.

3109. Chockful o' Chips / compiled, handwritten and designed by Peggy Seemann. Harrisonville, Mo.: PECS Pub., 1990. 96 p. 96 recipes.

see also Chocolate Chips *(Section I); and broader category:* Cookies

Chocolate Cookies

3110. Chocolate Lover's Cookies & Brownies. Lincolnwood, Ill.: Publications International; New York: Beekman House; Distributed by Crown Publishers, c1990. 96 p., 28 colored photos. Includes index.

see also Chocolate *(Section I);* Chocolate Chip Cookies; *and broader category:* Cookies

Chowders *see* Soups

Chutney

see entries 3577, 3581, 3586, 3678, 3681, 3683, 4412, 4421; and broader category: Condiments *(Section I)*

Coffee Cakes

3111. Easiest & Best Coffee Cakes & Quick Breads / Renny Darling. Beverly Hills, Calif.: Royal House Pub. Co., 1985. 301 p., illus. More than 500 recipes. Includes index.

see also entries 2730, 2790; and broader category: Cakes

Confectionery

3112. Candy Recipes & Other Confections / by May B. Van Arsdale and Ruth Parrish Casa Emellos; with an introduction by Natalie K. Fitch. New York: Dover Publications, 1975. 188 p. Includes index. Reprint of the 1941 ed. published by M. Barrows, New York, under title: Our Candy Recipes & Other Confections.

3113. Natural Sweets & Treats / Ruth Laughlin. Santa Barbara, Calif.: Woodbridge Press Pub. Co., 1975. 176 p.

3114. Sweet Treat Cookery Made with Your Favorite M&M/Mars Candies. Sea Cliff, N.Y.: Carbooks, Inc., 1980. 1 v.

3115. Sweets for Presents / Jenny Leggatt. Cambridge, Eng.: Dinosaur Publications, 1980. 1 v. (Althea Series).

3116. Sweets 'n' Treats / edited by Annette Gohlke. Milwaukee, Wis.: Reiman Publications, c1980. 68 p., illus. At head of title: Farm Wife News. Includes index.

3117. Holiday Sweets Without Sugar / Nina and Michael Shandler. 1st ed. New York: Rawson, Wade Publishers, c1981. 202 p. 234 recipes. Includes index.

3118. The New International Confectioner: Confectionery, Cakes, Pastries, Desserts and Ices, Savouries / edited by Wilfred J. Fance. 5th ed., metric revised by Michael Small. London, Eng.: Virtue, 1981. 891 p., illus. (some colored). Previous ed. published in 1968 under title: The International Confectioner.

Confectionery *(Continued)*

3119. The Old Fashioned Confectioner's Handbook / Darcy Williamson. Bend, Or.: Maverick Publications, 1982. 207 p.

3120. 100 Sweets & Candies / edited by Jo Barker. London, Eng.: Octopus, 1983. 64 p., illus. (some colored). Includes index.

3121. Sonia Allison's Sweets Book. Loughton, Eng.: Piatkus, 1983. 96 p. Includes index.

3122. The Book of Sweets / Patricia Lousada. London, Eng.: Ebury, 1984. 48 p., colored illus.

3123. Natural Sweets / Janet Hunt; illustrated by Clive Birch. Wellingborough, Eng.: Thorsons, 1984. 64 p., illus. Includes index.

3124. Sweets and Candies / Marguerite Patten. London, Eng.: Hamlyn, 1984. 128 p., illus. (some colored). (Hamlyn Cookshelf Series). Includes index. Originally published in 1964 under title: 500 Recipes for Sweets and Candies.

3125. Candies & Goodies / Allen D. Bragdon; edited by Marion Ham. New York: A.D. Bragdon, 1985? 64 p., illus. (Munchie Books).

3126. Mrs. Mary Eales's Receipts: Reproduced from the Edition of 1733. London, Eng.: Prospect Books, 1985. 100 p. Facsimile reprint. Originally published: London, Eng.: Printed for J. Brindley, 1733. "Confectioner to her late majesty Queen Anne."

3127. The Southern Heritage Gift Receipts Cookbook. Birmingham, Ala.: Oxmoor House, c1985. 143 p., illus. (some colored). (Southern Heritage Cookbook Library). Includes index.

3128. The Sweets Book: Home-Made Sweets, Chocolates and Candies / Shona Crawford Poole; photographs by Jasper Partington. London, Eng.: Collins, 1986. 96 p., illus. (some colored). Includes index.

Confectionery *(Continued)*

3129. Claire's Confectionery / Claire Attridge. London, Eng.: Macdonald Orbis, 1987. 44 p., colored illus. (Claire's Kitchen).

3130. The Complete Home Confectioner / Hilary Walden. London, Eng.: Macdonald in association with the kitchen of Silver Spoon, 1987. 160 p., colored illus. Includes index.

3131. Sweets & Candies. Tunbridge Wells, Eng.: Search, 1987. 32 p.

3132. Sugar Work: Blown-and Pulled-Sugar Techniques / Peter T. Boyle. New York: Van Nostrand Reinhold Co., c1988. 130 p., 16 p. of plates, illus. (some colored). "A CBI Book." Includes index.

3133. Candy and Gifts. Toronto, Ont.: Grolier, 1989. 1 v. (Microwave Magic).

3134. The Christmas Cook: Three Centuries of Yuletide Sweets / William Woys Weaver. New York: Harper Collins, 1990. ca. 255 p., illus., colored photos. 75 recipes taken from old cookbooks and updated. Includes bibliography and index.

CHILDREN'S COOKBOOKS

3135. Sweet Things / Angela Wilkes; illustrated by Stephen Cartwright. London, Eng.: Usborne, 1983. 24 p., illus. (some colored). (Usborne First Cookbooks).

3136. Sweetmaking for Children / Margaret Powell; illustrations by Karen Heywood. Rev. ed. London, Eng.: Piccolo, 1983. 93 p., illus. Includes index.

3137. Little Mouse Makes Sweets / Michelle Cartlidge. London, Eng.: Walker, 1986. 24 p., illus.

see also entry 2649; Candy; Desserts

Cookies

3138. Cookie Cookery / by John J. Zenker and Hazel G. Zenker. 1st ed. Philadelphia, Pa.: M. Evans; Distributed in association with Lippincott, 1969. 319 p., illus.

3139. Cookies from Many Lands / Josephine Perry. New York: Dover Publications, 1972. 157 p. Reprint of the 1940 ed., published under title: Around the World Making Cookies.

3140. Maida Heatter's Book of Great Cookies / drawings by Toni Evins. 1st ed. New York: Knopf, 1977. 277 p., illus. Includes index.

3141. German Cookie Recipes from Fredericksburg, Texas / collected by St. Barnabas Church, Fredericksburg. Fredericksburg, Tex.: Awani Press, 1978. 36 p., illus. (some colored).

3142. Around the World Cooky Book / by Lois Lintner Sumption and Marguerite Lintner Ashbrook. New York: Dover Publications, 1979. 182 p., illus. Includes index. Published in 1948 under title: Cookies and More Cookies.

3143. The Cookie and Cracker Cookbook: 150 Unusual and Mouth-Watering Temptations / by Anne Lanigan; book illustrations, Michael Emerson. New York: Quick Fox, c1980. 233 p., illus. Includes index.

3144. Cookies / by Lou Seibert Pappas; illustrated by Dorothy Cutright Davis. Concord, Calif.: Nitty Gritty Productions, c1980. 183 p., illus. Includes index.

3145. Farm Journal's Best-Ever Cookies / by Patricia A. Ward; book design by Michael P. Durning, illustrations by Merry Casino. Philadelphia, Pa: Farm Journal; Garden City, N.Y.: Distributed to the trade by Doubleday, 1980. 279 p., illus. Includes index.

3146. Munches / Peggy Dobbin. Kitchener, Ont.: Vision Pub., 1980. 39 p.

Cookies *(Continued)*

3147. The Woman's Day Great American Cookie Book / edited by Julie Houston; photography by Ben Calvo. New York: Fawcett Columbine, c1980. 160 p., 8 p. of plates, colored illus. "An original collection of best loved cookies from Woman's Day Magazine." Includes index.

3148. The Cookie Connection: A Cookbook for Cookies: American and International Recipes / by Lottye Gray Van Ness. 1st ed. Waverly, Iowa: G & R Pub. Co.; Louisville, Ky.: Additional copies L.G. Van Ness, 1981. 315 p. Includes index.

3149. Cookies by Bess / Bess Hoffman. Rev. and updated ed. New York: St. Martin's Press, 1981. 94 p.

3150. Homemade Cookies / by the food editors of Farm Journal; edited by Nell B. Nichols. 1st Ballantine Books ed. New York: Ballantine, 1981, c1971. 330 p., illus. Includes index.

3151. The Perfect Cookie. Skokie, Ill.: Consumer Guide, c1981. 32 p., colored illus. (Perfect Cookbooks).

3152. Sonia Allison's Biscuit Book. Loughton, Eng.: Piatkus, 1981. 95 p. Includes index.

3153. Bar Cookie Bonanza / Annette Gohlke. Milwaukee, Wis.: Reiman Associates, 1982. 68 p.

3154. A Baker's Dozen: A Sampler of Early American Cookie Cut-outs with Recipes / Susan Riecken. Cambridge, Mass.: Steam Press; New York: Distributed by Kampmann & Co., c1982. 26 p., illus.

3155. Cookies / Annette Laslett Ross, Jean Adams Disney. Toronto, Ont.: Forum House, c1982. 252 p., illus. (some colored). Includes index.

Cookies *(Continued)*

3156. Cookies & Crackers / by the editors of Time-Life Books. Alexandria, Va.: Time-Life Books, c1982. 176 p., illus. (The Good Cook, Techniques and Recipes). Includes index.

3157. Cookies from Amish and Mennonite Kitchens / collected and edited by Phyllis Pellman Good and Rachel Thomas Pellman. Lancaster, Pa.: Good Books, c1982. 32 p. (Pennsylvania Dutch Cookbooks).

3158. Pillsbury Cookies, Cookies, and More Cookies Cookbook: Over 100 Recipes. Minneapolis, Minn.: Pillsbury Co., c1982. 112 p., colored illus. Includes index.

3159. Traditional Biscuits / collected by Vera Segal. London, Eng.: Cottage, 1982. 32 p., illus.

3160. 32 Fabulous Cookies / by Marie Bianco. Woodbury, N.Y.: Barron's, c1983. 64 p., illus. (Easy Cooking). Includes index.

3161. 101 Tasty Treats: Squares, Bars & Cookies / by Adele Marks; illustrated by Klaus Schoenfeld. Weston, Ont.: Gadget Pub.: Distributed by General, 1983. 131 p., illus.

3162. The All Natural Cookie Cookbook / by Darcy Williamson. Bend, Or.: Maverick Publications, c1983. 113 p. Includes index.

3163. The Cookie Bookie / by Diane Fine and Ria Teale. 1st Quill ed. New York: Quill, c1983. 124 p., illus.

3164. Cookies / Natalie Hartanov Haughton. Tucson, Ariz.: HP Books, c1983. 160 p., colored illus. Includes index.

3165. The English Biscuit and Cookie Book / Sonia Allison. 1st U.S. ed. New York: St. Martin's Press, c1983. 72 p. Includes index.

3166. Favorite Cookies. Los Angeles, Calif.: Knapp Press, c1983. 87 p. (The Bon Appétit Kitchen Collection). Includes index.

Cookies *(Continued)*

3167. The Great Cookie Caper / compiled and written by Elizabeth Chatterton and Mary Chatterton. Southampton, Ont.: E. Chatterton, c1983. 61 p., illus.

3168. Ideals Hershey's Cookies, Bars, and Brownies. Milwaukee, Wis.: Ideals Pub. Corp., c1983. 80 p., colored illus. Spine title: Hershey's Cookies, Bars, and Brownies. Includes index.

3169. KMA Festival Cookie Book / edited by Evelyn Birkby. Shenandoah, Iowa (Box 500, Shenandoah 51603): KMA Radio, 1983. 143 p., illus. Cover title: Festival Cookie Book. Includes index.

3170. Mrs. Witty's Monster Cookies / by Helen Witty; illustrations by Ted Arnold. New York: Workman Pub., 1983. 128 p., illus. More than 50 recipes. Spine title: Monster Cookies. Includes index.

3171. Betty Crocker's Cookie Book / photography director, Remo Cosentino; illustrations, Ray Skibinski. New York: Golden Press, c1984. 96 p., illus. (some colored). Includes index. Published in 1963 under title: Cooky Book.

3172. Biscuits / Helen Thomas; illustrated by Kate Simunek. London, Eng.: Hale, 1984. 114 p., illus. (A Jill Norman Book). Includes index.

3173. Cookies: 80 Crunchy, Nutty, Chewy and Chocolatey Recipes from Old-Fashioned Favorites to New Taste Treats / Diane Rozas & Rosa Lee Harris. New York: Harmony Books, 1984. 128 p., illus.

3174. Cookies and Slices / Eva G. Fingas. Winnipeg, Man.: Frye Pub., 1984. 120 p., illus. Includes index.

3175. Just Cookies / compiled and tested by Gaye Hansen. North Vancouver, B.C.: Just Muffins, 1984. 56 p. (Just Series).

Cookies *(Continued)*

3176. Natural Biscuits / by Lorraine Whiteside; illustrated by Clive Birch. Wellingborough, Eng.: Thorsons, 1984. 64 p., illus. Includes index.

3177. The Shadow Hill Book of Squares, Bars & Brownies / written by Susan Ashby; illustrated by Pat Steiner. New Hope, Pa.: Woodsong Graphics, c1984. 137 p. Includes index.

3178. The WI Book of Biscuits / illustrated by Ann Rees; edited by Sue Jacquemier and Rosemary Wadey. London, Eng.: Ebury Press, 1984. 96 p., illus. Includes index.

3179. The Allergy Cookie Jar / by Carol Rudoff; foreword by Donald L. Unger. 1st ed. Menlo Park, Calif.: Prologue Publications, c1985. 116 p., illus. Includes index.

3180. The Baking Experience of Switzerland: Cookies the Easy and Simple Way: Hundreds of Varieties at Your Finger Tips: (run your own private cookie business by using the simple methods in this book) / by Gerard A. Voland. Palmdale, Calif.: G.A. Voland, c1985. 160 p., 17 p. of plates, illus.

3181. Better Homes and Gardens Cookies for Christmas / editor, Jill Johnson. 1st ed. Des Moines, Iowa: Meredith Corp., c1985. 96 p., colored illus. Includes index.

3182. Biscuits and Cookies / Nicola Diggins. Twickenham, Eng.: Hamlyn, 1985. 128 p., illus. (some colored). (Hamlyn Cookshelf Series). Includes index.

3183. Festive Cookies / drawn by Vee Guthrie; compiled by Edna Beilenson. White Plains, N.Y.: Peter Pauper Press, c1985. 61 p., illus. (some colored).

3184. Golden Bar Recipe Booklet / S. A. Prodaniuk. Sundre, Alta.: S.A. Prodaniuk, c1985. 8 p., illus.

Cookies *(Continued)*

3185. Magnificent Cookies Cookbook / Kathryn L. Ramsay. Richmond Hill, Ont.: Magnificent Cookbooks Pub., c1985. 124 p., colored illus.

3186. My Favorite Cookies from the Old Country: Loved Recipes / assembled by Olli Leeb. 1st ed. Munich, Germany: Kochbuch, Verlag O. Leb, 1985. 183 p., illus. (some colored). Translation of: Die Feinsten Plätchen Rezepte. Includes index.

3187. The Perfect Cookie / Bernice Hurst; illustrations by Ronald Hurst. Twickenham, Eng.: Hamlyn, 1985. 32 p., illus. (The Perfect Series). Originally published: Reading, Eng.: Elvendon, 1980.

3188. Smart Cookies: 80 Recipes for Heavenly, Healthful Snacking / Jane Kinderlehrer; illustrations by Claude Martinot. 1st ed. New York: Newmarket Press, c1985. 170 p., illus. Includes index.

3189. The Southern Heritage Cookie Jar Cookbook. Birmingham, Ala.: Oxmoor House, c1985. 143 p., illus. (some colored). (Southern Heritage Cookbook Library). Includes index.

3190. Sunset Cookies: Step-by-Step Techniques / by the editors of Sunset Books and Sunset Magazine. 1st ed. Menlo Park, Calif.: Lane Pub. Co., c1985. 96 p., colored illus. ca. 150 recipes. Includes index.

3191. Christmas Cookies / senior foods editor, Katherine M. Eakin, senior editor, Joan E. Denman; assistant editor, Ellen de Lathouder. Birmingham, Ala.: Oxmoor House, c1986. 91 p., illus. Includes index.

3192. The Cookie Lover's Cookie Book / Richard Sax; illustrations by William Joyce. 1st ed. New York: Perennial Library, c1986. 144 p., illus. More than 60 recipes. Includes index.

Cookies *(Continued)*

3193. Cookies and Bars: Family Favorites from Frankenmuth Bavarian Inn / by Dorothy Zehnder; book compiled by Judith Zehnder Keller. Caro, Mich.: Tuscola County Advertiser, c1986. 105 p., illus. Includes index.

3194. Cookies Supreme!/ by the Astrolabe Kids. Burnstown, Ont.: General Store Pub. House, 1986. 52 p., illus. Includes index.

3195. Country Cookies / Allen D. Bragdon. New York: A.D. Bragdon, 1986. 64 p., illus. (Munchie Books).

3196. The Art of Making Good Cookies / by Annette Laslett Ross and Jean Adams Disney. New York: Dover, 1987, c1963. 252 p., illus. Includes index. Reprint. Originally published: New York: Doubleday, 1963.

3197. Better Homes and Gardens Cookies / editor, Maureen Powers; photographers, Michael Jensen and Sean Fitzgerald; food stylists, Suzanne Finley and others. 1st ed. Des Moines, Iowa: Meredith Corp., c1987. 128 p., colored illus. (Great Cooking Made Easy). Includes index.

3198. Christmas Cookies: Scrumptious Recipes with Decoration Tips / by Linda Curtis; recipes created by Sassy Hall; photographs by John Pemberton. 1st ed. New York: Weidenfeld & Nicolson, 1987. 70 p., colored illus. "A Tern Book."

3199. Cookie Sampler: A Collection of Favorite Cookie Recipes / by Jan Siegrist. Shelburne, Vt.: New England Press, 1987. 48 p., illus.

3200. Cookies. Los Angeles, Calif.: Knapp Press, c1987. 119 p., 16 p. of plates, colored illus. (Cooking with Bon Appétit). Includes index. Recipes from Bon Appétit Magazine.

Cookies *(Continued)*

3201. Cookies / Cynthia Scheer, writer and food stylist; Janet Kessel Fletcher, contributing writer; Barbara Feller-Roth, editor; Michael Lamotte, photographer. San Francisco, Calif.: Ortho Information Services, c1987. 127 p., illus. (some colored). More than 140 recipes. (California Culinary Academy Series). Includes index.

3202. Country Sampler's Cookie Sampler. Glen Ellyn, Ill.: Sampler Publications, 1987. 120 p., illus.

3203. The Creative Cookie / by James David Rudoff; foreword by Oscar L. Frick. 1st ed. Menlo Park, Calif.: Allergy Publications Group, c1987. 100 p. (The Allergy Kitchen; v. 2). Includes index.

3204. Good for You Cookies! / Jane Marsh Dieckmann; edited by Andrea Chesman. Freedom, Calif.: Crossing Press, 1987. 126 p. More than 100 recipes. Includes index.

3205. Great American Cookies / Lorraine Bodger. New York: Warner Books, 1987, c1985. 168 p., illus. Includes index.

3206. The Joy of Cookies / Sharon Tyler Herbst. New York: Barron's, c1987. 220 p., 48 p. of plates, illus. (some colored). Includes index.

3207. KMA's Come Again Cookie Book / by Evelyn Birkby. Shenandoah, Iowa: KMA Broadcasting, c1987. 144 p., illus. Includes index.

3208. Blue Ribbon Cookies / edited by Maria Polushkin Robbins. 1st ed. New York: St. Martin's Press, c1988. 134 p.

3209. The Book of Cookies / Pat Alburey; photography by Jon Stewart. Tucson, Ariz.: HP Books, 1988. 128 p., colored illus. 100 recipes. Includes index.

Cookies *(Continued)*

3210. Company's Coming Cookies / by Jean Paré. 1st ed. Edmonton, Alta.: Company's Coming Pub., 1988. 156 p., colored illus. Includes index.

3211. Cookiemania: 100 Irresistible Recipes for Cookiemaniacs / Jeri Dry and Alix Engel. Chicago, Ill.: Contemporary Books, c1988. 118 p. Includes index.

3212. Dr. Cookie's Cookbook: Nutritious, Delicious Gourmet Cookies and Other Treats / Marvin A. Wayne. Cockeysville, Md.: Liberty Pub. Co., c1988. 93 p., illus.

3213. The International Cookie Cookbook / Nancy Baggett; photographs by Dennis M. Gottlieb. 1st ed. New York: Stewart, Tabori & Chang: Distributed by Workman Pub., c1988. 256 p., 53 colored plates. 152 recipes. Includes index.

3214. The Wellesley Cookie Exchange Cookbook / Susan Mahnke Peery. 1st Fireside ed. New York: Simon & Schuster, 1988, c1986. 243 p., illus. More than 200 recipes. "A Fireside Book." Includes index.

3215. 110 More Cookie Recipes. Minneapolis, Minn.: General Mills, 1989. 92 p., colored illus. (Betty Crocker Creative Recipes; no. 37). Includes index.

3216. Best Recipes for Cookies. New York: Prentice Hall Press, c1989. 112 p., colored illus. (Betty Crocker's Red Spoon Collection). Includes index.

3217. Better Homes and Gardens Homemade Cookies. 1st ed. Des Moines, Iowa: Meredith Corp., c1989. 80 p., colored illus. (Better Homes and Gardens Test Kitchen). Includes index.

3218. Brownies, Bars & Biscotti / Terri Henry. Freedom, Calif.: Crossing Press, c1989. 170 p. 80 recipes. (Specialty Cookbook Series). Includes index.

Specialty Cookbooks

Cookies *(Continued)*

3219. Canada Cooks!: Cookies & Squares / Angela Nilsen. North Vancouver, B.C.: Whitecap Books, 1989. 1 v.

3220. Cookies!: Crunchy, Chewy, Nutty, Crumbly, Chocolatey / edited by Marian Levine. Silver Spring, Md.: American Cooking Guild, 1989. 64 p., illus. (Collector's Series).

3221. Cookies Naturally: For Children of All Ages! / by Shirley Hartung. Rev. ed. Kitchener, Ont.: S. Hartung, c1989. 81 p.

3222. Cookies You Can Make: A Step-by-Step Illustrated Cookbook / Sachiko Moriyama. New York: Japan Publications Trading Co., Ltd., 1989. 48 p., illus. (some colored).

3223. 110 Cookie Recipes. Minneapolis, Minn.: General Mills, 1990. 91 p., colored illus. (Betty Crocker Creative Recipes; no. 49). Includes index.

3224. 365 Great Cookies You Can Bake / Lois Hill. New York: Weathervane Books: Distributed by Crown Publishers, 1990. 230 p. Includes index.

3225. The Christmas Cookie Book / Judy Knipe and Barbara Marks. 1st ed. New York: Fawcett Columbine, 1990. ca. 160 p., illus. 96 recipes. Includes index.

3226. Christmas Cookies / edited by Glorya Hale. New York: Avenel Books, 1990. 1 v.

3227. Christmas Cookies. Des Moines, Iowa: Meredith Corp., 1990. 104 p., colored illus. 157 recipes. (Better Homes and Gardens Creative Ideas). Includes index. "Better Homes and Gardens Special Interest Publications."

3228. Country Cookies: An Old-Fashioned Collection / Lisa Yockelson; illustrations by Wendy Wheeler. 1st ed. New York: Harper & Row, 1990. 144 p., illus. 60 recipes. Includes index.

Cookies *(Continued)*

3229. Golde's Homemade Cookies: A Treasured Collection of Timeless Recipes / by Golde Hoffman Soloway; illustrated by Loretta Trezzo. Expanded ed. Charlotte, Vt.: Williamson Pub. Co., c1990. 176 p., illus. Includes index.

3230. Land O' Lakes Cookie Collection. Lincolnwood, Ill.: Publications International, 1990. 96 p., colored illus. (Favorite Recipes; v. 5, no. 27). Includes index.

3231. Poppin' Fresh Homemade Cookies. Minneapolis, Minn.: Pillsbury Co., 1990. 93 p., colored illus. More than 100 recipes. (Classic Pillsbury Cookbooks; 104).

3232. Rose's Christmas Cookies / Rose Levy Beranbaum; photographs by Louis Wallach. New York: W. Morrow, 1990. 118 p., 57 colored photos. 60 recipes. Includes index.

CHILDREN'S COOKBOOKS

3233. My Brother and I Like Cookies / by Anna L. Carlson & Diana Wynne; illustrated by Diana Wynne. [n.p.]: Karwyn Enterprises, c1980. 86 p., illus. Easy-to-follow recipes for 50 different kinds of cookies.

3234. Better Homes and Gardens Cookies for Kids. 1st ed. Des Moines, Iowa: Meredith Corp., c1983. 96 p., illus. (some colored). Includes index. Text and photographs present detailed instructions for making a variety of cookies, including holiday, no-bake, and "natural" ones.

3235. Cookie Fun / by Judith Hoffman Corwin. New York: J. Messner, 1985. 63 p., illus. (some colored). (Messner Holiday Library). Recipes for holiday and everyday cookies, rated for difficulty.

see also entries 2777, 2961, 3528, 3530, 3690; Brownies; Cakes and Cookies; Candy and Cookies; Chocolate Chip Cookies

Crackers

3236. Crackers!: Fun, Easy Recipes for Baking Delicious Crackers / Linda Foust and Tony Husch. Oakland, Calif.: Gravity Pub., c1987. 167 p. Includes index.

see also entry 3143

Crepes and Pancakes

3237. Pancakes & Waffles: The Fine Art of Pancake, Waffle, Crepe, and Blintz Cooking / editor, Carol D. Brent; art director, Dick Collins; photography by Bill Miller. 1st ed. Chicago, Ill.: Tested Recipe Publishers; Garden City, N.Y.: Distribution by Doubleday, 1970. 80 p., colored illus.

3238. Crepes: The Fine Art of Crepe and Blintz Cooking / editor, Carol D. Brent; photography, Bill Miller. Chicago, Ill.: Tested Recipe Publishers; Garden City, N.Y.: Distribution by Doubleday, 1976. 84 p., colored illus. Includes index.

3239. Crepes & Omelets / by Bob and Coleen Simmons; illustrated by Craig Torlucci. Concord, Calif.: Nitty Gritty Productions, c1976. 88, 86 p., illus. Consists of two parts, Crepes & Omelets and Omelets & Crepes, inverted with respect to each other. Omelets & Crepes is illustrated by Mike Nelson. Includes indexes.

3240. Crepe Cookery: 15 Different Batters and 200 Delicious Recipes. Sea Cliff, N.Y.: Carbooks, Inc., 1980. 1 v.

3241. The Crepe and Pancake Cookbook / Cecilia Norman; colour photography by Roger Tuff. London, Eng.: Hutchinson, 1984, c1979. 96 p., illus. (some colored). Includes index.

3242. Pancakes & Crepes / Martha Lomask. 1st ed. New York: Tribeca Communications, 1984. 95 p., illus. Includes index.

Specific Dishes and Courses 415

Crepes and Pancakes *(Continued)*

3243. Pancakes from Vinegar Hill Farm / Susan Ashby. Nashville, Tenn.: Winston-Derek Publishers, 1984. 64 p.

3244. The Great Pancake Cookbook / George A. Zabriskie and Sherry LaFollette. Chicago, Ill.: Contemporary Books, 1985. 106 p., illus. 100 recipes. Includes index.

3245. You Can Do Anything with Crepes / Virginia Pasley and Jane Green. 1st Fireside ed. New York: Simon & Schuster, 1985, c1970. 174 p. "A Fireside Book." Includes index.

3246. Waffles & Wafers / Mary Barile. Margaretville, N.Y.: Heritage Publications, 1987. 1 v.

3247. The Book of Crepes & Omelets / Mary Norwak; photography by Jon Stewart. Tucson, Ariz.: HP Books, c1988. 120 p., colored illus. Includes index.

3248. Pancakes: From Flapjakes to Crepes / by Dorian Leigh Parker; illustrations by Sally Sturman. 1st ed. New York: C.N. Potter: Distributed by Crown, c1988. 120 p., illus. Includes index.

3249. True Grist: Buckwheat Flour and Cornmeal Recipes / Patricia B. Mitchell. Rev. ed. Chatham, Va.: P.B. Mitchell, c1989. 37 p.

see also entries 1705, 3717; and Grains *(Section I)*

Croissants

3250. The Quintessential Croissant / Pamella Z. Asquith, text; Michael Starkman, design and illustration. Millbrae, Calif.: Celestial Arts, c1982. 63 p., colored illus.

3251. The Perfect Croissant: Step-by-Step Instructions Plus Fabulous Fillings / Dee Coutelle. Chicago, Ill.: Contemporary Books, c1983. 106 p., illus. Includes index.

Specialty Cookbooks

Croissants *(Continued)*

3252. The Little Croissant Cookbook / Mary L. Green. Denver, Colo.: Giftstar, 1984. ca. 10 p., illus. (Little Cookbooks).

see also broader category: Bread

Desserts

3253. Festive Dessert Cookery / Evelyn Loeb. White Plains, N.Y.: Peter Pauper Press, 1967. 61 p.

3254. 101 Desserts to Make you Famous / Yvonne Young Tarr. New York: L. Stuart, 1970. 191 p.

3255. Family Circle's Great Desserts / editor, Nancy Hecht Fitzpatrick. New York: Family Circle, Inc. 1974. 144 p., colored illus. "A New York Times Company Publication."

3256. Maida Heatter's Book of Great Desserts / drawings by Toni Evins. 1st ed. New York: Knopf, 1974. 411 p., illus.

3257. A World of Desserts and Delicacies from Solor / prepared and produced by Rutledge Books. New York: Benjamin Co., c1976. 128 p., illus. Includes index. "Recipes developed by Sokol & Company."

3258. Just Desserts / Anita Borghese. New York: Stein and Day, 1977. 383 p. Includes index.

3259. Happy Endings. Cincinnati, Ohio: Happy Endings, 1978? 314 p., illus. Includes index. Title on spine: Desserts.

3260. Rodale's Naturally Delicious Desserts and Snacks / by Faye Martin; editor, Charles Gerras; photography, Carl Doney, Sally Ann Shenk, and Laura Hendry. Emmaus, Pa.: Rodale Press, c1978. 408 p., illus. Includes index.

Specific Dishes and Courses

Desserts *(Continued)*

3261. Deliriously Delightful Desserts / by the Better Weigh; recipes compiled by Brenda Wood. Egbert, Ont.: Better Weigh, 198-? 42 leaves.

3262. Victorian Desserts for Dinner and High Tea / compiled by Penelope Peck for the benefit of School Volunteers for New Haven, Inc. New Haven, Conn.: The Volunteers, 198-? 50 p., illus. Includes bibliography and index.

3263. Classic Desserts / by the editors of Time-Life Books. Alexandria, Va.: Time-Life Books; Morristown, N.J.: School and library distribution by Silver Burdett Co., c1980. 176 p., illus. (The Good Cook, Techniques and Recipes). Includes index.

3264. The Dessert Cookbook: A Tribute to Campaign 1980 / Deirdre McVey. [n.p.]: McVey, c1980. 112 p. Cover title: The American Statesmen and Honorary Citizen Dessert Cookbook.

3265. Ideals Desserts, Candy & Cookie Cookbook. New York: Bonanza Books, 1980. 3 v. in 1, illus. Contents: Nice & Easy Desserts Cookbook / by Cyndee Kannenberg.--Candy Cookbook / by Mildred Brand.--Cookie Cookbook / by Darlene Kronschnabel. First published separately in 1978, 1979, and 1977 respectively. Includes index.

3266. Indian Sweet Cookery / Jack Santa Maria; illustrated by Carmen Miranda. Boulder, Colo.: Shambala; New York: Distributed in the U.S. by Random House, 1980. 146 p., illus.

3267. Microwave Baking & Desserts / by Barbara Methven and Sylvia Ogren; photographers, Michael Jensen, Steven Smith. Minnetonka, Minn.: Publication Arts, c1980. 160 p., colored illus. (Microwave Cooking Library). Includes index.

3268. The Natural Sugarless Dessert Cookbook / Carole Collier. New York: Walker, 1980. 180 p., illus. Includes bibliography and index.

Desserts *(Continued)*

3269. Puddings & Desserts / edited by Valerie Creek. London, Eng.: Octopus Books, 1980. 92 p., illus. (chiefly colored). Includes index.

3270. Quick-to-Fix Desserts for Foodservice Menu Planning / Eulalia C. Blair. Boston, Mass.: CBI Pub. Co., c1980. 309 p., illus. Includes index.

3271. Sweets for Saints and Sinners / Janice Feuer; illustrations by Veronica de Rosa. San Francisco, Calif.: 101 Productions, c1980. 144 p., illus. Includes index.

3272. Wholefood Desserts. Sheffield, Eng. (Townhead, Dunford Bridge, Sheffield, S30 6TG): Lifespan Community Collective, c1980. 13 p., illus. Includes index.

3273. The Woman's Day Low-Calorie Dessert Cookbook / Carol Cutler. Boston, Mass.: Houghton Mifflin, 1980. 213 p., illus. 200 recipes. Includes index.

3274. C and H Sugar Complete Dessert Cookbook: 75 Years of Good Eating from the Famous C and H Sugar Kitchen / prepared under the direction of Nancy F. Newland. New York: Benjamin Co., c1981. 224 p., illus. (some colored). "A Benjamin Company/Rutledge Book." Includes index.

3275. Desserts / the Sir Mortimer B. Davis Jewish General Hospital Auxiliary; illustrated by Evelyn Schaffer. Montreal, Que.: The Auxiliary, 1981. 141 p., illus.

3276. Light Desserts: The Low Calorie, Low Salt, Low Fat Way / by Deborah Kidushim-Allen; illustrations by Heather Preston; photographs by Hans Albers. 1st ed. San Francisco, Calif.: Harper & Row, c1981. 182 p., 8 p. of plates, illus. (some colored). Includes index.

Desserts *(Continued)*

3277. The Sweet Life: Natural Macrobiotic Desserts / Marcea Weber. 1st ed. Tokyo, Japan: Japan Publications; New York: Distributors, United States, Kodansha International/USA through Harper & Row, 1981. 176 p., illus. Includes bibliography and index.

3278. Time for Dessert / Betty Yew. Singapore: Times Books International, c1981. 166 p., illus. (some colored).

3279. Treats for My Sweets / by Gail C. Jaye; illustrations and photography by Charlie and Brenda Culver. Bay Minette, Ala.: G.C. Jaye, 1981. 124 p., illus. Includes index.

3280. Vachon Desserts / written & edited by Margaret Gilmour. Montreal, Que.: L.E.L. Marketing, c1981. 95 p. Includes index. Issued also in French under title: Les desserts de Vachon.

3281. The Woman's Day Book of Delicious Desserts / edited by Julie Houston. New York: Fawcett Columbine, c1981. 160 p., colored illus. Includes index.

3282. Bishop Museum Salad and Dessert Cookbook, 1982-1983. Honolulu, Hawaii: Bishop Museum, 1982. 110 p., illus.

3283. Dessert Cooking Class Cookbook / by the editors of Consumer Guide. New York: Beekman House, 1982. 64 p., illus.

3284. Desserts / edited by Georgia Orcutt and Sandra Taylor. 1st ed. Dublin, N.H.: Yankee Books, c1982. 144 p., illus. (The Flavor of New England). "A Yankee Magazine Publication." Includes index.

3285. Desserts: Hundreds of Mouth-Watering Treats Sure to Be Perfect for any Occasion! Nashville, Tenn.: Favorite Recipes Press, c1982. 231 p., illus. (some colored). (Favorite Recipes of Home Economics Teachers). Includes index.

Desserts *(Continued)*

3286. Diabetic Candy, Cookie & Dessert Cookbook / Mary Jane Finsand. New York: Sterling Pub. Co., c1982. 160 p. Includes index.

3287. The Exchange Cookbook: Featuring Dessert & Casserole Recipes for Diabetic & Weight Control Programs / Pamela Gillispie Barbour, Norma Green Spivey; foreword by Paul C. Davidson; designed & illustrated by Susan F. Yakrus. Atlanta, Ga.: G&G Pub. Co., c1982. 197 p., illus. Spice chart inserted. Includes indexes.

3288. Favorite Brand Name Recipes: Desserts for All Occasions / by the editors of Consumer Guide. New York: Beekman House: Distributed by Crown Publishers, c1982. 80 p., colored illus. Includes index.

3289. The Fine Art of Delectable Desserts / by Camille Glenn; illustrations by William Hamby and Mary Walter. Louisville, Ky.: Nana Publications, c1982. 216 p., colored illus. "Published for the benefit of the Louisville Fund for the Arts Endowment." Includes index.

3290. Hamlyn All Colour Book of Puddings & Desserts / Carol Bowen. London, Eng.: Hamlyn, 1982. 124 p., illus. (some colored). Includes index.

3291. Just Desserts / Michael Smith. London, Eng.: British Broadcasting Corp., 1982. 56 p.

3292. Maida Heatter's New Book of Great Desserts / drawings by Toni Evins. 1st ed. New York: Knopf, 1982. 467 p., illus. Includes index.

3293. Parish Delights: A Collection of Sweets / editors, Shirley S. Siegel, Edna C. Manicas. Alexandria, Va.: St. Mary's Home & School Association, 1982. 89 p., illus.

Specific Dishes and Courses 421

Desserts *(Continued)*

3294. Slim Gourmet Sweets and Treats / Barbara Gibbons. 1st ed. New York: Harper & Row, c1982. 264 p. Includes index.

3295. Sweet & Natural: Desserts Without Sugar, Honey, Molasses, or Artificial Sweeteners / Janet Warrington; foreword by Lendon H. Smith. Trumansburg, N.Y.: Crossing Press, c1982. 143 p., illus. Includes index.

3296. Sweet and Sugarfree: An All Natural Fruit-Sweetened Dessert Cookbook / by Karen E. Barkie. 1st ed. New York: St. Martin's Press, c1982. 160 p. Includes bibliography and index.

3297. Unforbidden Sweets: More Than 100 Classic Desserts You Can Now Enjoy--Without Counting Calories / Jean Anderson. New York: Arbor House, c1982. 203 p. Includes index.

3298. Variations on a Dessert / Jean Conil. London, Eng.: New English Library, 1982. 144 p.

3299. 101 Allergy-Free Desserts / Frances Sheridan Goulart. New York: Simon & Schuster, c1983. 188 p. "A Wallaby Book." Includes index.

3300. The Best of Lenôtre's Desserts: Glorious Desserts from France's Finest Pastry Maker / translated and adapted by Philip and Mary Hyman; photos by Pierre Ginet. Woodbury, N.Y.: Barron's, 1983? 232 p., illus. Includes index. Combined and abridged edition from Lenôtre's Ice Cream and Candies, 1978, and Lenôtre's Desserts and Pastries, 1975.

3301. The Common Ground Dessert Cookbook: Recipes from the Common Ground Community Restaurant, Brattleboro, Vermont / created, compiled and written by Katherine Kohrman; graphics by Molly Forsythe and Meghan Merker; additional writing by Kevin Connors. Berkeley, Calif.: Ten Speed Press, c1983. 201 p., illus. Includes index.

Desserts *(Continued)*

3302. Cook with Me Sugar Free: Favorite Snacks, Sweets, and Desserts for Children and Grownups Too / Sharon M. Dregne Gerstenzang; illustrations by Rhoda Watel. New York: Simon and Schuster, c1983. 222 p., illus. "A Fireside Book." Includes index.

3303. Dazzling Desserts: Over 100 Delicious Recipes / by Miriam Canter. Iowa City, Iowa: Penfield Press, c1983. 40 p., illus. (some colored).

3304. Desserts from the Garden / Janet Ballantyne; illustrations by Elayne Sears. Charlotte, Vt.: Garden Way, c1983. 156 p., illus. Includes index.

3305. The Encyclopedia of Desserts / Emma Codrington, Michael Raffael. London, Eng.: Octopus Books, c1983. 192 p., illus. Includes index.

3306. The Festive Tradition, Table Decoration and Desserts in America, 1650-1900 / Louise Conway Belden. New York: W.W. Norton, c1983. 340, 8 p. of plates, illus. (some colored). Includes index.

3307. From Marina with Love /Marina Reed Gonzalez. San Antonio, Tex. (9714 Laurel Oaks, San Antonio 78240): M. Reed Gonzalez, c1983. 285 p., illus. (some colored). Includes index.

3308. Glorious Desserts / Carol Bowen; photography by Paul Williams; line illustrations by Marilyn Day. Woodbury, N.J.: Barron's Educational Series, 1983. 124 p., illus. (some colored). Includes index.

3309. The Great Dessert Book: Classic Light Desserts of the World / Christian Teubner, Sybil Grafin Schonfeldt. New York: Hearst Books, 1983. 192 p., colored illus. Includes index. Translation of: Das Grosse Buch der Desserts.

Desserts *(Continued)*

3310. I Can't Cook Desserts / Sonia Allison. London, Eng.: Hamilton, 1983. 64 p., illus. (some colored). Includes index.

3311. Josceline Dimbleby's Book of Puddings, Desserts and Savouries. Harmondsworth, Eng.: Penguin, 1983, c1979. 176 p. (Penguin Handbooks). Includes index.

3312. The Magic Mountain Natural Dessert Book / by Debi Fischer. Trumansburg, N.Y.: Crossing Press, c1983. 110 p., illus. Includes index.

3313. Old-Fashioned Desserts / Richard Sax; illustrated by Marc Rosenthal. New York: I. Chalmers Cookbooks, c1983. 84 p., illus.

3314. Pig-Out / by Christina Hanley. 1st ed. Secaucus, N.J.: Citadel Press, c1983. 93 p., colored illus.

3315. Sister Jennie's Shaker Desserts / by Arthur Tolve and James Bissland III; photography by Frank Breithaupt. Bowling Green, Ohio: Gabriel's Horn Pub. Co., c1983. 48 p., illus.

3316. Sweet Dreams: Puddings and Pies, Gateaux and Ices--and Lots More / Josceline Dimbleby. Cambridge, Eng.: Woodhead-Faulkner for J. Sainsbury, 1983. 96 p., illus. (some colored). (A Sainsbury Cookbook).

3317. Sweets & Puddings. Newton Abbot, Eng.: David & Charles, c1983. 64 p., colored illus. (Kitchen Workshop). Includes index. Translation of: Desserter.

3318. Viennese Desserts Made Easy / Georgina Gronner. Chicago, Ill.: Contemporary Books, c1983. 111 p., illus. Includes index.

3319. All Color Book of Delightful Desserts. New York: Arco Pub., 1984. 82 p., colored illus. ca. 80 recipes. (All Color Cookbooks). Includes index.

Desserts *(Continued)*

3320. Delicious Desserts: More Than 300 Recipes for Cookies, Cakes, Pies, Puddings, Ice Cream, and Other Irresistible Sweets / the editors of Family Circle. New York: Times Books, c1984. 326 p., illus. Includes index.

3321. The Dessert Cookbook / Frederick E. Kahn; edited by Betty Carol. New York: Nautilus Communications; Aurora, Ill.: Distributed by Caroline House, c1984. 196 p., illus. Includes index.

3322. Desserts and Pastries: A Professional Primer / Marion Blatsos Gilman, Richard Gilman. New York: Van Nostrand Reinhold, c1984. 225 p., illus. (some colored). "A CBI Book." Includes index.

3323. Desserts, Cheesecakes & Gateaux / by Jenny Allday; illustrated by Ian Jones. Wellingborough, Eng.: Thorsons, 1984. 160 p., illus. (A Thorsons Wholefood Cookbook). Includes index.

3324. Dinner Party Desserts / translated by Caroline Beamish; foreword by Arne Kruger. London, Eng.: Macdonald, 1984. 198 p., illus. (some colored). Includes index. Translated from the Japanese.

3325. Elegant Desserts / translated by Caroline Beamish. Tucson, Ariz.: HP Books, c1984. 199 p., colored illus. Translation of: I dolci. Includes index.

3326. Fast Fabulous Desserts / Jack Lirio. 1st ed. New York: E.P. Dutton, c1984. 292 p. More than 150 recipes. Includes index.

3327. Great Desserts / by Christine Koury. Woodbury, N.Y.: Barron's, c1984. 64 p., colored illus. (Easy cooking). Includes index.

Desserts *(Continued)*

3328. Hot Puddings and Cold Sweets / by Kate Hutchinson; photographs by Tim Clark. Loughborough, Eng.: Ladybird, c1984. 43 p., colored illus. (A Ladybird Cookery Book). Includes index.

3329. Light Desserts. Los Angeles, Calif.: Knapp Press, c1984. 120 p., 16 p. of plates, colored illus. (Cooking with Bon Appétit). Includes index.

3330. Miss Grimble Presents Delicious Desserts / Sylvia Balser Hirsch. New York: New American Library, 1984, c1983. 211 p. "A Plume Book." Includes index.

3331. Naughty but Nice / Michael Smith. London, Eng.: British Broadcasting Corp., 1984. 64 p., illus. (some colored). Includes index.

3332. The No Sugar Delicious Dessert Cookbook / Jeanne Moe, Karen Rubin, Sally Abrams. Berkeley, Calif.: Celestial Arts, c1984. 121 p.

3333. Plain Jane's Thrill of Very Fattening Foods Cookbook / by Linda Sunshine; illustrations by Alison Seiffer. 1st ed. New York: St. Martin's Press, c1984. 127 p., illus. Includes index.

3334. Serve It Forth!: Festive Desserts from the Nineteenth Century Adapted for Modern Times / compiled by Dorothy Duncan; with the assistance of Rowena Colman and others; designed and illustrated by Mary Ellen Perkins. Willowdale, Ont.: Ontario Historical Society, 1984. 28 p., illus. Includes index.

3335. The Southern Heritage Just Desserts Cookbook. Birmingham, Ala.: Oxmoor House, c1984. 143 p., illus. (some colored). (The Southern Heritage Cookbook Library). Includes index.

Desserts *(Continued)*

3336. The Supernatural Dessert Cookbook: A Book of Unreal Desserts / written by Lois Fishkin; illustrations & script by Susan DiMarco. Berkeley, Calif.: Creative Arts Book Co., 1984. 118 p., illus. Includes index.

3337. Sweet Surprises / presented by California Home Economics Teachers; editor, Gerry Henderson; graphics, Laura Pierce. Orange, Calif.: California Management Services, c1984. 149 p., 8 p. of plates, illus. (some colored). Includes index.

3338. Sweets and Desserts from the Middle East / Arto der Haroutunian. London, Eng.: Century Pub., 1984. 224 p., illus. Includes bibliography and index.

3339. The WI Book of Desserts / Janet Wier. London, Eng.: Ebury, 1984. 96 p., illus. Includes index.

3340. 101 Delicious Desserts / by Adele Marks; illustrated by Anthony Van Bruggen. Downsview, Ont.: Gadget Pub., 1985. 129 p., illus. Includes index.

3341. Chez Panisse Desserts / by Lindsey Remolif Shere; preface by Alice Waters; illustrations by Wayne Thiebaud. 1st ed. New York: Random House, c1985. 341 p., illus. Includes bibliography and index.

3342. Chicago's Sweet Tooth: Five Hundred Prominent Chicagoans Divulge Their Favorite Dessert Recipes / Ann Gerber. 1st ed. Chicago, Ill.: Chicago Review Press, c1985. 269 p., illus. Includes index.

3343. A Collection of Favorite Family Dessert Recipes Graciously Donated by the Famous, Near Famous & Friends to Help Refurbish Lady Liberty / compiled by the Albany, N.Y., Council of the Telephone Pioneers of America. Albany, N.Y.: Telephone Pioneers of America, Adirondack Empire Chapter, Albany Council, c1985. 366 p. Cover title: Lady Liberty's Celebrity Desserts. Spine title: Celebrity Desserts.

Desserts *(Continued)*

3344. The Complete Book of Desserts / edited by Linda Doeser. Feltham, Eng.: Newnes, c1985. 184 p., colored illus. Includes index.

3345. Delectable Desserts / Robert Carrier. London, Eng.: Marshall Cavendish, 1985. 112 p., colored illus. Includes index.

3346. Delicious Desserts / Jane Suthering. Tucson, Ariz.: HP Books, c1985. 80 p., colored illus. 100 recipes, including fresh fruits, baked goods, and frozen desserts. (Creative Cuisine). Includes index.

3347. The Dessert Lover's Cookbook / Marlene Sorosky; photographs by Robert Stein. 1st ed. New York: Harper & Row, c1985. 238 p., colored illus. More than 200 recipes and 120 step-by-step photos. Includes index. Republished 1990.

3348. Desserts, Cakes and Breads. London, Eng.: Reader's Digest Association, c1985. 104 p., illus. (some colored). Includes index.

3349. Famous Brands Desserts. St. Louis, Mo.: Brand Name Pub. Corp., 1985? 128 p., colored illus. (Famous Brands Cookbook Library). Includes index.

3350. Fancy, Sweet & Sugarfree / by Karen E. Barkie. 1st ed. New York: St. Martin's Press, c1985. 173 p., illus. Includes bibliography and index.

3351. Fast Desserts / Mary Berry. London, Eng.: Sphere, 1985. 192 p. Includes index.

3352. The Great International Dessert Cookbook: 80 Easy and Elegant Recipes--a Glorious Celebration of Global Delights / Honey & Larry Zisman with the help and cooperation of the U.S. Committee for UNICEF. 1st ed. New York: St. Martin's Press, c1985. 146 p., 8 p. of plates, colored illus. Includes index.

Desserts (Continued)

3353. The Great Microwave Dessert Cookbook / Thelma Pressman. Chicago, Ill.: Contemporary Books, c1985. 161 p., 8 p. of plates, colored illus. Includes index.

3354. Healthy Desserts / Janette Marshall. London, Eng.: Hamlyn, 1985. 125 p. (Here's Health).

3355. An Individualized Food Laboratory Approach to: Fancy Desserts / Barbara Kern Williams. Westbury, N.Y.: Westville Pub. Co., 1985. 1 v. [Publication of this book has not been verified].

3356. Irresistible Desserts. 1st U.S. and Canadian ed. Woodbury, N.Y.: Barron's, 1985, c1984. 160 p., illus. (some colored). (Step-by-Step Cooking Series). Includes index. Originally published: Desserts and Puddings. 1984.

3357. Maida Heatter's Book of Great American Desserts / drawings by Toni Evins. 1st ed. New York: Knopf, 1985. 385 p., illus. Includes index.

3358. The National Trust Book of Sorbets, Flummeries, and Fools / Colin Cooper English. Newton Abbot, Eng.; North Pomfret, Vt.: David & Charles, c1985. 95 p., illus. Includes index.

3359. Naturally Delicious Desserts / Cherie Baker. 1st ed. New York: Ballantine Books, c1985. 238 p., illus. ca. 150 recipes. Includes index.

3360. Rodale's Sensational Desserts / by Joan Bingham and Dolores Riccio. Emmaus, Pa.: Rodale Press, c1985. 288 p., colored illus. Includes index. British ed. published in 1986 under title: Sensational Desserts (entry 3379).

3361. Special Occasion Desserts. Los Angeles, Calif.: Knapp Press, c1985. 119 p., 16 p. of plates, colored illus. (Cooking with Bon Appétit). Includes index.

Desserts *(Continued)*

3362. Sweet Delights / editor, Mary Devine. Secaucus, N.J.: Chartwell Books, c1985. 119 p., illus.

3363. The Best of Desserts. Nashville, Tenn.: Favorite Recipes Press, c1986. 207 p., illus. (some colored). Includes index.

3364. Chinese Dessert, Dim Sum & Snack Cookbook / Wonona W. Chang and others. New York: Sterling, c1986. 160 p., colored illus. Includes index.

3365. Creative Desserts. Minneapolis, Minn.: General Mills, 1986. 92 p., colored illus. (Betty Crocker Creative Recipes; no. 3). Includes index.

3366. Delicious Desserts / text by Denise Jarrett-Macauley. Guildford, Eng.: Coombe, c1986. 64 p., illus. Includes index.

3367. Desserts / Christian Teubner; translation and Americanization by Anne Mendelson. 1st English-language ed. Woodbury, N.Y.: Barron's, 1986. 96 p., colored illus. (Cooking Magic). Includes index.

3368. Desserts / by Nancy Silverton in collaboration with Heidi Yorkshire; decorative paintings by Deborah Healy; technique drawings by Wendy Wray. 1st ed. New York: Harper & Row, c1986. 365 p., illus. Includes index.

3369. Desserts: The Perfect Finish / Mary Lou Arnold and others. London, Eng.: Bay Books, 1986. 96 p. Includes index.

3370. Diabetic Delights: Cakes, Biscuits and Desserts / by Jane Suthering and Sue Lousley. London, Eng.: Dunitz, 1986. 123 p., colored illus. (Positive Health Guide). Includes index.

3371. Divine Desserts / Bernice Hurst. London, Eng.: Apple, c1986. 128 p., illus. (some colored). (A Quintet Book). Includes index.

Specialty Cookbooks

Desserts *(Continued)*

3372. Fresh Ways with Desserts / by the editors of Time-Life Books. Alexandria, Va.: Time-Life Books, c1986. 144 p., colored illus. (Healthy Home Cooking). Includes index.

3373. Fruit Desserts / by Sarah Brown. London, Eng.: Dorling Kindersley, 1986. 96 p., colored illus. (Sainsbury's Healthy Eating Cookbooks). Includes index.

3374. Great Desserts from Ceil Dyer. New York: McGraw-Hill, c1986. 314 p. "McGraw-Hill Paperbacks."

3375. The Holiday Dessert Book: Nearly 200 Delectable Treats for a Year of Celebrations / Kathy Cutler; photographs by John Uher. New York: Macmillan, c1986. 262 p., illus. Includes index.

3376. Light & Easy Choice Desserts / Kay Spicer. Toronto, Ont.: Grosvenor House, 1986. 175 p., 10 leaves of colored plates. Includes index. "Published in co-operation with the Canadian Diabetes Association."

3377. Miniature Desserts / Pam Dotter. 1st ed. New York: Weidenfeld & Nicolson, 1986. 160 p., colored illus. Includes index.

3378. Puddings and Desserts / Carole Handslip. London, Eng.: Octopus, 1986, c1980. 93 p., colored illus. (The Kitchen Library). Includes index.

3379. Sensational Desserts / by Joan Bingham and Dolores Riccio; revised and edited for the United Kingdom by Lee Faber. Wellingborough, Eng.: Thorsons, 1986. 288 p., illus. Includes index. Originally published: Emmaus, Pa.: Rodale, 1985 (entry 3360).

3380. The Silver Palate Sweet Times Dessert Book / by Julee Rosso & Sheila Lukins, with Michael McLaughlin & Sarah Leah Chase. New York: Workman, c1986. 61 p., illus.

Desserts *(Continued)*

3381. Sweet & Natural Desserts: East West's Best and Most Wholesome, Sugar- and Dairy-Free Treats / from the editors of East West Journal; illustrations by James Steinberg. 1st ed. Brookline, Mass.: East West Health Books; New York: Distributed by Talman, c1986. 120 p., illus.

3382. Sweet Things / Claire Macdonald of Macdonald. London, Eng.: Corgi, 1986, c1984. 169 p., illus. Includes index.

3383. The American Baker: Exquisite Desserts from the Pastry Chef of the Stanford Court / by Jim Dodge, with Elaine Ratner; foreword by Maida Heatter; illustrations by Susan Mattmann, photographs by Michael Lamotte. New York: Simon and Schuster, c1987. 350 p., illus. Includes index.

3384. Better Homes and Gardens Desserts / editor, Joyce Trollope. 1st ed. Des Moines, Iowa: Meredith Corp., c1987. 128 p., colored illus. (Great Cooking Made Easy). Includes index.

3385. A Book of Welsh Puddings and Pies / Bobby Freeman. Talybont, Wales: Y Lolfa, 1987. 31 p.

3386. Cooking with Desserts / Veronica Bull. New York: Gallery Books, 1987. 73 p., colored illus. (Microwave Library). Includes index.

3387. Cranks Puddings & Desserts / compiled by Daphne Swann. Enfield, Eng.: Guinness, c1987. 80 p., illus. (some colored). Includes index.

3388. Desserts. Toronto, Ont.: Grolier, 1987. 109 p., illus. (Microwave Magic; 3). Includes index.

3389. Dolci, the Fabulous Desserts of Italy / Virginie and George Elbert; drawings by Glenn Wolff. New York: Simon and Schuster, c1987. 301 p., illus. Includes index.

Desserts *(Continued)*

3390. Gourmet's Best Desserts / from the editors of Gourmet. New York: Random House, c1987. 576 p., colored photos. More than 600 recipes from 25 years of Gourmet magazine. "Condé Nast Books." Includes index.

3391. Great Old-Fashioned American Desserts / Beatrice Ojakangas. 1st ed. New York: Dutton, c1987. 293 p. Includes index.

3392. Impossible-to-Resist Desserts / Maria Middlestead. London, Eng.: Hodder and Stoughton, 1987. 86 p.

3393. Mexican Desserts: The Sweet Side of Mexican Cooking! / by Socorro Muñoz Kimble and Irma Serrano Noriega. Phoenix, Ariz.: Golden West Publishers, 1987. 144 p. More than 200 desserts. Includes index.

3394. Sugar Free--Goodies / by Judith Soley Majors. Milwaukie, Or.: Apple Press, c1987. 159 p., illus. "Approved by American Diabetes Association, Inc., Hawaii Affiliate, Inc." Includes index.

3395. Summer Desserts / Carole Handslip. Mississauga, Ont.: Cupress, c1987. 79 p., colored illus. (A & P Creative Cooking Collection). Includes index.

3396. Sunset Light Desserts / by the editors of Sunset Books and Sunset Magazine. 1st ed. Menlo Park, Calif.: Lane Pub. Co., c1987. 96 p., colored illus. Includes index.

3397. Sweet Temptations: Natural Dessert Book / Frances Kendall; foreword by Ann Wigmore. Garden City Park, N.Y.: Avery Pub. Group, c1987. 160 p. Includes index.

3398. Winter Desserts / Sallie Morris. Mississauga, Ont.: Cupress, c1987. 79 p., colored illus. (A & P Creative Cooking Collection). Includes index.

Desserts *(Continued)*

3399. A Year of Diet Desserts: 365 Delectable Low-Calorie Treats--a Different One for Every Day / by Joan Bingham; photography by the Rodale Press Photography Department. Emmaus, Pa.: Rodale Press, c1987. 301 p., colored illus. Includes index.

3400. The All New Desserts Cookbook: Including Holiday Classics. Nashville, Tenn.: Favorite Recipes Press, c1988. 164 p., illus. (some colored). (Favorite Recipes of Home Economics Teachers). Includes index.

3401. A Dessert Cookbook / Digby Law. London, Eng.: Hodder and Stoughton, 1988. 194 p.

3402. The Dessert Scene: Toronto's Top Dessert Spots Reveal Their Secret Recipes / Rose Reisman. North York, Ont.: R. Reisman, c1988. 112 p., 8 p. of colored plates. Includes index.

3403. Desserts / Pol Martin. Montreal, Que.: Brimar, c1988. 64 p. (Smart & Simple Cooking).

3404. Desserts / Bonnie Stern. Toronto, Ont.: Random House of Canada, 1988. 192 p., illus. Includes index.

3405. Desserts II. Toronto, Ont.: Grolier, 1988. 110 p., colored illus. (Microwave Magic; 9). Includes index.

3406. Desserts and Pastries / Anne Willan. London, Eng.: Walker, 1988. 94 p.

3407. Desserts to Lower Your Fat Thermostat / written by Barbara W. Higa; introduction by Dennis W. Remington; illustrated by Janice K. Fritze. Provo, Utah: Vitality House International, c1988. 214 p., colored illus. Includes bibliography and index.

3408. The Free and Equal Sweet Tooth Cookbook / by Carole Kruppa. Chicago, Ill.: Surrey Books, c1988. 159 p. Includes index.

Specialty Cookbooks

Desserts *(Continued)*

3409. Gourmet Desserts. London, Eng.: Hamlyn, 1988. 96 p. (Vogue Cookery Collection).

3410. Great Desserts of the South / by Mary Leigh Furrh and Jo Barksdale; calligraphy by Doris Ann Spell. Gretna, La.: Pelican Pub. Co., 1988. 209 p., illus. Includes index.

3411. Lee Bailey's Country Desserts: Cakes, Cookies, Ice Creams, Pies, Puddings & More / by Lee Bailey; photographs by Joshua Greene; recipe development and research by Mardee Haidin Regan. 1st ed. New York: C.N. Potter: Distributed by Crown Publishers, c1988. 173 p., illus. (some colored). Includes index.

3412. Low Salt, Low Sugar, Low Fat Desserts / Penny Ballantyne and Maureen Egan. San Leandro, Calif.: Bristol Pub. Enterprises, c1988. 187 p., illus. (some colored).

3413. Macrobiotic Dessert Book / Anneliese Wollner; translated by Gabriele Kushi. 1st ed. Tokyo, Japan; New York: Japan Publications; New York: Distributor, Kodansha International/USA, through Harper & Row, Publishers, 1988. 107 p., illus. (some colored). Includes index. Translation of: Makrobiotik-Dessertbuch.

3414. Sugarless Desserts, Jams, and Salads Cookbook / Addie Gonshorowski; cover & illustrations by Susan Selander. Eugene, Or.: Ad-Dee Publishers, c1988. 150 p., illus. Includes index.

3415. Summer Desserts / Rosemary Stark, Emma Codrington and Michael Raffael. London, Eng.: Hamlyn, 1988, c1986. 79 p. (Cooking for Today).

3416. Sweet Mania / by Cathy Prange and Joan Pauli. Kitchener, Ont.: Muffin Mania Pub., c1988. 87 p., illus.

Desserts *(Continued)*

3417. Texas Sweets from Grandma's Kitchen: "Goodies of the Past" / recipes compiled by Donna Duncan Jomaa. Livingston, Tex.: Straw Hat Productions, 1988, c1987. 158 p. Includes index.

3418. The Worldwide Dessert Contest / by Dan Elish; illustrated by John Steven Gurney. New York: Orchard Books, c1988. 206 p., illus. "A Richard Jackson Book."

3419. Zero Calorie Desserts: The 7-Day Scratch & Sniff Diet / by Andy Mayer & Jim Becker; illustrations by Dick Witt. New York: Workman Pub., c1988. 14 p., colored illus.

3420. 52 Sugar Free Desserts / Joan Mary Alimonti. 1st ed. Pleasant Hill, Calif.: Quickline Publications, c1989. 121 p.

3421. Antoine Bouterin's Desserts from Le Perigord / by Antoine Bouterin with Ruth Gardner. New York: Putnam, c1989. ca. 224 p., illus. ca. 100 recipes. Includes index.

3422. The Artists & Mathematicians Dessert Book: Dessert Recipes from the School of Art & the Department of Mathematical Sciences, Montana State University / designed and produced by Michael D. Clark and others; design advisor, Anne Garner. Bozeman, Mont.: Bozarts Press, 1989? 27 p., illus. Includes index.

3423. David Wood Dessert Book / David Wood with Karen Barnaby and others. Vancouver, B.C.: Whitecap Books, 1989. 238 p., colored illus.

3424. Delicious Desserts / Mary Mouzar, Joane Uhlman. Halifax, N.S.: Periwinkle, c1989. 156 p., colored illus. (Kiss the Cook Who Microwaves).

3425. Desserts: Simple Ways to Prepare Imaginative Meals! Toronto, Ont.: Grolier, c1989. 90 p., colored illus. (The Creative Cook; 3).

Specialty Cookbooks

Desserts *(Continued)*

3426. Diabetic Desserts / Sue Hall. Wellingborough, Eng.: Thorsons, 1989. 112 p.

3427. Great Desserts / from the editors of Food & Wine Magazine; selected and edited by Mardee Haidin Regan; photography by Irvin Blitz; art direction by Leslie Smolan. New York, N.Y.: Stewart, Tabori & Chang, c1989. 248 p., colored illus. More than 200 recipes. Includes index. Originally published: New York: American Express Pub. Corp., c1987.

3428. Great Desserts / Lorenza de Medici Stucchi. New York: International Culinary Society; Distributed by Crown Publishers, 1989. 358 p. Includes index.

3429. Just Desserts: Recipes for Health and Well Being / Steve Parsons; illustrations by Alexis Hannah. Hantsport, N.S.: Lancelot Press, 1989. 61 p., illus.

3430. Light Desserts / Beatrice Ojakangas. Birmingham, Ala.: Oxmoor House, 1989. 256 p., 60 p. of colored photos. More than 350 recipes which have 200 or less calories. Includes index.

3431. Lite Sweet Delites: Delicious Treats Without Guilt / by Lee Mangione Cirillo; illustrated by Barbara L. Cirillo. Rochester, N.Y.: Specialty Cookbooks Publishers, c1989. 226 p., illus. "Recipes sweetened with sugar substitutes or fructose." Includes index.

3432. Manhattan's Dessert Scene: New York City's Top Dessert Spots Reveal Their Secret Recipes / by Rose Reisman. Chicago, Ill.: Lyman Publications; Distributed by Independent Publishers Group, 1989. 144 p., 12 p. of colored photos.

3433. Miniature Cakes, Pastries & Desserts / Pam Dotter. Godalming, Eng.: Peerage, 1989. 160 p.

Desserts *(Continued)*

3434. Virtuous Desserts / Lynn Bassler and Fran Raboff; illustrated by Lynn Bassler. Freedom, Calif.: Crossing Press, c1989. 216 p., illus. (some colored). Includes index. Contains recipes for low calorie desserts.

3435. Best Recipes for Sensational Desserts. 1st ed. New York: Prentice Hall, c1990. 112 p., illus. (some colored). (Betty Crocker's Red Spoon Collection). Includes index.

3436. The Book of Desserts / by Sally Taylor. Los Angeles, Calif.: HP Books, 1990. 120 p., more than 100 colored photos.

3437. Dessert Sensations: Grand Finales for Everyday Meals and Gala Occasions / Faye Levy; illustrations by Maureen Jensen; photographs by Gus Francisco. 1st ed. New York: Dutton, 1990. 406 p., 8 p. of plates, illus. (some colored). 225 recipes. (Fresh from France). Includes index.

3438. Desserts / Carole Handslip. London, Eng.: Hamlyn, 1990, c1980. 95 p., colored illus. (The Kitchen Library). Includes index.

3439. Fresh Fruit Desserts: Classic and Contemporary / Sheryl and Mel London. New York: Prentice Hall, 1990. 432 p., colored photos. 175 recipes. Includes index.

3440. Good Housekeeping Complete Book of Desserts / Janet Smith. London, Eng.: Ebury, 1990. 256 p.

3441. Granny's Sweet Things: With Recipes from the Collection of Ama Gae Wix Allgood / Pat Allgood. Lubbock, Tex.: Hinson Graphics, 1990. 1 v.

3442. The Great American Dessert Cookbook / Andrea Chesman and Fran Raboff. Freedom, Calif.: Crossing Press, 1990. ca. 176 p. Includes index.

Desserts *(Continued)*

3443. Great Italian Desserts / by Nick Malgieri; illustrated by Christine Buhr. Boston, Mass.: Little, Brown, 1990. 276 p., illus. More than 100 recipes. Includes bibliography and index.

3444. Just Naturally Sweet: Recipes Utilizing Honey, Molasses, Sorghum, and Maple Syrup, No Refined Sugar / Patricia B. Mitchell. Chatham, Va.: P.B. Mitchell, 1990. 37 p. (Patricia B. Mitchell Foodways Publications).

3445. Low Cholesterol Desserts! / Terri J. Siegel. Freedom, Calif.: Crossing Press, 1990. 183 p. (Specialty Cookbook Series). Includes index.

3446. Maida Heatter's Best Dessert Book Ever / drawings by Toni Evins. New York: Random House, 1990. ca. 448 p., illus. Includes index.

3447. Mrs. Beeton's Complete Book of Puddings & Desserts / consultant editor, Bridget Jones. London, Eng.: Ward Lock, 1990. 336 p.

3448. Naturally Sweet Desserts: The Sugarfree Dessert Cookbook / Marcea Weber. Garden City Park, N.Y.: Avery Pub. Group, 1990. 248 p., 16 p. of plates, illus. (some colored). More than 250 recipes.

3449. Spoon Desserts!: Custards, Cremes, & Elegant Fruit Desserts / by Lynn Nusom. Freedom, Calif.: Crossing Press, 1990. ca. 138 p. 100 recipes. (Specialty Cookbook Series). Includes index.

3450. Sweet Indulgences: Festive and Elegant Party Menus / Norman Kolpas. Los Angeles, Calif.: HP Books, 1990. 144 p., 100 colored photos. Contains menus and tips for dessert parties. Includes index.

3451. Sweet Success / Steven Wheeler. London, Eng.: Anaya, 1990. 192 p.

Desserts *(Continued)*

3452. The Wooden Spoon Dessert Book: The Best You Ever Ate / Marilyn Moore. 1st ed. New York: Harper & Row, c1990. 304 p., illus. 275 recipes. Contains many recipes from old cookbooks and favorite Midwestern specialties. Includes bibliography and index.

CHILDREN'S COOKBOOKS

3453. Desserts You Can Make Yourself: volume 1: A Children's Cookbook age 8 through 15. Tokyo, Japan: Ondorisha; New York: Distributed in the U.S. by Kodansha International through Harper & Row, c1983. 64 p., colored illus.

3454. Drinks and Desserts / S.J.A. de Villiers and Eunice van der Berg; illustrated by Marita Johnson. U.S. ed. Milwaukee, Wis.: G. Stevens, c1985. 31 p., colored illus. Includes index. "First published in It's Fun to Cook by Daan Retief Publishers."

3455. Dessert Recipes Children Love and Can Make / by Harlan B. Bebell. New York: Van Vliet Pub., 1989. 41 p., illus. Instructions for making cookies, cakes, pies, and other treats.

see also entries 1169, 1171, 1173, 1719, 2408, 3456; Appetizers and Desserts; Frozen Desserts; *specific kinds of desserts:* Cakes, Cookies, Ice Cream and Ices, Pastry, *etc.; and specific ingredients frequently used in Desserts, e.g.* Chocolate, Condensed Milk, Fruits, Honey, *etc. (Section I).*

Dim Sum

3456. Chinese Dessert and Pastry / Hsëh Hsiung-fei; edited by Xue Xiong Fei, Yan Mei. Hong Kong: Wan li shu tien, 1981, 1982 printing. 116 p., colored illus. In Chinese and English.

3457. Dim Sum and Chinese One-Dish Meals: A Contemporary Approach / Jean Yueh; illustrated by Donald Hendricks. New York: I. Chalmers Cookbooks, 1981. 84 p., illus.

Specialty Cookbooks

Dim Sum *(Continued)*

3458. Yum Cha: Dim Sums & Other Chinese Delights / Ella-Mei Wong; illustrated by Lorraine Hannay. London, Eng.: Angus & Robertson, c1981. 110 p., illus. Includes index.

3459. Dim Sum and Other Chinese Street Food / Mai Leung; drawings by Claude Martinot. 1st Harper colophon ed. New York: Harper & Row, 1982, c1979. 236 p., illus. (Harper Colophon Books). First published in 1979 under title: The Chinese People's Cookbook.

3460. The Dim Sum Book: Classic Recipes from the Chinese Teahouse / by Eileen Yin-fei Lo; drawings by Lauren Jarrett; calligraphy by San Yan Wong. 1st ed. New York: Crown Publishers, c1982. 180 p., illus. Includes index.

3461. Dim Sum, Fast and Festive Chinese Cooking / Ruth Law. Chicago, Ill.: Contemporary Books, c1982. 300 p., illus. Includes index.

3462. Chopsticks Recipes: Dim Sum / Ou-yang Jen-shih pien chu. Hong Kong: Chopsticks Publications, 1984, c1976. 128 p., colored illus. (Chopsticks Recipes / Cecilia J. Au-yeung; v. 2).

3463. Chinese Snacks / author, Huang Su-huei; translator, Lai Yen-jen; editors, Chen Chang-yen, Gloria C. Martinez. Taipei, Taiwan: The Author; Monterey Park, Calif.: Wei-Chuan's Cooking, c1985. 99 p., colored illus. (Wei-Chuan's Cookbook). In Chinese and English.

3464. Classic Deem Sum / Henry Chan, Yukiko and Bob Haydock. 1st ed. New York: Holt, Rinehart, and Winston, c1985. 120 p., illus. (some colored). 32 recipes. Includes index.

3465. Dimsum: Chinese Light Meals, Pastries and Delicacies / Margaret Leeming and May Huang Man-Hui. Topsfield, Mass.: Salem House, 1985. 160 p., illus. (some colored). Includes index.

Dim Sum *(Continued)*

3466. Tiny Delights: Cooking Dim Sum and Simple Chinese Dishes / Elizabeth Chong. Toronto, Ont.: Macmillan of Canada, 1987. 174 p., 16 p. of plates, colored illus. Includes index.

see also broader category: Appetizers

Dips

3467. Dips with a Difference / by Dorinda Bowers. Ripley, Ont.: c1984. 48 p., illus.

3468. Dip It!: 70 Quick and Easy Recipes for Simply Delicious Dips / Barry Bluestein and Kevin Morrissey. Chicago, Ill.: Contemporary Books, c1990. 106 p. 70 recipes. Includes index.

see also entry 3670; and broader category: Appetizers

Doughnuts

3469. The Donut Book: The Origins, History, Lore, Literature, Cuisine, Varieties ... / Sally Levitt Steinberg. 1st ed. New York: Knopf: Distributed by Random House, 1987. 225 p., illus. (some colored).

see also broader category: Cakes; Pastry

Drinks *see* Beverages

Empanadas *see* Turnovers

Entrées

3470. Delicious Main Course Dishes: 200 Recipes / Marian Tracy. New York: Dover Publications, 1978, c1964. 219 p. Reprint of the edition published by Scribner, New York under the title: 200 Main Course Dishes.

3471. Fast & Fancy: Main Dishes / Saddle River Day School Parents Guild Staff. Saddle River, N.J.: Saddle River Day School, 198-? 1 v.

3472. Helen Dollaghan's Best Main Dishes. New York: McGraw-Hill, c1980. 229 p. Includes index.

3473. Better Homes and Gardens Meatless Main Dishes / editors, Julia Martinusen, Marcia Stanley, Pat Teberg. 1st ed. Des Moines, Iowa: Meredith Corp., c1981. 96 p., colored illus. Includes index.

3474. Great Dinners with Less Meat / Dorothy Ivens; with illustrations by the author. Englewood Cliffs, N.J.: Prentice-Hall, c1981. 175 p., illus. Includes index.

3475. Variations on a Main Course: How to Create Your Own Original Dishes / Jean Conil and Hugh Williams. London, Eng.: New English Library, 1981. 144 p., illus. (New English Library Books for Cooks). Includes index.

3476. Farmhouse Feasts: Main Meal Recipes for Children / prepared by the National Dairy Council; illustrations by Gerry Greaves. Stevanhage, Eng.: Publications for Companies, 1982. 16 p., illus. (some colored).

3477. Meatless Main Dishes. New York: Golden Press, c1982. 64 p., colored illus. (A Betty Crocker Picture Cookbook; 2). "Selected from Betty Crocker's step-by-step recipe cards."

3478. Quick-to-Fix Mainstays. New York: Golden Press; Racine, Wis.: Western Pub. Co., c1982. 64 p., colored illus. (A Betty Crocker Picture Cookbook; 1).

Entrées *(Continued)*

3479. Festive Entrées. Los Angeles, Calif.: Knapp Press, c1983. 91 p., illus. (The Bon Appétit Kitchen Collection). Includes index.

3480. I Can't Cook Main Courses / Sonia Allison. London, Eng.: Hamilton, 1983. 64 p.

3481. All Color Book of Main Courses. New York: Arco Pub., 1984. 82 p., colored illus. Includes index.

3482. Famous Brands Main Dishes. St. Louis, Mo.: Brand Name Pub. Corp., 1985? 128 p., colored illus. (Famous Brands Cookbook Library). Includes index.

3483. Main Dishes for Every Occasion / Rosemary Wadey. Tucson, Ariz.: HP Books, c1985. 80 p., colored illus. 100 recipes. (Creative Cuisine). Contains recipes for meat, poultry, game, and fish.

3484. Recipes for Daily Living / Quezon City, Philippines: Nutrition Foundation of the Philippines, 1985. 74 p., illus.

3485. 300 and Under: Low-Calorie Entrées the Whole Family Will Enjoy / by Flo Niedermayer. Regina, Sask.: J.B. Pub., 1986. 142 p., colored illus. Includes index.

3486. Better Homes and Gardens Shortcut Main Dishes. 1st ed. Des Moines, Iowa: Better Homes and Gardens Books, c1986. 128 p., colored illus. Includes index.

3487. Signature Entrées: From 50 of America's Finest Restaurants / the Master Chefs Institute of America. New York (500 5th Ave., New York 10010): MCIA Pub., c1986. 100 p., colored illus. Includes index.

3488. Easy Entrées. Los Angeles, Calif.: Knapp Press, c1987. 118 p., 16 p. of plates, colored illus. 200 recipes. (Cooking with Bon Appétit). Includes index.

Specialty Cookbooks

Entrées *(Continued)*

3489. Microwaving One-Dish Dinners / Barbara Methven. 1st ed. New York: Prentice Hall Press, c1987. 159 p., colored illus. Originally published under title: Microwaving Fast & Easy Main Dishes. Includes index.

3490. Better Homes and Gardens Quick Main Dishes / editor, Rosemary C. Hutchinson. 1st ed. Des Moines, Iowa: Meredith Corp., c1989. 47 p., colored illus.

3491. Entrées, the Main Event / Eileen Dwillies and others. Vancouver, B.C.: Opus Productions, c1989. 160 p., colored illus. (The Easy Gorumet; v. 1). Includes index.

3492. Make It Light Main Dishes. Minneapolis, Minn.: General Mills, 1989. 92 p., colored illus. (Betty Crocker Creative Recipes; no. 33). Includes index.

see also entries 187, 2699; Casseroles; Stews

Fajitas

3493. The Official Fajita Cookbook / by Richard L. Miller. Houston, Tex.: Lone Star Books, 1990. 69 p., illus. Includes index. Reprint. Originally published: Austin, Tex.: Texas Monthly Press, c1988.

Flans

3494. Rose Elliot's Book of Savoury Flans and Pies. London, Eng.: Fontana Paperbacks, 1984. 64 p., illus. Includes index.

see also entries 3742, 3746-3748

Fondue

3495. Fondue: The Fine Art of Fondue, Chinese Wok, and Chafing Dish Cooking / editor, Carol D. Brent; photography by Bill Miller. New rev. ed. Chicago, Ill.: Tested Recipe Publishers; Garden City, N.Y.: Distribution by Doubleday, 1970. 64 p.

3496. Wok, Fondue & Chafing Dish Cookbook / the Culinary Arts Institute staff; Sherrill Weary, editor, Helen Lehman, assistant editor; illustrations by Laura Lee Lizak; photos. by Bob Scott Studios. New York: The Institute, c1980. 96 p., illus. (Adventures in Cooking Series). Includes index.

3497. Fondues from Around the World / Eva and Ulrich Klever. Woodbury, N.Y.: Barron's, 1984. 138 p., illus. "Nearly 200 recipes for fish, cheese and meat fondues, oriental hot pots, tempura, sukiyaki, dessert fondues." Includes index. Translation of: Das Grosse Buch der Fondues.

3498. The Book of Fondues / Lorna Rhodes; photography by Simon Butcher. Tucson, Ariz.: HP Books, 1988. 120 p., colored illus. Includes index.

3499. New International Fondue Cookbook / Ed Callahan. San Leandro, Calif.: Bristol Pub. Enterprises, 1990. 112 p., illus. "Cheese, meat, seafood, hot dips, baked fondues, desserts, Oriental mizutaki, poultry, tempura, rarebits."

Frostings see Icings for Cakes

Frozen Desserts

3500. All Frosty and Cool / illustrated by Aline Riquier; recipes by Isabelle Anargyros; adapted and translated by Julia Chalkley and Alexandra Campbell; lettering by Howard Walker. London, Eng.: Moonlight, 1981. 28 p., colored illus. Includes index. Translated from the French.

Specialty Cookbooks

Frozen Desserts *(Continued)*

3501. Ice Creams, Sorbets, Mousses & Parfaits: The Delicious Natural Way / by Jenny Allday; illustrated by Paul Turner. Wellingborough, Eng.: Thorsons, 1982. 128 p., illus. (A Thorsons Wholefood Cookbook). Includes index.

3502. Ice Creams & Cold Desserts / Mitzie Wilson. Twickenham, Eng.: Hamlyn, 1985. 63 p., colored illus. (Rainbow). Includes index.

3503. Ices Galore / Helge Rubinstein and Sheila Bush. Rev. and updated. Harmondsworth, Eng.: Penguin, 1986. 141 p., illus. (Penguin Handbooks). Includes index.

3504. Frozen Delights / Linda Burum. New York: Scribner, 1987. 225 p., illus. More than 300 recipes. Includes index.

3505. Iced Delights / Shona Crawford Poole. 1st ed. in U.S. Garden City, N.Y.: Doubleday, 1987, c1986. 80 p., colored illus. (The Conran Cookbooks). Includes index.

3506. Ice Cream & Frozen Desserts / Lonnie Gandara, writer; Elaine Ratner, editor; Victor Budnick, photographer. San Ramon, Calif.: Ortho Information Services, c1988. 127 p., colored illus. (California Culinary Academy Series). More than 40 recipes for syrups, toppings, and sauces. Includes index.

see also Ice Cream and Ices; *and broader category:* Desserts

Fudge

3507. Wild About Fudge / by Marilyn Myerly. New York: Barron's, c1989. 96 p., colored photos. Includes index.

3508. Oh Fudge!: A Celebration of America's Favorite Traditional Candy / by Lee Edwards Benning. 1st ed. New York: H. Holt, c1990. 289 p., illus. 297 recipes. Includes index.

see also broader categories: Candy; Chocolate Candy

Specific Dishes and Courses 447

Galantines

3509. Terrines, Patés, & Galantines / by the editors of Time-Life Books. Alexandria, Va.: Time-Life Books, c1982. 176 p., illus. (some colored). (The Good Cook, Techniques & Recipes). Includes index.

Garnishes

3510. Culinary Design and Decoration / William Emery; illustrations by Joyce Tuhill. Boston, Mass.: CBI, 1980. 135 p., illus.

3511. Japanese Garnishes: The Ancient Art of Mukimono / Yukiko and Bob Haydock; illustrations and photos. by Bob Haydock. 1st ed. New York: Holt, Rinehart, and Winston, c1980. 103 p., illus.

3512. Special Touches for Decorating Food / Laurette R. Rosenstrauch; with illustrations by Allys Palladino-Craig. Tallahassee, Fla.: Garland Press, c1981. 106 p., illus. Includes index.

3513. The Final Touch: Decorative Garnishes / Margo Kokko; illustrator, Buzz Gorder; photographer, Bruce Beauchamp. 2nd ed. Boston, Mass.: CBI Pub. Co., c1982. 160 p., illus. (some colored). Includes index.

3514. Elegant and Easy: Decorative Ideas for Food Presentations / Jean F. Nicolas. Boston, Mass.: CBI Pub. Co., c1983. 118 p., illus. (some colored).

3515. How to Garnish: Illustrated Step-by-Step Instructions / Harvey Rosen; Robert J. Rosen, editor. Elberon, N.J.: International Culinary Consultants, c1983. 96 p., illus. (some colored).

3516. More Japanese Garnishes / Yukiko and Bob Haydock. 1st ed. New York: Holt, Rinehart, and Winston, c1983. 118 p., illus. (some colored).

Garnishes *(Continued)*

3517. Mrs. Mayo's Book of Creative Foods: A Complete Guide to Fancy Food Decorating Anyone Can Do / written and illustrated by Esther Murphy. 1st ed. Denver, Colo.: Deco-Press Pub. Co., c1983. 175 p., illus. On spine: Book of Creative Foods.

3518. Garnishing: The Basics and Beyond / Constance Quan; designed and illustrated by S. Neil Fujita. Chicago, Ill.: Contemporary Books, c1984. 80 p., illus. (some colored). (Kitchen Masterpieces Series). "An Irena Chalmers Book."

3519. The Book of Garnishes / June Budgen; photography by Per Ericson. Tucson, Ariz.: HP Books, c1986. 128 p., colored illus. Includes index.

3520. Edible Art: Forty-Eight Garnishes for the Professional / David Paul Larousse. New York: CBI, c1987. 94 p., 8 p. of plates, illus. (some colored). Includes index.

3521. Garnishing / Francis Talyn Lynch. Tucson, Ariz.: HP Books, c1987. 143 p., illus. (mostly colored). Includes index.

3522. Garnishing and Decoration / Rudolf Biller. London, Eng.: Virtue, 1987. 159 p., colored illus. Includes index. Translation of: Garnieren und Verzieren.

3523. Food Garnishes and Decorations / Beryl Childs, Sue Alexander. London, Eng.: Hamlyn, 1989. 95 p.

3524. Garnishing: Step-by-Step Instructions in the Art of Preparing Gorgeous Food / Dr. Oetker; translated from the German by John M. Kleeberg and adapted for the American kitchen by Lois Hill. New York: Weathervane Books: Distributed by Crown Publishers, 1989. 1 v. Translation of: Garnieren, Verzieren, Dekorieren. [Publication of this book has not been verified].

Garnishes *(Continued)*

3525. Step by Step Garnishing / Wendy Veale. Seacaucus, N.J.: Chartwell Books, c1989. 112 p., colored illus. Includes index.

3526. Fun Foods: Clever Ideas for Garnishing & Decorating / by Wim Kros. New York: Sterling, c1990. 128 p., illus. (some colored). Translation of: Sierlijk Smullen.

see also entries 27, 1253, 2615, 3955

Gingerbread

3527. The Book of Gingerbread / Carla Capalbo. London, Eng.: Ebury, 1984. 47 p., illus. (some colored).

3528. Gingerbread Delights: A Collection of Holiday Cookie Recipes / calligraphy & illustrations by Elizabeth Walsh. Limited ed. Olympia, Wash. (2929 Hoffman Rd., Olympia 98501): E. Walsh, c1983. 99 p., illus. Includes bibliography and index.

3529. Making & Baking Gingerbread Houses / written and illustrated by Lauren Jarrett & Nancy Nagle. 1st ed. New York: Crown Publishers, c1984. 127 p., illus. 14 designs.

3530. Holiday Cookies & Centerpieces: Creative Ways with Gingerbread / editor in chief, Allen D. Bragdon. New York: A.D. Bragdon Publishers: Distributed by Kampmann, c1986. 167 p. Rev. ed. of: The Gingerbread Book. c1984.

3531. Gingerbread Tales / Allen D. Bragdon; edited by David Gamon [and others]. New York: A.D. Bragdon Publishers, 1986. 64 p., illus. (Munchie Books).

3532. Sweet Dreams of Gingerbread / Jann Johnson. New York: Sedgewood Press: Distributed by Macmillan, c1986. 144 p., illus. (some colored). Includes index.

Gingerbread *(Continued)*

3533. Gingerbread: Ninety-Nine Delicious Recipes from Sweet to Savory / Linda Merinoff. New York: Simon & Schuster, 1989. 191 p., illus. "A Fireside Book." Includes bibliography.

3534. Gingerbread Art / Vi and Ed Whittington. Fort Wayne, Ind.: Country Kitchen Retail Mailorder, 1990. 63 p., illus. Includes index.

see also broader categories: Cakes; Cookies

Herbal Teas

3535. Herbal Teas, Tisanes and Lotions / by Ceres; line illustrations by Juliet Remy and Alison Ross; colour photography by Paul Turner. Wellingborough, Eng.: Thorsons Publishers; New York: Distributed by Sterling Pub. Co., 1981. 128 p., illus. (some colored).

3536. The Complete Book of Herbal Teas / Marietta Marshall Marcin. 1st ed. New York: Congdon & Weed: Distributed by St. Martin's Press, c1983. 224 p., illus. "A Roundtable Press Book." Includes index.

3537. A Garden of Miracles: Herbal Drinks for Pleasure, Health, and Beauty / Jill Davies; with a foreword by Kitty Campion. 1st American ed. New York: Beaufort Books, c1985. 144 p., illus. Includes index.

3538. The Healing Power of Herbal Teas / by Ceres; line illustrations by Juliet Renny and Alison Ross; colour photography by Paul Turner. New York: Thorsons, c1985. 128 p., illus. (some colored). Includes index.

3539. Herbal Teas for Health and Healing / by Ceres; illustrated by Alison Ross. 1st U.S. ed. Rochester, Vt.: Healing Arts Press; New York: Distributed to the book trade in the U.S. by Harper and Row, c1988. 96 p., illus. Includes indexes.

Herbal Teas *(Continued)*

3540. Teas & Tisanes / Jill Norman, Gwen Edmonds. Bantam ed. Toronto, Ont.; New York: Bantam Books, c1989. 41 p., illus. (some colored). (The Bantam Library of Culinary Arts). Includes index. On cover: "Everyday & unusual teas & tisanes flavoured with them."

see also broader categories: Beverages; and Herbs *(Section I).*

Hors d'Oeuvres *see* Appetizers

Ice Cream and Ices

3541. Heavenly Home Made Ice Cream / by Sifto Salt; written and compiled by Anne Borella. Montreal, Que.: Comtar Chemicals Group, Sifto Salt Division,[between 1979-1982] 16 p., illus.

3542. The Baskin-Robbins Book of Ice Cream, Entertaining, and Fun / text by Mary Ann O'Roark. New York: Simon and Schuster, c1980. 222 p., illus.

3543. The Ice Cream Book / by Shona Crawford Poole and Jasper Partington. London, Eng.: Octopus Books, 1980. 92 p., illus. (some colored). Includes index.

3544. Ice Cream / by Mable & Gar Hoffman. Tucson, Ariz.: HP Books, c1981. 160 p., colored illus. Includes index.

3545. The Little Ice Cream Book / by W.S. Arbuckle. [n.p.]: W.S. Arbuckle, c1981. 141 p., illus.

3546. The Haagen-Dazs Book of Ice Cream / by Steven Sherman. 1st ed. New York: St Martin's Press, c1982. 108 p.

3547. Ice Cream & Ices / Nancy Arum; illustrated by Isadore Seltzer. 1st Harper & Row ed. New York: Harper & Row: I. Chalmers Cookbooks, c1983. 83 p., illus.

Ice Cream and Ices *(Continued)*

3548. The Little Ice Cream Cookbook / Mary L. Green. Denver, Colo.: Giftstar, 1984. ca. 10 p., illus. (Little Cookbooks).

3549. Making Ice Cream, Ices & Sherbets / by Phyllis Hobson. Pownal, Vt.: Garden Way Pub., 1984, c1977. 76 p., illus. Cover title: Garden Way Publishing's Making Ice Cream, Ices & Sherbets. Includes index. Reprint. Originally published: Making Your Own Ice Cream, Ices & Sherbets. Charlotte, Vt.: Garden Way Pub., c1977.

3550. Old-Fashioned Homemade Ice Cream: With 58 Original Recipes / Thomas R. Quinn. New York: Dover Publications, 1984. 31 p., illus.

3551. Victorian Ices & Ice Cream: 117 Delicious and Unusual Recipes Updated for the Modern Kitchen: Original Recipes from The Book of Ices by A.B. Marshall, London, 1885 / introduction and annotations by Barbara Ketcham Wheaton; foreword by A. Hyatt Mayor. New York: Metropolitan Museum of Art: Scribner, 1984, c1976. 44 p., 15 p. of plates, illus. Reprint. Originally published: The Book of Ices. London, Eng.: Marshall's School of Cookery, 1885. With new introd. and annotations.

3552. Ice Cream: Over 400 Variations, from Simple Scoops to Spectacular Desserts, from Fresh Fruit Sorbets to Parfaits and Bombés, with Meringues and Sauces Plus Low Calorie and Special Recipes / Hilary Walden. New York: Simon and Schuster, c1985. 159 p., colored illus. "A Fireside Book." Includes index.

3553. The Joy of Ice Cream / Matthew Klein. Woodbury, N.Y.: Barron's, c1985. 218 p., 32 p. of plates, colored illus. More than 100 recipes. Contains recipes for homemade ice cream, parfaits, ice cream drinks, and ice cream cakes. Includes index.

3554. Wild About Ice Cream / by Sue Spitler. Woodbury, N.Y.: Barron's, c1985. 101 p., colored illus. Includes index.

Ice Cream and Ices *(Continued)*

3555. Ice Cream / by Jill Neimark; illustrated by Karen Milone-Dugan. New York: Hastings House, c1986. 64 p., illus. (some colored). Includes index.

3556. Ben & Jerry's Homemade Ice Cream & Dessert Book / by Ben Cohen and Jerry Greenfield with Nancy J. Stevens; design & illustration by Lyn Severance. New York: Workman Pub., 1987. 125 p., colored illus. 90 recipes. Includes index.

3557. The Book of Ice Creams & Sorbets / Jackie Passmore. Tucson, Ariz.: HP Books, 1987. 128 p., colored photos. More than 90 recipes.

3558. Ice Cream / created for Donvier by Irena Chalmers & friends. New York: Penguin, 1987. 91 p., illus. Cover title: Donvier Ice Cream.

3559. Homemade Ice Cream Naturally / Mark Young & Lesley Howard Murdoch. London, Eng.: Bay Books, 1987. 96 p.

3560. The Donvier Ice Cream Dessert Book / by Anna Creery. Norfolk, Va.: Donning, c1988. 122 p., colored illus. Includes index.

3561. Sorbets! / by Jim Tarantino. Freedom, Calif.: Crossing Press, c1988. 176 p. More than 120 recipes. (Speciality Cookbook Series). Includes index.

CHILDREN'S COOKBOOKS

3562. I Love Ice Cream / by Carolyn Vosburg Hall and the food editors of Farm Journal; illustrations by the author. 1st ed. Garden City, N.Y.: Doubleday, 1976. 64 p., illus. (some colored). Facts about ice cream with recipes for a variety of flavors as well as for related yummies such as floats, sodas, sundaes, and sauces.

see also entry 3851; and broader category: Frozen Desserts

Icings for Cakes

3563. Woman's Realm Cake Icing / Christine France. London, Eng.: Hamlyn, c1982. 125 p., illus. (some colored). Includes index.

3564. Successful Icing / Nicola Astell-Burt. London, Eng.: Willow, 1985. 128 p., illus. Includes index.

3565. Royal Icing / Brenda Purton. London, Eng.: Merehurst, 1987. 127 p., illus. (some colored). Includes index.

3566. Icing the Cake: 66 Fast and Fabulous Frostings, Icings, Glazes, Toppings, and Fillings for Every Kind of Cake / Jill Van Cleave. Chicago, Ill.: Contemporary Books, 1990. 112 p. Contains recipes for six basic cakes. Includes index.

see also broader category: Cake decoration; Cakes

Jams and Jellies

3567. Jams and Jellies: 543 Recipes / May Byron. New York: Dover Publications, 1975. 276 p. Originally published in 1917 under title: May Byron's Jam Book.

3568. The Forgotten Art of Making Old-Fashioned Jellies, Jams, Preserves, Conserves, Marmalades, Butters, Honeys, and Leathers / prepared by the staff of Yankee, Inc.; illustrated by Margo Letourneau; designed by Carl F. Kirkpatrick; Clarissa M. Silitch, editor. 1st ed. Dublin, N.H.: Yankee, 1977. 64 p., illus. Recipes selected from those submitted to the Old Farmers Almanac and Yankee Magazine.

3569. Wild Preserves: Illustrated Recipes for Over 100 Natural Jams and Jellies / Joe Freitus. Boston, Mass.: Stone Wall Press, c1977. 192 p., illus.

3570. Home Made Jams, Jellies and Marmalades / Winifred Graham. Wakefield, Eng.: EP Pub., 1980. 121 p., illus.

Jams and Jellies *(Continued)*

3571. Ivy Hall's Book of Jams and Jellies. Flimwell, Eng. (6 High Street, Flimwell): Mervyn W. Passmore, 1980. 48 p., illus. Includes index.

3572. The Quest for Wild Jelly / by Kathryn G. March, Andrew L. March. Bailey, Colo.: Meridian Hill Publications, c1981. 60 p., illus.

3573. The Art of Preserving / by Jacqueline Wejman; essays by Charles St. Peter; drawings by Holly Zapp. San Francisco, Calif.: 101 Productions; New York: Distributed to the book trade in the U.S. by Scribner, c1983. 192 p., illus. Includes index. Enlarged edition of: Jams & Jellies. 1975.

3574. How to Make Jellies, Jams, and Preserves at Home. Baton Rouge, La.: Louisiana State University and Agricultural and Mechanical College, Cooperative Extension Service, 1983? 34 p., illus.

3575. Jams, Jellies & Relishes: From Amish and Mennonite Kitchens / collected and edited by Phyllis Pellman Good and Rachel Thomas Pellman. Lancaster, Pa.: Good Books, c1983. 32 p. (Pennsylvania Dutch Cookbooks).

3576. Traditional Gifts / collected by Vera Segal. London, Eng.: Cottage, 1983. 32 p., illus.

3577. Aunt Freddie's Pantry: Southern-Style Preserves, Jellies, Chutneys, Conserves, Pickles, Relishes, Sauces--and What Goes with Them / by Freddie Bailey, text with Mardee Haidin Regan; photographs by Brigitte Lacombe; foreword by Lee Bailey, a word from Liz Smith. 1st ed. New York: C.N. Potter: Distributed by Crown, c1984. 73 p., illus. Includes index. Previously published under title: Freddie Bailey's Favorite Southern Recipes.

Jams and Jellies *(Continued)*

3578. Jams and Preserves / Olive Odell; foreword by Theodora FitzGibbon. London, Eng.: Century, 1984. 1 v. (loose leaf). (The Recipe Store). Includes index.

3579. The WI Book of Jams and Other Preserves / Pat Hesketh. London, Eng.: Ebury, 1984. 96 p., illus. Includes index.

3580. How to Make Jellies, Jams, and Preserves at Home. Raleigh, N.C.: North Carolina State University at Raleigh, 1985? 34 p., illus.

3581. Jams, Jellies, Pickles & Chutneys / Mary Norwak. London, Eng.: Ward Lock, 1985. 80 p., illus. (some colored). Includes index.

3582. Fine Preserving: M.F.K. Fisher's Annotated Edition of Catherine Plagemann's Cookbook / illustrations by Earl Thollander. Berkeley, Calif.: Aris Books, 1986. 132 p., illus. Includes index.

3583. From Juice to Jelly / by Barbara Willenberg and Karla Hughes. Columbia, Mo.: University of Missouri, Columbia, Extension Division, 1985? 7 p., illus.

3584. The Illustrated Book of Preserves / Simonetta Lupi, Angelo Sorzio. Garden City, N.Y.: Doubleday, 1986. 205 p., colored illus. Translation of: Le Nostre Conserve. Includes index.

3585. Robert's Famous Jams & Jellies: Okanagan Valley / by Barbara McClure Robert. Summerland, B.C.: Barrob Pub., 1986. 98 p.

3586. Harrods Book of Jams, Jellies & Chutneys / by Rosamond Richardson. New York: Arbor House, 1987, c1986. 96 p., colored illus. Includes index.

Jams and Jellies *(Continued)*

3587. Jams & Preserves: Delicious Recipes for Jams, Jellies, and Sweet Preserves / Jill Norman. Bantam ed. New York: Bantam Books, 1990. 48 p., colored illus. Includes index. (The Bantam Library of Culinary Arts). "Dorling Kindersley edition published in Great Britain in 1989."

see also entry 3680; Condiments *(Section I);* Fruits *(Section I);* Marmalade; *and* Canning and Preserving *(Section IV)*

Jellies *see* Jams and Jellies

Main Dishes *see* Entrées

Marinades

3588. Marinade Magic: Cooking with Homemade Marinades / Dona Meilach. Chicago, Ill.: Contemporary Books, c1981. 163 p., illus. Includes index.

3589. The Book of Dressings & Marinades / Janice Murfitt. Los Angeles, Calif.: HP Books, 1989. 120 p., colored photos. 100 recipes, each accompanied by step-by-step colored photos.

see also entry 3864

Marmalade

3590. The Book of Marmalade: Its Antecedents, Its History, and Its Role in the World Today, Together with a Collection of Recipes for Marmalades & Marmalade Cookery / C. Anne Wilson. 1st U.S. ed. New York: St. Martin's/Marek, c1985. 184 p., illus. Includes bibliography and index.

see also broader category: Jams and Jellies

Marzipan

3591. The Complete Book of Marzipan. London, Eng.: Elsevier Applied Science, 1984. 167 p.

3592. Marzipan / Pat Ashby. London, Eng.: Merehurst, 1986. 127 p. (The Art of Sugarcraft).

see also broader category: Candy

Meringue

3593. The Meringue Cookbook / Margaret N. Shakespeare. New York; London, Eng.: Van Nostrand Reinhold, c1982. 240 p., illus. More than 200 recipes for desserts, cakes, tortes, pies, tarts, cookies, custards, and dishes made of meringue. Includes index.

see also broader categories: Confectionery; Desserts

Molded Foods

3594. Soufflés, Mousses, Jellies & Creams / Robert Ackart; drawings by Marjorie Zaum. 1st ed. New York: Atheneum, 1980. 210 p., illus. Includes index.

3595. Edible Architecture / by Margot Coatts; drawings by Ian Beck. Marlborough, Eng.: Libanus Press, 1987. 38 p., colored illus. "This edition is limited to three hundred copies."

see also Gelatin *(Section I);* Mousses

Mousses

3596. The Ultimate Mousse Cookbook / Jack Stone and Janet Cassidy. Chicago, Ill.: Contemporary Books, 1990. 8 leaves. 12 recipes.

see also entries 364, 3501, 3920; and broader categories: Desserts; Molded Foods

Muffins

3597. Everybody's Favorite Orthomolecular Muffin Book / by Rose Hoffer and Muriel Warrington; drawings by Lawrie Kaplan; with an introduction by Abram Hoffer. New Canaan, Conn.: Keats Pub., c1980. 120 p. (A Keats Original Health Book).

3598. 101 Marvelous Muffins / by Adele Marks; text lettered by Martin Marks; ilustrated by Klaus Schoenfeld. Willowdale, Ont.: Gadget Pub., 1982. 129 p., illus. Includes index.

3599. Muffins: A Cookbook / by Joan Bidinosti and Marilyn Wearring. London, Ont.: Joan & Marilyn, 1982. 48 p., illus.

3600. The Complete Muffin and Quick Bread Encyclopedia: 291 Quick Bread and Muffin Recipes with Fruit, Nuts, and Vegetables / by Carol James Thrower. Wooster, Ohio?: C.J. Thrower, c1983. 110 p. Includes index.

3601. The Muffin Baker's Guide / by Bruce Koffler. Scarborough, Ont.: Firefly Books, 1983. 135 p., illus.

3602. Muffins / from Annie. White Rock, B.C.: A.L. Wolverton, 1983. 135 p., illus.

3603. The Marvelous Muffin / by Colleen M. Zickert-Poulos; illustrations by Gina Blickenstaff. [n.p.]: Marvelous Muffin, c1984. 101 p., illus.

Muffins *(Continued)*

3604. Mostly Muffins / Barbara Albright and Leslie Weiner; illustrations by Leslie Nelson. 1st ed. New York: St. Martin's Press, c1984. 104 p., illus. More than 75 recipes for muffins and spreads. Includes index.

3605. Muffin Madness / compiled, edited and tested by Jean Kelley and Arlene Kelley-McGregor. Winnipeg, Man.: Gateway Pub. Co., 1984. 76 p.

3606. Muffins, Nut Breads and More / by Barbara Kanerva Kyte, Katherine Hayes Greenberg. Benicia, Calif.: Nitty Gritty Productions, c1985. 185 p., illus. Includes index.

3607. Muffins: Sixty Sweet and Savory Recipes from Old Favorites to New / by Elizabeth Alston; illustrations by Sally Sturman. 1st ed. New York: C.N. Potter: Distributed by Crown Publishers, c1985. 90 p., illus. Includes index. Reprinted in 1990.

3608. Wild About Muffins / by Angela Clubb; color photographs by Karen Leeds. 1st U.S. ed. Woodbury, N.Y.: Barron's, 1985, c1982. 95 p. Previously published as: Mad About Muffins. Includes index.

3609. Muffins & Cupcakes / by Lawrence Rosenberg. Silver Spring, Md.: American Cooking Guild, c1986. 64 p. (The Collector's Series; v. 18).

3610. Delicious Quick Breads and Muffins / Dimetra Makris. 1st ed. New York: Fawcett Columbine, 1987, c1986. 140 p. Includes index.

3611. Smart Muffins: 83 Recipes for Heavenly, Healthful Eating / Jane Kinderlehrer; illustrations by Claude Martinot. 1st ed. New York: Newmarket Press, c1987. 170 p., illus. Includes index.

3612. Muffin Memories / Ellen Dohan. Woodbury, Conn.: Muffin Memories, 1988. 188 p. More than 180 recipes.

Muffins *(Continued)*

3613. The Joy of Muffins: The International Muffin Cook Book / by Genevieve Farrow and Diane Dreher. Phoenix, Ariz.: Golden West Publishers, c1989. 120 p., illus. 150 recipes. Includes index.

3614. The Muffins are Coming / by Theresa Nell Millang. Minneapolis, Minn.: Waldman House Press, c1989. 20 leaves.

3615. The Muffin Cookbook: Muffins for All Occasions. Lincolnwood, Ill.: Publications International, 1990. 96 p., colored illus. More than 100 recipes. Includes index.

3616. Muffins and Quick Breads with Schmecks Appeal / Edna Staebler. Montreal, Que.: McGraw-Hill Ryerson, c1990. 88 p., illus. (Schmecks Appeal Cookbook Series).

see also entry 2717; broader category: Bread; *and* Baking *(Section IV)*

Omelets

3617. The 40-Second Omelet Guaranteed: The Gourmet Way to Breakfast, Brunch, Lunch, Dinner, and Dessert / Howard Helmer with Joan O'Sullivan. 1st ed. New York: Atheneum, 1982. 135 p., illus. Includes index.

3618. Omelettes & Soufflés / Anne Byrd; illustrated by Dana Burns. 1st Harper & Row ed. New York: Harper & Row: I. Chalmers Cookbooks, c1982. 82 p., illus.

3619. The Omelette Book / Narcissa G. Chamberlain. Boston, Mass.: D.R. Godine, Publisher, 1990, c1955. 175 p., illus. More than 300 recipes. Reprint. Originally published: New York: Knopf, 1956, c1955.

see also entries 3239, 3247; and Eggs *(Section I)*

462   Specialty Cookbooks

One-Dish Meals *see* **Casseroles**

Pancakes *see* **Crepes and Pancakes**

Pastry

3620. The Viennese Pastry Cookbook, from Vienna with Love / Lilly Joss Reich. New York: Macmillan, 1970. 335 p., illus. More than 200 recipes. Reprinted.

3621. Patisserie: Professional Pastry and Dessert Preparation / L.J. Hanneman. New York: Van Nostrand Reinhold, 1977, c1971. 349 p., illus. Includes index.

3622. Chinese Refreshment Illustrated: Chinese-English / Hsëh Hsiung-fei; edited by Xue Xiong Fei, Yan Mei. Hong Kong: Wan li shu tien, 1981. 118 p., colored illus.

3623. The Complete Book of Pastry, Sweet and Savory / Bernard Clayton, Jr.; illustrations by Tom Stoerrle. New York: Simon & Schuster, c1981. 411 p., illus. Includes index.

3624. Pies & Pastries / by the editors of Time-Life Books. Alexandria, Va.: Time-Life Books; Morristown, N.J.: School and library distribution by Silver Burdett Co., c1981. 176 p., illus. Includes index.

3625. Good Housekeeping Perfect Pastry / Good Housekeeping Institute. London, Eng.: Ebury, c1982. 160 p., illus. (some colored). Includes index.

3626. Pies & Pastries: Appetizers, Main Dishes & Desserts / Janet Pittman. Tucson, Ariz.: HP Books, c1982. 192 p., colored illus. Includes index.

3627. Under the Crust / by Sifto Salt; written and compiled by Anne Borella. Montreal, Que.: Domtar Chemicals, Sifto Salt Division, 1982? 16 p.

Specific Dishes and Courses

Pastry *(Continued)*

3628. Caribbean Pastry Delights / by Edward Beharry. Mount Lambert, Trinidad, W.I.: RLL Enterprises, c1983. 98 p., illus. Includes index.

3629. The Complete Pastry Cook / Carol Bowen. London, Eng.: Century, 1983. 206 p., illus. Includes index.

3630. The Modern Pâtissier: A Complete Guide to Pastry Cookery / William Barker. 2nd ed. London, Eng.: Hutchinson, 1983, c1978. 285 p., illus. (some colored). Includes index. Originally published: London, Eng.: Northwood, 1978.

3631. The Pastry Chef / William J. Sultan. Westport, Conn.: AVI Pub. Co., c1983. 674 p., illus. Includes index.

3632. The Pie and Pastry Cookbook / Cecilia Norman. London, Eng.: Granada, 1983. 274 p., illus. Includes index.

3633. 101 Delicious Danish / Adele Marks. Weston, Ont.: Gadget Pub., 1984. ca. 130 p., illus.

3634. 101 Tempting Tarts / by Adele Marks; illustrated by Anthony Van Bruggen; text by Martin Marks. Downsview, Ont.: Gadget Pub., 1984. 129 p., illus. Includes index.

3635. Basic Pastrywork Techniques / L.G. Nicolello. London, Eng.: Edward Arnold, 1984. 212 p., illus. Includes bibliography and index.

3636. The Little Pastry Cookbook / Mary L. Green. Denver, Colo.: Giftstar, 1984. ca. 10 p., illus. (Little Cookbooks).

3637. Mastering the Art of French Pastry: An Illustrated Course / by Bruce Healy & Paul Bugat; with drawings by Paul Bugat, photographs by Pierre Ginet. Woodbury, N.Y.: Barron, c1984. 450 p., 32 p. of plates, illus. (some colored). Includes indexes.

Pastry *(Continued)*

3638. The Pies and Pastries Cookbook: Favorite Recipes of Home Economics Teachers. Nashville, Tenn.: Favorite Recipes Press, c1984. 128 p., illus. Includes index.

3639. The Southern Heritage Pies and Pastry Cookbook. Birmingham, Ala.: Oxmoor House, c1984. 143 p., illus. (some colored). (The Southern Heritage Cookbook Library). Includes index.

3640. The WI Book of Pastry / Janet Wier; edited by Sue Jacquemier and Rosemary Wadey. London, Eng.: Women's Institute, 1984. 96 p., illus. Includes index. Also published: London, Eng.: Ebury, 1984.

3641. French Tarts / compiled by Jo Gosling. London, Eng.: Octopus, 1985. 95 p., colored illus. Includes index.

3642. Fresh Tarts / Susan Mendelson & Deborah Roitberg. Vancouver, B.C.: Douglas & McIntyre, 1985. 112 p., 8 p. of plates, colored illus. Includes index.

3643. Italian Pastry Book / by Alfredo Croce; editor, Nancy Wagner. Saratoga, Calif.: A.P.C. Enterprize, 1985. 51 p.

3644. The Joy of Pastry / David Munn. Woodbury, N.Y.: Barron's, c1985. 227 p., illus. Includes index.

3645. The Pastry Book / Rosemary Wadey. Harmondsworth, Eng.: Penguin, 1985, c1982. 209 p., illus. Includes index. Originally published: Newton Abbot, Eng.: David & Charles, 1982.

3646. Pastrywork and Confectionery Handbook / Douglas Sutherland. London, Eng.: Batsford Academic and Educational, 1985. 160 p., illus. (Catering). Includes index.

3647. Sunset Pies & Pastries: Step-by-Step Techniques / by the editors of Sunset Books and Sunset Magazine. Menlo Park, Calif.: Lane Pub. Co., c1985. 96 p., illus. (some colored).

Pastry *(Continued)*

3648. The New Pastry Cook: Modern Methods for Making Your Own Classic and Contemporary Pastries / Helen S. Fletcher; color photography by T. Mike Fletcher. 1st ed. New York: W. Morrow, c1986. 352 p., illus. (some colored). 100 recipes for cakes, cookies, and pastries with many variations. Includes index.

3649. Pastry Without Tears / Donna Thacker; illustrated by David Shaw. 1st ed. Ottawa, Ont.: D.A. Cameron, c1986. 77 p., illus.

3650. The Roux Brothers on Patisserie / Michel & Albert Roux; photographs by Anthony Blake. New York: Prentice Hall Press, 1986. 256 p., illus. Includes index.

3651. The National Trust Book of Tuck Box Treats / Geraldene Holt. Newton Abbot, Eng.: David & Charles, c1987. 95 p., illus. Includes index.

3652. Fresh Ways with Pastries & Sweets / by the editors of Time-Life Books. Alexandria, Va.: Time-Life Books, 1988. 144 p., illus. (Healthy Home Cooking). Includes index.

3653. La Nouvelle Patisserie: The Art & Science of Making Beautiful Pastries & Desserts / Jean-Yves Duperret and Jacqueline Mallorca. New York: Viking, 1988. 256 p., illus. (some colored). Includes index.

3654. Patisserie of Italy / Jeni Wright. New York: McGraw-Hill, c1988. 128 p., colored illus. Includes index.

3655. Patisserie of Vienna / Josephine Bacon. New York: McGraw-Hill, 1988. 128 p. "A MacDonald Orbis Book."

Pastry *(Continued)*

3656. The Professional French Pastry Series / Roland Bilheux and Alain Escoffier; under the direction of Pierre Michalet; translated by Rhona Poritzky-Lauvand and James Peterson. Paris, France: CICEM (Compagnie internationale de consultation education et media); New York: Van Nostrand Reinhold, c1988. 4 v., colored illus. Translation of: Traité de pâtisserie artisanale. Includes index. v. 1. Doughs, batters, and meringues. v. 2. Creams, confections, and finished desserts. v. 3. Petits fours, chocolate, frozen desserts, and sugar work. v. 4. Decorations, borders and letters, marzipan, and modern desserts.

3657. Nick Malgieri's Perfect Pastry. New York: Macmillan; London, Eng.: Collier Macmillan, c1989. 338 p., 150 photos. ca. 200 recipes. Includes bibliography and index.

3658. Patisserie of France / Hilary Walden. New York: McGraw-Hill, 1989, c1988. 128 p., colored illus. Includes index.

3659. Patisserie of Scandinavia / J. Audrey Ellison. London, Eng.: Macdonald Orbis, 1989. 128 p., colored illus. Includes index.

3660. Patisserie of the Eastern Mediterranean / Arto der Haroutunian. New York: McGraw-Hill, 1989. 128 p., colored photos. Includes index.

3661. Sweet Temptation / Wendy Majerowicz & Patricia Bourne. London, Eng.: Treasure, 1989. 80 p.

3662. In Praise of Cake & Pastry Flour. Willowdale, Ont.: Robin Hood Multifoods, 1990? 14 p., colored illus.

3663. The Professional Pastry Chef / Bo Friberg; charts, cake decorating designs, chocolate figurines, marzipan designs, and templates designed and drawn by Bo Friberg; all other illustrations by Joyce Hasselbeck; photography by Bo Friberg. 2nd ed. New York: Van Nostrand Reinhold, c1990. 626 p., illus. (some colored).

Pastry *(Continued)*

see also entries *2728, 2740, 2996;* Desserts; Dim Sum; Pies; Quiches; and Baking *(Section IV)*

Pâtés

3664. Pâtés and Terrines with Magimix / recipes written by Brian and Vanessa Binns for food processors. Sunbury, Eng.: ICTC, 1982. 33 p.

3665. The Cuisinart Food Processor Pâté Cookbook / Carmel Berman Reingold. New York: Perigee Books, c1983. 224 p. "A GD/Perigee Book." Includes index.

3666. Pâté: The New Main Course for the '80s: A Menu Cookbook / Carol Cutler; illustrations by Joan McGurren. 1st ed. New York: Rawson, 1983. 242 p., illus. Includes index.

3667. The Little Brown Pâté Book / Jo Marcangelo. Wellingborough, Eng.: Thorsons, 1984. 56 p.

3668. Pâtés & Terrines / Friedrich W. Ehlert and others. 1st U.S. ed. New York: Hearst Books, 1984. 192 p., colored illus. Several hundred recipes. Includes index. Translation of: Das Grosse Buch der Pasteten.

3669. The Perfect Pâté / Bernice Hurst; illustrations by Ronald Hurst. Twickenham, Eng.: Hamlyn, 1985. 32 p., illus.

3670. Vegetarian Pâtés & Dips: For Parties, First Courses, Quick Lunches or Late Night Snacks / by Janet Hunt. Wellingborough, Eng.: Thorsons, 1986. 112 p., illus. (A Thorsons Wholefood Cookbook). Includes index.

3671. Fresh Ways with Terrines & Pâtés / by the editors of Time-Life Books. Alexandria, Va.: Time-Life Books, c1989. 144 p., colored illus. (Healthy Home Cooking). Includes index.

see also entries *1763, 1774, 3509, 3744, 4409*

Specialty Cookbooks

Patisserie see Pastry

Pestos

3672. Pestos!: Cooking with Herb Pastes / by Dorothy Rankin. Trumansburg, N.Y.: Crossing Press, c1985. 140 p., illus. 29 recipes for pesto and 60 for using them in appetizers, breads, entrées, marinades, salad dressings, sauces, and soups. Includes index.

3673. Pesto Manifesto / Lorel Nazzaro. 1st ed. Chicago, Ill.: Chicago Review Press, c1988. 110 p. Includes index.

see also Herbs *(Section I); and broader category:* Sauces

Pickles and Relishes

3674. The Willow Farm Pickle Book / John McKinney. Santa Fe, N.M.: Lightening Tree, 1973. 80 p. (A Lightening Tree Cook Book).

3675. Homemade Pickles & Relishes / by Betsy McCracken, with the food editors of Farm Journal. Philadelphia, Pa.: Countryside Press; New York: Distributed by Two Continents Pub. Group, c1976. 128 p. Includes index.

3676. All About Pickling / James K. McNair. Edinburgh, Scot.: Bartholomew, 1980. 96 p. Originally published: San Francisco, Calif.: Ortho Books, 1975.

3677. Making Pickles and Relishes at Home. Baton Rouge, La.: Louisiana State University and Agricultural and Mechanical College, Cooperative Extension Service, 1983? 33 p., illus.

3678. Pickles and Chutneys: (Confined to Guntar and Krishna Districts of Andhra Pradesh, India) / C.R. Chevendra and Varalakshmi Chevendra. London, Ont.: C.R. Chevendra, c1983. 102 leaves.

Pickles and Relishes *(Continued)*

3679. Pickles and Relishes: 150 Recipes, from Apples to Zucchinis / by Andrea Chesman. Charlotte, Vt.: Garden Way Pub., c1983. 150 p., illus. Includes index.

3680. Summer in a Jar: Making Pickles, Jams & More / Andrea Chesman; illustrated by Loretta Trezzo. Charlotte, Vt.: Williamson Pub., c1985. 160 p., illus. 120 recipes. Includes index.

3681. A Pickle and Chutney Cookbook / Digby Law. London, Eng.: Hodder and Stoughton, 1986. 232 p. Includes index.

3682. Blue-Ribbon Pickles & Preserves / edited by Maria Polushkin Robbins. 1st ed. New York: St. Martin's Press, c1987. 116 p., illus. Includes index.

3683. Pickles & Chutneys. Tunbridge Wells, Eng.: Search Press, 1987. 32 p.

3684. The Perfect Pickle Book / David Mabey and David Collison. London, Eng.: BBC, 1988. 160 p.

see also entries 3575, 3577, 3581, 3719, 4433; Condiments *(Section I);* Canning and Preserving *(Section IV)*

Pies

3685. Pies Aplenty / Annette Gohlke. Milwaukee, Wis.: Reiman Associates, 1975. 64 p.

3686. The Book of Pies / Elisabeth Orsini. London, Eng.: Pan, 1981. 191 p., illus. (Pan Original). Includes bibliography and index.

3687. Farm Journal's Best-Ever Pies / by Patricia A. Ward. Philadelphia, Pa.: Farm Journal; Garden City, N.Y.: Distributed to the trade by Doubleday, c1981. 278 p., 8 p. of plates, colored illus. Includes index.

Pies *(Continued)*

3688. The Perfect Pie. Skokie, Ill.: Consumer Guide, c1981. 32 p., colored illus. (Perfect Cookbooks).

3689. Pies from Amish and Mennonite Kitchens / collected and edited by Phyllis Pellman Good and Rachel Thomas Pellman. Lancaster, Pa.: Good Books, c1982. 31 p. (Pennsylvania Dutch Cookbooks).

3690. Farm Journal's Homemade Pies, Cookies & Bread / by the food editors of Farm Journal. New York: Greenwich House: Distributed by Crown Publishers, 1983. 794 p., illus. Includes index. Originally published in three volumes as: Complete Pie Cookbook, Homemade Cookies, and Homemade Bread.

3691. The Pie's the Limit: Savoury Pies for All Occasions / Judy Wells and Rick Johnson. Harmondsworth, Eng.; New York: Penguin Books, 1983. 158 p., 8 p. of plates, illus. (some colored). (Cooking & Dining). Includes index.

3692. American Pie / by Teresa Kennedy; illustrations by Elizabeth Koda-Callan. New York: Workman Pub., c1984. 94 p., illus. 45 recipes for fillings. Includes index.

3693. The Great American Pie Book / by Judith Choate; illustrated by Bob Johnson. 1st ed. Dublin, N.H.: Yankee Books, c1984. 144 p., illus. "A Yankee Magazine Publication." Includes index.

3694. The Little Pie Cookbook / Mary L. Green. Denver, Colo.: Giftstar, 1984. ca. 10 p., illus. (Little Cookbooks).

3695. The Perfect Pie Book / Anne Marshall. Ware, Eng.: Omega, 1984, c1979. 112 p., illus. (some colored). Includes index. Originally published: Sydney, Australia: Summit, 1979 under the title: Anne's Perfect Piebook.

3696. The Complete Book of Pies / Maria Luisa Scott and Jack Denton Scott. New York: Bantam Books, c1985. 191 p. Includes index.

Pies *(Continued)*

3697. Keebler Ready-Crust Recipe Book. Elmhurst, Ill.: Keebler Co., 1985. 1 v. 100 recipes.

3698. Martha Stewart's Pies & Tarts / photographs by Beth Galton; designed by Henrietta Condak. 1st ed. New York: C.N. Potter: Distributed by Crown Publishers, c1985. 216 p., colored illus. More than 100 recipes. Includes index.

3699. Pamella Z. Asquith's Sweet & Savory Pies / by Pamella Z. Asquith. 1st ed. New York: Harmony Books, c1985. 141 p., illus. 130 recipes. Includes index.

3700. The Perfect Pie / Bernice Hurst; illustrations by Ronald Hurst. Twickenham, Eng.: Hamlyn, 1985. 31 p., illus.

3701. Perfect Pies: A Complete Savory & Sweet Fare of Unique Wholesome Pies / Diane Fine. 1st ed. New York: Quill, c1985. 206 p., illus. More than 100 recipes. Includes index.

3702. Pies and Tarts. Los Angeles, Calif.: Knapp Press, c1986. 118 p., 16 p. of plates, colored illus. (Cooking with Bon Appétit). Includes index.

3703. Traditional Pies and Pasties / collected by Vera Segal. London, Eng.: Cottage Press, 1986. 32 p., illus. Includes index.

3704. Blue-Ribbon Pies / edited by Maria Polushkin Robbins. 1st ed. New York: St. Martin's Press, c1987. 131 p., illus. Includes index.

3705. The National Trust Book of Pies / Sara Paston-Williams. Newton Abbot, Eng.: David & Charles, 1987. 128 p., illus. Includes index.

3706. Country Pies: A Seasonal Sampler / Lisa Yockelson; illustrations by Wendy Wheeler. 1st ed. New York: Harper & Row, c1988. 143 p., illus. Includes index.

Pies *(Continued)*

3707. James McNair's Pie Cookbook / photography by Patricia Brabant. San Francisco, Calif.: Chronicle Books, c1989. 96 p., colored photos. More than 35 recipes. Includes index.

3708. 4 & 20 Blackbirds, Cooking in Crust / Nancy Fair McIntyre; illustrations by Maxwell Moray. Portland, Or.: Cobble & Mickle Books, 1990. 93 p., illus. Includes index.

3709. As Easy as Pie / Susan G. Purdy; drawings by Sidonie Coryn; diagrams by the author. 1st Collier Books ed. New York: Collier Books, 1990, c1984. 426 p., illus. More than 300 recipes. Includes index. Reprint. Originally published: From Basic Apple to Four and Twenty Blackbirds It's as Easy as Pie. 1st ed. New York: Atheneum, 1984.

3710. Borden Great American Pies. Lincolnwood, Ill.: Publications International, 1990. 96 p., colored photos. More than 100 recipes. Includes index.

3711. Pies and Tarts with Schmecks Appeal / Edna Staebler. Montreal, Que.: McGraw-Hill Ryerson; Toronto, Ont.: McClelland & Stewart, 1990. 92 p., illus. (Schmecks Appeal Cookbook Series). Includes index.

see also entries 754, 890, 2991, 2996, 3494; Quiches; *and broader category:* Pastry

Pita Bread

3712. Pocket Bread Potpourri: Meals in Minutes / by Madelain Farah and Leila Habib. Memphis, Tenn.: Wimmer Brothers Books, c1984. 108 p., illus. Includes index.

3713. Pita Breads and Pocket Fillings / Darcy Williamson and John Allgair. Bend, Or.: Maverick, 1986, c1981. 134 p.

Specific Dishes and Courses 473

Pita Bread *(Continued)*

3714. Pita the Great / by Virginia T. Habeeb; illustrations by Emanuel Schongut. New York: Workman Pub., c1986. 176 p., illus. 100 recipes for all varieties of pita and dips, fillings, and toppings. Includes index.

3715. Vegetarian Pitta Bread Recipes: Delicious Wholefood Meals-in-a-pocket. / Leah Leneman; illustrated by Juliet Breese. Wellingborough, Eng.: Thorsons, 1987. 111 p., illus. Includes index.

see also broader category: Bread

Pizza

3716. The Complete Book of Pizza / Louise Love. Evanston, Ill.: Sassafras Press, 1980. 100 p.

3717. Pizzas and Pancakes / by Janet Hunt; illustrated by Clive Burch. Wellingborough, Eng.: Thorsons, 1982. 128 p., illus. Includes index.

3718. The Great Chicago-Style Pizza Cookbook / by Pasquale Bruno, Jr. Chicago, Ill.: Contemporary Books, c1983. 130 p., illus. Includes index.

3719. Pizzas, Hamburgers & Relishes / Martha Lomask. Loughton, Eng.: Piatkus, 1983. 96 p., illus.

3720. Zesty Pizza / Beverly Bennett & Kim Upton. Woodbury, N.Y.: Barron's, 1983. 1 v., colored photos. 32 recipes. (Easy Cooking Series).

3721. The Joy of Pizza / Pamella Z. Asquith; illustrations by Michael Starkman. 1st ed. New York: Random House, c1984. 165 p., illus. Includes index.

Pizza *(Continued)*

3722. Pizza / by Vincenzo Buonassisi. 1st American ed. Boston, Mass.: Little, Brown, c1984. 183 p., illus. (some colored). Includes index. Translated from the Italian.

3723. The Pizza Book: Everything There Is to Know About the World's Greatest Pie / written and illustrated by Evelyne Slomon. New York: Times Books, c1984. 276 p., illus. Includes index and bibliography.

3724. Pizza Cookery / Ceil Dyer. New York: McGraw-Hill, c1984. 202 p. Includes index.

3725. Pizza Pizzaz (Basic to Gourmet) / Richard Erickson. Silver Spring, Md.: American Cooking Guild, 1985. 64 p., illus. (Collector's Series).

3726. Italian Pizza and Hearth Breads / written and illustrated by Elizabeth Romer. 1st American ed. New York: C. N. Potter: Distributed by Crown Publishers, c1987. 157 p., illus. (some colored.) 90 recipes for pizza, calzone, and other breads. Contains information on cheese and herbs. Includes index and bibliography.

3727. Pizza / James McNair; photography by Patricia Brabant. San Francisco, Calif.: Chronicle Books, c1987. 96 p., colored illus.

3728. All the Best Pizzas / by Joie Warner. Scarborough, Ont.: Prentice-Hall Canada, 1988. 96 p., illus. 50 recipes.

3729. The Book of Pizzas & Italian Breads / Sarah Bush. Los Angeles, Calif.: HP Books, c1988. 120 p., colored photos. More than 100 recipes. Includes index.

3730. The Pizza Gourmet / Robert Arlett; featuring recipes by Carl Oshinsky. 1st ed. New York: Carroll & Graf; Distributed by Publishers Group West, 1988. 103 p., colored illus. Includes index. Prepared in conjunction with the 13 part PBS television series of the same title.

Pizza *(Continued)*

3731. Pizza California Style: More Than 80 Fast & Easy Recipes for Delicious Gourmet Pizza / Norman Kolpas. Chicago, Ill.: Contemporary Books, c1989. 133 p., colored illus. Includes index.

see also Pasta and Pizza; *and broader category:* Bread

Preserves

see Condiments *(Section I)*; Jams and Jellies; Pickles and Relishes; and Canning and Preserving *(Section IV)*

Pretzels

3732. The Pretzel Book / by Phyllis Raybin Emert. New Hope, Pa.: Woodsong Graphics, c1984. 152 p., illus.

3733. Making Soft Pretzels / Liz Martin. New York: Viking Kestrel, 1986. 1 v. (Little Chef Series).

Puddings

3734. Glorious Puds / Mary Berry. London, Eng.: Dent, 1980. 168 p. Includes index.

3735. The Pudding Book / by Helen Thomas; decorations by Kate Simunck. London, Eng.: Hutchinson, 1980. 241 p., illus. (chiefly colored). Includes index.

3736. Traditional Puddings / collected by Vera Segal. London, Eng.: Cottage, 1983. 32 p., illus. Includes index.

3737. English Puddings: Sweet and Savoury / Mary Norwak. London, Eng.: Sphere, 1984, c1981. 215 p., illus. Includes index.

Puddings *(Continued)*

3738. Hot Puddings / edited by Susan Dixon. London, Eng.: Ward Lock, 1986. 63 p., illus. (some colored). (Mrs. Beeton's Home Cooking). Includes index. Contains recipes selected from Mrs. Beeton's Cookery and Household Management.

3739. The National Trust Book of Traditional Puddings / Sara Paston-Williams. Harmondsworth, Eng.: Penguin, 1986, c1983. 130 p., illus. (Penguin Cookery Library). Includes index.

3740. The WI Book of Puddings / Janet Wier; illustrated by Vanessa Luff; edited by Sue Jacquemeir and Rosemary Wadey. London, Eng.: Women's Institute, 1986. 96 p., illus. Includes index.

3741. Hot Puddings / Patricia Payne. London, Eng.: Hamlyn, 1987. 64 p.

3742. Puddings, Custards, and Flans: 43 Sweet and Savory Recipes, from Old-Fashioned Favorites to New Creations / by Linda Zimmerman. 1st ed. New York: C.N. Potter: Distributed by Crown Publishers, c1990. 114 p.

see also broader category: Desserts

Quiches

3743. Quiche and Salad Made Easy / Eileen Barth. Sherman Oaks, Calif.: Alfred Pub., 1981. 64 p. (An Alfred Handy Guide).

3744. Quiche & Pâté / Peter Kump; illustrated by Susan Gray. 1st Harper & Row ed. New York: Harper & Row: I. Chalmers Cookbooks, c1982. 84 p., illus.

3745. Quiche & Soufflé Cookbook / Paul Mayer; illustrated by Mike Nelson. rev. Concord, Calif.: Nitty Gritty Productions, 1982, c1972. 85, 86 p., illus. (Nitty Gritty Cookbooks). Includes index. The author's Quiche and Soufflé with separate title pages.

Specific Dishes and Courses 477

Quiches *(Continued)*

3746. Quiches and Flans / by Janet Hunt; illustrated by Clive Burch. Wellingborough, Eng.: Thorsons; New York: Distributed by Sterling Pub., 1982. 128 p., illus. (A Thorsons Wholefood Cookbook). Includes index. At head of cover title: The Best of Vegetarian Cooking.

3747. Quiches, Flans, and Tarts / Mary Norwak. London, Eng.: Ward Lock, 1985. 80 p., illus. (some colored). Includes index.

3748. Quiches, Pies, Tarts, and Flans / Ginette Hell-Girod. Tunbridge Wells, Eng.: Costello, 1985. 143 p., illus. (some colored). Includes index. Translation of: Le livre des tartes.

see also entry 3929; Pastry; Pies

Relishes *see* **Pickles and Relishes**

Salad Dressings

3749. Not for Salads Only--from Wish-Bone: Tested Recipes from the Lipton Kitchens. New York: Benjamin Co., c1980. 128 p., illus. (some colored), and microwave recipe supplement (19 p.). "A Benjamin Company/Rutledge Book." Includes index.

3750. Salad Dressings! / Jane Marsh Dieckmann; edited by Andrea Chesman. Freedom, Calif.: Crossing Press, c1987. 151 p. More than 100 recipes. (The Crossing Press Specialty Cookbook Series). Includes index.

3751. The Ultimate Salad Dressing Book / by Claire Stancer. New York: McGraw-Hill, c1989. 110 p., line drawings. 100 recipes. Includes index.

see also entries 2613, 3589, 3864, 3872, 3875; and broader category: Salads

Salads

3752. Greens 'n Things / by Sifto Salt; written and compiled by Anne Borella. Montreal, Que.: Domtar Chemicals Group, Sifto Salt Division, [between 1979 and 1982]. 16 p.

3753. Book of Salads / Fylde Rugby Club; compiled by Ann Graham Elwell. Lytham St. Anne's, Eng.: (Blackpool Rd., Ansdell, Lytham St. Anne's): The Club, 1980. 36 p.

3754. A Salad a Day / Ruth Moorman & Lalla Williams. Brandon, Miss.: Quail Ridge Press, 1980. 78 p. (Cookbook Series; no. 3).

3755. Salads from Beginning to Endive / from Kraft; recipes and editorial, the Kraft Kitchens; photography, Kraft, Inc., Creative Services. New York: Benjamin Co., c1980. 160 p., illus. Includes index.

3756. The Woman's Day Book of Salads / Carol Truax; recipes tested and edited by Bonnie Levine. 1st ed. New York: Dutton, c1980. 234 p. Includes index.

3757. The Complete Book of Salads / created and designed by the editorial staff of Ortho Books; written by Cynthia Scheer; photography by Fred Lyon; illustrations by Ellen Blonder. San Francisco, Calif.: Ortho Books, c1981. 94 p., colored illus. Includes index.

3758. Salads for All Occasions / Elke Fuhrmann; translated from German by Helen Feingold. Woodbury, N.Y.: Barron's 1981. 1 v. Includes index. Translation of: Salate. [Publication of this book has not been verified].

3759. A World of Salads / Rosalie Swedlin. 1st American ed. New York: Holt, Rinehart and Winston, 1981. 216 p., illus. Includes index.

3760. All Kinds of Salads. New York: Golden Press, c1982. 64 p., colored illus. (A Betty Crocker Picture Cookbook).

Salads *(Continued)*

3761. The All Natural Salad Book / by Darcy Williamson and John Allgair. Bend, Or.: Maverick Publications, c1982. 100 p.

3762. Book of Salads and Summer Dishes / Jacqui Hine. Poole, Eng.: Blandford, 1982. 95 p., illus. (some colored). Includes index.

3763. Contemplation and the Art of Saladmaking / Jeanne Heiberg. New York: Crossroad, 1982. 234 p., illus. Includes index.

3764. How to Book of Salads and Summer Dishes / Jacqui Hine. London, Eng.: Blandford Press; New York: Distributed by Sterling Pub. Co., 1982. 95 p., illus. (some colored). Includes index. Probably a reprint of: Book of Salads and Summer Dishes (entry 3762).

3765. Miriam B. Loo's Salads for All Seasons. Colorado Springs, Colo.: Current Inc., 1982. 92 p.

3766. Salads for All Seasons / Barbara Gibbons. New York: Macmillan; London, Eng.: Collier Macmillan, c1982. 247 p. Includes index.

3767. Salads for Every Season / Roz Denny. Cambridge, Eng.: Martin, 1982. 96 p., colored illus. Includes index.

3768. Salads of All Kinds / by the editors of Consumer Guide. New York: Beekman House: Distributed by Crown Publishers, c1982. 80 p., illus. (some colored). (Favorite Brand Name Recipes). Includes index.

3769. 32 Super Salads. Woodbury, N.Y.: Barron's, c1983. 63 p., colored illus. (Easy Cooking). Includes index.

3770. Best of Salads and Buffets / Christian Teubner & Annette Wolter. Tucson, Ariz.: HP Books, c1983. 224 p., colored illus. Includes index. Translation of: Kalte Köstlichkeiten Wie Noch Nie.

Salads *(Continued)*

3771. Good Housekeeping Salads / Good Housekeeping Institute. London, Eng.: Ebury, 1983. 128 p., illus. (some colored). Includes index.

3772. Rose Elliot's Book of Salads. London, Eng.: Fontana, 1983. 64 p., illus. Includes index.

3773. Salads / by Desda Crockett; illustrated by Clive Birch. 1st American ed. New York: Thorsons Publishers: Distributed to the trade by Inner Traditions International, 1983. 128 p., illus. (A Thorsons Wholefood Cookbook). Includes index. British ed. reprinted in 1987 under title: Sensational Vegetarian Salads (entry 3806).

3774. Salads & Dressings. Newton Abbot, Eng.: David & Charles, 1983. 64 p., colored illus. (Kitchen Workshop). Includes index. Translation of: Salater.

3775. Salads of India / by Varsha Dandekar; drawings by Jyotsna Raj. Trumansburg, N.Y.: Crossing Press, c1983. 94 p., illus. Includes index.

3776. The Grand Salad / from John Evelyn's Acetaria (1699); compiled and edited by Madeleine Mason; pen drawings and water colour illustrations, calligraphy and the present day salads, Joan Wolfenden. Bonchurch, Eng.: Peacock Vane, c1984. 96 p., illus. (some colored). Includes index.

3777. The Salad Garden / Elisabeth Arter; line drawings by David Henderson. London, Eng.: Croom Helm, c1984. 187 p., illus. Includes index.

3778. The Salad Garden / Joy Larkcom; photographs by Roger Phillips. New York: Viking Press, 1984. 168 p., illus. (some colored). "Published in cooperation with the New York Botanical Garden Institute of Urban Horticulture." Most of the book is on gardening but one chapter is devoted to salad making and contains ca. 100 recipes. Includes indexes.

Specific Dishes and Courses 481

Salads *(Continued)*

3779. Salads / Pamela Westland. London, Eng.: Ward Lock, 1984. 80 p., illus. (some colored). Includes index.

3780. Salads: A Cookbook / by Joan Bidinosti and Marilyn Wearring. London, Ont.: Bidinosti & Wearring, 1984. 48 p.

3781. Salads and Dressings for All Seasons, Hot and Cold, Fruits and Vegetables, Meats and Fish / by Georgina. London, Ont.: G. MacGregor, 1984. 64 p., illus.

3782. Betty Crocker's Salads. Rev. ed. New York: Golden Press, c1985. 96 p., colored illus. Includes index.

3783. Four Seasons Salads / Jackie Burrow. Tucson, Ariz.: HP Books, c1985. 80 p., colored illus. 100 recipes. Includes index. Also published: London, Eng.: Hamlyn, 1988 (entry 3814).

3784. The Perfect Salad / Bernice Hurst; illustrations by Ronald Hurst. Twickenham, Eng.: Hamlyn, 1985. 32 p., illus. (The Perfect Series). Includes index.

3785. Salad / by Amy Nathan; foreword by Barbara Tropp; text by Kelly McCune and Amy Nathan; photographs by Kathryn Kleinman. San Francisco, Calif.: Chronicle Books, c1985. 119 p., colored photos. Almost 50 recipes. Includes index.

3786. Salad Menus. Alexandria, Va.: Time-Life Books, c1985. 105 p., illus. (some colored). (Great Meals in Minutes). Includes index.

3787. Salads / Mary Norwak. London, Eng.: Bell & Hyman, 1985. 91 p., illus. (some colored). (New & Natural). Includes index.

3788. Salads / Cynthia Scheer, writer; Fred Lyon, photographer. San Francisco, Calif.: California Culinary Academy, c1985. 128 p., colored illus. ca. 100 recipes. Includes index.

Salads *(Continued)*

3789. Sensational Salads / Lionel Martinez. London, Eng.: Macdonald, 1985. 127 p., colored illus. Includes index.

3790. Better Homes and Gardens Make-a-Meal Salads / editor, Mary Jo Plutt. 1st ed. Des Moines, Iowa: Meredith Corp., c1986. 96 p., colored illus. Includes index.

3791. Better Homes and Gardens Salads. 1st ed. Des Moines, Iowa: Meredith Corp., c1986. 128 p., colored illus. (Great Cooking Made Easy). Includes index.

3792. Fresh Salad Ideas / Allen D. Bragdon. New York: A.D. Bragdon Publishers, 1986? 64 p., illus. (Munchie Books).

3793. Fresh Ways with Salads / by the editors of Time-Life Books. Alexandria, Va.: Time-Life Books, c1986. 144 p., colored illus. (Healthy Home Cooking). Includes index.

3794. New Salads: Quick, Healthy Recipes from Japan / salads by Shinko Shimizu; introduction by Michio Kushi; photographs by Masaya Suzuki. 1st ed. Tokyo, Japan; New York: Kodansha International; New York: Distributed through Harper & Row, 1986. 124 p., illus. (some colored). Includes index.

3795. The Salad Book / Carole Handslip; illustrated by Mike Dodd. London, Eng.: Pan, 1986. 192 p., illus. Includes index.

3796. Salads & Cold Dishes / Annette Wolter. Twickenham, Eng.: Hamlyn, 1986. 64 p., colored illus. (Hamlyn Favourite Cook Books). Includes index. Translation of: Bunte Happen, Kalte Platten.

3797. Salads and Summer Dishes. Woodbury, N.Y.: Barron's, 1986, c1984. 160 p., illus. (some colored). (Step-by-Step Cooking Series). Includes index.

3798. Salads for All Occasions / Vo Bacon. London, Eng.: Tiger Books International, 1986. 79 p., illus. Includes index.

Salads *(Continued)*

3799. Seasonal Salads: From Around the World / David Scott and Paddy Byrne. 1st U.S. ed. Pownal, Vt.: Storey Communications, c1986. 153 p., illus. "A Garden Way Publishing Book." Includes index.

3800. Better Homes and Gardens Light Salad Meals / editor, Elizabeth Woolever. 1st ed. Des Moines, Iowa: Meredith Corp., c1987. 48 p., colored illus. Includes index.

3801. The Salad Bowl / Sonia Allison. London, Eng.: Futura, 1987. 176 p., illus. (some colored). Includes index.

3802. Salad Days / Zune and Heather Bampfylde. London, Eng.: Sackville, in association with Tupperware, 1987. 128 p.

3803. Salad Recipes from the School of Music and the Department of Entomology, Montana State University / designed and produced by Kara Armstrong and others; design advisor, Stephanie Newman. Bozeman, Mont.: Bozarts Press, c1987. 28 p., illus. Includes index. Cover title: Entomologists & Musicians Salad Recipes.

3804. Salads / Mary Cadogan. Mississauga, Ont.: Cupress, c1987. 79 p., colored illus. (A & P Creative Cooking Collection).

3805. Salads / Gilly Cubitt and Judy Williams. Twickenham, Eng.: Hamlyn, 1987. 64 p., colored illus. Includes index.

3806. Sensational Vegetarian Salads: Crisp, Colourful and Nutritious Dishes for All Seasons Food Preparation / by Desda Crockett; styling and colour photography by Paul Turner and Sue Pressley; illustrated by Clive Birch. Wellingborough, Eng.: Thorsons, 1987. 128 p., illus. (some colored). Includes index. First published in 1983 under title: Salads (entry 3773).

3807. Sunset Fresh Ways with Salads / by the editors of Sunset Books and Sunset Magazine. 5th ed. Menlo Park, Calif.: Lane Pub. Co., c1987. 96 p., colored illus.

Salads *(Continued)*

3808. A Taste of Summer / Beverley Sutherland Smith; photography by Ray Joyce. Topsfield, Mass.: Salem House, 1987, c1983. 151 p., colored illus. Includes index.

3809. All the Best: Salads and Salad Dressings / by Joie Warner. Scarborough, Ont.: Prentice-Hall Canada, 1988. 96 p., illus. Includes index.

3810. Book of Salads / Anna Moore. Los Angeles, Calif.: HP Books, c1988. 120 p. More than 100 colored photos. More than 100 recipes. Includes index.

3811. Canada Cooks!: Salads / Edena Sheldon. North Vancouver, B.C.: Whitecap Books, c1988. 160 p., colored illus. Includes index.

3812. Christopher Idone's Salad Days / wine suggestions by Yves-Andre Istel; calorie counts by Patricia F. Messing. First ed. New York: Random House, 1988. 192 p., colored illus. 75 recipes. Includes index.

3813. Cranks Salads & Dressings / Daphne Swann. London, Eng.: Guinness, c1988. 89 p., illus. (some colored). Includes index.

3814. Four Seasons Salads / Jackie Burrow. London, Eng.: Hamlyn, 1988. 79 p. (Cooking for Today). Originally published in 1985 (entry 3783).

3815. Salads / by Cheri Lambourne; edited by Martina Boudreaux. Silver Spring, Md.: American Cooking Guild, 1988. 64 p., illus. (Collector's Series).

3816. Salads for Foodservice Menu Planning / Eulalia C. Blair. New York: Van Nostrand Reinhold Co., c1988. 201 p., colored illus. "A CBI Book." Includes index.

3817. Summer Salads. Minneapolis, Minn.: General Mills, 1988. 92 p., colored illus. (Betty Crocker Creative Recipes; no. 17).

Salads *(Continued)*

3818. Aveline Kushi's Wonderful World of Salads / Aveline Kushi and Wendy Esko. 1st ed. Tokyo, Japan; New York: Japan Publications, 1989. 178 p., illus. Includes bibliography and index.

3819. The Book of Salads / Lorna Rhodes. London, Eng.: Salamander, 1989. 120 p.

3820. The Complete Book of Salads / Allesandra Avallone; photographs by Franco Pizzochero. New York : Gallery Books, W.H. Smith Publishers, 1989. 144 p., colored photos. More than 130 recipes. Translated from the Italian by Elaine Hardy.

3821. Hearty Salads / Nina Graybill and Maxine Rapoport. Washington, D.C.: Farragut Pub. Co., c1989. 167 p. Includes index.

3822. Michele Evans' Sensational Salads: Main Course Salads for Every Season. New York: New American Library, c1989. 216 p. "NAL Books." Includes index.

3823. Salads / by Veronika Müller. English language ed. New York: Van Nostrand Reinhold, 1989. 169 p., colored illus. Includes index. Translation of: Salate.

3824. Salads Cookbook / Annette Wolter. New York: Crescent Books, 1989. 128 p., colored illus. (Good Cook's Library). Includes index. "Published originally under the title: Salate / by Gräfe und Unzer, München."

3825. Summer Salads and Barbecue Cookouts. Vancouver, B.C.: Opus Productions, 1989. 1 v. (The Easy Gourmet; v. 2). Includes index.

3826. The Whole Meal Salad Book / Frances Sheridan Goulart. New York: D.I. Fine, 1989. ca. 200 p. More than 200 recipes. Includes index.

Salads *(Continued)*

3827. Wild About Salads / by Marie Bianco. New York: Barron's, c1989. 96 p., 16 p. of plates, colored illus. 75 recipes for salads and dressings. Includes index.

3828. Seasonal Salads / Paddy Byrne & David Scott. London, Eng.: Grafton, 1990. 181 p.

3829. Super Salads & Vegetables. Minneapolis, Minn.: Pillsbury Co., 1990. 93 p., colored illus. More than 100 recipes. (Classic Pillsbury Cookbooks; #89).

see also entries 887, 958, 1648, 1666, 1817, 2328, 2349, 2373, 2419, 2426, 2449, 2498, 2613, 2644, 2660, 2671, 2826, 3282, 3743; Greens *(Section I);* Vegetables *(Section I);* and Salad Dressings

Salsas

3830. Salsas! / by Andrea Chesman. Trumansburg, N.Y.: Crossing Press, c1985. 137 p. More than 90 recipes. Includes index.

see also entry 4421; and broader category: Sauces

Sandwiches

3831. Danish Open Sandwiches / by Mette Herborg; translated by Kathleen and Erik Brondal. Copenhagen, Denmark: Host, c1980. 76 p., colored illus. Includes indexes.

3832. The Sandwich Cookbook. Secaucus, N.J.: Chartwell Books, 1980. 104 p., illus. (some colored). Includes index.

3833. Snacks & Sandwiches / by the editors of Time-Life Books. Alexandria, Va.: Time-Life Books, c1980. 176 p., colored illus. Includes indexes.

Sandwiches *(Continued)*

3834. The 1,000 Fabulous Sandwiches Cookbook / by Doris McFerran Townsend. New York: Gramercy Pub. Co.: Distributed by Crown Publishers, 1982, c1965. 256 p. Includes index. Reprint. Originally published: New York: Nelson, c1965.

3835. The Breville Toasted Sandwiches Book / Judy Ridgway. Cambridge, Eng.: Martin Books in association with Breville Europe, 1982. 96 p., colored illus.

3836. The Complete International Sandwich Book: Hundreds of World-Tested Recipes for Lunch, Brunch, or Breakfast, Between-Meal Snacks, Supper, the Cocktail Hour, Picnics, and Cookouts / Sonia Uvezian. New York: Stein and Day, 1982. 283 p. Includes index.

3837. The Original Sandwich Maker's Sandwich Guide: 260 Recipes to Build Better Sandwiches / by Pamela McDowell. Ottawa, Ont.: Hanover Press, c1982. 96 p., illus. (some colored). Includes index.

3838. The Ultimate Sandwich Book: With Over 700 Delicious Sandwich Creations / by Louis De Gouy, and others. Philadelphia, Pa.: Running Press, c1982. 155 p., illus. Includes index.

3839. The Woman's Day Book of Great Sandwiches / Diane Harris. 1st ed. New York: Holt, Rinehart, and Winston, c1982. 180 p., illus. Includes index.

3840. 500 Recipes for Sandwiches and Packed Meals / by Catherine Kirkpatrick. London, Eng.: Hamlyn, 1984, c1964. 96 p.

3841. The Book of Sandwiches / Gwen Robyns. London, Eng.: Macdonald, 1984. 174 p.

3842. The Complete Book of Sandwiches for the Professional Chef / Terence Janericco. Boston, Mass.: CBI Pub. Co., c1984. 134 p., 12 p. of colored photos. Includes index.

Sandwiches *(Continued)*

3843. The Sandwich Cookbook / Frederick E. Kahn; edited by Naomi Silverman. New York: Nautilus Communications; Aurora, Ill.: Distributed by Caroline House, c1984. 175 p., illus.

3844. Tasty Toasties / Gill McCormick. London, Eng.: Foulsham, c1984. 78 p., illus. (some colored). Includes index.

3845. A Bit Between the Teeth / Molly Parkin; sandwich recipes by Topsy Fryers. London, Eng.: Ward Lock, 1985. 96 p., colored illus. Includes index.

3846. Sandwiches, Sandwiches / from Barbara Lynn. Zephyr, Ont.: Sandwiches, Sandwiches, 1985. 72 p.

3847. Upper Crust / Brenda Bell. Chicago, Ill.: Contemporary Books, c1986. 80 p., colored illus. "The Great American Sandwich Book"--Cover. Includes index.

3848. Better Homes and Gardens Savory Sandwiches. 1st ed. Des Moines, Iowa: Meredith Corp., c1988. 47 p., colored illus. 40 recipes. Includes index.

3849. The Sandwich Book: A Complete Guide to America's Favorite Food- from Child-Pleasers to Classics to Calzones and Other Dagwood Dreams / Judy Gethers. 1st ed. New York: Vintage Books, 1988. 210 p., illus. More than 130 recipes. Includes index.

3850. The Book of Sandwiches / Louise Steele; photography by Paul Grater. Los Angeles, Calif.: HP Books, c1989. 120 p., colored illus. Includes index.

3851. Luncheonette: Ice Cream, Beverage, and Sandwich Recipes from the Golden Age of the Soda Fountain / by Carol Vidinghoff and Patricia M. Kelly. New York: Crown, 1989. 96 p., illus. Includes index. "Portions of this book were previously published in Soda Fountain and Luncheonette Drinks and Recipes by Louis De Gouy."

Sandwiches *(Continued)*

3852. The Real Sandwich Book / edited by Miriam Polunin. London, Eng.: Ebury, 1989. 128 p.

3853. The Sophisticated Sandwich: Exotic, Eclectic, Ethnic Eatables / Janet Hazen. Reading, Mass.: Aris Books, c1989. 144 p. (Kitchen Edition). Includes indexes.

3854. The Art of the Sandwich / by Jay Harlow; photography by Viktor Budnik. San Francisco, Calif.: Chronicle Books, 1990. 104 p., colored illus.

3855. Sensational Sandwiches / by Roy Passin. Gaithersburg, Md.: American Cooking Guild, 1990. 64 p., illus. (Collector's Series).

3856. Susan Costner's Book of Great Sandwiches: Sensational Recipes from Uptown, Down Home, and Around the World / by Susan Costner, with Camilla Turnbull; photographs by Faith Echtermeyer. New York: Crown, 1990. 150 p., 130 colored photos.

see also entries 1719, 2772, 3941, 3979, 3982; Pita Bread; and Lunches in a Bag or Box *(Section III)*

Sauces

3857. The Easy Harvest Sauce & Puree Cookbook / Marjorie Blanchard. Charlotte, Vt.: Garden Way Pub., c1980. 171 p., illus. Includes index. Reprint. Originally published: Sauce It. Charlotte, Vt.: Garden Way Pub., c1979.

3858. The Secret Sauce Book of the Hungry Monk / written by Ken Austin, Nigel and Susan MacKenzie. Jevington, Eng. (Willingdon La., Jevington, Nr. Posegate, Sussex): Hungry Monk, 1982. 84 p., illus.

Sauces *(Continued)*

3859. The Unofficial Florida Bar-B-Que Sauces & Chili Recipes / D.L. & P.A. Jackson. St. Cloud, Fla.: Jaxon's Pub. Co., 1982. 40 p.

3860. Sauces / by the editors of Time-Life Books. Alexandria, Va.: Time-Life Books, c1983. 176 p., illus. (some colored). (The Good Cook, Techniques & Recipes). Includes index.

3861. Preparing Sauces / Frederick E. Kahn. New York: Nautilus Communications; Aurora, Ill.: Distributed by Caroline House, c1984. 152 p., illus.

3862. The Sauce Book / Pepita Aris. New York: McGraw-Hill, c1984. 176 p., colored illus. "A Phoebe Phillips Editions Book." Includes index.

3863. Simply Sauces / Linda Gassenheimer. London, Eng.: Foulsham, c1984. 96 p., illus. (some colored). Includes index.

3864. Sauces, Dressings and Marinades / Celia Norman. London, Eng.: Macdonald, 1985. 160 p., colored illus. Includes index.

3865. Lady Maclean's Book of Sauces and Surprises / Lady Veronica Maclean. London, Eng.: Collins, 1986, c1978. 192 p. Includes index.

3866. All the Best: Pasta Sauces / Joie Warner. Scarborough, Ont.: Prentice-Hall Canada, 1987. 96 p., illus. More than 50 recipes.

3867. The Book of Sauces / Gordon Grimsdale. Tucson, Ariz.: HP Books, 1987. 128 p., colored photos.

3868. The Top One Hundred Pasta Sauces / Diane Seed; illustrations by Robert Budwig. Berkeley, Calif.: Ten Speed Press, 1987. 123 p., colored illus.

3869. Sauces / edited by Rosemary Wilkinson. London, Eng.: Bloomsbury, 1988. 104 p.

Sauces *(Continued)*

3870. Sauces and Soups. Toronto, Ont.: Grolier, 1988. (Microwave Magic; 11).

3871. Secrets of French Sauces: Over 100 Authentic Sauce Recipes / general editor, Beverly LeBlanc. London, Eng.: Macdonald Orbis, 1988. 95 p., illus. Includes index.

3872. Sauces and Dressings: 84 Light and Easy Recipes from Nouvelle to New American / by Diane Rozas. 1st ed. New York: Harmony Books, c1989. 95 p., illus. "A Particular Palate Cookbook." Includes index.

3873. Sumptuous Sauces in the Microwave / Patricia Tennison. Chicago, Ill.: Contemporary Books, c1989. 128 p. More than 80 recipes. Includes index.

3874. Classic Sauces and Their Preparation / Raymond Oliver. London, Eng.: Robinson, 1989. 208 p. Originally published under title: Wine and Food Society's Guide to Classic Sauces and Their Preparation.

3875. The Complete Book of Sauces / Sallie Y. Williams; produced by the Philip Lief Group, Inc. New York: Macmillan; London, Eng.: Collier Macmillan, c1990. 264 p., illus. "Recipes for more than 300 sauces and dressings for poultry, meat, fish, pasta, salads, vegetables, and desserts." Includes index.

3876. Pasta Light: 80 Low-Fat, Low Calorie, Fast & Fabulous Pasta Sauces / Norman Kolpas. Chicago, Ill.: Contemporary Books, 1990. 134 p. Includes index.

3877. Sauces for Pasta! / by Kristie Trabant with Andrea Chesman. Freedom, Calif.: Crossing Press, 1990. 111 p. (Specialty Cookbook Series).

see also entries 442, 448, 599, 1234, 1645, 1680, 1845, 2030, 2074, 2409, 3942, 4421, 4423; and Salsas

Scones

3878. Simply Scones / Leslie Weiner and Barbara Albright; illustrations by Janet Nelson. 1st ed. New York: St. Martin's Press, c1988. 128 p., illus. "Quick and easy recipes for more than 70 delicious scones and spreads." Includes index.

see also entries 2716, 2992; and broader category: Bread

Snacks

3879. How to Survive Snack Attacks...Naturally / Judi & Shari Zucker. Santa Barbara, Calif.: Woodbridge Press Pub. Co., 1980. 105 p.

3880. The Junk Food Alternative / Linda Burum; illustrations by Andra Rudolph. San Francisco, Calif.: 101 Productions; New York: Distributed to the book trade in the U.S. by Scribner, c1980. 186 p., illus. Includes index.

3881. T.N.T. Cookbook: A Dynamite Cookbook for Nutritional Treats / by Wendy Morrison. Calgary, Alta.: Detselig Enterprises, c1980. 72 p. On cover: Treats Nutritional Treats.

3882. The Whole Thing: An Alternative Snackfood Cookbook / edited by Catherine Mumaw and Marilyn Voran. Scottdale, Pa.: Herald Press, 1980. 23 p., illus. Includes index.

3883. Woman's Day Snack Cookbook / by Lyn Stallworth. 1st Collier Books ed. New York: Collier Books, 1980. 118 p., illus. "A Media Projects Incorporated Book." Includes index.

3884. Nutritious Nibbles: Quality Snacks for Kids. Mound, Minn.: Quality Child Care Press, c1981. 122 p. Includes menus and index.

3885. The Snack and Bag Lunch Idea Book / prepared and published by the Edmonton City Centre Church Corporation. Edmonton, Alta.: The Corp., 1981. 110 p., illus. Includes index.

Snacks *(Continued)*

3886. The Boozer's Late Night Cook Book, or, "Sorry I'll Eat That Again" / recipes by Caralan Butcher; artwork by Mollusc. New Barnet, Eng.: Chalk and Cheese, 1982. 48 p., illus. Includes index.

3887. Cocktails & Snacks / edited by Helen Chester. London, Eng.: Ward Lock, 1982. 96 p., illus. (some colored). Includes indexes.

3888. Kinder-Krunchies: Healthy Snack Recipes for Children / by Donna Austin. Pleasant Hill, Calif.: Distributed by Discovery Toys, c1982. 121 p., illus.

3889. The Midnight Snack Cookbook / Chris Hibbard. Evanston, Ill.: Sassafras Press, 1982. 100 p.

3890. My Munch Book / by Gretchen Bartlett and Luann Williams; artist, Ray Packard. 2nd ed. Hudson, Ohio: Nourishing Thoughts Enterprises, 1982. 100 p., illus.

3891. Slim Snacks: More than 200 Delectable Low-Calorie Snacks That Can Be Made in Minutes / Sharon Sanders. Chicago, Ill.: Contemporary Books, c1982. 216 p., illus. Includes index.

3892. Super Snacks: Seasonal Sugarless Snacks for Young Children: No Sugar, No Honey, No Artificial Sweeteners / by Jean Warren. Alderwood Manor, Wash.: Warren Pub. House; Mt. Rainier, Md.: Distributed by Gryphon House, c1982. 63 p., illus. Includes index.

3893. Tom Thumb Treats: Snack Recipes for Children / prepared by the National Dairy Council; illustrations by Gerry Greaves. Stevenage, Eng.: Publications for Companies, 1982. 16 p., illus. (some colored).

3894. Does Your Lunch Pack Punch?: A Cookbook for the Crunch & Munch Bunch / by Robin Toth & Jacqueline Hostage. White Hall, Va.: Betterway Publications; Stockbridge, Mass.: Distributed by Berkshire Traveller Press, c1983. 160 p., illus.

Snacks *(Continued)*

3895. Guilt-Free Snacking / Yvonne G. Baker. Denver, Colo.: Accent Books, c1983. 160 p., illus. Includes index.

3896. Healthy Snacks for Kids / by Penny Warner. 1st ed. Concord, Calif.: Nitty Gritty Productions, c1983. 190 p., illus. (some colored). Includes index.

3897. Nifty Nibbles / by Cathy Prange and Joan Pauli; sketches by Miriam Stanbury. Kitchener, Ont.: Muffin Mania Pub., 1983. 66 p., illus.

3898. Going Crackers: Great Recipes for Homemade Snacks / by Becky Lee Hirdman. San Luis Obispo, Calif.: Padre Productions, c1984. 64 p., illus. Includes bibliography and index.

3899. S.N.A.C.K.S.: Speedy, Nutritious, and Cheap Kids' Snacks / by Jan Brink and Melinda Ramm; illustrated by Roberta Simanowitz. New York: New American Library, c1984. 199 p., illus. "A Plume Book." Includes index.

3900. Fast & Easy Company Treats / Nicole Parton. Toronto, Ont.: McClelland and Stewart, c1985. 113 p. Includes index.

3901. Nutritious Seasonal Snacks: Fall, Winter, Spring, Summer. Charleston, W.Va.: West Virginia Dept. of Education, Child Nutrition Division, 1985. 13 p., colored illus.

3902. Super Snacks for Kids / Penny Warner; illustrations by Constance Pike; food styling by Terry Paetzold; photography by Jim Ketsdever. 1st ed. New York: St. Martin's Press, c1985. 176 p., illus. (some colored). Includes index.

3903. Magnificent Snacks Cookbook / written & edited by Kathryn L. Ramsay. Richmond Hill, Ont.: Magnificent Cookbooks Pub., c1986. 124 p., colored illus.

Snacks *(Continued)*

3904. Party Pieces: Cocktail Food with a Difference / Polly Tyrer. London, Eng.: Macdonald, 1986. 160 p., colored illus. Includes index.

3905. Snacks: Tasty Tidbits from Around the World / Lorenzo Nicoletti; translated by Ardele Dejey. London, Eng.: W.H. Allen, 1986. 188 p., colored illus. Translated from the Italian.

3906. The Joy of Snacks / Nancy Cooper. Minnetonka, Minn.: Diabetes Center, c1987. 269 p., illus. Includes index.

3907. Munchies Minus Mom: A Collection of Healthy Snacks and Meals Compiled Especially for Sitters or Latch Key Kids. Charleston, W.Va.: West Virginia Dept. of Education, Child Nutrition Division, 1987. 14 p., illus.

3908. Fresh Ways with Snacks & Party Fare / by the editors of Time-Life Books. Alexandria, Va.: Time-Life Books, c1988. 144 p., colored illus. (Healthy Home Cooking). Includes index.

3909. The Official Couch Potato Cookbook / by Mary Beth Jung, Melinda Corey, and Jackie Ogburn; illustrated by Robert Armstrong; foreword by Jack Mingo. New York: Warner Books, c1988. 128 p., illus. "Blue Cliff Editions Book." Includes index.

3910. Street Food / Rose Grant. Freedom, Calif.: Crossing Press, c1988. 165 p., illus. More than 100 recipes. Includes index.

3911. Good Nature's Wholesome Snacks & Lunches for Kids / by Lori B. Huff; illustrated by Sherri Datres. Pleasant Valley, N.Y.: Good Nature, c1989. 36 leaves.

3912. Holiday Snack Sampler. Minneapolis, Minn.: General Mills, 1989. 92 p., colored illus. (Betty Crocker Creative Recipes; no. 32). Includes index.

Specialty Cookbooks

Snacks *(Continued)*

3913. The Snack Bar Gourmet: Versatile Treats for People on the Go / Marsha Eines, Elliott Katz. Toronto, Ont.: Great North Books; Willowdale, Ont.: Trade distribution by Firefly Books, c1989. 78 p., illus. Includes index.

3914. Snacks You Can Say Yes To! / written by Cheryl Beck; illustrated by Shirley Davies. Calgary, Alta.: Kids Care International, c1989. 71 p., illus.

3915. Summertime Snacks: Recipes and Menu Ideas for the Michigan Summer Food Service Program / compiled and edited by Julie Swenson. Chicago, Ill.: USDA Food and Nutrition Service, Midwest Regional Office of Public Affairs and State Funding and Summer Section, Child Nutrition Progams, 1989. 102 p., illus. Includes index.

3916. Wild About Munchies / by Dotty Griffith. New York: Barron's, c1989. 96 p., 16 p. of plates, colored illus. 65 recipes.

3917. The Mennonite Girl Presents Smackin' Snacks: 50 Recipes for Wholesome Snacks from Mennonite Kitchens / compiled by Isaac R. Horst. Mt. Forest, Ont.: I.R. Horst, c1990. 32 p.

3918. Snack Food / edited by R. Gordon Booth. New York: Van Nostrand Reinhold, 1990. 401 p., illus. "An AVI Book." Includes bibliography and index.

CHILDREN'S COOKBOOKS

3919. Weekly Reader Books Presents Andy and Sandy's Yummy Summer Snack Book / by Kathy Bieger Roche; illustrations by Blanche Sims. Middletown, Conn.: Weekly Reader Books, c1985. 36 p., colored illus. Spine title: Yummy Summer Snack Book. Easy-to-follow instructions for preparing cold drinks, frozen treats, cookies, and picnic and party snacks.

see also entries 402, 1719, 2691, 2794, 2833, 2836, 3012, 3991, 3995, 4118, 4134, 4196, 4200; Appetizers and Snacks; Dim Sum

Specific Dishes and Courses

Sorbets *see* Ice Cream and Ices

Soufflés

3920. Soufflés, Quiches, Mousses & the Random Egg. 1st ed. New York: Harper & Row, 1971. 138 p.

3921. Soufflés: Forty Savory and Sweet Recipes--from Baked to Frozen / by Ann Amernick and Richard Chirol; illustrations by Sally Sturman. New York: C.N. Potter: Distributed by Crown Publishers, 1989. 128 p., illus. Includes index.

3922. The Soufflé Cookbook / Myra Waldo. New York: Dover Publications, 1990, c1982. 190 p. Reprint. Originally published: Serve at Once: The Soufflé Cookbook. New York: Crowell, 1954.

see also entries 3594, 3618, 3745; and Eggs *(Section I)*

Soups

3923. The Soup Book: 770 Recipes / by Louis P. De Gouy. New York: Dover Publications, 1974, c1949. 414 p. Includes index. "Unabridged republication of the work originally published in 1949 by Greenberg."

3924. The Book of Chowder / Richard J. Hooker; illustrated by Anna Baker. Harvard, Mass.: Harvard Common Press, c1978. 135 p. illus. Includes bibliography and index.

3925. The Complete International Soup Cookbook / Kay Shaw Nelson. New York: Stein and Day, 1980. 314 p. More than 280 recipes for soups, appetizers, snacks, one-dish meals, salads, and sandwiches. Includes index.

3926. Galley Soups for All Seasons. New York: Mayflower Books, c1980. 63 p., illus. (some colored). Includes index.

Soups *(Continued)*

3927. Soup Wisdom / by Frieda Arkin and the editors of Consumer Reports Books. Mount Vernon, N.Y.: Consumers Union, c1980. 142 p., illus.

3928. Birds Eye Super Soups Booklet. White Plains, N.Y.: General Foods, 1981. 1 booklet, colored photos. Contains recipes for soups using frozen vegetables.

3929. The Master Book of Soups: Featuring 1001 Titles and Recipes / Henry Smith. New York: Gordon Press, 1981. 232 p. Includes index. Reprint. Originally published: London, Eng.: Spring Books.

3930. Super Soups Made Easy / Eileen Barth. Sherman Oaks, Calif.: Alfred Pub., 1981. 64 p. (An Alfred Handy Guide).

3931. Unusual Soups: Hot and Cold Soups for All Occasions / Cheryl Brooks. Englewood Cliffs, N.J.: Prentice Hall, c1981. 164 p., illus. "A Spectrum Book." Includes index.

3932. A Celebration of Soups / by Robert Ackart; illustrations by Ron Becker. 1st ed. Garden City, N.Y.: Doubleday, 1982. 260 p., illus. "Dolphin Books." Includes index.

3933. A Feast of Soups / Jacqueline Heriteau. New York: Dial Press, c1982. 424 p., illus. More than 500 recipes. Includes index.

3934. A Soup Cookbook / Digby Law. London, Eng.: Hodder & Stoughton, 1982. 239 p.

3935. Soups from Amish and Mennonite Kitchens / collected and edited by Phyllis Pellman Good and Rachel Thomas Pellman. Lancaster, Pa.: Good Books, 1982. 32 p. (Pennsylvania Dutch Cookbooks).

Specific Dishes and Courses

Soups *(Continued)*

3936. Soups of Hakafri Restaurant: Original Version / by Rena Franklin; drawings, Daniel; translator, Yehudit Venezia. Gainesville, Fla.: Triad Pub. Co., c1982. 125 p. English and Hebrew. Includes index.

3937. Follow Your Heart's Vegetarian Soup Cookbook / by Janice Cook Migliaccio; illustrated by Donna Wright. Santa Barbara, Calif.: Woodbridge Press, c1983. 127 p., illus. Includes index.

3938. Gallery Buffet Soup Cookbook. Rev. 4th ed. Dallas, Tex.: Dallas Museum of Art, 1983. 141 p., colored illus. Includes index.

3939. Soup Time! / by Bob McNeil. Lumsden, Sask.: Soup Time! Pub. Co., 1983. 122 p., colored illus. Includes index.

3940. Soups / Jeannette Seaver; illustrated by Nathalie Seaver. New York: Seaver Books: Distributed by Arbor House Pub. Co., 1983, c1978. 214 p., illus. Includes index.

3941. Soups & Sandwiches / by Sue and Bill Deeming. Tucson, Ariz.: HP Books, c1983. 160 p., colored illus. Includes index.

3942. Soups & Sauces. Newton Abbot, Eng.: David & Charles, c1983. 62 p., colored illus. (Kitchen Workshop). Includes index. Translation of: Supper og Sauser.

3943. Soups Supreme / by the editors of Rodale Books. Emmaus, Pa.: Rodale Press, c1983. 98 p., illus. (Rodale's High Health Cookbook Series). Includes index.

3944. Truly Unusual Soups / Lu Lockwood. 2nd ed. Chester, Conn.: Globe Pequot Press, c1983. 144 p. More than 125 recipes. Includes index.

3945. All Color Book of Soups and Appetizers. New York: Arco Pub., 1984. 82 p., colored illus.

Soups *(Continued)*

3946. Simply Souper / by Carol Martin and Jane Romagnoli. Breslau, Ont.: Simply Souper, c1984. 44 p.

3947. Souped Up / text, illustrations, Terri Fuglem. Edmonton, Alta.: Alberta Association for Adult Literacy, c1984. 32 p., illus. Includes bibliography.

3948. The All Natural Soup Cookbook / by Darcy Williamson. Bend, Or.: Maverick Publications, c1985. 138 p. Includes index.

3949. The Little Gumbo Book: Twenty-Seven Carefully Created Recipes That Will Enable Everyone to Enjoy the Special Experience of Gumbo / by Gwen McKee; illustrations by Tupper Davidson. Baton Rouge, La.: Quail Ridge Press, c1986. 64 p., illus.

3950. More Soup Anyone?: A Souper Collection / garnered by Leigh Boyle Coffin. Ormstown, Que.: L.B. Coffin, 1985. 93 p. Includes bibliography and index.

3951. The Perfect Soup / Bernice Hurst; illustrations by Ronald Hurst. Twickenham, Eng.: Hamlyn, 1985. 32 p., illus.

3952. Soup, Beautiful Soup / Felipe Rojas-Lombardi. 1st ed. New York: Random House, c1985. 166 p. Includes index.

3953. Souper Type: 28 Soup Recipes from Some Super Restaurants and Friends, all typeset on Grenville's new CRS system. Toronto, Ont.: Grenville, 1985. 32 p.

3954. Soups / Hannah Wright; illustrations by Vivien Ashley. London, Eng.: Hale, 1985. 299 p., illus. (A Jill Norman Book). Includes index.

3955. Soups and Garnishes / Jehane Benoît. Saint-Lambert, Que.: Héritage, 1985. 100 p., colored illus. (Encyclopedia of Microwave Cooking; 2). Includes index. Issued also in French under title: Les soupes et leurs garnitures.

Soups *(Continued)*

3956. Soups & Starters / Robert Carrier. London, Eng.: Marshall Cavendish, 1985. 112 p., colored illus. (Robert Carrier's Kitchen). Includes index.

3957. Soup's On / Nancy Baggett & Ruth Glick. New York: Macmillan, c1985. 339 p., illus. More than 200 recipes. "A Bobbs-Merrill Book." Includes index.

3958. Sunset Homemade Soups / by the editors of Sunset Books and Sunset Magazine. 1st ed. Menlo Park, Calif.: Lane Pub. Co., c1985. 96 p., colored illus. Includes index.

3959. Microwave Magic: Soups, Chowders and Vegetables / Jean Tweddle. Harris, Sask.: Microwave Magic, c1986. 142 p., colored illus. Includes index.

3960. A Soup for All Seasons / Rosalie Fefergrad & Micki Bregman. Toronto, Ont.: Methuen, 1986. 1 v. Includes index. [Publication of this book has not been verified].

3961. Soups / edited by Susan Dixon. London, Eng.: Ward Lock, 1986. 63 p., illus. (some colored). (Mrs. Beeton's Mini Series). Contains recipes selected from Mrs. Beeton's Cookery and Household Management.

3962. Super Soups / by Sally Meddock; edited by Jeannine Winquist. Silver Spring, Md.: American Cooking Guild, 1986. 64 p., illus.

3963. Cranks Soups & Starters / compiled by Daphne Swann. Enfield, Eng.: Guinness, c1987. 85 p., 8 p. of plates, illus. (some colored). Includes index.

3964. Favorite Recipes for Soups / Ch'en Min-liang pien chu. Hong Kong: Yin shih t'ien ti ch'u pan she, 1987. 96 p., illus. (some colored).

Soups *(Continued)*

3965. The Philosophers & Microbiologists Soup Book: Soup Recipes from the Department of Microbiology & the Philosophy & Religious Studies faculty, Montana State University / illustrated, lettered & produced by Robert Rath and others; design advisor, Anne Garner. Bozeman, Mont.: Bozarts Press, c1987. 28 p., illus.

3966. Soups and Starters / Nichola Palmer. Twickenham, Eng.: Hamlyn, 1987. 64 p., colored illus. (Rainbow). Includes index.

3967. Soups for All Seasons / Brad McCrorie. Toronto, Ont.: Doubleday Canada; Garden City, N.Y.: Doubleday, 1987. 123 p., illus. Includes index.

3968. The Allergy Kitchen: Savory Soups / by Ellen Ratner; foreword by Oscar L. Frick. 1st ed. Menlo Park, Calif.: Allergy Publications, c1988. 116, illus. "Milk-free, egg-free, corn-free, soy-free." Includes index.

3969. Cold Soups / Nina Graybill and Maxine Rapoport. Washington, D.C.: Farragut Pub. Co., c1988. 181 p.

3970. Lee Bailey's Soup Meals: Main Events in Year-Round Menus / by Lee Bailey; photographs by Tom Eckerle. New York: C.N. Potter: Distributed by Crown, 1988. 164 p., 118 colored photos. 32 menus with soups as the main course. Contains sections on appetizers, salads, and desserts. Includes index.

3971. Soup / Coralie Castle; illustrated by Roy Killeen. Rev. ed. San Ramon, Calif.: Chevron Chemical Co., 1988. 192 p., illus. Includes index.

3972. Soups and Borschts from Hutterite, Amish, Mennonite, Dutch, Ukrainian and Russian Kitchens / compiled by Sam Hofer. 1st ed. Calgary, Alta.: Hofer Pub., c1988. 100 p., illus.

3973. Soups for the Professional Chef / Terence Janericco. New York: Van Nostrand Reinhold, c1988. 211 p., colored illus.

Soups *(Continued)*

3974. The Book of Soups / Lorna Rhodes; photography by Jon Stewart, assisted by Kay Small. Los Angeles, Calif.: HP Books, 1989. 120 p. More than 100 recipes. Includes index.

3975. Herbs & Imagination: A Season for Soups / by Jean S. Fisher; cover design by Marcia Romashko. Madison, Wis.?: Wisconsin Unit of the Herb Society of America, c1989. 45 p., illus.

3976. The Best of Cold Soups / by Sandy Hall. Tempe, Ariz.: Graham-Conley Press, c1990. 1 v.

3977. James McNair's Soups / photography by Patricia Brabant. San Francisco, Calif.: Chronicle Books, 1990. 96 p., colored photos.

CHILDREN'S COOKBOOKS

3978. Grandmother Soup / by Stacy & Judith Bosley; illustrations by Gary Nowak. Middleton, Mich. (P.O. Box 7, Middleton 48856): Grand Books, 1985. 31 p., colored illus. 8 recipes.

see also entries 2660, 2766, 2772, 2826, 3870; Soups and Salads; Soups and Stews; Stocks

Soups and Salads

3979. Small Feasts: Soups, Salads, & Sandwiches / edited by Marilee Matteson. New York: C.N. Potter; Distributed by Crown, 1980. 288 p., illus. Includes index.

3980. Rodale's Soups and Salads Cookbook and Kitchen Album: Nearly 300 Kitchen-Tested Recipes, plus some surprising facts about foods, nutritional tips, and entertaining visits with some remarkable cooks / editor, Charles Gerras; assistant editor, Carol Meinhardt Hopkins; recipes, Carole Collier; additional recipes and recipe testing, Joanne Benedict and Linda Gilbert; personal profiles, Carol Meinhardt Hopkins; editorial assistant, Camille Bucci. Emmaus, Pa.: Rodale Press, c1981. 278 p., illus. (some colored). Includes index.

Soups and Salads *(Continued)*

3981. Soup and Salad Bars / edited by Patricia Moore Kolb and the editors of Restaurant Business Magazine; photographs by Don Kushnick. Boston, Mass.: CBI Pub. Co., c1981. 56 p., colored illus.

3982. Soup, Salad, Sandwich Cookbook / by June Turner and Naomi Arbit. Milwaukee, Wis.: Ideals Pub. Corp., c1981. 63 p.

3983. Soup, Salad & Pasta: A Collection of Recipes / by Ursel Norman; designed and illustrated by Derek Norman. New York: Galley Press, c1982. 176 p., illus. (some colored). Includes index.

3984. Annie Lerman's New Salad and Soup Book / newly edited by Laura Fortenbaugh; drawings by Teresa Anderko. Philadelphia, Pa.: Running Press, c1983. 190 p., illus. Includes index.

3985. Creative Soups & Salads / by Lou Seibert Pappas; editor, Jackie Walsh; photographer, Glen Millward. 1st ed. Concord, Calif.: Nitty Gritty Productions, c1983. 191 p., illus. (some colored). Includes index.

3986. Soups and Salads. Los Angeles, Calif.: Knapp Press, c1983. 119 p., colored illus. (Cooking with Bon Appétit). Includes index.

3987. Soups & Salads / Sandi Cooper; illustrated by Joan Blume. 1st ed. New York: Harper & Row: Chalmers Cookbooks, c1983. 82 p., illus.

3988. The Soups and Salads Cookbook / Lillian Langseth-Christensen and Carol Sturm Smith; illustrations by Lillian Langseth-Christensen. Walker large print ed. New York: Walker, 1984, c1968. 96 p., illus. Includes index.

3989. Famous Brands Soups & Salads. St. Louis, Mo.: Brand Name Pub. Corp., 1985? 128 p., colored illus. Includes index.

Soups and Salads *(Continued)*

3990. Soup, Salad, and Pasta Innovations / by Karen Lee; written with Alaxandra Branyon; illustrations by Lauren Jarrett. 1st ed. Garden City, N.Y.: Doubleday, 1987. 196 p., illus. Includes index.

3991. Soups, Salads, and Snacks: Favorite Recipes from Home Economics Teachers. Nashville, Tenn.: Favorite Recipes Press, c1988. 128 p., illus. Includes index.

3992. Dr. Jensen's Real Soup & Salad Cookbook / Bernard Jensen; original illustrations, Vicki Hudon. Garden City Park, N.Y.: Avery Pub. Group, c1989. 172 p., illus. (some colored). Includes index.

3993. Cold Soups, Warm Salads / Irene Rothschild. 1st ed. New York: Dutton, c1990. 144 p., illus. Includes index.

3994. Soups and Salads with Schmecks Appeal / Edna Staebler. Montreal, Que.: McGraw-Hill Ryerson, c1990. 87 p.

3995. Soups, Salads and Snacks / Caroline Ellwood. London, Eng.: Hamlyn, 1990, c1980. 93 p., colored illus. (The Kitchen Library). Includes index.

see also entries 2626, 4194; and Salads

Soups and Stews

3996. Soups, Chowders, and Stews / by Georgia Orcutt; illustrated by Pamela Carroll. 1st ed. Dublin, N.H.: Yankee, Inc., c1981. 143 p., illus. More than 220 recipes for hot and cold soups, chowders, and stews, together with noodles, dumplings, and croutons. (The Flavor of New England). Includes index.

3997. Stews and Soups and Go-with Breads. New York: Golden Press, c1982. 64 p., colored illus. (A Betty Crocker Picture Cookbook).

Soups and Stews *(Continued)*

3998. 32 Soups and Stews / by Jan Aaron. Woodbury, N.Y.: Barron's, c1983. 64 p., colored illus. (Easy cooking). Includes index.

3999. Main-Course Soups & Stews / Dorothy Ivens. 1st ed. New York: Harper & Row, c1983. 336 p. Includes index.

4000. The Complete Book of Soups and Stews / Bernard Clayton, Jr.; illustrations by Stephanie Fleischer Osser. New York: Simon and Schuster, c1984. 441 p., illus. Includes index.

4001. Dave Maynard's Soups, Stews & Casseroles: And Many Other Tried and True Recipes for Chilis, Chowders, and Other Hearty Fare. 1st ed. New York: St. Martin's Press, c1984. 221 p., illus. Includes index.

4002. Betty Crocker's Soups and Stews Cookbook. New York: Golden Press, c1985. 96 p., colored illus. Includes index.

4003. The Good Food: Soups, Stews, and Pastas / Daniel Halpern and Julie Strand. New York: Viking, 1985. 249 p. Includes index.

4004. Soup & Stew Menus. Alexandria, Va.: Time-Life Books, c1985. 105 p., illus. (some colored). (Great Meals in Minutes). Includes index.

4005. The Southern Heritage Soups and Stews Cookbook. Birmingham, Ala.: Oxmoor House, 1985. 143 p., illus. (some colored). (The Southern Heritage Cookbook Library). Includes index.

4006. Fresh Ways with Soups & Stews / by the editors of Time-Life Books. Alexandria, Va.: Time-Life Books, c1986. 144 p., colored illus. (Healthy Home Cooking). Includes index.

Soups and Stews *(Continued)*

4007. Soups & Stews / Cynthia Scheer, writer and food stylist; Karin Shakery, editor; Linda Hinrichs, Carol Kramer, designers; Michael Lamotte, photographer; Sara Slavin, photographic stylist. San Francisco, Calif.: Ortho Information Services, 1986. 127 p., colored illus. (California Culinary Academy series). Includes index.

4008. Better Homes and Gardens Soups & Stews. 1st ed. Des Moines, Iowa: Meredith Corp., c1987. 128 p., colored illus. (Great Cooking Made Easy). Includes index.

4009. Hearty Vegetarian Soups & Stews / Jeanne Marie Martin. Madeira Park, B.C.: Harbour Pub., 1989. 64 p., illus.

4010. Soups and Stews. London, Eng.: Treasure, 1989. 128 p.

4011. Recipes from the Night Kitchen: A Practical Guide to Spectacular Soups, Stews, and Chilies / Sally Nirenberg. New York: Simon & Schuster, 1990. 141 p., illus. "A Fireside Book." Recipes from the Night Kitchen restaurant in Brookline, Mass. Most of the recipes are for soups with a small number for stews and chilies. Includes index.

4012. Soups, Stews and Casseroles. New York?: Dial Pub. Co., c1990. 160 p. (Food Writers' Favorites). Includes index.

4013. Soups, Stews & Oven Lovin' Breads. Minneapolis, Minn.: Pillsbury Co., 1990. 93 p., colored illus. More than 100 recipes. (Classic Pillsbury Cookbooks; #109). "One-pot meals to team with warm hearty breads."

see also entry 935; Casseroles; Stews

Starters *see* **Appetizers**

Stews

4014. The Stew Cookbook / by Johnrae Earl and James McCormick. Los Angeles, Calif.: Price/Stern/Sloan, 1974. 158 p.

4015. Glorious Stew / by Dorothy Ivens; illustrated by the author; with wine notes and comment by William E. Massee. Rev. ed. New York: Harper & Row, c1976. 272 p., illus. Includes index.

4016. 500 Super Stews / Carol Truax. 1st ed. New York: Ballantine Books, 1977. 291 p. Includes index.

4017. This is Potjiekos / Matie Brink; with illustrations by Cora Coetzee; English translation by Willem Steenkamp. Cape Town, South Africa: Human & Rousseau, c1983. 59 p., illus. Includes index.

see also Casseroles; Soups and Stews

Stocks

4018. Out of the Stockpot / William J. Dunn. New York: Scribner, 1971. 295 p. illus.

4019. The Simmering Pot Cookbook / Alice Devine Loebel; photographs by Herbert Loebel; illustrations by Vladimir F. Hervert. Rev. and enl. ed. New York: Macmillan, 1974. 341 p., illus. Published in 1969 under title: The Stockpot and Steamer Cookbook.

see also Soups

Stuffed Foods

4020. The Roll 'em & Stuff 'em Cookbook: The Art of Filling & Saucing Gourmet Food / by Carol Reuter & Susan Freelund. New York: Sea Cliff Press, 1974. 305 p., illus.

Stuffed Foods *(Continued)*

4021. The Ready Aim Cookbook / Jo-ann Schoenfeld. New York: Hopkinson and Blake, c1976. 149 p., illus. Includes index.

Sushi

4022. The Book of Sushi / Kinjiro Omae, Yuzuru Tachibana; foreword by Jean-Pierre Rampal. 1st ed. Tokyo, Japan; New York: Kodansha International; New York: Distributed through Harper & Row, 1981. 127 p., illus. (some colored). Includes index.

4023. Sushi / Mia Detrick; photographs by Kathryn Kleinman. San Francisco, Calif.: Chronicle Books, 1981. 95 p., illus. (some colored). Includes index. A guide to the origins, varieties, customs, and etiquette of sushi.

4024. Sushi Made Easy / by Nobuko Tsuda; foreword by Donald Richie. 1st ed. New York: Weatherhill, 1982. 128 p., illus. (some colored). Includes indexes.

4025. The Sushi Handbook: A Guide to Eating Japan's Favorite Delicacy / by Kenji Kumagai. South San Francisco, Calif.: Heian International, 1983. 88 p., illus. (chiefly colored).

4026. Sushi at Home / edited by Kay Shimizu. Tokyo, Japan: Shufunotomo: Japan Publications; New York: Distributors, United States, Kodansha International/USA, c1984. 140 p., colored illus. Includes index.

4027. Sushi / Masuo Yoshino. Tokyo, Japan: Gakken Co., c1986. 96 p., illus. (some colored). Includes index.

4028. Sushi: A Light and Right Diet / Asako Kishi. Newly revised edition. Tokyo, Japan: Japan Publications Trading Co.; New York: Distributed by Harper & Row, 1986. 135 p.

Sushi *(Continued)*

4029. Step-by-Step Sushi: How to Prepare & Present a Host of Beautiful Japanese Dishes / Katsuji Yamamoto and Roger W. Hicks. New York: Gallery Books, 1990. 96 p., illus., colored photos. Includes index.

see also: Fish; *and* Rice *(Section I)*

Tapas

4030. Tapas: The Little Dishes of Spain / Penelope Casas; photographs by Tom Hopkins. 1st ed. New York: Knopf, 1985. 219 p., colored photos. More than 300 recipes. Includes index.

4031. Tapas, Wines & Good Times / Don and Marge Foster. Chicago, Ill.: Contemporary Books, c1986. 204 p., 8 p. of plates, colored illus. On cover: More than 200 recipes for entertaining. Includes index.

4032. Tapas and Appetizers / by Jose Sarrau; translated by Francesca Piemonte Slesinger. New York: Simon and Schuster, c1987. 192 p., illus. "A Fireside Book." Includes index. Translation of: Tapas y Aperitivos.

see also Appetizers; Snacks

Tarts *see* **Pastry; Pies**

Terrines *see* **Pâtés**

Tisanes *see* **Herbal Teas**

Specific Dishes and Courses

Tortillas

4033. The Tortilla Book / Diana Kennedy; drawings by Sidonie Coryn. 1st ed. New York: Harper & Row, 1975. 158 p., illus. 80 recipes. Includes index.

4034. The Art of Making Tortillas / by Mary Jasso. Likely, Calif.: Casa de Maria, c1982. 18 p.

4035. The Well-Filled Tortilla Cookbook / by Victoria Wise and Susanna Hoffman; illustrated by Lisa Henderling. New York: Workman Pub., 1990. 256 p., illus. More than 200 recipes, including tacos, burritos, tostadas, quesadillas, chimichangas, and enchiladas.

see also entry 452; and broader category: Bread

Turnovers

4036. Empanadas & Other International Turnovers: 60 Easy Low-Salt, Low-Fat Recipes / George & Sherry LaFollette Zabriskie. 1st ed. New York: C.N. Potter, c1983. 95 p., illus. Includes index.

see also broader category: Pastry

Waffles *see* Crepes and Pancakes

SECTION III

FROM BREAKFAST TO SUPPER
COOKBOOKS FOR SPECIFIC MEALS

Breakfasts

4037. The Breakfast Book / Kay Applegate. Santa Fe, N.M.: Lightning Tree, c1975. 80 p.

4038. The Good Breakfast Book / by Nikki and David Goldbeck; illustrated by Merle Cosgrove; foreword by Beatrice Trum Hunter. New York: Links: Distributed by Quick Fox, c1976. 206 p., illus. Includes index.

4039. The Good Morning Cook Book / Jill M. Phillips. Gretna, La.: Pelican Pub. Co., 1976. 134 p. Includes index.

4040. The Breakfast Book / David St. John Thomas. Newton Abbot, Eng.; North Pomfret, Vt.: David & Charles, c1980. 96 p., illus. Includes index.

4041. Sunrise: A Breakfast Cookbook Using Natural Foods and Whole Grains / by Diana Scesny Greene. Trumansburg, N.Y.: Crossing Press, c1980. 215 p., illus.

4042. Workday Breakfasts / by John W. Hansen; illustrations by Jodie Lucey Ahern. 1st ed. Minneapolis, Minn.: Hopewood Press, c1980. 128 p., illus. Includes index.

4043. Breakfasts for Lovers / Lu Lockwood; illustrated by Jill Coykendall Callaway. Old Saybrook, Conn.: Peregrine Press, c1981. 71 p., illus.

Breakfasts *(Continued)*

4044. The Great British Breakfast / Jan Read and Maite Manjon. London, Eng.: Joseph, 1981. 128 p., illus. (some colored).

4045. Better Breakfasts: A Healthy Wholefood Start to the Day / by Rachael Holme; illustrated by Clive Birch. Wellingborough, Eng.: Thorsons, 1982. 160 p., illus. (A Thorsons Wholefood Cookbook). Includes index.

4046. Rise and Shine: Breakfast Recipes for Children / prepared by the National Dairy Council; illustrations by Gerry Greaves. Stevenage, Eng.: Publications for Companies, 1982. 16 p., illus. (some colored).

4047. Glynn Christian's Best of Breakfast Time Cook Book. London, Eng.: British Broadcasting Corp., 1984. 64 p.

4048. Bread & Breakfast: The Best Recipes from North America's Bed & Breakfast Inns / Linda Kay Bristow; illustrations, Roy Killeen & others. San Francisco, Calif.: 101 Productions; New York: Distributed to the book trade in the U.S. by Scribner, c1985. 134 p., illus. 150 recipes. Includes index.

4049. The Breakfast Book / Diana Troy; illustrated by Belinda Murphy. London, Eng.: Allison & Busby, c1985. 160 p., illus. Includes index.

4050. The Breakfast Book / Diana Terry; with illustrations by Jean Saxby. London, Eng.: Futura, 1985, c1983. 127 p., illus. Includes index.

4051. Breakfasts, Ozark Style / compiled by Kay Cameron; edited by Patricia Brown; illustrated by Pat Crone. Point Lookout, Mo. (P.O. Box 526, Point Lookout 65726): KATYDID Publications, c1986. 165 p., illus. Includes index.

4052. Sunny Side Up / by Valiska Gregory; pictures by Jeni Bassett. 1st American ed. New York: Four Winds Press, c1986. 24 p., colored illus.

Breakfasts *(Continued)*

4053. Why Not Stay for Breakfast? / by Penny Dann. London, Eng.: Elm Tree Books/H. Hamilton, 1986. 57 p., colored illus.

4054. The American Country Inn and Bed & Breakfast Cookbook / Kitty and Lucian Maynard; Julia M. Pitkin, editor. Vol. 1. Nashville, Tenn.: Rutledge Hill Press, c1987. 510 p., illus. ca. 1700 recipes from more than 500 inns throughout the U.S. Vol. 2, 1990 contains 1850 recipes from 600 inns.

4055. The Breakfast Book / Marion Cunningham; illustrated by Donnie Cameron. 1st ed. New York: Knopf: Distributed by Random House, 1987. 320 p., illus. 288 recipes. Contains quotations relating to breakfast. Includes index.

4056. Cooking Inn Style: A Bed & Breakfast Guide & Bed & Breakfast Recipe Cookbook / by Sonnie Imes and the Bed & Breakfast Innkeepers of Northern California. Calistoga, Calif.: BBINC, c1987. 352 p., illus. Includes index.

4057. The Ultimate Breakfast / Phillip Scully and Annie Gilbar. 1st ed. New York: Weidenfeld & Nicolson, c1987. 200 recipes and menus. 288 p. Includes index.

4058. The London Ritz Book of English Breakfasts / Helen Simpson. 1st U.S. ed. New York: Arbor House/W. Morrow, c1988. 64 p., illus.

4059. What's for Breakfast? / Mary Anne Bauer. San Leandro, Calif.: Bristol Pub. Enterprises, c1988. 187 p., illus. (some colored). Includes index.

4060. Country Living, Country Mornings Cookbook / edited by Lucy Wing. New York: Hearst Books, 1989. 192 p., illus. (some colored). Includes index.

4061. Smart Breakfasts: 101 Delicious, Healthy Ways to Start the Day / Jane Kinderlehrer. New York: Newmarket Press, c1989. 192 p. Includes index.

Breakfasts *(Continued)*

4062. Ten Late Breakfasts / Alexandra Carlier. New York: Interlink Books, 1989, c1988. 128 p. Includes index.

4063. The Good Morning Macrobiotic Breakfast Book / Aveline Kushi, Wendy Esko. Garden City Park, N.Y.: Avery, 1990. 1 v. Includes bibliography and index.

4064. Popovers, Peaches, and Four-Poster Beds: A Hill Country Sampler of Delicious Ways to Start the Day / Patsy Swendson; illustrations by Debbie Little. 1st ed. Austin, Tex.: Eakin Press, c1990. 138 p., illus. More than 200 recipes from resorts, inns, and bed and breakfasts in East Texas. Includes index.

CHILDREN'S COOKBOOKS

4065. Breakfast / Tom and Jenny Watson. American ed. Chicago, Ill.: Childrens Press International, 1983, c1982. 64 p., colored illus. (What the World Eats). Includes index. Introduces breakfast habits in various countries around the world and includes several recipes and a brief discussion of food and health.

see also entry 2773

Breakfasts and Brunches

4066. Dinner in the Morning: A Collection of Breakfast and Brunch Recipes / by Elizabeth N. Shor, with lots of help from George G. Shor, Jr.; editor, Elizabeth Rand; illustrations, Dana Wooster. San Diego, Calif.: Tofua Press, 1977. 85 p., illus.

4067. Ideas & Recipes for Breakfast & Brunch. Menlo Park, Calif.: Lane Pub. Co., c1980. 96 p., illus.

4068. The Complete International Breakfast/Brunch Cookbook / Kay Shaw Nelson. New York: Stein and Day, 1982. 269 p. Includes index.

Specialty Cookbooks

Breakfasts and Brunches *(Continued)*

4069. Becky's Brunch & Breakfast Book: Recipes & Menus to Get Your Day Off to Its Very Best Start / Rebecca J. Walker. Austin, Tex.: R.J. Walker, 1983. 127 p., illus. Includes index.

4070. The Book of Great Breakfasts and Brunches / Terence Janericco. Boston, Mass.: CBI Pub. Co., c1983. 217 p., illus. Includes index.

4071. Breakfast & Brunch Dishes for the Professional Chef / Terence Janericco. Boston, Mass.: CBI Pub. Co., c1983. 106 p., colored illus. Includes index.

4072. Breakfasts and Brunches. Los Angeles, Calif.: Knapp Press, c1983. 119 p., colored photos. More than 200 recipes. (Cooking with Bon Appétit). Includes index.

4073. The Breakfast & Brunch Cookbook / Frederick E. Kahn; edited by Carla Neville Ciofalo. New York: Nautilus Communications; Aurora, Ill.: Distributed by Caroline House, c1984. 132 p., illus. (Preparing Food the Healthy Way Series).

4074. The Southern Heritage Breakfast and Brunch Cookbook. Birmingham, Ala.: Oxmoor House, c1984. 143 p., illus. (some colored). (The Southern Heritage Cookbook Library). Includes index.

4075. The American Bed & Breakfast Cookbook / the Bed Post Writers Group. Charlotte, N.C.: East Woods Press, c1985. 189 p., illus. Includes index.

4076. Bed & Breakfast Cookbook / by Pamela Lanier. Philadelphia, Pa.: Running Press, c1985. 138 p., illus. More than 165 recipes. Includes index.

4077. Breakfasts & Brunches / Cynthia Scheer, writer and food stylist; Jill Fox, project editor; Dennis Gray, photographer. San Francisco, Calif.: California Culinary Academy, c1985. 128 p., 70 colored illus. More than 170 recipes. Includes index.

Breakfasts and Brunches *(Continued)*

4078. Diabetic Breakfast & Brunch Cookbook / Mary Jane Finsand; foreword by James D. Healy. New York: Sterling Pub. Co, c1987. 160 p. More than 275 recipes. Includes index.

4079. Fresh Ways with Breakfasts & Brunches / by the editors of Time-Life Books. Alexandria, Va.: Time-Life Books, c1987. 144 p., colored illus. (Healthy Home Cooking). Includes index.

4080. Good Mornings: A Breakfast Cookbook / C. Lee Crawford. 1st ed. Toronto, Ont.: Doubleday Canada Ltd.; Garden City, N.Y.: Doubleday, 1987. 107 p., illus.

4081. James McNair's Breakfast / photography by Patricia Brabant. New York, Arbor House, c1987. 96 p., colored illus. 100 recipes. Includes index.

4082. Breakfast & Brunch Book / by Norman Kolpas. Los Angeles, Calif.: HP Books, c1988. 144 p., colored illus. Includes index.

4083. Wake Up and Smell the Coffee / Laura Zahn. St. Paul, Minn.: Down to Earth Publications; Stillwater, Minn.: Distributed by Voyageur Press, 1988. 223 p., illus. "Favorite breakfast and brunch recipes from the upper Midwest's best bed and breakfast inns where you can lie in bed and smell breakfast cooking."

4084. Better Homes and Gardens Brunches and Breakfasts. 1st ed. Des Moines, Iowa: Meredith Corp., 1989. 80 p., colored illus. (Better Homes and Gardens Test Kitchen). Includes index.

4085. Breakfast & Lunches. Minneapolis, Minn.: Pillsbury Co., 1989. 93 p., colored illus. (Classic Pillsbury Cookbooks; #103).

4086. Breakfast with Friends / by Elizabeth Alston. New York: McGraw-Hill, c1989. 224 p., colored illus. Includes menus.

Breakfasts and Brunches *(Continued)*

4087. Morning Food: From Café Beaujolais / by Margaret Fox & John Bear. Berkeley, Calif.: Ten Speed Press, c1989. 256 p., illus. 150 recipes. Includes index. "Favorite breakfast and brunch recipes from the legendary Café Beaujolais."

4088. The Book of Breakfasts & Brunches / by Kerenza Harries; photographed by Alan Newnham. Los Angeles, Calif.: HP Books, 1990. 120 p., colored illus. Includes index.

4089. Wake Up and Smell the Coffee / Pacific Northwest edition collected by Laura Zahn. St. Paul, Minn.: Down to Earth Publications, 1990. 175 p., illus. "Favorite breakfast and brunch recipes from the Pacific Northwest's best bed and breakfast inns where you can lie in bed and smell breakfast cooking."

see also Breakfasts; Brunches

Brunches

4090. Brunch / by Christie Williams; photographs by Glen Millward; illustrations by Mike Nelson. Concord, Calif.: Nitty Gritty Productions, c1981. 177 p., illus. (some colored). Includes index.

4091. Brunch Menus. Alexandria, Va.: Time-Life Books, c1984. 103 p., illus. (some colored). (Great Meals in Minutes). Includes index.

4092. All New Brunch Cookbook. Minneapolis, Minn.: Pillsbury Co., 1990. 93 p., colored illus. (Classic Pillsbury Cookbooks; #112).

see also Breakfasts and Brunches

Specific Meals 519

Buffets

4093. Better Homes and Gardens Best Buffets Cook Book. 1st ed. Des Moines, Iowa: Meredith Corp., 1974. 112 p., illus.

4094. Buffets and Receptions / Pierre Mengelatte, Walter Bickel, Albin Abelanet; editor, Michael Small; assistant editor, Mabel Quin. 3rd ed. London, Eng.: Virtue, 1980. 1221 p., illus. (some colored). Provides information on menu planning and serving suggestions as well as recipes. Includes indexes. Translation of: Buffets & Receptions.

4095. Country Inn Buffets: A Selection of Favorite Recipes from The Country Inns of America Cookbook. Los Angeles, Calif.: Knapp Press, c1980. 22 p., colored illus.

4096. The Woman's Day Buffet Cookbook / by Carol Truax. New York: Fawcett Columbine, 1982. 160 p., illus.

4097. The Art of Buffet Entertaining / Diana and Paul von Welanetz; illustrations by Adrienne Picchi. Los Angeles, Calif.: J.P. Tarcher; Boston, Mass.: Distributed by Houghton Mifflin, 1984, c1978. 228 p., illus. Includes index.

4098. Betty Crocker's Buffets. New York: Random House, c1984. 192 p., colored illus. 270 recipes and 67 menus. Includes index.

4099. Buffets. Los Angeles, Calif.: Knapp Press, c1984. 119 p., illus. (Cooking with Bon Appétit). Includes index.

4100. More Thoughts for Buffets. Boston, Mass.: Houghton Mifflin, 1984. 440 p. 775 recipes and 114 menus. Includes index.

4101. The Professional Chef's Book of Buffets / by George K. Waldner and Klaus Mitterhauser; edited by Jule Wilkinson. New York: CBI, 1985, 1971. 224 p., illus. Includes index.

4102. Buffets: A Guide for Professionals / Georges C. St. Laurent, Jr., Chet Holden. New York: Wiley, c1986. 368 p., 24 photos. More than 300 recipes. Includes bibliography and indexes.

Specialty Cookbooks

Buffets *(Continued)*

4103. Feasting with a Fork / Joan Wolfenden. Ventor, Isle of Wight, Eng.: Peacock Vane, 1986. 96 p.

4104. Buffets / Mary Berry. London, Eng.: Sphere, 1988. 189 p., illus. Includes index.

4105. Party Eats / Yan-Kit So and Paul Bloomfield. London, Eng.: Piatkus, 1988. 128 p.

4106. The Professional Chef's Art of Garde Manger / Frederic Sonnenschmidt, John F. Nicolas. 4th ed. New York: Van Nostrand Reinhold, c1988. 276 p., 16 p. of plates, illus. (some colored). Updated ed. of: Art of Garde Manger. Includes index.

4107. Family Buffet & Cocktail / Kuo Shu-hsien chu. Hong Kong: Po i ch'u pan chi t'uan yu hsien kung ssu, 1989. 126 p., colored illus. In Chinese and English.

4108. Successful Buffet Management / Ronald A. Yudd. New York: Van Nostrand Reinhold, 1989. 288 p. More than 100 photos and drawings and 130 menus. Includes index.

4109. Successful Cold Buffets / Peter Grotz; foreword by Raymond Blanc. English language ed. New York: Van Nostrand Reinhold, 1990. 175 p., colored photos. 108 recipes for appetizers, fish, fruit, game, and other foods. Contains information on purchasing, equipment, and schedules. Includes index.

see also entry 2663, 3770

Lunches

4110. Easy, Elegant Luncheon Menus / Beverly Barbour. Radnor, Pa.: Chilton Book Co., c1980. 264 p., 12 p. of plates, colored illus. Includes index.

Lunches *(Continued)*

4111. The Twelve-to-One Habit: Noon-Time Recipes for the Harried Cook and the Successful Hostess / by Ruth McPherson and Marilyn Cassidy. St. Catharines, Ont.: Stonehouse Publications, c1980. 106 p., illus. Includes index.

4112. The Perfect Sunday Lunch / Mary Berry. London, Eng.: Century, 1982. 224 p., illus. (some colored). Includes index.

4113. Marguerite Patten's Sunday Lunch Cookbook. Newton Abbot, Eng.: David & Charles, c1983. 120 p., illus. (some colored). Includes index.

4114. The Sunday Lunch Book / Elisabeth Ayrton. London, Eng.: Macdonald, 1984. 128 p.

4115. Better Homes and Gardens Kids' Lunches. 1st ed. Des Moines, Iowa: Meredith Corp., c1986. 80 p., colored illus. "Better Homes and Gardens Books." Includes index.

4116. Naked Ladies' Lunches: An Orgy of Eating / by Marina Beebe. San Francisco, Calif.: Gateway Books, c1987. 171 p., illus. Includes index.

4117. Ten Vineyard Lunches / Richard Olney. New York: Interlink Books, 1988. 128 p., colored illus. (The Ten Menus Series). Includes index.

4118. Lunches and Snacks / editor, Wendy Lazar. New York: Modern Publishing Division of Unisystems Inc., c1990. 64 p., illus. (Convenient Cooking). Includes index.

see also entry 4085

Lunches in a Bag or Box

4119. Sack It and Pack It / by Darcy Williamson. Bend, Or.: Maverick Publications, 1980. 268 p., illus.

Specialty Cookbooks

Lunches in a Bag or Box *(Continued)*

4120. Packed Lunches / Janet Ford. Wendover, Eng.: John Goodchild, 1983. 96 p.

4121. Packed Lunches / by Kate Hutchinson; photographs by Tim Clark. Loughborough, Eng.: Ladybird, 1983. 51 p., colored illus. (A Ladybird Cookery Book). Includes index.

4122. The Brown Bag Cookbook: Nutritious Portable Lunches for Kids and Grown-ups / by Sara Sloan; illustrated by Loretta Trezzo. Charlotte, Vt.: Williamson Pub. Co., c1984. 192 p., illus. Includes index.

4123. Lunch Box / Rosemary Povey. Dereham, Eng.: Rix, 1984. 35 p., illus.

4124. The Lunch Box Book / by Anne Gilbar. New York: Simon and Schuster, c1984. 95 p., illus. Includes index.

4125. Lunches to Go / by Janeen Sarlin. Woodbury, N.Y.: Barron's, c1984. 64 p., colored illus. (Easy Cooking). Includes index.

4126. The Natural Lunchbox / Runa and Victor Zurbel. 1st ed. New York: Holt, Rinehart and Winston, c1984. 148 p., illus. "An Owl Book." Includes index.

4127. Nutritious Brown Bag Lunches / Margaret E. Happel; edited by Leslie R. Keylock. Elgin, Ill.: Brethren Press, c1984. 160 p. 200 recipes. Includes index.

4128. Nutritious Packed Lunches for Children / Janet Ford. Wendover, Eng.: Bookward, 1984. 83 p.

4129. Better Homes and Gardens Brown Bagger's Cook Book / editor, Molly Culbertson. 1st ed. Des Moines, Iowa: Meredith Corp., c1985. 80 p., illus. (some colored). Includes index.

4130. The Box Lunch / Ingrid Juliana. Myers Flat, Calif.: I. Juliana, 1985. 40 p., illus.

Specific Meals

Lunches in a Bag or Box *(Continued)*

4131. The Lunchbox Book / by Patricia D. Exter; illustrated by Elizabeth Cawood Freeman. Ithaca, N.Y.: McBooks Press, c1985. 159 p., illus. Includes index.

4132. Packed Lunches and Picnics / Miranda Hall. London, Eng.: Piatkus, 1985. 96 p., illus. Includes index.

4133. The All Natural Brown Bagger's Cookbook / Darcy Williamson. Bend, Or.: Maverick Publications, 1986. 160 p., illus. (The All Natural Cookbook Series).

4134. Packed Lunches & Snacks: Delicious Recipes for the Diabetic's Lunch Box / Sue Hall. Wellingborough, Eng.: Thorsons, 1986. 112 p., illus. Includes index.

4135. The Vegetarian Lunchbox: Nutritious Packed Lunches and Hot Snacks / by Janet Hunt. Rev. ed. Wellingborough, Eng.: Thorsons, 1987. 128 p., illus. (some colored). Includes index. Previous ed. published as: The Wholefood Lunchbox, 1983.

4136. The Lunchbox Book / Emma-Lee Gow & Janet Smith. London, Eng.: Ebury, 1988. 63 p.

4137. The Penny Whistle Lunch Box Book / Meredith Brokaw & Annie Gilbar; designed and illustrated by Jill Weber. 1st ed. New York: Weidenfeld & Nicolson, c1989. 112 p., illus. Includes index.

4138. Lunch Box. Toronto, Ont.: Grolier, 1989. 1 v. (Microwave Magic). Includes index.

4139. Lunch Box Treats: 120 Recipes for Healthy, Fun Lunches That Really Make the Grade / Nancy Shodack. Austin, Tex.: Texas Monthly Press, c1989. 224 p., illus.

Specialty Cookbooks

Lunches in a Bag or Box *(Continued)*

4140. The Vegetarian Lunchbasket: 225 Easy, Nutritious Recipes for the Quality-Conscious Family on the Go / by Linda Haynes. Willow Springs, Mo.: NUCLEUS Publications, 1990. 200 p., illus. Includes bibliographical references.

see also entry 3885; and Sandwiches *(Section II)*

Afternoon Teas

4141. The National Trust & the West Country Tourist Board's Book of Afternoon Tea / edited by Marika Hanbury Tenison; with research by Jackie Gurney and Warren Davis. Newton Abbot, Eng.: David and Charles, 1980. 96 p., illus. Spine title: Book of Afternoon Tea. Includes index.

4142. The Afternoon Tea Cookbook / Linda Hewitt; illustrations by Robert G. Hewitt. New York: Stein and Day, 1982. 335 p., illus. Includes indexes.

4143. Crumpets and Scones / Iris Ihde Frey. 1st ed. New York: St. Martin's Press, c1982. 161 p., illus. Includes bibliography and index.

4144. Just for Tea / compiled by Gaye Hansen. North Vancouver, B.C.: Just Muffins, 1982, c1978. 61 p. (Just Series).

4145. Come for Tea: Ideas & Recipes for Casual & Festive Occasions / writing, collection, book design & illustrations by Jacquelyn Smyers. Abernathy, Tex.: The Very Idea, c1985. 122 p., illus.

4146. The London Ritz Book of Afternoon Tea: The Art and Pleasure of Taking Tea / Helen Simpson. New York: Arbor House, c1986. 64 p., illus. Includes index.

Specific Meals

Afternoon Teas *(Continued)*

4147. Boston Tea Parties: Recipes from the Museum of Fine Arts, Boston / compiled and edited by Judith F. Chamberlain and Janet R. Sears. Boston, Mass.: The Museum, c1987. 162 p., illus. (some colored). Includes index.

4148. Having Tea: Recipes & Table Settings / Tricia Foley; photographs by Keith Scott Morton; written by Catherine Calvert; design by Rita Marshall. 1st ed. New York: C.N. Potter: Distributed by Crown Publishers, c1987. 87 p., illus. (some colored). Includes index.

4149. The Pleasures of Afternoon Tea / Angela Hynes. Tucson, Ariz.: HP Books, c1987. 160 p., colored illus. Includes index.

4150. A Proper Tea / devised and illustrated by Joanna Isles. 1st U.S. ed. New York: St. Martin's Press, c1987. 95 p., colored illus. Includes index.

4151. Taking Tea: The Essential Guide to Brewing, Serving, and Entertaining with Teas from Around the World / Andrea Israel; with original recipes by Pamela Mitchell. 1st ed. New York: Weidenfeld & Nicolson, 1987. 144 p., colored illus.

4152. Jane Pettigrew's Tea Time: A Complete Collection of Traditional Recipes. London, Eng.: Dorling Kindersley, 1988, c1986. 144 p., illus. (some colored). Includes index.

4153. Ridgways: The Complete Tea Book. London, Eng.: Ebury, 1988. 95 p.

4154. Teatime at Airthrey / edited by Susan Ward and Barbara Waddell for the Airthrey Gardens Group of the University of Stirling. Stirling, Scot.: The Group, 1988. 56 p.

4155. Teatime Celebrations / Patricia Gentry, author; Jane Horn, editor; Craig Mohr, principal photographer. San Ramon, Calif.: 101 Productions: Distributed by Ortho Information Services, c1988. 143 p., illus. (some colored). Includes index.

Afternoon Teas *(Continued)*

4156. The Afternoon Tea Book / Michael Smith; illustrations by Michael R.P. Bartlett. 1st Collier Books ed. New York: Collier Books, 1989, c1986. 275 p., illus. Contains recipes for sandwiches, buns, scones, and crumpets. Includes index.

4157. The Book of Tea / by John Beilenson; illustrated by Michel Design. White Plains, N.Y.: Peter Pauper Press, c1989. 63 p., illus.

4158. The Complete Book of Teas / Marguerite Patten. London, Eng.: Piatkus, 1989. 144 p.

4159. A Little English Book of Teas / by Rosa Mashiter; illustrated by Milanda Lopez. San Francisco, Calif.: Chronicle Books, 1989. 60 p., colored illus. 30 recipes. Includes index.

4160. Tea with Mrs. Beeton. London, Eng.: Ward Lock, 1990. 47 p.

Dinners

4161. Sunday Dinner: Meals from Family Kitchens / Lora Lee Parrott; illustrated by Crandall Vail. Kansas City, Mo.: Beacon Hill Press of Kansas City, c1979. 302 p., illus.

4162. Dinner Can be a Picnic All Year Round: Meatless Recipes / by Sharon Elliot; illustrations by Tonia Macneil. 1st ed. Palo Alto, Calif.: Fresh Press, 1981. 128 p., illus. Includes index.

4163. Dinner for Two: Recipes, Menus & Techniques for the Easy Preparation of Elegant Dinners for Two / by Rick Leed. 1st ed. San Francisco, Calif.: Gay Sunshine Press, 1981. 157 p.

4164. Dining Customs Around the World: With Occasional Recipes / by Alice Bonzi Mothershead; with illustrations by Marilena Perrone. Garrett Park, Md.: Garrett Park Press, c1982. 150 p., illus. Includes index.

Specific Meals 527

Dinners *(Continued)*

4165. Dining in: 52 Dinner Menus from the Herald's Mike Henderson / illustrated by Glen Oberg. Everett, Wash.: Daily Herald Co., c1982. 110 p., illus. Includes index.

4166. The San Francisco Dinner Party Cookbook / Judith Ets-Hokin; illustrated by Maryanne Regal Hoburg. Millbrae, Calif.: Celestial Arts, c1982. 254 p., illus. Includes index.

4167. Bon Appétit Dinner Party Cookbook. Los Angeles, Calif.: Knapp Press, c1983. 276 p., colored illus. Includes index.

4168. Dinner Menus with Wine / by Emily Chase; editor, Marjorie Kent Jacobs; assistant editor, Elizabeth Bannerman; illustrator, Nancy J. Kennedy. San Francisco, Calif.: Wine Appreciation Guild, c1983. 126 p., illus. Includes index. Rev. ed. of: Wine Cookbook of Dinner Menus / by Emily Chase. c1978.

4169. Dinners in a Scottish Castle / The Lady Glentruim. Edinburgh, Scot.: Harris, 1983. 72 p., illus. (some colored).

4170. Quick and Easy 10 Minute Dinners / by Barbara Tucker-Pursley. 1st ed. New York: Tribeca Communications, 1983. 90 p., illus. Includes index.

4171. Betty Crocker's Dinner for Two Cookbook. Rev. ed. New York: Golden Press; Racine, Wis.: Western Pub. Co., c1984. 96 p., colored illus. Includes index. Rev. ed. of: Betty Crocker's Dinner for Two. c1977.

4172. Betty Crocker's Family Dinners in a Hurry. Rev. ed. with recipes selected from the original edition. New York: Golden Press, c1984. 96 p., illus. (some colored). Includes index.

4173. Vegetarian Dinner Parties / by Leon Lewis. 1st U.S. ed. New York: Thorsons Publishers: Distributed to the trade by Inner Traditions International, 1984. 160 p., illus. Includes index.

Dinners *(Continued)*

4174. Christopher Idone's Glorious American Food / photographs by Tom Eckerle; food assistant, Rena Coyle; wine consultant, Penelope Wisner. 1st ed. New York: Random House, c1985. 359 p., colored illus. "A Welcome Book." Includes index.

4175. Prue Leith's Dinner Parties / illustrated by Vivien Ashley. London, Eng.: Macmillan, 1985, c1984. 192 p., illus. Includes index.

4176. Successful Dinner Parties / Robert Carrier. London, Eng.: Marshall Cavendish, 1985. 112 p., colored illus. (Robert Carrier's Kitchen). Includes index.

4177. Cooking for Dinner Parties / Janice Murfitt. London, Eng.: Orbis: 1986, c1984. 95 p., colored illus. Includes index.

4178. Dinner Parties / Theodor Bottiger. Twickenham, Eng.: Hamlyn, 1986. 64 p., colored illus. (Hamlyn Favourite Cookbooks). Includes index. Translation of: Gourmet Menus für Gäste und Feste.

4179. The Dinner Party Book: Planned Menus for Busy Gourmets / Alexandra Carlier. London, Eng.: Collins, 1986. 200 p., illus. Includes index.

4180. Florence Fabricant's Pleasures of the Table: Innovative Menus for Entertaining, Easily Prepared Recipes, and the Wines to Serve with Them / introduction by Sam Aaron; with photographs by Matthew Klein. New York: Abrams, 1986. 175 p., colored illus. Includes index.

4181. The International Dinner Party Cookbook / by Jan Bilton. London, Eng.: Piatkus, 1986, c1985. 15 p. Includes index. Originally published: The New Zealand Dinner Party Cookbook. Auckland, N.Z.: Endeavour, 1985.

4182. Tiffany Taste / by John Loring. 1st ed. Garden City, N.Y.: Doubleday, 1986. 223 p., illus.

Specific Meals

Dinners *(Continued)*

4183. Ann Long's Dinner Party Book. London, Eng.: Hodder and Stoughton, 1987. 224 p., illus.

4184. Dinner's Ready / Daphne Metaxas Hartwig. New York: Macmillan; London, Eng.: Collier Macmillan, c1987. 230 p. "A Bobbs-Merrill Book." Includes index.

4185. Feasts of Wine and Food / William Rice; photography, Rudy Muller. 1st ed. New York: Morrow, c1987. 159 p., illus. (some colored). Includes indexes.

4186. Good Friends, Great Dinners: 32 Menus for Casual Entertaining / Susan Costner, with Camilla Turnbull; photographs by Faith Echtermeyer. 1st ed. New York: Crown Publishers, c1987. 224 p., colored illus. Includes index.

4187. Ten Dinner Parties for Two / Frances Bissell. London, Eng.: Ebury, 1988. 128 p. Includes menus.

4188. Come for Dinner II. Minneapolis, Minn.: Pillsbury Co., 1989. 93 p., colored illus. Contains recipes for 10 meals. (Classic Pillsbury Cookbooks; #95).

4189. Dinner Inspirations: Classic, Country, & Contemporary Entrees Made Simple / Faye Levy. 1st ed. New York: Dutton, c1989. ca. 400 p., illus. More than 150 recipes. (Fresh from France). Includes index.

4190. Enjoy!: Make-ahead Dinner Menus / Nina Graybill and Maxine Rapoport. Washington, D.C.: Farragut Pub. Co., 1989. 192 p.

4191. Serve it Forth / M.F.K. Fisher. San Francisco, Calif.: North Point Press, 1989, c1937. 146 p. Originally published: New York: Harper, 1937.

Dinners *(Continued)*

4192. Dinner Party: The New Entertaining / Jane Freiman; photographs by Jerry Simpson. 1st ed. New York: Harper & Row, c1990. 477 p., illus. (some colored). More than 200 recipes and 150 menus. Includes index.

Suppers

4193. Easy Suppers / by Pat Jester. Tucson, Ariz.: HP Books, c1980. 160 p., colored illus. Includes index.

4194. Super Suppers: Soup, Salad, and Pasta / a collection of recipes by Ursel Norman; designed and illustrated by Derek Norman. London, Eng.: Collins, 1982. 176 p., illus. (chiefly colored). Includes index.

4195. The Supper Book / Elizabeth Kent; illustrations by David Green. London, Eng.: Fontana, 1983, c1982. 256 p., illus. Includes index.

4196. Suppers & Snacks. Newton Abbot, Eng.: David & Charles, c1983. 64 p., colored illus. (Kitchen Workshop). Includes index. Translation of: Smaretter.

4197. Fast Suppers / Mary Berry. London, Eng.: Sphere, 1984, c1982. 192 p. Includes index.

4198. Late-Night Supper Menus. Alexandria, Va.: Time-Life Books, c1985. 105 p., colored illus. (Great Meals in Minutes). Includes index.

4199. The Supper Book / Diana Terry; with illustrations by Jean Saxby. Christchurch, N.Z.; London, Eng.: Whitcoulls, 1985, c1983. 127 p., illus. Includes index.

4200. Suppers and Snacks / Carol Bowen. Tucson, Ariz.: HP Books, c1985. 80 p., colored illus. ca. 100 recipes. (Creative Cuisine). Includes index.

Suppers *(Continued)*

4201. Sunday Suppers: Informal American Home Cooking / Melanie Barnard and Brooke Dojny. 1st ed. New York: Prentice Hall Press, c1988. 276 p., 20 line drawings. Includes index.

4202. Let's Eat In: Quick and Delicious Weekday Meals / Brooke Dojny and Melanie Barnard. 1st ed. New York: Prentice Hall Press, 1990. 257 p. Includes index.

SECTION IV

BAKING...FREEZING...STIR-FRYING COOKBOOKS FOR SPECIAL TECHNIQUES

Baking

4203. Food Processor Baking Magic / by Mary Moon Hemingway and Suzanne De Lima; illustrations by Sheilia Camera. New York: Hastings House, c1978. 222 p., illus. Includes index.

4204. Baking / edited by Jean Prince. London, Eng.: Octopus Books, 1980. 92 p., colored illus. Cover title: The Colour Book of Baking. Includes index.

4205. Best of Baking / Annette Wolter, Christian Teubner. Tucson, Ariz.: HP Books, c1980. 224 p., colored illus. Includes index. Translation of: Backvergnugen wie Noch Nie.

4206. Dutch Baking and Pastry / H. Menkveld. London, Eng.: Applied Science Publishers, 1980. 159 p., illus. Includes index.

4207. The Whole Grain Bake Book / by Gail L. Worstman. 2nd ed. Seattle, Wash.: Pacific Search Press, c1980. 119 p. Includes index. First ed. published in 1976 under title: You Knead It.

4208. Amish Treats from My Kitchen / by Sallie Lapp; illustrations by Rodger Melnick. Gordonville, Pa.: S. Lapp, c1981. 47 p., illus. Includes index.

4209. The Any Oven Cookbook: Microwave/Conventional Recipes from Saran Wrap. New York: Benjamin Co., c1981. 160 p., colored illus. Includes index.

Baking *(Continued)*

4210. The Baker's Formula and Procedure Manual: The Success of Baking / by Lennart Erik Jansson. San Diego, Calif.: Sea Lion Publications, 1981. 118 p., colored illus. Includes index.

4211. Baking / Mala Young. Newton Abbot, Eng.: David & Charles, c1981. 48 p., illus. (Health Food Cooking).

4212. The Baking Book / Lloyd Moxon; illustrations, Joseph D'Addetta. New York: Culinary Arts Institute, c1981. 255 p., illus. Includes index.

4213. Blue Ribbon Winner's Bakebook / by Fredlyn Kruglak; illustrations by Bruce Radtke. Milwaukee, Wis.: Bakebooks & Cookbooks, 1981, c1980. 320 p., illus. 275 recipes, some of which won blue ribbons at the Wisconsin State Fair.

4214. The Complete All-in-the-Oven Cookbook / Dolores Riccio & Joan Bingham. New York: Stein and Day, 1981. 381 p.

4215. The Robin Hood Canadian Flour Cook Book: A Collection of New and Traditional Canadian Baking Recipes Made from Canadian Flour. Vancouver, B.C.: Robin Hood Multifoods Limited, 1981, c1967. 183 p. in various pagings, colored illus.

4216. Baking at Home / Christian Teubner. London, Eng.: Hamlyn, c1982. 79 p., colored illus. (Hamlyn Kitchen Shelf). Includes index. Translation of: Back-Vergnugen Leicht Gemacht.

4217. Favorite Home Baking Recipes. London, Eng.: Sedgewood Press, 1982. 215 p., illus. (some colored). Includes index.

4218. The Great Day Cookbook. Doylestown, Pa.: Quixott Press, 1982. 91 p., illus. Introduction signed: Velia Dean and Barbara B.J. Zimmerman. Available from Women's International League for Peace and Freedom, Box 147, Richboro, Pa. 18954.

Baking *(Continued)*

4219. The Italian Bakery / by Lee Mangione Cirillo; illustrated by Barbara Cirillo. Rochester, N.Y. (P.O. Box 17160, Rochester 14617): Cirillo's Cooking School, 1982. 208 p., illus. Includes index.

4220. Saskatchewan Ethnic Baking: Published for the Town of Humboldt's 75th Anniversary 1907-1982: A Collection of Ethnic Recipes from Saskatchewan Kitchens / edited by Clara Eckert. Humboldt, Sask.: Humboldt Journal, 1982. 216 p., colored illus. Includes index.

4221. All Colour Home Baking / Elizabeth Pomeroy. London, Eng.: Octopus, 1983, c1979. 159 p., colored illus. Includes index.

4222. Baking is Fun. Mississauga, Ont.: Oetker, c1983-. 6 v., colored illus. Includes indexes.

4223. Breads, Pastries, Pies and Cookies: Quantity Baking Recipes / Nathan S. Cotton. Boston, Mass.: CBI Pub. Co., c1983. 292 p. Includes index.

4224. Gottlieb's Bakery Since 1884: 100 Years of Recipes or 100 Years of "Is it Fresh?" / compiled and tested by Sarah Gaede; with Irving and Isser Gottlieb. Savannah, Ga.: Gottlieb's Bakery, c1983. 131 p., illus. More than 150 recipes.

4225. Hamlyn All Colour Book of Home Baking / Carol Bowen. London, Eng.: Hamlyn, c1983. 125 p., colored illus. Includes index.

4226. Sedgewood Book of Baking. New York: Sedgewood Press: Distributed by Van Nostrand Reinhold, c1983. 191 p., colored illus. Includes index.

4227. Sonia Allison's Home Baking Book / Sonia Allison. Newton Abbot, Eng.; North Pomfret, Vt.: David & Charles, c1983. 255 p., illus. (some colored). Includes index.

Baking *(Continued)*

4228. The Sugarless Baking Book: The Natural Way to Prepare America's Favorite Breads, Pies, Cakes, Puddings, and Desserts / Patricia Terris Mayo; illustrated by Richard Spencer. Boulder, Colo.: Shambhala; New York: Distributed in the U.S. by Random House, 1983, c1979. 116 p., illus. Includes index. Originally published: Brookline, Mass.: Autumn Press, c1979.

4229. Sweet Remembrances: Recipes to Treasure: A Friends of Bon Ami Cookbook / edited & compiled by Cathy Beaham. Kansas City, Mo.: Faultless Starch/Bon Ami Co., c1983. 101 p.

4230. The Art of Fine Baking / Paula Peck; drawings by Grambs Miller. New York: Simon & Schuster, 1984, c1961. 320 p., illus. "A Fireside Book." Includes index.

4231. The Bakers' Manual / by Bert J. Phillips. 3rd ed. Burnaby, B.C.: Pacific Vocational Institute, 1984, c1983. 1 v. (various pagings), illus. Includes index.

4232. Bakery Specialities / A.B. Barrows. London, Eng.; New York: Elsevier Applied Science Publishers, c1984. 324 p., illus.

4233. Baking Easy & Elegant. Tucson, Ariz.: HP Books, c1984. 240 p., colored illus. Includes index. Translation of: Das Beste Dr. Oetker Backbuch.

4234. The Fannie Farmer Baking Book / by Marion Cunningham; illustrated by Lauren Jarrett. 1st ed. New York: Knopf: Distributed by Random House, c1984. 624 p., illus. 800 recipes. Includes index.

4235. Farm Journal's Country Fair Cookbook: Prizewinning Recipes / edited by Elise W. Manning. New York: Gramercy Pub. Co.: Distributed by Crown Publishers, 1984, c1975. 225 p. Includes index. Originally published: Country Fair Cookbook. 1st ed. Garden City, N.Y.: Doubleday, c1975.

Baking *(Continued)*

4236. Keys to Successful Baking / by Diane Phillips. Silver Spring, Md.: American Cooking Guild, c1984. 64 p.

4237. Marguerite Patten's Successful Baking. London, Eng.: Collins, 1984. 219 p., illus. (some colored). Includes index.

4238. Recipes from the Raleigh Tavern Bake Shop. Williamsburg, Va.: Colonial Williamsburg Foundation, c1984. 29 p.

4239. The Upper Canada Village Flour and Grist Mill Cookbook / Gay Cook. Toronto, Ont.: NC Press, 1984. 1 v.

4240. Whole Grain Baking / Diana Scesny Greene. Trumansburg, N.Y.: Crossing Press, c1984. 183 p., illus. Includes bibliography and index.

4241. Wholefood Baking / Sarah Bounds; illustrations by Elaine Hill; photography by Dave Jordan. Feltham, Eng.: Hamlyn, c1984. 124 p., illus. (some colored). (Here's Health). Includes index.

4242. Busy Mum's Baking Book / Wendy Craig. Twickenham, Eng.: Hamlyn, 1985. 144 p., illus. (some colored). Includes index.

4243. Danish Home Baking: Traditional Danish Recipes / compiled by Kaj Viktor og Kirsten Hansen and edited by Karen Berg. 8th ed. Copenhagen, Denmark: Host, 1985. 85 p., colored illus. Includes index.

4244. Delicious Baking / Mary Cadogan. Tucson, Ariz.: HP Books, c1985. 80 p., colored illus. (Creative Cuisine). Includes index.

4245. The Italian Baker / by Carol Field. 1st ed. New York: Harper & Row, c1985. 443 p., illus. Includes index.

4246. Italian Baking and Pastry Book / by A. Croce; editor, Pauline Orr. Saratoga, Calif.: A.P.C. Enterprize, 1985. 57 p.

Baking *(Continued)*

4247. Kelly's Kitchen Presents Pride of America: Featuring Recipes from State and County Fairs / by Kelly Herman. Tallahassee, Fla. (Rt. 19, Box 1152, Tallahassee 32308): Hall Herman Promotions, c1985. 1 v., illus. Cover title: Pride of America. Includes index.

4248. Professional Baking / Wayne Gisslen. New York: Wiley, c1985. 346 p., ca. 200 illus. and colored photos. More than 400 recipes. Includes index. Originally published as a college and vocational school textbook.

4249. The Simple Art of Perfect Baking / Flo Braker; illustrations by Kristee Kreitman. 1st ed. New York: Morrow, c1985. 506 p., illus. 112 recipes. Contains complete instructions for all aspects of baking. Includes index.

4250. Bake Your Way to a Better Diet / Jane Inglis. 2nd ed. Potters Bar, Eng.: Oakroyd, c1986. 15 p.

4251. Baking for Health / Linda Edwards; illustrations by Lyn Giles. Bridport, Eng.: Prism, c1986. 207 p., illus. Includes bibliography and index.

4252. Baking: Practice Tested Techniques and Achieve Perfection. Twickenham, Eng.: Hamlyn, 1986. 287 p., colored illus. Includes index. Translated from the German.

4253. The Complete Book of Baking. New York: Crescent Books: Distributed by Crown Publishers, 1986, c1985. 320 p., illus. (some colored). Includes index.

4254. The Country Fare Cookbook / by Judie MacBeath-Howes. Saint John, N.B.: J. MacBeath-Howes, c1986. 89 p., illus.

4255. Favourite Recipes from the U.B.C. Bakeshop, "Home of the Famous Cinnamon Bun" / editor, Shirley Louie: graphic design, Heather Aston Moore. Vancouver, B.C.: University of British Columbia, Food Services, 1986. 26 p., illus.

Baking *(Continued)*

4256. The Greyston Bakery Cookbook / by Helen Glassman and Susan Postal; photographs by Lou Manna; illustrations by Lynn Wohlers. 1st ed. Boston, Mass.: Shambhala; New York: Distributed by Random House, 1986. 148 p., illus. (some colored). More than 80 recipes, from the Zen Community's New York bakery. Includes index.

4257. The Joy of Baking / by Barbara Grunes. Nashville, Tenn.: Ideals, c1986. 238 p., colored illus. Includes index. Translation of: Backen Macht Freude.

4258. Julia Aitken's Baker's Secret: Quick & Easy Baking. Toronto, Ont.: Grosvenor House Press, 1986. 152 p., illus. (some colored).

4259. Mrs. McLintock's Receipts for Cookery and Pastry-Work: First published 1736 / reproduced from the original with an introduction and glossary by Iseabail Macleod. Aberdeen, Scot.: Aberdeen University Press, 1986. 62 p.

4260. The Wholegrain Oven / Christopher & Jean Conil. London, Eng.: Foulsham, c1986. 126 p., illus. (some colored).

4261. Baking: Cakes, Cookies, Breads, Pastries / Arnold Zabert, originator and photographer; Martina Meuth, recipe format, writer of text. Tucson, Ariz.: HP Books, 1987. 277 p., colored illus. Includes index. Translation of: Backen, die Neue Grosse Schule.

4262. Baking and Roasting / Li Tseng P'eng-chan chu. Ch'u pan. Hong Kong: Po i ch'u pan chi t'uan yu hsien kung sau, 1987. 124 p., colored illus. In Chinese and English.

4263. Baking Treasures from Grandma's Farm Kitchen: Delicious Breads, Luscious Cakes and Frostings, Variety of Loaf Cakes, Fruit Cakes and Muffins with Detailed Step by Step Instructions / by Carole Baraniski Wells. Calgary, Alta.: Grandma's Farm Kitchen Pub., c1987. 216 p., colored illus.

Baking *(Continued)*

4264. Best of Bazaar Baking--and More / compiled by Doris Rauch; illustrated by Judy Budovitch. Fredericton, N.B.: Lillian Freiman Chapter of Hadassah-Wizo, 1987. 36 p., illus.

4265. Easy Baking / by Libuse Schraeder; illustrated by Mary Ward. Sault Ste. Marie, Ont.: Tyro Pub., c1987. 151 p., illus.

4266. Get Your Buns in Here: Recipes for Mouthwatering Buns / Laurel A. Wicks. Berkeley, Calif.: Ten Speed Press, c1987. 134 p., illus. 100 recipes for cake, candy, cookies, desserts, muffins, pastries, rolls, etc.

4267. Jim Fobel's Old-Fashioned Baking Book: Recipes from an American Childhood. 1st ed. New York: Ballantine Books, 1987. 207 p., illus. Includes index.

4268. McDougalls Better Baking. Reading, Eng.: McDougalls Home Baking Advisory Service, 1987. 62 p.

4269. The McVitie's Book of Better Baking / Mary Norwak. Cambridge, Eng.: Martin Books in association with UB (Biscuits), 1987. 128 p., illus. (some colored). More than 150 recipes. Includes index.

4270. Baking Cookbook. New York: Crescent Books, 1988. 128 p., 145 colored photos. (Good Cook's Library). "More than 150 tempting recipes for creating breads, cakes, cookies, and pastries with a guide to selecting and using natural ingedients, grains, and flours". Includes index.

4271. The Country Bakehouse / Christopher Conil. Wiltshire, Eng.: Crowood, 1988. 192 p., illus.

4272. The Farmhouse Kitchen Baking Book / Grace Mulligan. London, Eng.: Collins, 1988. 275 p.

Baking *(Continued)*

4273. Festive Baking: Holiday Classics in the Swiss, German, and Austrian Tradition / Sarah Kelly Iaia. 1st ed. in the U.S. New York: Doubleday, 1988. 352 p., illus. Includes index. Revision of: Festive Baking in Austria, Germany, and Switzerland.

4274. From a Baker's Kitchen: Techniques and Recipes for Professional Quality Baking in the Home Kitchen / by Gail Sher; illustrated by Mimi Osborne. Berkeley, Calif.: Aris Books; Reading, Mass.: Addison-Wesley Pub. Co., 1988, c1984. 219 p., illus. Includes index.

4275. The Great Scandinavian Baking Book / by Beatrice Ojakangas; illustrated by Rudy Luoma. 1st ed. Boston, Mass.: Little, Brown, c1988. 318 p., illus. Includes index.

4276. Cookies and Conversation: Tasty and Nutritious Baking from Judy's Kitchen / recipes and hand-lettering by Judy Wandschneider. Enterprise, Or.: Pika Press, c1988. 112 p., illus. Includes index.

4277. The New Baking / Caroline Liddell. London, Eng.: Bloomsbury, 1988. 192 p.

4278. The Best of Baking: Includes More Than 400 Easy and Delicious Recipes for Bread, Cakes, Cookies, Pies, and Pastries with 200 Full-Color Photographs. New York: International Culinary Society, 1989. 336 p. Includes index. Translated by Judith Geerke from the original German edition: Backen Leicht und Gut das Ganze Jahr.

4279. The Gift Giver's Cookbook / Judith Choate, Jane Green. Rev. ed., 1st ed. New York: Weidenfeld & Nicolson, 1989. 144 p., colored illus. Includes index. Authors' names in reverse order in 1971 ed.

4280. Good Housekeeping Complete Book of Home Baking. London, Eng.: Ebury, 1989. 234 p.

Baking *(Continued)*

4281. Martha White's Southern Sampler: Ninety Years of Baking Tradition. Nashville, Tenn.: Rutledge Hill Press, 1989. 222 p., illus. (some colored). Recipes from Martha White Foods.

4282. Perfect Yeast Baking / by Winnie. Morris, Man.: Maple Grove, 1989. 32 p., illus.

4283. Practical Baking / William J. Sultan. 5th ed. New York: Van Nostrand Reinhold, 1989. 822 p. Includes bibliography and index.

4284. The WI Book of Baking. London, Eng.: Ebury, 1989. 256 p. (Women's Institute Cookery Series).

4285. The Allergy Baker / by Carol Rudoff; foreword by Vincent A. Marinkovich; cover by Deborah Cotter. 3rd ed. Menlo Park, Calif.: Allergy Publications, c1990. 114 p., illus. Includes index.

4286. Baking with Yeast with Schmecks Appeal / Edna Staebler. Toronto, Ont.: McClelland & Stewart, c1990. 1 v.

4287. Better Homes and Gardens Old-Fashioned Home Baking. Des Moines, Iowa: Meredith Corp., 1990. 312 p., 112 colored photos, and 57 instructive photos. More than 300 recipes with step-by-step directions. Includes index and charts listing calories, protein, carbohydrates, fats, cholesterol, and sodium content for each recipe.

4288. Betty Crocker's Baking Classics. 1st ed. New York: Prentice Hall, c1990. 112 p., colored photos. More than 120 recipes. Includes index. "Originally published in 1979 by General Mills, Inc., as the Gold Medal Century of Success Cookbook and distributed in response to Gold Medal flour offers."

4289. Biscuits, Spoonbread, and Sweet Potato Pie: The Glories of 300 Years of Southern Baking / by Bill Neal. 1st ed. New York: Knopf, 1990. 312 p., 60 photos. 300 recipes. (Knopf Cooks American Series; 2). Includes index.

Baking *(Continued)*

4290. Christmas Baking: Traditional Recipes Made Easy / Christian Teubner. Hauppage, N.Y.: Barron's, 1990. 96 p., 40 colored photos.

4291. Country Baking: Simple Home Baking with Wholesome Grains and the Pick of the Harvest / Ken Haedrich. New York: Bantam Books, c1990. 352 p. More than 250 recipes.

4292. Country Baking: Delicious Pies, Cakes, Cookies, Breads, and More for All Occasions. Alexandria, Va.: Time-Life Books, 1990. 175 p., illus. (American Country). "A Rebus Book."

4293. Home Baking: 36 Holiday Make-Ahead Recipes. Minneapolis, Minn.: Pillsbury Co., 1990. 94 p., colored illus. (Classic Pillsbury Cookbooks; #117).

4294. Home Bakings: Recipes for Cakes, Cookies, Pastry, and Breads / Carole Handslip, Brian Binns. London, Eng.: Hamlyn, 1990, c1980. 95 p., colored illus. (The Kitchen Library). Includes index.

4295. Kathleen's Bake Shop Cookbook / Kathleen King. New York: St. Martin's Press, 1990. 128 p., illus. 100 recipes. The best recipes from Kathleen's Bake Shop in Southampton, N.Y.

4296. The Pillsbury Bake-Off Cookbook. New York: Doubleday, 1990. 1st ed. 192 p., colored illus. Includes index. Collection of 40 years of contest recipes.

4297. The Professional Bakers' Manual / John Gnos [and others]. 2nd ed. Vancouver, B.C.: Vancouver Community College Press, 1990. 1 v.

4298. Uprisings: The Whole Grain Bakers' Book / by the Cooperative Whole Grain Education Association. Rev. ed. Summertown, Md.: Book Pub. Co., c1990. 288 p., illus. 200 recipes for breads, cakes, muffins, and granolas from 32 bakeries. Includes bibliography and index.

Baking *(Continued)*

CHILDREN'S COOKBOOKS

4299. My First Baking Book / by Rena Coyle; illustrated by Tedd Arnold. New York: Workman Pub., c1988. 142 p., illus. (some colored). (Bialosky & Friends). Includes index. Simple directions and step-by-step drawings for 50 treats.

see also ingredients in Section I used in baking, e.g.: Flour, Grains, Yeast; *and dishes in Section II requiring baking, e.g.:* Bread, Cakes, Cookies, Pastry, Pies, etc.

Barbecuing, Broiling, and Grilling

4300. Barbeque: The Fine Art of Charcoal, Gas, and Hibachi Cooking / editor, Carol D. Brent; art director, Dick Collins; photography by Bill Miller. 1st ed. Chicago, Ill.: Tested Recipe Publishers; Garden City, N.Y.: Distribution by Doubleday, 1971. 64 p., colored illus.

4301. Barbecuing the Weber Covered Way / editor, Carol D. Brent; art director, Dick Collins; photography by Bill Miller. 1st ed. Chicago, Ill.: Published for the Weber-Stephen Products Co. by Tested Recipe Publishers, 1972. 80 p., illus.

4302. The Pleasures of Gas Grilling / contributing recipe consultants, Penny Peterson and others. Des Moines, Iowa: Meredith Pub. Services, c1980. 96 p., illus. Includes index.

4303. The Outdoor Barbecue / prepared by H.L. Orr and W.R. Usborne. Toronto, Ont.: Ontario Ministry of Agriculture and Food, 1981. 14 p., illus.

4304. Betty Crocker's Barbecue Cookbook / photography director, Remo Cosentino; illustrations, Ray Skibinski. New York: Golden Press, c1982. 72 p., illus. (some colored). Includes index.

Barbecuing, Broiling, and Grilling *(Continued)*

4305. Bradley's Complete Gas Grill Cookbook / by Nancy Elmont. Boston, Mass.: Dorison House Publishers, c1982. 144 p., illus. Includes index.

4306. Finger Lickin', Rib Stickin', Great Tastin', Hot & Spicy Barbecue / by Jane Butel; illustrations by Jerry Joyner. New York: Workman Pub. Co., c1982. 96 p., illus. 40 recipes. Title on cover: A Passionate Cookbook. Includes index.

4307. 32 Better Barbecues / by Helen Feingold. Woodbury, N.Y.: Barron's, c1983. 63 p., colored illus. (Easy Cooking). Includes index.

4308. Barbecue: And the Joy of Cooking on an Open Fire / Heinz and Geneste Kurth. London, Eng.: Batsford, 1983. 80 p., colored illus. Includes index. Also published: Braai Book: The Joy of Cooking on an Open Fire. Cape Town, South Africa: Tafelberg, 1983.

4309. Barbecue!: From the Reynolds Wrap Kitchens. 1st ed. New York: Random House, c1983. 112 p., colored illus. Includes index. "Originally published by Reynolds Metals Company in 1982."

4310. Barbecue: With an International Flavour / by Maggie Black. London, Eng.: Foulsham, c1983. 80 p., illus. (some colored). (Know-How Books). Includes index.

4311. Barbecue & Smoke Cookery / by Maggie Waldron; drawings by Erni Young. San Francisco, Calif.: 101 Productions; New York: Distributed to the book trade in the U.S. by Scribner, c1983. 192 p., illus. Includes index. New ed. of: Fire & Smoke.

4312. Barbecues / Judy Ridgway. London, Eng.: Ward Lock, 1983. 80 p., illus. (some colored). Includes index.

4313. Barbecues & Grills. Newton Abbot, Eng.: David & Charles, 1983. 64 p. (Kitchen Workshop). Translation of: Grillmat.

Barbecuing, Broiling, and Grilling *(Continued)*

4314. The Complete Barbecue Cookbook: Recipes for the Gas Grill and Water Smoker / Charmglow. Chicago, Ill.: Contemporary Books, c1983. 152 p., illus. (some colored). Includes index.

4315. The Complete Gas Barbecue Cookbook / by Jo-Anne Bennett. Burnstown, Ont.: General Store Pub. House, 1983. 130 p., illus. (some colored). Includes index.

4316. Cooking with Flare: An Easy and Complete Barbecue Guide / by Walter Zogar. Sooke, B.C.: Quint Marketing Ltd., 1983. 64 p., illus.

4317. Picnics and Barbecues / Clare Payne. Cambridge, Eng.: Woodhead-Faulkner for J. Sainsbury, 1983. 96 p., illus. (some colored). (A Sainsbury Cookbook).

4318. Barbecue Cookery / Cecilia Norman. London, Eng.: Granada, 1984. 222 p., illus. Includes index.

4319. Barbecues / James F. Marks. 2nd ed. Harmondsworth, Eng.: Penguin, 1984. 190 p., illus. (A Penguin Handbook). Includes index. First edition published 1977.

4320. Barbecues & Summer Cooking / Robert Carrier. London, Eng.: Marshall Cavendish, 1984. 112 p., colored illus. (Robert Carrier's Kitchen). Includes index.

4321. Farm Journal's Picnic & Barbecue Cookbook / by the food editors of Farm Journal; edited by Patricia A. Ward. New York: Greenwich House: Distributed by Crown Publishers, 1984, c1982. 150 p. Includes index.

4322. Gas Grill Cookouts: Simple to Sensational. Evansville, Ind.: Preway Industries, c1984. 96 p., colored illus. Includes index.

4323. Quick & Easy Gas Grill Cookbook / by Structo. Elmsford, N.Y.: Benjamin Co., c1984. 144 p., illus.

Barbecuing, Broiling, and Grilling *(Continued)*

4324. Wonderful Ways to Prepare Barbecue & Picnic Meals / by Marion Mansfield. 1st U.S. ed. Orlando, Fla.: H.C. Pub., 1984, c1979. 96 p., colored illus. Includes index.

4325. All About Bar-b-q Kansas City Style / Shifra Stein & Rich Davis. Kansas City, Mo.: Barbacoa Press, c1985. 184 p., illus.

4326. Barbecue and Summer Party Cookbook. Secaucus, N.J.: Chartwell Books, c1985. 118 p., colored illus. Includes index.

4327. The Barbecue Book: Everything You Need to Know About Barbecues / Gail Duff. Sherborne, Eng.: Prism; San Leandro, Calif.: Distributed by Interbook, 1985. 165 p., colored photos. ca. 200 recipes. Includes descriptions of barbecue equipment and index.

4328. Barbecue Recipes / Mitzie Wilson. Twickenham, Eng.: Hamlyn, 1985. 64 p., colored illus. Includes index.

4329. Better Homes and Gardens Hot off the Grill. 1st ed. Des Moines, Iowa: Meredith Corp., c1985. 96 p., illus. (some colored). 75 recipes. Includes menus and index.

4330. The Great American Barbeque Instruction Book / C. Clark "Smoky" Hale; illustrated by Greg Harbison; edited by Judy Black Frank; photos by T. Douglas Hale. McComb, Miss.: Abacus Pub. Co., 1985. 1 v., illus. Includes index. [Publication of this book has not been verified].

4331. Kingsford's Best Barbecues: A Tour of American Regional Favorites. Kingsford, Mich.: Kingsford; Chicago, Ill.: Distributed by Chicago Review Press, c1985. 48 p.

4332. The Vegetarian Barbecue: A Guide to Gourmet Eating Outdoors / by David Eno; illustrated by Kim Blundell. 1st U.S. ed. New York: Thorsons Publishers, 1985. 128 p., illus. Includes index.

Special Techniques 547

Barbecuing, Broiling, and Grilling *(Continued)*

4333. Bar & Grill Cookbook: Exciting New Recipes from San Francisco's Bar & Grill Restaurants / James McNair; photography by Tom Tracy. San Francisco, Calif.: Chronicle Books, c1986. 107 p., colored illus. Includes index.

4334. Barbecue Cookbook / Carol Bowen. 2nd ed. London, Eng.: Hamlyn, 1986. 127 p., illus. (some colored). Includes index.

4335. The Barbecue Cookbook / Arto der Haroutunian. London, Eng.: Pan, 1986. 266 p., illus. Includes index.

4336. Barbecue Cooking the Gourmet Way / Patrice Dard. 1st English ed. Toronto, Ont.; New York: Methuen, 1986. 116 p. Includes index. Translation of: Le Barbecue.

4337. Barbecues and Outdoor Living / editor, Helen Davies. Greenford, Eng.: Ura Editions, c1986. 120 p., colored illus. Includes index.

4338. Cooking with Fire and Smoke / Phillip Stephen Schulz; illustrations by Richard Pracher. New York: Simon and Schuster, c1986. 335 p., illus. Includes index.

4339. The Gourmet Barbecue / Pip Bloomfield, Annie Mehra & Kay Spicer; photography by Peter Johnson. Toronto, Ont.: Key Porter Books, 1986. 173 p., colored illus. Includes index.

4340. Grill Book / text by Kelly McCune; design by Thomas Ingalls; produced by David Barich. 1st ed. New York: Perennial Library, 1986. 106 p., colored photos. 75 recipes for meat poultry, and seafood. Includes index.

4341. Grilling & Barbecuing / John Phillip Carroll & Charlotte Walker. Tucson, Ariz.: HP Books, c1986. 160 p., colored illus.

4342. Justin Wilson's Outdoor Cooking--with Inside Help / photographs by Jeannine Meeds Wilson. Gretna, La.: Pelican Pub. Co., 1986. 160 p., colored illus. Includes index.

Barbecuing, Broiling, and Grilling *(Continued)*

4343. The New Barbecue Cookbook: Better Recipes for Outdoor Eating / edited by Maggie Black. London, Eng.: Foulsham, c1986. 96 p., illus. Includes index.

4344. Picnics and Barbecues. Los Angeles, Calif.: Knapp Press, c1986. 113 p., 16 p. of plates, colored illus. (Cooking with Bon Appétit). Includes index.

4345. Sunset Barbecue Cook Book / by the editors of Sunset Books and Sunset Magazine; research & text, Joan Griffiths, Mary Jane Swanson; illustrations, Sally Shimizu; photographers, Glenn Christiansen and others. 6th ed. Menlo Park, Calif.: Lane Pub. Co., c1986. 96 p., colored illus. Includes index.

4346. The Barbecue Book / Audrey Ellis. New York: Crescent, c1987. 128 p., illus. Includes index.

4347. Barbecue, Indoors and Out / Linda West Eckhardt. 1st ed. Los Angeles, Calif.: J.P. Tarcher; New York: Distributed by St. Martin's Press, c1987. 157 p., illus. Includes index.

4348. Barbecue with Beard: Outdoor Recipes from a Great Cook / James Beard. Warner Books ed. New York: Warner Books, 1987 printing, c1975. 277 p. Includes index. Reprint. Originally published: New York: Golden Press, c1975.

4349. Better Homes and Gardens Great Cookouts. 1st ed. Des Moines, Iowa: Meredith Corp., c1987. 47 p., illus. (some colored). Includes index.

4350. The Little Gourmet Gas Barbecue Cookbook / May Sadkowski and Judith Whitehead. Burnstown, Ont.: General Store Pub. House, 1987. 108 p., illus. Includes index.

4351. Vegetarian Barbecue and Summer Cooking / Felicity Jackson. London, Eng.: Windward, c1987. 124 p.

Special Techniques

Barbecuing, Broiling, and Grilling *(Continued)*

4352. The All-American Barbecue Book / Rich Davis and Shifra Stein. 1st ed. New York: Vintage Books, 1988. 241 p., illus.

4353. The Barbecue Cookbook / senior editor, Joan Erskine Denman; illustrator, Caroline Wellesley. Birmingham, Ala.: Oxmoor House, c1988. 60 p. Over 150 recipes. "Recipes adapted from Southern Living Cookbooks."

4354. Barbecues and Summer Food / Rosamond Man. London, Eng.: Hamlyn, 1988. 79 p. (Cooking for Today).

4355. Barbecuing, Grilling & Smoking / Ron Clark, Bruce Aidells, Carole Latimer, writers; Jill Fox, editor; Ernie Friedlander, photographer; Joanne Dexter, food stylist; Janet Nusbaum, photographic stylist. San Ramon, Calif.: Chevron Chemical Co., c1988. 127 p., colored illus. (California Culinary Academy series). Includes index.

4356. Barbeque'n with Bobby / Bobby Seale. Berkeley, Calif.: Ten Speed Press, 1988. 142 p.

4357. Canada Cooks!: Barbecue / by Edena Sheldon. North Vancouver, B.C.: Whitecap Books, c1988. 160 p., colored illus.

4358. The Complete Australian Barbecue Kettle Cookbook / Ross McDonald, Margaret Kirkwood. Dulwich, South Aust.: McDonald-Kirkwood Pub. Co., 1988? 216 p., colored illus.

4359. The Joy of Grilling / Joe Famularo. New York: Barron's, c1988. 330 p., colored illus. Includes indexes.

4360. New Vegetarian Barbecue / Maggie Black. London, Eng.: Foulsham, c1988. 96 p.

4361. Real Barbecue / Greg Johnson and Vince Staten. 1st ed. New York: Perennial Library, c1988. 261 p., illus. Includes index. Chiefly reviews of restaurants in the U.S. that offer the best barbecue food, with only a few recipes.

Barbecuing, Broiling, and Grilling *(Continued)*

4362. Best Recipes for Grilling. 1st Prentice Hall Press ed. New York: Prentice Hall Press, c1989. 112 p., illus. (some colored). More than 100 recipes. (Betty Crocker's Red Spoon Collection). Includes index.

4363. Better Homes and Gardens Best Barbecue Recipes / editor, Marcia Stanley. 1st ed. Des Moines, Iowa: Meredith Corp., c1989. 80 p., illus. (some colored). (Better Homes and Gardens Test Kitchen).

4364. The Book of Grilling & Barbecuing / Cecilia Norman; photography by Paul Grater. Los Angeles, Calif.: HP Books, c1989. 120 p. More than 100 colored illus. Includes index.

4365. The Complete Book of Outdoor Cookery / by James A. Beard and Helen Evans Brown; foreword by Jeremiah Tower. 1st Perennial Library ed. New York: Harper & Row, 1989, c1955. 254 p.

4366. Cooking with Gas: From the Grill / recipes, Sue Spitler. 1st ed. Chappaqua, N.Y.: Genesis Promotions, 1989. 1 v., illus.

4367. Fresh Ways with Picnics & Barbecues / by the editors of Time-Life Books. Alexandria, Va.: Time-Life Books, c1989. 144 p., colored illus. (Healthy Home Cooking). Includes index.

4368. Great Grilling: Easy & Elegant Entertaining All Year Round / Hillary Davis; principal photographer, Michael Grand. 1st ed. New York: Weidenfeld & Nicolson, 1989. 128 p., 100 photos, some colored. "A Friedman Group Book." Includes index.

4369. The Grilling Book: The Techniques, Tools, and Tastes of the New American Grill / by A. Cort Sinnes; with recipes by Jay Harlow; illustrated by Earl Thollander. Reading, Mass.: Aris Books, 1989, c1985. 191 p., illus. More than 75 recipes. Includes index.

Barbecuing, Broiling, and Grilling *(Continued)*

4370. The Random House Barbecue and Summer Foods Cookbook / by Margaret Fraser. New York: Random House/Madison Press Book, c1989. 159 p., colored illus. Originally published: The Canadian Living Barbecue and Summer Foods Cookbook / by Margaret Fraser and the food writers of Canadian Living Magazine, 1988.

4371. The Ultimate Grill Book / by the editors of Sunset Books and Sunset Magazine; research & text, Joan Griffiths, Mary Jane Swanson; coordinating editor, Deborah Thomas Kramer; illustrations, Guy Porfirio, Sally Shimizu; photography by Tom Wyatt. 1st ed. Menlo Park, Calif.: Lane Pub. Co., c1989. 208 p., colored illus. More than 300 recipes. At head of title: Sunset. "Favorite barbecue recipes from the pages of Sunset Magazine and Sunset's Popular Barbecue Cook Book." Includes index.

4372. 365 Great Barbecue & Grilling Recipes / by Lonnie Gandara with Peggy Fallon. 1st ed. New York: Harper & Row, c1990. 240 p.

4373. The Art of Grilling: 75 New Recipes from the Authors of The Grill Book / Kelly McCune, T. Ingall. New York: Harper & Row, 1990. 108 p. Contains 25 menus and information on various kinds of grills. Includes bibliography and index.

4374. Barbecue Hints and Tips / Bridget Jones. London, Eng.: Ward Lock, 1990. 127 p.

4375. Barbecued Ribs, Smoked Butts, and Other Great Feeds / Jeanne Voltz. Rev. ed. New York: Knopf: Distributed by Random House, 1990. 272 p., illus. 235 recipes. (Knopf Cooks American). Includes bibliography and index. Rev. ed. of: Barbecued Ribs and Other Great Feeds. 1985.

4376. Gas Barbecuing / Jim Marks. London, Eng.: Simon & Schuster, 1990. 144 p.

Specialty Cookbooks

Barbecuing, Broiling, and Grilling *(Continued)*

4377. Gourmet Grilling / Charmaine Solomon; illustrations by Toula Antonakos. 1st Perigee ed. New York: Perigee Books, 1990. 112 p., illus. Includes index. Originally published as: Gourmet Barbecue Cookery. 1986.

4378. James McNair's Grill Cookbook / photography by Patricia Brabant. San Francisco, Calif.: Chronicle Books, c1990. 96 p., colored photos.

4379. Jerk: Barbecue from Jamaica / Helen Willinsky. Freedom, Calif.: Crossing Press, 1990. 150 p. Contains more than 100 recipes for the Jamaican way of barbecuing meat, poultry, and seafood, together with accompaniments. Includes index.

4380. Kingsford Barbecue. Lincolnwood, Ill.: Publications International, 1990. 96 p., colored illus. (Favorite Recipes; v. 5, no. 20). Includes index.

4381. The Passion of Barbeque / presented by the Kansas City Barbeque Society. Kansas City, Mo.: Pig Out Publications, 1990, c1989. 159 p., illus. Includes index. Reprint. Originally published: Kansas City, Mo.: Westport Publishers, c1988.

4382. The Thrill of the Grill: Techniques, Recipes & Down-Home Barbecue / Chris Schlesinger & John Willoughby; line drawings by Laura Hartman Maestro; photography by Vincent Lee. 1st ed. New York: W. Morrow, c1990. 395 p., 32 colored photos. 200 recipes. Includes index.

see also entries 91, 596, 628, 2060, 2070, 2107, 2148, 3859; and Mesquite Cooking

Boiling

4383. Boiled, Poached, and Steamed Foods. Garden City, N.Y.: Doubleday, 1972. 112 p., illus. (Cooking Adventures with Michael Field).

Braising

see entry 4481

Broiling see Barbecuing, Broiling, and Grilling

Canning and Preserving

4384. Home Canning / compiled by Blue Flame Kitchen Economists. Edmonton, Alta.: Alberta Agriculture, Print Media Branch, 1980. 1 v.

4385. Home Preserving / Judy Ridgway; illustrated by Vanessa Pancheri. London, Eng.: Teach Yourself, 1980. 184 p., illus. Includes index.

4386. Ball Blue Book: The Guide to Home Canning and Freezing / Ball Corp. Muncie, Ind.: Ball Corp., 1981. 96 p.

4387. The Complete Book of Home Preserving / Mary Norwak. London, Eng.: New English Library, 1981, c1979. 236 p., illus. (New English Library Books for Cooks). Includes index.

4388. Food for Keeps: Everything You Need to Know About Preserving / Pamela Westland. London, Eng.: Granada, 1981. 224 p. Includes index.

4389. Good Housekeeping Complete Book of Home Preserving / Good Housekeeping Institute. London, Eng.: Ebury, 1981. 192 p., illus. (some colored). Includes index.

4390. Home Food Systems: Rodale's Catalog of Methods and Tools for Producing, Processing, and Preserving Naturally Good Foods / Corliss A. Bachman and others; edited by Roger B. Yepsen, Jr. Emmaus, Pa.: Rodale Press, c1981. 475 p., illus. Includes bibliographical references and index.

Specialty Cookbooks

Canning and Preserving *(Continued)*

4391. Making Your Own Preserves / Jane and Rob Avery; illustrated by Trevor Aldous. Dorchester, Eng.: Prism, c1981. 112 p., illus. Includes index.

4392. Preserving / by the editors of Time-Life Books. Alexandria, Va.: Time-Life Books; Morristown, N.J.: School and library distribution by Silver Burdett, c1981. 176 p., illus. (The Good Cook Techniques & Recipes). Includes index.

4393. The Sainsbury Book of Preserves & Pickles / Heather Lambert. London, Eng.: Published for J. Sainsbury by Cathay, 1981. 93 p., colored illus. Includes index.

4394. Sunset Canning, Freezing & Drying / by the editors of Sunset Books and Sunset Magazine. Menlo Park, Calif.: Lane Pub. Co., c1981. 128 p., illus. (some colored). Includes index.

4395. Basic Preserve Making / by Brian Leverett. Evershot, Eng.: Gavin, 1982. 88 p., illus. Includes index.

4396. Better Homes and Gardens Home Canning and Freezing. Large-format ed. Des Moines, Iowa: Meredith Corp., 1982, c1973. 96 p., illus. (some colored). Includes index. Originally published: Better Homes and Gardens Home Canning Cookbook. 1st ed. Des Moines: Meredith Corp., 1973.

4397. The Busy Person's Guide to Preserving Food / Janet Bachand Chadwick; illustrations by Elayne Sears. Charlotte, Vt.: Garden Way Pub., c1982. 132 p., illus. Includes bibliography and index.

4398. The Complete Guide to Canning / created and designed by the editorial staff of Ortho Books; edited by Susan M. Lammers; written by Charlotte Walker Pisinski. San Francisco, Calif.: Ortho Books, c1982. 96 p., illus.; Cover title: The Complete Book of Canning. Includes index.

Canning and Preserving *(Continued)*

4399. Home Preserving / editor, Renny Harrop; art editor, Judith Robertson; illustrator, Caroline Austin. London, Eng.: Marshall Cavendish, c1982. 64 p., colored illus. Includes index.

4400. The Pleasures of Preserving and Pickling / Jeanne Lesem; illustrations by Julie Maas. 1st Vintage Books ed. New York: Vintage Books, 1982, c1975. 227 p., illus. 117 recipes. Includes indexes.

4401. Canning / by Sue & Bill Deeming. Tucson, Ariz.: HP Books, c1983. 192 p., colored illus. Includes index.

4402. Home-Canning Made Easy / A. Borella. Toronto, Ont.: Royce Pub., c1983. 128 p., illus. Includes index. Reprint. Originally published: Home-Canning Handbook. New York: Benjamin Co., c1974.

4403. Seasonal Gifts from the Kitchen / Emily Crumpacker; illustrated by Vivienne Flesher. 1st ed. New York: W. Morrow, 1983. 94 p., illus. (some colored). Includes index.

4404. Canning & Preserving Foods / Frederick E. Kahn; edited by Debra Bock-Woo and Mitchell Woo. New York: Nautilus Communications, c1984. 121 p., illus. (Preparing Food the Healthy Way Series). Includes index.

4405. The Giant Handbook of Food Preserving Basics / by Elizabeth & Robert Williams. 1st ed. Blue Ridge Summit, Pa.: Tab Books, c1984. 214 p., illus. Includes index.

4406. How to Can Food the Right Way / prepared by Gerald D. Kuhn and Elizabeth L. Andress. University Park, Pa.: Pennsylvania State University, College of Agriculture, Extension Service, c1984. 63 p., illus. Includes index.

Specialty Cookbooks

Canning and Preserving *(Continued)*

4407. Jean Anderson's Green Thumb Preserving Guide: How to Can and Freeze, Dry and Store, Pickle, Preserve, and Relish Home-grown Vegetables and Fruits / drawings by Lauren Jarrett. 1st Quill ed. New York: Quill, c1984. 241 p., illus. Contains directions for preserving 40 vegetables and 30 fruits and berries as well as recipes. Includes index. Rev. ed. of: The Green Thumb Preserving Guide. 1976.

4408. NEFCO Canning Book / edited by William C. Hurst. 1st ed. Athens, Ga. (786 E. Broad St., Athens 30601): Dixie Canner Equipment Co., 1984. 142 p., illus. At head of cover title: Nutrition Education and Food Conservation. "A non-technical reference book for NEFCO Center personnel." Includes bibliography.

4409. The Pantry Gourmet: Over 250 Recipes for Mustards, Vinegars, Relishes, Pâtés, Cheeses, Breads, Preserves, and Meats to Stock Your Pantry, Freezer, and Refrigerator / by Jane Doerfer. Emmaus, Pa.: Rodale Press, c1984. 290 p., illus. Includes index.

4410. The National Trust Book of the Country Kitchen Store Cupboard / Sara Paston Williams. Newton Abbot, Eng.; North Pomfret, Vt.: David & Charles, c1985. 112 p., illus. Includes index.

4411. Saving the Plenty: Pickling & Preserving / Richard Humphrey. Kingston, Mass.: Teaparty Books, 1985. 126p.

4412. The Book of Preserves, Jams, Chutneys, Pickles, Jellies / Mary Norwak; photography by Jon Stewart. Tucson, Ariz.: HP Books, c1986. 128 p., colored photos.

4413. Fancy Pantry / by Helen Witty; illustrated by Pierre Le-Tan. New York: Workman Pub., c1986. 351 p., illus. (some colored). 250 recipes. Includes index.

Canning and Preserving *(Continued)*

4414. Food Preservation / compiled by the Homemaking Division, Dept. of Education and Culture, Administration: House of Assembly. Rev. metricated ed. Pretoria, South Africa: Govt. Print., 1986. 129 p., illus. Includes index.

4415. Blue Ribbon Winners: America's Best State Fair Recipes / Catherine Hanley. Tucson, Ariz.: HP Books, c1987. 232 p., illus. Includes index.

4416. The Book of Gifts from the Pantry / Annette Grimsdale. Tucson, Ariz.: HP Books, 1987. ca. 120 p., colored photos.

4417. Gifts from the Kitchen. Los Angeles, Calif.: Knapp Press, c1987. 119 p., 16 p. of plates, colored illus. (Cooking with Bon Appétit). Includes index.

4418. Canning and Preserving Without Sugar / by Norma M. MacRae. 2nd ed. Chester, Conn.: Globe Pequot Press, 1988. 230 p. "Includes the latest USDA canning recommendations and the most recent diabetic exchange list from the American Diabetes Association." Includes indexes.

4419. The Complete Book of Home Preserving / Mary Norwak. London, Eng.: Ward Lock, 1988. 160 p., illus. (some colored). (WI Life & Leisure). Includes index.

4420. Complete Guide to Home Canning. Washington, D.C.: U.S. Dept. of Agriculture, Extension Service; Supt. of Docs., U.S. G.P.O., distributor, 1988. 1 v., colored illus. (Agriculture Information Bulletin; no. 539). Supersedes four USDA Home and Garden Bulletins: no. 8, "Home Canning of Fruits and Vegetables"; no. 56, "How to Make Jellies, Jams, and Preserves at Home"; no. 92, "Making Pickles and Relishes at Home"; no. 106, "Home Canning of Meat and Poultry."

Canning and Preserving *(Continued)*

4421. Easy Microwave Preserving: The Shortcut Way to Jams, Jellies, Fruits, Sauces, Pickles, Chutneys, Relishes, Salsas, Blanching Vegetables, Drying Herbs, and Special Extras! / by Cynthia Fischborn and Cheryl Long. Portland, Or.: Culinary Arts Ltd., c1988. 95 p., illus. Includes index.

4422. Putting Food By / Janet Greene, Ruth Hertzberg, Beatrice Vaughan. 4th ed. Lexington, Mass.: Stephen Greene Press, 1988. 420 p., illus. Hertzberg's name appears first on the previous ed. Includes bibliography and index. Contains information on canning, drying, freezing, and smoking.

4423. Gourmet Preserves: Sweet or Savory, Spread, Sauce, or Condiment, a Complete Guide to Delicious and Unique Preserving / Judith Choate. New York: Weidenfeld & Nicolson, c1989. ca. 176 p., illus. Includes index.

4424. Kerr Kitchen Cookbook: Home Canning and Freezing Guide. Los Angeles, Calif. (P.O. Box 76961, Los Angeles 90076): Kerr, c1990. 112 p., colored illus. Includes index.

4425. Perfect Preserves: Provisions from the Kitchen Garden / by Nora Carey; photographs by Mick Hales. New York: Stewart, Tabori & Chang: Distributed in the U.S. by Workman Pub., c1990. 256 p., ca. 150 colored photos. 150 recipes. Includes bibliography and index. Contains information on preserving fruits and vegetables.

4426. Stocking Up: The Third Edition of the Classic Preserving Guide / edited by Carol Hupping and the staff of the Rodale Food Center. 1st Fireside ed. New York: Simon & Schuster, 1990, c1986. 627 p., illus. ca. 300 recipes. Reprint. Originally published: Stocking Up III. Emmaus, Pa.: Rodale Press, c1986.

see also entries 726, 735, 781, 790, 1093, 1101, 1591, 4449; and dishes in Section II that are often canned or preserved, e.g. Jams and Jellies; Pickles and Relishes

Deep Fat Frying

4427. Mable Hoffman's Mini Deep-fry Cookery / co-author, Gar Hoffman. Tucson, Ariz.: HP Books, c1977. 176 p., illus. Includes index.

4428. Mac Meals in Minutes / by June Roth. New York: Dorison House Publishers, c1977. 160 p., illus. Includes index.

4429. Mini Deep Fry Cookery: Appetizers to Desserts. Sea Cliff, N.Y.: Carbooks, Inc., 1980. 1 v. 216 recipes.

4430. Frying Tonight / Judy Ridgway. London, Eng.: Piatkus, 1984. 96 p., illus.

4431. Get More from Your Deep Fat Fryer / Petra Kuhne. London, Eng.: Foulsham, 1987. 96 p.

see also broader category: Frying

Drying

4432. Home Food Dehydrating: Economical "Do-It-Yourself" Methods for Preserving, Storing & Cooking / Jay and Shirley Bills. Bountiful, Utah: Horizon Publishers, 1974. 151 p.

4433. Don Holm's Book of Food Drying, Pickling & Smoke Curing / by Don and Myrtle Holm. Caldwell, Idaho: Caxton Printers, 1978. 160 p., illus.

4434. How to Dry Foods / by Deanna DeLong. Tucson, Ariz.: HP Books, c1979. 160 p., illus. Includes bibliography and index.

4435. How to Dry Food: Fruit, Vegetables, Meats, Fish + 100 Recipes. Sea Cliff, N.Y.: Carbooks, Inc., 1980. 1 v.

4436. Garden Way's Guide to Food Drying / by Phyllis Hobson. Charlotte, Vt.: Garden Way Pub., c1980. 216 p., illus. Includes index.

Drying *(Continued)*

4437. The Food Dryer Handbook / Pamela G. Wubben. Boulder, Colo.: One Percent Pub., 1981. 27 p.

4438. Home Drying of Fruits and Vegetables / B.J. Edwards and G.E. Strachan. Ottawa, Ont.: Agriculture Canada, c1982. 37 p., illus. (some colored). Issued also in French under title: La déhydratation chez soi des fruits et des légumes.

4439. New Concepts in Dehydrated Food Cookery: Hundreds of New Ideas and Tested Recipes for Enjoying Home Dehydrated Foods / Barbara Densley. Bountiful, Utah: Horizon, c1982. 191 p., illus. Includes index.

4440. Preserve it Naturally: A Complete Guide to Food Dehydration / text prepared and book designed by Robert Scharff and Associates. Reston, Va.: Reston Pub. Co., c1983. 140 p., illus. (some colored). Includes index.

4441. Drying Vegetables, Fruits & Herbs / by Phyllis Hobson. Pownal, Vt.: Storey Communications, 1984, c1975. 60 p., illus. (The Country Kitchen Library). Includes index. Reprint. Originally published: Home Drying Vegetables, Fruits & Herbs. Charlotte, Vt.: Garden Way Pub., 1975.

4442. Let's Dry It / Bernice Neff; edited by Brett Wescott. Surrey, B.C.: Hancock House, c1984. 112 p., illus. (some colored).

see also entries 4394, 4407, 4457

Freezing

4443. Freezer Cookery / by Gerry Bernstein. 1st ed. Chicago, Ill.: Chicago Review Press, c1980. 115 p., illus. Includes index.

4444. What to Freeze and How / text by Rosemary Wadey; illustrations by J. Arbeau with Jane Griffin. London, Eng.: Mirror Books, 1980. 128 p., illus. (Step by Step Guides).

Special Techniques 561

Freezing *(Continued)*

4445. The Wholefood Freezer Book: The First Freezer Book for Wholefooders and Vegetarians / by Pamela Brown; illustrated by Clive Birch. Wellingborough, Eng.: Thorsons, 1980. 160 p., illus. (A Thorsons Wholefood Cookbook). Includes index.

4446. The Freezer Cookbook / edited by Gill Edden & Wendy James; home economist, Gilly Cubitt. London, Eng.: Orbis, 1981. 189 p., colored illus. Includes index.

4447. Marika Hanbury Tenison's Freezer Cookbook. Rev. and updated. London, Eng.: Pan, 1981. 288 p. Includes index. Previous ed. published as: Deep Freeze Sense. 1976.

4448. Pocket A to Z Guide to Freezing Food / by Sally Major. London, Eng.: Arlington, 1981. 151 p.

4449. Farm Journal's Freezing & Canning Cookbook: Prized Recipes from the Farms of America / edited by Nell B. Nichols and Kathryn Larson. New rev. ed. New York: Ballantine Books, 1982. 484 p. Includes index. Edition for 1973 published under title: Freezing & Canning Cookbook.

4450. Making the Most of Your Freezer. London, Eng.: Consumers' Association, c1982. 144 p., illus. (A Consumer Publication). Includes index.

4451. Mary Norwak's Guide to Home Freezing. London, Eng.: Ward Lock, 1982. 224 p., illus. (some colored). Includes index.

4452. The Microwave & Freezer / by Barbara Methven; photographers, Buck Holzemer, Graham Brown, Jill Greer. Minnetonka, Minn. (5700 Green Circle Dr., Minnetonka 55343): Publication Arts, c1982. 160 p., colored illus. (Microwave Cooking Library). Includes index. Also published as: Microwave Cooking, from the Freezer. Minneapolis, Minn.: Litton Microwave Cooking Products, c1982.

Freezing *(Continued)*

4453. Will it Freeze? / compiled for Home & Freezer Digest by Joan Hood, with additional research by Vivian Donald. New York: Scribner, 1982, c1980. 192 p., illus.

4454. Seasonal Freezer Cookbook / Caroline Ellwood...and others. London, Eng.: Octopus Books, 1983. 207 p., colored illus. Includes index.

4455. Betty Crocker's Do-ahead Cookbook / photography director, George Ancona. Rev. ed. New York: Golden Press, c1984. 95 p., illus. (some colored). Includes index.

4456. The Freezer Cookbook / Mary Berry. London, Eng.: Piatkus, 1984. 80 p., colored illus. Includes index.

4457. Freezing & Drying / created and designed by the editorial staff of Ortho Books; project editors, Anne Coolman, Sally W. Smith; writer, Charlotte Walker; designers, Linda Hinrichs, Karen Berndt; photographer, Michael Lamotte; photographic stylist, Sara Slavin; associate editor, Beverley DeWitt. San Francisco, Calif.: Chevron Chemical Co., c1984. 96 p., illus. (some colored). (Ortho Library). Includes index.

4458. Mary Berry's New Freezer Cookbook. London, Eng.: Piatkus, 1984. 192 p., colored illus. Includes index.

4459. The Practical Freezer Handbook / Jill McWilliam. London, Eng.: Octopus in association with Bejam, 1984. 80 p., colored illus. Includes index.

4460. Rodale's Complete Book of Home Freezing / by Marilyn Hodges. Emmaus, Pa.: Rodale Press, c1984. 375 p., illus. Includes index.

4461. Slimming Magazines Freezer Owner's Diet Book / edited by Glynis McGuinness and Sybil Greatbatch. London, Eng.: Fontana, 1984. 224 p. Includes index.

Special Techniques   563

Freezing *(Continued)*

4462. Cooking from Your Freezer / Mary Berry. Cambridge, Eng.: Martin, 1985. 96 p., colored illus. (An Iceland Guide). Includes index.

4463. The New Freezer Cookbook / Mary Norwak. London, Eng.: Ward Lock, 1985. 1 v., illus. Includes index.

4464. Better Homes and Gardens Fix & Freeze Cookbook. 1st ed. Des Moines, Iowa: Meredith Corp., c1986. 96 p., colored illus. Includes index.

4465. The Freezer Companion / Michelle Berriedale-Johnson. London, Eng.: Macdonald, 1986. 192 p., colored illus.

4466. Good Food from Your Freezer / Helge Rubinstein and Sheila Bush. Harmondsworth, Eng.: Penguin, 1986. 202 p. (Penguin Handbooks). Includes index.

4467. A-Z of Home Freezing / Mary Norwak. 2nd rev. ed. London, Eng.: Sphere, 1988. 363 p.

4468. The Complete Guide to Freezer and Microwave Cooking / Jill McWilliam in association with Bejam. London, Eng.: Hamlyn, 1989. 188 p.

4469. Farmhouse Kitchen Freezer & Microwave / Marie Emmerson. London, Eng.: Yorkshire Television Enterprises, 1989. 136 p.

4470. The Gourmet's Freezer / Glynn Christian, Sue Ross. London, Eng.: Simon & Schuster, 1989. 223 p.

4471. Fresh from the Freezer / Michael Roberts; edited by Janet Speigel. New York: Morrow, 1990. 384 p. More than 250 recipes. Contains directions on cooking, freezing, and defrosting basic dishes, and then using them in new preparations. Includes index.

see also entries 790, 4386, 4394, 4396, 4407, 4409

Specialty Cookbooks

Frying

4472. The Cook and Serve Book: 250 Recipes for Electric Frypan and Cooker Fryer / Sunbeam. Boston, Mass.: Dorison House Publishers, c1980. 160 p., illus. (some colored).

4473. Farm Journal's Speedy Skillet Meals / by Patricia A. Ward; book design by Michael P. Durning; illustrations by Wendy Biggins. Philadelphia, Pa.: Farm Journal, c1980. 216 p., illus. Includes index.

4474. Skillet Cookery / by Joanne Lindeman; illustrated by Craig Torlucci. Concord, Calif.: Nitty Gritty Productions, c1980. 183 p., illus. Includes index.

4475. Fabulous Fry Pan Favorites: The Complete Electric Fry Pan Cookbook / by Patricia Phillips. Eau Clair, Wis.: National Presto Industries, c1984. 160 p., colored illus. Includes index.

4476. Deep-Frying & Pan-Frying / text, Hae Sung Hwang [and others]; translator, Miyoung Kim Lee. Seoul, Korea: Ju Bu Saeng & Hak Won, 1985. 62 p., colored illus. (Korean Card Cook; 4).

4477. Out of the Frying Pan: A Collection of Recipes from Members and Friends of the Faversham Society / compiled and typed by Dorothy Percival; foreword by Anthony Swaine. Faversham, Eng.: Faversham Society, 1985. 29 p., illus.

4478. Secrets of Sauté Cooking: The Procedures, Apparatus and Gourmet Recipes / Leonard F. Kruze. Lanham, Md.: Liberty Pub., 1989. 84 p.

see also Deep Fat Frying; Stir Frying

Grilling *see* **Barbecuing, Broiling, and Grilling**

Special Techniques 565

Mesquite Cooking

4479. Beinhorn's Mesquite Cookery / by Courtenay Beinhorn; with wine suggestions by Gerald Asher, wine editor of Gourmet Magazine. Austin, Tex.: Texas Monthly Press, c1986. 137 p. Includes index.

4480. Mesquite Cookery / by John "Boog" Powell. New York: McGraw-Hill, c1986. 148 p., illus. Includes index.

see also broader category: Barbecuing, Broiling, and Grilling

Poaching

see entry 4383

Preserving *see* Canning and Preserving

Roasting

4481. Roasted and Braised Dishes / by Helen McCully. Garden City, N.Y.: Doubleday, 1972. 112 p., illus. (Cooking Adventures with Michael Field).

see also entry 4262

Sautéing *see* Frying

Smoking

4482. Home Book of Smoke-Cooking Meat, Fish & Game / Jack Sleight & Raymond Hull. Harrisburg, Pa.: Stackpole Books, 1971. 160 p., illus.

Smoking *(Continued)*

4483. The Easy Art of Smoking Food / Chris Dubbs and Dave Heberle; illustrated by Jay Marcinowski; photographs by Gary Thomas Sutto. New York: Winchester Press, 1977. 180 p., illus. Includes index.

4484. Cook'n Ca'jun Water Smoker Cookbook: Recipes for the Water Smoker & Grill / by Sondra Hester. Shreveport, La. (P.O. Box 3726, Shreveport 71133): Cook'n Ca'jun Products, c1984. 192 p., illus. (some colored). Includes index.

4485. Smoking Food at Home / Maggie Black. Newton Abbot, Eng.; North Pomfret, Vt.: David & Charles, c1985. 176 p., illus.

4486. Home Smoking and Curing: How You Can Smoke, Cure, Salt and Preserve Fish, Meat and Game / Keith Erlandson. 3rd ed. London, Eng.: Century, 1989. 128 p., illus.

see also 1930, 1956, 2066, 4311, 4355, 4433

Steaming

4487. Steam Cooking Now! / By Barbara Swift Brauer; illustrated by Dennis Redmond; editor, Susan H. Herbert. San Francisco, Calif.: Owlswood Productions, c1980. 64 p., illus. "An Owlswood Productions Cookbook." Includes index.

4488. All About Steam Cooking / Carol Truax; illustrated by Lauren Jarrett. 1st ed. Garden City, N.Y.: Doubleday, 1981. 264 p., illus. 300 recipes and menus. Includes index.

4489. Cooking with Steamers / Randye Rappaport; illustrated by Scott Berkson. New York: I. Chalmers Cookbooks, c1981. 48 p., illus.

4490. The Yip Recipes: Steam Cooking / Victoria Yip, Lin Yip. Pickering, Ont.: Lin Leaf Pub., 1982. 64 p., illus. "Over 80 North American and Chinese recipes."

Steaming *(Continued)*

4491. Steam Cooking / Li Tseng P'eng-chan chu. Hong Kong: Hsiang-kang tien shih ch'u pan yu hsien kung ssu; Fa hsing Hsiao t'ai yang yu hsien kung ssu, 1984. 126 p., colored illus. In Chinese and English.

4492. The Complete Book of Steam Cookery: Tasty and Healthful Dishes from Around the World: With Instructions on Equipment and Technique / Coralie Castle; illustrations by Jeanette Lendino Gurney. 1st ed. Los Angeles, Calif.: J.P. Tarcher; New York: Distributed by St. Martin's Press, c1985. 248 p., illus. More than 200 recipes. Includes index.

4493. Innovations in Cooking: A Revolutionary Concept in Food Preparation / written by Stephen E. Elinsky; illustrated by Barbara L. Summy. West Chester, Pa. (Box 90, West Chester 19381): Elins Laboratories, c1986. 72 leaves in various foliations, illus.

4494. Steam Cuisine / Annette Annechild; written with and illustrated by Laura Johnson. New York: Collier Books; London, Eng.: Collier Macmillan, c1987. 197 p., illus. Includes index.

4495. Steam Cuisine / Tessa Hayward. London, Eng.: Dorling Kindersley, 1988. 168 p.

4496. Steaming Cookbook / Hilary Walden. London, Eng.: Grafton, 1990. 240 p., illus. Includes index.

see also entry 4383

Stir Frying

4497. Better Homes and Gardens Stir-Fry Recipes / editor, Lynn Hoppe. 1st ed. Des Moines, Iowa: Meredith Corp., c1985. 80 p., colored illus. Includes index.

Stir Frying *(Continued)*

4498. Better Homes and Gardens Easy Stir-Fry Recipes. 1st ed. Des Moines, Iowa: Meredith Corp., c1988. 80 p., illus. (some colored). Includes index.

4499. Sunset Stir-Fry Cook Book / by the editors of Sunset Books and Sunset Magazine. 1st ed. Menlo Park, Calif.: Lane Pub. Co., c1988. 96 p., colored photos. More than 130 recipes. Includes index.

4500. Wok & Stir Fry Cooking / Joyce Jue. San Ramon, Calif.: Chevron Chemical Co., 1989. 128 p., colored illus.

see also broader category: Frying

Author Index

1006 Summit Avenue Society. 2539
Aamodt, Jo Ann. 14
Aaron, Jan. 3998
Abernathy, Estelle K. 1864
Ackart, Robert C. 574, 2555, 3594, 3932
Adams, Doug. 1614
Adams, Gerry. 38
Adams, Joan. 1614
Adamson, Jean. 332
Ager, Anne. 896, 1477, 1642
Agliano, Sal. 629
Aho, Katherine K. 146
Aidells, Bruce. 1954
Aitken, Julia. 4258
Akel, D'Ann Ausherman. 1315
Akins, Harold D.T. 1911
Alaska Magazine. 129
Alaska Seafood Marketing Institute. 2055
Alba, Felipe Padilla de
 see Padilla de Alba, Felipe
Albert, Rachel. 1503
Alberta Beekeepers' Association. 1104, 1116
Albright, Barbara. 2850, 3604, 3878
Albright, Nancy. 1222, 1391, 1484
Alburey, Pat. 2965, 3209
Alda, Flora. 1625
Alda, Robert. 1625
Alexander, Agnes. 712
Alexander, Jane. 154
Alexander, Sharon Kay. 13, 2217
Alexander, Sue. 3523
Alimonti, Joan M. 3420
Allday, Jenny. 3323, 3501
Allen, Charles F. 960
Allen, Christine. 2304
Allen, Deborah Kidushim
 see Kidushim-Allen, Deborah
Allen, Jana. 2316
Allen, Ruth N. 960
Allgair, John. 1341, 3713, 3761
Allgood, Ana G.W. 3441
Allgood, Pat. 3441
Allison, Sonia. 1068, 1166, 1213, 1570, 2621, 2770, 3054, 3121, 3152, 3165, 3310, 3480, 3801, 4227

Allman, Ruth. 2165
Allsop, Michael. 789, 2188
Alston, Elizabeth. 2716, 3607, 4086
Amana Refrigeration, Inc. 1091
American Association of University Women. New Brunswick Area Branch. 2665
American Association of University Women. Wilmington Branch. 1293
American Dairy Association of Illinois. 509
American Dairy Association. 212
American Egg Board. 527, 531
American Honey Institute. 1114, 1119
American National CowBelles. 88
American Rabbit Breeders Association. 1873
Amernick, Ann. 3921
Ammon, Richard. 403
Amsden, Pat. 1574
Amsterdam, Morey. 1164
Ananda, Sita. 2205
Anargyros, Isabelle. 3500
Andersen, Arthur W. 1090
Andersen, Juel. 192, 486, 583, 1202, 2127, 2253, 2259, 2260, 2265
Andersen, Paula. 2129
Andersen, Sigrid. 192, 486, 583, 2117, 2265
Anderson, Beth. 2537
Anderson, Gail. 150
Anderson, Henry L.N. 1886
Anderson, Jean. 3297, 4407
Anderson, Kenneth. 2014
Anderson, Linda T. 1165
Anderson, Marcie. 2466
Anderson, William D. 2160
Andersson, Billie V. 557
Andoh, Elizabeth. 2087
Andrews, Gillian. 2356
Andrews, S.W. 1210
Andrews, Sheila. 713
Angier, Bradford. 822
Annechild, Annette. 2025, 4494
Annie. 3602
Anton, Liz. 136
Aoyagi, Akiko. 1133, 1258, 2174, 2246, 2263
Apicius. 996

Specialty Cookbooks

Applegate, Kay. 4037
Araldo, Josephine. 2443
Arasaki, Seibin. 1203
Arasaki, Teruko. 1203
Arbit, Naomi. 934, 3982
Arbuckle, W.S. 3545
Aris, Pepita. 3862
Arkava, Mort. 555
Arkin, Frieda. 3927
Arlett, Robert. 3730
Armitage, Yvonne N. 446
Armstrong, Miriam. 1413
Arnold, Mary-Lou. 1440, 2287, 2648, 3369
Arora, Renu. 482
Arter, Elisabeth. 3777
Arum, Nancy. 3547
Ash, Janet. 1470
Ashbrook, Marguerite L. 2750, 3142
Ashby, Pat. 2901, 3592
Ashby, Susan. 2343, 2953, 3177
Asher, Jane. 2850, 2870
Asher, Sandy F. 1724
Ashmore, Gwyneth. 723
Asoliva. 1596
Asquith, Pamella Z. 330, 754, 3095, 3250, 3699, 3721
Astell-Burt, Nicola. 3564
Astrolabe Kids. 3194
Atalanta Corp. 954
Atkins, Barbara. 1848
Atkinson, Pauline H. 3016
Atlas, Nava. 1533
Attridge, Claire. 2709, 2970, 3129
Au-Yeung, Cecilia J. 81
Aughenbaugh, Anna. 86
Austin, Donna. 3888
Austin, Ken. 3858
Avallone, Allesandra. 3820
Avery, Jane and Rob. 4391
Axcell, Claudia. 1485
Ayala, Mitzi. 1235, 1846
Ayotte, Ellen. 175, 2602
Ayrton, Elisabeth. 2364, 4114
B & B/Benedictine Liqueurs. 1177
Babbar, Purobi. 2820
Bachman, Corliss A. 4390
Back, Phillipa. 970, 980, 981
Backus, David. 635

Bacon, Josephine. 411, 756, 1242, 2423, 3077, 3655
Bacon, Lisa. 2302
Bacon, Vo. 3798
Badenhorst, Judy. 776
Bagel, Marilyn and Tom. 2689
Baggett, Nancy. 1411, 1577, 2385, 2783, 3213, 3957
Bailey, Adrian. 785
Bailey, Freddie. 3577
Bailey, Lee. 3411, 3970
Bailey, Tom. 463
Baird, Elizabeth. 127
Bajor, Dottie. 1144
Baker, Cherie. 3359
Baker, Elizabeth and Elton. 1407, 1881
Baker, Jenny. 624, 2227
Baker, Jill. 471
Baker, Yvonne G. 1328, 3895
Balasuriya, Heather J. 2196
Baljo, Wallace. 704
Ball Corp. 4386
Ballantyne, Janet. 2282, 2375, 3304
Ballantyne, Penny. 3412
Ballard, Patricia. 2550, 2567
Ballenger, Bruce P. 1184
Ballister, Barry. 792
Bambiger, Michael. 1309
Bampfylde, Heather. 1381, 1383, 3802
Bampfylde, Zune. 1381, 1383, 1508, 3802
Banks, Jane. 1321
Bannock, Bill. 669
Barbe, Marilyn. 2756
Barber, James. 1288
Barber, Linda L. 2269, 2276
Barbour, Beverly. 4110
Barbour, Judy. 554
Barbour, Pamela G. 3287
Barclay, Gwen. 1023
Bard, Rachel. 2208
Bardwell, Flora. 2468
Bareham, Lindsey. 1826
Barile, JoAnne B. Cats see Cats-Barile, JoAnne B.
Barile, Mary. 3246
Barker, Alex. 1904
Barker, Jo. 3120
Barker, William. 3630

Author Index

Barkie, Karen E. 3296, 3350
Barksdale, Jo. 2620, 3410
Barnaby, Karen. 3423
Barnard, Melanie. 4201, 4202
Barrett, Joanne. 1096
Barrett, Judith. 1912
Barrett, Valerie. 350
Barrow, Mary R. 2015
Barrows, A.B. 4232
Barry, Aldonna Kaulius
 see Kaulius-Barry, Aldonna
Barry, Bob and Lynn. 197
Barsky, Ruth. 1379
Barth, Eileen. 3743, 3930
Bartiromo, Sandra. 1638
Bartlett, Gretchen. 3890
Bashline, Sylvia G. 568, 830, 2487
Bass, Lorena L. 1109
Bassett, Barbara. 1355, 1368
Bassler, Lynn. 3434
Bastrya, Judy. 763
Batchelder, Dorothy. 2079
Batcheller, Barbara. 877
Bateman, Michael. 1362, 2754
Bates, Dorothy R. 1540, 2247
Batten, Marion. 1895
Bauer, Cathy. 2253
Bauer, Mary Anne. 4059
Baumann, Paul. 573
Baxter, Kathleen M. 1346
Baylis, Maggie. 2827
Beadle, B. Gayle. 521
Beaham, Cathy. 4229
Beanstalk, Jack. 69
Bear, John. 4087
Beard, James. 609, 1634, 1856, 2635, 2736, 4348, 4365
Beard, Lisa M. 565
Beasley, Sonia. 2204
Beaton, Jane. 3032
Beatty, Bill. 2517
Beazley, Mitchell. 2711
Bebell, Harlan B. 3455
Beck, Anna R. 2473
Beck, Bruce. 2106
Beck, Cheryl. 3914
Beck, Howard. 2473
Beck, Phillips. 981

Becker, Jim. 3419
Bed & Breakfast Innkeepers of Northern California. 4056
Bed Post Writers Group. 4075
Beebe, Marina. 4116
Beef Industry Council. 95
Beef Information Centre. 89, 91, 92, 941
Beeton, Mrs. 861, 1237, 1852, 2404, 2406, 2998, 3447, 3961, 4160
Beharry, Edward. 3628
Beilenson, Edna. 3183
Beilenson, John. 4157
Beinhorn, Courtenay. 4479
Belden, Louise C. 3306
Bell, Brenda. 1807, 3847
Bell, Tracy. 101
Belsinger, Susan. 692, 989
Beltz, Muriel. 1466
Benjamin, Phyllis. 1398
Bennett, Beverly. 2624, 2630, 3720
Bennett, Cheryl. 289
Bennett, D.W. 152
Bennett, Jo-Anne. 4315
Bennett, Kim H. 818
Benning, Lee E. 3508
Benoît, Jehane. 1234, 1667, 1845, 1902, 2030, 2409, 3955
Beranbaum, Rose L. 390, 2935, 2977, 3232
Berger, Lesly. 341
Bergeron, Victor J. 1924
Berkley, Robert. 138
Berkowitz, George. 2085
Berman, Connie. 2688
Bernachon, Jean-Jacques. 390
Bernachon, Maurice. 390
Bernstein, Gerry. 4443
Berriedale-Johnson, Michelle. 1739, 4465
Berry, Mary. 209, 370, 730, 1238, 1469, 2944, 2974, 2986, 3351, 3734, 4104, 4112, 4197, 4456, 4462, 4958
Berthe, Sister. 2583
Bertling, Terry S. 1734
Beta Sigma Phi International. 3032
Better Weigh. 3261
Beutel, Mary. 1131
Bevan, David. 2707
Beyle, Noel W. 2054

Bianco, Marie. 1808, 1913, 1990, 3160, 3827
Bickerstaff, Patsy Anne. 2703
Bidinosti, Joan. 3599, 3780
Bier, Olga. 2311
Bilheux, Roland. 2830, 3656
Biller, Rudolf. 3522
Billmeyer, Pat. 636, 646
Bills, Jay. 4432
Bills, Shirley. 4432
Bilton, Jan. 1232, 4181
Bilton, Rhonda. 1929
Bingham, Joan. 2371, 3360, 3379, 3399, 4214
Binns, Brian. 3664, 4294
Binns, Vanessa. 3664
Birkby, Evelyn. 3169, 3207
Bishop Museum, Honolulu. 3282
Bissell, Frances. 4187
Bissland, James. 3315
Bjornskov, Elizabeth. 2097
Black-Crowley, Linda. 504
Black, Dana Yuen. 56
Black, Maggie. 1323, 1472, 2419, 3072, 4310, 4343, 4360, 4485
Black, Naomi. 2067
Black, Sonia. 404
Blackburn, Ferdie. 275
Blackman, Jackson F. 1549
Blair, Bevelyn. 2949
Blair, Eulalia C. 3270, 3816
Blair, Mary. 2636
Blanc, Georges. 1509
Blanchard, Marjorie P. 782, 3857
Blate, Michael. 1400
Blazek, Mark. 1735
Blessing, Marlene. 1795
Bloch, Barbara. 1211, 1272, 1302
Bloom, Leslie. 298
Bloomfield, Paul. 4105
Bloomfield, Pip. 4339
Blue Diamond Growers. 3
Blue Flame Kitchen Economists. 4384
Bluestein, Barry. 3468
Bodger, Lorraine. 2973, 3205
Boehmer, Peggy M. 856
Boehmer, Raquel. 2089, 2497
Boely, Patrice. 2083
Bollen, Constance. 1795
Bolton, Shelly. 3026
Bonar, Ann. 1010, 1021
Bond, Shirley. 1588
Bonomo, Giuliana. 2121
Boorman, Sylvia. 2522
Boot, William. 2591
Booth, R. Gordon. 3918
Bord, Janet. 1108
Borden, Inc. 155, 156, 439-441, 1153, 1161, 1257
Borella, Anne. 3541, 3627, 3752, 4402
Borghese, Anita. 1559, 2301, 3258
Borland, Barbara D. 2402
Bosker, Gideon. 1352
Bosley, Judith. 24, 233, 257, 3978
Bosley, Stacy. 3978
Bothwell, Jean. 1600
Bottiger, Theodor. 4178
Bottrell, Donna. 2557
Boudreau, Marina. 17
Bounds, Sarah. 1438, 1474, 1556, 4241
Bourne, Patricia. 2387, 3661
Bouterin, Antoine. 3421
Bovbjerg, Dana. 3069
Bove, Eugene. 2843
Bowen, 'Asta. 1126
Bowen, Carol. 3290, 3308, 3629, 4200, 4225, 4334
Bowers, Dorinda. 3467
Bowler, Printer, 2465
Boxer, Arabella. 970, 1065, 2643, 2646
Boyd, Ina C. 2604
Boyle, Peter T. 3132
Boze, Arthur. 1716
Braden, Michele. 2653
Bradford, Montse. 1206
Bradford, Peter. 1206
Bradshaw, L.J. 2922
Brady, Pamela L. 2821
Bragdon, Allen D. 3004, 3125, 3192, 3530, 3531
Bragg, Patricia and Paul. 1344, 1442
Braida, Charlene A. 876
Braker, Flo. 4249
Brand, Elizabeth. 752, 2392
Brand, Mildred. 3010, 3265
Brandt, Linda. 3031
Brandt, Jane. 2699

Author Index

Brass, Betty J. 1714
Brassel, Helen. 1419
Brauer, Barbara S. 933, 4487
Braun, Linda. 668
Bray, Elizabeth H. 2077
Bregman, Micki. 3960
Bremer, Kathy. 2798
Bremner, Moyra. 1647
Bremness, Lesley. 1024
Brennan, Barbara. 1132
Brennan, Georgeanne. 1744, 2428
Brennan, Jennifer. 3053
Brenner, Shauna C. 2370
Brent, Carol D. 526, 3238, 3239, 3495, 4300, 4301
Bridges, Bill. 3083
Brigande, Pat. 404
Brink, Jan. 3899
Brink, Matie. 4017
Bristow, Linda K. 4048
Brody, Lora. 398
Brokaw, Meredith. 4137
Brooks, Cheryl. 3931
Brooks, Jeffree S. 447
Brooks, Karen G. 1352
Browder, Robyn. 2015
Brower, Millicent. 2696
Brown, Angela. 2905
Brown, Colin. 844
Brown, Edward E. 2805
Brown, Elizabeth B. 2447
Brown, Helen E. 4365
Brown, Judy A. 1540
Brown, Lynda. 1524, 2442
Brown, Marlene. 804
Brown, Pamela. 1457, 4445
Brown, Sarah. 1151, 1888, 2800, 3373
Brownlee, Sue. 2641
Bruce, James G. 2495
Brucken, Robert T. 1758
Bruno, Pasquale. 3718
Bryant, Jim. 654
Buchanan, Marian. 1827
Buchmann, Cindy. 1876
Budd, Mavis. 1112
Budgen, June. 2638, 3519
Buffler, Rob. 632
Bugat, Paul. 3637

Bugg, Judy. 2954
Bugialli, Giuliano. 1679
Buishand, Tjerk. 2397
Bull, Veronica. 1241, 3386
Bumgarner, Marlene A. 903, 1335
Bunch, Bryan H. 995
Buonassisi, Vincenzo. 1653, 3722
Burbidge, Cile B. 2884
Burleigh, Ian. 1705
Burley, G. Lamont. 651
Burmeister, Jill. 2183, 2871
Burpee, Lois. 2363
Burrow, Jackie. 1375, 1382, 3783, 3814
Burrows, Lois M. 2324
Burtis, Jean. 1960
Burum, Linda. 1689, 2849, 3504, 3880
Bush, Sarah. 3729
Bush, Sheila. 3503, 4466
Bush, T.L. 98
Buszek, Beatrice R. 23, 145, 468, 1192, 2223
Butcher, Caralan. 3886
Butel, Jane. 2194, 3082, 4306
Butler, JoNett. 2633
Butterfield, M.J. 232, 552
Buyers, Rebecca. 1188
Byrd, Anita. 710
Byrd, Anne. 3618
Byrne, Paddy. 3799, 3828
Byrne, Susan O. 2307
Byron, May. 3567
Cadogan, Mary. 253, 1588, 2150, 3804, 4244
Cain, Doris B. 2433
Calella, John R. 1313
California Almond Growers Exchange. 2, 3
California Apricot Advisory Board. 36
California Culinary Academy. 3506, 4007, 4077
California Home Economics Teachers. 3337
California Olive Industry. 1594
California Wine Advisory Board. 2546, 2558, 2565, 2566
California Winemakers. 2546, 2547
Calingaert, Efrem F. 1643
Callahan, Ed. 3499
Callen, Anna T. 1688
Calvert, Rita. 1304

Specialty Cookbooks

Cambruzzi, Doris. 2841
Cameron, Angus. 649
Cameron, Kay. 4051
Cameron, Myra. 1329
Cameron, Nonnie. 2623
Camp, Raymond R. 852
Campbell, Diane. 1317
Campbell, Mary M. 685
Campbell Soup Co. 180, 184-189, 2297
Canadian Egg Marketing Agency. 532, 544
Canadian Living Magazine. 4370
Canadian Pork Council. 1770
Candler, Teresa. 2336
Candy, Robert. 671
Canino, Thomas L. 2456
Canning, Julia. 763
Cannon, Minuha. 708, 709
Cannon, Poppy. 182
Canter, David. 1434
Canter, Miriam. 3303
Capalbo, Carla. 3527
Capossela, Jim. 461, 868
Capozzo, Bette M. 749, 2596
Carcione, Joe. 764
Carder, Shirl. 1569
Cardiff, Cheryl. 2541
Cardigan, Rosamond. 1748
Carey, Mary. 2764
Carey, Nora. 4425
Carlier, Alexandra. 4062, 4179
Carlisle, Joyce. 49
Carlman, Susan F. 799
Carlson, Anna L. 3233
Carlson, Shirlee C. 1809
Carluccio, Antonio. 1294
Carlyle, William D. 753
Carmack, Robert. 1173
Carpenter, David. 580
Carr, Ann. 39, 51, 418, 551, 1754, 2228, 2425, 2426
Carrier, Robert. 99, 696, 1140, 2390, 3345, 3956, 4176, 4320
Carroll, David. 1431
Carroll, John P. 4341
Carstarphen, Dee. 437
Carswell, E.W. 1607
Carter, Hugh. 1725
Cartlidge, Michelle. 3137

Cary, Pam. 242, 758
Casa Emellos, Ruth P. 3112
Casas, Penelope. 4030
Casella, Dolores. 2361
Cassidy, Janet. 3596
Cassidy, Marilyn. 4111
Casson, Chris. 1155
Castelvetro, Giacomo. 803
Castle, Coralie. 2655, 2827, 3971, 4492
Cats-Barile, JoAnne B. 3061
Cavage, Betty. 1606
Cavalier, Victoria P. 1493
Cawley, Richard. 1468
Cayce, Edgar. 1311
Caywood, Zoe M. 915
Ceirin, Cyril O. see O Ceirin, Cyril
Celebrity Kitchen. 766
Celli, Elisa. 1646
Center for Self Sufficiency. 25, 135, 1710, 2286
Central Florida Wildlife Adoption Society. 198
Ceres. 3535, 3538, 3539
Cestnik, Lisa. 1550
Ch'en, Min-liang. 3964
Chadwick, Janet B. 4397
Chalmers, Irena. 3558
Chamberlain, Judith F. 4147
Chamberlain, Narcissa G. 3619
Chan, Henry. 3464
Chang, Wonona W. 3364
Chanin, Myra. 3081
Chapman, Nan T. 74
Chapman, Pat. 489, 492
Chapman, Tom. 2147
Charmglow. 4314
Charmine, Susan E. 1884
Chase, Cora G. 2493
Chase, Emily. 4168
Chase, Karen. 101
Chatham, Russell. 2229
Chatterton, Elizabeth. 3167
Chatterton, Mary. 3167
Cheek, Chandler S. 519
Chelgren, Paul. 1264
Chenel, Laura. 240, 900
Cheney, Susan. 2833
Cherniske, Stephen S. 2254

Author Index

Chesman, Andrea. 2233, 3442, 3679, 3680, 3830
Chester, Helen. 3887
Chetwood, Doreen. 2729
Chevendra, C.R. 3678
Chevendra, Varalakshmi. 3678
Chilcote, Ann. 541
Child, Pauline G. 312
Childs, Beryl. 3523
Childs, Sarah K. 93
Chirich, Nancy. 2553
Chirol, Richard. 3921
Chittenden, Russ. 674
Chitty, Cordelia. 284
Choate, Judith. 3693, 4279, 4423
Chocolate News. 358
Chocolatier Magazine. 386
Chong, Elizabeth. 3466
Choronzey, Darryl. 601, 613, 1939
Christensen, Janet M. 10
Christensen, Lillian Langseth
 see Langseth-Christensen, Lillian
Christian, Glynn. 4047, 4470
Church, Jennifer. 1927
Church, Virginia A. Strong
 see Strong-Church, Virginia A.
Chute, Kathy. 29
Cirillo, Lee M. 3431, 4219
Cituk, Kathy. 1542
Claessens, Sharon. 1363, 1417, 3215, 3223
Claiborne, Craig. 1064, 2319
Clark, Ann. 2056
Clark, Bettie. 955
Clark, John. 438
Clark, Marge. 1028
Clark, Maxine. 2912
Clark, Ron. 4355
Clarke, Charlotte B. 2484
Clarke, Christina. 2255
Clarke, Ethne. 2420
Clayton, Bernard. 2802, 2807, 3623, 4000
Clements, Julia. 1920
Cleveland-Peck, Patricia. 498
Clifton, Claire. 687
Clingerman, Polly. 1695, 2647
Clubb, Angela. 218, 3608
Clute, Robin. 192
Coatts, Margot. 3595

Cobb, Brenda. 790
Cochran, Debby. 2210
Cockburn, Amy. 1060
Cockburn-Smith, Beth. 2577
Codrington, Emma. 3305
Cofacci, Gino. 1173
Coffin, Leigh B. 3950
Cohen, Ben. 3556
Colbin, Annemarie. 1376, 1543
Cole, Gwyneth. 2880
Coleman, Gill. 765
Collier, Carole. 886, 2887, 3268
Collier, Diana. 2809
Collingwood, Deborah. 2767
Collins, Bill and Pam. 2053
Collins, Tom. 637
Collins, Val. 575, 768, 1446
Collison, David. 3684
Collister, Linda. 1799
Colman, Rowena. 3334
Colonial Williamsburg Foundation. 4238
Colorado Division of Wildlife. 661
Comfort, Judith. 29
Compañía Bananera de Costa Rica. 53
Cone, Joan. 641, 813
Conil, Christopher. 2268, 4260, 4271
Conil, Jean. 757, 2046, 2268, 2609, 3030, 3298, 3475, 4260
Connor, Marlene K. 346
Conran, Terence. 2376
Conrod, Hugh. 415
Conrod, Suzanne. 415
Consumer Guide. 265, 273, 317, 2009, 2355, 2673, 2732, 3151, 3283, 3288, 3688, 3768
Consumer Reports Books. 297, 1910, 2096, 3927
Consumers' Association (Gt. Brit.). 1502, 4450
Conte, Susan. 1704
Cook, Gay. 4239
Cook, Sid F. 2131
Cookbook Consortium. 430
Cooper, Carole. 946
Cooper, Guy. 975
Cooper, Nancy. 3906
Cooper, Sandi. 3987
Cooper, Thelma B. 31

Cooperative Whole Grain Education Association. 4298
Corlett, Jim. 1310
Cornell University, Division of Nutritional Sciences. 2327
Corning, Elizabeth. 2413
Cornish, Elizabeth. 602
Cornog, Mary W. 125, 1788
Corran, Janet. 1012
Corry, Grace and John. 2333
Corsi, Pietro. 743
Corwin, Judith H. 3235
Cost, Bruce. 897
Costner, Susan. 3856, 4186
Cotrez, David. 3101
Cottenceau, Marcel. 1778
Cotton, Nathan S. 2941, 4223
Cottrell, Edyth Y. 1358
Courrege, Keith. 1733
Coutelle, Dee. 3251
Cox, Dee. 1001
Cox, Jill. 2711
Cox, Nicola. 862
Cox-Lloyd, Barbara. 668
Coxe, Antony
 see Hippisley Coxe, Antony
Coxe, Araminta
 see Hippisley Coxe, Araminta
Coyle, Rena. 4299
Craig, Miranda. 1207
Craig, Wendy. 4242
Crane, Eva. 1094
Crawford, C. Lee. 4080
Creasy, Rosalind. 2421
Creations Lac Brome of Knowlton. 2606
Creek, Valerie. 3269
Creery, Anna. 3560
Cremeans, Lola M. 1928
Cristofano, Lois M. 1702
Croce, Alfredo. 1680, 3643, 4246
Crocker, Betty
 see Betty Crocker in Title Index
Crockett, Desda. 3773, 3806
Cronin, Isaac. 2072, 2215
Cross, Billy Joe. 643
Cross, Pamela. 1640
Cross, Rena. 1121, 2332
Crossman, Elizabeth. 1243

Crouch, Dorothy. 2705
Crowley, Kathleen. 104
Crowley, Linda Black
 see Black-Crowley, Linda
Crown, G.H. 2619
Crownover, Mary H. 3080
Crumpacker, Emily. 4403
Cubitt, Gilly. 3805
Culbertson, Molly. 4129
Culinary Arts Institute. 117, 172, 216, 374, 936, 1997, 2942, 3025, 3496
Cullen, Frank. 1167
Cullen, Mary Anne. 1167
Cumbria Seafoods. 571
Cummings, Joy. 2221
Cunningham, Marci. 1479
Cunningham, Marion. 4055, 4234
Curle, Judie. 1425, 2500
Currie, Heather. 2048
Curtis, Linda. 3198
Cusumano, Camille. 2179
Cutler, Carol. 2096, 2789, 3273, 3666
Cutler, Kathy. 2748, 3375
Cutts, Su. 3035
Cuyler, Margery. 1872
Czarnecki, Jack. 1292
D'Ermo, Dominique. 640
Da Costa, Ayee Mendes. 1303
Dadant & Sons. 1103
Dahlem, Ted. 1956
Dahlen, Martha. 746, 2365
Dairy Bureau of Canada. 497
Dairy Farmers of Wisconsin. 507
Dairy Goat Journal. 902
Daisley, Gilda. 986
Dalby, Barbara. 1120
Dalison, Patrick. 3101
Dallas Museum of Art. 3938
Dalsass, Diana. 1345, 2939
Dameron, Peggy. 1387
Dandar, Emil B. and Helen O. 1712, 1871, 2597, 2600
Dandekar, Varsha. 3775
Daniels, Joe. 1621
Dann, Peggy. 4053
Dansby, Patti Jon. 2257
Dard, Patrice. 4336
Dark, Robert. 515

Author Index

Darling, Renny. 2666, 3111
Davenport, Dana T. 3102
Davenport, Rita. 2168
David, Elizabeth. 1052, 2751
Davidson, Alan. 1982, 2105, 2109
Davies, Helen. 4337
Davies, Jill. 3537
Davis, Frank. 1999
Davis, Hillary. 4368
Davis, May H. 423
Davis, Rich. 4352
Davis, Sandra. 2481
Davy, Pamela. 1194
Dawson, Adele G. 969
Day, Bunny. 1968
Day, Glenn. 2159
Day, Harvey. 491
De Alba, Felipe Padilla
see Padilla de Alba, Felipe
De Angeli, Tony. 1249
De Angioy, Rossella. 1655
De Burnay, China. 1518
De Gouy, Louis P. 663, 3838, 3851, 3923
De Langre, Jacques. 164, 738
De Langre, Yvette. 164
De Lima, Suzanne. 4203
De Medici, Lorenza
see Medici, Lorenza de
De Saulles, Denys. 800
De Verteuil, Maurice. 714
De Villiers, S.J.A. 2448, 2840, 3022, 3068, 3454
Deeming, Bill and Sue. 61, 3941, 4401
Del Corte, Anna. 1675
Del Giudice, Paula J. 656
Del Nero, Constance A. 1909
Del Nero, Rosario. 1909
Delahunty, Millie. 2631
Della Croce, Julia. 1673
DeLong, Deanna. 4434
Delver and Weston. 801
DeMers, John. 436
Dempsey, Jim. 854
Denman, Joan E. 4353
Dennis, Tina. 1748
Dennon, Jerry. 1935
Denny, Roz. 617, 2230, 3767
Densley, Barbara. 4439
Der Haroutunian, Arto. 2382, 2584, 3338, 3660, 4335
Detrick, Mia. 4023
Deugo, Shirley. 1194
Development Academy of the Philippines. 2345
Devi, N. Maheswari
see Maheswari Devi, N.
Devine, Mary. 3362
Dewhurst, Yvonne. 1483
DeWitt, Dave. 1746, 2185, 2640
Diamond, Denise. 684
Diamond, Marilyn. 1512
Dickson, Tom. 632
Dieckmann, Jane M. 3204, 3750
Dietz, Juanita. 2470
Diggins, Nicola. 3182
Dikshit, Madhvi. 1423
Dille, Carolyn. 989
Dilsaver, Willene. 2930
DiMarco, Susan. 1544
Dimbleby, Josceline. 481, 937, 3311, 3316
Dinaburg, Kathy. 1315
Dinnage, Paul. 719
Director, Anne. 2542
Disney, Jean A. 3196
Dixon-Hudson, Suzanne. 1176
Dixon, Pamela. 1145
Dixon, Steve. 1585
Dixon, Susan. 770, 1237, 1852, 2404, 2641, 3738, 3961
Dobbin, Peggy. 3146
Dobrin, Arnold. 1558
Dobson, Sue. 2915
Dodge, Jim. 3383
Doerfer, Jane. 2085, 4409
Doerper, John. 2145
Doeser, Linda. 46, 3344
Dohan, Ellen. 3612
Dojny, Brooke. 4201, 4202
Dolamore, Anne. 1597
Dollaghan, Helen. 3472
Donkin, Maria. 43, 524, 1743, 1870
Donna, Natalie. 1729
Donnelly, Hallie. 2634
Donnelly, Nell. 1816
Dooley, Beth. 136, 1745

Dore, Ian. 633, 2013
Dotter, Pamela. 773, 2881, 3377, 3433
Doty, Walter L. 2279, 2283, 2441
Dowling, Kim. 171
Downie, Mary A. 1519
Drachman, Linda. 924
Drake, Bill. 1201
Dreher, Diane. 3613
Dribin, Lois. 2232, 3336
Drinkwater, Penny. 869
Drouin, Renata. 762
Dry Bean Advisory Board. 69
Dry, Jeri. 3211
Drysdale, Julia. 653
Dubbs, Chris. 4483
Ducks Unlimited. 832
Dueland, Joy V. 1180
Duff, Gail. 1079, 1319, 1441, 1448, 1537, 2494, 3059, 4327
Duffala, Sharon. 644
Dugas, Ronald. 1613
Duke, James A. 1003
Dunbar, Patricia. 323, 336, 401
Duncan, Dorothy. 3334
Duncann, Geraldine. 2190
Dunn, Norma. 2872, 2876
Dunn, William J. 4018
Duperret, Jean-Yves. 3653
DuSablon, Mary A. 2256
Duval, Thérèse. 762
Dvorak, Barbara B. 2569
Dwillies, Eileen. 3062, 3063, 3491
Dworkin, Floss and Stan. 2822
Dyer, Ceil. 269, 1672, 3374, 3724
Dykeman, Peter A. 2496
Eakin, Katherine. 3191
Eales, Mary. 3126
Earl, Johnrae. 4014
Early, Howard. 2804
Earnest, Barbara. 1589, 1599
Easlea, Kate. 2573
East West Journal. 3381
Eastman, Margaret C. 1567
Eberly, Carole. 11, 254, 733, 1274, 2846
Ebling, Ruth. 1616
Eccleshare, Julia. 2824
Eckert, Clara. 4220

Eckhardt, Linda W. 4347
Edden, Gill. 3103, 4446
Edelman, Edward. 235
Edington, Sarah. 1554
Edmonds, Gwen. 3540
Edmonton City Centre Church Corporation. 3885
Edmunds, Hunter. 116
Edwards, B.J. 4438
Edwards, John. 996
Edwards, Linda. 4251
Edwinn, Gloria. 2611
Egami, Tomi. 1897
Egan, Jeanette P. 1575
Egan, Maureen. 3412
Ehlert, Friedrich W. 3668
Eines, Marsha. 3913
Elbert, George. 3389
Elbert, Virginie. 3389
Elias, Thomas S. 2496
Elinsky, Stephen E. 4493
Elish, Dan. 3418
Elkon, Juliette
  see Hamelecourt, Juliette Elkon
Ellicott, Margaret. 1453
Elliot, Rose. 75, 734, 1146, 1651, 2768, 2952, 3494, 3772
Elliot, Sharon. 1377, 4162
Ellis, Audrey. 357, 1644, 2810, 2893, 4346
Ellison, J. Audrey. 3659
Ellsworth, Lorna. 296
Ellwood, Caroline. 3995, 4454
Elmont, Nancy. 4305
Emellos, Ruth P. Casa see Casa Emellos, Ruth P.
Emert, Phyllis R. 3732
Emery, William. 3510
Emmerson, Marie. 4469
Emmons, Vicki. 2002
Enderson, Mary Beth. 2862
Engel, Alix. 3211
English, Colin C. 3358
English, Sandal. 720
Eno, David. 72, 163, 538, 2763, 4332
Enright, Nancy. 1011
Episcopal Church Women. Diocese of Southern Virginia. 283
Erickson, Jack. 123

Author Index

Erickson, Richard. 3725
Erlandson, Keith. 4486
Erschen, Olivia. 3003
Eschmann, Clara. 255
Escoffier, Alain. 3656
Eshbach, Charles E. 1979
Esko, Wendy. 3818, 4063
Estella, Mary. 1450
Ets-Hokin, Judith. 4166
Evans, Brenda. 1338
Evans, Margaret M. 1266
Evans, Michele. 3822
Evelyn, John. 3776
Everglades City High School. 718
Evergreen Foundation. 1552
Eversole, Arnold G. 2160
Exter, Patricia D. 4131
Fabricant, Florence. 4180
Fadala, Sam. 857
Fairbairn, Kay. 13
Fairweather, Barbara. 787
Fallon, Peggy. 1859, 4372
Family Circle. 1843, 3320
 see also Title Index
Famularo, Joe. 1635, 2394, 4359
Fance, Wilfred J. 3118
Farah, Madelain. 3712
Farm Journal. 3150, 3562
 see also Title Index
Farmer, Fannie. 4234
Farnsworth, Ruth. 726
Farr, Barbara. 2173
Farrell, Kenneth T. 2200
Farrow, Genevieve. 3613
Farrow, Joanna. 2065, 2899
Farwell, Bea. 2633
Fast, Barry. 201
Fast, Julius. 612
Faubion, Nina. 1268
Faversham Society. 4477
Fawcett, Ingrid N. 1742, 2280
Fears, J. Wayne. 652
Feder, Jack. 2741
Feder, Patti. 2741
Fefergrad, Rosalie. 3960
Feingold, Helen. 4307
Fell, Derek. 2181
Ferguson, Bernadine. 879

Ferguson, Judith. 1080, 2041
Ferndock, Malfred. 1265
Ferrary, Jeannette. 1031
Fessler, Stella Lau. 1831, 1974
Feuer, Janice. 3271
Field, Carol. 4245
Field, Michael. 534, 4383
Field, Pat. 545
Field, Ray A. 831
Fielder, Mildred. 737
Filippini, Liz. 1647
Filut, Marie A. 1747
Findlater, Evelyn. 1412, 1436, 1445, 1482, 1510, 1523
Fine, Diane. 3163, 3701
Fingas, Eva G. 3174
Finnegan, John. 1542
Finsand, Mary Jane. 340, 2683, 3286, 4078
Firkaly, Susan T. 1418
Fischborn, Cynthia. 4421
Fischer, Al. 410, 3086
Fischer, Debi. 3312
Fischer, Mildred. 410, 3086
Fischer, Robert. 701
Fisher, Donald E. 2828
Fisher, Jean S. 3975
Fisher, Jeffrey A. 1980
Fisher, M.F.K. 1620, 3582, 4191
Fishkin, Lois. 1544, 3336
Fishman, Eleanor. 1584
Fitzpatrick, Nancy H. 258, 3255
Flack, Dora D. 2775
Flagg, William G. 421, 1278, 2155
Fleetwood, Jenni. 3055
Fleming, Susan. 750, 1040, 1814
Fletcher, Anne M. 626, 930
Fletcher, Helen S. 3648
Fletcher, Janet K. 920, 2634
Fletcher, Nichola. 666, 2454
Florida Dept. of Citrus. 412, 413
Floris, Christopher. 2934
Flournoy, Barbara D. 1394
Floyd, Keith. 586
Fobel, Jim. 4267
Fohring, Sharon. 1895
Foley, Joan and Joe. 100, 2073
Foley, Tricia. 4148
Fontaine, Bertha V. 2063

Specialty Cookbooks

Food & Wine Magazine. 3427
Ford, Cathy. 432
Ford, Janet. 4120, 4128
Ford, Mary. 2868, 2888, 2896, 2900, 2902, 2909
Ford, Richard. 1202
Forsell, Mary. 137
Foster, Don. 4031
Foster, Frank. 1723
Foster, Gertrude B. 973
Foster, Marge. 4031
Foust, Linda. 3236
Fox, Margaret S. 4087
Foxwell, Mike. 1529
France, Christine. 3563
Francis, Claude. 1095
Franey, Pierre. 2050, 2319
Frank, Dorothy C. 1720
Franklin, Fay. 757, 2046
Franklin, Linda C. 2739
Franklin, Rena. 3936
Fraser, Linda. 493
Fraser, Margaret. 4370
Frazier, Barbara. 1403
Frederick, J. George. 1957
Freedman, Louise. 1295
Freedman, William. 1295
Freeland, Susan. 4020
Freeman, Bobby. 2808, 2968, 3385
Freeman, John A. 1455
Freiman, Jane. 4192
Freitus, Joe. 2490, 3569
French, Alison. 2920
French, Jack. 846
Frey, Iris I. 4143
Friberg, Bo. 3663
Friday, Sandra K. 1365
Friedland, Susan R. 204, 1771
Friedman, Sara Ann. 1290
Froud, Nina. 608
Fryers, Topsy. 3845
Fuglem, Terri. 3947
Fuhrmann, Elke. 3758
Fukuhara, Janice M. 292
Fuller, Lucy. 1489
Fulwiler, Kyle D. 12, 134, 2353
Furlong, Marjorie. 2028, 2488
Furrh, Mary L. 2620, 3410

Fuzzetti, Mike. 1718
Fylde Rugby Club. 3753
Gabbott, Pegge. 1428
Gaede, Sarah. 4224
Gaida, Urban. 667
Gail, Peter A. 513
Gandara, Lonnie. 1859, 2029, 3506, 4372
Garcia, Helen L. 950
Gardner, Jo Ann. 760
Gardner, Ruth. 3421
Garfield, Sandy. 2982
Garland, Sarah. 1055
Garraghan, Leonard Ty. 1878
Gassenheimer, Linda. 3863
Gault, Lila. 406
Gautron, Louis J. 2483
Gay, Kathlyn and Martin. 1324
Gay, W. Lee. 449
Gayle. 1892
Geiskopf, Susan. 1093, 1101, 1380
Gelles, Carol. 922
Genders, Roy. 2524
Gennis, Rita. 40
Gentry, Patricia. 4055
George, Jean C. 2499
George, Susan. 2585
Georgia Agricultural Commodity Commission for Milk. 1256
Georgia Apple Commission. 20
Georgia Peach Commission. 1708
Georgina. 3781
Gerber, Ann. 3342
Gerlach, Nancy. 1746, 2185, 2640
Gerras, Charles. 1545, 1880, 3980
Gerstenzang, Sharon M.D. 3302
Gethers, Judy. 3849
Gewanter, Vera. 2334
Gibbons, Barbara. 2198, 2303, 3294, 3766
Gibbons, Euell. 2519, 2532
Gibson, Karen J. 1254
Gilbar, Annie. 4057, 4124, 4137
Gilberg, R.L. 1866
Gilbertie, Sal. 1029
Gill, Cathy. 355, 376
Gill, Janice M. 2734
Gill, Shirley. 228, 542
Gillespie, William H. 2513
Gilletz, Norene. 222

Gilman, Marion B. 3322
Gilman, Richard. 3322
Gilmour, Margaret. 3280
Gin, Margaret. 2316, 3023
Gina Marie Corp. 1857, 2080
Giobbi, Ed. 1598
Girod, Ginette Hall
 see Hell-Girod, Ginette
Gisslen, Wayne. 4248
Glassman, Helen. 4256
Glenn, Camille. 3289
Glenn, Charlotte. 1744
Glentruim, Sandra MacPherson, Lady. 4169
Glentworth, Marjorie. 2940
Glick, Ruth. 1577, 3957
Glynn, Joanne. 1681
Gnos, John. 4297
Godfrey, Thomas G. 1797
Goetz, Eleanor. 1781
Gohlke, Annette. 2322, 2723, 2928, 3116, 3153, 3685
Gokay, Nancy H. 1198
Gold, Kerry Rose
 see Rose-Gold, Kerry
Gold, Robert. 607
Goldbeck, David and Nikki. 1395, 4038
Goldbeck, Nikki. 1395, 4038
Golden Dipt Co. 1998
Goldrick, Richard. 2095
Gonshorowski, Addie. 3414
Gontier, Fernande. 1095
Gonzales, Marina R. 3307
Gonzalez, Elaine. 324
Good Housekeeping Institute (Gt. Brit.) 3044, 3625, 3771, 4280, 4389
Good, Phyllis Pellman. 1223, 3012, 3157, 3575, 3689, 3935
Goodbody, Mary. 386, 2921
Goode, John. 794, 2125
Goode, Onagh. 2777
Goodfellow, Amanda. 1539
Goodsell, Jeffrey A. 115
Goodwin, Michael. 2191
Goolsby, Sam. 817
Gordon, Karen E. 1330
Gordon, Lesley. 967
Gordon, Monteen. 993

Gordon, Teri. 50
Gore, Sheila. 2988
Gorman, Judy. 2400, 2818
Gorman, Marion. 728, 2248
Gorton, Audrye A. 2450
Gorton's. 705
Gorzalka, Ann. 859
Gosling, Jo. 3641
Goulart, Frances S. 190, 191, 1396, 3299, 3826
Gould, Judith. 122
Gow, Emma-Lee. 4136
Gow, Rosalie. 2479
Graham, Frances K. 2508
Graham, Jill. 697
Graham, Peter. 239
Graham, Winifred. 3570
Granger, Jean. 1273
Grant, Doris. 1535
Grant, Rose. 3910
Gray, Carmen. 2300
Gray, Rebecca. 597, 835
Graybill, Nina. 1648, 3821, 3969, 4190
Green, Delores. 865
Green, Jane. 3245, 4279
Green, Marie. 1454
Green, Mary L. 4, 21, 37, 41, 48, 119, 200, 223, 256, 278, 343, 409, 435, 540, 942, 1113, 1157, 1182, 1286, 1605, 1611, 1740, 1753, 1796, 2154, 2222, 2284, 2554, 2950, 3073, 3252, 3548, 3636, 3694
Greenberg, Ellen. 3097
Greenberg, Hal. 3097
Greenberg, Katherine H. 2337, 3606
Greenberg, Margaret H. 1989
Greene, Bert. 443, 921, 928
Greene, Diana S. 4041, 4240
Greene, Janet. 4422
Greene, Karen. 1513
Greenfield, Jerry. 3556
Greer, Rita. 516
Gregory, Patricia R. 73
Gregory, Valiska. 4052
Grieve, M. 957
Griffis, Nixon. 438
Griffith, Dotty. 3089, 3916
Griffith, Terry. 638, 1988
Griffiths, Joan. 797, 4345, 4371

Grigson, Jane. 732, 793, 1284, 1763, 2342
Grijalva, Priscilla. 1082
Grimsdale, Annette. 4416
Grimsdale, Gordon. 3867
Grochowski, Nita. 761
Grodnick, Susan. 235
Groen, Elaine. 1384
Groll, Helen. 2733
Gronner, Georgina. 3318
Grotz, Peter. 4109
Groves, Phyll. 2161
Groves, Roy. 2161
Grunes, Barbara. 596, 628, 1858, 2117, 2148, 4257
Gubin, Margaret. 32
Gubser, Mary. 2784, 2794, 2834
Gunderson, Jeffrey. 581
Gunn, Bill. 3087
Gunst, Kathy. 442
Gustard, Valerie. 1460
Gwaltney, Frances. 850
Habeeb, Virginia T. 3714
Habib, Leila. 3712
Hadley, Saroj. 488
Haedrich, Ken. 1193, 1196, 2744, 4291
Haessler, John. 2126
Hagen, Autumn D.I. 1406
Hagiwara, Yoshihide. 927
Hagler, Louise. 2271, 2275
Haigh, Rachel. 1481
Haines, M.J. 2575
Hale, C. Clark. 4330
Hale, Glorya. 3017, 3226
Hale, Helen. 839
Hale, Sophie. 882, 2193
Hall, Carolyn V. 3562
Hall, Dorothy. 1392
Hall, Ivy. 3571
Hall, Jeanne and John. 2773
Hall, Lyn. 1860, 2916
Hall, Miranda. 4132
Hall, Nancy. 2491
Hall, Sandy. 3976
Hall, Sue. 3426, 4134
Hall, Walter. 2491
Hallgarten, Elaine. 503, 1163
Halpern, Daniel. 4003
Halpin, Anne Moyer. 2341

Halsey, Johanna. 779
Halsey, Patricia. 779
Ham, Marion. 2801
Hamelecourt, Juliette Elkon. 354, 1089
Hamerstrom, Frances. 2533
Hamilton, Mary. 1143
Hamilton, Tricia. 195
Hampstead, Marilyn. 59
Hanbury Tenison, Marika. 560, 562, 572, 1991, 2331, 4141, 4447
Handslip, Carole. 397, 1361, 1490, 2713, 2951, 3378, 3395, 3438, 3795, 4294
Handwerker, Murray. 703
Hanford, Margaret. 1461
Hanle, Zack. 683
Hanley, Catherine. 4415
Hanley, Christina. 3314
Hannan, Pamela. 1360
Hanneman, L.J. 2855, 2856, 2956, 3621
Hansen, Evie. 2103, 2123
Hansen, Gaye. 2084, 3175, 3033, 4144
Hansen, John W. 4042
Hansen, Kirsten. 4243
Hanssen, Maurice. 968, 1259, 2457, 2578
Happel, Margaret. 4127
Harbo, Rick M. 2075
Hardesty, Corrinne. 1762
Hardwick, Geraline B. 2613
Hargreaves, Barbara. 672
Harlow, Jay. 3854, 4369
Harlow, Julian. 2157
Harrell, Monette R. 953
Harrell, Robert W. 953
Harries, Kerenza. 4088
Harris, Ben C. 956
Harris, Beth. 2126
Harris, Diane. 3839
Harris, Gertrude. 1698
Harris, Jessica B. 1741
Harris, Lloyd J. 878, 881
Harris, Marilyn R. 1191
Harris, Marjorie. 1183
Harris, Rosa Lee. 3173
Harris, Valentina. 1650
Harris, Woodman. 1995
Harrison, John B. 1308
Harrison, Shirley. 407
Harrop, Renny. 999, 4399

Author Index

Harrowsmith Kitchens. 3061
Harsila, Janis. 2103, 2123
Harter, Lynda. 142
Hartung, Shirley. 3221
Hartwell, Stella. 2958
Hartwig, Daphne M. 4184
Harvey, Jacques. 1630
Harvey, L. Wallace. 682
Harvey, Martha. 302
Haskell, Patricia. 225
Hastrop, Kate. 1601
Haughton, Natalie H. 3064, 3164
Hauksson, Sigmar B. 2032
Hauser, Nao. 319, 1759
Hawkes, Alex D. 1923, 2378
Hawkins, Arthur. 2136
Hawkins, Nancy. 2136
Hayden, Barbara Jo. 814
Haydock, Bob and Yukiko. 2632, 3511, 3516
Hayes, Elizabeth S. 1050
Hayes, Kirby M. 1979
Hayes, Patricia A. 2292
Haynes, Linda. 4140
Hayward, Tessa. 2957, 4495
Hayward Zucchini Festival. 2598
Hazelton, Nika. 1641, 2323
Hazen, Janet. 867, 3853
Heal, Carolyn. 789, 2188
Healy, Bruce. 3637
Heath, Veronica. 843
Heatter, Maida. 314, 3140, 3256, 3292, 3357, 3446
Hebbring, Judi. 169
Heberle, Dave. 4483
Hebert, Malcolm R. 159, 2544, 2549, 2551
Hecht, Nancy A.
see Fitzpatrick, Nancy H.
Heetland, Rick I. 512
Heiberg, Jeanne. 3763
Heinerman, John. 1058
Helgeland, Glenn. 836
Helgeland, Judy. 836
Hell-Girod, Ginette. 3748
Helmer, Howard. 3617
Hemingway, Mary M. 4203
Hemmings, Pauline. 1454
Hemphill, John. 992, 1063
Hemphill, Rosemary. 985, 992, 1063, 1070
Hemzö, Károly. 660, 2994
Henderson, Gerry. 3337
Henderson, Janice W. 2482
Henderson, Mike. 4165
Hendrickson, Audra and Jack. 199, 419, 2434
Hendrickson, Robert. 128, 2285
Henrick, Shaun Nelson
see Nelson-Henrick, Shaun
Henry, Linda. 945, 3013
Henry, Terri. 3218
Hensperger, Beth. 2815
Herb Society of America. Chattahoochee, Ga., Unit. 997
Herb Society of America. Southern Ontario Unit. 1022
Herb Society of Greater Cincinnati. 979
Herbert, Susan. 2927
Herborg, Mette. 3831
Herbst, Sharon T. 2760, 3206
Heriteau, Jacqueline. 224, 775, 1287, 1879, 2016, 3933
Herman, Kelly. 4247
Herskowitz, Joel. 1761
Hesketh, Pat. 698, 3579
Hester, Sondra. 4484
Hewitt, Jean. 1373
Hewitt, Linda. 4142
Hiatt, Judith M. 174
Hibbard, Chris. 3889
Hibler, Jane F. 827, 2008
Hickman, Mark. 1494
Hicks, Roger W. 4029
Hicks, Susan. 605, 2049
Higa, Barbara W. 3407
Hildebrand, June. 681
Hill, Lois. 3224
Hill, Madalene. 1023
Hillman, Libby. 2362
Himalayan International Institute of Yoga Science and Philosophy. 1340
Hinde, Thomas. 284
Hine, Jacqui. 3762, 3764
Hinman, Bobbie. 1580
Hippisley Coxe, Antony and Araminta. 1948
Hirasuna, Delphine. 2393

Hirdman, Becky L. 3898
Hirsch, Sylvia B. 353, 3330
Hoag, Nancy. 1122
Hoare, Jean. 84
Hobson, Phyllis. 22, 502, 815, 2780, 3549, 4436, 4441
Hodge, Helene. 1452
Hodges, Anne. 351
Hodges, Marilyn. 4460
Hodgson, Moira. 2197
Hofer, Sam. 3972
Hoffer, Rose. 3597
Hoffman, Bess. 3149
Hoffman, Gar. 2650, 3544, 4427
Hoffman, Mable. 327, 2650, 3544, 4427
Hoffman, Marian. 372
Hoffman, Susanna. 4035
Hoffman, Willa M. 1922
Hoffpauer, Betty. 473
Hogan, Julie. 1791
Hoge, Tom. 1785, 2477
Hoglund, Linette. 2082
Hokin, Judith Ets
 see Ets-Hokin, Judith
Holahan, James. 1963
Holden, Chet. 4102
Holding, Audrey. 2908
Hollander, Mary Kay. 266
Holloway, Malcolm. 2742
Holm, Don and Myrtle. 2164, 4433
Holme, Rachael. 2186, 2755, 2992, 4045
Holmes, Ferne. 670
Holmes, Meredith. 1573
Holt, Geraldene. 806, 1036, 2929, 3651
Holthaus, Fusako. 2262
Hom, Ken. 1678
Homan, Carla. 2627
Honey, Babs. 2694
Honig, Kim. 2308
Hood, Joan. 4453
Hooker, Richard J. 3924
Hope, Dorothy. 2300
Hopfer, Dave. 2074
Hopkinson, Judith. 1034
Hopkinson, Simon. 1034
Hoppe, Lynn. 3050
Horn, Jane. 788, 1841

Horsley, Janet. 66, 611
Horst, Isaac R. 1805, 2502, 3065, 3917
Horton, Eliza Mears. 1709
Hoshijo, Kathy. 1357
Hostage, Jacqueline. 3894
Houdret, Jessica. 1041
Houston, Alice W. 1966
Houston, Julie. 3147, 3281
Hovey, Eddy. 2130
Howard, Pat. 1323
Howarth, A. Jan. 1992, 1994
Howes, Judie MacBeath
 see MacBeath-Howes, Judie
Howkins, Morris. 2883
Howlett, Lorraine Sorby
 see Sorby-Howlett, Lorraine
Hsëh, Hsiung-fei. 3456, 3622
Huang, May Man-hui. 3465
Huang, Su-huei. 2006, 2615, 3463
Huber, Carrie. 3096
Huberty, Kay. 1374
Hudson, Suzanne Dixon
 see Dixon-Hudson, Suzanne
Huff, Lori B. 3911
Hughes, Joyce. 2761
Hughes, Karla. 3583
Hull, Raymond. 4482
Hum, Nellie G. 755
Human Nutrition Information Service. 1138, 1766, 1833, 2357
Humphrey, Richard. 4411
Humphreys, Angela. 845
Humphries, Carolyn. 361
Hunsberger, Eydie M. 1314
Hunt, Bernice. 2836
Hunt, Janet. 1475, 1499, 1674, 2677, 3123, 3670, 3717, 3746, 4135
Hunt, Linda. 1561
Hunt, Rachel. 1557
Hunt-Wesson Foods. 2234, 2277
Hunter, Alice. 657
Hunter, Carol. 1451
Hupping, Carol. 4426
Hurd, Frank J. 1439
Hurd, Rosalie. 1439
Hurlburt, Sarah. 1297
Hurley, Judith Benn. 796

Author Index

Hurst, Bernice. 285, 490, 1659, 2637, 2795, 2960, 3076, 3187, 3371, 3669, 3700, 3784, 3951
Hurst, Jacqui. 1296
Hurst, William C. 4408
Hurwitz, Heidi S. 1365
Husch, Tony. 3236
Hushaw, Glenda. 44
Huson, Paul. 959
Hutchinson, Ann B. 3074
Hutchinson, Kate. 3328, 4121
Hutchinson, Rosemary C. 237, 3490
Hutson, Lucinda. 1017
Huxley, Alyson. 981
Hwang, Hae Sung. 97, 4476
Hyman, Mary. 3300
Hyman, Philip. 3300
Hynes, Angela. 4149
Iaia, Sarah K. 4273
Idone, Christopher. 3812, 4174
Iggers, Jeremy. 3069
Illinois Dairy Farmers. 509
Imes, Sonnie. 4056
Immegart, Mavis. 2257
Imperiale, Louise. 1635, 2394
Indelicato, Dorothy. 2556
Ingall, T. 4373
Inglis, Jane. 4250
Innes, Dorothy H. 786
International Culinary Society. 4278
International Institute of Yoga Science and Philosophy. 1340
International Marine Publishing Co. 2021
International Rice Festival & Dry Bean Jubilee. 1908
Iowa Honey Producers Association. 1119
Iris Garden Club of Wakulla County. 1970
Ishida, Eiwan. 167
Isles, Joanna. 4150
Israel, Andrea. 4151
Ivens, Dorothy. 3474, 3999, 4015
Ivey, Judy. 772
Jabara, Mary L. 1086
Jackson, D.L. 3859
Jackson, Felicity. 1487, 4351
Jackson, Judy. 2438
Jackson, Lee. 19
Jackson, Margaret. 1528
Jackson, P.A. 3859
Jacobs, Andrea. 1379
Jacobs, Barbara. 2474
Jacobs, Greta. 154
Jacobs, Leonard. 2474
Jacquemier, Sue. 3178
Jaeger, James. 573
James, Theodore. 774
James, Wendy. 4446
Jana. 2264
Janericco, Terence. 748, 2661, 2772, 3842, 3973, 4070, 4071
Janes, Garcia. 736
Janson, Betty L. 1160
Jansson, Lennart E. 4210
Jarratt, Enrica and Vernon. 1623
Jarrett, Lauren. 1623, 3529
Jarrett-Macauley, Denise. 352, 2892, 3366
Jasso, Mary. 4034
Jauman, Elaine. 130, 131
Jaxson, Jay. 645
Jaye, Gail C. 3279
Jeanneret, Beatrice. 1022
Jenner, Alice. 1152
Jennie, Sister. 3315
Jennings, Suzanne C. 1465
Jensen, Bernard. 3992, 4092
Jervey, Phyllis. 1896
Jesper, Anne. 2701
Jester, Pat. 4193
Jewell, C. Thomas. 1576
Jewell, Dina R. 1576
Joeb, Joseph M. 547
John, Sue. 2839
Johner, Martin. 316
Johns, Leslie. 745
Johnson, Alison. 1516
Johnson, Cathy. 2534
Johnson, Ellen F. 2725
Johnson, Greg. 4361
Johnson, Jackie. 3025
Johnson, Jann. 3532
Johnson, Jill. 3181
Johnson, L.W. Bill. 811
Johnson, Laura. 4494
Johnson, Michelle Berriedale
  see Berriedale-Johnson, Michelle
Johnson, Rebecca H. 1732

Johnson, Rick. 1804, 3691
Johnson, Roberta B. 1426
Johnston, Elaine. 721
Johnston, Martha P. 2460
Johnstone, Bruce. 2325
Joice, Jean. 1535
Jolly, Martine. 349
Jomaa, Donna D. 3417
Jones, Bridget. 1106, 4374
Jones, Constance. 1696
Jones, Elizabeth. 160
Jones, Evan. 205, 2796, 2837
Jones, Jeanne. 1495, 1792
Jones, Judith. 649, 2796, 2837
Jones, Katharine. 1464
Jones, Marge. 7
Jones, Marian. 2910
Jones, Miriam L. 838
Jones, Sachiye. 1137
Jones, Sonia. 2586
Jones, Stan. 158, 1925, 2249
Jordan, Elaine B. 2094
Jordan, Marynor. 2601
Joshua Morris, Inc. 1840, 2792
Jue, Joyce. 4500
Juliana, Ingrid. 4130
Jung, Mary Beth. 3909
Junior League of Stamford-Norwalk. 2088
Kafka, Barbara. 1553
Kahn, Frederick E. 579, 741, 940, 1839, 2020, 2622, 2702, 2774, 3321, 3843, 3861, 4073, 4404
Kalson, Steven S. 1356
Kannenberg, Cyndee. 3265
Kansas City Barbeque Society. 4381
Kansas Wheat Commission. 2472
Kaplan, Jane. 926
Katz, Carol. 124
Katz, Elliott. 3913
Katz, Nancy B. 2352
Katzen, Mollie. 1312
Kaufman, Sheilah. 2391
Kaufman, William I. 183, 375, 1717
Kaulius-Barry, Aldonna. 1318
Kavasch, E. Barrie. 2492
Kay, Sophie. 265, 1624, 3041
Kaylor, John D. 630
Keeshen, Jan. 2042

Keith, Velma J. 993
Kelley, Jean. 3605
Kelley-McGregor, Arlene. 3605
Kellogg, Caroline. 2208
Kelly, Denis. 1954
Kelly, Patricia M. 3851
Kempfer, Carolyn. 93
Kenda, Margaret E. 1370
Kendall, Frances. 3397
Kendrick, Ruth A. 3016
Kennedy, Diana. 4033
Kennedy, Robert L. 2613
Kennedy, Teresa. 3692
Kenney, Pamela S. 304
Kent, Elizabeth. 4195
Kenton, Leslie. 1885
Kenton, Susannah. 1885
Kenyon, Janice. 1541
Kerby, Mona. 1124
Kerhulas, George. 2024
Kerr, Don. 2343
Kerr Glass Manufacturing Corp. 4424
Kerr, Rose G. 1960
Kerr, Vivian. 2343
Kery, Patricia F. 545
Keyes, Jane. 2607
Khalsa, Baba S. 2445
Khalsa, Siri V. K. 2437
Kibbey, Heather. 1179
Kidston, Jocelyne. 1893
Kidushim-Allen, Deborah. 3276
Kimble, Socorro M. 3393
Kinderlehrer, Jane. 1378, 3188, 3611, 4061
King, Caroline B. 2967
King, Kathleen. 4295
King, Shirley. 599, 2119
Kinmont, Vikki. 1485
Kirkpatrick, Catherine. 2999, 3840
Kirkwood, Margaret. 4358
Kirsta, Alix. 1536
Kishi, Asako. 4028
Kisslinger, Juanita. 1917
Klarie, Anne. 2012
Klebba, Louise. 474
Kleiman, Evan. 1684
Klein, Maggie B. 1593
Klein, Matthew. 3553
Klein, Vera. 1817

Kleinman, Kathryn. 690
Klever, Eva. 3497
Klever, Ulrich. 3497
Klingel, Ruth. 321
Kloepper, Elisabeth. 434
Kloss, Jethro. 1342
Kluger, Marilyn. 2505
KMA Radio, Shenandoah, Iowa. 3169, 3207
Knickelbine, Scott. 1389
Knight, Jacqueline E. 823
Knipe, Judy. 3225
Knode, Sandi. 1107
Knox Gelatine Co. 888, 892
Knox, Gerald M. 2038, 2411
Knox, Maxine. 1940
Koffler, Bruce. 3601
Kohrman, Katherine. 3301
Kokko, Margo. 3513
Kolb, Patricia Moore. 3981
Kolpas, Norman. 1685, 1719, 2663, 3450, 3731, 3876, 4082
Koretsky, Ruth. 122
Koshkin, Naomi. 2696
Kosoff, Susan. 2984
Koufas, Theo. 1443
Koury, Christine. 279, 3327
Kovash, Arlene. 2466
Kowbel, Anne K. 2599
Kraft, Inc. 206, 207, 211, 213, 214, 476, 563, 1199, 2347, 3755
Kraft, Ken and Pat. 2321
Krajeski, Anita. 118
Kramer, Rene. 1227
Kranzdorf, Hermie. 1061
Krause, Steven A. 2700
Krech, Inez M. 64, 1602, 1789, 2281
Kreitzman, Sue. 871, 1824
Kroll, Maria. 2376
Kronschnabel, Darlene. 248, 3265
Kros, Wim. 3526
Kruglak, Fredlyn. 4213
Krumm, Bob. 139
Kruppa, Carole. 3408
Kruze, Leonard F. 4478
Kuhn, Gerald D. 4406
Kuhne, Petra. 4431
Kumagai, Kenji. 4025
Kump, Peter. 3744

Kuntz, Bernie. 1547
Kuo, Shu-hsien. 4107
Kurth, Geneste and Kurth. 4308
Kurth, Heinz. 4308
Kushi, Aveline. 3818, 4063
Kutas, Rytek. 1949
Kutner, Lynn. 2749
Kuyper, Frances. 2878
Kybal, Jan. 1049
Kyler, Vicki. 106
Kyte, Barbara K. 2337, 3606
La Follette, Sherry. 3244
La Leche League International. 1426
La Place, Viana. 1684
Lacerte-Neumann, Geraldine. 1062
Lacy, Barbara L. 121
Laffal, Florence. 2722
LaFray-Young, Joyce. 2004
Lagowski, Barbara J. 2706
Lajos, Mari. 660, 2994
Lamagna, Joseph. 826
Lamba, Vishwa. 874
Lambert, Heather. 433, 4393
Lambert, Henry A. 227
Lambert, Robert. 378
Lambeth, Joseph A. 2860
Lambourne, Cheri. 3815
Lambrecht, Helga. 918
LaMere, Shirley. 583
Lammers, Susan A. 4398
Lammie, Ron. 2068
Lampert, Junko. 2269, 2270, 2276
Landgrebe, Gary. 2251, 2258
Langseth-Christensen, Lillian. 8, 181, 274, 338, 1228, 3049, 3988
Lanier, Pamela. 4076
Lanigan, Anne. 3143
Lanner, Ronald M. 1750
Lapp, Sallie Y. 4208
Larkcom, Joy. 3778
Larousse, David P. 3520
Larsen, Phyllis. 329
Larson, Kathryn. 4449
Lashford, Stephanie. 1563
Lassalle, George. 567, 627, 2058
Latorre, Dolores L. 962
Laughlin, Ruth. 3113
Lavis, Sally. 873

Law, Digby. 3401, 3681, 3934
Law, Ruth. 3461
Lawrence, Paul A. 315
Lazar, Wendy. 4118
Leach, Alison. 2712
Leach, Peter. 1265
Learson, Robert J. 630
LeBlanc, Beverly. 1248, 1687, 2657, 3871
Lebrecht, Elbie. 2961
Leclair, Normand. 293
Lee, Deborah. 2529
Lee, Gary. 2675
Lee, Hilde G. 2561
Lee, Karen. 3990
Lee, Susan. 1155
Lee, William H. 1883
Leeb, Ollie. 3186
Leed, Rick. 4163
Leeming, Margaret. 3465
Leggatt, Jenny. 689, 693, 3115
Lehrer, Stephen M. 309
Leibenstein, Margaret. 1291
Leith, Prue. 4175
Leman, Pat. 2904
Lemley, Jo and Virg. 2172, 2589
Lemon, Julianne. 1726
Leneman, Leah. 47, 2180, 2267, 3715
Lenôtre, Gaston. 3300
Lentz, Ginny. 1998, 2027
Leonard, Thom. 2832
LeRiche, Susanne. 325
Lerman, Annie. 3984
Lesem, Jeanne. 4400
Letellier, Phyllis M. 475
Leung, Mai. 3459
Leverett, Brian. 4395
Levin, Betty B. 10
Levine, Marian. 2195, 3220
Levitt, Eleanor. 1316
Levitt, JoAnn. 1332
Levy-Bacon, Josephine
 see Bacon, Josephine
Levy, Faye. 365, 1692, 2417, 3437, 4189
Lewis, Cynthia. 2897
Lewis, Janet. 2590
Lewis, Leon. 4173
Lewis, Sam. 1221
Leyel, C.F., Mrs. 1014

Li Tseng, P'eng-chan. 3039, 4262, 4491
Libby, McNeill, Libby. 1867
Liddell, Caroline. 1339, 4277
Liebman, Malvina W. 1047
Lifespan Community Collective. 3272
Lin, Florence. 2803, 3040
Lindeman, Joanne W. 4474
Lindsay Olives International. 1595
Ling, Amy. 2976
Lipton, Inc. 517, 518, 3749
Lirio, Jack. 3326
Little, Billie. 363
Little, Carolyn. 866
Littlebee, Cy. 662
Littlewood, Alan. 2799
Litton Systems. 767
Liu, Christine Y.C. 2266
Living Springs Retreat. 1393
Livingston, A.D. 673
Lloyd, Barbara Cox
 see Cox-Lloyd, Barbara
Lo, Eileen Yin-Fei. 3460
Lo, Kenneth. 2401
Lo, Tamara. 608
Lobel, Leon and Stanley. 1217, 1252
Locke, Susan. 433, 2379
Lockett, Patricia. 2959
Lockie, Gillian. 1483
Lockwood, Lu. 3944, 4043
Lodge, Nicholas. 2926
Loeb, Evelyn. 3253
Loebel, Alice D. 4019
Loeffler, Chris. 1314
Loewenfeld, Claire. 980
Lomask, Martha. 3028, 3242, 3719
Lombardi, Felipe Rojas
 see Rojas-Lombardi, Felipe
London, Mel. 910, 1075, 2011, 2758, 2776, 3439
London, Sheryl. 910, 1075, 2011, 3439
Long, Ann. 4183
Long, Cheryl. 1179, 4421
Longacre, Doris. 1507
Longo, Nancy. 2061
Lonik, Larry J. 1097, 1263
Loo, Miriam B. 2753, 3765
Loomis, Susan H. 2081
Lorenz, Klaus. 2930

Lorenzo, Henry R. 132, 1130
Loring, John. 4182
Louden, Rosemary F. 973
Louie, Shirley. 4255
Louisiana Dept. of Wilflife and Fisheries. 1613
Louisiana Sea Grant College Program. 2047
Louisiana State University & Agricultural & Mechanical College. 3574, 3677
Lousada, Patricia. 335, 858, 1025, 1631, 3122
Love, Louise. 3716
Lovejoy, Ann. 1042
Lovers of the Stinking Rose. 878
Lowery, Joseph. 1531
Lubrina, François. 1125
Lucas, Karen A. 2649
Luckett, Pete. 807
Lukins, Sheila. 3380
Lumpkin, Julie. 2531
Lund, Duane R. 1289, 1372, 2538
Lupi Vada, Simonetta. 1645, 1652, 1658, 3584
Luther Burbank Home & Gardens. 1806
Lynch, Francis Talyn. 3521
Lynn, Barbara. 3846
Mabbutt, Anita and Bill. 576, 824
Mabey, David. 1301, 1946, 3684
Macadam, Robert K. 1269
Macauley, Denise Jarrett
  see Jarrett-Macauley, Denise
MacBeath-Howes, Judie. 4254
MacCallum, Anne C. 1869
MacCarthy, Daphne. 1021, 3030
Macdonald, Claire, Lady. 381, 591, 3382
Macgregor, Elaine. 2890, 2925
MacIlquham, Frances. 647
Mackay, Muriel H. 2548
Mackley, Lesley. 397, 1669, 2713
Maclean, Lady Veronica. 3865
MacLennan, Gill. 15
MacNeil, Karen. 1343
MacRae, Norma M. 4418
Madlener, Judith C. 891
Madsen, Sandra. 2092
Maffin, June M. 1350
Magel, Werner O. 662

Magida, Phyllis. 596, 628, 1858, 2117, 2148, 2864
Maher, Barbara. 2882, 2946, 2995, 3002, 3075
Maheswari Devi, N. 487
Mahnken, Jan. 2384
Maine Bureau of Agricultural Marketing. 30
Maisner, Heather. 2754
Majerowicz, Wendy. 3661
Major, Mary. 3060
Major, Sally. 4448
Majors, Judith S. 3394
Makris, Dimetra. 3610
Malgieri, Nick. 3443, 3657
Mallorco, Jacqueline. 3653
Mallos, Tess. 60, 1150
Man, Rosamond. 616, 4354
Manderson, Emma. 52
Mandry, Kathy. 1728
Manicas, Edna C. 3293
Manion, Timothy E. 650, 665
Manjon, Maite. 4044
Mann, Lynn. 2962
Mann, Sue. 2895
Manning, Elise W. 4235
Mansfield, Marion. 4324
Manteris, Jimmy. 1876
Manthei, George. 676
Marcangelo, Jo. 226, 236, 3667
March, Andrew L. and Kathryn G. 1280, 2515, 2535, 3572
Marchello, Martin. 667
Marcin, Marietta M. 3536
Marcus, George and Nancy. 771
Marina, Denise. 2232
Marks, Adele. 3161, 3340, 3598, 3633, 3634
Marks, Barbara. 3225
Marks, James F. 4319
Marks, Jim. 4376
Marquardt, Suzanne. 1486
Marquis, Vivienne. 225
Marrone, Teresa. 849
Marsh, Carole S. 1134
Marshall, A.B. 3551
Marshall, Anne. 3695
Marshall, Janette. 194, 1402, 1427, 1474, 1488, 1586, 3354

Marshall, Mel. 658
Marteka, Vincent J. 1276
Martha White's Foods. 4281
Martin, Carol. 3946
Martin, Dale. 1527
Martin, Faye. 3260
Martin, Franklin W. 2238
Martin, Jeanne M. 1366, 4009
Martin, Kathy. 1526
Martin, Liz. 3107, 3733
Martin, Pol. 1671, 2060, 2107, 2644, 2671, 3403
Martin, Rux. 3061
Martindale, Carolyn. 1027
Martinez, Lionel. 3789
Martinson, Linda. 1932
Martinusen, Julia. 3473
Maruska, P. 2403
Maryland Seafood Marketing Authority. 1958
Mashiter, Rosa. 4159
Mason, Anne. 260
Mason, Madeleine. 3776
Massie, Georgia M. 2388
Master Chefs Institute of America. 3487
Matney, Jim. 6
Matteson, Marilee. 2669, 3979
Maureau, Paul. 1809
May, Betty M. 2645
May, Bill. 2869
Mayer, Andrew. 3419
Mayer, Paul. 3745
Mayes, Angela. 120
Maynard, Dave. 4001
Maynard, Kitty and Lucian. 1578, 4054
Maynard, Moya. 2328
Mayo, Patricia T. 4228
Mazza, Irma G. 961
McAndrew, Ian. 604, 700
McCay, Clive M. and Jeanette B. 2730
McClane, A.J. 615, 1961, 1971
McConnaughey, Evelyn. 1205
McCormick & Co. 2187
McCormick, Gill. 3844
McCormick, James. 4014
McCracken, Betsy. 3675
McCreary, Susan A. 2216, 2219
McCristall, Marion. 2626

McCrorie, Brad. 3967
McCully, Helen. 4481
McCune, Kelly. 2078, 4340, 4373
McDonald, Camille. 1894
McDonald, Karen. 904
McDonald, Kendall. 1969
McDonald, Ross. 4358
McDougalls Home Baking Advisory Service. 4268
McDowell, Pamela. 3837
McEnery, Sheila. 501
McGregor, Arlene Kelley
  see Kelley-McGregor, Arlene
McGruter, Patricia Gaddis. 2252
McGuinness, Glynis. 4461
McIlhenny Co. 2240
McIlvaine, Charles. 1269
McIntyre, Nancy F. 3708
McIntyre, Pam. 1603
McKee, Gwen. 3949
McKinney, John. 3674
McKnight, Brenda. 1711
McLaughlin, Michael. 3090
McLintock, Mrs. 4279
McMichael, Betty. 904
McNair, James K. 113, 230, 243, 291, 456, 1515, 1654, 1694, 1822, 1907, 1933, 2211, 3676, 3707, 3727, 3977, 4081, 4333, 4378
McNamara, John. 2877, 2886
McNaught, Chriss. 111
McNeil, Bob. 3939
McNulty, Henry. 2708
McPherson, Gail. 1707
McPherson, Ruth. 4111
McVey, Deirdre. 3264
McWilliam, Jill. 1496, 4459, 4468
Mead, Chris. 1005, 1033
Meadows, Hank. 1829
Meat and Livestock Commission. 1135, 1218, 2317
Meche, Shirley. 2235
Meddock, Sally. 3962
Medici, Lorenza de'. 3428
Medrich, Alice. 396
Medve, Mary Lee and Richard J. 2536
Meilach, Dona Z. 1162, 1175, 3588
Meilach, Mel. 1162, 1175
Meintjes, Ria. 2857

Author Index

Meller, Eric. 926
Mellody, Peggy. 405
Mellor, Isha. 1099
Melvin, Shelley. 2588
Mendelson, Lynn. 281
Mendelson, Susan. 369, 3642
Mendes da Costa, Ayee
 see Da Costa, Ayee Mendes
Mengelatte, Pierre. 4094
Menghi, Umberto. 1661, 2068
Menkveld, H. 4206
Menzies, Robert H. 976
Menzies, Yve. 2652
Merinoff, Linda. 1663, 1951, 3533
Merris, Mary. 1154
Merrison, Lynne. 1915
Mességué, Maurice. 994
Messinger, Lisa. 2274
Metcalf, Sheila. 2294
Metcalfe, Kathleen. 2869
Methven, Barbara. 769, 949, 1212, 1851, 2687, 3267, 3489, 4452
Metland, Daphne. 1115, 1147
Meuninck, Jim. 2523
Meyer, Carolyn. 428
Meyer, Clarence. 964, 1030
Meyer, Susan J. 1666
Meyers, Perla. 2422, 2430
Michael, Pamela. 966, 2510
Michaelson, Mike. 2278
Michigan Grape and Wine Industry Council. 2543
Michigan United Conservation Clubs. 820
Microwave Cooking Institute. 295, 948, 2062, 2685
Microwave Times. 3058
Middione, Carlo. 1633
Middlestead, Maria. 1433, 3392
Middleton, Lynette M. 2937
Migliaccio, Janice C. 3937
Mikkelson, Anne. 1265
Miles, Karen. 1081
Millang, Theresa N. 3614
Miller, Bryan. 2050
Miller, Carol Lee. 1731
Miller, Elna. 533
Miller, Lani. 1337
Miller, Richard L. 3493

Miller, Rita. 784
Millner, Cork. 2152
Miloradovich, Milo. 582, 1074, 1084
Minnesota Conservation Officers Association. 860
Mirel, Elizabeth P. 1754
Mitchamore, Pat. 2478, 2480
Mitchell, Howard. 2151
Mitchell, Jess. 313
Mitchell, Patricia B. 9, 34, 2717, 2825, 2829, 3249, 3444
Mitterhauser, Klaus. 4101
Mock, Lonnie. 259
Moe, Jeanne. 3332
Mohlenbrock, Beverly K. 724
Mohney, Russ. 514
Moll, Judy. 1420
Monaco, Steve. 1718
Monroe, Elvira. 3070
Montagard, Jean. 2964
Montana Dept. of Fish, Wildlife, and Parks. 863
Montana State University. 3422, 3803, 3965
Montoya-Welsh, Sharon. 1615
Moore, Anna. 3810
Moore, C. Teresa Kennedy. 1367
Moore, Eva. 57
Moore, Lolita D. 971
Moore, Marilyn M. 2747, 2814, 3452
Moore, Suzanne T. 431
Moorman, Ruth. 311, 3754
Moosewood Collective. 1511, 1555
Morash, Marian. 2358
Mordengren, Fritz. 2564
Morehead, Judith and Richard. 842
Morgan, Jan. 3011
Morgan, Lane. 2446
Morgan, Sarah. 2721
Morin, Rita. 3093
Moriyama, Sachiko. 2981, 3222
Moriyama, Yukiko. 2261
Morley, Laurene. 2642
Morris, Ann. 2845
Morris, Dan. 590
Morris, Glenda. 2804
Morris, Inez. 580
Morris, Mary. 2863, 3035
Morris, Sallie. 1067, 3398

Morris, Sally M. 2099
Morrisey, Kevin. 3468
Morrison, Wendy. 3881
Mortimer B. Davis Jewish General Hospital Auxiliary. 2610, 3275
Moscovitz, Judy. 1905
Mosimann, Anton. 614, 631, 1467, 2146
Mother Earth News. 1414
Mothershead, Alice B. 4164
Mottram, Angela. 1239, 1245
Moulton, LeArta. 899
Mouzar, Mary. 3066, 3424
Moxon, Lloyd. 4212
Moyer, Anne. 2356
Mr. Bratwurst Meats & Sausages. 1947
Mueller, Arlene. 2556
Mueller, Jo. 1275, 1285
Mueller, T.G. 1774
Muenscher, Minnie W. 965
Muessen, H.J. 270
Muir, Reginald L. 1610
Muller, John. 2595
Müller, Veronika. 3823
Mulligan, Grace. 4272
Mullin, John M. 856
Mumaw, Catherine. 3882
Munn, David. 3644
Munshower, Suzanne. 2668
Munson, Shirley. 35
Murdoch, Lesley H. 3559
Murfitt, Janice. 384, 2917, 3589, 4177
Murphy, Esther. 2907, 3517
Murphy, Margaret D. 2026
Murray, Rose. 706, 2366
Museum of Fine Arts, Boston. 4147
Mycological Society of San Francisco. 1295
Myerly, Marilyn. 3507
Myers, Barbara. 326
Myers, Laura G. 2324
Na Lima Kokua. 429, 2236, 2241
Nabisco, Inc. 114, 1306, 2574
Naftalin, Rose. 2996
Nagel, Werner O. 662
Nagle, Nancy. 3529
Naldrett, Frances. 2335
Nalepa, Jan. 589
Nathan, Amy. 759, 2656, 3785

National Dairy Council. 501, 2695, 3476, 3893, 4046
National Fish & Seafood Promotional Council. 210
National Gardening Magazine. 479, 525, 929, 2888
National Live Stock and Meat Board. 1216
National Marine Fisheries Service Gloucester Laboratory. 630
National Meat Institute. 1262
National Pork Producers Council. 1765, 1769
Natural Food Institute. 2813
Nature's Nook (Co-op). 1333
Nault, Leona M. 2592
Nazzaro, Lorel. 3673
Neal, Bill. 4289
Nearing, Helen. 1336
Neely, Martina and William. 3084
Neff, Bernice. 4442
Neimark, Jill. 3555
Nelson, A.E. 1197
Nelson-Henrick, Shaun. 2576
Nelson, Jo. 35
Nelson, Joan. 875
Nelson, Kay Shaw. 3024, 3925, 4068
Nelson, R. Smith. 1197
Nelson, William H. 115
Nettleton, Joyce A. 2064
Neumann, Geraldine Lacerte see Lacerte-Neumann, Geraldine
Neuville, Christiane. 2964
New Mexico State University, Las Cruces, Cooperative Extension Service. 3091
Newland, Nancy F. 3274
Newman, Rhona. 1798
Newton, Marceline A. 1311
Ney, Tom. 2102
Nibeck, Cecilia G. 952, 1937
Nichol, Kathleen M. 2715
Nichols, J.L. 1172
Nichols, Lew. 500
Nichols, Nell B. 3150, 4449
Nickell, Estelle B. 1260
Nickerson, Dorothy. 939
Nickerson, Doyne. 939
Nicol, Ann. 795
Nicolas, Jean F. 2118, 3514

Nicolello, L.G. 3635
Nicoletti, Lorenzo. 3905
Niedermayer, Flo. 3485
Niethammer, Carolyn J. 2520
Nilsen, Angela. 3219
Nilsson, Anne. 496
Nirenberg, Sally. 4011
Nixon, Iona. 267
No, Chin-hwa. 1231
Noble, Rudolf. 261
Nocentini, Alberta. 1691
Nodl, L. 2403
Noepel, Penny. 2424
Nordengren, Fritz and Mary. 2564
Nordstrom, Jane. 2719, 2735
Noriega, Irma S. 3393
Norman, Cecilia. 244, 3241, 3632, 3864, 4318, 4364
Norman, Jill. 394, 1037, 2199, 2201, 2202, 2203, 3540, 3587
Norman, Ursel. 3983, 4194
North American Hunting Club. 829
North American Maine-Anjou Association. 103
North American Truffling Society. 2293
North Carolina State Beekeepers Association. 1117
North Carolina State University, Raleigh. 3580
North Dakota Wheat Commission. 2471
Norton, Ann M. 1565
Norwak, Mary. 52, 393, 711, 2069, 2330, 2782, 2788, 2947, 2993, 3247, 3581, 3737, 3747, 3787, 4269, 4387, 4412, 4419, 4451, 4463, 4467
Nova Scotia Dept. of Fisheries. 1987
Novak, Jane. 305
Novak, Paul. 2823
Null, Gary. 2418
Nusom, Lynn. 3449
Nusz, Frieda H. 1307
Nutrition Foundation of the Philippines. 3484
Nyerges, Christopher. 2498
O Ceirin, Cyril and Kit. 2511
O'Brien, Claudia. 2092
O'Brien, Jane. 2175
O'Brien, Marian M. 1066

O'Connor, Lois. 1078
O'Leary, Helen. 2676
O'Roark, Mary Ann. 3542
O'Sullivan, Joan. 3617
Oakland, Ann. 170
Oberrecht, Kenn. 564
Oberrecht, Pat. 564
Ocean Spray Cranberries. 469
Odell, Carol. 1392
Odell, Olive. 3578
Oetker, Dr. 3524, 4233
Ogden, Ellen. 2435
Ogden, Shepherd. 2435
Ogren, Sylvia. 2724, 2838, 3267
Ohrbach, Barbara M. 691
Ohsawa, George. 738
Ojakangas, Beatrice. 2540, 2778, 2835, 3051, 3391, 3430, 4275
Oklahoma Peanut Commission. 1727
Oklahoma State Society of Washington, D.C. 3085
Older, Julia. 2826
Oldham, Jan. 3047
Olds, Nancy J. 1989
Olin, Leon. 2530
Olin, Sylvia. 2530
Oliver, Martha H. 1347
Oliver, Raymond. 3874
Olney, Judith. 321, 2793
Olney, Richard. 4117
Olson, Carol K. 133
Omae, Kinjiro. 4022
Ontario Beekeepers' Association. 1118
Ontario Egg Producers' Marketing Board. 530, 537, 546
Ontario Milk Marketing Board. 1255
Ontario Ministry of Agriculture and Food. 2746, 4303
Oosthuizen, Juliet. 1622
Orchard, Jan. 2525
Orcutt, Georgia. 1832, 2740, 3284, 3996
Organic Gardening Magazine. 2341
Orlando, Joseph. 1972
Orr, H.L. 4303
Orr, Suezanne Tangerose. 777
Orsini, Elisabeth. 3686
Ortho Books. 2279, 2283, 2441, 3757, 4007, 4398, 4457

Ortiz, Elisabeth Lambert. 783
Ortman, Donna M. 385, 392
Orton, Ellen and Vrest. 907
Osterhaug, Kathryn. 1960
Ou-yang, Jen-shih. 3462
Ouzinkie Botanical Society. 2508
Owen, Millie. 963, 2363
Paananen, Eloise. 173
Padilla de Alba, Felipe. 2248
Pahlow, Mannfried. 1882
Paimblanc, Jean-Jacques. 2035
Paino, John. 2274
Painter, Gillian. 729, 984
Palmer, Joyce. 2627
Palmer, Nichola. 362, 2806, 3966
Pandya, Michael. 444, 484
Panton, Cindy. 1371
Pappas, Lou S. 548, 788, 2044, 2354, 2562, 2720, 3144, 3985
Paré, Jean. 2987, 3210
Parke, Gertrude. 318
Parker, Dorian L. 3248
Parker, Dorothy. 751, 1825
Parkhill, Joe M. 1092, 1098, 1105, 1107
Parkin, Molly. 3845
Parks, Frederick J. 1617
Parrott, Lora L. 4161
Parsonage, Sally. 916
Parsons, Steve. 3429
Partain, Katherine. 1110
Partington, Jasper. 2579, 3543
Parton, Nicole. 3900
Pasley, Virginia. 3245
Passin, Roy. 3855
Passmore, Jacki. 2672, 3557
Paston-Williams, Sara. 623, 3705, 3739, 4410
Paterson, Wilma. 2690, 2698
Patten, Marguerite. 96, 566, 1534, 3100, 3124, 4113, 4158, 4237
Pauli, Joan. 2410, 2680, 3416, 3897
Pay, Joanna. 1522
Payne, Clare. 4317
Payne, Patricia. 3741
Peanut Museum, Plains, Ga. 1722
Pearse, John. 2563

Peck, Patricia Cleveland see Cleveland-Peck, Patricia
Peck, Paula. 4230
Peck, Penelope. 3262
Peck, Tombi. 2901
Pederson, Rolf A. 695, 825
Peery, Susan M. 3214
Pellegrini, Angelo M. 2436
Pellman, Rachel Thomas. 1223, 3012, 3157, 3575, 3689, 3935
Penner, Lucille R. 1123
Peplow, Elizabeth. 978, 1053
Percival, Dorothy. 4477
Pereira, Anna S. 2242
Perkins, Romi. 659
Perl, Lila. 1560
Perry, Josephine. 3139
Perry, Rick. 1525
Pertwee, Ingeborg. 2625
Peter, Madeleine. 994
Peterson, Penny. 4302
Pettigrew, Jane. 4152
Pfeifer, Diane. 1760
Pfeiffer, Carl C. 1321
Phillipps, Karen. 746, 2365
Phillips, Bert J. 4231
Phillips, Diane. 2623, 4236
Phillips, Jill M. 4039
Phillips, Patricia. 4475
Phillips, Roger. 2512
Piccinardi, Antonio. 1670, 2045, 2093
Pickard, Mary Ann. 1326
Pierce, Gail. 162, 165
Pietschmann, Richard. 814
Pijpers, Dick. 747
Pill, Virginia. 2028, 2488
Pinder, Polly. 383, 1386, 2811, 2894, 2906
Pinelands Folklife Project. 467
Pinneys Smokehouses. 578
Pisinski, Charlotte W. 4398.
Pitchford, Polly. 1530
Pittman, Janet. 3626
Pitzer, Sara. 67, 906, 1837, 2225
Pizzico, William A. 1225, 1857, 2080
Plageman, Karen. 2927, 3027
Plagemann, Catherine. 3582
Planters Lifesavers Co. 1564
Plastino, Maxine. 2594

Author Index 595

Plotkin, Fred. 1690
Plumb, Barbara. 2590
Plutt, Mary Jo. 2013, 3790
Pointing, Keith. 2714
Pollio Dairy Products Corp. 229, 1918
Polunin, Miriam. 917, 2469, 3852
Polushkin, Maria. 454
Pomeroy, Elizabeth. 1830, 4221
Poole, Shona C. 2579, 3128, 3505, 3543
Poppke, William R. 460
Porter, Suzanne. 1476, 1517
Postal, Susan. 4256
Potato Marketing Board. 1780, 1793, 1800, 1801, 1811, 1818-1820
Potter, Betty M. 364
Potts, Evangela. 1045
Potts, Leanna K. 1038, 1045
Poulos, Colleen M. Zickert
 see Zickert-Poulos, Colleen M.
Poulton, Lucy. 2911
Povey, Rosemary. 4123
Powell, John. 4480
Powell, Margaret. 3136
Powers, Judy. 1111
Powers, Maureen. 3197
Powling, Suzy. 2918
Prange, Cathy. 2410, 2680, 3416, 3897
Predika, Jerry. 1943
Prenis, John. 1043, 1076
Prescott, Elaine. 1813
Prescott, Ellen G. 485
Prescott, Lawrence M. 485
Pressman, Thelma. 3353
Preston, George and Marianne. 2143
Preway Industries. 4322
Prichard, Anita. 3007, 3099
Pride, Colleen. 2245
Prince, Jean. 4204
Prince Rupert 75th Birthday Committee. 2019
Pringle, Laurence. 2485
Prodaniuk, S.A. 3184
Prop Roots Organization. 718
Proulx, E. Annie. 500
Pryor, Mandy. 2975
Puget Sound Mycological Society. 1267, 1282

Pulse Growers Association of Alberta. 1149
Purdy, Susan G. 2980, 3709
Pursley, Barbara Tucker
 see Tucker-Pursley, Barbara
Purton, Brenda. 3565
Quadra Island Child Care Society. 1981
Quan, Constance. 3518
Quick, Clifford. 1359
Quick, Vivien. 1359
Quigley, Delia. 1530
Quinn, Elizabeth. 2704
Quinn, Thomas R. 3550
Raab, Carolyn A. 831
Rabbit Breeders Association. 1874
Raboff, Fran. 3434, 3442
Radecka, Helena. 740
Raffael, Michael. 3305
Rago, Linda O. 990, 1026
Rain, Patricia. 42, 2315
Ralston, Nancy C. 2601
Ralston Purina Company. 1272, 2296
Ramm, Melinda. 3899
Ramp, Wilma. 1583
Ramsay, Kathryn L. 3057, 3185, 3903
Randlesome, Geraldine. 2923
Rankin, Dorothy. 3672
Rapoport, Maxine. 1648, 3821, 3969, 4190
Rapp, Irene. 1384
Rapp, Joel. 2344
Rappahannock Community College. 2018
Rappaport, Randye. 4489
Rare Fruit Council International. 725
Ratner, Ellen. 3968
Rauch, Doris. 4264
Ravenhill Herb Farm, Saanichton, B.C. 988
Rawls, Sarah. 2305
Rawson, Judie. 294
Raymond, Dick and Jan. 161, 451, 479, 525, 929, 1730, 2351
Raymond, Jennifer. 2350
Read, Jan. 4044
Reader's Digest Association (Canada). 1847
Reader's Digest Association (Gt. Brit.). 655, 781, 1233, 2395, 2408, 3348
Reader's Digest Association (U.S.). 594
Reardon, Joan. 1616

Reaske, Christopher R. 425, 466
Reavis, Charles. 1950, 1952
Rebollo, Deborah L. 300
Rechner, Bernardine M. 1942
Recycling Consortium. 18, 455, 510, 550, 1158, 1612, 1823, 1921, 2462
Red River Edible Bean Growers Association. 76
Ree. 1159
Reece, Byron H. 998
Reed, Ruth. 3102
Reekie, Jennie. 337, 345, 368, 1775, 1887
Reeve, Cintra. 597
Reeves, Janet. 1815
Regan, Mardee Haidin. 3427
Regardz, Beth. 2214
Reich, Lilly J. 3620
Reichert, Katherine D. 1649
Reid, Shirley. 1006
Reider, Freda. 2812
Reidpath, Stewart. 522
Reingold, Carmel B. 3665
Reisman, Rose. 3402, 3432
Renaud, Julie. 1841
Renwick, Ethel H. 1397
Reppert, Bertha. 1007, 1013
Restino, Susan. 1501
Reuter, Carol. 4020
Reynolds, Mary. 1214
Reynolds Wrap Kitchens. 4309
Rhodes, Lorna. 1508, 3498, 3819, 3974
Riccio, Dolores. 2371, 3360, 3379, 4214
Riccuiti, Edward R. 2138
Rice, William. 4185
Richardson, Julia. 808
Richardson, Noel. 1016, 1044
Richardson, Rosamond. 870, 1283, 1566, 1676, 2415, 2489, 3586
Richert, Barbara. 1351
Ricketts, Verne. 356
Ridgeway, Don. 1385
Ridgway, Judy. 71, 219, 234, 290, 339, 539, 1538, 1571, 1636, 1794, 1900, 1901, 1983, 2405, 2765, 3835, 4312, 4385, 4430
Ridgwell, Jenny. 549, 1538
Riecken, Susan. 3154
Rinzler, Carol Ann. 1087
Rippon, Sadhya. 2412
Rivers, Patrick. 1348
Rivers, Shirley. 1348
Rizzuto, Shirley. 595
Robbins, Maria P. 454, 3208, 3682, 3704
Robert, Barbara M. 358
Roberts, Ada Lou. 2169, 2743
Roberts, Dulcie. 1470
Roberts, Margaret. 987, 1083
Roberts, Michael. 1032, 4471
Robertson, Barbara. 1519
Robertson, Dale H. 864
Robertson, Laurel. 2779
Robertson, Phyllis M. 864
Robin Hood Multifoods. 3662, 4215
Robinson, Greg. 2919
Robinson, Jan. 2108
Robinson, Kathleen. 807
Robinson, Robert H. 422, 2137, 2140
Robyns, Gwen. 1784, 3841
Roche, Kathy B. 3919
Rochfort, D'Oyly. 2769
Rockwell, Anne. 3021
Rodale Books. 908, 1369, 3943
Rodale, R. 1353
Rodgers, Diane. 1337
Rodgers, Rick. 2314
Rodnitzky, Donna. 1862
Rodriguez, Mary. 1940
Rodway, Avril. 2528
Rogers, Annie. 715, 2037
Rogers, Evelyn C.M. 1604
Rogers, Jean. 983
Rogers, Jenny. 1456
Rohde, Eleanour S. 958, 1919
Rohe, Fred. 1480
Roitberg, Deborah. 369, 3642
Rojas-Lombardi, Felipe. 812, 3952
Romagnoli, Jane. 3946
Romer, Elizabeth. 3726
Root, Waverley. 1069
Rose, Jeanne. 1035
Rose, Peter G. 367
Rose-Gold, Kerry. 607
Rosen, Harvey. 27, 1253, 3515
Rosen, Samuel R. 1279
Rosenbaum, Helen. 1751
Rosenberg, Barbara S. 277
Rosenberg, Lawrence M. 2891, 3609

Author Index

Rosenbloom, Linda. 405
Rosengarten, Frederic. 1568
Rosenstrauch, Laurette R. 3512
Rosenvall, Vernice. 2464
Rosina. 452
Ross, Annette L. 3155, 3196
Ross, Shirley. 1462, 1962
Ross, Sue. 2963
Rosso, Julee. 3380
Roth, Alex. 2133
Roth, Harriet. 1410
Roth, June. 495, 1048, 1665, 4428
Rothschild, Irene. 3993
Rousseau, Sharon K. 1730
Roux, Albert and Michel. 3650
Rozas, Diane. 280, 310, 3173, 3872
Rubin, Cynthia and Jerome. 1721
Rubinstein, Helge. 333, 3503, 4466
Rudoff, Carol. 3179, 4285
Rudoff, James D. 3203
Runyon, Linda. 2507, 2509
Rush, Eva. 2231
Rutherford, Lyn. 1296
Rutledge Books. 884, 1129, 2295, 3257
Ryan, Tom. 147
Rycroft, Christine. 3056
Ryder, Beverly. 1444
Rywell, Martin. 809
Sable, Myra. 445
Sabotin, Irene E. 1388, 1421
Saddle River Day School Parents Guild Staff. 3471
Sadkowski, May. 4350
Sagstetter, Brad. 2451
Saha, N.N. 1889
Sahni, Julie. 914
Saiff, Bill. 625
Sakamoto, Mike. 621
Salaman, Rena. 2427
Saling, Ann. 196, 1891
Saltonstall, Maxine J. 535, 1142
Saltzman, Joanne. 923
Sams, Ann and Craig. 166
Samuels, Nettie Lou. 1266
Sanders, Sharon. 3891
Sanecki, Kay N. 1000
Santa Maria, Jack. 1072, 2439, 3266
Sarlin, Janeen. 4125
Sarrau, Jose. 4032
Sarvis, Shirley. 1, 1924
Savina, Gail. 1478
Sawyer, Helene. 1305
Sax, Richard. 3192, 3313
Schaffer, Mac. 2465
Schapira, Joel. 2693
Scharff, Robert. 4440
Scheele, Charel. 2819
Scheer, Cynthia. 1699, 2787, 3201, 3757, 3788, 4077
Schemenauer, Elma. 2816
Scherer, San Dee. 1813
Scherie, Strom. 1562
Schioler, Gail. 2692
Schlesinger, Chris. 4382
Schlesinger, Sarah. 1589, 1599
Schlichter, Tom. 427
Schmevelyn, Evelyn. 1200
Schmidt, Michelle. 5
Schmidt, R. Marilyn. 143, 148, 153, 202, 424, 426, 465, 470, 584, 677, 1186, 1189, 1190, 1261, 1299, 1608, 1618, 1938, 1955, 2039, 2051, 2057, 2066, 2122, 2128, 2132, 2142, 2158, 2212, 2213, 2239, 2250, 2299, 2459, 2463
Schmidt, Whitey. 464
Schneider, Carol. 802
Schneider, Elizabeth. 791
Schnell, Greg and Jeff. 1128
Schoen, Dolores F. 1861
Schoenfeld, Jo-ann. 4021
Schofield, Max. 2919
Schonfeldt, Sybil G. 3309
School Volunteers for New Haven. 3262
Schoon, Louise S. 1762
Schraeder, Libuse. 4265
Schultz, Joseph. 2214
Schulz, Phillip S. 4338
Schwanz, Lee. 1875
Schwartz, Elizabeth. 2218
Schwartz, Florence. 2348
Scicolone, Michele. 620, 2149
Scobey, Joan. 534
Scott, Anna Lee. 679
Scott, David. 1331, 1497, 3799, 3828
Scott, Jack D. and Maria L. 264, 1247, 1656, 1782, 1910, 3696

Specialty Cookbooks

Scott, Michael. 1009
Scott, Noni. 2710
Scott, Philippa. 675
Scott, Shirley. 1009
Scott, Sue. 1491
Scully, Phillip. 4057
Seabrook, Peter. 773
Seale, Bobby. 4356
Seaman, Dorothy. 577
Sears, Janet R. 4147
Seaver, Jeannette. 3940
Seay, Bill. 2703
Sedaker, Cheryl. 286
Seddon, George. 1375
Seed, Diane. 3868
Seemann, Peggy. 3109
Segal, Vera. 2936, 3159, 3576, 3703, 3736
Segreto, John J. 3071
Sekules, Veronica. 1327
Self, Elaine. 869
Self, R.A. 837
Selinger, Bertie M. 1942
Sellman, Gita. 2206
Sellmann, Per. 2206
Selph, Annabelle D. 1117
Seranne, Ann. 536
SerVaas, Cory. 905
Serwer, Jacquelyn D. 1643
Sestrap, Betsy. 406
Shakespeare, Margaret N. 3593
Shandler, Michael. 898, 3117
Shandler, Nina. 898, 3117
Shannon, Bette. 1738
Shapiro, Bernard. 1443
Sharrigan, Patricia. 1514
Shaudys, Phyllis V. 1008, 1015, 1039, 2181
Shaulov, Hana. 2966
Shaver, Elizabeth. 26
Sheldon, Edena. 3811, 4357
Shelter Against Violent Environments. 331
Shepard, Judith. 1349, 1390
Shepard, Reba E. 55
Shepard, Sigrid M. 1405
Shepherd, Renee. 2416
Sher, Gail. 4274
Shere, Lindsey R. 3341
Sherman, Elaine. 344
Sherman, Steve. 215, 2826, 3546

Shibles, Loana. 715, 2037
Shimizu, Kay. 1271, 4026
Shimizu, Shinko. 3794
Shinn, Florene R. 2885
Shipp, Robert L. 592
Shodack, Nancy. 4139
Shor, Elizabeth N. and George C. 4066
Shou, Tuan-hsi. 1993, 2360
Shulman, Martha R. 872, 1004, 1088, 2831
Shurtleff, William. 1133, 1258, 2174, 2246, 2263
Sickler, Roberta. 1447
Siegel, Shirley S. 3293
Siegel, Terri J. 3445
Siegfried, Linda. 240, 900
Siegrist, Jan. 28, 151, 508, 2113, 2226, 3199
Siewertsen, Virginia. 417
Sifto Salt Division, Comtar Chemicals Group. 3541, 3621, 3752
Sigler, Doris D. 853
Silverszweig, Mary Z. 805
Silverton, Nancy. 3368
Simmons, Adelma G. 1019, 1020
Simmons, Bob and Coleen. 1639, 2313, 3239
Simmons, Leon F. 2861
Simmons, Marie. 1677, 2706
Simmons, Paula. 2593
Simmons, Rhonda. 459
Simms, A.E. 1964, 1978
Simon, Andre L. 1270
Simpson, Helen. 4058, 4146
Simpson, Jane. 15
Sinnes, A. Cort. 2279, 2283, 4369
Sir Mortimer B. Davis Jewish General Hospital Auxiliary. 2610, 3275
Sirota, Golda. 1415
Skramstad, Gene L. 2452
Skumavc, Michael T. 1936
Slack, Margaret. 1460
Slack, Susan F. 2684
Slavin, Sara. 690
Sleight, Jack. 4482
Sloan, Sara. 4122
Slomon, Evelyne. 3723
Smitch, Curt and Margie. 1931

Author Index

Smith, Beth Cockburn
see Cockburn-Smith, Beth
Smith, Beverley S. 2797, 3098, 3808
Smith, Carol S. 8, 181, 274, 338, 1228, 3049, 3988
Smith College Club of New York City. 1736
Smith, Delia. 2978
Smith, Henry. 3929
Smith, James A. 833
Smith, Jane Wilton
see Wilton-Smith, Jane
Smith, Janet. 610, 3440, 4136
Smith, Jeff. 2559
Smith, Jo. 678
Smith, John A. 848
Smith, Leona W. 688
Smith, Michael. 561, 3291, 3331, 4156
Smith, Paula. 577
Smith, Sheryn. 2932, 2938
Smithson, Rosemary. 1865
Smoler, Roberta W. 1779
Smoot, Deborah S. 2370
Smyers, Jacquelyn. 4145
Snyman, Lannice. 2012
So, Yan-Kit. 4105
Soares, Manuela. 885
Society of St. Andrew. 1827
Sokol & Company. 3257
Solmson, Jane. 2990
Solomon, Charmaine. 480, 4377
Solomon, Jay. 448
Solomon, Reuben. 480
Soloway, Golde H. 3229
Sonnenschmidt, Frederic. 4106
Sonntag, Linda. 2272
Soothill, Eric. 2501
Sorby-Howlett, Lorraine. 2910
Sorosky, Marlene. 3347
Sorzio, Angelo. 3584
Sotebeer, Titia. 2340
Sousanis, Marti. 558
South Africa Dept. of Education and Culture. Homemaking Division. 4414
South Carolina Wildlife Magazine. 2531
South Dakota Dept. of Game, Fish, and Parks. 648
Southeastern Fisheries Association. 2091
Southern Living Magazine. 991
Spear, Ruth A. 2007, 2381
Speare-Yerxa, Marjorie. 1615
Spector, Sherri. 972
Speir, Elizabeth. 414
Spencer, Colin. 1430, 1500, 1551
Spencer, Louise. 2865
Spender, Lizzie. 1686
Sperry, Shirley L. 1579
Spicer, Kay. 3376
Spieler, Marlena. 2189
Spinazzola, Anthony. 2035
Spitler, Sue. 1759, 3554, 4366
Spivack, Ellen S. 1459, 3043
Spivey, Norma G. 3287
Spoczynska, Joy O.I. 2516
St. Barnabas Church, Fredericksburg, Tex. 3141
St. Laurent, Georges C. 4102
St. Mary's Home & School Association, Alexandria, Va. 3293
Sta Maria, Connie. 1984
Stacey, Jane. 2921
Stacey, Sarah. 2898
Staebler, Edna. 3616, 3711, 3994, 4286
Stafford, Julie. 1506, 1546
Stallworth, Lyn. 3883
Stancer, Claire. 3751
Standish, Marjorie. 2005
Stanley, Marcia. 1967, 4363
Stapley, Patricia. 85
Star Kist Seafood Co. 2298
Starchild, Adam. 1963, 2022
Stark, Rosemary. 3415
Stat, Bob. 3105
Stat, Suzanne. 3105
Staten, Vince. 4361
Stauts, Betty L. 2853
Stead, Jennifer. 2034
Steege, Gwen. 3108
Steel, Jennifer. 1821
Steele, Louise. 2192, 2444, 3850
Steeves, Julie. 102
Steffanides, George F. 1592
Stein, Gerald M. 203
Stein, Richard. 2076
Stein, Shifra. 4325, 4352
Steinberg, Sally L. 3469

Specialty Cookbooks

Steindler, Geraldine. 840
Stelzer, John and Kelly. 1002
Stephenson, Bee. 1018
Stern, Bonnie. 2660, 3404
Stern, Gai. 1504
Stetson, Marguerite. 2602
Steuer, Joan. 2851
Stevenson, Violet. 745
Stewart, Alan. 1528
Stewart, Anita. 2086
Stewart, Martha. 2628, 3698
Stewart, Winnie. 828
Stibolt, Hoppie. 70
Stidham, Martin. 2348
Stobart, Tom. 1057
Stockton Asparagus Festival. 44, 45
Stoffer, Judith A. 1492
Stokely-Van Camp of Canada. 82
Stone, Jack. 3596
Stone, Lucas L. 819
Stone, Marie. 2339
Stone, Marilyn. 925, 2587, 2588, 2667
Stone, Martin. 80, 1300
Stone, Sally. 80, 1300
Stovel, Edith. 1071
Stover, Annette A. 117
Strachan, G.E. 4438
Strand, Julie. 4003
Strauss, Sandra C. 778
Street, Myra. 585, 1437, 1629, 1903
Strong-Church, Virginia A. 1927
Structo. 4323
Stuart, Charles E. 821
Stuart, Malcolm. 974
Stubbs, Ansel H. 1277
Stucchi, Lorenza de Medici
 see Medici, Lorenza de
Studley, Helen. 297
Stuhlman, Daniel D. 2726
Sturmanis, Dona. 432
Styler, Christopher. 2659
Suddendorf, Carol. 87
Sullivan, Eugene T. and Marilynn C. 2852, 2854, 2858, 2859, 2873, 2874, 2889, 3009
Sultan, William J. 3631, 4283
Sumption, Lois L. 2750, 3142
Sun Maid Growers of California. 1877
Sunbeam Corp. 4472

Sunset Books. 231
 see also Title Index
Sunshine, Linda. 3333
Sunzeri, John. 1680
Suthering, Jane. 2971, 3346, 3370
Sutherland, Douglas. 3646
Sutton, Robert. 2714
Swann, Daphne. 2817, 2997, 3387, 3813, 3963
Swanson Chunk Chicken. 180
Swanson, Mary Jane. 797, 4345, 4371
Swedlin, Rosalie. 3759
Swendson, Ole. 391
Swendson, Patsy. 391, 4064
Swenson, Julie. 3915
Sykes, Gerald. 2221
Szczawinski, Adam F. 2338
Szilard, Paula. 1325
Tachibana, Yuzuru. 4022
Taeuber, Dick. 1169
Tambouri, Armand. 1664
Tan, Terry. 982
Taneja, Meera. 483
Tanner, Lisa. 1810, 2848
Tarantino, Jim. 3561
Tarr, Yvonne Y. 1985, 2209, 3254
Tatum, Billy Joe. 2506
Taylor, Barbara H. 2718
Taylor, Gordon. 975
Taylor, Grace. 2036
Taylor, Joyce. 2104
Taylor, Peter. 1183
Taylor, Rick. 2291
Taylor, Ronald L. 1127
Taylor, Sally. 3436
Taylor, Sandra. 1832, 2740, 3284
Tea Council of Canada. 2244
Teale, Ria. 3163
Teberg, Pat. 276
Tedone, David. 2134
Tee, Susanna. 1471
Telephone Pioneers of America. 3343
Templeman, Kristine H. 951
Tenison, Marika Hanbury
 see Hanbury Tenison, Marika
Tennison, Patricia. 2101, 2414, 3873
Terry, Diana. 4050, 4199
Terry, Norene R. 1388

Author Index

Teubner, Christian. 593, 1703, 2407, 3000, 3005, 3309, 3367, 3770, 4205, 4216, 4290
Texas Dept. of Agriculture. 529, 1100, 1790, 2752
Thacker, Donna. 2759, 3649
Thomas, Art. 634
Thomas, David S. 4040
Thomas, Helen. 3172, 3735
Thomas, Michael J. 2501
Thompson, Illa D. 58
Thompson, Pat. 702
Thoms, Sara Jean. 769
Thomson, Ruth. 2842
Thorne, John. 3088
Thornton, Claire. 2841
Thrower, Carol J. 3600
Time-Life Books. 68, 94, 107, 112, 268, 520, 559, 731, 1136, 1141, 1626, 1637, 1764, 1773, 1776, 1828, 1850, 2010, 2043, 2139, 2318, 2377, 2399, 2552, 2616, 2654, 2697, 2737, 2931, 2979, 3008, 3624, 3652, 3372, 3509, 3671, 3786, 3793, 3833, 3860, 3908, 4006, 4079, 4091, 4198, 4367, 4392
Timperley, Carol. 244
Tipping, Jill. 2913
Tobias, Doris. 1154
Todd, Jane. 247, 943
Toews-Andrews, Agnes. 1803
Tolbert, Frank X. 3092
Tolley, Emelie. 1005, 1033
Tolley, Lynne. 2478, 2480
Tolve, Arthur. 3315
Tomikel, John. 2486
Tomnay, Susan. 1527
Toms, Laraine. 1408
Toomay, Mindy. 1380
Topper, Suzanne. 717
Toth, Robin. 3894
Tovey, John. 2389
Townsend, Doris M. 208, 1056, 3834
Trabant, Kristie. 3877
Tracy, Marian. 1898, 3034, 3470
Trainer, Antoinette. 373
Treadwell, Peggy. 1737
Trewby, Mary. 1085
TritiRich Products. 2289, 2290
Trollope, Joyce. 3384
Trombold, Mary Ann. 2309
Troy, Diana. 4049
Truax, Carol. 3756, 4016, 4096, 4488
Truman, Danielle. 1494
Tryon, Diana. 2989
Tsuda, Nobuko. 4024
Tucker, Dean. 2166
Tucker, Margaret E. 1532
Tucker-Pursley, Barbara. 4170
Tull, Delena. 2518
Turgeon, Charlotte. 2373
Turnbull, Camilla. 3856, 4186
Turner, Ainslie. 1965
Turner, Dorothy. 553, 2844
Turner, James H. 1786
Turner, June. 934, 3982
Turner, Nancy J. 2338
Tweddle, Jean. 3048, 3959
Twin City Herb Society. 977
Tyler, Margie F. 83
Tyrer, Polly. 2679, 3904
U.B.C. Bakeshop. University of British Columbia. 4255
U.S. Bureau of Commercial Fisheries. 1756
U.S. Dept. of Agriculture. 2310, 4420
U.S. Fish and Wildlife Service. 1960
Ubaldi, Jack. 1243
Udesky, James. 2162
Uhlman, Joane. 3424
Ullman, Phyllis. 1156
Umlauff, Susy. 1596
Uncle Ben's, Inc. 1906
Underhill, J.E. 126
United Fresh Fruit and Vegetable Association. 766
Universal Food Corp. 2571
Upson, Norma. 65, 262, 523, 1868
Upton, Kim. 2624, 2630, 3720
Ursell, Martin. 2824
Usborne, W.R. 4303
Utah State University Cooperative Extension Service. 533, 2467, 2468
Uvezian, Sonia. 2629, 3836
Vada, Simonetta Lupi
  see Lupi Vada, Simonetta
Van Arsdale, May B. 3112
Van Cleave, Jill. 3566
Van der Berg, Eunice. 2840, 3022, 3068, 3454

Van Kersbergen, Wilma G. 1812
Van Ness, Lottye Gray. 3148
Van Roden, Joanne. 2135
Van Wyk, Magdaleen
see Wyk, Magdaleen van
Vanderniet, Deborah Pedersen. 909
Vary, Colin. 1181
Vaughn, Reese. 1591
Veale, Wendy. 308, 3525
Vernon Community Arts Council. 359
Veronelli, Luigi. 1657
VeuCasovic, Edith M. 54
Vidinghoff, Carol. 3851
Viktor, Kaj. 4243
Vinegar Institute. 2458
Vinegrad, Berit. 2651
Voland, Gerard A. 3180
Vollsted, Maryana. 2017
Voltz, Jeanne. 4375
Von Welanetz, Diana and Paul. 4097
Voran, Marilyn. 3882
Voth, Norma Jost. 2731, 2762, 2933
Waddell, Barbara. 4154
Wade, Mary L. 450
Wadey, Rosemary. 2728, 2917, 2948, 3483, 3645, 4444
Wagenvoord, James. 1995, 2545
Wake, Susan. 420, 2449
Waldegrave, Caroline. 1473
Walden, Hilary. 3130, 3552, 3658, 4496
Waldner, George K. 4101
Waldo, Myra. 3922
Waldron, Maggie. 4311
Walker, Charlotte. 4341, 4457
Walker, Clare. 765
Walker, Fern. 149
Walker, Lorna. 2761
Walker, Marilyn. 2504
Walker, Rebecca J. 4069
Walnut Marketing Board. 2461
Walrod, Dennis. 2453
Walsh, Elizabeth. 3528
Walther, Lynnette. 462, 2156
Walton, Sally. 217
Wandschneider, Judy. 4276
Ward, Patricia A. 3145, 3687, 4321, 4473
Ward, Ruth. 33
Ward, Susan. 4154

Warner, Joie. 282, 306, 3728, 3809, 3866
Warner, Penny. 3896, 3902
Warren, Jean. 3892
Warrington, Janet. 3295
Warrington, Muriel. 3597
Warwick, Paul. 1174, 1178
Wary, Carol V. 664, 855
Wary, William G. 664
Waskey, Frank H. 79
Wasserman, Norma. 1912
Watanabe, Tokuji. 2176
Waters, Alice. 1700
Watson, Gail C. 1364, 1400
Watson, Jenny. 4065
Watson, Julie V. 1185, 1298, 2001, 2070, 2124
Watson, Tom. 4065
Wayne, Marvin A. 3212
Wearring, Marilyn. 3599, 3780
Weary, Sherrill. 3496
Weatherbee, Ellen E. 2495
Weaver, A.T. 1609, 1752
Weaver, William W. 3134
Weber, Marcea. 1401, 3277, 3448
Weber, Marlis. 911, 1404, 1449
Weikersheim, Princess. 1783, 1787
Weimar Institute Kitchen. 1424
Weinberg, Julia. 2273, 2605
Weiner, Leslie. 2850, 3604, 3878
Weinreich, Moira. 2243
Weiss, John. 642, 2455
Wejman, Jacqueline. 3573
Welch, Adrienne. 3094
Wells, Carole B. 4263
Wells, Joyce. 2003
Wells, Judy. 1804, 3691
Welsh, Ferrilyn M. 408
Welsh, Sharon Montoya
see Montoya-Welsh, Sharon
Welsh, Virginia. 2920
West Virginia Child Nutrition Division. 3901, 3907
Westland, Pamela. 63, 238, 744, 1422, 1435, 1587, 3029, 3779, 4388
Whalen, Nana. 1986, 2220
Wheeler, Steven. 3078, 3451
Whelan, Jack. 1930
Whitaker, Donald R. 1394

Author Index

White, Alan. 1478
White, Beverly. 1458
White, Charles. 2033, 2144
White, Connie. 865
White, Hollie. 2237
White, Marjorie. 1168
White, Merry. 1628
White, Patrick. 925
White, Susan K. 1187
Whiteaker, Stafford. 2224
Whitehead, Judith. 4350
Whiteman, Kate. 622
Whiteside, Lorraine. 193, 739, 3176
Whittington, Ed and Vi. 3534
Wicks, Laurel A. 4266
Wiener, Joan. 2809
Wier, Janet. 3339, 3640, 3740
Wigmore, Ann. 2207, 2476
Wilford, Charles D. 2163
Wilkes, Angela. 3135
Wilkinson, Alicia. 1975
Wilkinson, Faye. 217
Wilkinson, Jule. 2182
Wilkinson, Rosemary. 3869
Willan, Anne. 3406
Willard, John. 810
Willenberg, Barbara. 3583
Williams, Anne. 603, 798
Williams, Barbara K. 3355
Williams, Christie. 4090
Williams, Elizabeth. 4405
Williams, Hugh. 3475
Williams, Judy. 3805
Williams, Karen. 798
Williams, Kim. 1505, 2503
Williams, Lalla. 311, 3754
Williams, Lonnie. 1619
Williams, Luann. 3890
Williams, Pam. 3093
Williams, Phyllis S. 1370
Williams, Robert. 4405
Williams, Sallie Y. 3875
Williams, Sara Paston
  see Paston-Williams, Sara
Williamson, Darcy. 1341, 1463, 2514, 2526, 3119, 3162, 3713, 3761, 3948, 4119, 4133
Willinsky, Helen. 4379
Willoughby, John. 4382
Willson, Carol. 794, 2125
Wilson, C. Anne. 3590
Wilson, Justin. 4342
Wilson, Lisa. 2649
Wilson, Mitzie. 362, 2806, 3502, 4328
Wilson, Robyn. 619
Wiltens, James S. 2527
Wilton-Smith, Jane. 43, 524, 1743, 1870
Wimmer's Meat Products. 1945
Wine Advisory Board
  see California Wine Advisory Board
Wine, Cynthia. 2184
Wine Institute. 2560
Winegar, Karin. 2196
Wing, Lucy. 4060
Winkelman, Babe and Charlie. 587
Winnie. 4282
Winquist, Jeannine. 358
Winterflood, James. 2866
Wisconsin Milk Marketing Board. 507
Wise, Naomi. 1246
Wise, Victoria. 1240, 4035
Withee, John E. 62
Wittenberg, Margaret M. 1498
Wittich, Boris. 1102
Witty, Helen. 3170, 4413
WNPE-TV, Nashville, Tenn. 625
Wöckinger, Klaus. 699
Wolf, Stanley. 271
Wolfe, Ken. 2311
Wolfe, Robert W. 77
Wolfenden, Joan. 4103
Wollner, Anneliese. 3413
Wolter, Annette. 1250, 2120, 3006, 3770, 3796, 3824, 4205
Woman's Day. 2329
  see also Title Index
Women's Institute. 241, 1239, 1461, 1548, 2069, 2419, 2782, 2962, 3178, 3339, 3579, 3640, 3740, 4284
Women's International League for Peace and Freedom. 4218
Wong, Ella-Mei. 3458
Wongrey, Jan. 694, 1959, 2346
Wood, Brenda. 3261
Wood, David. 3423
Wood, Deone R. 1195

Wood, Ed. 2170
Wood, Marion N. 1916
Wood, Ron. 834
Woodard, Elaine R. 1399
Woodier, Olwen. 16, 453, 1660, 2581
Woodin, G.B. 1046
Woolever, Elizabeth. 2989
Worstman, Gail L. 727, 1334, 4207
Wright, Carol. 1215
Wright, Charlotte. 569
Wright, Hannah. 3954
Wright, Jeni. 3654
Wubben, Pamela G. 1890, 4437
Wunderle, Steve L. 472
Wunderlich, Elinor. 1322
Wyk, Magdaleen van. 735
Wylie, Betty Jane. 221
Wynne, Diana. 3234
Wynne, Peter. 924
Wyssenbach, Willy. 1934
Yamaguchi, Eri. 2432
Yamamoto, Katsuji. 4029
Yan-Kit So
  see So, Yan-Kit
Yan, Stephen. 2052
Yankee, Inc. 3568
Yarbrough, John L. 841
Yerxa, Marjorie Speare
  see Speare-Yerxa, Marjorie
Yew, Betty. 3278
Yip, Lin. 4490
Yip, Victoria. 4490
Yockelson, Lisa. 2983, 3228, 3706
Yoder, Lois. 2177
Yorkshire, Heidi. 3368
Yoshida, Shizuko. 2110, 2111
Yoshino, Masuo. 4027
Young, Joyce LaFray
  see LaFray-Young, Joyce
Young, Mala. 1054, 2349, 2691, 4211
Young, Mark. 3559
Young, Yvonne T. 2766
Youngson, Jeanne. 288
Yudd, Ronald A. 4108
Yueh, Jean. 3457
Zabert, Arnold. 4261
Zabriski, Sherry L. 4036
Zabriskie, George A. 3244, 4036

Zachary, Hugh. 1973
Zahn, Laura. 4083, 4089
Zebroff, Karen. 1428
Zebroff, Sylvie. 543
Zehnder, Dorothy. 3193
Zelman, Milton. 358
Zenker, Hazel G. and John J. 3138
Zickert-Poulos, Colleen M. 3603
Zimmerman, Dina. 1051
Zimmerman, Linda. 3742
Zinn, Donald J. 2141
Zisman, Honey and Larry. 377, 947, 1713, 3014, 3106, 3352
Zogar, Walter. 4316
Zucker, Judi and Shari. 3879
Zumbo, Jim and Lois. 847
Zurbel, Runa and Victor. 4126

Title Index

100 Coffee Dishes. 433
100 Great Cakes. 2954
100 Luscious Diet Drinks. 2696
100 Sweets & Candies. 3120
100 Vegetable Dishes. 2379
1000 Fabulous Sandwiches Cookbook. 3834
1001 Nights of Seafood Delights. 2094
101 Allergy-Free Desserts. 3299
101 Cake Designs. 2868
101 Cherry Recipes. 254
101 Delicious Danish. 3633
101 Delicious Desserts. 3340
101 Desserts to Make You Famous. 3254
101 Favorite Mushroom Recipes. 1289
101 Favorite Wild Rice Recipes. 2538
101 Marvelous Muffins. 3598
101 Pretentious Hors d'Oeuvres. 2619
101 Quick Ways with Chicken. 290
101 Simple Seafood Recipes. 2053
101 Tasty Treats. 3161
101 Tempting Tarts. 3634
101 Ways to Fix Venison. 2452
104 Ontario Game Fish Recipes. 601
110 Cookie Recipes. 3223
110 More Cookie Recipes. 3215
141 and One-Half Chinese-Style Chicken Recipes. 259
150 Potato Recipes. 1809
16 Classic Recipes. 2240
20-Minute Natural Foods Cookbook. 1363
200 Main Course Dishes. 3470
3-in-1 Cook Book. 1712
300 and Under. 3485
32 Better Barbecues. 4307
32 Fabulous Cookies. 3160
32 Seafood Dishes. 1990
32 Soups and Stews. 3998
32 Super Salads. 3769
365 Easy One-Dish Meals. 3064
365 Great Barbecue & Grilling Recipes. 4372
365 Great Cookies You Can Bake. 3224
365 Ways to Cook Chicken. 286
365 Ways to Cook Hamburger. 939
365 Ways to Cook Pasta. 1630, 1677
37 Best Chocolate Chip Cookies in America. 3104
4 & 20 Blackbirds, Cooking in Crust. 3708

40-Second Omelet Guaranteed. 3617
47 Best Chocolate Chip Cookies in the World. 3106
49 North Cooks Wild. 818
500 Recipes for Cakes & Pastries. 2999
500 Recipes for Fish Dishes. 566
500 Recipes for Sandwiches and Packed Meals. 3840
500 Recipes for Sweets and Candies. 3124
500 Recipes for Vegetables and Salads. 2328
500 Super Stews. 4016
50th Anniversary Cookbook. 1945
52 Sugar Free Desserts. 3420
60-Minute Bread Book. 2783
77 Ways to Use Rice & Beans. 1908
80 Proof Cookbook. 1167
80 Quick 'n Easy Polish Ham Recipes 954.
99 Biscuits and Cakes. 2994
99 Game and Fish Dishes. 660
99 Ways to Cook Pasta. 1625
A is for Apple. 26
A-Z of Favorite Fruits. 742
A-Z of Home Freezing. 4467
A-Z of Vegetable Variety. 2380
ABC of Natural Cooking. 1428
About Crawfish. 474
Acetaria. 3776
Adam's Luxury and Eve's Cookery. 2359
Adventures in Sourdough Cooking and Baking. 2163
Adventures in Wine Cookery. 2557
Adventurous Fish Cook. 567
After-School Cooking. 2681
After the Hunt Cookbook. 832
Afternoon Tea Book. 4156
Afternoon Tea Cookbook. 4142
Alaska Sourdough. 2165
Alaska Trappers Cookin' Book. 837
Alaska Wild Berry Guide and Cookbook. 129
Alaska's Seafood Cookbook. 2055
Alaskan Grown Cabbage. 175
Alaskan Halibut Recipes. 952
Alcohol-free Entertaining. 2703
Aldonna's Wholesome Delights. 1318
Alice Hunter's North Country Cookbook. 657

Specialty Cookbooks

All About Bar-b-q Kansas City Style. 4325
All About Blueberries. 148
All About Caviar. 202
All About Mead. 1210
All About Monkfish. 1261
All About Pickling. 3676
All About Steam Cooking. 4488
All About Tomatoes. 2279, 2283
All About Vegetables. 2441
All American Apple Cookbook. 13
All-American Barbecue Book. 4352
All-American Bean Book. 79
All-American Potato Cookbook. 1791
All-Around Pumpkin Book. 1872
All Beef Cookbook. 88
All Canadian Meat Book. 1224
All Color Book of Delightful Desserts. 3319
All Color Book of Main Courses. 3481
All Color Book of Soups and Appetizers. 3945
All Color Book of Vegetable Dishes. 2372
All-Colour Cake Decorating Course. 2890
All Colour Cake Making and Decorating. 2958
All Colour Home Baking. 4221
All Frosty and Cool. 3500
All Good Things Around Us. 966
All Kinds of Salads. 3760
All Maine Fruit Cookbook. 715
All-Maine Seafood Cookbook. 2037
All Natural Baby Cookbook. 1492
All Natural Brown Bagger's Cookbook. 4133
All Natural Cookie Cookbook. 3162
All Natural International Vegetarian Entrée Cookbook. 1463
All Natural Salad Book. 3761
All Natural Seed & Grain Cookbook. 1341
All Natural Soup Cookbook. 3948
All New Brunch Cookbook. 4092
All New Desserts Cookbook. 3400
All-Occasion Casseroles Cookbook. 3042
All the Best Pasta Sauces. 3866
All the Best Pizzas. 3728
All the Best Salads. 3809
All-Time Favorite Cake & Cookie Recipes. 2989
All-Time Favorite Cranberry Recipes. 469
All-Time Favorite Fish & Seafood Recipes. 1967
All-Time Favorite Fruit Recipes. 716
All-Time Favorite Hamburger & Ground Meat Recipes. 932
All Trout Cookbook. 2291
All You Need Is Under the Peel. 53
All You Need to Know About Herbs & Spices. 1046
Allergy Baker. 4285
Allergy Cookie Jar. 3179
Allergy Kitchen: Savoury Soups. 3968
Allergy Recipes: Baking with Amaranth. 7
Almond Paste Recipe Book. 2
Amazing Avocado. 47
Amazing Grains. 923
Amazing Legume. 1152
Amazing Magical Jell-O Brand Desserts. 883
Amazing Tomato Cookbook. 2287
America's Best Appetizers. 2633
America's Bread Book. 2784
America's Favorites, Naturally. 1493
American Baker. 3383
American Bed & Breakfast Cookbook. 4075
American Charcuterie. 1240
American Corn. 454
American Country Cheese. 240
American Country Inn and Bed & Breakfast Cookbook. 4054
American Egg Board Food Service Manual. 527
American Heritage Book of Fish Cookery. 1966
American Honey Institute's Old Favorite Honey Recipes. 1114, 1119
American Pie. 3692
American Rice Cookbook. 1904
American Seafood Cooking. 2024
American Statesmen and Honorary Citizen Dessert Cookbook. 3264
American Wholefoods Cuisine. 1395
Amish Treats from My Kitchen. 4208
And More Squid. 2213
Andy and Sandy's Yummy Summer Snack Book. 3919

Title Index

Angler's Guide to Fish as Food. 630
Angler's Only Cookbook. 613
Anglers' Cookbook. 522
Anita Prichard's Complete Candy Cookbook. 3007
Ann Clark's Fabulous Fish. 2056
Ann Long's Dinner Party Book. 4183
Anna Teresa Callen's Menus for Pasta. 1688
Annapolis Diet. 1254
Anne's Perfect Piebook. 3695
Annette Annechild's Seafood Wok. 2025
Annie Lerman's New Salad and Soup Book. 3984
Answering the Call to Duck Cookery. 519
Antipasto Feasts. 2649
Antoine Bouterin's Desserts from Le Perigord. 3421
Anton Mosimann's Fish Cuisine. 631
Antony & Araminta Hippisley Coxe's Book of Sausages. 1948
Any Oven Cookbook. 4209
Anytime Appetizers. 2678
Anytime is Dairytime. 497
Appealing Potatoes. 1787
Appetizer Cookbook. 2622
Appetizers. 2612, 2650, 2660, 2664
Appetizers & Hors d'Oeuvres. 2634
Appetizers and Salads. 2644
Appetizers and Side Dishes. 2686
Appetizers, Salad Dressings, and Salads. 2613
Appetizers, Salads and Desserts. 2671
Apple Book. 15
Apple Connection. 23
Apple Cookbook. 12, 16
Apple Country Cooking. 34
Apple Garnishing. 27
Apple-Lovers' Cook Book. 35
Apple Magic. 17
Apple Orchard Cook Book. 10
Apple Sampler. 28
Apples. 18
Apples, Apples, Apples. 29
Apples Everyday. 31
Apples for Every Season. 14
Armadillo Cook-off Cookbook. 1221
Aromatic Herbs. 1037

Around the World Cooky Book. 3142
Around the World Making Cookies. 3139
Art and Secrets of Making Bratwurst the Old Fashion Way. 1947
Art of Accompaniment. 447
Art of Buffet Entertaining. 4097
Art of Catching & Cooking Crabs. 462
Art of Catching and Cooking Shrimp. 2156
Art of Charcuterie. 1763
Art of Cheesemaking. 496
Art of Cooking. 1552
Art of Cooking with Certified Angus Beef. 109
Art of Cooking with Herbs and Spices. 1084
Art of Decorating Cakes. 2861
Art of Filo Cookbook. 558
Art of Fine Baking. 4230
Art of Fish Cookery. 582
Art of Garde Manger. 4106
Art of Grilling. 4373
Art of Making Good Cookies. 3196
Art of Making Sausages. 1763
Art of Making Tortillas. 4034
Art of Preserving. 3573
Art of the Kitchen Garden. 2420
Art of the Sandwich. 3854
Artichoke Cookbook. 42
Artists & Mathematicians Dessert Book. 3422
As Easy as Pie. 3709
Asian Food Feasts. 1405
Asian Pasta. 1689
Asian Vegetarian Feast. 1678
Asparagus. 43
Asparagus, All Ways--Always. 44
Asparagus Cookbook. 45
At the Dainty Rice Sign. 1902
Atlanta Herb Sampler. 997
Atora Family Suet Cookery. 2230
Aubergine. 524
Aunt Freddie's Pantry. 3577
Authentic Pasta Book. 1690
Autumn's Country Heritage Cookbook. 1406
Avalon Dairy Cookbook. 504
Aveline Kushi's Wonderful World of Salads. 3818

Specialty Cookbooks

Avocado Lovers' Cookbook. 49
Avocado Recipes, etc. 50
Award-Winning Chicken Recipes. 307
Back to Eden Cookbook. 1342
Backroom Cooking Secrets. 637
Bagel Book. 2689
Bagelmania. 2688
Bake Breads from Frozen Dough. 2724
Bake Shop in a Book. 176
Bake Your Own Bread. 2822
Bake Your Way to a Better Diet. 4250
Baker's Book of Chocolate Riches. 347
Baker's Dozen. 3154
Baker's Dozen of Daily Breads & More. 2823
Baker's Formula and Procedure Manual. 4210
Baker's Secret. 4258
Bakers' Manual. 4231
Bakery Specialities. 4232
Baking. 4204, 4211, 4252, 4261
Baking and Bread. 2806
Baking and Roasting. 4262
Baking at Home. 4216
Baking Better Breads. 2755
Baking Book. 4212
Baking Classics. 4288
Baking Cookbook. 4270
Baking Country Breads and Pastries. 2728
Baking Easy & Elegant. 4233
Baking Experience of Switzerland. 3180
Baking for Health. 4251
Baking is Fun. 4222
Baking Treasures from Grandma's Farm Kitchen. 4263
Baking with American Dash. 178
Baking with Yeast with Schmecks Appeal. 4286
Baking Your Own. 2747
Ball Blue Book. 4386
Banana Book. 56
Banana Cookbook. 55
Bananas by the Bunch. 54
Bandwagon to Health. 1407
Bang! 1758
Bar & Grill Cookbook. 4333
Bar Cookie Bonanza. 3153
Barbecue. 4308-4310, 4357

Barbecue & Smoke Cookery. 4311
Barbecue and Summer Foods Cookbook. 4370
Barbecue and Summer Party Cookbook. 4326
Barbecue Book. 4327, 4346
Barbecue Cook Book. 4345
Barbecue Cookbook. 4304, 4334, 4335, 4353
Barbecue Cookery. 4318
Barbecue Cooking the Gourmet Way. 4336
Barbecue Hints and Tips. 4374
Barbecue, Indoors and Out. 4347
Barbecue Recipes. 4328
Barbecue with Beard. 4348
Barbecued Ribs, Smoked Butts, and Other Great Feeds. 4375
Barbecues. 4312, 4319
Barbecues & Grills. 4313
Barbecues & Summer Cooking. 4320
Barbecues and Outdoor Living. 4337
Barbecues and Summer Food. 4354
Barbecuing Atlantic Seafood. 2070
Barbecuing, Grilling & Smoking. 4355
Barbecuing the Weber Covered Way. 4301
Barbeque. 4300
Barbeque'n with Bobby. 4356
Bargain Seafoods. 2057
Barmy Bread Book. 2719
Barron's the Festive Bread Book. 2748
Barry Ballister's Fruit and Vegetable Stand. 792
Basic Essentials of Edible Wild Plants & Useful Herbs. 2523
Basic Pastrywork Techniques. 3635
Basic Preserve Making. 4395
Basically Beans. 1147
Basically Blue. 149
Basically Bread. 2756
Basics of Cake Baking, Decorating and Serving. 2937
Basil Book. 59
Baskin-Robbins Book of Ice Cream. 3542
Batch of Biscuits. 2715
Beachcomber's Handbook of Seafood Cookery. 1973
Bean & Lentil Cookbook. 1145
Bean Banquets. 73

Title Index

Bean Cookbook. 60, 65
Bean Cookery. 61
Bean Cuisine. 66, 74
Bean Feast. 63
Beanfest. 75
Beans & Peas. 64
Beans, Greens and Other Things. 2433
Beans in My Boots. 70
Beans, Nuts and Lentils. 1151
Beard on Birds. 1856
Beard on Bread. 2736
Beard on Pasta. 1634
Bears in My Kitchen. 87
Beautiful Bridal Cakes the Wilton Way. 2854
Beaver Tails and Dorsal Fins. 651
Becky's Brunch & Breakfast Book. 4069
Bed & Breakfast Cookbook. 4076
Bee Prepared with Honey. 1090
Beef. 105, 106
Beef & Veal. 90
Beef & Veal Menus. 94
Beef and Veal. 110
Beef Cookbook. 113
Beef Dishes. 97
Beef II. 108
Beef Jerky Recipes. 115
Beef, Light Lean Beef Recipes for Contemporary Lifestyles. 101
Beef Lover's Guide to Weight Control and Lower Cholesterol. 111
Beef Recipe Round-up. 102
Beef Sounds Good, Good Value Cookbook. 91
Beef Sounds Good, on a Barbecue. 92
Beef, Veal, Lamb & Pork. 1226
Before & After. 2665
Beginner's Guide to Meatless Casseroles. 3043
Beginning Again. 2614
Being Social with Tea. 2244
Beinhorn's Mesquite Cookery. 4479
Ben & Jerry's Homemade Ice Cream & Dessert Book. 3556
Benny Cooker Crock Book for Drinkers. 1164
Bernard Clayton's New Complete Book of Breads. 2807

Berried Treasures Cookbook. 130
Berries. 137, 138
Berries Beautiful. 133
Berry Book. 128
Berry Cookbook. 124, 132, 134
Bert Greene's Kitchen Bouquets. 443
Best Barbecue Recipes. 4363
Best Buffets Cook Book. 4093
Best Chicken Recipes. 296
Best Dessert Book Ever. 3446
Best-Ever Brownies. 2851
Best-Ever Chicken Recipes. 279
Best-Ever Cookies. 3145
Best-Ever Pies. 3687
Best-Ever Vegetable Recipes. 2374
Best Kept Secrets of Chocolate Drinks & Life. 373
Best Little Hors d'Oeuvres in Kansas. 2645
Best Main Dishes. 3472
Best of Bacon Cookbook. 52
Best of Baking. 4205, 4278
Best of Barley. 58
Best of Bazaar Baking. 4264
Best of Breakfast Time Cook Book. 4047
Best of Cold Soups. 3976
Best of Desserts. 3363
Best of Jenny's Kitchen. 2350
Best of Lenôtre's Desserts. 3300
Best of Marjorie Standish Seafood Recipes. 2005
Best of Salads and Buffets. 3770
Best of Strawberries. 2218
Best of Thai Seafood. 2095
Best of the "Fest". 2598
Best of the Pumpkin Recipes Cookbook. 1871
Best of the Spirit of Cooking. 1178
Best of the Zucchini Recipes Cookbook. 2600
Best of Vegetarian Cooking. 3746
Best of Wild Rice Recipes. 2540
Best of Zucchini Time. 2594
Best Recipes for Appetizers. 2658
Best Recipes for Chicken. 299
Best Recipes for Cookies. 3216
Best Recipes for Fish and Shellfish. 2116
Best Recipes for Grilling. 4362
Best Recipes for Pasta. 1693

Specialty Cookbooks

Best Recipes for Sensational Desserts. 3435
Best Vegetable Recipes from Woman's Day. 2329
Bette McClure Capozzo Presents Just Zucchini Cook Book. 2596
Better a Dinner of Herbs. 998
Better Baking. 4268
Better Bean Microwave Recipes. 82
Better Breakfasts. 4045
Better Health with Culinary Herbs. 956
Better Homes and Gardens
After-School Cooking. 2681
All-Time Favorite Cake & Cookie Recipes. 2989
All-Time Favorite Fish & Seafood Recipes. 1967
All-Time Favorite Fruit Recipes. 716
All-Time Favorite Hamburger & Ground Meats Recipes. 932
Anytime Appetizers. 2678
Best Barbecue Recipes. 4363
Best Buffets Cook Book. 4093
Bigger Better Burgers. 945
Brown Bagger's Cook Book. 4129
Brunches and Breakfasts. 4084
Candy. 3013
Cheese Recipes. 237
Chocolate. 334
Christmas Cookies. 3227
Cookies & Candies. 3020
Cookies for Christmas. 3181
Cookies for Kids. 3234
Cookies. 3197
Cooking with Whole Grains. 912
Creative Cake Decorating. 2871
Desserts. 3384
Easy Stir-Fry Recipes. 4498
Fast-Fixin' Chicken. 287
Fast-Fixin' Meat Recipes. 1244
Favorite Meat Recipes. 1230
Fish & Seafood. 2038, 2071
Fix & Freeze Cookbook. 4464
Fresh Fish Cook Book. 588
Great Cookouts. 4349
Home Canning and Freezing. 4396
Home Canning Cookbook. 4396
Homemade Cookies. 3217

Better Homes and Gardens (Continued)
Hot & Spicy Cooking. 2183
Hot Off the Grill. 4329
Kids' Lunches. 4115
Light Salad Meals. 3800
Make-a-Meal Salads. 3790
Meatless Main Dishes. 3473
Microwave Vegetables. 2396
New Casserole Cook Book. 3060
Old-Fashioned Home Baking. 4287
One-Dish Microwave Meals. 3050
Pasta. 1668
Poultry. 1848
Quick Main Dishes. 3490
Salads. 3791
Savory Sandwiches. 3848
Shortcut Main Dishes. 3846
Soups & Stews. 4008
Stir-Fry Recipes. 4497
Super Snacks. 2682
Vegetables. 2411
Betty Cooker's Crock Book. 1164
Betty Crocker Creative Recipes. 141, 399, 680, 2112, 2312, 2429, 3215, 3223, 3365, 3492, 3817, 3912
Betty Crocker Picture Cookbook. 722, 2991, 3037, 3478, 3760, 3997
Betty Crocker's
Baking Classics. 4288
Barbecue Cookbook. 4304
Best Recipes for Appetizers. 2658
Best Recipes for Chicken. 299
Best Recipes for Fish and Shellfish. 2116
Breads. 2785
Buffets. 4098
Cake Decorating. 2924
Cake Decorating with Cake Recipes for Every Occasion. 2879
Casserole Cookbook. 3046
Chicken Cookbook. 272
Chocolate Cookbook. 348
Cookie Book. 3171
Cooking with American Wine. 2568
Creative Recipes with Bisquick. 140
Dinner for Two Cookbook. 4171
Do-Ahead Cookbook. 4455
Family Dinners in a Hurry. 4172
Fruit Desserts. 722

Title Index

Betty Crocker's (Continued)
Hamburger Cookbook. 944
Red Spoon Collection. 299, 1693, 2116, 2658, 3216, 3435, 4362
Salads. 3782
Soups and Stews Cookbook. 4002
Betty Jane Wylie Cheese Cookbook. 221
Beverage Cookbook. 2702
Beverages. 2697
Bible Herb Cook. 1066
Big Beautiful Book of Hors d'Oeuvres. 2605
Big Chocolate Cookbook. 318
Big, Fat, Red, Juicy Apple Cook Book. 24
Big Little Peanut Butter Cookbook. 1719
Bigger Better Burgers. 945
Bill & Bev Beatty's Wild Plant Cookbook. 2517
Bill Saiff's Rod & Reel. 625
Billy Joe Tatum's Wild Foods Field Guide and Cookbook. 2506
Birds Eye Magic Moments in Minutes Cookbook. 707
Birds Eye Super Soups Booklet. 3928
Birthday Cakes. 2896
Biscuit Book. 3152
Biscuits. 3172
Biscuits and Cookies. 3182
Biscuits and Scones. 2716
Biscuits, Spoonbread, and Sweet Potato Pie. 4289
Bishop Museum Salad and Dessert Cookbook. 3282
Bisquick Classics Collection. 141
Bisto Book of Meat Cookery. 1213
Bit Between the Teeth. 3845
Black Sheep Newsletter Cookbook. 1137
Blackberry Delights. 142
Blackfish-Tautog. 143
Blue Crab. 465
Blue Ribbon Cookies. 3208
Blue-Ribbon Pickles & Preserves. 3682
Blue-Ribbon Pies. 3704
Blue Ribbon Winners. 4415
Blue Ribbon Winner's Bakebook. 4213
Blueberry Connection. 145
Blueberry Cookbook. 144
Blueberry Sampler. 151

Blueberry Thrills. 146
Bluefish. 153
Bluefish Cookbook. 154
Body and Soul. 1464
Boiled, Poached, and Steamed Foods. 4383
Bon Appétit Dinner Party Cookbook. 4167
Book of Afternoon Tea. 4141
Book of Appetizers. 2638
Book of Baking. 4284
Book of Beans and Lentils. 1146
Book of Biscuits. 3178
Book of Bread. 2796, 2824
Book of Bread and Buns. 2782
Book of Breads. 2768
Book of Breakfasts & Brunches. 4088
Book of Cakes. 2952, 2978
Book of Cauliflower, Broccoli & Cabbage. 161
Book of Cheesecakes. 3078
Book of Chocolate. 335
Book of Chocolates & Petits Fours. 3098
Book of Chowder. 3924
Book of Coffee and Tea. 2693
Book of Cookies. 3209
Book of Corn Cookery. 450
Book of Creative Foods. 3517
Book of Crepes & Omelets. 3247
Book of Cucumbers, Melons, & Squash. 479
Book of Curries & Indian Foods. 493
Book of Decorative Cakes. 2880
Book of Desserts. 3436
Book of Dressings & Marinades. 3589
Book of Edible Nuts. 1568
Book of Eggplant, Okra & Peppers. 525
Book of Flowers. 681
Book of Fondues. 3498
Book of Food Drying, Pickling & Smoke Curing. 4433
Book of Fruit and Fruit Cookery. 719
Book of Fruits. 734
Book of Fruits and Flowers. 686
Book of Garlic. 881
Book of Garnishes. 3519
Book of Gifts from the Pantry. 4416
Book of Gingerbread. 3527
Book of Great American Desserts. 3357

Book of Great Breakfasts and Brunches. 4070
Book of Great Chocolate Desserts. 314
Book of Great Cookies. 3140
Book of Great Desserts. 3256
Book of Great Hors d'Oeuvre. 2661
Book of Great Sandwiches. 3856
Book of Great Soups, Sandwiches, and Breads. 2772
Book of Grilling & Barbecuing. 4364
Book of Herbs. 987, 999, 1000
Book of Herbs & Spices. 1063, 1079
Book of Honey. 1094, 1095
Book of Hot & Spicy Foods. 2192
Book of Ice Creams & Sorbets. 3557
Book of Ices. 3551
Book of Jams and Jellies. 3571
Book of Jams and Other Preserves. 3579
Book of Kudzu. 1133
Book of Lettuce & Greens. 929
Book of Marmalade. 3590
Book of Miso. 1258
Book of Pasta. 1651, 1669
Book of Pastry. 3640
Book of Pies. 3686
Book of Pizzas & Italian Breads. 3729
Book of Preserves. 4412
Book of Puddings. 3740
Book of Puddings, Desserts, and Savouries. 3311
Book of Raw Fruit and Vegetable Juices and Drinks. 1883
Book of Rose Arrangements. 1920
Book of Salads. 3753, 3772, 3810, 3819
Book of Salads and Summer Dishes. 3762
Book of Sandwiches. 3841, 3850
Book of Sauces. 3867
Book of Sauces and Surprises. 3865
Book of Sausages. 1948
Book of Savoury Flans and Pies. 3494
Book of Soba. 2162
Book of Soups. 3974
Book of Soybeans. 2176
Book of Sushi. 4022
Book of Sweets. 3122
Book of Tea. 4157
Book of Tempeh. 2246
Book of the Lobster. 1180

Book of Tofu. 2263
Book of Tomatoes. 2288
Book of Vegetables and Salads. 2419
Book of Welsh Bread. 2808
Book of Welsh Country Cakes and Buns. 2968
Book of Welsh Puddings and Pies. 3385
Book of Whole Foods. 1343
Book of Whole Grains. 903
Book of Whole Meals. 1376
Boozer's Late Night Cook Book. 3886
Boozy Chef. 1176
Borden Great American Pies. 3710
Boston Tea Parties. 4147
Bouillon is Basic. 155
Bountiful Bread. 2749
Bounty of the Earth Cookbook. 2487
Bouquet of Flowers. 691
Bourbon Cookbook. 2477
Bowl of Red. 3092
Box Lunch. 4130
Braai Book. 4308
Bradley's Complete Gas Grill Cookbook. 4305
Bragg Health Food Cook Book. 1344
Bread. 2721, 2809, 2815, 2844
Bread & Beyond. 2797
Bread & Breakfast. 4048
Bread & Cake Cookbook. 2774
Bread & Yeast Cookery. 2757
Bread and Breakfasts. 2773
Bread Baking. 2720
Bread Baking Made Easy. 2775
Bread Bonanza. 2798
Bread Book. 2770, 2810, 2831, 2832
Bread, Bread, Bread. 2845
Bread Winners Cookbook. 2758
Bread Winners Too. 2776
Bread without Tears. 2759
Breadbasket Cookbook. 2839
Breadcraft. 2799
Breadmaking and Yeast Cookery. 2729
Breads. 2737, 2738, 2760, 2781, 2785-2787, 2800
Breads & Biscuits. 2739
Breads & Breadmaking. 2788
Breads & Muffins. 2801
Breads 2. 2811

Title Index 613

Breads and Biscuits. 2840
Breads and Coffee Cakes with Homemade Starters. 2169
Breads and More Breads. 2750
Breads from Many Lands. 2750
Breads of France. 2802
Breads of Many Lands. 2722
Breads of New England. 2818
Breads, Pastries, Pies and Cookies. 4223
Breads, Rolls, and Pastries. 2740
Breadspeed. 2816
Breadtime Stories. 2833
Breakfast. 4065, 4081
Breakfast & Brunch Book. 4082
Breakfast & Brunch Cookbook. 4073
Breakfast & Brunch Dishes for the Professional Chef. 4071
Breakfast & Lunches. 4085
Breakfast Book. 4037, 4040, 4049, 4050, 4055
Breakfast with Friends. 4086
Breakfasts & Brunches. 4077
Breakfasts and Brunches. 4072
Breakfasts for Lovers. 4043
Breakfasts, Ozark Style. 4051
Breville Toasted Sandwiches Book. 3835
Brew Cuisine. 122
Bride's Choice. 2857
Brilliant Bean. 80
Bring Out the Basic. 156
Bristol Recipe Book. 2412
British Charcuterie. 1775
British Country Cheeses. 238
Broccoli & Company. 2434
Brown Bag Cookbook. 4122
Brown Bagger's Cook Book. 4129
Brown Rice Cookbook. 164-166
Brownie Experience. 2848
Brownie Recipes. 2846
Brownies. 2849
Brownies, Bars & Biscotti. 3218
Brunch. 4090
Brunch Menus. 4091
Brunches and Breakfasts. 4084
Buffalo at Steak. 170
Buffalo Cook Book. 171
Buffalo Cookbook. 169
Buffets. 4098, 4099, 4102, 4104

Buffets and Receptions. 4094
Bugialli on Pasta. 1679
Bulgur Wheat Recipes. 2467
Bumper Crop. 798
Bundt Cakes. 2927
Burger Book. 931, 947
Busy Mum's Baking Book. 4242
Busy People's Naturally Nutritious, Decidedly Delicious Fast Foodbook. 1377
Busy Person's Guide to Preserving Food. 4397
But I Love Fruits. 738
Butter 'em While They're Hot!. 2717
Buying and Cooking Fish and Seafood. 1991
Buying and Cooking Meat. 1214
Buying and Cooking Vegetables. 2330
C and H Sugar Complete Dessert Cookbook. 3274
Cabbage. 174
Caboodle Cookbook. 1550
Cadbury's Cocoa Recipes. 322
Cadbury's Creative Chocolate Cookbook. 336
Cadbury's Novelty Cookbook. 323
Cajun Yam Cuisine. 2235
Cake Bible. 2977
Cake Calendar. 2862
Cake Crafts. 2938
Cake Decor. 2897
Cake Decorating. 2863, 2910, 2924, 2925
Cake Decorating Book. 2864
Cake Decorating for All Seasons. 2911
Cake Decorating Ideas & Designs. 2865
Cake Decorating Ornaments. 2872
Cake Decorating Simplified. 2891
Cake Decorating with Cake Recipes for Every Occasion. 2879
Cake Design and Decorating Course. 2918
Cake Design and Decoration. 2855
Cake Designs. 2888
Cake Designs and Ideas. 2869
Cake Icing and Decorating. 2881
Cake Magic. 2920
Cake Making & Decorating. 2882
Cake Making and Decorating. 2958
Cake Shop Bread Book. 2741
Cake Stall. 2929

Specialty Cookbooks

Cakemaking and Decoration. 2916
Cakes. 2931, 2946, 2947, 2969
Cakes & Cake Decoration. 2892
Cakes & Cookies. 2993
Cakes & Pastries. 3000, 3003
Cakes & Pies. 3004
Cakes & Sponges. 2943
Cakes and Cake Decorating. 2948
Cakes and Pastries Cookbook. 3006
Cakes Aplenty. 2928
Cakes for Kids. 2898
Cakes, Icings, and Cheese Cakes. 2941
Cakes, Scones and Biscuits. 2992
Cakes You Can Make. 2981
Calamari Cookbook. 2214
California Apricot Growers' Favorite Recipes. 36
California Brandy Cuisine. 159
California Seafood Cookbook. 2072
California State Grange Recipes Are Naturally Good Eating. 1429
California Walnuts. 2461
California Wine Lovers' Cookbook. 2551
Campbell's Creative Cooking with Soup. 188, 189
Can I Make One? 919
Can-Opener Cookbook. 182
Canada Cooks! 3062, 3219, 3811, 4357
Canadian Bread Book. 2734
Canadian Fish Cook Book! 1992
Canadian Herb Cookbook. 1011
Canadian Living Barbecue and Summer Foods Cookbook. 4370
Canapés. 2651
Canapés--Appetizers--for Your Party. 2606
Candies & Goodies. 3125
Candies, Beverages & Snacks. 3012
Candy. 3008, 3013
Candy and Candy Molding Cookbook. 3010
Candy and Gifts. 3133
Candy Cookbook. 3015, 3265
Candy Recipes & Other Confections. 3112
Candymaking. 3016
Canned Fish Cookbook. 181
Canned Salmon Delicacies. 1928
Canning. 4401

Canning & Preserving Foods. 4404
Canning and Preserving Without Sugar. 4418
Canning, Freezing & Drying. 4394
Cape Cod Seafood Cookbook. 2026, 2054
Care & Cooking of Fish & Game. 642
Caribbean Pastry Delights. 3628
Caribbean Rum Book. 1926
Carob Cookbook. 193, 195
Carob Primer. 192
Carob Way to Health. 191
Carol Cutler's Great Fast Breads. 2789
Carol Wright's Complete Meat Cookery. 1215
Carousing in the Kitchen. 1165
Carrot Cookbook. 196, 197, 199
Carton Full of Texas Eggs. 529
Cashews and Lentils, Apples and Oats. 1345
Casserole Book. 3031
Casserole Cook Book. 3031
Casserole Cookbook. 3025, 3046, 3047
Casserole Cookery. 3044
Casseroles. 3037, 3055
Casseroles & Stews. 3026, 3045, 3062
Casseroles and Bakes. 3056
Casseroles and One-Dish Meals. 3041
Casseroles Cookbook. 3038
Catch 'em, Hook 'em, and Cook 'em. 1968
Catch of the Day. 2027, 2096
Catchin' & Cookin' Freshwater Fish. 589
Caterers' Guide to Potatoes. 1780
Catfish Cookbook. 201
Caviar. 204
Caviar! Caviar! Caviar! 203
Celebrate! VI. 2859
Celebrate! Wedding Cakes. 2873
Celebrate! With Party Spectaculars from A to Z. 2874
Celebrated Oysterhouse Cookbook. 1617
Celebrating the Wild Mushroom. 1290
Celebration Cakes. 2883
Celebration of Soups. 3932
Celebrity Desserts. 3343
Champagne Cookbook. 2544
Champneys Cookbook. 1494
Character Cakes. 2982
Charcuterie & French Pork Cookery. 1763

Title Index

Charlie the Tuna's Recipe Booklet. 2298
Cheese. 230, 231
Cheese & Wine Anytime. 214
Cheese and Cheese Making. 241
Cheese and Dairy Sampler. 508
Cheese Book. 225
Cheese Cheese. 232
Cheese Cookbook. 221, 242, 243
Cheese Cookery. 208
Cheese Please! 233
Cheese Recipes. 237
Cheese Sweets and Savories. 215
Cheesecake Extraordinaire. 3080
Cheesecake Madness. 3071
Cheesecake Only. 3074
Cheesecakes. 3072, 3075, 3077
Chef Recommends. 571
Chef Wolfe's New American Turkey Cookery. 2311
Cherries Galore. 255
Cherry Time! 257
Chesapeake Bay Fish & Fowl Cookbook. 2073
Cheval a Toutes les Sauces. 1125
Chevon (Goat Cheese) Recipes. 902
Chevre! 900
Chez Panisse Desserts. 3341
Chez Panisse Pasta, Pizza & Calzone. 1700
Chic Chicken Book. 300
Chicago's Sweet Tooth. 3342
Chicken 'n Quick Fixin's. 301
Chicken. 291, 292
Chicken & Game Hen Menus. 268
Chicken & Other Poultry. 1841
Chicken & Poultry Cookbook. 1836
Chicken and Egg Cookbook. 274
Chicken and Fowl. 1840
Chicken and Poultry. 1842, 1857
Chicken and Poultry Cookbook. 1829
Chicken and the Egg Cookbook. 264
Chicken Breasts. 280
Chicken Cook Book. 308
Chicken Cookbook. 260, 265, 272, 273, 1830
Chicken Cookery. 269
Chicken Expressions. 293
Chicken Favorites. 266

Chicken for Every Occasion Cookbook. 297
Chicken for Every Pot. 261
Chicken Gourmet. 275
Chicken Just for You! 276
Chicken Little Cookbook. 302
Chicken of the Sea Tempting Tuna Cookbook. 2295
Chicken of the Sea Tuna Recipes. 2296
Chicken on the Run. 298
Chicken Only, Only Chicken. 262
Chicken! Chicken! Chicken! 281
Child's Garden. 1465
Children's Party Cake Book. 2903
Children's Party Cakes. 2912
Chili Cookbook. 3087
Chili Madness. 3082
Chili-Lovers' Cook Book. 3086
Chinese Appetizers and Garnishes. 2615
Chinese Dessert and Pastry. 3456
Chinese Dessert, Dim Sum & Snack Cookbook. 3364
Chinese One-Dish Meals. 3040
Chinese People's Cookbook. 3459
Chinese Poultry Cooking. 1831
Chinese Refreshment Illustrated. 3622
Chinese Seafood. 1993, 2006
Chinese Seafood Cooking. 1974
Chinese Snacks. 3463
Chinese Style Casserole Dishes Recipe. 3039
Chinese Vegetarian Dishes. 2360
Chockful o' Chips. 3109
Chocolate. 334, 337, 361, 384, 385, 394
Chocolate and Candy Cookbook. 3011
Chocolate and Coffee Cookbook. 338
Chocolate Artistry. 324
Chocolate Book. 325, 333, 350, 351, 381
Chocolate Candy. 3099
Chocolate, Chocolate, Chocolate. 326, 404
Chocolate Cookbook. 348, 354, 374, 375, 383
Chocolate Cookery. 327, 362
Chocolate Cooking. 339, 352, 376
Chocolate Crazy. 353
Chocolate Delights. 355, 370
Chocolate Desserts. 328

Specialty Cookbooks

Chocolate Fantasies. 356, 371, 377
Chocolate Lover's Cookbook. 363
Chocolate Lover's Cookies & Brownies. 3110
Chocolate Lovers Cookbook. 357
Chocolate Lovers IV. 395
Chocolate Lovers' Cookbook. 346
Chocolate Mousse. 364
Chocolate Quick Fix. 358
Chocolate Recipes. 359
Chocolate Sensations. 365
Chocolate Truffles. 3096
Chocolates and Sweets. 3100
Chopsticks Recipes. 81, 3462
Chosen, Appetizers & Desserts. 2667
Christmas Baking. 4290
Christmas Candy. 3017
Christmas Cook. 3134
Christmas Cookie Book. 3225
Christmas Cookies. 3191, 3198, 3226, 3227
Christopher Idone's Glorious American Food. 4174
Christopher Idone's Salad Days. 3812
Churche's [sic] Banquet. 2777
Cider Book. 406
Cider Vinegar and Molasses Recipe Book. 2457
Cinnamon Cook Book. 408
Citrus Cookbook. 411
Citrus Fruits. 417, 420
Citrus Recipes. 410
Citrus Recipes from Florida Restaurants. 413
Claire's Cakes. 2970
Claire's Cocktails & Party Drinks. 2709
Claire's Confectionery. 3129
Clam Lover's Cookbook. 421
Clambakes Sans Sand in Pots & Woks. 422
Clams, Mussels, Oysters, Scallops, & Snails. 2151
Classic Book of Pasta. 1653
Classic Cake Recipes. 2942
Classic Cakes and Cookies. 2995
Classic Cheese Cookery. 239
Classic Deem Sum. 3464
Classic Desserts. 440, 3263
Classic Egg Dishes. 528

Classic Fish Dishes. 585
Classic Game Cookery. 653
Classic Indian Vegetarian and Grain Cooking. 914
Classic Liqueurs. 1179
Classic Sauces. 3874
Classic Vegetable Cookbook. 2381
Classic Vegetable Cookery. 2382
Classic Wheat for Man Cookbook. 2464
Classical Cake Decorating. 2904
Cleaning & Cooking Fish. 568
Cocktail Party Nibbles. 2676
Cocktails & Hors d'Oeuvres. 2604
Cocktails & Snacks. 3887
Cocolat. 396
Coconut. 428-430
Coffee. 431
Coffee for Every Occasion. 434
Coffee Lover's Handbook. 432
Cold Pasta. 1654
Cold Soups. 3969
Cold Soups, Warm Salads. 3993
Colin Spencer's Vegetarian Wholefood Cookbook. 1430
Collection of Favorite Family Dessert Recipes. 3343
Collectors Goat Milk Cook Book. 901
Collins' Backroom Cooking Secrets. 637
Color Book of Chocolate Cooking. 339
Colorado Catch Cookbook. 661
Colour Book of Baking. 4204
Come and Get It. 1346
Come for Dinner II. 4188
Come for Tea. 4145
Common Ground Dessert Cookbook. 3301
Community Kitchens Complete Guide to Gourmet Coffee. 436
Company's Coming Cakes. 2987
Company's Coming Cookies. 3210
Compleat Angler's Wife. 672
Compleat Clammer. 425
Compleat Crab and Lobster Book. 466
Compleat Fish Cook. 2117
Compleat Lemon. 1155
Compleat McClane. 615
Compleat Strawberry. 2224
Complete All-in-the-Oven Cookbook. 4214
Complete Apricot Cookbook. 38

Title Index

Complete Australian Barbecue Kettle Cookbook. 4358
Complete Barbecue Cookbook. 4314
Complete Book of American Fish and Shellfish Cookery. 2097
Complete Book of Baking. 4253
Complete Book of Breads. 2807
Complete Book of Cakes and Biscuits. 2998
Complete Book of Canning. 4398
Complete Book of Chicken Wings. 282
Complete Book of Chinese Noodles. 2803
Complete Book of Desserts. 3344
Complete Book of Egg Cookery. 536
Complete Book of Fruit. 745, 747
Complete Book of Herbal Teas. 3536
Complete Book of Herbs. 1024
Complete Book of Herbs & Spices. 1055
Complete Book of Herbs, Spices, and Condiments. 1087
Complete Book of Home Preserving. 4387, 4419
Complete Book of Marzipan. 3591
Complete Book of Natural Foods. 1431, 1480
Complete Book of Outdoor Cookery. 4365
Complete Book of Pasta. 1623
Complete Book of Pastry. 3623
Complete Book of Pies. 3696
Complete Book of Pizza. 3716
Complete Book of Puddings & Desserts. 3447
Complete Book of Salads. 3757, 3820
Complete Book of Sandwiches for the Professional Chef. 3842
Complete Book of Sauces. 3875
Complete Book of Soups and Stews. 4000
Complete Book of Spices. 1058, 2199
Complete Book of Starters. 2652
Complete Book of Steam Cookery. 4492
Complete Book of Teas. 4158
Complete Book of Vegetables. 2397
Complete Book of Yogurt. 2576
Complete Bread Book. 2761
Complete Cake Cookbook. 2955
Complete Cake Decorating Book. 2875
Complete Candy Cookbook. 3007
Complete Cheese Cookbook. 206, 234

Complete Chocolate Chip Cookie Book. 3105
Complete Cookbook of American Fish and Shellfish. 2118
Complete Curry Cookbook. 480
Complete Dairy Foods Cookbook. 500
Complete Encyclopedia of Wild Game & Fish Cleaning & Cooking. 646
Complete Fish and Game Cookery of North America. 647
Complete Fish Cookbook. 590, 1994
Complete Garlic Lovers' Cookbook. 880
Complete Gas Barbecue Cookbook. 4315
Complete Guide to Canning. 4398
Complete Guide to Freezer and Microwave Cooking. 4468
Complete Guide to Fresh Fruits & Vegetables. 807
Complete Guide to Game Care & Cookery. 857
Complete Guide to Game Cookery. 816
Complete Guide to Home Canning. 4420
Complete Health Food Cookbook. 1432
Complete Home Confectioner. 3130
Complete Idaho Potato Cookbook. 1813
Complete International Breakfast/Brunch Cookbook. 4068
Complete International One-Dish Meal Cookbook. 3024
Complete International Sandwich Book. 3836
Complete International Soup Cookbook. 3925
Complete Meat Cookbook. 1245
Complete Meat Cookery. 1215
Complete Muffin and Quick Bread Encyclopedia. 3600
Complete Pastry Cook. 3629
Complete Peanut Cook-Book. 1722
Complete Pie Cookbook. 3690
Complete Pork Cookbook. 1762
Complete Poultry Cookbook. 1859
Complete Rabbit Cook Book. 1876
Complete Raw Juice Therapy. 1884
Complete Rice Cookbook. 1903
Complete Seafood Book. 1995
Complete Shellfisherman's Guide. 2134
Complete Sourdough Cookbook. 2164

Complete South African Fish & Seafood Cookbook. 1975
Complete Sprouting Book. 2206
Complete Turkey Cookbook. 2302
Complete Vegetable Cookbook. 2361, 2383
Complete Whole Grain Cookbook. 922
Complete Wholefood Cuisine. 1395
Complete Wilton Book of Candy. 3009
Comstock Year Full of Special Event Treats. 1749
Conch Book. 437
Condiments. 442, 448
Consider the Oyster. 1620
Contemplation and the Art of Saladmaking. 3763
Cook and Serve Book. 4472
Cook Gourmet Everyday. 1001
Cook It Light. 1495
Cook Milk in Any Flavour You Like. 1255
Cook with Me Sugar Free. 3302
Cook with Tofu. 2255
Cook'n Ca'jun Water Smoker Cookbook. 4484
Cook's Book. 2131
Cook's Garden. 2384, 2435, 2442
Cook's Guide to Growing Herbs, Greens, and Aromatics. 963
Cook's Wine Book. 2564
Cookbook & Commentary. 1505
Cookbook & Guide to Fresh Fruits & Vegetables. 807
Cookbook for Drinkers. 1164
Cookbook for Vegetarians. 2340
Cookbook of North American Truffles. 2293
Cookery Magic with Spices and Herbs. 1082
Cookie and Cracker Cookbook. 3143
Cookie Book. 3171
Cookie Bookie. 3163
Cookie Connection. 3148
Cookie Cookbook. 3265
Cookie Cookery. 3138
Cookie Fun. 3235
Cookie Lover's Cookie Book. 3192
Cookie Sampler. 3199
Cookiemania. 3211

Cookies. 3144, 3155, 3164, 3173, 3190, 3197, 3200, 3201, 3220
Cookies & Crackers. 3156
Cookies & Squares. 3219
Cookies and Bars. 3193
Cookies and Cakes. 2990
Cookies and Candies. 3020
Cookies and Conversation. 4276
Cookies and More Cookies. 3142
Cookies and Slices. 3174
Cookies by Bess. 3149
Cookies, Cakes, and Candies. 3022
Cookies, Cakes, and Pies. 2991
Cookies, Candies & Confections. 3019
Cookies for Christmas. 3181
Cookies for Kids. 3234
Cookies from Amish and Mennonite Kitchens. 3157
Cookies from Many Lands. 3139
Cookies Naturally. 3221
Cookies Supreme! 3194
Cookies You Can Make. 3222
Cooking Against Cancer. 777
Cooking Among Friends. 2668
Cooking and Baking with Dried Fruit. 516
Cooking and Curing with Mexican Herbs. 962
Cooking Conch. 438
Cooking Fish and Shellfish. 2007
Cooking for Compliments. 499
Cooking for Dinner Parties. 4177
Cooking for Health. 1520
Cooking for Health II. 1521
Cooking for Kids the Healthy Way. 1522
Cooking for Your Baby the Natural Way. 1408
Cooking for Your Hunter. 838
Cooking Frankly. 704
Cooking from the Garden. 2421
Cooking from Your Freezer. 4462
Cooking in Style with British Potatoes. 1800
Cooking Inn Style. 4056
Cooking Kosher. 1378
Cooking Lite, Feeling Right Cookbook. 2234
Cooking Naturally. 1313, 1433

Title Index

Cooking Naturally for Pleasure and Health. 1364
Cooking Over Coals. 658
Cooking the Natural Way. 1319
Cooking the Shore Catch. 2039
Cooking the Sportsman's Harvest II. 648
Cooking the Wild Harvest. 652
Cooking Wild Game & Fish Mississippi Style. 643
Cooking with American Wine. 2568
Cooking with Apples Every Season. 14
Cooking with Bacardi Rum. 1925
Cooking with BC Fruit. 749
Cooking with Beer. 116, 117, 120, 121
Cooking with Booze. 1172
Cooking with Bran Cookbook. 157
Cooking with Carob. 190
Cooking with Cheese. 209, 216
Cooking with Chinese Herbs. 982
Cooking with Cilantro. 449
Cooking with Confidence in Your Microwave. 184
Cooking with Cream. 475
Cooking with Culinary Herbs. 1002
Cooking with Curry. 482
Cooking with Dates. 511
Cooking with Desserts. 3386
Cooking with Dried Beans. 67
Cooking with Exotic Mushrooms. 1271
Cooking with Fire and Smoke. 4338
Cooking with Fish. 602, 616
Cooking with Flare. 4316
Cooking with Flowers. 683
Cooking with Fresh Sausage. 1952
Cooking with Fructose. 710
Cooking with Fruit. 711, 728
Cooking with Fruit and Preserving. 726
Cooking with Fruits & Wines. 743
Cooking with Gas. 4366
Cooking with Grains, Nuts and Seeds. 913
Cooking with Great American Chefs. 1906
Cooking with Herbs. 989, 1025, 1033
Cooking with Herbs & Spices. 1064, 1067, 1073, 1080
Cooking with Herbs and Spices. 1064, 1084
Cooking with Honey. 1096, 1111
Cooking with Jalapeños. 1128
Cooking with Jam. 1130

Cooking with Love & Cereal. 904
Cooking with Love and Honey. 1122
Cooking with Maple Syrup. 1197
Cooking with Marijuana. 1200
Cooking with Meat. 1241
Cooking with Natural Foods As You Search for Abundant Health. 1466
Cooking with Nuts & Cereals. 1571
Cooking with Oat Bran. 1572, 1574
Cooking with Old Bay. 2195
Cooking with Oysters and other Shellfish. 2143
Cooking with Pasta & Fine Sauces. 1680
Cooking with Pecans. 1734, 1736
Cooking with Potatoes. 1825
Cooking with Scotch Whisky. 2479
Cooking with Sea Vegetables. 1206
Cooking with Seitan. 2474
Cooking with Sour Cream and Buttermilk. 172
Cooking with Spices. 2188
Cooking with Spices & Herbs. 1051
Cooking with Steamers. 4489
Cooking with Stone Ground Flour. 2466
Cooking with Sun-Dried Tomatoes. 2232
Cooking with Sunshine. 416
Cooking with Taro and Poi. 2242
Cooking with Tequila Sauza. 2249
Cooking with the "Protein Twins" Dry Peas and Lentils. 1160
Cooking with the Chicken Breast. 309
Cooking with the Christian Brothers Brandy. 158
Cooking with the Healthful Herbs. 983
Cooking with the Vegetable Aloe Vera. 6
Cooking with Tofu. 2256
Cooking with Vegetables. 2331, 2413
Cooking with Vitamins. 1347
Cooking with Whole Grains. 912
Cooking with Wholegrains. 907
Cooking with Wine. 2563
Cooking with Wine & Spirits. 2569
Cooking with Wines and Spirits. 1163
Cooking with Yoghurt. 503
Cooking with Yogurt. 2577, 2581, 2583
Cooking with Zucchini. 2590
Cooking Without Additives. 1496
Cooking Your Own Mushrooms. 1285

Specialty Cookbooks

Cooks with Herbs & Spices. 1083
Cooky Book. 3171
Cordial Cookery. 1168
Corn. 453, 455
Corn Cookbook. 456
Corn Means Tamales. 452
Cornell Bread Book. 2730
Cottonseed Cookery. 459
Count Dracula Chicken Cookbook. 288
Country Bakehouse. 4271
Country Baking. 4291, 4292
Country Cakes. 2949, 2983
Country Cookies. 3195, 3228
Country Cooking. 839
Country Cooking with A-peel. 32
Country Cup. 2690
Country Desserts. 3411
Country Fair Cookbook. 4235
Country Fare Cookbook. 4254
Country Harvest. 2510
Country Herbal. 967
Country Inn Buffets. 4095
Country Kitchen. 2343
Country Kitchen Recipes with Herbs. 968
Country Kitchen Recipes with Molasses. 1259
Country Kitchen Recipes with Yogurt. 2578
Country Kitchen Store Cupboard. 4410
Country Life Natural Foods Cookbook. 1409
Country Life Recipes. 1409
Country Living, Country Mornings Cookbook. 4060
Country Mouse. 217
Country Pies. 3706
Country Sampler's Cookie Sampler. 3202
Country Winemaking & Wine Cookery. 2548
Country Wines & Cordials. 2698
Countryside Cookbook. 2494
Covent Garden Cookbook. 2339
Cowboy's Cookbook. 98
Crab. 463
Crab & Abalone. 1
Crackers! 3236
Cranberries. 467
Cranberry Connection. 468
Cranberry Cookery. 470
Cranks Breads & Teacakes. 2817
Cranks Cakes & Biscuits. 2997
Cranks Puddings & Desserts. 3387
Cranks Recipe Book. 1434
Cranks Salads & Dressings. 3813
Cranks Soups & Starters. 3963
Crappie Cookbook. 472
Crawfish House Cookbook. 473
Cream Cakes & Gateaux. 2963
Create a Difference. 1153
Creative Cake Baking and Decorating. 2893
Creative Cake Decorating. 2871, 2899
Creative Cakes. 2932
Creative Cheese Cookery. 226
Creative Chicken. 303
Creative Cook. 185
Creative Cookie. 3208
Creative Cooking with Grains & Pasta. 910
Creative Cooking with Soup. 188, 189
Creative Desserts. 3365
Creative Gardener's Cookbook. 780
Creative Hamburger Cookery. 931
Creative Kitchen: Poultry. 1847
Creative Party Cakes for Children. 2905
Creative Recipes with Bisquick. 140
Creative Soups & Salads. 3985
Crepe and Pancake Cookbook. 3241
Crepe Cookery. 3240
Crepes. 3238
Crepes & Omelets. 3239
Crisco's Good Cooking Made Easy Cookbook. 2153
Crown Valley Natural Food Reserve Cookbook. 1320
Crumpets and Scones. 4143
Cuisinart Food Processor Paté Cookbook. 3665
Cuisine Naturelle. 1467
Culinary and Salad Herbs. 958
Culinary Creations. 2543
Culinary Design and Decoration. 3510
Culinary Herbs. 1003
Culinary Herbs and Condiments. 957
Cultured Mussel Cookbook. 1298
Curious Morel. 1263
Curries and Oriental Cookery. 481

Title Index

Curry Club Favourite Restaurant Curries. 492
Curry Every Sunday. 485
Curry Primer. 486
Cy Littlebee's Guide to Cooking Fish & Game. 662
Cynthia Wine's Hot & Spicy Cooking. 2184
Dairy Food Cookery. 499
Dandelion. 510
Danish Home Baking. 4243
Danish Open Sandwiches. 3831
Dannon Yogurt Cookbook. 2582
Daring Dairy Cookbook. 505
Date Recipes. 512
Dave Hopfer's Fresh-water Fish Cookbook. 2074
Dave Maynard's Soups, Stews & Casseroles. 4001
David Wood Dessert Book. 3423
Dazzling Desserts. 3303
Dear James Beard. 95
Decorated Cakes. 2900
Decorating Cakes for Children's Parties. 2894
Decorating Cakes for Special Occasions. 2906
Decorative Cakes. 2917
Deep Freeze Sense. 4447
Deep-Frying & Pan-Frying. 4476
Delectable Desserts. 3345
Delia Smith's Book of Cakes. 2978
Delicious and Easy Rice Flour Recipes. 1916
Delicious Baking. 4244
Delicious Desserts. 3320, 3346, 3366, 3424
Delicious Desserts Made Easy with Eagle Brand Sweetened Condensed Milk. 439
Delicious Fish. 591
Delicious Home-Made Chocolates. 3101
Delicious Home-Made Petits Fours. 2964
Delicious Main Course Dishes. 3470
Delicious Quick Breads and Muffins. 3610
Deliciously Decadent. 2500
Deliciously Different. 1818
Deliciously Low. 1410
Delightful Delicious Daylily. 513
Deliriously Delightful Desserts the Better Weigh. 3261
Demiveg. 1468
Demiveg Cookbook. 1497
Derrydale Cook Book of Fish and Game. 663
Dessert Book. 3423
Dessert Cookbook. 3264, 3321, 3401
Dessert Cooking Class Cookbook. 3283
Dessert Lover's Cookbook. 3347
Dessert Recipes Children Love and Can Make. 3455
Dessert Scene. 3402
Dessert Sensations. 3437
Desserts. 3275, 3284, 3285, 3367-3369, 3384, 3388, 3403, 3404, 3425, 3438
Desserts and Pastries. 3300, 3322, 3406
Desserts and Puddings. 3356
Desserts, Cakes and Breads. 3348
Desserts, Cheesecakes & Gateaux. 3323
Desserts from Le Perigord. 3421
Desserts from the Garden. 3304
Desserts II. 3405
Desserts to Lower Your Fat Thermostat. 3407
Desserts with Spirit! 1173
Desserts You Can Make Yourself. 3453
Diabetic Breakfast & Brunch Cookbook. 4078
Diabetic Candy, Cookie & Dessert Cookbook. 3286
Diabetic Chocolate Cookbook. 340
Diabetic Delights. 3370
Diabetic Desserts. 3426
Diabetic Snack & Appetizer Cookbook. 2683
Diet for a Small Island. 1348
Diet for the Young at Heart. 457
Different Kettle of Fish. 1976
Dilettante Book of Chocolate and Confections. 3102
Dim Sum and Chinese One-Dish Meals. 3457
Dim Sum and Other Chinese Street Food. 3459
Dim Sum Book. 3460, 3462
Dim Sum, Fast and Festive Chinese Cooking. 3461
Dimsum. 3465
Dining Customs Around the World. 4164

Specialty Cookbooks

Dining in. 4165
Dinner Can be a Picnic All Year Round. 4162
Dinner for Two. 4163
Dinner for Two Cookbook. 4171
Dinner in the Morning. 4066
Dinner Inspirations. 4189
Dinner Menus with Wine. 4168
Dinner Parties. 4175, 4178
Dinner Party. 4192
Dinner Party Book. 4179, 4183
Dinner Party Desserts. 3324
Dinner's Ready. 4184
Dinners in a Scottish Castle. 4169
Dip It! 3468
Dips with a Difference. 3467
Discover the Fun of Cake Decorating. 2858
Discover Turkey. 2306
Divine Desserts. 3371
Diving for Crayfish in South Africa. 1181
Do-Ahead Cookbook. 4455
Dock to Dish. 1977, 2098
Does Your Lunch Pack Punch? 3894
Dogfish Cookbook. 514
Dolci, the Fabulous Desserts of Italy. 3389
Dominique's Famous Fish, Game & Meat Recipes. 640
Don Holm's Book of Food Drying, Pickling & Smoke Curing. 4433
Don't Tell 'em It's Good for 'em. 1411
Donut Book. 3469
Donvier Ice Cream. 3558
Donvier Ice Cream Dessert Book. 3560
Dooryard Herb Cookbook. 1026
Dooryard Herbs. 990, 1026
Down to Earth Cookbook. 1559
Down to Earth with British Potatoes. 1801
Dr. Bob Shipp's Guide to Fishes of the Gulf of Mexico. 592
Dr. Cookie's Cookbook. 3212
Dr. Jensen's Real Soup & Salad Cookbook. 3992
Dr. Pfeiffer's Total Nutrition. 1321
Dress 'em Out. 833
Dressing & Cooking Wild Game. 849
Dried Beans & Grains. 68
Dried Fruit. 515
Drinks & Snacks. 2691

Drinks and Desserts. 3454
Drinks for All Seasons. 2694
Drinks without Liquor. 2699
Dry Peas and Lentils. 1160
Drying Vegetables, Fruits & Herbs. 4441
Duncan Hines Bake Shop in a Book. 176
Duncan Hines Baking with American Dash. 178
Duncan Hines Celebrates Baking. 179
Durkee Spice and Herb Cookbook. 1059
Dutch Baking and Pastry. 4206
Early Summer Garden. 2422
Easiest & Best Coffee Cakes & Quick Breads. 3111
East-West Book of Rice Cookery. 1898
Eastern Oysters. 1618
Easy & Elegant Hors d'Oeuvres. 2623
Easy & Elegant Seafood. 2008
Easy Appetizers. 2624
Easy Art of Smoking Food. 4483
Easy Baking. 4265
Easy Can Opener Cookbook. 183
Easy, Elegant Luncheon Menus. 4110
Easy Entrées. 3488
Easy Game Cookery. 815
Easy Game Cooking. 813
Easy Gourmet Vegetables & Salads. 2373
Easy Harvest Sauce & Puree Cookbook. 3857
Easy Microwave Preserving. 4421
Easy Recipes for Wild Game and Fish. 670
Easy Recipes of California Winemakers. 2565
Easy Stir-Fry Recipes. 4498
Easy Suppers. 4193
Easy Way to the Fascinating Art of Cake Decorating. 2853
Easy Whole-Food Recipes. 1322
Eat Fish, Live Better. 626
Eat Well. 1435
Eat Well, Stay Well. 1534
Eat Your Vegetables! 2385
Eating Meat and Staying Healthy. 1242
Eating Naturally. 1323
Eating What Grows Naturally. 1324
Eating Wild Plants. 2503
Eats with Oats. 1586

Title Index

Edible and Useful Plants of California. 2484
Edible Architecture. 3595
Edible Art. 3520
Edible Flowers. 687
Edible Mushroom. 1291
Edible Seashore. 2075
Edible Wild Plants. 2495, 2524
Edible Wild Plants of Pennsylvania and Neighboring States. 2536
Edible? Incredible! 2028
Edible? Incredible! Pondlife. 2488
Egg & Cheese Dishes. 253
Egg & Cheese Menus. 250
Egg and Cheese Cookbook. 247
Egg Cookbook. 534
Egg Cookery. 548
Egg Primer. 530
Eggcyclopedia. 531
Eggplant Cookbook. 523
Eggs. 550, 553
Eggs & Cheese. 246, 249
Eggs and Cheese. 252
Eggs by the Dozen. 546
Eggs Only. 543
Eggsinstead. 537
Electric Vegetarian. 1325
Elegant and Easy. 3514
Elegant Desserts. 3325
Elegant Economical Egg Cookbook. 548
Elegant Elk, Delicious Deer. 554
Elegant Entertaining Cookbook. 445
Elegant Onion. 1606
Empanadas & Other International Turnovers. 4036
Encyclopedia of Desserts. 3305
Encyclopedia of Fish Cookery. 1961
Encyclopedia of Herbs and Herbalism. 974
Encyclopedia of Herbs, Spices, and Flavourings. 1065
Encyclopedia of Wild Game Cleaning and Cooking. 636
English Biscuit and Cookie Book. 3165
English Bread and Yeast Cookery. 2751
English Puddings. 3737
English Seafood Dishes. 2076
Enjoy B.C. Brand Fruit the Diabetic Way. 721

Enjoy! 4190
Entertaining Chicken. 304
Entertaining with Appetizers. 2639
Entertaining with Eggs. 532
Entertaining with Insects. 1127
Entertaining Without Alcohol. 2705
Entrées, the Main Event. 3491
Epicure's Book of Steak and Beef Dishes. 96
Epicurean Recipes of California Winemakers. 2558
Episcopal Chicken. 283
Essential Book of Shellfish. 2140
Essential Olive Oil Companion. 1597
Ethnic Is Now. 2471
European Recipes for American Fish & Game. 635
European Wild Boar Cookbook. 2483
Evelyn Findlater's
  Natural Foods Primer. 1436
  Wholefood Cookery Course. 1412
  Wholefood Cookery School. 1523
Every Day - Serve Eggs - Some Way. 533
Everybody's Favorite Orthomolecular Muffin Book. 3597
Everybody's Natural Foods Cookbook. 1379
Everyday Recipes with Home Grown Potatoes. 1820
Everywoman's Wholefood Cookbook. 1359
Exchange Cookbook. 3287
Exclusively Chocolate Cookbook. 312
Exclusively Eggs. 552
Exotic Curries. 488
Exotic Fruits & Vegetables. 793
Exotic Fruits A-Z. 756
Exotic Pasta. 1655
Exotic Vegetables A-Z. 2423
Exotic Yam. 2237
Experiencing Quality. 1498
Explore the Magic World of California Beans. 69
Exploring Nature's Uncultivated Garden. 2529
Eydie Mac's Natural Recipes. 1314
F for Fish. 603
Fabulous Cooking with Zucchini, Pumpkin and Squash. 2599

Fabulous Desserts of Italy. 3389
Fabulous Fiber Fixings. 2472
Fabulous Fish. 2056
Fabulous French Fruit Cuisine. 757
Fabulous Fruit Desserts. 748
Fabulous Fry Pan Favorites. 4475
Fair Game. 827
Family Buffet & Cocktail. 4107
Family Circle Great Chicken Recipes. 258
Family Circle Great Ground-Beef Recipes. 930
Family Circle's Great Desserts. 3255
Family Cookbook for Fishes and Seafoods Recipes. 1984
Family Dinners in a Hurry. 4172
Family Fish Cookbook. 617
Famous Brands
  Breads, Quick Breads. 2790
  Chicken & Poultry. 1849
  Chocolate Classics. 366
  Cooking with Eggs and Cheese. 251
  Desserts. 3349
  Fish & Seafood Cookbook. 2040
  Great Vegetable Dishes. 2386
  Main Dishes. 3482
  Meat Cookbook. 1236
  Pasta Dishes. 1662
  Soups & Salads. 3989
Famous Jams & Jellies. 3585
Fancy Fruits and Extraordinary Vegetables. 778
Fancy Pantry. 4413
Fancy, Sweet & Sugarfree. 3350
Fannie Farmer Baking Book. 4234
Fantastic Cakes. 2895
Fantastic Oatmeal Recipes. 1583
Fantasy Chocolate Desserts. 378
Farm Journal's
  Best-Ever Cookies. 3145
  Best-Ever Pies. 3687
  Best-Ever Vegetable Recipes. 2374
  Complete Cake Decorating Book. 2875
  Country Fair Cookbook. 4235
  Freezing & Canning Cookbook. 4449
  Ground Beef Roundup. 935
  Homemade Breads. 2791
  Homemade Pies, Cookies & Bread. 3690
  Picnic & Barbecue Cookbook. 4321

Farm Journal's (Continued)
  Speedy Skillet Meals. 4473
Farm Wife News Sweets 'n' Treats. 3116
Farmers Market Cookbook. 799
Farmhouse Feasts. 3476
Farmhouse Kitchen Baking Book. 4272
Farmhouse Kitchen Freezer & Microwave. 4469
Fashionable First Courses. 2646
Fast & Easy Company Treats. 3900
Fast & Easy Oat Bran Cookbook. 1575
Fast & Fabulous Hors d'Oeuvres. 2647
Fast & Fancy. 3471
Fast & Flashy Hors d'Oeuvres. 2653
Fast & Natural Cuisine. 1380
Fast and Easy Vegetarian Cooking. 1499
Fast and Healthy Ways to Cook Vegetables. 2424
Fast Breads! 2804
Fast Cakes. 2944
Fast Desserts. 3351
Fast Fabulous Desserts. 3326
Fast-Fixin' Chicken. 287
Fast-Fixin' Meat Recipes. 1244
Fast Suppers. 4197
Favorite Blueberry Recipes. 147
Favorite Brand Name Recipes
  Appetizers. 2673
  Desserts. 3288
Favorite Cookies. 3166
Favorite Gold Medal Flour Recipes. 680
Favorite Home Baking Recipes. 4217
Favorite Homemade Cookies and Candies. 3018
Favorite Meat Recipes. 1230
Favorite Recipes for Soups. 3964
Favorite Recipes of California Winemakers. 2546
Favorite Seafood Recipes. 2099
Favorite Southern Recipes. 3577
Favourite Cakes. 2971
Favourite Recipes from the U.B.C. Bakeshop. 4255
Faye Levy's Chocolate Sensations. 365
Feast for Health. 1500
Feast of Fish. 604
Feast of Fishes. 2077
Feast of Soups. 3933

Title Index 625

Feast of the Olive. 1593
Feast of Vegetables. 2332, 2389
Feasting Naturally from Your Own Recipes. 1326
Feasting on Raw Foods. 1880
Feasting with a Fork. 4103
Feasts of Wine and Food. 4185
Feed Your Family the Healthier Way. 1469
Feed Your Family with Love. 2340
Festival Cookie Book. 3169
Festive and Novelty Cakes. 2972
Festive Baking. 4273
Festive Breads of Christmas. 2762
Festive Breads of Easter. 2731
Festive Cakes of Christmas. 2933
Festive Chocolate. 367
Festive Cookies. 3183
Festive Dessert Cookery. 3253
Festive Entrées. 3479
Festive Tradition. 3306
Fiber & Bran Better Health Cookbook. 905
Fibre-Plan Cookbook. 1437
Field Guide to North American Edible Wild Plants. 2496
Fiery Appetizers. 2640
Fiery Cuisines. 2185
Fifty Delightfully Different Ways to Cook Potatoes. 1781
Fifty Squash Recipes. 2210
Filo File for Filophiles. 557
Final Touch. 3513
Fine Art of Cake Decorating. 2884
Fine Art of Delectable Desserts. 3289
Fine Art of Egg, Omelet & Souffle Cooking. 526
Fine Kettle of Fish. 561
Fine Preserving. 3582
Fine Wine in Food. 2567
Finger Lickin', Rib Stickin', Great Tastin', Hot & Spicy Barbecue. 4306
Finishing Touches. 2901
Fire & Smoke. 4311
Fire and Spice. 2196
First American Peanut Growing Book. 1728
First Course Dishes. 2641
First You Take a Leek. 1142

Fish. 559, 593, 618, 619, 2119
Fish & Seafood. 2009, 2038, 2041, 2071
Fish & Seafood Made Easy. 2100
Fish & Shellfish. 1996, 2029, 2114
Fish & Shellfish Cookbook. 1997
Fish & Shellfish Menus. 2010
Fish and Fowl Cookery. 664
Fish and Game Cooking. 641
Fish and Meat. 594
Fish and Seafood. 2120
Fish and Shell-fish. 1978
Fish and Shellfish. 1964, 2058
Fish and Shellfish for Your Table. 1979
Fish and Their Sauces. 2030
Fish Book. 1980, 2078
Fish Cookbook. 579, 597
Fish Cookery. 609
Fish Cookery with Magimix. 562
Fish Course. 605
Fish Cuisine. 614
Fish Dishes of the Pacific. 595
Fish Feast. 569
Fish for Health. 570
Fish in My Life. 627
Fish-Lovers' Cookbook. 2011
Fish on the Grill. 596
Fish, Poultry and Game. 655
Fish Recipe Book. 572
Fish Steaks and Fillets. 620
Fish Without Fuss. 1998
Fishing for Buffalo. 632
Fishing for Compliments. 2042
Fishing in the West. 580
Fishing is for Me. 634
Fishmonger Cookbook. 2079
Fitness from Food. 1413
Fix & Freeze Cookbook. 4464
Fixin' Fish. 581
Flavored Vinegars. 2459
Fleischmann's Bake-it-easy Yeast Book. 2572
Flo Sez Have Fun with Cake and Icing. 2885
Floral Cake Decorating. 2876
Florence Fabricant's Pleasures of the Table. 4180
Florence Lin's Chinese One-Dish Meals. 3040

Florence Lin's Complete Book of Chinese Noodles. 2803
Florida Citrus Cookbook. 414
Florida CowBelles Cookbook. 93
Floris Book of Cakes. 2934
Flounder and Other Flat Fish. 677
Flour Cooking, Naturally. 678
Flowers in the Kitchen. 692
Flowery Food & Drink. 693
Floyd on Fish. 586
Follow Your Heart's Vegetarian Soup Cookbook. 3937
Fondue. 3495
Fondues from Around the World. 3497
Food & Wine Great Desserts. 3427
Food Combining for Health. 1535
Food Dryer Handbook. 4437
Food for Health and Vitality. 1438
Food for Keeps. 4388
Food from the Countryside. 2530
Food from the Seashore. 1969
Food from Your Garden. 781
Food Garnishes and Decorations. 3523
Food-Lover's Garden. 2436
Food of My Friends. 1349
Food Preservation. 4414
Food Processor Baking Magic. 4203
Food Processor Bread Book. 2732
Food Service Manual. 527
Food Sleuth Handbook. 1365
For Popcorn Lovers Only. 1759
For Starters. 2625
For the Love of Food. 1366
Foraging Vacation. 2497
Forbidden Fruits & Forgotten Vegetables. 771
Forgotten Art of Flower Cookery. 688
Forgotten Art of Making Old-Fashioned Jellies. 3568
Four Seasons Salads. 3783
Fowl and Game Bird Cookery. 1856
Fowl Play. 294
Fragrance and Flavour. 1070
Fragrant Vegetable. 2398
Frango Chocolate Cookbook. 382
Frank Davis Seafood Notebook. 1999
Freddie Bailey's Favorite Southern Recipes. 3577

Free and Equal Sweet Tooth Cookbook. 3408
Free Cookbook. 1350
Free From the Sea. 2012
Free Hand Figure Piping. 2877
Freezer Companion. 4465
Freezer Cookbook. 4446, 4447, 4456
Freezer Cookery. 4443
Freezing & Canning Cookbook. 4449
Freezing & Drying. 4457
French Fish Cuisine. 2046
French Tarts. 3641
French Vegetable Cookery. 2387
French Way with Vegetables. 2439
Fresh Fish Cook Book. 588
Fresh Fish Cookbook. 606
Fresh Foods Country Cookbook. 1414
Fresh from the Country. 1501
Fresh from the Freezer. 4471
Fresh from the Garden. 784
Fresh-from-the Oven Breads. 2753
Fresh Fruit and Vegetable Book. 766
Fresh Fruit Cookbook. 758
Fresh Fruit Desserts. 3439
Fresh Fruit Drinks. 739
Fresh Garden Vegetables. 2362
Fresh Ideas for Fish 'n Poultry. 563
Fresh Ideas for Vegetable Cooking. 2388
Fresh Ideas with Mushrooms. 1272
Fresh Produce. 797
Fresh Salad Ideas. 3792
Fresh Salmon. 1938
Fresh Seafood. 2013
Fresh Tarts. 3642
Fresh Thoughts on Food. 1524
Fresh Tuna. 2299
Fresh Turkey Ideas. 2312
Fresh-Water Fish Cookbook. 2074
Fresh Ways with Appetizers. 2654
Fresh Ways with Beef & Lamb. 107
Fresh Ways with Beef & Veal. 112
Fresh Ways with Breakfasts & Brunches. 4079
Fresh Ways with Cakes. 2979
Fresh Ways with Chicken. 1853
Fresh Ways with Desserts. 3372
Fresh Ways with Fish & Shellfish. 2043
Fresh Ways with Lamb. 1141

Title Index

Fresh Ways with Pasta. 1699
Fresh Ways with Pastries & Sweets. 3652
Fresh Ways with Picnics & Barbecues. 4367
Fresh Ways with Pork. 1776
Fresh Ways with Poultry. 1850
Fresh Ways with Salads. 3793, 3807
Fresh Ways with Snacks & Party Fare. 3908
Fresh Ways with Soups & Stews. 4006
Fresh Ways with Terrines & Patés. 3671
Fresh Ways with Vegetables. 2399
Fresh: A Greenmarket Cookbook. 802
Freshwater Fisherman's Companion. 573
Friendly Bees, Ferocious Bees. 1124
Friends of the Earth Cookbook. 1327
Friends of the Essex Youth Orchestras Present Overtures & Encores. 2670
From a Baker's Kitchen. 4274
From a Breton Garden. 2443
From Basic Apple to Four and Twenty Blackbirds. 3709
From Caravan to Casserole. 1047
From God's Natural Storehouse. 1328
From Juice to Jelly. 3583
From Marina with Love. 3307
From Sea & Stream. 2044
From Sea to Shining Sea. 2081
From Seed to Serve. 1038
From the Apple Orchard. 19
From the Night Kitchen. 4011
From the Strawberry Patch. 2217
From Vegetables with Love. 2437
Frozen Delights. 3504
Frozen Hors d'Oeuvre Cookbook. 2607
Fructose Cookbook. 708
Frugal Fish. 574
Frugal Gourmet Cooks with Wine. 2559
Fruit. 744, 759
Fruit and Nut Book. 740
Fruit and Vegetables of the World. 794
Fruit Book. 732
Fruit Cookbook. 717, 729, 741
Fruit Desserts. 722, 751, 3373
Fruit Fare. 730
Fruit for the Home and Garden. 745
Fruit from Your Garden. 752
Fruit, Herbs & Vegetables of Italy. 803

Fruit Tart Cookbook. 754
Fruits. 731
Fruits & Vegetables. 769
Fruits of the Desert. 720
Fruits of the Earth. 785
Frying Tonight. 4430
Fun Foods. 3526
Further Guide to Chinese Market Vegetables. 2365
Gale's Honey Book. 1106
Gallery Buffet Soup Cookbook. 3938
Galley Soups for All Seasons. 3926
Game. 699, 851
Game and Fish Menu Cookbook. 665
Game Cookbook. 821, 840, 844, 866
Game Cookery. 812, 816, 845, 858, 861, 862
Game Cookery Book. 653
Game Cookery in America and Europe. 852
Game for All. 666
Game for All Seasons. 853
Game Gourmet. 834
Game in Good Taste. 859
Game in Season. 659
Game is Good Eating. 810
Garden-Fresh Cooking. 796
Garden of Eternal Swallows. 1330
Garden of Miracles. 3537
Garden to Table. 2325
Garden Way Bread Book. 2725
Garden Way Publishing Bulletin. 815
Garden Way Publishing's Making Apple Pies & Crusts. 22
Ice Cream, Ices & Sherbets. 3549
Whole-Grain Breads. 2780
Garden Way's
Guide to Food Drying. 4436
Joy of Gardening Cookbook. 2375
Red & Green Tomato Cookbook. 2282
Zucchini Cookbook. 2601
Gardener's Companion and Cookbook. 2363
Gardener's Kitchen. 2333
Gardens for All Book of
Cauliflower, Broccoli & Cabbage. 161
Corn. 451
Cucumbers, Melons, Squash. 479
Eggplant, Okra & Peppers. 525

Specialty Cookbooks

Gardens for All Book of (Continued)
Lettuce & Greens. 929
Peas & Peanuts. 1730
Potatoes. 1802
Garlic. 871
Garlic Cookery. 872, 1004
Garlic for Health! and for Taste! 874
Garlic Gourmet. 875
Garlic Lovers' Cookbooks. 880
Garnishing. 3518, 3521, 3524
Garnishing and Decoration. 3522
Gas Barbecuing. 4376
Gas Grill Cookouts. 4322
Gateaux & Pastries. 3001
Gateaux and Torten. 2956
Gelatin Cook Book. 885
Genmai. 167
Georgia Apple Recipes. 20
Georgia Cooking with Sweet Vidalia Onions. 1604
Georgia Milk Recipes. 1256
Georgia Peach Recipes. 1708
Geraldene Holt's Cake Stall. 2929
German Cookie Recipes from Fredericksburg, Texas. 3141
Get More from Your Deep Fat Fryer. 4431
Get Your Buns in Here. 4266
Getting the Most from Your Game and Fish. 671
Getting Your Kids to Eat Right. 1351
Ghirardelli Original Chocolate Cookbook. 329
Giant Handbook of Food Preserving Basics. 4405
Gift Giver's Cookbook. 4279
Gifts from the Kitchen. 4417
Ginger Cookbook. 896
Ginger East to West. 897
Gingerbread. 3533
Gingerbread Art. 3534
Gingerbread Book. 3530
Gingerbread Delights. 3528
Gingerbread Tales. 3531
Give Yourself a Treat! 506
Global Kitchen. 1352
Glorious American Food. 4174
Glorious Chocolate. 386

Glorious Desserts. 3308
Glorious Fish in the Microwave. 2101
Glorious Garlic. 876
Glorious Noodle. 1663
Glorious Puds. 3734
Glorious Stew. 4015
Glorious Vegetables in the Microwave. 2414
Glut of Apricots & Peaches. 39
Glut of Avocados. 51
Glut of Citrus Fruit. 418
Glut of Courgettes & Marrows. 2425
Glut of Plums. 1754
Glut of Strawberries & Soft Fruit. 2228
Glut of Tomatoes and Salad Vegetables. 2426
Gluten Book. 899
Glynn Christian's Best of Breakfast Time Cook Book. 4047
GNC Gourmet Vitamin Cookbook. 1329
Going Crackers. 3898
Going Wild. 667, 668
Gold Medal Century of Success Cookbook. 4288
Golda Sirota's Love Food. 1415
Golde's Homemade Cookies. 3229
Golden Bar Recipe Booklet. 3184
Golden Lemon. 1154
Good and Healthy. 1551
Good and Wholesome Honey Recipes. 1114
Good Breakfast Book. 4038
Good Cake Book. 2939
Good Cook -- Ten Talents. 1439
Good Fat Diet. 607
Good Food. 4003
Good Food from Your Freezer. 4466
Good Food Gardening. 773
Good Food Ideas Cheese Cookbook. 207
Good Food Naturally. 1308, 1381
Good for You Cookies! 3204
Good Friends, Great Dinners. 4186
Good Grains. 908
Good Health Cook Book. 1382
Good Health Cookbook. 1440
Good Health Cookery Book. 1502
Good Healthy Food. 1441

Title Index

Good Housekeeping
  Complete Book of Desserts. 3440
  Complete Book of Home Baking. 4280
  Complete Book of Home Preserving. 4389
  Eating for a Healthy Skin. 1536
  Perfect Pastry. 3625
  Salads. 3771
  Wholefood Cookery. 1537
Good Ideas Keep Popping Up. 213
Good Life Natural Cooking from Teresa Kennedy Moore's Kitchen. 1367
Good Morning Cook Book. 4039
Good Morning Macrobiotic Breakfast Book. 4063
Good Mornings. 4080
Good Nature's Wholesome Snacks & Lunches for Kids. 3911
Good Old-Fashioned Cakes. 2984
Good Ole Boys Wild Game Cookbook. 674
Good Spirits. 2706
Gottlieb's Bakery Since 1884. 4224
Gourmet Barbecue. 4339
Gourmet Barbecue Cookery. 4377
Gourmet Carrot Cookbook. 198
Gourmet Desserts. 3409
Gourmet Fish on the Grill. 628
Gourmet Food Naturally. 1383
Gourmet Food on a Wheat-Free Diet. 1916
Gourmet Game. 675
Gourmet Garden. 774, 806
Gourmet Gardening. 2341
Gourmet Goobers. 1723
Gourmet Grilling. 4377
Gourmet Health Recipes. 1442
Gourmet Mustards. 1305
Gourmet Preserves. 4423
Gourmet Seafood Entrees. 2080
Gourmet Vegetarian Feasts. 872, 1004
Gourmet Vinegars. 2460
Gourmet Whole Foods. 1503
Gourmet Wine Cooking the Easy Way. 2566
Gourmet's Best Desserts. 3390
Gourmet's Book of Mushrooms & Truffles. 1296
Gourmet's Freezer. 4470

Gourmet's Guide to Cheese. 244
Gourmet's Guide to Chocolate. 341, 397
Gourmet's Guide to Coffee & Tea. 2713
Gourmet's Guide to Fish and Shellfish. 2014
Gourmet's Guide to Fruit. 763
Gourmet's Guide to Herbs and Spices. 1085
Gourmet's Guide to Shellfish. 2150
Gourmet's Guide to Vegetables. 2444
Grain Gastronomy. 920
Grains and Fibres for Optimum Health. 918
Grains and Vegetables. 1552
Grains, Beans & Pulses. 1148
Grains Cookbook. 921
Grains, Nuts and Seeds. 913
Grains! Beans! Nuts! 1331
Grand Central Oyster Bar & Restaurant Seafood Cookbook. 2059
Grand Finales. 1169
Grand Performer. 892
Grand Salad. 3776
Grandma Rose's Book of Sinfully Delicious Cakes. 2996
Grandmother Soup. 3978
Granny's Sweet Things. 3441
Granola Cookbook. 926
Gray's Fish Cookbook. 597
Gray's Wild Game Cookbook. 835
Great American Barbeque Instruction Book. 4330
Great American Cakes. 2973
Great American Chili Book. 3083
Great American Chocolate Cookbook. 379
Great American Cookbook. 1732
Great American Cookies. 3205
Great American Dessert Cookbook. 3442
Great American Peanut Book. 1724
Great American Peanut Butter Book. 1713
Great American Pie Book. 3693
Great American Sandwich Book. 3847
Great American Seafood Cookbook. 2081
Great American Tofu Cookbook. 2252
Great American Tomato Book. 2285
Great Banana Cookbook. 57
Great Beginnings. 2626
Great Beginnings & Happy Endings. 2666

Specialty Cookbooks

Great Book of Seafood Cooking. 2121
Great Bread! 2836
Great British Breakfast. 4044
Great British Lamb Guide. 1135
Great British Potato Recipes. 1793
Great Cakes & Pastries. 3005
Great Casseroles! 3027
Great Chicago-Style Pizza Cookbook. 3718
Great Chicken Dishes. 305
Great Cookie Caper. 3167
Great Cooking with Beer. 123
Great Cooking with Dairy Products. 494
Great Cookouts. 4349
Great Day Cookbook. 4218
Great Dessert Book. 3309
Great Desserts. 3327, 3427, 3428
Great Desserts from Ceil Dyer. 3374
Great Desserts of the South. 3410
Great Dinners with Less Meat. 3474
Great East Coast Seafood Book. 1985
Great Fast Breads. 2789
Great Garlic Cookbook. 882
Great Grains. 924
Great Grilling. 4368
Great Ground-Beef Recipes. 930
Great International Dessert Cookbook. 3352
Great Italian Desserts. 3443
Great Meat Cookery. 1249
Great Microwave Dessert Cookbook. 3353
Great Oklahoma Congressional Chile Cook-Off. 3085
Great Old-Fashioned American Desserts. 3391
Great Pancake Cookbook. 3244
Great Pasta Dishes. 1670
Great Potato Cookbook. 1782, 1821
Great Pumpkin Cookbook. 1867, 1868
Great Sausage Recipes. 1949
Great Scandinavian Baking Book. 4275
Great Seafood Dishes. 2045
Great Seafood Recipes. 2059
Great Southern Wild Game Cookbook. 817
Great Taste of Virginia Seafood. 2015
Great Tasting Health Foods. 1353
Great Tomato Cookbook. 2278
Great Vegetable Dishes. 2386

Great Vegetables from the Great Chefs. 2445
Great Whole Grain Breads. 2778
Great Year-Round Turkey Cookbook. 2301
Green Banana Recipes. 53
Green Barley Essence. 927
Green Chili. 1738
Green Thumb Cookbook. 2356
Green Thumb Harvest. 779
Green Thumb Preserving Guide. 4407
Greene on Greens. 928
Greengrocer Cookbook. 764
Greens 'n Things. 3752
Grey Poupon. 1306
Greyston Bakery Cookbook. 4256
Grill Book. 4340
Grill Cookbook. 4378
Grilled Fish and Seafood. 2060
Grilling & Barbecuing. 4341
Grilling Book. 4369
Ground Beef Cookbook. 938
Ground Beef Favorites. 933
Ground Beef Microwave Meals. 949
Ground Beef Roundup. 935
Ground Beef Sounds Good. 941
Ground Meat Cookbook. 934, 936, 940
Ground Turkey Cookbook. 951
Ground Turkey Lover's Cookbook. 950
Grow it, Cook it. 775
Growing and Cooking Beans. 62
Growing and Cooking Berries. 125
Growing and Cooking Potatoes. 1788
Growing and Using Herbs and Spices. 1074
Growing and Using Herbs with Confidence. 1013
Growing Up on the Chocolate Diet. 398
Growing Vegetables & Herbs. 991
Guide to Chinese Market Vegetables. 2365
Guide to Common Whelks. 2160
Guide to Cooking Fish & Game. 662
Guide to Fishes of the Gulf of Mexico. 592
Guide to Food Drying. 4436
Guide to Home Freezing. 4451
Guide to Market Fruits of Southeast Asia. 746
Guide to Natural Foods Cooking. 1540
Guide to Northeastern Wild Edibles. 2492

Title Index

Guilt-Free Snacking. 3895
Gulden's Makes Good Food Taste Great. 1302
Gulf Fare. 1970
Haagen-Dazs Book of Ice Cream. 3546
Hallah Book. 2812
Ham Book. 953
Ham for All Seasons. 955
Hamburger Cookbook. 944
Hamlyn All Colour
  Book of Home Baking. 4225
  Book of Puddings & Desserts. 3290
  Cakes and Baking. 2985
Hamlyn Cake Design and Decorating Course. 2918
Hamlyn Chicken Cookbook. 1830
Hamlyn Curry Cookbook. 483
Happiness is Junk-Free Food. 1470
Happy Eating Recipe Book. 977
Happy Endings. 3259
Hard Clams. 426
Harriet's Zucchini Lovers' Cookbook. 2591
Harrods Book of Cakes & Desserts. 2965
Harrods Book of Chocolates & Other Edible Gifts. 3103
Harrods Book of Jams, Jellies & Chutneys. 3586
Harrowsmith Cookbook. 1354
Harrowsmith Fish & Seafood Cookbook. 2031
Harrowsmith Pasta Cookbook. 1640
Harvest of Apples. 33
Harvesting the Northern Wild. 2504
Having Tea. 4148
Healing Power of Herbal Teas. 3538
Healing with Whole Foods. 1552
Health Food Cook Book. 1344
Health Food, Fruit and Nuts, Seafood. 1416
Health, Happiness, and the Pursuit of Herbs. 969
Health-Lover's Guide to Super Seafood. 2102
Healthful Korean Cooking. 1231
Healthy Bean Dishes. 81
Healthy Cooking. 1417
Healthy Cooking on the Run. 1384
Healthy Desserts. 3354

Healthy Eating. 1471, 1538
Healthy Eating on a Low Budget. 1472
Healthy Gourmet. 1473
Healthy Gourmet Cookbook. 1355
Healthy Gourmet International Cookbook. 1368
Healthy Peasant Gourmet. 1385
Healthy Snacks for Kids. 3896
Healthy Taste of Honey. 1097
Hearty Salads. 3821
Hearty Vegetarian Soups & Stews. 4009
Hearty Winter Stews and Casseroles. 3063
Heaven on the Half Shell. 2147
Heavenly Home Made Ice Cream. 3541
Hedgerow Cookery. 2489
Hedgerow Harvest. 2525
Helen Dollaghan's Best Main Dishes. 3472
Helen Groll's Homemade Bread, Fun and Foolproof. 2733
Hellmann's Mayonnaise Best Foods. 1209
Hellmann's Real Mayonnaise Seasonal Cookbook. 1208
Helping Hand. 1886
Herb & Spice Cookbook. 1075
Herb & Spice Handbook. 1081
Herb and Honey Cookery. 872, 1004
Herb Book. 970, 978
Herb Cookbook. 965, 984
Herb Cuisine with Added Spice. 1086
Herb Garden Cookbook. 1017
Herb Grower's Guide. 1076
Herbal Delights. 1014
Herbal Fare. 1027
Herbal Guide to Food. 1035
Herbal Recipes. 964
Herbal Secrets from a Kenya Garden. 1018
Herbal Teas for Health and Healing. 3539
Herbal Teas, Tisanes and Lotions. 3535
Herbal Treasures. 1039
Herbs. 992, 1005, 1034, 1040
Herbs & Cooking. 1042
Herbs & Imagination. 3975
Herbs & Spices. 1068
Herbs and Comfort Cooking. 1044
Herbs and Spices. 1049, 1060, 1069
Herbs and Spices of the Bible. 1066
Herbs and Spices of the World. 1061
Herbs Are Good Companions. 1019

Herbs for All Seasons. 985
Herbs for Better Body Beauty. 981
Herbs for Cooking, Cleaning, Canning, and Sundry Household Chores. 981
Herbs for Health and Cookery. 980
Herbs for the Home and Garden. 1006
Herbs for the Kitchen. 961
Herbs, from Cultivation to Cooking. 979
Herbs, Health, and Cookery. 980
Herbs in Healthy Home Cooking. 1041
Herbs, Spices & Flavorings. 1056
Herbs, Spices, and Flavorings. 1057
Herbs Through the Seasons at Caprilands. 1020
Herbs Today. 1007
Here's Health Alternative Chocolate Book. 194
Here's Health Wholefood Cookery Course. 1474
Here's to You Honey! 1098
Hershey's
   Chocolate and Cocoa Cookbook. 320
   Chocolate Cookbook. 387
   Chocolate Memories Through the Years Cookbook. 319
   Chocolate Recipe Collection. 388
   Chocolate Treasury. 342
   Cookies, Bars, and Brownies. 3168
   Fabulous Desserts. 389
   Kidsnacks. 402
   Simply Chocolate. 380
   Timeless Desserts. 360
Hobbying with Herbs. 1008
Hodgson Mill Oat Bran Cookbook. 1573
Holiday Appetizers. 2662
Holiday Cookies & Centerpieces. 3530
Holiday Dessert Book. 3375
Holiday Snack Sampler. 3912
Holiday Sweets Without Sugar. 3117
Holistic Cook. 1475
Holistic H.E.L.P. Handbook. 1356
Home Baking. 4293
Home Baking Book. 4227
Home Bakings. 4294
Home Book of Cooking Venison. 822
Home Book of Smoke-Cooking Meat, Fish & Game. 4482
Home Canning. 4384

Home Canning and Freezing. 4396
Home Canning Cookbook. 4396
Home Canning Handbook. 4402
Home Canning Made Easy. 4402
Home Canning of Fruits and Vegetables. 4420
Home Canning of Meat and Poultry. 4420
Home Cookbook of Wild Meat and Game. 822
Home Drying of Fruits and Vegetables. 4438
Home Drying Vegetables, Fruits & Herbs. 4441
Home Food Dehydrating. 4432
Home Food Systems. 4390
Home Garden Book of Herbs and Spices. 1074
Home Garden Cookbook. 2321
Home Gardener's Cookbook. 765
Home Gardener's Month-by-Month Cookbook. 782
Home Gardening Wisdom. 2351
Home Grown. 800
Home Is My Garden. 786
Home-Made. 1386
Home Made Jams, Jellies and Marmalades. 3570
Home Pickling of Olives. 1591
Home Preserving. 4385, 4399
Home Sausage Making. 1950
Home Smoking and Curing. 4486
Homemade Bread, Fun and Foolproof. 2733
Homemade Breads. 2723, 2791, 2792, 3690
Homemade Cookies. 3150, 3217, 3690
Homemade Cream Liqueurs. 1175
Homemade Ice Cream Naturally. 3559
Homemade Liqueurs. 1162
Homemade Pickles & Relishes. 3675
Homemade Pies, Cookies & Bread. 3690
Homemade Sausage Cookbook. 1942
Homemade Soups. 3958
Hometown Celebration Cookbook. 2480
Honey. 1099, 1107, 1108, 1115
Honey & Spice. 1109
Honey Book. 1123
Honey Cookbook. 1089
Honey Delights. 1110

Honey Kitchen. 1103
Honey Microwave Cookery Recipes. 1120
Honey of a Cookbook. 1100, 1104, 1116
Honey Recipes. 1117
Honey Recipes Book. 1119
Honey Recipes from Amana. 1091
Hook 'em and Cook 'em. 1968
Hooked on Seafood. 1986
Hors d'Oeuvre. 2616
Hors d'Oeuvre and Canapes. 2635
Hors d'Oeuvre Book. 2655
Hors d'Oeuvre Cookbook. 2636
Hors d'Oeuvre Etc. 2655
Hors d'Oeuvres. 2603, 2610, 2618, 2627, 2628, 2642, 2663
Hors d'Oeuvres and Party Snacks. 2674
Hors d'Oeuvres Everybody Loves. 2620
Hot & Spicy. 2189
Hot & Spicy Cooking. 2183, 2184
Hot and Spicy Cookbook. 2193, 2197
Hot Dog! 701
Hot Drink Book. 2710
Hot Links & Country Flavors. 1954
Hot off the Grill. 4329
Hot Pepper Cookbook. 1742
Hot Puddings. 3738, 3741
Hot Puddings and Cold Sweets. 3328
Hot Stuff. 1741
Hotter Than Hell. 2194
Household Legacy. 1539
How Do We Eat It? 909
How Steak Is Done. 114
How the World Cooks Chicken. 270
How to Air Brush Cakes-Arts-Crafts. 2878
How to Book of Bread. 2742
How to Book of Salads and Summer Dishes. 3764
How to Buy More Meat for Less Money. 1225
How to Can Food the Right Way. 4406
How to Catch a Crab. 460
How to Catch Clams by the Bushel! 427
How to Catch Crabs by the Bushel! 461
How to Catch Shellfish. 2144
How to Cook 'Possum and Other Varmints Good. 674
How to Cook and Use Whole Kernel Wheat. 2468

How to Cook Clams. 1960
How to Cook Halibut. 1960
How to Cook Oysters. 1960
How to Cook Salmon. 1960
How to Cook Shrimp. 1960
How to Cook with Herbs, Spices & Flavorings. 1056
How to Dry Food. 4435
How to Dry Foods. 4434
How to Garnish. 3515
How to Grapple with the Pineapple. 1751
How to Grow and Cook It Book of Vegetables, Herbs, Fruits, and Nuts. 775
How to Grow and Use Herbs. 1021
How to Herb Book. 993
How to Hook and Cookbook. 621
How to Improve Your Cooking with Canned Salmon. 1929
How to Make All the "Meat" You Eat Out of Wheat. 898
How to Make Jellies, Jams, and Preserves at Home. 3574, 3580, 4420
How to Make Love to a Lobster. 1183
How to Make Pasta One Hundred and One Different Ways. 1664
How to Make Sprouted Wheat Bread. 2813
How to Prepare Common Wild Foods. 2526
How to Smoke Seafood Florida Cracker Style. 1956
How to Succeed with Chicken Without Even Frying. 277
How to Survive Snack Attacks. 3879
How to Use Hawaiian Fruit. 712
Howard Mitchell's Clams, Mussels, Oysters, Scallops, & Snails. 2151
Huckleberry Book. 1126
Hugh Carter's Peanut Cook-Book. 1725
Humble Crumb. 160
Humpty Dumpty Cook Book. 547
Hundreds of the Best Recipes from The Art of Fish Cookery. 582
Hunt's Tomato Paste Recipe Collection. 2277
Hunter's Game Cookbook. 823
Hurricane Kitchen. 1525
I Can't Cook Desserts. 3310
I Can't Cook Main Courses. 3480

Specialty Cookbooks

I Can't Cook Starters. 2621
I Love Hot Dogs. 702
I Love Ice Cream. 3562
I Love Peanut Butter Cookbook. 1717, 1718
Ian McAndrew on Poultry and Game. 700
Ice Cream. 3544, 3552, 3555, 3558
Ice Cream & Frozen Desserts. 3506
Ice Cream & Ices. 3547
Ice Cream and Candies. 3300
Ice Cream Book. 3543
Ice Creams & Cold Desserts. 3502
Ice Creams, Sorbets, Mousses & Parfaits. 3501
Iced Delights. 3505
Iced Follies. 2913
Icelandic Seafood. 2032
Ices Galore. 3503
Icing on the Cake. 2919
Icing the Cake. 3566
Ideal Cheese Book. 235
Ideals Dannon Yogurt Cookbook. 2582
Ideals Desserts, Candy & Cookie Cookbook. 3265
Ideals Egg and Cheese Cookbook. 248
Ideals Hershey's Chocolate and Cocoa Cookbook. 320
Ideals Hershey's Cookies, Bars, and Brownies. 3168
Ideas & Recipes for Breakfast & Brunch. 4067
Illustrated Book of Herbs. 986
Illustrated Book of Preserves. 3584
Impossible-to-Resist Desserts. 3392
In Love with Chocolate. 399
In Praise of Cake & Pastry Flour. 3662
In Praise of Chocolate. 315
In Praise of the Potato. 1826
In Search of the Wild Dewberry. 2700
In the Beginning. 2617
In the Chips. 405
Incipient Elk Hunter. 555
Incredible Edible Egg. 527
Incredible Potato. 1803
Incredible Tofu Cookbook. 2257
Indian Chutneys, Raitas, Pickles & Preserves. 444
Indian Curries. 484, 491

Indian Sweet Cookery. 3266
Indian Vegetarian Curries. 491
Individualized Food Laboratory Approach to Bake Someone Happy. 3355
Innards and Other Variety Meats. 2316
Innovations in Cooking. 4493
Inside Chocolate. 3097
International Appetizer Cookbook. 2629
International Chili Society Official Chili Cookbook. 3084
International Confectioner. 3118
International Cook. 185
International Cookie Cookbook. 3213
International Curry Cooking. 487
International Dinner Party Cookbook. 4181
International Fish Cookbook. 608
International Gourmet Uses of Ground Beef. 930
International Produce Cookbook & Guide. 804
International Squid Cookbook. 2215
International Tofu Cookery Book. 2267
International Whole Meals. 1504
Into the Mouths of Babes. 1418
Introspection by Observation. 753
Irresistible Desserts. 3356
Island Cookery. 1981
It's About Thyme! 1028
It's All Fish. 577
It's Easy to Be a Gourmet with Peanuts. 1727
It's Only Natural. 1476
It's the Berries! 136
Italian Baker. 4245
Italian Bakery. 4219
Italian Baking and Pastry Book. 4246
Italian Delights. 1703
Italian Herb Cooking. 971
Italian Pastry Book. 3643
Italian Pizza and Hearth Breads. 3726
Itinerant Ripe Olive. 1594
Ivy Hall's Book of Jams and Jellies. 3571
Jack Daniel's Cookbook. 2478
Jack Daniel's Hometown Celebration Cookbook. 2480
Jack Daniel's The Spirit of Tennessee Cookbook. 2478

Title Index

Jack Ubaldi's Meat Book. 1243
Jam Book. 3573
James Beard's Fowl and Game Bird Cookery. 1856
James Beard's New Fish Cookery. 609
James McNair's Beef Cookbook. 113
James McNair's Breakfast. 4081
James McNair's Cheese Cookbook. 243
James McNair's Corn Cookbook. 456
James McNair's Grill Cookbook. 4378
James McNair's Pasta Cookbook. 1694
James McNair's Pie Cookbook. 3707
James McNair's Potato Cookbook. 1822
James McNair's Rice Cookbook. 1907
James McNair's Salmon Cookbook. 1933
James McNair's Soups. 3977
James McNair's Squash Cookbook. 2211
Jams & Preserves. 3587
Jams and Jellies. 3567
Jams and Preserves. 3578
Jams, Jellies & Relishes. 3575
Jams, Jellies, Pickles & Chutneys. 3581
Jane Asher's Party Cakes. 2870
Jane Grigson's Fruit Book. 732
Jane Grigson's Vegetable Book. 2342
Jane Pettigrew's Tea Time. 4152
Janice Murray Gill's Canadian Bread Book. 2734
Japanese Garnishes. 3511
Jean Anderson's Green Thumb Preserving Guide. 4407
Jean Conil's French Fish Cuisine. 2046
Jean's Beans. 84
Jeanne Rose's Herbal Guide to Food. 1035
Jell-O Brand Fun and Fabulous Recipes. 893
Jell-O Gelatin Salad Selector. 887
Jell-O Pages Recipe Book. 894
Jerk. 4379
Jewel Lake Seafood Market Cookbook. 2082
Jewish Holiday Cakes. 2966
Jim Fobel's Old-Fashioned Baking Book. 4267
Jimmy Dean 20th Anniversary Recipe Book. 1953
Joe's Book of Mushroom Cookery. 1292
John McNamara's Shaped & Cut-Out Cakes. 2886
John Tovey's Feast of Vegetables. 2389
Josceline Dimbleby's Book of Puddings, Desserts and Savouries. 3311
Journey for Health. 1443
Joy of Baking. 4257
Joy of Cheesecake. 3069
Joy of Chocolate. 321
Joy of Cocktails & Hors d'Oeuvre. 2630
Joy of Cookies. 3206
Joy of Cooking Naturally. 1387
Joy of Gardening Cookbook. 2375
Joy of Gluten-Free Cooking. 1917
Joy of Grilling. 4359
Joy of Ice Cream. 3553
Joy of Muffins. 3613
Joy of Pasta. 1632, 1635
Joy of Pastry. 3644
Joy of Pizza. 3721
Joy of Seafood. 2083
Joy of Snacks. 3906
Joy of Wellness Cookbook. 1444
Joys of Jell-O Brand Gelatin. 889
Judge Judges Mushrooms. 1279
Judith Olney on Bread. 2793
Judy Brown's Guide to Natural Foods Cooking. 1540
Judy Gorman's Breads of New England. 2818
Judy Gorman's Vegetable Cookbook. 2400
Juel Andersen's Carob Primer. 192
Juel Andersen's Curry Primer. 486
Juel Andersen's Sea Green Primer. 1202
Juel Andersen's Seafood Primer. 583
Juel Andersen's Sesame Primer. 2127
Juel Andersen's Tofu Fantasies. 2259
Juel Andersen's Tofu Kitchen. 2260
Juel Andersen's Tofu Primer. 2265
Julia Aitken's Baker's Secret. 4258
Julia Clements Book of Rose Arrangements. 1920
Junk Food Alternative. 3880
Junk Food, Fast Food, Health Food. 1560
Just a Bite. 2679
Just Another Bowl of Texas Red. 3088
Just Casseroles. 3033
Just Chicken. 284

Specialty Cookbooks

Just Cookies. 3175
Just Desserts. 3258, 3391, 3429
Just for Starters. 2611
Just for Tea. 4144
Just Hooked. 2084
Just Naturally Sweet. 3444
Just Oranges. 1609
Just Pineapples. 1752
Just Zucchini Cook Book. 2596
Justin Wilson's Outdoor Cooking--with Inside Help. 4342
Kake Brand Cookbook. 313
Karo Cook Book. 458
Kathleen's Bake Shop Cookbook. 4295
Kathy Cooks--Naturally. 1357
Keebler Ready-Crust Recipe Book. 3697
Keeping the Catch. 564
Kelly's Kitchen Presents Pride of America. 4247
Kenner O.K.R.A. Festival Cookbook. 1590
Kerr Kitchen Cookbook. 4424
Kerr's Country Kitchen. 2343
Kettle of Fish. 565
Keys to Successful Baking. 4236
Kid Power. 1388
Kids' Book of Chocolate. 403
Kids' Lunches. 4115
Kikkoman Cookbook. 2171
Kim Williams' Cookbook. 1505
Kinder-Krunchies. 3888
Kingsford Barbecue. 4380
Kingsford's Best Barbecues. 4331
Kitchen Bouquets. 443
Kitchen Bread Book. 2779
Kitchen Crew. 1563
Kitchen Garden Heritage. 787
Kitchen Herbal. 994
Kitchen Herbs. 1029
Kiwifruit Collection. 1132
KMA Festival Cookie Book. 3169
KMA's Come Again Cookie Book. 3207
Knead It, Punch It, Bake It! 2837
Know Your Onions. 1601
Knox Gelatine Cookbook. 884
Kraft Philadelphia Brand Cream Cheese Cheesecakes. 3079
Kripalu Kitchen. 1332
Kudzu Cookbook. 1134

L.L. Bean Game and Fish Cookbook. 649
La Leche League International Cookbook. 1426
Lady Liberty's Celebrity Desserts. 3343
Lady Macdonald's Chocolate Book. 381
Lady Maclean's Book of Sauces and Surprises. 3865
Laird's Kitchen. 828
Lamb. 1136
Lamb & Mutton. 1139
Lamb in Family Meals. 1138
Lambeth Method of Cake Decoration and Practical Pastries. 2860
Land O Lakes Chicken & Seafood Cookbook. 263
Land O Lakes Cookie Collection. 3230
Largely Lobster. 1185
Late-Night Supper Menus. 4198
Laurel's Kitchen Bread Book. 2779
Lawn Food Cook Book. 2507
Le Chocolat. 349
Lea & Perrins Appetizer, Soup, Main Dish, Vegetable, and Salad Cookbook. 2570
Lean Cuisine. 1477
Learning with Numbers. 2841
Lee Bailey's Country Desserts. 3411
Lee Bailey's Soup Meals. 3970
Leek Cookbook. 1143
Legal Sea Foods Cookbook. 2085
Lemon. 1158
Lemon Twist. 1159
Lenôtre's Desserts and Pastries. 3300
Lenôtre's Ice Cream and Candies. 3300
Lessons on Meat. 1216
Let's Cook Fish. 598
Let's Dry It. 4442
Let's Eat In. 4202
Let's Talk Turkey. 2309
Lettering for Cake Decoration. 2922
Liberated Man's Natural Foods Cookbook. 1309
Liberty Cookbook. 222
Life with Wine. 2553
Light & Easy Choice Desserts. 3376
Light & Spicy. 2198
Light Desserts. 3276, 3329, 3396, 3430
Light Fantastic. 1541

Title Index

Light-Hearted Seafood. 2103
Light Salad Meals. 3800
Light'n Fruity Pies. 890
Lighthouse Cookbook. 2086
Lilies of the Kitchen. 877
Lipton Creative Cookery. 518
Liquid Sunshine, Naturally Yours. 2704
Lisa Bacon's Complete Turkey Cookbook. 2302
Lite Sweet Delites. 3431
Little Almond Cookbook. 4
Little Apple Cookbook. 21
Little Apricot Cookbook. 37
Little Artichoke Cookbook. 41
Little Avocado Cookbook. 48
Little Bean Book. 71, 83
Little Bean Cookbook. 85
Little Beer Cookbook. 119
Little Book of Recipes for Cooking with Herbs. 1009
Little Brown Bean Book. 72
Little Brown Bread Book. 2763
Little Brown Egg Book. 538
Little Brown Paté Book. 3667
Little Brown Rice Book. 163
Little Brown Spice Book. 2186
Little Cake Cookbook. 2950
Little Cashew Cookbook. 200
Little Cheese Cookbook. 223
Little Cheesecake Cookbook. 3073
Little Cherry Cookbook. 256
Little Chicken Cookbook. 278
Little Chocolate Book. 368
Little Chocolate Cookbook. 343
Little Cinnamon Cookbook. 409
Little Coffee Cookbook. 435
Little Croissant Cookbook. 3252
Little Curry Book. 489
Little Egg Book. 549
Little Egg Cookbook. 540
Little English Book of Teas. 4159
Little Exotic Fruit Book. 750
Little Exotic Vegetable Book. 2415
Little Garlic Book. 870
Little Gourmet Gas Barbecue Cookbook. 4350
Little Green Avocado Book. 46
Little Gumbo Book. 3949

Little Hamburger Cookbook. 942
Little Honey Book. 1112
Little Honey Cookbook. 1113
Little Ice Cream Book. 3545
Little Ice Cream Cookbook. 3548
Little Lemon Cookbook. 1157
Little Lobster Cookbook. 1182
Little Meat Goes a Long Way. 1222
Little Mouse Makes Sweets. 3137
Little Mushroom Book. 1283
Little Mushroom Cookbook. 1286
Little Mustard Book. 1301
Little Nut Book. 1566
Little Onion Cookbook. 1605
Little Orange Cookbook. 1611
Little Pastry Cookbook. 3636
Little Pepper Book. 1739
Little Pepper Cookbook. 1740
Little Pie Cookbook. 3694
Little Pineapple Cookbook. 1753
Little Potato Book. 1814
Little Potato Cookbook. 1796
Little Rice Book. 1901
Little Shrimp Cookbook. 2154
Little Strawberry Cookbook. 2222
Little Tofu Book. 2272
Little Tomato Cookbook. 2284
Little Wine Cookbook. 2554
Living Medicine. 1882
Living Off the Sea. 2033
Living Well. 1527
Living with the Flowers. 684
Loaf Magic. 2764
Loaves and Fishes. 1561
Loaves of Love. 2825
Lobel Brothers' Complete Guide to Meat. 1252
Lobel Brothers' Meat Cookbook. 1217
Lobster Almanac. 1184
Lobster in Every Pot. 1187
Lois Burpee's Gardener's Companion and Cookbook. 2363
London Ritz Book of Afternoon Tea. 4146
London Ritz Book of English Breakfasts. 4058
Long Island Seafood Cook Book. 1957
Lots of 'Cots. 40
Louisiana Oyster. 1613

Specialty Cookbooks

Louisiana Seafood Cookbook. 2047
Love Enterprises Presents Creative Cakes. 2932
Love Food. 1415
Love That Tuna and Other Gamefish. 2300
Love the Sunshine in with Sprouts! 2205
Low Calorie, High Nutrition Vegetables from the Sea. 1203
Low Cholesterol Desserts! 3445
Low-Cholesterol Oat Plan. 1589
Low Cholesterol Olive Oil Cookbook. 1599
Low-Cost Natural Foods. 1369
Low-Salt Cookery. 1077
Low Salt, Low Sugar, Low Fat Desserts. 3412
Low, Slow, Delicious. 3028
Low-Cost No-Fuss, All-Natural, Food Guide for Students. 1389
Lunch Box. 4123, 4138
Lunch Box Book. 4124
Lunch Box Treats. 4139
Lunchbox Book. 4131, 4136
Luncheonette. 3851
Lunches and Snacks. 4118
Lunches to Go. 4125
Lyman's Wild Gourmet. 814
Mable Hoffman's Chocolate Cookery. 327
Mable Hoffman's Mini Deep-Fry Cookery. 4427
Mac Meals in Minutes. 4428
Mackerel. 1189
Macmillan Treasury of Herbs. 1010
Macrobiotic Dessert Book. 3413
Mad About Cheddar. 218
Mad About Fish & Seafood. 2016
Mad About Muffins. 3608
Mad About Mushrooms. 1287
Mad About Pastas & Cheese. 224
Mad About Raspberries & Strawberries. 1879
Madam LaZong's Chicken Breast Recipes. 289
Madame Chocolate's Book of Divine Indulgences. 344
Magic Mountain Natural Dessert Book. 3312
Magic of Tofu and Other Soybean Products. 2175

Magical Art of Cake Decorating. 2887
Magimix Cake Book. 2957
Magnificent Casserole Cookbook. 3057
Magnificent Cookies Cookbook. 3185
Magnificent Snacks Cookbook. 3903
Mahi-Mahi. 1190
Maida Heatter's
  Best Dessert Book Ever. 3446
  Book of Great American Desserts. 3357
  Book of Great Chocolate Desserts. 314
  Book of Great Cookies. 3140
  Book of Great Desserts. 3256
  New Book of Great Desserts. 3292
Main-Course Soups & Stews. 3999
Main Dishes for Every Occasion. 3483
Maine-Anjou Association Cookbook. 103
Maine Apples, Blue Ribbon Recipes. 30
Maine Potato Cookbook. 1809
Make-a-Meal Salads. 3790
Make Bread-in-a-Bag with Texas Wheat Flour. 2752
Make It Light. 1333
Make It Light Main Dishes. 3492
Make It with Meat. 1218
Making & Baking Gingerbread Houses. 3529
Making Apple Pies & Crusts. 22
Making Bread. 2842
Making Breads with Home-Grown Yeasts & Home-Ground Grains. 2780
Making Cheese and Butter. 502
Making Cheeses, Butters, Cream, and Yogurt at Home. 498
Making Chocolate Chip Cookies. 3107
Making Homemade Apple Pies & Crusts. 22
Making Ice Cream, Ices & Sherbets. 3549
Making Pickles and Relishes at Home. 3677, 4420
Making Soft Pretzels. 3733
Making the Most of Beef & Veal. 99
Making the Most of Bread. 2765
Making the Most of Cheese. 219
Making the Most of Chicken, Poultry & Game. 696
Making the Most of Eggs. 539
Making the Most of Lamb & Pork. 1140
Making the Most of Meat. 1232

Title Index

Making the Most of Pasta. 1636
Making the Most of Potatoes. 1794
Making the Most of Rice. 1900
Making the Most of Vegetables. 2390
Making the Most of Your Catch. 633
Making the Most of Your Freezer. 4450
Making Whole-Grain Breads. 2780
Making Your Own Home Proteins. 1445
Making Your Own Ice Cream, Ices & Sherbets. 3549
Making Your Own Preserves. 4391
Mako Shark. 2132
Malfred Ferndock's Morel Cookbook. 1265
Mama's Fruits & Vegetables Cookbook. 772
Mangos, Mangos, Mangos. 1191
Manhattan Chili Co. Southwest-American Cookbook. 3090
Manhattan's Dessert Scene. 3432
Maple Syrup Baking and Dessert Cookbook. 1193
Maple Syrup Cookbook. 1196
Margaret Roberts Cooks with Herbs & Spices. 1083
Margaret Roberts' Book of Herbs. 987
Marguerite Patten's Successful Baking. 4237
Marguerite Patten's Sunday Lunch Cookbook. 4113
Marijuana Food. 1201
Marika Hanbury Tenison's Freezer Cookbook. 4447
Marinade Magic. 3588
Marine Mollusks of Cape Cod. 2141
Marshall Field's Frango Chocolate Cookbook. 382
Martha Stewart's Hors d'Oeuvres. 2628
Martha Stewart's Pies & Tarts. 3698
Martha White's Southern Sampler. 4281
Marvelous Macadamia Nut. 1188
Marvelous Meals with Mince. 932
Marvelous Muffin. 3603
Mary Berry's New Book of Meat Cookery. 1238
Mary Berry's New Cake Book. 2986
Mary Berry's New Freezer Cookbook. 4458
Mary Blair's Hors d'Oeuvre Cookbook. 2636

Mary Ford's Cake Designs. 2888
Mary Norwak's Guide to Home Freezing. 4451
Mary's Bread Basket and Soup Kettle. 2794
Mary's Quick Breads, Soups, and Stews. 2834
Maryland Seafood Cookbook. 1958
Marzipan. 3592
Master Book of Soups. 3929
Mastering Herbalism. 959
Mastering the Art of French Pastry. 3637
Maurice's Tropical Fruit Cook Book. 714
May Byron's Jam Book. 3567
Mazola Diet for the Young at Heart. 457
McClane's North American Fish Cookery. 1971
McCormick Spices of the World Cookbook. 2187
McDougalls Better Baking. 4268
McVitie's Book of Better Baking. 4269
Meal-in-a-Loaf Cookbook. 2574
Meat & Game Cookery. 1246
Meat & Potatoes Too. 1251
Meat and Game Cookbook. 1250
Meat and Potatoes Cookbook. 1247
Meat Board Meat Book. 1211
Meat Book. 1243
Meat Dishes. 1233, 1237
Meat Dishes in the International Cuisine. 1227
Meat Hunter. 841
Meat Meals in Minutes. 1219
Meatless Main Dishes. 3473, 3477
Meats and Sauces. 1234
Meats from Amish and Mennonite Kitchens. 1223
Meats, Including Poultry & Seafood. 1220
Mediterranean Gold. 1927
Mediterranean Seafood. 1982
Mediterranean Vegetable Cooking. 2427
Melon Garnishing. 1253
Mennonite Girl Presents Ovenly Fare. 3065
Smackin' Snacks. 3917
Menus à Trois. 2826
Menus for Pasta. 1688
Meringue Cookbook. 3593

Specialty Cookbooks

Mesquite Cookery. 4479, 4480
Mexican Desserts. 3393
Mexico: Her Daily & Festive Breads. 2718
Michael Field Egg Cookbook. 534
Michele Evans' Sensational Salads. 3822
Mickey's Zucchini Recipes. 2592
Microegg Meets the Munch Bunch. 544
Microwave & Freezer. 4452
Microwave Baking & Desserts. 3267
Microwave Cooking, from the Freezer. 4452
Microwave Cooking, Fruits & Vegetables. 767
Microwave Cuisine Cooks Appetizers. 2631
Microwave Fish Cookbook. 575, 610
Microwave Fish Cooking. 622
Microwave Fruit & Vegetable Cookbook. 768
Microwave Game & Fish Cookbook. 656
Microwave Gourmet Healthstyle Cookbook. 1553
Microwave Lite One-Dish Meals. 3058
Microwave Magic Casseroles. 3048
Microwave Magic: Soups, Chowders and Vegetables. 3959
Microwave Vegetable Cooking. 2438
Microwave Vegetables. 2396
Microwave Wholefood Cookbook. 1446
Microwaved Maple. 1194
Microwaving Fast & Easy Main Dishes. 3489
Microwaving Fruits & Vegetables. 769
Microwaving Light Meals & Snacks. 2687
Microwaving Meats. 1212
Microwaving One-Dish Dinners. 3489
Microwaving Poultry & Seafood. 1851
Midnight Snack Cookbook. 3889
Mighty Mince Cookbook. 943
Mile-High Cakes. 2930
Minced Beef Cookbook. 946
Mini Deep Fry Cookery. 4427, 4429
Miniature Cakes, Pastries & Desserts. 3433
Miniature Desserts. 3377
Minnesota Game Warden's Cookbook. 860
Minnie Muenscher's Herb Cookbook. 965
Minute Rice. 1914
Miriam B. Loo's Fresh-from-the-Oven Breads. 2753

Miriam B. Loo's Salads for All Seasons. 3765
Miso Production. 1258
Miss Grimble Presents Delicious Desserts. 3330
Mitchell Beazley Pocket Guide to Non-alcoholic Drinks. 2711
Modern Cake Decoration. 2856
Modern Pâtissier. 3630
Molluscan Melange. 2133
Monster Cookies. 3170
Moose From Forest to Table. 1262
Moosewood Cookbook. 1312
More Barmy Breads. 2735
More Berried Treasures. 131
More Chicken Breasts. 310
More Fast Cakes. 2974
More Food of My Friends. 1390
More Japanese Garnishes. 3516
More Soup Anyone? 3950
More Taste of Life. 1506
More Than a Trophy. 2453
More Than Chicken Cookbook. 1837
More Than Soup. 86
More Thoughts for Buffets. 4100
More with Less Cookbook. 1507
Morel Cookbook. 1265
Morelling. 1266
Morey Amsterdam's Benny Cooker Crock Book for Drinkers. 1164
Morey Amsterdam's Cookbook for Drinkers. 1164
Morning Food. 4087
Most for the Money Main Dishes. 187
Mostly Muffins. 3604
Mostly Vegetable Menu Cookbook. 2352
Mother Earth's Hassle-Free Vegetable Cookbook. 2344
Mother Goose Cookie-Candy Book. 3021
Mother Wonderful's Cheesecakes and Other Goodies. 3081
Mountain Harvest Cookbook. 1447
Mountain Indian Recipes. 850
Mountain Man Cookbook. 2456
Mountains of Chocolate. 316
Mr. Boston Cordial Cooking Guide. 1170
Mr. Boston Spirited Dessert Guide. 1171
Mr. Dudley's Peppermill Cookbook. 1737

Title Index

Mrs. Beeton's
 Complete Book of Cakes. 2998
 Complete Book of Puddings. 3447
 Cookery and Household Management.
   1852, 2404, 3961
 Game Cookery. 861
 Home Cooking. 1237, 1852, 2404
 Mini Series. 2406, 3961
Mrs. Cottrell's Stretching-the-Food-Dollar Cookbook. 1358
Mrs. Mary Eales's Receipts. 3126
Mrs. Mayo's Book of Creative Foods. 3517
Mrs. Mayo's How to Make a Wedding Cake. 2907
Mrs. McLintock's Receipts for Cookery and Pastry-Work. 4259
Mrs. Witty's Monster Cookies. 3170
Muffin Baker's Guide. 3601
Muffin Cookbook. 3615
Muffin Madness. 3605
Muffin Memories. 3612
Muffins. 3599, 3602, 3607
Muffins & Cupcakes. 3609
Muffins and Quick Breads with Schmecks Appeal. 3616
Muffins are Coming. 3614
Muffins, Nut Breads and More. 3606
Multitude of Mints. 975
Munches. 3146
Munchies Minus Mom. 3907
Mushroom Basket. 1280
Mushroom Cookery. 1275
Mushroom Feast. 1284
Mushroom Lover's Cookbook. 1293, 1278
Mushroom Matings. 1273
Mushroom Recipes. 1270
Mushroom Time. 2594
Mushrooms Are Marvelous. 1288
Mushrooms, Mushrooms. 1281
Mushrooms, Wild and Edible. 1276
Mussel Cookbook. 1297
Mussels. 1299
Mustard Cookbook. 1300
My Brother and I Like Cookies. 3233
My Cake. 2988
My Favorite Cookies from the Old Country. 3186
My Favorite Molasses Recipes. 1260

My First Baking Book. 4299
My Munch Book. 3890
Mystic Seaport's Seafood Secrets Cookbook. 1965
NAHC Wild Game Cookbook. 829
Naked Ladies' Lunches. 4116
Nancy Enright's Canadian Herb Cookbook. 1011
Nathan's Famous Hot Dog Cookbook. 703
National Trust Book of
 Afternoon Tea. 4141
 Fish Cookery. 623
 Healthy Eating. 1554
 Pies. 3705
 Sorbets, Flummeries, and Fools. 3358
 The Country Kitchen Store Cupboard. 4410
 Traditional Puddings. 3739
 Tuck Box Treats. 3651
Natural Baby Food Cookbook. 1370
Natural Biscuits. 3176
Natural Cook. 1508
Natural Cookbook. 1448
Natural Cuisine. 1509
Natural Entertainer. 1510
Natural Fast Food Cookbook. 1334
Natural Food Cookery. 1316
Natural Foods and Good Cooking. 1542
Natural Foods Blender Cookbook. 1307
Natural Foods Cookbook. 1449, 1450
Natural Foods East and West. 1478
Natural Foods Epicure. 1391
Natural Foods Healthy Baby Cookbook. 1451
Natural Foods Primer. 1436
Natural Foods Recipe Book. 1419
Natural Fruit Cookbook. 727
Natural Gourmet. 1371, 1543
Natural Health Cookbook. 1392
Natural Lunchbox. 4126
Natural Recipes. 1314
Natural Remedies, Recipes & Realities. 1479
Natural Sugarless Dessert Cookbook. 3268
Natural Sweets. 3123
Natural Sweets & Treats. 3113
Natural World Cookbook. 2490
Naturally Delicious Desserts. 3359

Specialty Cookbooks

Naturally Delicious Desserts and Snacks. 3260
Naturally Good Wheat Germ Cookbook. 2475
Naturally Sweet Desserts. 3448
Naturally Wild Rice. 2541
Nature's Banquet. 1393
Nature's Bounty for Your Table. 1372
Nature's Kitchen. 1394, 1480
Nature's Wild Harvest. 2501
Naughty but Nice. 3331
Neal Yard Bakery Wholefood Cookbook. 1481
NEFCO Canning Book. 4408
New 365 Ways to Cook Hamburger. 939
New Adventures in Wine Cookery. 2547
New Age Brown Rice Cookbook. 162
New Almond Cookery. 5
New American Turkey Cookery. 2311
New American Vegetable Cookbook. 2428
New and Classic Cocktails Without Alcohol. 2714
New and Easy Yeast Recipes. 2571
New Baking. 4277
New Barbecue Cookbook. 4343
New Book of Favorite Breads from Rose Lane Farm. 2743
New Book of Great Desserts. 3292
New Book of Meat Cookery. 1238
New Cake Book. 2986
New Casserole Cook Book. 3060
New Casserole Cookery. 3034
New Chinese Vegetarian Cookery. 2401
New Complete Book of Breads. 2807
New Complete Book of Chicken Wings. 306
New Complete Book of Pasta. 1656
New Concepts in Dehydrated Food Cookery. 4439
New Domestic Rabbit Cook Book. 1873
New England Aquarium. 2077
New England Berry Book. 139
New England Butt'ry Shelf Almanac. 685
New Favorite Honey Recipes. 1114
New Fish Cookbook. 611
New Fish Cookery. 560, 609
New Food. 1452
New Freezer Cookbook. 4458, 4463

New Game Cuisine. 867
New Harvest. 788
New Herb Cook Book. 1022
New Honey & Yogurt Recipes. 1121
New Ideas for Casseroles. 3051
New International Confectioner. 3118
New International Fondue Cookbook. 3499
New Joys of Jell-O. 895
New Life Cookbook. 1311
New Look of Beef. 104
New Mexico Favorites. 3091
New New Can-Opener Cookbook. 182
New Pasta Cookbook. 1681
New Pastry Cook. 3648
New Recipes from Moosewood Restaurant. 1511
New Salad and Soup Book. 3984
New Salads. 3794
New Texas Wild Game Cookbook. 842
New Treasury of Almond Recipes. 3
New Vegetarian Barbecue. 4360
New Wave in Cooking. 972
New Way of Eating. 1512
New Ways to Eat Well. 1527
New Ways to Enjoy Chicken. 271
New Ways with Fresh Fruit and Vegetables. 770
New York Times Bread and Soup Cookbook. 2766
New York Times New Natural Foods Cookbook. 1373
New Zealand Dinner Party Cookbook. 4181
New Zealand Fish and Shellfish Cookbook. 2048
New Zucchini Cookbook. 2601
Newest, Easiest, Most Exciting Recipes and Menus for Fish and Game Cooking. 641
Newnes All Colour Cake Making and Decorating. 2958
Nibble Mania. 2680
Nice & Easy Desserts Cookbook. 3265
Nick Malgieri's Perfect Pastry. 3657
Nicola Cox on Game Cookery. 862
Nifty Nibbles. 3897
Nika Hazelton's Pasta Cookbook. 1641
Nika Hazelton's Way with Vegetables. 2323

Nikki & David Goldbeck's American Wholefoods Cuisine. 1395
No-Cooking Fruitarian Recipe Book. 713
No Fuss Chicken Recipe Booklet. 180
No Knead Baking with Fermipan. 2767
No Ordinary Clam Book. 423
No-Salt Seafood. 2104
No Sugar Delicious Dessert Cookbook. 3332
No Weenie Cookbook. 1420
Noble Potato. 1783
Noble Spud. 1804
Nobody Loves Me Cookbook. 521
Non-alcoholic Cocktail Book. 2707
Non-alcoholic Cocktails. 2701
Non-alcoholic Pocket Bartender's Guide. 2711
Non-drinker's Drink Book. 2692
Noodles Galore. 1628
North American Fish Cookery. 1971
North American Game Fish Cookbook. 576
North American Lobster. 1186
North American Wild Game Cookbook. 824
North Atlantic Seafood. 2105
North Cooks Wild! 818
North Country Cookbook. 657
Northeast Saltwater Fisherman's International Cookbook. 629
Northeast Upland Hunting Guide. 868
Northwestern Wild Berries. 126
Not for Salads Only. 3749
Not Just Cheesecake! 2587
Not Quite Vegetarian. 1468
Not-Strictly Vegetarian Cookbook. 1544
Nouvelle Patisserie. 3653
Nova Scotia Seafood Cookery. 1987
Novelty Cakes. 2914
Nut Cookbook from Planters. 1564
Nutlovers' Cookbook. 1569
Nutrition Education and Food Conservation Canning Book. 4408
Nutrition Survival Kit. 1315
Nutritional Cooking with Tofu. 2266
Nutritious Brown Bag Lunches. 4127
Nutritious Nibbles. 3884

Nutritious Packed Lunches for Children. 4128
Nutritious Seasonal Snacks. 3901
Nuts About Chocolate. 369
Nuts! 1570
Nuts! Nuts! Nuts! 1565
O Taste and See. 2959
Oat and Wheat Bran Health Plan. 1576
Oat Bran Baking Book. 1577
Oat Bran Cookbook. 1578
Oat Bran Recipes. 1579
Oat Cookbook. 1588
Oat Cuisine. 1580, 1587
Oatcake Cookbook. 1585
Ocean of Flavor. 2087
Ode to the Oysters. 1614
Odyssey Cookbook. 2549
Of Cabbages and the King. 173
Of Tarragon, Thyme & Tauvirg. 1078
Off the Hook. 2088
Off the Shelf. 1482
Official Couch Potato Cookbook. 3909
Official Crab Eater's Guide. 464
Official Eating to Win Cookbook. 1396
Official Fajita Cookbook. 3493
Official Fulton Fish Market Cookbook. 2106
Official Garlic Lovers Handbook. 878
Official Rice & Dry Bean Cookbook. 1908
Oft Told Mushroom Recipes. 1267
Oh Fudge! 3508
Oh Truffles by Au Chocolat. 3093
Okanagan Harvest. 801
Old Cape Farmstall Cookbook. 776
Old-Fashioned
  Baking Book. 4267
  Confectioner's Handbook. 3119
  Desserts. 3313
  Fruit Garden. 760
  Home Baking. 4287
  Homemade Ice Cream. 3550
  Pumpkin Recipes. 1863
Old Favorite Honey Recipes. 1119
Old Ways Rediscovered. 1030
Old World Breads! 2819
Olive Oil from Italy. 1598
Olives and Olive Oil for the Gourmet. 1592

Specialty Cookbooks

Omega-3 Breakthrough. 612
Omelets & Crepes. 3239
Omelette Book. 3619
Omelettes & Souffles. 3618
On Flowers. 690
On Poultry and Game. 700
Once Upon a Recipe. 1513
One-Dish Meals. 3052, 3066, 3068
One-Dish Meals of Asia. 3053
One Dish Microwave Meals. 3050
One for the Road. 2708
One Hundred and One Apple Recipes. 11
One Hundred and One Fruit Recipes. 733
One-Pot Cookbook. 3049
One-Pot Cooking. 3029, 3035
One Pot Meals. 3023, 3059
One-Pot Meals to Team with Warm Hearty Breads. 3067
One Potato, Two Potato. 1795, 1815
One Potato, Two Potato, Three Potato--Four. 1797
Onion Cookbook. 1600
Onions. 1602
Onions Without Tears. 1600
Ontario Honey Recipe Book. 1118
Ontario Salmon Fishing. 1939
Openers. 2656
Orange. 1612
Orange Cook Book. 1610
Orange Fantasia. 415
Orange Roughy. 1608
Ordinary and Extraordinary Fruits & Vegetables. 805
Organic Cooking for Mothers. 1335
Oriental Appetizers. 2632
Oriental Appetizers & Light Meals. 2684
Oriental Snacks and Appetizers. 2672
Original All Prune Recipe Book. 1861
Original Sandwich Maker's Sandwich Guide. 3837
Original Vidalia Onion Cookbook. 1603
Orvis Cookbook. 659
Oscar Mayer Celebration Cookbook. 1767
Other Half of the Egg. 541
Our Candy Recipes. 3112
Our Dairy Specialties. 509
Our Wild Harvest. 825
Out of the Frying Pan. 4477

Out of the Stockpot. 4018
Outdoor Barbecue. 4303
Outdoor Cooking and Grilled Fish. 2107
Outdoor Cooking--with Inside Help. 4342
Outdoor Life's Complete Fish and Game Cookbook. 673
Ova Easy. 535
Oyster Cookery. 1615, 1621
Oysters. 1615, 1616, 1619
Pacific Fresh Seafood Cookbook. 2017
Pacific Northwest Salmon Cookbook. 1931
Packed Lunches. 4120, 4121
Packed Lunches & Snacks. 4134
Packed Lunches and Picnics. 4132
Pamella Asquith's Ultimate Chocolate Cake Book. 330
Pamella Z. Asquith's Fruit Tart Cookbook. 754
Pamella Z. Asquith's Sweet & Savory Pies. 3699
Pancakes. 3248
Pancakes & Crepes. 3242
Pancakes & Waffles. 3237
Pancakes from Vinegar Hill Farm. 3243
Pantry Gourmet. 4409
Papino Papaws Please. 1622
Paradise Preserves. 446
Parish Delights. 3293
Park's Success with Herbs. 973
Parkay Margarine Cookbook. 1199
Party Cakes. 2866, 2870, 2920, 2951
Party Eats. 4105
Party Pieces. 3904
Pass the Salt. 1156
Passion for Bread. 2744
Passion for Chocolate. 390
Passion for Garlic. 869
Passion for Mushrooms. 1294
Passion for Pasta. 1695
Passion for Peaches Cookbook. 1707
Passion for Vegetables. 2334
Passion of Barbeque. 4381
Passionate Cookbook. 4306
Pasta. 1626, 1633, 1642, 1668, 1696, 1697
Pasta & Budget Cooking. 1671
Pasta & Cheese. 227
Pasta & Pizza with Pizazz. 1706
Pasta al Dente-Recipes. 1691

Title Index

Pasta and Noodles. 1628
Pasta and Other Special Salads. 1672
Pasta and Pizza. 1701
Pasta and Rice. 1682, 1683
Pasta and Rice Italian Style. 1643
Pasta Book. 1644, 1645, 1657
Pasta Classica. 1673
Pasta Cook Book. 1627
Pasta Cookbook. 1629, 1641, 1694
Pasta Cookery. 1624
Pasta Cooking. 1630
Pasta Diet. 1646
Pasta Dishes. 1674
Pasta for Pleasure. 1647
Pasta Fresca. 1684
Pasta International. 1698
Pasta Italian Style. 1631
Pasta Light. 3876
Pasta-Lover's Diet Book. 1665
Pasta Menus. 1637
Pasta Perfect. 1675
Pasta Plus. 1658
Pasta Presto. 1685
Pasta Salad Book. 1648
Pasta Salads! 1666
Pasta with a Flair. 1649
Pastability. 1686
Pastas, Rice and Dried Beans. 1667
Pastry Book. 3645
Pastry Chef. 3631
Pastry Without Tears. 3649
Pastrywork and Confectionery Handbook. 3646
Pâté. 3666
Pâtés & Terrines. 3664, 3668
Patisserie. 3621
Patisserie of France. 3658
Patisserie of Italy. 3654
Patisserie of Scandinavia. 3659
Patisserie of the Eastern Mediterranean. 3660
Patisserie of Vienna. 3655
Patty Cakes. 1514
Paula Smith & Dorothy Seaman's It's All Fish. 577
Peach Sampler. 1709
Peaches 'n Cream. 1711
Peanut Butter Madness. 1714

Peanut Butter Plus. 1715
Peanut Cook-Book. 1725
Peanut Cookbook. 1720, 1729
Peanut One Goes to Washington. 1721
Peanutty Food. 1725
Pecan Lovers' Cook Book. 1735
Pecan Lovers' Cookbook. 1731
Pecans, From Soup to Nuts! 1733
Penguin Book of Herbs and Spices. 1070
Peninsula Farm Yogurt Cookbook. 2586
Penny Whistle Lunch Box Book. 4137
People Pleasing Persimmon Recipes. 1747
People Power. 1421
Peppers. 1743
Peppers Hot & Chile. 1744
Peppers, Hot and Sweet. 1745
Perfect Bread. 2795
Perfect Cake. 2960
Perfect Cheesecake. 3076
Perfect Chicken. 285
Perfect Chocolate Dessert. 317
Perfect Cookie. 3151, 3187
Perfect Cooking with Chicken. 285
Perfect Cooking with Exotic Fruit & Vegetables. 783
Perfect Cooking with Game. 843
Perfect Cooking with Garlic. 873
Perfect Cooking with Herbs. 1012
Perfect Cooking with Mustard. 1303
Perfect Cooking with Pasta. 1659
Perfect Cooking with Seafood. 2034
Perfect Cooking with Wholefoods. 1453
Perfect Croissant. 3251
Perfect Curry. 490
Perfect Pasta. 1650
Perfect Pastry. 3625, 3657
Perfect Pâté. 3669
Perfect Pickle Book. 3684
Perfect Pie. 3688, 3700
Perfect Pie Book. 3695
Perfect Pies. 3701
Perfect Poultry. 1843
Perfect Preserves. 4425
Perfect Pulses. 1149
Perfect Salad. 3784
Perfect Soup. 3951
Perfect Starter. 2637
Perfect Sunday Lunch. 4112

Specialty Cookbooks

Perfect Yeast Baking. 4282
Pesto Manifesto. 3673
Pestos! 3672
Pete Luckett's Cookbook & Guide to Fresh Fruits & Vegetables. 807
Peter Rabbit's Natural Foods Cookbook. 1558
Phabulous Philly Cookbook. 476
Pheasant Cook. 1748
Philadelphia Cream Cheese Cookbook. 477
Philadelphia Cream Cheese Summer Sensations. 478
Philosophers & Microbiologists Soup Book. 3965
Pick Your Own
  Apples, Oranges, and Pears. 25
  Blueberries, Raspberries, and Other Berries. 135
  Cook Book. 795
  Peaches, Melons, and Grapes. 1710
  Tomatoes, Plums, and Avocadoes. 2286
Pickle and Chutney Cookbook. 3681
Pickles & Chutneys. 3683
Pickles and Chutneys. 3678
Pickles and Relishes. 3679
Picnic & Barbecue Cookbook. 4321
Picnics and Barbecues. 4317, 4344
Pie and Pastry Cookbook. 3632
Pie Cookbook. 3707
Piece of Cake. 2980
Pies & Pastries. 3624, 3626, 3647
Pies & Tarts. 3698
Pies and Pastries Cookbook. 3638
Pies and Tarts. 3702
Pies and Tarts with Schmecks Appeal. 3711
Pies Aplenty. 3685
Pies from Amish and Mennonite Kitchens. 3689
Pie's the Limit. 3691
Pig-Out. 3314
Pillsbury Bake-Off Cookbook. 4296
Pillsbury Chocolate Lovers Cookbook. 400
Pillsbury Cookies, Cookies, and More Cookies Cookbook. 3158
Pillsbury Plus Recipe Cookbook. 177
Pinch of This, a Grain of That. 1062
Piñon Pine. 1750

Pioneer Heritage Wild Game Cookbook. 846
Pita Breads and Pocket Fillings. 3713
Pita the Great. 3714
Pizza. 3722, 3727
Pizza and Pasta. 1704
Pizza Book. 3723
Pizza California Style. 3731
Pizza Cookery. 3724
Pizza Gourmet. 3730
Pizza Pizzaz. 3725
Pizzas and Pancakes. 3717
Pizzas, Hamburgers & Relishes. 3719
Pizzas, Pasta and Pancakes. 1705
Plain & Fancy Mustard Cookbook. 1304
Plain & Fancy Vegetables. 2429
Plain Jane's Thrill of Very Fattening Foods Cookbook. 3333
Plant Lore of an Alaskan Island. 2508
Plants Your Mother Never Told You About. 2527
Please Pass the Potatoes. 1827
Pleasure of Herbs. 1015
Pleasure of Vegetables. 2364
Pleasures of Afternoon Tea. 4149
Pleasures of Gas Grilling. 4302
Pleasures of Preserving and Pickling. 4400
Pleasures of the Table. 4180
Pleasures of Wine with Food. 2560
Plum Crazy. 1754
Pocket A to Z Guide to Freezing Food. 4448
Pocket Book of Fruit and Nut Cooking. 723
Pocket Book of Simple Starters. 2608
Pocket Book on Cheese. 228
Pocket Book on Eggs. 542
Pocket Book on Potatoes. 1798
Pocket Book on Pure Food. 1454
Pocket Bread Potpourri. 3712
Pocket Guide to Non-alcoholic Drinks. 2711
Polly-O Cooking with Cheese Cookbook. 229
Polly Pinder's Chocolate Cookbook. 383
Popcorn and Peanuts. 1726
Popcorn Cookery. 1757
Popcorn Lover's Book. 1759

Title Index

Popcorn Plus Diet. 1761
Popovers, Peaches, and Four-Poster Beds. 4064
Poppin' Fresh Homemade Cookies. 3231
Popular Guide to Chinese Vegetables. 2365
Pork. 1764, 1777
Pork & Ham Menus. 1773
Pork Facts. 1769
Pork, Ham & Bacon. 1768
Pork in Family Meals. 1766
Pork, Perfect Pork. 1770
Portraits with Pollock. 1756
Positively Pasta. 1638
Possum Cookbook. 1607
Pot Luck. 1816, 3054
Potato Cookbook. 1784, 1822
Potato Cookery. 1785, 1799
Potato Experience. 1810
Potato Potential. 1805
Potatoes. 1789, 1823, 1824
Potpourri of Poultry & Seafood Favorites. 1844
Potter County Leek Cookbook. 1144
Poultry. 1828, 1838, 1848, 1854
Poultry II. 1855
Poultry and Game. 700
Poultry and Game Birds. 1832, 1860
Poultry and Game Cookbook. 697
Poultry and Sauces. 1845
Poultry Cookbook. 1839
Poultry Dishes. 1834, 1852
Poultry in Family Meals. 1833
Poultry on the Grill. 1858
Poultry, Stuffing, and Sauces. 1845
Power Food. 1515
Power of Pasta. 1660
Practical Baking. 4283
Practical Freezer Handbook. 4459
Practical Guide to Edible & Useful Plants. 2518
Practical Guide to Health Foods. 1422
Practical Herb Gardening with Recipes. 995
Practice of Royal Icing. 2908
Prairie Farmer Meat Cookbook. 1235
Prairie Farmer Poultry Cookbook. 1846
Predominantly Fish. 2061

Preparing and Cooking Various Seafoods. 1960
Preparing Sauces. 3861
Preserve It Naturally. 4440
Preserving. 4392
Pretty Cakes. 2921
Pretzel Book. 3732
Pride of America. 4247
Primi Piatti. 2659
Primitive Maple-Sugaring. 1195
Professional Bakers' Manual. 4297
Professional Baking. 4248
Professional Charcuterie Series. 1778
Professional Chef's Art of Garde Manger. 4106
Professional Chef's Book of Buffets. 4101
Professional Chef's Book of Charcuterie. 1774
Professional French Pastry Series. 3656
Professional Pastry Chef. 3663
Proper Tea. 4150
Prue Leith's Dinner Parties. 4175
Prune Gourmet. 1862
Pudding Book. 3735
Puddings & Desserts. 3269
Puddings and Desserts. 3378
Puddings, Custards, and Flans. 3742
Pulse Cookery. 1145
Pumpkin Cookbook. 1866
Pumpkin Corner. 1864
Pumpkin Eaters Cook Book. 1865
Pumpkin, Pumpkin! 1869
Pumpkins & Squashes. 1870
Pure Pasta. 1676
Purity All-Purpose Flour Cook Book. 679
Purity Cook Book. 679
Putting Food By. 4422
Putting It Up with Honey. 1093
Quaker Oat Bran Cookbook. 1581
Quaker Oat Bran Favorite Recipes. 1582
Queer Gear. 789
Quest for Wild Jelly. 3572
Quiche & Paté. 3744
Quiche & Souffle Cookbook. 3745
Quiche and Salad Made Easy. 3743
Quiches and Flans. 3746
Quiches, Flans, and Tarts. 3747
Quiches, Pies, Tarts and Flans. 3748

Specialty Cookbooks

Quick & Easy Gas Grill Cookbook. 4323
Quick & Easy Microwaving Chicken. 295
Quick & Easy Microwaving Ground Beef. 948
Quick & Easy Microwaving Seafood. 2062
Quick & Easy Microwaving Snacks & Appetizers. 2685
Quick & Easy Pasta Recipes. 1639
Quick and Easy 10 Minute Dinners. 4170
Quick and Easy Tofu Cook Book. 2261
Quick and Easy Ways with Beef. 89
Quick and Easy Yeast Recipes. 2573
Quick Breads. 2835
Quick Breads, Soups, and Stews. 2834
Quick Main Dishes. 3490
Quick Meals. 1399
Quick Meats Cookbook. 1228
Quick-to-Fix Desserts for Foodservice Menu Planning. 3270
Quick-to-Fix Mainstays. 3478
Quintessential Croissant. 3250
Rabbit, a Taste of Tradition! 1874
Rabbits for Food and Profit. 1875
Random House Barbecue and Summer Foods Cookbook. 4370
Rappahannock Seafood Cookbook. 2018
Raquel's Main Guide to New England Seafoods. 2089
Rasoi. 1423
Raspberry Tyme. 1878
Raw Energy Recipes. 1885
Raw Food Cookbook. 1887
Raw Foods. 1888
Reader's Digest, the Creative Kitchen: Poultry. 1847
Ready Aim Cookbook. 4021
Real Barbecue. 4361
Real Bill Bannock Cookbook. 669
Real Bread. 2829
Real Food Cookbook. 1359, 1397
Real Sandwich Book. 3852
Real Soup & Salad Cookbook. 3992
ReaLime Recipe Booklet. 1161
Receipts for Cookery and Pastry-Work. 4259
Recipes for Daily Living. 3484
Recipes for Extra Brownie Points. 2847
Recipes for Healthy Eating. 1483

Recipes for Kiwifruit Lovers. 1131
Recipes from a French Herb Garden. 1036
Recipes from a Kitchen Garden. 2416
Recipes from the Mangrove Country. 718
Recipes from the Night Kitchen. 4011
Recipes from the Raleigh Tavern Bake Shop. 4238
Recipes from the Third Annual Chocolate Tasting Fair. 331
Recipes from the Weimar Kitchen. 1424
Recipes of the Deep. 1988
Recipes of the Wild. 638
Recipes, the Great Oklahoma Congressional Chili Cook-off. 3085
Recipes We Use at King John's Hunting Lodge. 2940
Red Star Centennial Bread Sampler. 2745
Revised Seafood Secrets. 2122
Rhubarb. 1895
Rhubarb Cookbook. 1890
Rhubarb for Good Measure. 1893
Rhubarb Recipes. 1892
Rhubarb Renaissance. 1891
Ribs. 1771
Rice. 1910, 1911, 1915
Rice and Spice. 1896
Rice Cookbook. 1907
Rice Cookery. 1899
Rice Diet Report. 1905
Rice Flour Cookbook. 1917
Rice Recipes from Around the World. 1897
Ricotta Recipes from Polly-O. 1918
Ridgways, the Complete Tea Book. 4153
Rise and Shine. 4046
Rise to the Occasion with Yeast Breads. 2828
Risotto. 1909, 1912
Roasted and Braised Dishes. 4481
Robert's Famous Jams & Jellies. 3585
Robin Hood Canadian Flour Cook Book. 4215
Rocky Mountain Cache. 644
Rod & Reel. 625
Rodale's
  Basic Natural Foods Cookbook. 1545
  Complete Book of Home Freezing. 4460
  Garden-Fresh Cooking. 796

Title Index 649

Rodale's (Continued)
Naturally Delicious Desserts and Snacks. 3260
Naturally Great Foods Cookbook. 1391, 1484
Sensational Desserts. 3360
Soups and Salads Cookbook. 3980
Rolf's Collection of Wild Game Recipes. 695
Roll 'em & Stuff 'em Cookbook. 4020
Roman Cookery of Apicius. 996
Romance of West Coast Cooking. 1425
Romantic and Classic Cakes. 2935
Roon. 1264
Rootcrops. 2345
Roots & Tubers. 2353
Rose Elliot's Book of
Beans and Lentils. 1146
Breads. 2768
Cakes. 2952
Fruits. 734
Pasta. 1651
Salads. 3772
Savoury Flans and Pies. 3494
Rose Murray's Vegetable Cookbook. 2366
Rose Recipes from Olden Times. 1919
Rose's Christmas Cookies. 3232
Roses. 1921
Rotis and Naans of India. 2820
Roux Brothers on Patisserie. 3650
Royal Icing. 3565
R-r-rhubarb. 1894
Rum Cookbook. 1922, 1923
Runner's World Natural Foods Cookbook. 1360
Rural and Native Heritage Cookbook. 2521
S.N.A.C.K.S. 3899
Sable & Rosenfeld, Elegant Entertaining Cookbook. 445
Sack It and Pack It. 4119
Sainsbury Book of
Preserves & Pickles. 4393
Wholefood Cooking. 1361
Salad. 3785
Salad a Day. 3754
Salad and Dessert Cookbook. 3282
Salad Book. 3795
Salad Bowl. 3801

Salad Days. 3802, 3812
Salad Dressings! 3750
Salad Garden. 3777, 3778
Salad Menus. 3786
Salad Recipes. 3803
Salads. 3771, 3773, 3779, 3780, 3782, 3787, 3788, 3791, 3804-3806, 3815, 3823
Salads & Cold Dishes. 3796
Salads & Dressings. 3774
Salads and Dressings for All Seasons. 3781
Salads and Summer Dishes. 3797
Salads Cookbook. 3824
Salads for All Occasions. 3758, 3798
Salads for All Seasons. 3765, 3766
Salads for Every Season. 3767
Salads for Foodservice Menu Planning. 3816
Salads from Beginning to Endive. 3755
Salads of All Kinds. 3768
Salads of India. 3775
Salmon. 1934
Salmon Cookbook. 1933, 1935
Salmon Is King. 1936
Salmon Recipes. 1937
Salsas! 3830
Salt-Free Cooking with Herbs & Spices. 1048
Salt-Free Herb Cookery. 1071
Salute to the Great American Chefs. 1177
San Francisco Dinner Party Cookbook. 4166
San Giorgio Pasta. 1697
Sandwich Book. 3849
Sandwich Cookbook. 3832, 3843
Sandwiches, Sandwiches. 3846
Saran Wrap Any Oven Cookbook. 4209
Sargento Cheese Recipe Booklet. 210
Saskatchewan Ethnic Baking. 4220
Sauce Book. 3862
Sauce It. 3857
Sauces. 3860, 3869
Sauces and Dressings. 3872
Sauces and Soups. 3870
Sauces, Dressings and Marinades. 3864
Sauces for Pasta! 3877
Saucing the Fish. 599
Sausage Book. 1941

Sausage-Making Cookbook. 1943
Sausages. 1946
Sausages & Mince. 1944
Saving the Plenty. 4411
Savoring the Wild. 863
Savory Game Cookbook. 830
Savory Sandwiches. 3848
Savory Sausage. 1951
Savory Shellfish Recipes of the Shore. 2135
Savory Soups. 3968
Savoy Food and Drink Book. 2712
Say Cheesecake--and Smile. 3070
Scallops. 1955
Scarista Style. 1516
Sea Green Primer. 1202
Sea to Shore. 2108
Sea Vegetable Gelatin Cookbook. 891
Sea Vegetables. 1205
Seafish Cookbook. 2049
Seafood. 2000, 2090, 2109, 2123
Seafood Adventures. 2063
Seafood and Health. 2064
Seafood As We Like It. 2035
Seafood Book. 1962
Seafood Celebration. 2019
Seafood Cook Book. 2115
Seafood Cookbook. 1963, 2020, 2050, 2068
Seafood Cookery. 2001, 2110
Seafood Cooking for Your Health. 2111
Seafood Favorites. 2021
Seafood Heritage Cookbook. 2022
Seafood Kitchen. 1983
Seafood Lover's Cookbook. 2112
Seafood Menus for the Microwave. 2124
Seafood Microwave Cookery. 2065
Seafood Notebook. 1999
Seafood of Australia & New Zealand. 2125
Seafood Primer. 583
Seafood Sampler. 2113
Seafood Secrets. 2051
Seafood Secrets Cookbook. 1965
Seafood Smoking. 2066
Seafood Wok. 2025
Seafood Wokbook. 2052
Sealtest Great Cooking with Dairy Products. 494
Search for the Perfect Chocolate Chip Cookie. 3108

Seashore Entertaining. 2067
Season to Taste. 1031
Seasonal Freezer Cookbook. 4454
Seasonal Gifts from the Kitchen. 4403
Seasonal Salads. 3799, 3828
Seasonings Cookbook for Quantity Cuisine. 2182
Seaweed and Vegetables. 1204
Second Bite of the Cherry. 1528
Secret Ingredients. 1032
Secret Sauce Book of the Hungry Monk. 3858
Secrets of Bluefishing. 152
Secrets of French Hors d'Oeuvres. 2657
Secrets of French Sauces. 3871
Secrets of Italian Meat and Poultry Dishes. 1248
Secrets of Italian Pasta. 1687
Secrets of Potfishing. 2138
Secrets of Sauté Cooking. 4478
Secrets of the Sea. 706
Secrets of Tofu. 2268
Sedgewood Book of Baking. 4226
Seed and Nut Cookery. 1567
Self-Sufficient Larder. 1529
Sensational Desserts. 3379
Sensational Pasta. 1692
Sensational Salads. 3789, 3822
Sensational Sandwiches. 3855
Sensational Vegetarian Salads. 3773, 3806
Separate Egg. 545
Serve at Once. 3922
Serve It Forth. 3334, 4191
Sesame Primer. 2127
Seven Chocolate Sins. 311
Shad and Shad Roe. 2128
Shadow Hill Book of Mix-Easy Cakes. 2953
Shadow Hill Book of Squares. 3177
Shaker Desserts. 3315
Shaklee Family Favorites Cookbook. 1398
Shape It & Bake It. 2838
Shaped & Cut-out Cakes. 2886
Shark Cookbook. 2129
Shark, Sea Food of the Future. 2130
Shellfish. 2139, 2146, 2149
Shellfish Cookbook. 2136

Title Index

Shellfish Cookery. 2145
Shellfish Heritage Cookbook. 2137
Shellfish on the Grill. 2148
Sherry, the Golden Wine of Spain. 2152
Sheryl & Mel London's Creative Cooking with Grains & Pasta. 910
Shirley's Cajun Yam Cuisine. 2235
Shopwell's Dairy Lovers' Cookbook. 495
Short Course with King Arthur Flour in Baking with Yeast. 2727
Shortcut Main Dishes. 3486
Shrimp. 2157
Shrimp Lover's Cookbook. 2155
Signature Entrees. 3487
Silver Palate Sweet Times Dessert Book. 3380
SIMAC's Cuisine Collection. 1632
Simmering Pot Cookbook. 4019
Simmering Suppers. 3061
Simple and Speedy Whole Food Cookery. 1499
Simple Art of Perfect Baking. 4249
Simple Feasts. 2669
Simple Food for the Good Life. 1336
Simple Foods for the Pack. 1485
Simple Sanibel Seafood. 1989
Simply Delicious Desserts. 441
Simply Elegant. 1595, 2923
Simply Fish. 624
Simply Healthy. 1517
Simply Salmon. 1932
Simply Sauces. 3863
Simply Scones. 3878
Simply Seafood Cookbook of East Coast Fish. 584
East Coast Shellfish. 2142
Simply Seafood, Seafood Cookery Made Easy. 2002
Simply Shrimp. 2158, 2159
Simply Souper. 3946
Simply Strawberries. 2225
Sinlessly Sweet Recipes. 888
Sister Jennie's Shaker Desserts. 3315
Skillet Cookery. 4474
Slim Gourmet Sweets and Treats. 3294
Slim Snacks. 3891
Slimming Magazines Freezer Owner's Diet Book. 4461

Small Feasts. 3979
Small Potatoes. 1806
Smart Breakfasts. 4061
Smart Cookies. 3188
Smart Muffins. 3611
Smell That Bread. 2769
Smoked Fish Recipes. 578
Smoking Food at Home. 4485
Smoking Salmon & Trout. 1930
Smucker's Cookbook. 1129
Snack and Bag Lunch Idea Book. 3885
Snack Bar Gourmet. 3913
Snack Food. 3918
Snack to Your Heart's Content! 2588
Snacks. 3905
Snacks & Sandwiches. 3833
Snacks You Can Say Yes To! 3914
Soda Fountain and Luncheonette Drinks and Recipes. 3851
Soft Shell Clams-Steamers. 424
Solid Chocolate. 391
Some Edible Mushrooms. 1268
Some Like It Hotter. 2190
Something Cranberry. 471
Something Strawberry. 2227
Sonia Allison's Biscuit Book. 3152
Sonia Allison's Bread Book. 2770
Sonia Allison's Home Baking Book. 4227
Sonia Allison's Sweets Book. 3121
Sophie Kay's Casseroles. 3041
Sophisticated Sandwich. 3853
Sorbets! 3561
Souffle Cookbook. 3922
Souffles. 3921
Souffles, Mousses, Jellies & Creams. 3594
Souffles, Quiches, Mousses & the Random Egg. 3920
Soup. 3971
Soup & Stew Menus. 4004
Soup and Salad Bars. 3981
Soup, Beautiful Soup. 3952
Soup Book. 3923
Soup Cookbook. 3934
Soup for All Seasons. 3960
Soup Meals. 3970
Soup, Salad & Pasta. 3983
Soup, Salad, and Pasta Innovations. 3990
Soup, Salad, Sandwich Cookbook. 3982

Specialty Cookbooks

Soup Time! 3939
Soup Wisdom. 3927
Soup's On. 3957
Souped Up. 3947
Souped Up Recipes. 517
Souper Tuna Cook Book. 2297
Souper Type. 3953
Soups. 3940, 3954, 3961, 3977
Soups & Salads. 3987
Soups & Sandwiches. 3941
Soups & Sauces. 3942
Soups & Starters. 3956
Soups & Stews. 4007, 4008
Soups and Borschts from Hutterite Kitchens. 3972
Soups and Garnishes. 3955
Soups and Salads. 3986
Soups and Salads Cookbook. 3988
Soups and Salads with Schmecks Appeal. 3994
Soups and Starters. 3966
Soups and Stews. 4010
Soups and Stews Cookbook. 4002
Soups, Chowders, and Stews. 3996
Soups for All Seasons. 3967
Soups for the Professional Chef. 3973
Soups from Amish and Mennonite Kitchens. 3935
Soups of Hakafri Restaurant. 3936
Soups, Salads, and Snacks. 3991, 3995
Soups, Stews & Casseroles. 4001
Soups, Stews & Oven Lovin' Breads. 4013
Soups, Stews and Casseroles. 4012
Soups Supreme. 3943
Sourdough Breads and Coffee Cakes. 2169
Sourdough Cookery. 2167, 2168
Sourdough Cookin'. 2166
South African Fruit Cooking. 735
South Carolina Wildlife Cookbook. 2531
Southeastern Wildlife Cookbook. 2531
Southern Born and Bread. 2829
Southern Fish and Seafood Cookbook. 1959
Southern Herb Growing. 1023
Southern Heritage
  All Pork Cookbook. 1772
  Beef, Veal & Lamb Cookbook. 1229
  Breads Cookbook. 2771

Southern Heritage (Continued)
  Breakfast and Brunch Cookbook. 4074
  Cakes Cookbook. 2945
  Cookie Jar Cookbook. 3189
  Gift Receipts Cookbook. 3127
  Just Desserts Cookbook. 3335
  Pies and Pastry Cookbook. 3639
  Plain and Fancy Poultry Cookbook. 1835
  Sea and Stream Cookbook. 2023
  Soups and Stews Cookbook. 4005
  Vegetables Cookbook. 2367
Southern Sampler. 4281
Southern Seafood Classics. 2091
Southern Vegetable Cooking. 2346
Southern Wildfowl and Wild Game Cookbook. 694
Soy for the 21st Century. 2177
Soya Foods Cookery. 2180
Soybean Cookery. 2172
Soybeans and Soybean Products. 2178
Special and Decorative Breads. 2830
Special Occasion Desserts. 3361
Special Offal. 2317
Special Touches for Decorating Food. 3512
Speedy, Nutritious, and Cheap Kids' Snacks. 3899
Speedy Skillet Meals. 4473
Sphinx Ranch Date Recipes. 512
Spice of Vegetarian Cooking. 1088
Spices and Herbs Around the World. 1050
Spices and Herbs, Lore & Cookery. 1050
Spices and Savour. 1070
Spices, Condiments, and Seasonings. 2200
Spices of the World Cookbook. 2187
Spices, Salt and Aromatics in the English Kitchen. 1052
Spices, Roots & Fruit. 2201
Spices, Seeds & Barks. 2202
Spicy Vegetarian Feasts. 1088
Spilling the Beans. 76
Spirit of Cooking. 1174
Spirit of Tennessee Cookbook. 2478
Spirited Cooking. 1166, 2555
Spirulina Cookbook. 2204
Spoon Desserts! 3449
Sporting a Healthier Image for Chocolate Cookbook. 392
Sporting Wife. 672

Title Index 653

Spotlight on Bread. 2746
Spring Garden. 2430
Sprouting Book. 2207
Spud Book. 1786
Spuds. 1807
Squash. 2208
Squash Cookbook. 2209, 2211
Squid. 2212
Staffordshire Oatcake Recipe Book. 1584
Stalking the Healthful Herbs. 2532
Stalking the Wild Asparagus. 2519
Stan Jones' Cooking with
 Bacardi Rum. 1925
 Tequila Sauza. 2249
 The Christian Brothers Brandy. 158
Standard Wine Cookbook. 2542
Star Herbal. 976
Starchild & Holahan's Seafood Cookbook. 1963
Starters as a Main Meal. 2648
Starters with Style. 2643
Starting Over. 1530
Stay Slim with Herbs and Spices. 1053
Steakhouse Cookbook. 100
Steam Cooking. 4491
Steam Cooking Now! 4487
Steam Cuisine. 4494, 4495
Steaming Cookbook. 4496
Steinbeck's Street, Cannery Row. 1940
Step by Step Garnishing. 3525
Step-by-Step Pasta Cookbook. 1652
Step-by-Step Sushi. 4029
Step-by-Step to Natural Food. 1317
Stephen Yan's Seafood Wokbook. 2052
Stew Cookbook. 4014
Stews & Casseroles. 3030
Stews and Soups and Go-with Breads. 3997
Stir-Fry Cook Book. 4499
Stir-Fry Recipes. 4497
Stocking Up. 4426
Stockpot and Steamer Cookbook. 4019
Stone Age Diet. 925
Strawberries. 2220
Strawberry Connection. 2223
Strawberry Delights. 2221
Strawberry Patchwork. 2216
Strawberry Sampler. 2226
Strawberry Sportcake. 2219

Street Food. 3910
Stretching-the-Food-Dollar Cookbook. 1358
Strictly Fish Cookbook. 587
Striped Bass on the Fly. 2229
Stuffed Spuds. 1792
Stuffin' Muffin. 1562
Successful Baking. 4237
Successful Buffet Management. 4108
Successful Cold Buffets. 4109
Successful Dinner Parties. 4176
Successful Icing. 3564
Sugar Bush. 1198
Sugar Bush Connection. 1192
Sugar Flowers from Around the World. 2926
Sugar Free Cakes and Biscuits. 2961
Sugar Free, Goodies. 3394
Sugar Work. 3132
Sugarless Baking Book. 4228
Sugarless Cookbook. 755
Sugarless Desserts, Jams, and Salads
 Cookbook. 3414
Summer Berries. 127
Summer Cook's Book. 790
Summer Delights. 988, 1016
Summer Desserts. 3395, 3415
Summer in a Jar. 3680
Summer Salads. 3817, 3825
Summertime Cookbook. 2092
Summertime Snacks. 3915
Summit Casserole Cookbook. 3047
Sumptuous Sauces in the Microwave. 3873
Sun-Dried Tomatoes! 2233
Sun Maid Cookbook. 1877
Sunburst Tropical Fruit Co. Cookbook. 761
Sunday Dinner. 4161
Sunday Lunch Book. 4114
Sunday Lunch Cookbook. 4113
Sunday Suppers. 4201
Sunday Times Book of Real Bread. 2754
Sunday Times Guide to the World's Best
 Food. 1362
Sundays at Moosewood Restaurant. 1555
Sunny Side Up. 4052
Sunrise. 4041
Sunset Appetizers. 2664

Specialty Cookbooks

Sunset Barbecue Cook Book. 4345
Sunset Breads. 2781
Sunset Canning, Freezing & Drying. 4394
Sunset Casserole Cook Book. 3031
Sunset Cookies. 3190
Sunset Fish & Shellfish. 2114
Sunset Fresh Produce. 797
Sunset Fresh Ways with Chicken. 1853
Sunset Fresh Ways with Pasta. 1699
Sunset Fresh Ways with Salads. 3807
Sunset Homemade Soups. 3958
Sunset Hors d'Oeuvres. 2618
Sunset Light Desserts. 3396
Sunset Pasta Cook Book. 1627
Sunset Pies & Pastries. 3647
Sunset Quick Meals. 1399
Sunset Seafood Cook Book. 2115
Sunset Stir-Fry Cook Book. 4499
Sunset Ultimate Grill Book. 4371
Sunset Vegetable Cook Book. 2368
Sunshine Coast Seafood. 2036
Sunshine Cookbook. 412
Sunshine Larder. 1101
Super Chicken Cookbook. 267
Super Natural Cookery. 1310
Super Salads & Vegetables. 3829
Super Snacks. 2682, 3892
Super Snacks for Kids. 3902
Super Soups. 3962
Super Soups Made Easy. 3930
Super Soy! 2173
Super Suppers. 4194
Super Sweets. 3014
Supercook Cakes & Cake Decorating. 2975
Supernatural Dessert Cookbook. 3336
Supper Book. 4195, 4199
Suppers & Snacks. 4196
Suppers and Snacks. 4200
Surprising Citrus. 419
Survival Acre. 2509
Survival Gardening Cookbook. 1455
Susan Costner's Book of Great Sandwiches. 3856
Sushi. 4023, 4027, 4028
Sushi at Home. 4026
Sushi Handbook. 4025
Sushi Made Easy. 4024
Suzanne's Natural Food Cookbook. 1486

Sweet 'n' Slow. 9
Sweet & Natural. 3295
Sweet & Natural Desserts. 3381
Sweet & Savory Pies. 3699
Sweet and Sugarfree. 3296
Sweet Delights. 3362
Sweet Dreams. 3316
Sweet Dreams of Gingerbread. 3532
Sweet Flavorings. 2203
Sweet Indulgences. 3450
Sweet Life. 3277
Sweet Mania. 3416
Sweet Potato. 2236
Sweet Potato Cookbook. 2238
Sweet Remembrances. 4229
Sweet Seduction. 3094
Sweet Success. 3451
Sweet Surprises. 3337
Sweet Temptation. 3661
Sweet Temptations. 3397
Sweet Things. 3135, 3382
Sweet Touch in Family Cooking. 2231
Sweet Treat Cookery. 3114
Sweetmaking for Children. 3136
Sweets 'n' Treats. 3116
Sweets & Candies. 3131
Sweets & Puddings. 3317
Sweets and Candies. 3124
Sweets and Desserts from the Middle East. 3338
Sweets Book. 3121, 3128
Sweets for Presents. 3115
Sweets for Saints and Sinners. 3271
Sweets Without Guilt. 709
Sweets Without Sugar. 762
Swordfish. 2239
Sylvia Bashline's Savory Game Cookbook. 830
T.N.T. Cookbook. 3881
Take the E Out of Eating. 1487
Taking Tea. 4151
Talkin' Turkey. 2305
Talking About Turkey. 2310
Tapas. 4030
Tapas and Appetizers. 4032
Tapas, Wines & Good Times. 4031
Taro. 2241
Tassajara Bread Book. 2805

Title Index

Taste Niagara. 736
Taste of Blueberries. 150
Taste of Chocolate. 401
Taste of Cider. 407
Taste of Health. 1456
Taste of Honey. 1102
Taste of Life Cookbook. 1546
Taste of Pasta. 1670
Taste of Seafood. 2093
Taste of Summer. 1819, 3808
Taste of the Tropics. 2003
Taste of the West from Coors. 118
Tasty Toasties. 3844
Tea Lover's Handbook. 2243
Tea Time. 4152
Tea with Mrs. Beeton. 4160
Teas & Tisanes. 3540
Teatime at Airthrey. 4154
Teatime Celebrations. 4155
Tempeh Cookbook. 2247
Tempeh Cookery. 2245
Tempeh Production. 2246
Tempting Cheesecakes. 3075
Tempting Tuna Cookbook. 2295
Ten Dinner Parties for Two. 4187
Ten Late Breakfasts. 4062
Ten Talents. 1439
Ten Vineyard Lunches. 4117
Tequila Book. 2248
Terrines, Pâtés & Galantines. 3509
Texas Family's Cookbook. 1531
Texas Potatoes. 1790
Texas Sweets from Grandma's Kitchen. 3417
Texas Wild Game Cookbook. 842
Texas Wild Game Recipes Cookbook. 864
That Amazing Ingredient. 1207
That Special Touch. 2481
This is Potjiekos. 4017
This Is the Way My Garden Grows. 2402
Thistle Greens and Mistletoe. 2527
Thomas' Best. 556
Thorsons Green Cookbook. 1556
Thorsons Guide to Entertaining with Wholefood. 1488
Thrill of the Grill. 4382
Through Thick & Thin. 1374

Thursday Night Feast and Good Meals Cookbook. 1405
Thyme for Kids. 1045
Tiffany Taste. 4182
Tilefish. 2250
Time for Dessert. 3278
Tiny Delights. 3466
To Cook a Snail. 2161
To Everything There Is a Season. 1532
To Hell with Gravy! 836
Toadstools, Mushrooms, Fungi. 1269
Today's Pork Goes to School. 1765
Tofu. 2254, 2264, 2269
Tofu at Center Stage. 2258
Tofu Book. 2274
Tofu Cookbook. 2253, 2270
Tofu Cookery. 2262, 2275
Tofu Fantasies. 2259
Tofu Goes West. 2251
Tofu Gourmet. 2276
Tofu Kitchen. 2260
Tofu Magic. 2273
Tofu Primer. 2265
Tofu Quick & Easy. 2271
Tofu, Tempeh, & Other Soy Delights. 2179
Tom Thumb Treats. 3893
Tomato Cookbook. 2278
Tomatoes. 2280, 2281, 2283
Tomatoes, Cheese, and Anchovies Cookbook. 8
Too Many Tomatoes. 2324
Tootie Frootie. 2695
Top One Hundred Pasta Sauces. 3868
Topsy and Tim's Chocolate Cook Book. 332
Tortilla Book. 4033
Total Nutrition. 1321
Totally Hot! 2191
Touch of Taste. 1257
Trader Vic's Rum Cookery and Drinkery. 1924
Traditional Biscuits. 3159
Traditional Cakes. 2936
Traditional Cakes and Pastries. 3002
Traditional Gifts. 3576
Traditional Herb & Spice Cookery. 1072
Traditional Pies and Pasties. 3703
Traditional Puddings. 3736

Specialty Cookbooks

Treasury of A.J. McClane's Classic Angling Adventures. 615
Treasury of Chicken Cookery. 305
Treats for My Sweets. 3279
Treats Nutritional Treats. 3881
Triticale Cook Book. 2289
Triticale New Harvest Recipes. 2290
Tropical Fruit Desserts. 724
Tropical Fruit Recipes. 725
Trout Cookbook. 2292
True Grist. 3249
Truffles and Other Chocolate Confections. 3095
Truly Unusual Soups. 3944
Trust in British Potatoes Recipe Book. 1811
Trust the Gorton's Fisherman for Delicious Recipe Ideas. 705
Tumbleweed Gourmet. 2520
Tuna Cookbook. 2294
Turkey. 2313
Turkey & Duck Menus. 520
Turkey All Year. 2307
Turkey Cookbook. 2314
Twelve Days of Turkey. 2304
Twelve-to-One Habit. 4111
Twenty-two Common Herbs and How to Use Them. 960
Two-in-One Herb Book. 981
Uala. 2236
Ultimate Breakfast. 4057
Ultimate Chocolate Cake. 333
Ultimate Chocolate Cake Book. 330
Ultimate Chocolate Cookbook. 337, 345
Ultimate Grill Book. 4371
Ultimate Mousse Cookbook. 3596
Ultimate Peanut Butter Cookbook. 1716
Ultimate Salad Dressing Book. 3751
Ultimate Sandwich Book. 3838
Umberto Menghi Seafood Cookbook. 2068
Umberto's Pasta Book. 1661
Unabridged Vegetable Cookbook. 2323
Uncle Gene's Breadbook for Kids! 2843
Uncle Russ Chittenden's Good Ole Boys Wild Game Cookbook. 674
Uncommon Fruits & Vegetables. 791
Uncook Book. 1881
Under the Crust. 3627

Under the Influence of Bright Sunbeams. 1518
Underwater Gourmet. 2004
Unforbidden Sweets. 3297
Unique Potato Salad Cookbook. 1817
Unofficial Florida Bar-B-Que Sauces & Chili Recipes. 3859
Unusual Soups. 3931
Unusual Vegetables. 2341
Upper Canada Village Flour and Grist Mill Cookbook. 4239
Upper Crust. 3847
Uprisings. 4298
Useful Pig. 1779
Uses of Tubes. 2852
Using Herbs & Spices. 1054
Using Tofu, Tempeh & Other Soyfoods. 2174
Vachon Desserts. 3280
Vanilla Cookbook. 2315
Variations of Vegetables. 2347
Variations on a Dessert. 3298
Variations on a Main Course. 3475
Variations on a Starter. 2609
Variety Meats. 2318
Variety with Venison and Other Wild Game. 865
Veal and Lamb. 2320
Veal Cookery. 2319
Vegetable Book. 2342, 2376
Vegetable Bounty. 2322
Vegetable Cook Book. 2368
Vegetable Cookbook. 2366, 2400
Vegetable Cookery. 2335, 2354, 2403
Vegetable Cooking of All Nations. 2348
Vegetable Creations. 2417
Vegetable Dishes. 2369, 2404
Vegetable Gardening Encyclopedia. 2355
Vegetable Juice Therapy. 1889
Vegetable Lover's Cookbook. 2370
Vegetable Magic. 2391
Vegetable Menus. 2377
Vegetable Spaghetti Cookbook. 2181
Vegetable Year Cookbook. 2405
Vegetables. 2326, 2356, 2392, 2393, 2394, 2406, 2407, 2411, 2431, 2447, 2449
Vegetables & Salads. 2349
Vegetables and Desserts. 2408

Title Index

Vegetables and Salads. 2448
Vegetables and Their Sauces. 2409
Vegetables in Family Meals. 2357
Vegetables, Pasta and Rice. 2395
Vegetables the French Way. 2439
Vegetables the Italian Way. 2336
Vegetarian Barbecue. 4332, 4351
Vegetarian Cheese Cookery. 236
Vegetarian Cooker-Top Cookery. 1457
Vegetarian Dinner Parties. 4173
Vegetarian Handbook. 2418
Vegetarian Lunchbasket. 4140
Vegetarian Lunchbox. 4135
Vegetarian Patés & Dips. 3670
Vegetarian Pitta Bread Recipes. 3715
Vegetarian Snacks and Starters. 2677
Vegetarian Wholefood Cookbook. 1430
Veggie Mania. 2410
Velveeta Cookbook. 211
Velveeta Creative Cooking. 245
Venison. 2454
Venison Book. 2450
Venison Cookbook. 847
Venison--from Field to Table. 2455
Venison Handbook. 2451
Versatile Vegetable. 2327
Versatile Vegetable Cookbook. 2371
Versatile Vegetables. 2337, 2440
Victorian Cakes. 2967
Victorian Desserts. 3262
Victorian Ices & Ice Cream. 3551
Victory Garden Cookbook. 2358
Viennese Desserts Made Easy. 3318
Viennese Pastry Cookbook. 3620
Vintner's Choice. 2561
Virtues of Vinegar. 2458
Virtuous Desserts. 3434
Waffles & Wafers. 3246
Wainscott Seafood Shop Cookbook. 2126
Wake Up and Smell the Coffee. 4083, 4089
War Eagle Mill Wholegrain Cookbook. 915
Warm Weather Recipes Featuring Yogurt. 2585
Waterfront Cookbook. 1972
Watermelon. 2462
Way of Eating for Pleasure and Health. 1400
Way with Vegetables. 2323

We Love Your Body. 1337
Weakfish-Sea Trout. 2463
Wedding Cakes. 2902
Weed Eater's Cook Book. 2493
Weekly Reader Books. 3919
Well Cooked Egg. 551
Well-Filled Tortilla Cookbook. 4035
Well-Flavored Vegetable. 2432
Well-Filled Cupboard. 1519
Wellesley Cookie Exchange Cookbook. 3214
Western Bean Cookery. 77
Western-Style Cakes. 2976
What to Freeze and How. 4444
What's for Breakfast? 4059
Wheat, Farm to Feast. 2470
Wheat Flowers. 2465
Wheat for Man. 2464
Wheatgrass Book. 2476
Wheeler's New Fish Cookery. 600
Whisk It, Beat It, Cook It, Eat It!. 501
White Chocolate. 2482
Whitman's Chocolate Cookbook. 372
Whole Chile Pepper Book. 1746
Whole Foods Cookery. 1458
Whole Foods Experience. 1459
Whole Foods for the Whole Family. 1426
Whole Foods for Whole People. 1489
Whole Foods Kitchen Journal. 1547
Whole Grain Bake Book. 4207
Whole Grain Baking. 4240
Whole Grain Recipe Book. 911
Whole Grains. 906
Whole Meal Salad Book. 3826
Whole Meals. 1401
Whole Thing. 3882
Whole Wheat Bread Recipes. 2726
Whole Wheat Cookery. 2473
Wholefood Baking. 4241
Wholefood Book. 1375
Wholefood Catalog. 1533
Wholefood Cookery Course. 1402, 1412
Wholefood Cookery School. 1523
Wholefood Cookery with Beans, Peas and Lentils. 1150
Wholefood Cooking. 1490
Wholefood Desserts. 3272
Wholefood for Beginners. 1338

Specialty Cookbooks

Wholefood for the Whole Family. 1491
Wholefood Freezer Book. 4445
Wholefood Harvest Cookbook. 1557
Wholefood Lunch Box. 4135
Wholefood Party Cookbook. 1427, 1488
Wholefoods Book. 1460
Wholefoods Cookbook. 1339
Wholefoods Menu Book. 1403
Wholegrain, Health-Saver Cookbook. 2469
Wholegrain Oven. 4260
Wholegrain Recipe Book. 1404
Wholegrains. 916
Wholemeal Kitchen. 917
Why Not Stay for Breakfast? 4053
WI Book of
  Baking. 4284
  Biscuits. 3178
  Bread and Buns. 2782
  Cakes. 2962
  Desserts. 3339
  Fish and Seafood. 2069
  Healthy Family Cookery. 1548
  Jams and Other Preserves. 3579
  Meat Cookery. 1239
  Pastry. 3640
  Poultry and Game. 698
  Puddings. 3740
  Vegetables and Salads. 2419
  Wholefood Cookery. 1461
WIC Bean Book. 78
Wicked Chocolate Book. 393
Wild & Famous Fish & Game Cookbook. 676
Wild About Brownies. 2850
Wild About Chili. 3089
Wild About Fudge. 3507
Wild About Ice Cream. 3554
Wild About Muffins. 3608
Wild About Munchies. 3916
Wild About Mushrooms. 1295
Wild About Pizza and Pasta. 1702
Wild About Potatoes. 1808
Wild About Rice. 1913
Wild About Salads. 3827
Wild and Free. 2511
Wild Country All Game and Fish Recipes. 645
Wild Flavor. 2505

Wild Food. 2512
Wild Food Cookbook. 2533
Wild Foods. 2485, 2528
Wild Foods Cookbook. 2506, 2534
Wild Foods Cookery. 2486
Wild Foods Field Guide and Cookbook. 2506
Wild Foods of Appalachia. 2513
Wild Foods of the Desert Cookbook. 2514
Wild Fruits. 737
Wild Game and Country Cooking. 650
Wild Game and Fish Cookbook. 654
Wild Game Cook Book. 639, 809
Wild Game Cookbook. 811, 819, 826, 835, 848, 854
Wild Game Cookery. 855
Wild Green Vegetables of Canada. 2338
Wild Greens and Salads. 2498
Wild Mushroom Recipes. 1274, 1282
Wild Mushrooms of the Central Midwest. 1277
Wild Mushrooms Worth Knowing. 1277
Wild Palate. 2491
Wild Plant Companion. 2515
Wild Plant Cookbook. 2517
Wild Plums in Brandy. 2522
Wild Preserves. 3569
Wild Rice for All Seasons Cookbook. 2537
Wild Rice, Star of the North. 2539
Wild Taste. 2535
Wild, Wild Cookbook. 2499
Wildfoods Cookbook. 2516
Wildlife Chef. 820
Wildlife Harvest Game Cookbook. 856
Wildlife Vittles. 2502
Will It Freeze? 4453
Willacrick Farm French Giant Elephant Garlic Cookbook. 879
Willow Farm Pickle Book. 3674
Wilton Book of Wedding Cakes. 2867
Wilton Celebrates the Rose in Cake and Food Decorating. 2889
Wilton Way of Cake Decorating. 2852
Windowsill Herb Garden. 1043
Wine. 2552
Wine and Food Society's Guide to Classic Sauces. 3874
Wine Book. 2545

Title Index

Wine Cookbook of Dinner Menus. 4168
Wine, Food & the Good Life. 2556
Wine in Everyday Cooking. 2550
Winemakers Cookbook. 2562
Winning Ways with Cheese. 220
Winter Desserts. 3398
Winter Harvest Cookbook. 2446
Winter Pleasures. 1044
Wisconsin Dairy Country Recipes. 507
Wish-Bone Not for Salads Only. 3749
With a Touch of Olive Oil. 1596
Wok & Stir Fry Cooking. 4500
Wok Appetizers and Light Snacks. 2675
Wok, Fondue & Chafing Dish Cookbook. 3496
Wolff's Buckwheat Cookbook. 168
Woman and Home Celebration Cakes. 2915
Woman's Day
  Book of Delicious Desserts. 3281
  Book of Great Sandwiches. 3839
  Book of Great Turkey Feasts. 2308
  Book of Salads. 3756
  Buffet Cookbook. 4096
  Chocolate Lovers' Cookbook. 346
  Gelatin Cookery. 886
  Great American Cookie Book. 3147
  Low-Calorie Dessert Cookbook. 3273
  Snack Cookbook. 3883
Woman's Own Book of Casserole Cookery. 3032
Woman's Realm Cake Icing. 3563
Wonderful Ways to Prepare Barbecue & Picnic Meals. 4324
Wonderful World of Bee Pollen. 1105
Wonderful World of Cheese. 212
Wonderful World of Honey. 1092
Wonderful World of Natural-Food Cookery. 1316
Wonderful World of Salads. 3818
Wooden Spoon Bread Book. 2814
Wooden Spoon Dessert Book. 3452
Workday Breakfasts. 4042
Working Chef's Cookbook for Natural Whole Foods. 1549
World Almanac Guide to Natural Foods. 1462
World of Cheese. 205

World of Desserts and Delicacies from Solor. 3257
World of Potatoes. 1812
World of Salads. 3759
World of Vegetable Cookery. 2378
World Sourdoughs from Antiquity. 2170
World Wide Selection of Exotic Produce. 808
Worldly Taste of Seasonings, Herbs and Flowers. 682
Worldwide Dessert Contest. 3418
Writing in Icing. 2909
Wyler's New Idea Book. 155, 156
Year of Diet Desserts. 3399
Year-Round Turkey Cookbook. 2303
Yeast Bread and Rolls. 2821
Yip Recipes. 4490
Yoga Way Cookbook. 1340
Yoghurt Book. 2584
Yogurt Cookbook. 2579
Yogurt Cookery. 2586
You and Your Wild Game. 831
You Can Do Anything with Crepes. 3245
You Can Make Cornell Bread. 2730
You Knead It. 4207
Your First 100 Recipes for Nutritional Yeast. 2575
Yum Cha. 3458
Yummy Summer Snack Book. 3919
Zero Calorie Desserts. 3419
Zesty Pizza. 3720
Zucchini Cook Book. 2597
Zucchini Cookbook. 2593
Zucchini Cookery. 2589
Zucchini from A to Z. 2602
Zucchini Monster Cookbook. 2595
Zucchini Recipes. 2592
Zucchini Time. 2594

About the Authors

Harriet Ostroff has been editor of the *National Union Catalog of Manuscript Collections* and head of the Manuscripts Section, Special Materials Cataloging Division, Library of Congress, since 1975. She has a bachelor's degree in business administration from the City College of New York and an M.S. from Columbia University's School of Library Service. She is also an avid collector of recipes and is in the process of preparing a classification scheme and detailed computerized index to the recipes in her files and in her cookbook collection. Her home is in Rockville, Md.

Tom Nichols is a senior audiovisual librarian in the Special Materials Cataloging Division, Library of Congress, in Washington, D.C. Prior to this position, he worked as an editor of audiovisual cataloging records in the U.S. Copyright Office. He received a B.A. in history from Palm Beach Atlantic College in West Palm Beach, Fla., and a masters in library science from Catholic University in Washington, D.C. Privately he has compiled copyright bibliographies for the estate of the late Benny Goodman as well as for other famous American musicians. He lives on Capitol Hill.